4th Workshop on Representation Learning for NLP (RepL4NLP-2019)

Florence, Italy
2 August 2019

ISBN: 978-1-5108-9114-2

ACL 2019

The 4th Workshop on Representation Learning for NLP (RepL4NLP-2019)

Proceedings of the Workshop

August 2, 2019
Florence, Italy

Sponsors:

facebook

amazon

LABS
NAVER LABS
EUROPE

Introduction

The 4th Workshop on Representation Learning for NLP (RepL4NLP) will be hosted by ACL 2019 and held on 2 August 2019. The workshop is being organised by Isabelle Augenstein, Spandana Gella, Sebastian Ruder, Katharina Kann, Burcu Can, Alexis Conneau, Johannes Welbl, Xian Ren and Marek Rei; and advised by Kyunghyun Cho, Edward Grefenstette, Karl Moritz Hermann, Chris Dyer and Laura Rimell. The workshop is organised by the ACL Special Interest Group on Representation Learning (SIGREP) and receives generous sponsorship from Facebook AI Research, Amazon, and Naver.

The 4th Workshop on Representation Learning for NLP aims to continue the success of the 1st Workshop on Representation Learning for NLP (about 50 submissions and over 250 attendees; second most attended collocated event at ACL'16 after WMT), 2nd Workshop on Representation Learning for NLP and 3rd Workshop on Representation Learning for NLP. The workshop was introduced as a synthesis of several years of independent *CL workshops focusing on vector space models of meaning, compositionality, and the application of deep neural networks and spectral methods to NLP. It provides a forum for discussing recent advances on these topics, as well as future research directions in linguistically motivated vector-based models in NLP.

Organizers:

Isabelle Augenstein, University of Copenhagen
Burcu Can, Hacettepe University
Alexis Conneau, Facebook AI Research Paris, Université Le Mans
Spandana Gella, Amazon AI
Katharina Kann, New York University
Marek Rei, University of Cambridge
Xiang Ren, University of Southern California
Sebastian Ruder, DeepMind
Johannes Welbl, University College London

Senior Advisors:

Kyunghyun Cho, NYU and Facebook AI Research
Chris Dyer, DeepMind
Edward Grefenstette, Facebook AI Research
Karl Moritz Hermann, DeepMind
Laura Rimell, DeepMind

Program Committee:

Eneko Agirre, University of the Basque Country (UPV/EHU)
Yoav Artzi, Cornell University
Jonathan Berant, Tel Aviv University and AI2
Johannes Bjerva, Department of Computer Science, University of Copenhagen
Samuel R. Bowman, New York University
Jan Buys, University of Washington
Andrew Caines, University of Cambridge
Claire Cardie, Cornell University
Xilun Chen, Cornell University
Danqi Chen, Stanford University
Heeyoul Choi, Handong Global University
Eunsol Choi, University of Washington
Manuel Ciosici, Aarhus University
Stephen Clark, DeepMind
Marco Damonte, The University of Edinburgh
Miryam de Lhoneux, Uppsala University
Desmond Elliott, University of Copenhagen
Orhan Firat, Google AI
Lucie Flekova, Amazon Research
Daniela Gerz, University of Cambridge
Kevin Gimpel, Toyota Technological Institute at Chicago
Gholamreza Haffari, Monash University
Mareike Hartmann, University of Copenhagen
Mohit Iyyer, University of Massachusetts Amherst

Arzoo Katiyar, Cornell University
Yova Kementchedjhieva, University of Copenhagen
Douwe Kiela, Facebook
Bill Yuchen Lin, USC/ISI
Suresh Manandhar, University of York
Ana Marasovic, Allen Institute for Artificial Intelligence (AI2)
Sebastian J. Mielke, Johns Hopkins University
Todor Mihaylov, Heidelberg University
Pasquale Minervini, UCL
Nikita Nangia, New York University
Jason Naradowsky, Johns Hopkins
Shashi Narayan, Google
Thien Huu Nguyen, University of Oregon
Inkit Padhi, IBM Research
Chris Quirk, Microsoft Research
Roi Reichart, Technion - Israel Institute of Technology
Alan Ritter, The Ohio State University
Hinrich Schütze, Center for Information and Language Processing, University of Munich
Minjoon Seo, University of Washington
Tianze Shi, Cornell University
Vered Shwartz, Bar-Ilan University
Daniil Sorokin, UKP Lab, Technische Universität Darmstadt
Mark Steedman, University of Edinburgh
Karl Stratos, Toyota Technological Institute at Chicago
Jörg Tiedemann, University of Helsinki
Ivan Titov, University of Edinburgh / University of Amsterdam
Eva Maria Vecchi, University of Cambridge
Ivan Vulić, University of Cambridge
Dirk Weissenborn, Google AI, Berlin
Yadollah Yaghoobzadeh, Microsoft Research Montreal
Yi Yang, ASAPP
Helen Yannakoudakis, University of Cambridge
Wenpeng Yin, University of Pennsylvania
Luke Zettlemoyer, University of Washington
Wenxuan Zhou, University of Southern California
Diarmuid Ó Séaghdha, Apple
Robert Östling, Department of Linguistics, Stockholm University

Keynote Speakers:

Mohit Bansal, UNC Chapel Hill
Marco Baroni, Facebook AI Research
Raquel Fernandez, University of Amsterdam
Yulia Tsvetkov, Carnegie Mellon University

Table of Contents

Workshop Program

Friday, August 2, 2019

09:30–09:45   Welcome and Opening Remarks

09:45–14:45   Keynote Session

09:45–10:30   *Invited Talk 1*
Marco Baroni

10:30–11:00   Coffee Break

11:00–11:45   *Invited Talk 2*
Mohit Bansal

11:45–12:30   *Invited Talk 3*
Raquel Fernández

12:30–14:00   Lunch

14:00–14:45   *Invited Talk 4*
Yulia Tsvetkov

14:45–15:00   Outstanding Papers Spotlight Presentations

15:00–16:30   **Poster Session (including Coffee Break from 15:30-16:00) + Drinks Reception**

Deep Generalized Canonical Correlation Analysis
Adrian Benton, Huda Khayrallah, Biman Gujral, Dee Ann Reisinger, Sheng Zhang and Raman Arora

CBOW Is Not All You Need: Combining CBOW with the Compositional Matrix Space Model
Florian Mai, Lukas Galke and Ansgar Scherp

To Tune or Not to Tune? Adapting Pretrained Representations to Diverse Tasks
Matthew E. Peters, Sebastian Ruder and Noah A. Smith

Generative Adversarial Networks for Text Using Word2vec Intermediaries
Akshay Budhkar, Krishnapriya Vishnubhotla, Safwan Hossain and Frank Rudzicz

An Evaluation of Language-Agnostic Inner-Attention-Based Representations in Machine Translation
Alessandro Raganato, Raúl Vázquez, Mathias Creutz and Jörg Tiedemann

Multilingual NMT with a Language-Independent Attention Bridge
Raúl Vázquez, Alessandro Raganato, Jörg Tiedemann and Mathias Creutz

Efficient Language Modeling with Automatic Relevance Determination in Recurrent Neural Networks
Maxim Kodryan, Artem Grachev, Dmitry Ignatov and Dmitry Vetrov

MoRTy: Unsupervised Learning of Task-specialized Word Embeddings by Autoencoding
Nils Rethmeier and Barbara Plank

Pitfalls in the Evaluation of Sentence Embeddings
Steffen Eger, Andreas Rücklé and Iryna Gurevych

Learning Bilingual Sentence Embeddings via Autoencoding and Computing Similarities with a Multilayer Perceptron
Yunsu Kim, Hendrik Rosendahl, Nick Rossenbach, Jan Rosendahl, Shahram Khadivi and Hermann Ney

Specializing Distributional Vectors of All Words for Lexical Entailment
Aishwarya Kamath, Jonas Pfeiffer, Edoardo Maria Ponti, Goran Glavaš and Ivan Vulić

Deep Generalized Canonical Correlation Analysis

Adrian Benton[‡][*]   **Huda Khayrallah**[◇]   **Biman Gujral**[◇†]
Dee Ann Reisinger[◇]   **Sheng Zhang**[◇]   and   **Raman Arora**[◇]
[‡]Bloomberg LP
[◇]Johns Hopkins University
abenton10@bloomberg.net

Abstract

We present Deep Generalized Canonical Correlation Analysis (DGCCA) – a method for learning nonlinear transformations of arbitrarily many views of data, such that the resulting transformations are maximally informative of each other. While methods for nonlinear two-view representation learning (Deep CCA, (Andrew et al., 2013)) and linear many-view representation learning (Generalized CCA (Horst, 1961)) exist, DGCCA combines the flexibility of nonlinear (deep) representation learning with the statistical power of incorporating information from many sources, or views. We present the DGCCA formulation as well as an efficient stochastic optimization algorithm for solving it. We learn and evaluate DGCCA representations for three downstream tasks: phonetic transcription from acoustic & articulatory measurements, recommending hashtags, and recommending friends on a dataset of Twitter users.

1   Introduction

Multiview representation learning refers to settings where one has access to many "views" of data at train time. Views often correspond to different modalities about examples: a scene represented as a series of audio and image frames, a social media user characterized by the messages they post and who they friend, or a speech utterance and the configuration of the speaker's tongue. Multiview techniques learn a representation of data that captures the sources of variation common to all views.

Multiview representation techniques are attractive since a representation that is able to explain many views of the data is more likely to capture meaningful variation than a representation that is a good fit for only one of the views. These methods are often based on canonical correlation analysis (CCA), a classical statistical technique proposed by Hotelling (1936). CCA-based techniques cannot currently model nonlinear relationships between arbitrarily many views. Either they are able to model variation across many views, but can only learn linear mappings to the shared space (Horst, 1961), or they can learn nonlinear mappings, but they cannot be applied to data with more than two views using existing techniques based on Kernel CCA (Hardoon et al., 2004) and Deep CCA (Andrew et al., 2013).

We present Deep Generalized Canonical Correlation Analysis (DGCCA). DGCCA learns a shared representation from data with arbitrarily many views and simultaneously learns nonlinear mappings from each view to this shared space.Our main methodological contribution is the derivation of the gradient update for the Generalized Canonical Correlation Analysis (GCCA) objective (Horst, 1961).[1] We evaluate DGCCA-learned representations on three downstream tasks: (1) phonetic transcription from aligned speech & articulatory data, (2) Twitter hashtag and (3) friend recommendation from six text and network feature views. We find that features learned by DGCCA outperform linear multiview techniques on these tasks.

2   Prior Work

Some of the most successful techniques for multiview representation learning are based on canonical correlation analysis and its extension to the nonlinear and many view settings (Wang et al., 2015b,a).

---

[*] Work done while at Johns Hopkins University.
[†] Now at Google.

[1]See   https://bitbucket.org/adrianbenton/ dgcca-py3 for an implementation of DGCCA along with data from the synthetic experiments.

Proceedings of the 4th Workshop on Representation Learning for NLP (RepL4NLP-2019), pages 1–6
Florence, Italy, August 2, 2019. ©2019 Association for Computational Linguistics

Canonical correlation analysis (CCA) Canonical correlation analysis (CCA) (Hotelling, 1936) is a statistical method that finds maximally correlated linear projections of two random vectors. It is a fundamental multiview learning technique. Given two input views, $X_1 \in \mathbb{R}^{d_1}$ and $X_2 \in \mathbb{R}^{d_2}$, with covariance matrices, Σ_{11} and Σ_{22}, respectively, and cross-covariance matrix Σ_{12}, CCA finds directions that maximize the correlation between these two views:

$$(u_1^*, u_2^*) = \underset{u_1 \in \mathbb{R}^{d_1}, u_2 \in \mathbb{R}^{d_2}}{\operatorname{argmax}} \ corr(u_1^\top X_1, u_2^\top X_2)$$

Since this formulation is invariant to affine transformations of u_1 and u_2, we can write it as the following constrained optimization formulation:

$$(u_1^*, u_2^*) = \underset{u_1 \in \mathbb{R}^{d_1}, u_2 \in \mathbb{R}^{d_2}}{\operatorname{argmax}} \ u_1^\top \Sigma_{12} u_2 \quad (1)$$

such that $u_1^\top \Sigma_{11} u_1 = u_2^\top \Sigma_{22} u_2 = 1$. This technique has two limitations that have led to significant extensions: (1) it is limited to learning representations that are *linear* transformations of the data in each view, and (2) it can only leverage two input views.

Deep Canonical Correlation Analysis (DCCA) Deep CCA (DCCA) (Andrew et al., 2013) addresses the first limitation by finding maximally correlated *non-linear* transformations of two vectors. It passes each of the input views through neural networks and performs CCA on the outputs.

Let us use $f_1(X_1) = Z_1$ and $f_2(X_2) = Z_2$ to represent the network outputs. The weights, W_1 and W_2, of these networks are trained through standard backpropagation to maximize the CCA objective:

$$(u_1^*, u_2^*, W_1^*, W_2^*) = \underset{u_1, u_2}{\operatorname{argmax}} \ corr(u_1^\top Z_1, u_2^\top Z_2)$$

Generalized Canonical Correlation Analysis (GCCA) Generalized CCA (GCCA) (Horst, 1961) addresses the limitation on the number of views. It solves the optimization problem in Equation 2, finding a shared representation G of J different views, where N is the number of data points, d_j is the dimensionality of the jth view, r is the dimensionality of the learned representation, and $X_j \in \mathbb{R}^{d_j \times N}$ is the data matrix for the jth view.

$$\underset{U_j \in \mathbb{R}^{d_j \times r}, G \in \mathbb{R}^{r \times N}}{\operatorname{minimize}} \sum_{j=1}^{J} \|G - U_j^\top X_j\|_F^2 \quad (2)$$
$$\text{subject to} \quad GG^\top = I_r$$

Solving GCCA requires finding an eigendecomposition of an $N \times N$ matrix, which scales quadratically with sample size and leads to memory constraints.

Unlike CCA and DCCA, which only learn projections or transformations on each of the views, GCCA also learns a view-independent representation G that best reconstructs all of the view-specific representations simultaneously. The key limitation of GCCA is that it can only learn *linear* transformations of each view.

3 Deep Generalized Canonical Correlation Analysis (DGCCA)

We present Deep GCCA (DGCCA): a multiview representation learning technique that benefits from the expressive power of deep neural networks and can leverage statistical strength from more than two views. More fundamentally, Deep CCA and Deep GCCA have very different objectives and optimization problems, and it is not immediately clear how to extend deep CCA to more than two views.

DGCCA learns a nonlinear map for each view in order to maximize the correlation between the learned representations across views. In training, DGCCA passes the input vectors in each view through multiple layers of nonlinear transformations and backpropagates the gradient of the GCCA objective with respect to network parameters to tune each view's network. The objective is to train networks that reduce the GCCA reconstruction error among their outputs. New data can be projected by feeding each view through its respective network.

Problem Consider a dataset of J views and let $X_j \in \mathbb{R}^{d_j \times N}$ denote the jth input matrix. The network for the jth view consists of K_j layers. Assume, for simplicity, that each layer in the jth view network has c_j units with a final (output) layer of size o_j. The output of the kth layer for the jth view is $h_k^j = s(W_k^j h_{k-1}^j)$, where $s : \mathbb{R} \to \mathbb{R}$ is a nonlinear activation function and $W_k^j \in \mathbb{R}^{c_k \times c_{k-1}}$ is the weight matrix for the kth layer of the jth view network. We denote the output of the final layer as $f_j(X_j)$.

DGCCA can be expressed as the following optimization problem: find weight matrices $W^j = \{W_1^j, \ldots, W_{K_j}^j\}$ defining the functions f_j, and linear transformations U_j (of the output of the jth

network), for $j = 1, \ldots, J$, that

$$\operatorname*{minimize}_{U_j \in \mathbb{R}^{o_j \times r}, G \in \mathbb{R}^{r \times N}} \sum_{j=1}^{J} \| G - U_j^\top f_j(X_j) \|_F^2 \quad (3)$$

where $G \in \mathbb{R}^{r \times N}$ is the shared representation we are interested in learning, subject to $GG^\top = I_r$.

Optimization We solve the DGCCA optimization problem using stochastic gradient descent (SGD) with mini-batches. In particular, we estimate the gradient of the DGCCA objective in Equation 3 on a mini-batch of samples that is mapped through the network and use backpropagation to update the weight matrices, W^j's. Because DGCCA optimization is a constrained optimization problem, it is not immediately clear how to perform projected gradient descent with backpropagation. Instead, we characterize the objective function of the GCCA problem at an optimum and compute its gradient with respect to the inputs to GCCA (i.e. with respect to the network outputs), which are subsequently backpropagated through the network to update W^js.

Gradient Derivation The solution to the GCCA problem is given by solving an eigenvalue problem. In particular, define $C_{jj} = f(X_j)f(X_j)^\top \in \mathbb{R}^{o_j \times o_j}$, to be the scaled empirical covariance matrix of the jth network output, and $P_j = f(X_j)^\top C_{jj}^{-1} f(X_j) \in \mathbb{R}^{N \times N}$ to be the corresponding projection matrix that whitens the data; note that P_j is symmetric and idempotent. We define $M = \sum_{j=1}^{J} P_j$. Since each P_j is positive semi-definite, so is M. One can then check that the rows of G are the top r (orthonormal) eigenvectors of M, and $U_j = C_{jj}^{-1} f(X_j)G^\top$. Thus, at the minimum of the objective, we can rewrite the reconstruction error as follows:

$$\sum_{j=1}^{J} \| G - U_j^\top f_j(X_j) \|_F^2 = rJ - \operatorname{Tr}(GMG^\top)$$

Minimizing the GCCA objective (with respect to the weights of the neural networks) means maximizing $\operatorname{Tr}(GMG^\top)$, which is the sum of eigenvalues $L = \sum_{i=1}^{r} \lambda_i(M)$. Taking the derivative of L with respect to each output layer $f_j(X_j)$ gives:

$$\frac{\partial L}{\partial f_j(X_j)} = 2U_j G - 2U_j U_j^\top f_j(X_j)$$

Thus, the gradient is the difference between the r-dimensional auxiliary representation G embedded

Figure 1: Three synthetic views are displayed in the top row, and the bottom rows displays the matrix G learned by GCCA (left) and DGCCA (right).

into the subspace spanned by the columns of U_j (the first term) and the projection of the actual data in $f_j(X_j)$ onto said subspace (the second term).

4 Experiments

4.1 Synthetic Multiview Mixture Model

We apply DGCCA to a small synthetic data set to show how it preserves the generative structure of data sampled from a multiview mixture model. The three views of the data we use for this experiment are plotted in the top row of Figure 1. Points that share the same color across different views are sampled from the same mixture component.

Importantly, in each view, there is no linear transformation of the data that separates the two mixture components. This point is reinforced by Figure 1 (bottom left), which shows the two-dimensional representation G learned by applying linear GCCA to the data in plotted in the top row. The learned representation completely loses the structure of the data. In contrast, the representation G learned by DGCCA (bottom right) largely preserves the structure of the data, even after projection onto the first coordinate. In this case, the input neural networks for DGCCA had three hidden layers with ten units each, with randomly-initialized weights.

4.2 Phoneme Classification

We perform experiments on the University of Wisconsin X-ray Microbeam Database (XRMB) (Westbury, 1994), a collection of acoustic & articulatory recordings along with phonemic labels. We present phoneme classification results on the acoustic vectors projected using DCCA, GCCA, and DGCCA. Acoustic and articulatory data are set as the first two views and phoneme labels are set as the third view for GCCA and DGCCA, and

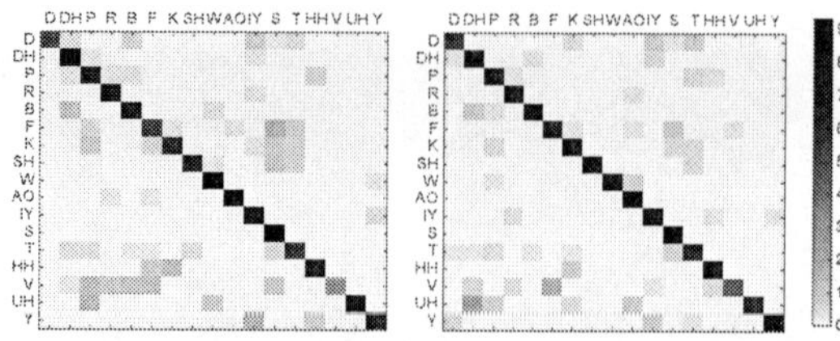

Figure 2: Confusion matrices over phonemes for speaker-dependent GCCA (left) and DGCCA (right).

Table 1: KNN phoneme classification performance.

| | CROSS-SPEAKER | | SPEAKER-DEPENDENT | |
| | DEV/TEST ACC | REC ERR | DEV/TEST ACC | REC ERR |
METHOD				
MFCC	48.9/49.3		66.3/66.2	
DCCA	45.4/46.1		65.9/65.8	
GCCA	49.6/50.2	40.7	69.5/69.8	40.4
DGCCA	**53.8/54.2**	**35.9**	**72.6/72.3**	**20.5**

K-nearest neighbor classification (Cover and Hart, 1967) is then run on the projected result.

Data We use the same split of the data as Arora and Livescu (2014). To limit experiment runtime, we use a subset of speakers for our experiments. We run a set of *cross-speaker* experiments using the male speaker JW11 for training and two splits of JW24 for tuning and testing. We also perform parameter tuning for the third view with 5-fold cross validation using a *single speaker*, JW11. For both experiments, we use acoustic and articulatory measurements as the two views in DCCA. Following the pre-processing in Andrew et al. (2013), we get 273 and 112 dimensional feature vectors for the first and second view respectively. Each speaker has ~50,000 frames. For the third view in GCCA and DGCCA, we use 39-dimensional one-hot vectors corresponding to the labels for each frame, following Arora and Livescu (2014).

Parameters We use a fixed network size and regularization for the first two views, each containing three hidden layers. Hidden layers for the acoustic view were all width 1024, and layers in the articulatory view all had width 512 units. L2 penalty constants of 0.0001 and 0.01 were placed on the acoustic and articulatory view networks, with 0.0005 on the label view. The output layer dimension of each network is set to 30 for DCCA and DGCCA. For the 5-fold speaker-dependent experiments, we performed a grid search for the network sizes in $\{128, 256, 512, 1024\}$ and covariance matrix regularization in $\{10^{-2}, 10^{-4}, 10^{-6}, 10^{-8}\}$ for the third view in each fold. We fix the hyperparameters for these experiments optimizing the networks with minibatch stochastic gradient descent with a step size of 0.005, and a batch size of 2,000.

Results DGCCA improves upon both the linear multiview GCCA and the non-linear 2-view DCCA for both the cross-speaker and speaker-dependent cross-validated tasks (Table 1). In addition to accuracy, we examine the reconstruction error (i.e. the objective in Equation 3) obtained from the objective in GCCA and DGCCA. The sharp improvement in reconstruction error shows that a non-linear algorithm can better model the data.

In this experimental setup, DCCA underperforms the baseline of simply running KNN on the original acoustic view. Prior work considered the output of DCCA stacked on to the central frame of the original acoustic view (39 dimensions). This poor performance, in the absence of original features, indicates that it was not able to find a more informative projection than original acoustic features based on correlation with the articulatory view within the first 30 dimensions.

To highlight the improvements of DGCCA over GCCA, Figure 2 presents a subset of the the confusion matrices on speaker-dependent test data. We observe large improvements in the classification of D, F, K, SH, V and Y. For instance, DGCCA rectifies the frequent misclassification of V as P, R and B by GCCA. In addition, commonly incorrect classification of phonemes such as S and T is corrected by DGCCA, which enables better performance on other voiceless consonants such as like F, K and SH. Vowels are classified with almost equal accuracy by both the methods.

4.3 Hashtag & Friend Recommendation

Linear multiview techniques are effective at recommending hashtag and friends for Twitter users (Benton et al., 2016). In this experiment, six views of a Twitter user were constructed by applying principal component analysis (PCA) to the bag-of-words representations of (1) tweets posted by the ego user, (2) other mentioned users, (3) their friends, and (4) their followers, as well as one-hot encodings of the local (5) friend and (6) follower networks. We learn and evaluate DGCCA models on identical training, development, and test sets as Benton et al. (2016), and evaluate

Table 2: Dev/test performance at Twitter friend and hashtag recommendation tasks.

	FRIEND		HASHTAG	
ALGORITHM	P@1K	R@1K	P@1K	R@1K
PCA[T+N]	**.445/.439**	**.149/.147**	.011/.008	.312/.290
GCCA[T]	.244/.249	.080/.081	.012/.009	.351/.326
GCCA[T+N]	.271/.276	.088/.089	**.012/.010**	.359/.334
DGCCA[T+N]	.297/.268	.099/.090	**.013/.010**	**.385/.373**
WGCCA[T]	.269/.279	.089/.091	.012/.009	.357/.325
WGCCA[T+N]	.376/.364	.123/.120	.013/.009	.360/.346

the DGCCA representations on macro precision at 1,000 (P@1K) and recall at 1,000 (R@1K) for the hashtag and friend recommendation tasks described there.

We trained 40 different DGCCA model architectures, each with identical network architectures across views, where the width of the hidden and output layers, c_1 and c_2, for each view are drawn uniformly from $[10, 1000]$, and the auxiliary representation width r is drawn uniformly from $[10, c_2]$.[2] All networks used rectified linear units in the hidden layer, and were optimized with Adam (Kingma and Ba, 2014) for 200 epochs. Networks were trained on 90% of 102,328 Twitter users, with 10% of users used as a tuning set to estimate held-out reconstruction error for model selection. We report development and test results for the best performing model on the downstream task development set. The learning rate was set to 10^{-4} with regularization of $\ell_1 = 10^{-2}$, $\ell_2 = 10^{-4}$.

Table 2 displays the precision and recall at 1000 recommendations of DGCCA compared to PCA[T+N] (PCA applied to concatenation of text and network view feature vectors), linear GCCA applied to the four text views *[T]*, and all text and network views *[T+N]*, along with a GCCA variant with discriminative view weighting (WGCCA). We learned PCA, GCCA, and WGCCA representations of width $r \in [10, 1000]$, and select embeddings based on development set R@1K.

There are several points to note: First is that DGCCA outperforms linear methods at hashtag recommendation by a wide margin in terms of recall. This is exciting because this task was shown to benefit from incorporating more than just two views from Twitter users. These results suggest that a nonlinear transformation of the in-

put views can yield additional gains in performance. In addition, WGCCA models sweep over every possible weighting of views with weights in $\{0, 0.25, 1.0\}$. The fact that DGCCA is able to outperform WGCCA at hashtag recommendation is encouraging, since WGCCA has much more freedom to discard uninformative views. As noted in Benton et al. (2016), only the friend network view was useful for learning representations for friend recommendation (corroborated by performance of PCA applied to friend network view), so it is unsurprising that DGCCA, when applied to all views, cannot compete with WGCCA representations learned on the single useful friend network view.

5 Discussion

There has also been strong work outside of CCA-related methods to combine nonlinear representation and learning from multiple views. Kumar et al. (2011) outlines two main approaches to learn a joint representation from many views: either by (1) explicitly maximizing similarity/correlation between view pairs (Masci et al., 2014; Rajendran et al., 2015) or by (2) alternately optimizing a shared, "consensus" representation and view-specific transformations (Kumar et al., 2011; Xiaowen, 2014; Sharma et al., 2012). Unlike the first class of methods, the complexity of solving DGCCA does not scale quadratically with number of views, nor does it require a privileged pivot view (G is learned). Unlike methods that estimate a "consensus" representation, DGCCA admits a globally optimal solution for both the view-specific projections $U_1 \ldots U_J$, and the shared representation G. Local optima arise in the DGCCA objective only because we are also learning nonlinear transformations of the input views.

We present DGCCA, a method for non-linear multiview representation learning from an arbitrary number of views. We show that DGCCA clearly outperforms prior work in phoneme recognition when using labels as a third view, and can successfully exploit multiple views to learn Twitter user representations useful for downstream tasks, such as hashtag recommendation. To date, CCA-style multiview learning techniques were either restricted to learning representations from no more than two views, or strictly linear transformations of the input views. This work overcomes these limitations.

---

[2]We only consider architectures with single-hidden-layer networks identical across views so as to avoid a fishing expedition. If DGCCA is an appropriate method for learning Twitter user embeddings, then it should require little architecture exploration.

References

Galen Andrew, Raman Arora, Jeff Bilmes, and Karen Livescu. 2013. Deep canonical correlation analysis. In *Proceedings of the 30th International Conference on Machine Learning*, pages 1247–1255.

Raman Arora and Karen Livescu. 2014. Multi-view learning with supervision for transformed bottleneck features. In *Acoustics, Speech and Signal Processing (ICASSP), 2014 IEEE International Conference on*, pages 2499–2503. IEEE.

Adrian Benton, Raman Arora, and Mark Dredze. 2016. Learning multiview embeddings of twitter users. In *The 54th Annual Meeting of the Association for Computational Linguistics*, page 14.

Thomas M Cover and Peter E Hart. 1967. Nearest neighbor pattern classification. *Information Theory, IEEE Transactions on*, 13(1):21–27.

David R Hardoon, Sandor Szedmak, and John Shawe-Taylor. 2004. Canonical correlation analysis: An overview with application to learning methods. *Neural computation*, 16(12):2639–2664.

Paul Horst. 1961. Generalized canonical correlations and their applications to experimental data. *Journal of Clinical Psychology*, 17(4).

Harold Hotelling. 1936. Relations between two sets of variates. *Biometrika*, pages 321–377.

Diederik Kingma and Jimmy Ba. 2014. Adam: A method for stochastic optimization. *arXiv preprint arXiv:1412.6980*.

Abhishek Kumar, Piyush Rai, and Hal Daume. 2011. Co-regularized multi-view spectral clustering. In *Advances in neural information processing systems*, pages 1413–1421.

Jonathan Masci, Michael M Bronstein, Alexander M Bronstein, and Jürgen Schmidhuber. 2014. Multimodal similarity-preserving hashing. *IEEE transactions on pattern analysis and machine intelligence*, 36(4):824–830.

Janarthanan Rajendran, Mitesh M Khapra, Sarath Chandar, and Balaraman Ravindran. 2015. Bridge correlational neural networks for multilingual multimodal representation learning. *arXiv preprint arXiv:1510.03519*.

Abhishek Sharma, Abhishek Kumar, Hal Daume, and David W Jacobs. 2012. Generalized multiview analysis: A discriminative latent space. In *Computer Vision and Pattern Recognition (CVPR), 2012 IEEE Conference on*, pages 2160–2167. IEEE.

Weiran Wang, Raman Arora, Karen Livescu, and Jeff Bilmes. 2015a. On deep multi-view representation learning. In *Proc. of the 32nd Int. Conf. Machine Learning (ICML 2015)*.

Weiran Wang, Raman Arora, Karen Livescu, and Jeff Bilmes. 2015b. Unsupervised learning of acoustic features via deep canonical correlation analysis. In *Proc. of the IEEE Int. Conf. Acoustics, Speech and Sig. Proc. (ICASSP'15)*.

John R. Westbury. 1994. X-ray microbeam speech production database user's handbook. In *Waisman Center on Mental Retardation & Human Development University of Wisconsin Madison, WI 53705-2280*.

Dong Xiaowen. 2014. *Multi-View Signal Processing and Learning on Graphs*. Ph.D. thesis, École Polytechnique Fédérale de Lausanne.

To Tune or Not to Tune?
Adapting Pretrained Representations to Diverse Tasks

Matthew E. Peters[1,]* Sebastian Ruder[2,3][†,]* and Noah A. Smith[1,4]

[1]Allen Institute for Artificial Intelligence, Seattle, USA
[2]Insight Research Centre, National University of Ireland, Galway, Ireland
[3]Aylien Ltd., Dublin, Ireland
[4]Paul G. Allen School of CSE, University of Washington, Seattle, USA
{matthewp,noah}@allenai.org, sebastian@ruder.io

Abstract

While most previous work has focused on different pretraining objectives and architectures for transfer learning, we ask how to best adapt the pretrained model to a given target task. We focus on the two most common forms of adaptation, feature extraction (where the pretrained weights are frozen), and directly fine-tuning the pretrained model. Our empirical results across diverse NLP tasks with two state-of-the-art models show that the relative performance of fine-tuning vs. feature extraction depends on the similarity of the pretraining and target tasks. We explore possible explanations for this finding and provide a set of adaptation guidelines for the NLP practitioner.

1 Introduction

Sequential inductive transfer learning (Pan and Yang, 2010; Ruder, 2019) consists of two stages: *pretraining*, in which the model learns a general-purpose representation of inputs, and *adaptation*, in which the representation is transferred to a new task. Most previous work in NLP has focused on pretraining objectives for learning word or sentence representations (Mikolov et al., 2013; Kiros et al., 2015).

Few works, however, have focused on the adaptation phase. There are two main paradigms for adaptation: *feature extraction* and *fine-tuning*. In feature extraction (❄) the model's weights are 'frozen' and the pretrained representations are used in a downstream model similar to classic feature-based approaches (Koehn et al., 2003). Alternatively, a pretrained model's parameters can be unfrozen and fine-tuned (🔥) on a new task (Dai and Le, 2015). Both have benefits: ❄ enables use of task-specific model architectures and may be

---

*The first two authors contributed equally.
†Sebastian is now affiliated with DeepMind.

Conditions			Guidelines
Pretrain	Adapt.	Task	
Any	❄	Any	Add many task parameters
Any	🔥	Any	Add minimal task parameters, 🔥 Hyper-parameters
Any	Any	Seq. / clas.	❄ and 🔥 have similar performance
ELMo	Any	Sent. pair	use ❄
BERT	Any	Sent. pair	use 🔥

Table 1: This paper's guidelines for using feature extraction (❄) and fine-tuning (🔥) with ELMo and BERT. Seq.: sequence labeling. Clas.: classification. Sent. pair: sentence pair tasks.

computationally cheaper as features only need to be computed once. On the other hand, 🔥 is convenient as it may allow us to adapt a general-purpose representation to many different tasks.

Gaining a better understanding of the adaptation phase is key in making the most use out of pretrained representations. To this end, we compare two state-of-the-art pretrained models, ELMo (Peters et al., 2018) and BERT (Devlin et al., 2018) using both ❄ and 🔥 across seven diverse tasks including named entity recognition, natural language inference (NLI), and paraphrase detection. We seek to characterize the conditions under which one approach substantially outperforms the other, and whether it is dependent on the pretraining objective or target task. We find that ❄ and 🔥 have comparable performance in most cases, except when the source and target tasks are either highly similar or highly dissimilar. We furthermore shed light on the practical challenges of adaptation and provide a set of guidelines to the NLP practitioner, as summarized in Table 1.

2 Pretraining and Adaptation

In this work, we focus on pretraining tasks that seek to induce *universal* representations suitable for any downstream task.

Proceedings of the 4th Workshop on Representation Learning for NLP (RepL4NLP-2019), pages 7–14
Florence, Italy, August 2, 2019. ©2019 Association for Computational Linguistics

Word representations Pretrained word vectors (Turian et al., 2010; Pennington et al., 2014) have been an essential component in state-of-the-art NLP systems. Word representations are often fixed and fed into a task specific model (❄), although 🔥 can provide improvements (Kim, 2014). Recently, contextual word representations learned supervisedly (e.g., through MT; McCann et al., 2017) or unsupervisedly (typically through language modeling; Peters et al., 2018) have significantly improved over noncontextual vectors.

Sentence embedding methods Such methods learn sentence representations via different pretraining objectives such as previous/next sentence prediction (Kiros et al., 2015; Logeswaran and Lee, 2018), NLI (Conneau et al., 2017), or a combination of objectives (Subramanian et al., 2018). During the adaptation phase, the sentence representation is typically provided as input to a linear classifier (❄). LM pretraining with 🔥 has also been successfully applied to sentence-level tasks. Howard and Ruder (2018, ULMFiT) propose techniques for fine-tuning a LM, including triangular learning rate schedules and discriminative fine-tuning, which uses lower learning rates for lower layers. Radford et al. (2018) extend LM-🔥 to additional sentence and sentence-pair tasks.

Masked LM and next-sentence prediction BERT (Devlin et al., 2018) combines both word and sentence representations (via masked LM and next sentence prediction objectives) in a single very large pretrained transformer (Vaswani et al., 2017). It is adapted to both word and sentence level tasks by 🔥 with task-specific layers.

3 Experimental Setup

We compare ELMo and BERT as representatives of the two best-performing pretraining settings. This section provides an overview of our methods; see the supplement for full details.

3.1 Target Tasks and Datasets

We evaluate on a diverse set of target tasks: named entity recognition (NER), sentiment analysis (SA), and three sentence pair tasks, natural language inference (NLI), paraphrase detection (PD), and semantic textual similarity (STS).

NER We use the CoNLL 2003 dataset (Sang and Meulder, 2003), which provides token level annotations of newswire across four different entity types (`PER`, `LOC`, `ORG`, `MISC`).

SA We use the binary version of the Stanford Sentiment Treebank (SST-2; Socher et al., 2013), providing sentiment labels (`negative` or `positive`) for sentences of movie reviews.

NLI We use both the broad-domain MultiNLI dataset (Williams et al., 2018) and Sentences Involving Compositional Knowledge (SICK-E; Marelli et al., 2014).

PD For paraphrase detection (i.e., decide whether two sentences are semantically equivalent), we use the Microsoft Research Paraphrase Corpus (MRPC; Dolan and Brockett, 2005).

STS We employ the Semantic Textual Similarity Benchmark (STS-B; Cer et al., 2017) and SICK-R (Marelli et al., 2014). Both datasets provide a similarity value from 1 to 5 for each sentence pair.

3.2 Adaptation

We now describe how we adapt ELMo and BERT to these tasks. For ❄ we require a task-specific architecture, while for 🔥 we need a task-specific output layer. For fair comparison, we conduct an extensive hyper-parameter search for each task.

Feature extraction (❄) For both ELMo and BERT, we extract contextual representations of the words from all layers. During adaptation, we learn a linear weighted combination of the layers (Peters et al., 2018) which is used as input to a task-specific model. When extracting features, it is important to expose the internal layers as they typically encode the most transferable representations. For SA, we employ a bi-attentive classification network (McCann et al., 2017). For the sentence pair tasks, we use the ESIM model (Chen et al., 2017). For NER, we use a BiLSTM with a CRF layer (Lafferty et al., 2001; Lample et al., 2016).

Fine-tuning (🔥): ELMo We max-pool over the LM states and add a softmax layer for text classification. For the sentence pair tasks, we compute cross-sentence bi-attention between the LM states (Chen et al., 2017), apply a pooling operation, then add a softmax layer. For NER, we add a CRF layer on top of the LSTM states.

Fine-tuning (🔥): BERT We feed the sentence representation into a softmax layer for text classification and sentence pair tasks following Devlin

Pretraining	Adaptation	NER CoNLL 2003	SA SST-2	Nat. lang. inference		Semantic textual similarity		
				MNLI	SICK-E	SICK-R	MRPC	STS-B
Skip-thoughts	❄	-	81.8	62.9	-	86.6	75.8	71.8
ELMo	❄	91.7	**91.8**	**79.6**	**86.3**	**86.1**	**76.0**	**75.9**
	🔥	**91.9**	91.2	76.4	83.3	83.3	74.7	75.5
	Δ=🔥-❄	0.2	-0.6	-3.2	-3.3	-2.8	-1.3	-0.4
BERT-base	❄	92.2	93.0	**84.6**	84.8	86.4	78.1	82.9
	🔥	**92.4**	**93.5**	**84.6**	**85.8**	**88.7**	**84.8**	**87.1**
	Δ=🔥-❄	0.2	0.5	0.0	1.0	2.3	6.7	4.2

Table 2: Test set performance of feature extraction (❄) and fine-tuning (🔥) approaches for ELMo and BERT-base compared to one sentence embedding method. Settings that are good for 🔥 are colored in red (Δ=🔥-❄ > 1.0); settings good for ❄ are colored in blue (Δ=🔥-❄ < -1.0). Numbers for baseline methods are from respective papers, except for SST-2, MNLI, and STS-B results, which are from Wang et al. (2018). BERT fine-tuning results (except on SICK) are from Devlin et al. (2018). The metric varies across tasks (higher is always better): accuracy for SST-2, SICK-E, and MRPC; matched accuracy for MultiNLI; Pearson correlation for STS-B and SICK-R; and span F_1 for CoNLL 2003. For CoNLL 2003, we report the mean with five seeds; standard deviation is about 0.2%.

et al. (2018). For NER, we extract the representation of the first word piece for each token and add a softmax layer.

4 Results

We show results in Table 2 comparing ELMo and BERT for both ❄ and 🔥 approaches across the seven tasks against with Skip-thoughts (Kiros et al., 2015), which employs a next-sentence prediction objective similar to BERT.

Both ELMo and BERT outperform the sentence embedding method significantly, except on the semantic textual similarity tasks (STS) where Skip-thoughts is similar to ELMo. The overall performance of ❄ and 🔥 shows small differences except for a few notable cases. For ELMo, we find the largest differences for sentence pair tasks where ❄ consistently outperforms 🔥. For BERT, we obtain nearly the opposite result: 🔥 significantly outperforms ❄ on all STS tasks, with much smaller differences for the others.

Discussion Past work in NLP (Mou et al., 2016) showed that similar pretraining tasks transfer better.[1] In computer vision (CV), Yosinski et al. (2014) similarly found that the transferability of features decreases as the distance between the pretraining and target task increases. In this vein, Skip-thoughts—and Quick-thoughts (Logeswaran and Lee, 2018), which has similar performance— which use a next-sentence prediction objective similar to BERT, perform particularly well on STS tasks, indicating a close alignment between the pretraining and target task. This strong alignment also seems to be the reason for BERT's strong relative performance on these tasks.

In CV, 🔥 generally outperforms ❄ when transferring from ImageNet supervised classification pretraining to other classification tasks (Kornblith et al., 2018). Recent results suggest 🔥 is less useful for more distant target tasks such as semantic segmentation (He et al., 2018). This is in line with our results, which show strong performance with 🔥 between closely aligned tasks (next-sentence prediction in BERT and STS tasks) and poor performance for more distant tasks (LM in ELMo and sentence pair tasks). Confounding factors may be the suitability of the inductive bias of the model architecture for sentence pair tasks and ❄'s potentially increased flexibility due to a larger number of parameters, which we will both analyze next.

5 Analyses

Modelling pairwise interactions LSTMs consider each token sequentially, while Transformers can relate each token to every other in each layer (Vaswani et al., 2017). This might facilitate 🔥 with Transformers on sentence pair tasks, on which ELMo-🔥 performs comparatively poorly. We additionally compare different ways of encoding the sentence pair with ELMo and BERT. For ELMo, we compare encoding with and without cross-sentence bi-attention in Table 3. When

---

[1] Mou et al. (2016), however, only investigate transfer between classification tasks (NLI → SICK-E/MRPC).

	SICK-E	SICK-R	STS-B	MRPC
ELMo-🔥 +bi-attn.	83.8	84.0	80.2	77.0
w/o bi-attn.	70.9	51.8	38.5	72.3

Table 3: Comparison of ELMO-🔥 cross-sentence embedding methods on dev. sets of sentence pair tasks.

	SICK-E	SICK-R	STS-B	MRPC
BERT-❄, joint enc.	**85.5**	86.4	**88.1**	**83.3**
separate encoding	81.2	**86.8**	86.8	81.4

Table 4: Comparison of BERT-❄ cross-sentence embedding methods on dev. sets of sentence pair tasks.

Model configuration	F_1
❄ + BiLSTM + CRF	**95.5**
❄ + CRF	91.9
🔥 + CRF + gradual unfreeze	**95.5**
🔥 + BiLSTM + CRF + gradual unfreeze	95.2
🔥 + CRF	95.1

Table 5: Comparison of CoNLL 2003 NER development set performance (F_1) for ELMo for both feature extraction and fine-tuning. All results averaged over five random seeds.

	TE	GO	TR	FI	SL
BERT-❄	84.4	86.7	86.1	84.5	80.9
Δ=🔥-❄	-1.1	-0.2	-0.6	0.4	-0.6
JS div	0.21	0.18	0.14	0.09	0.09

Table 6: Accuracy of feature extraction (❄) and difference compared to fine-tuning (🔥) with BERT-base trained on training data of different MNLI domains and evaluated on corresponding dev sets. TE: telephone. FI: fiction. TR: travel. GO: government. SL: slate.

adapting the ELMo LSTM to a sentence pair task, modeling the sentence interactions by fine-tuning through the bi-attention mechanism provides the best performance.[2] This provides further evidence that the LSTM has difficulty modeling the pairwise interactions during sequential processing—in contrast to a Transformer LM that can be fine-tuned in this manner (Radford et al., 2018).

For BERT-❄, we compare joint encoding of the sentence pair with encoding the sentences separately in Table 4. The latter reduces performance, which shows that BERT representations encode cross-sentence relationships and are therefore particularly well-suited for sentence pair tasks.

Impact of additional parameters We evaluate whether adding parameters is useful for both adaptation settings on NER. We add a CRF layer (as used in 🔥) and a BiLSTM with a CRF layer (as used in ❄) to both and show results in Table 5. We find that additional parameters are key for ❄, but hurt performance with 🔥.[3] In addition, 🔥 requires gradual unfreezing (Howard and Ruder, 2018) to match performance of feature extraction.

ELMo fine-tuning We found fine-tuning the ELMo LSTM to be initially difficult and required careful hyper-parameter tuning. Once tuned for one task, other tasks have similar hyper-parameters. Our best models used slanted triangular learning rates and discriminative fine-tuning (Howard and Ruder, 2018) and in some cases gradual unfreezing.

Impact of Target Domain Pretrained language model representations are intended to be universal. However, the target domain might still impact the adaptation performance. We calculate the Jensen-Shannon divergence based on term distributions (Ruder and Plank, 2017) between the domains used to train BERT (books and Wikipedia) and each MNLI domain. We show results in Table 6. We find no significant correlation. At least for this task, the distance of the source and target domains does not seem to have a major impact on the adaptation performance.

Representations at different layers In addition, we are interested how the information in the different layers of the models develops over the course of fine-tuning. We measure this information in two ways: a) with diagnostic classifiers (Adi et al., 2017); and b) with mutual information (MI; Noshad et al., 2018). Both methods allow us to associate the hidden activations of our model with a linguistic property. In both cases, we use the mean of the hidden activations of BERT-base[4] of each token / word piece of the sequence(s) as

---

[2]This is similar to text classification tasks, where we find max-pooling to outperform using the final hidden state, similar to (Howard and Ruder, 2018).

[3] 🔥 in fact optimizes a larger number of parameters than ❄, so a reduced expressiveness does not explain why it underperforms 🔥 on dissimilar settings.

[4]We show results for BERT as they are more inspectable due to the model having more layers. Trends for ELMo are similar.

the representation.[5]

With diagnostic classifiers, for each example, we extract the pretrained and fine-tuned representation at each layer as features. We use these features as input to train a logistic regression model (linear regression for STS-B, which has real-valued outputs) on the training data of two single sentence (CoLA[6] and SST-2) and two pair sentence tasks (MRPC and STS-B). We show its performance on the corresponding dev sets in Figure 1.

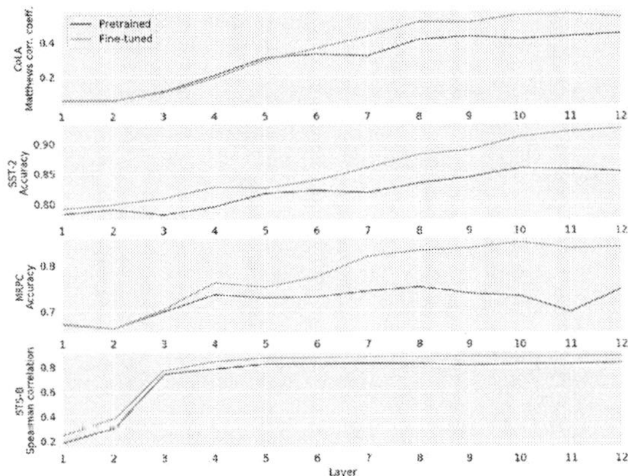

Figure 1: Performance of diagnostic classifiers trained on pretrained and fine-tuned BERT representations at different layers on the dev sets of the corresponding tasks.

For all tasks, diagnostic classifier performance generally is higher in higher layers of the model. Fine-tuning improves the performance of the diagnostic classifier at every layer. For the single sentence classification tasks CoLA and SST-2, pretrained performance increases gradually until the last layers. In contrast, for the sentence pair tasks MRPC and STS-B performance is mostly flat after the fourth layer. Relevant information for sentence pair tasks thus does not seem to be concentrated primarily in the upper layers of pretrained representations, which could explain why fine-tuning is particularly useful in these scenarios.

Computing the mutual information with regard to representations of deep neural networks has only become feasible recently with the development of more sophisticated MI estimators. In our experiments, we use the state-of-the-art ensemble dependency graph estimator (EDGE; Noshad et al., 2018) with default hyper-parameter values. As a sanity check, we compute the MI between hidden activations and random labels and random representations and random labels, which yields 0 in every case as we would expect.[7]

We show the mutual information $I(H; Y)$ between the pretrained and fine-tuned mean hidden activations H at each layer of BERT and the output labels Y on the dev sets of CoLA, SST-2, and MRPC in Figure 2.

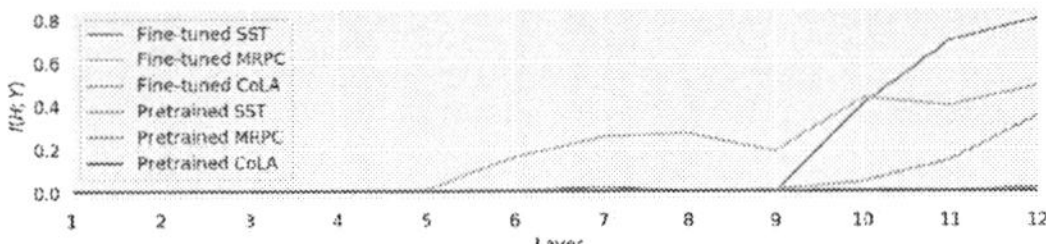

Figure 2: The mutual information between fine-tuned and pretrained mean BERT representations at different layers and the labels on the dev set of the corresponding tasks.

The MI between pretrained representations and labels is close to 0 across all tasks and layers, except for SST. In contrast, fine-tuned representations display much higher MI values. The MI for fine-tuned representations rises gradually through the intermediate and last layers for the sentence pair task MRPC, while for the single sentence classification tasks, the MI rises sharply in the last layers. Similar to our findings with diagnostic classifiers, knowledge for single sentence classification tasks thus seems mostly concentrated in the last layers, while pair sentence classification tasks gradually build up information in the intermediate and last layers of the model.

6 Conclusion

We have empirically analyzed fine-tuning and feature extraction approaches across diverse datasets, finding that the relative performance depends on the similarity of the pretraining and target tasks. We have explored possible explanations and provided practical recommendations for adapting pretrained representations to NLP practicioners.

---

[5]We observed similar results when using max-pooling or the representation of the first token.

[6]The Corpus of Linguistic Acceptability (CoLA; Warstadt et al., 2018) consists of examples of expert English sentence acceptability judgments drawn from 22 books and journal articles on linguistic theory. It uses the Matthews correlation coefficient (Matthews, 1975) for evaluation and is available at: nyu-mll.github.io/CoLA

[7]For the same settings, we obtain non-zero values with earlier estimators (Saxe et al., 2018), which seem to be less reliable for higher numbers of dimensions.

References

Yossi Adi, Einat Kermany, Yonatan Belinkov, Ofer Lavi, and Yoav Goldberg. 2017. Fine-grained analysis of sentence embeddings using auxiliary prediction tasks. In *Proceedings of ICLR*.

Daniel M. Cer, Mona T. Diab, Eneko Agirre, Iñigo Lopez-Gazpio, and Lucia Specia. 2017. Semeval-2017 task 1: Semantic textual similarity multilingual and crosslingual focused evaluation. In *Proceedings of SemEval*.

Qian Chen, Xiaodan Zhu, Zhenhua Ling, Si Wei, Hui Jiang, and Diana Inkpen. 2017. Enhanced LSTM for natural language inference. In *Proceedings of ACL*.

Alexis Conneau, Douwe Kiela, Holger Schwenk, Loïc Barrault, and Antoine Bordes. 2017. Supervised learning of universal sentence representations from natural language inference data. In *Proceedings of EMNLP*.

Andrew M. Dai and Quoc V. Le. 2015. Semi-supervised sequence learning. In *NIPS*.

Jacob Devlin, Ming-Wei Chang, Kenton Lee, and Kristina Toutanova. 2018. BERT: Pre-training of deep bidirectional transformers for language understanding. In *Proceedings of NAACL*.

William B. Dolan and Chris Brockett. 2005. Automatically constructing a corpus of sentential paraphrases. In *Proceedings of the Third International Workshop on Paraphrasing*.

Matt Gardner, Joel Grus, Mark Neumann, Oyvind Tafjord, Pradeep Dasigi, Nelson F. Liu, Matthew Peters, Michael Schmitz, and Luke S. Zettlemoyer. 2017. AllenNLP: A deep semantic natural language processing platform.

Kaiming He, Ross Girshick, and Piotr Dollár. 2018. Rethinking ImageNet pre-training. *arXiv preprint arXiv:1811.08883*.

Jeremy Howard and Sebastian Ruder. 2018. Universal language model fine-tuning for text classification. In *Proceedings of ACL*.

Yoon Kim. 2014. Convolutional neural networks for sentence classification. *Proceedings of EMNLP*, pages 1746–1751.

Diederik P. Kingma and Jimmy Ba. 2015. Adam: A method for stochastic optimization. In *Proceedings of ICLR*.

Ryan Kiros, Yukun Zhu, Ruslan Salakhutdinov, Richard S. Zemel, Antonio Torralba, Raquel Urtasun, and Sanja Fidler. 2015. Skip-thought vectors. In *NIPS*.

Philipp Koehn, Franz Josef Och, and Daniel Marcu. 2003. Statistical phrase-based translation. In *Proceedings of NAACL*.

Simon Kornblith, Jonathon Shlens, Quoc V Le, and Google Brain. 2018. Do better ImageNet models transfer better? *arXiv preprint arXiv:1805.08974*.

John D. Lafferty, Andrew McCallum, and Fernando Pereira. 2001. Conditional random fields: Probabilistic models for segmenting and labeling sequence data. In *Proceedings of ICML*.

Guillaume Lample, Miguel Ballesteros, Sandeep Subramanian, Kazuya Kawakami, and Chris Dyer. 2016. Neural architectures for named entity recognition. In *Proceedings of NAACL-HLT*.

Lajanugen Logeswaran and Honglak Lee. 2018. An efficient framework for learning sentence representations. In *Proceedings of ICLR*.

Ilya Loshchilov and Frank Hutter. 2017. Fixing weight decay regularization in Adam. *CoRR*, abs/1711.05101.

Marco Marelli, Stefano Menini, Marco Baroni, Luisa Bentivogli, Raffaella Bernardi, Roberto Zamparelli, et al. 2014. A SICK cure for the evaluation of compositional distributional semantic models. In *Proceedings of LREC*.

Brian W. Matthews. 1975. Comparison of the predicted and observed secondary structure of t4 phage lysozyme. *Biochimica et Biophysica Acta (BBA)-Protein Structure*, 405(2):442–451.

Bryan McCann, James Bradbury, Caiming Xiong, and Richard Socher. 2017. Learned in translation: Contextualized word vectors. In *NIPS*.

Tomas Mikolov, Ilya Sutskever, Kai Chen, Greg S Corrado, and Jeff Dean. 2013. Distributed representations of words and phrases and their compositionality. In *NIPS*.

Lili Mou, Zhao Meng, Rui Yan, Ge Li, Yan Xu, Lu Zhang, and Zhi Jin. 2016. How transferable are neural networks in NLP applications? *Proceedings EMNLP*.

Morteza Noshad, Yu Zeng, and Alfred O. Hero III. 2018. Scalable mutual information estimation using dependence graphs. *arXiv preprint arXiv:1801.09125*.

Sinno Jialin Pan and Qiang Yang. 2010. A survey on transfer learning. *IEEE Transactions on Knowledge and Data Engineering*, 22(10):1345–1359.

Jeffrey Pennington, Richard Socher, and Christopher D. Manning. 2014. GloVe: Global vectors for word representation. In *Proceedings of EMNLP*.

Matthew E. Peters, Mark Neumann, Mohit Iyyer, Matt Gardner, Christopher Clark, Kenton Lee, and Luke Zettlemoyer. 2018. Deep contextualized word representations. In *Proceedings of NAACL-HLT*.

Alec Radford, Karthik Narasimhan, Tim Salimans, and Ilya Sutskever. 2018. Improving language understanding by generative pre-training.

Sebastian Ruder. 2019. *Neural Transfer Learning for Natural Language Processing*. Ph.D. thesis, National University of Ireland, Galway.

Sebastian Ruder and Barbara Plank. 2017. Learning to select data for transfer learning with Bayesian optimization. In *Proceedings EMNLP*.

Erik F. Tjong Kim Sang and Fien De Meulder. 2003. Introduction to the CoNLL-2003 shared task: Language-independent named entity recognition. In *Proceedings of CoNLL*.

Andrew M Saxe, Yamini Bansal, Joel Dapello, Madhu Advani, Artemy Kolchinsky, Brendan D Tracey, and David D Cox. 2018. On the Information Bottleneck Theory of Deep Learning. In *Proceedings of ICLR 2018*.

Richard Socher, Alex Perelygin, Jean Y. Wu, Jason Chuang, Christopher D. Manning, Andrew Y. Ng, and Christopher Potts. 2013. Recursive deep models for semantic compositionality over a sentiment treebank. In *Proceedings of EMNLP*.

Sandeep Subramanian, Adam Trischler, Yoshua Bengio, and Christopher J Pal. 2018. Learning general purpose distributed sentence representations via large scale multi-task learning. In *Proceedings of ICLR*.

Joseph P. Turian, Lev-Arie Ratinov, and Yoshua Bengio. 2010. Word representations: A simple and general method for semi-supervised learning. In *Proceedings of ACL*.

Ashish Vaswani, Noam Shazeer, Niki Parmar, Jakob Uszkoreit, Llion Jones, Aidan N. Gomez, Lukasz Kaiser, and Illia Polosukhin. 2017. Attention is all you need. In *NIPS*.

Alex Wang, Amanpreet Singh, Julian Michael, Felix Hill, Omer Levy, and Samuel R. Bowman. 2018. GLUE: A multi-task benchmark and analysis platform for natural language understanding.

Alex Warstadt, Amanpreet Singh, and Samuel R Bowman. 2018. Neural network acceptability judgments. *arXiv preprint arXiv:1805.12471*.

Adina Williams, Nikita Nangia, and Samuel Bowman. 2018. A broad-coverage challenge corpus for sentence understanding through inference. In *Proceedings of NAACL*.

Jason Yosinski, Jeff Clune, Yoshua Bengio, and Hod Lipson. 2014. How transferable are features in deep neural networks? In *NIPS*.

A Experimental Details

For fair comparison, all experiments include extensive hyper-parameter tuning. We tuned the learning rate, dropout ratio, weight decay and number of training epochs. In addition, the fine-tuning experiments also examined the impact of triangular learning rate schedules, gradual unfreezing, and discriminative learning rates. Hyperparameters were tuned on the development sets and the best setting evaluated on the test sets.

All models were optimized with the Adam optimizer (Kingma and Ba, 2015) with weight decay fix (Loshchilov and Hutter, 2017).

We used the publicly available pretrained ELMo[8] and BERT[9] models in all experiments. For ELMo, we used the original two layer bidirectional LM. In the case of BERT, we used the BERT-base model, a 12 layer bidirectional transformer. We used the English uncased model for all tasks except for NER which used the English cased model.

A.1 Feature Extraction

To isolate the effects of fine-tuning contextual word representations, all feature based models only include one type of word representation (ELMo or BERT) and do not include any other pretrained word representations.

For all tasks, all layers of pretrained representations were weighted together with learned scalar parameters following Peters et al. (2018).

NER For the NER task, we use a two layer bidirectional LSTM in all experiments. For ELMo, the output layer is a CRF, similar to a state-of-the-art NER system (Lample et al., 2016). Feature extraction for ELMo treated each sentence independently.

In the case of BERT, the output layer is a softmax to be consistent with the fine-tuned experiments presented in Devlin et al. (2018). In addition, as in Devlin et al. (2018), we used document context to extract word piece representations. When composing multiple word pieces into a single word representation, we found it beneficial to run the biLSTM layers over all word pieces before taking the LSTM states of the first word piece in each word. We experimented with other pooling operations to combine word pieces into a

---

[8]https://allennlp.org/elmo
[9]https://github.com/google-research/bert

single word representation but they did not provide additional gains.

SA We used the implementation of the bi-attentive classification network in AllenNLP (Gardner et al., 2017) with default hyper-parameters, except for tuning those noted above. As in the fine-tuning experiments for SST-2, we used all available annotations during training, including those of sub-trees. Evaluation on the development and test sets used full sentences.

Sentence pair tasks When extracting features from ELMo, each sentence was handled separately. For BERT, we extracted features for both sentences jointly to be consistent with the pretraining procedure. As reported in Section 5 this improved performance over extracting features for each sentence separately.

Our model is the ESIM model (Chen et al., 2017), modified as needed to support regression tasks in addition to classification. We used default hyper-parameters except for those described above.

A.2 Fine-tuning

When fine-tuning ELMo, we found it beneficial to use discriminative learning rates (Howard and Ruder, 2018) where the learning rate decreased by $0.4\times$ in each layer (so that the learning rate for the second to last layer is $0.4\times$ the learning rate in the top layer). In addition, for SST-2 and NER, we also found it beneficial to gradually unfreeze the weights starting with the top layer. In this setting, in each epoch one additional layer of weights is unfrozen until all weights are training. These settings were chosen by tuning development set performance.

For fine-tuning BERT, we used the default learning rate schedule (Devlin et al., 2018) that is similar to the schedule used by Howard and Ruder (2018).

SA We considered several pooling operations for composing the ELMo LSTM states into a vector for prediction including max pooling, average pooling and taking the first/last states. Max pooling performed slightly better than average pooling on the development set.

Sentence pair tasks Our bi-attentive fine-tuning mechanism is similar to the the attention mechanism in the feature based ESIM model. To apply it, we first computed the bi-attention between all words in both sentences, then applied the same "enhanced" pooling operation as in (Chen et al., 2017) before predicting with a softmax. Note that this attention mechanism and pooling operation does not add any additional parameters to the network.

Generative Adversarial Networks for text using word2vec intermediaries

Akshay Budhkar[1,2,4], Krishnapriya Vishnubhotla[1], Safwan Hossain[1,2] and Frank Rudzicz[1,2,3,5]

[1]Department of Computer Science, University of Toronto
{abudhkar, vkpriya, frank}@cs.toronto.edu
[2]Vector Institute
safwan.hossain@mail.utoronto.ca
[3]St Michael's Hospital
[4]Georgian Partners
[5]Surgical Safety Technologies Inc.

Abstract

Generative adversarial networks (GANs) have shown considerable success, especially in the realistic generation of images. In this work, we apply similar techniques for the generation of text. We propose a novel approach to handle the discrete nature of text, during training, using word embeddings. Our method is agnostic to vocabulary size and achieves competitive results relative to methods with various discrete gradient estimators.

1 Introduction

Natural Language Generation (NLG) is often regarded as one of the most challenging tasks in computation (Murty and Kabadi, 1987). It involves training a model to do language generation for a series of abstract concepts, represented either in some logical form or as a knowledge base. Goodfellow introduced generative adversarial networks (GANs) (Goodfellow et al., 2014) as a method of generating synthetic, continuous data with realistic attributes. The model includes a discriminator network (D), responsible for distinguishing between the real and the generated samples, and a generator network (G), responsible for generating realistic samples with the goal of fooling the D. This setup leads to a minimax game where we maximize the value function with respect to D, and minimize it with respect to G. The ideal optimal solution is the complete replication of the real distributions of data by the generated distribution.

GANs, in this original setup, often suffer from the problem of mode collapse - where the G manages to find a few modes of data that resemble real data, using them consistently to fool the D. Workarounds for this include updating the loss function to incorporate an element of multi-diversity. An optimal D would provide G with

the information to improve, however, if at the current stage of training it is not doing that yet, the gradient of G vanishes. Additionally, with this loss function, there is no correlation between the metric and the generation quality, and the most common workaround is to generate targets across epochs and then measure the generation quality, which can be an expensive process.

W-GAN (Arjovsky et al., 2017) rectifies these issues with its updated loss. Wasserstein distance is the minimum cost of transporting *mass* in converting data from distribution P_r to P_g. This loss *forces* the GAN to perform in a min-max, rather than a max-min, a desirable behavior as stated in (Goodfellow, 2016), potentially mitigating mode-collapse problems. The loss function is given by:

$$L_{critic} = \min_{G} \max_{D \in \mathcal{D}} (E_{x \sim p_r(x)}[D(x)] \\ - E_{\tilde{x} \sim p_g(x)}[D(\tilde{x})]) \tag{1}$$

where $\mathcal{D}$ is the set of 1-Lipschitz functions and P_g is the model distribution implicitly defined by $\tilde{x} = G(z), z \sim p(z)$. A differentiable function is 1-Lipschtiz *iff* it has gradients with norm at most 1 everywhere. Under an optimal D minimizing the value function with respect to the generator parameters minimizes the $\mathcal{W}(p_r, p_g)$, where $\mathcal{W}$ is the Wasserstein distance, as discussed in (Vallender, 1974). To enforce the Lipschitz constraint, the authors propose clipping the weights of the gradient within a compact space $[-c, c]$.

(Gulrajani et al., 2017) show that even though this setup leads to more stable training compared to the original GAN loss function, the architecture suffers from exploding and vanishing gradient problems. They introduce the concept of *gradient penalty* as an alternative way to enforce the Lipschitz constraint, by penalizing the gradient norm

Proceedings of the 4th Workshop on Representation Learning for NLP (RepL4NLP-2019), pages 15–26
Florence, Italy, August 2, 2019. ©2019 Association for Computational Linguistics

directly in the loss. The loss function is given by:

$$L = L_{critic} + \lambda E_{\hat{x} \sim p(\hat{x})}[(||\nabla_{\hat{x}} D(\hat{x})||_2 - 1)^2] \quad (2)$$

where $\hat{x}$ are random samples drawn from $P_{\hat{x}}$, and L_{critic} is the loss defined in Equation 1.

Empirical results of GANs over the past year or so have been impressive. GANs have gotten state-of-the-art image-generation results on datasets like ImageNet (Brock et al., 2018) and LSUN (Radford et al., 2015). Such GANs are fully differentiable and allow for back-propagation of gradients from D through the samples generated by G. However, if the data is discrete, as, in the case of text, the gradient cannot be propagated back from D to G, without some approximation. Workarounds to this problem include techniques from reinforcement learning (RL), such as policy gradients to choose a discrete entity and reparameterization to represent the discrete quantity in terms of an approximated continuous function (Williams, 1992; Jang et al., 2016).

1.1 Techniques for GANs for text

SeqGAN (Yu et al., 2017) uses policy gradient techniques from RL to approximate gradient from discrete G outputs, and applied MC rollouts during training to obtain a loss signal for each word in the corpus. MaliGAN (Che et al., 2017) rescales the reward to control for the vanishing gradient problem faced by SeqGAN. RankGAN (Lin et al., 2017) replaces D with an *adversarial ranker* and minimizes pair-wise ranking loss to get better convergence, however, is more expensive than other methods due to the extra sampling from the original data. (Kusner and Hernández-Lobato, 2016) used the Gumbel-softmax approximation of the discrete one-hot encoded output of the G, and showed that the model learns rules of a context-free grammar from training samples. (Rajeswar et al., 2017), the state of the art in 2017, forced the GAN to operate on continuous quantities by approximating the one-hot output tokens with a softmax distribution layer at the end of the G network.

MaskGAN (Fedus et al., 2018) uses policy gradient with REINFORCE estimator (Williams, 1992) to train the model to predict a word based on its context, and show that for the specific blank-filling task, their model outperforms maximum likelihood model using the perplexity metric. LeakGAN (Guo et al., 2018) allows for long sentence generation by *leaking* high-level information from D to G, and generates a latent representation from the features of the already generated words, to aid in the next word generation. TextGAN (Zhang et al., 2017) adds an element of diversity to the original GAN loss by employing the Maximum Mean Discrepancy objective to alleviate mode collapse.

In the latter half of 2018, (Zhu et al., 2018) introduced *Texygen*, a benchmarking platform for natural language generation, while introducing standard metrics apt for this task. (Lu et al., 2018) surveys all these new methods along with other baselines, and documents model performance on standard corpus like EMNLP2017 WMT News[1] and Image COCO[2].

2 Motivation

2.1 Problems with the Softmax Function

The final layer of nearly all existing language generation models is the softmax function. It is usually the slowest to compute, leaves a large memory footprint and can lead to significant speedups if replaced by approximate continuous outputs (Kumar and Tsvetkov, 2018). Given this bottleneck, models usually limit the vocabulary size to a few thousand and use an unknown token (*unk*) for the rare words. Any change in the allowed vocabulary size also means that the researcher needs to modify the existing model architecture.

Our work breaks this bottleneck by having our G produce a sequence (or stack) of continuous distributed word vectors, with n dimensions, where $n << V$ and V is the vocabulary size. The expectation is that the model will output words in a semantic space, that is produced words would either be correct or close synonyms (Mikolov et al., 2013; Kumar and Tsvetkov, 2018), while having a smaller memory footprint and faster training and inference procedures.

2.2 GAN2vec

In this work, we propose GAN2vec - GANs that generate real-valued word2vec-like vectors (as opposed to discrete one-hot encoded outputs). While this work mainly focuses specifically on word2vec-based representation, it can be easily extended to other embedding techniques like GloVe and fastText.

---

[1] http://www.statmt.org/wmt17/
[2] http://cocodataset.org/

Expecting a neural network to generate text is, intuitively, expecting it to learn all the nuances of natural language, including the rules of grammar, context, coherent sentences, and so on. Word2vec has shown to capture parts of these subtleties by capturing the inherent semantic meaning of the words, and this is shown by the empirical results in the original paper (Mikolov et al., 2013) and with theoretical justifications by (Ethayarajh et al., 2018). GAN2vec breaks the problem of generation down into two steps, the first is the word2vec mapping, with the following network expected to address the other aspects of sentence generation. It also allows the model designers to swap out word2vec for a different type of word representation that is best suited for the specific language task at hand.

As a manifestation of the similar-context words getting grouped in word embedding space - we expect GAN2vec to have synonymic variety in the generation of sentences. Generating real-valued word vectors also allows the G architecture to be vocabulary-agnostic, as modifying the training data would involve just re-training the word embedding with more data. While this would involve re-training the weights of the GAN network, the initial architectural choices could remain consistent through this process. Finally, as discussed in Section 2.1, we expect a speed-up and smaller memory footprint by adapting this approach.

All the significant advances in the adaptation of GANs since its introduction in 2016, has been focused in the field of images. We have got to the point, where sometimes GAN architectures have managed to generate images even *better* than real images, as in the case of BigGAN (Brock et al., 2018). While there have been breakthroughs in working with text too, the rate of improvement is no-where close to the success we have had with images. GAN2vec attempts to bridge this gap by providing a framework to swap out image representations with word2vec representations.

3   The Architecture

Random normal noise is used as an input to the G which generates a sequence of word2vec vectors. We train the word2vec model on a real text corpus and generate a stack word vector sequences from the model. The generated and the real samples are then sent to D, to identify as real or synthetic. The generated word vectors are converted to text at

regular intervals during training and during inference for human interpretation. A nearest-neighbor approach based on cosine similarity is used to find the closest word to the generated embedding in the vector space.

4   The Algorithm

The complete GAN2vec flow is presented in Algorithm 1.

Algorithm 1 GAN2vec Framework

1: Train a word2vec model, e, on the train corpus

2: Transform text to a stack of word2vec vectors using e
3: Pre-train D for t iterations on real data
4: **for** k iterations **do**
5:    Send minibatch of real data to D
6:    $G(z)$ = Sample random normal z and feed to G
7:    Send minibatch of G generated data, $G(z)$, to D
8:    Update D using gradient descent
9:    Update G using gradient ascent
10: end **for**
11: $G(z)$ = Sample random normal z and feed to G
12: $w_{generated} = \underset{w}{argmin}\{d(\hat{e}, e(w))\}$, for every $\hat{e}$ in $G(z)$ and every w in the corpus

---

4.1   Conditional GAN2vec

We modify GAN2vec to measure the adaptability of GAN2vec to conditions provided *a priori*, as seen in (Mirza and Osindero, 2014). This change can include many kinds of conditions like positive/negative, question/statement or dementia/controls, allowing for the ability to analyze examples from various classes on the fly during inference. Both the G (and D) architectures get passed the condition at hand as an input, and the goal of G now is to generate a realistic sample given the specific condition.

5   Environmental Setup

All the experiments are run using Pytorch (Paszke et al., 2017). Word2vec training is done using the *gensim* library (Řehůřek and Sojka, 2010). Unless specified otherwise, we use the default parameters for all the components of these libraries, and all

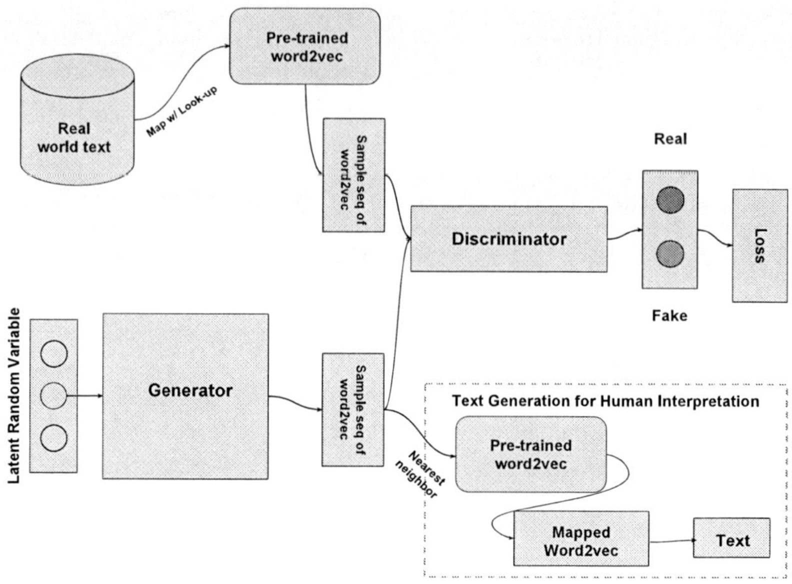

Figure 1: Structure of the GAN2vec model. Random normal noise is given as input to the generator network G. The discriminator network D is responsible for determining whether a sample originated from G or from the training set. At inference time, we use a nearest-neighbor approach to convert the output from G into human-readable text.

our models are trained for **100** epochs. The word embedding dimensions are set to 64. The learning rate for the ADAM optimizers for D and G are set to 0.0001, with the exponential decay rates for the first and second moments set to 0.5 and 0.999 respectively.

All our Ds take the word2vec-transformed vectors as an input and apply two 2-D convolutions, followed by a fully connected layer to return a single value. The dimensions of the second 2-D convolution are the only things varied to address the different input dimensions. Similarly, our Gs take a random normal noise of size 100 and transform it to the desired output by passing it through a fully-connected layer, and two 2-D fractionally-strided convolution layers. Again, the dimensions of the second fractionally-strided convolution are the only variables to obtain different output dimensions.

Normalizing word vectors after training them has no significant effect on the performance of GAN2vec, and all the results that we present do not carry out this step. Keeping in punctuation helped improve performance, as expected, and none of the experiments filter them out.

To facilitate stable GAN training, we make the following modifications, covered by (Chintala et al., 2016), by running a few preliminary tests on

a smaller sample of our dataset:

- Use LeakyRELU instead of RELU

- Send generated and real mini-batches to D in separate batches

- Use label smoothing by setting the target labels to 0.9 and 0.1 instead of 1 and 0 for real and fake samples respectively (for most of our experiments).

6 Metrics

6.1 BLEU

BLEU (Papineni et al., 2002) originated as a way to measure the quality of machine translation given certain ground truth. Many text generation papers use this as a metric to compare the quality of the generated samples to the target corpus. A higher n-gram coverage will yield a higher BLEU score, with the score reaching a 100% if all the generated n-grams are present in the corpus. The two potential flaws with this metric are: 1) It does not take into account the diversity of the text generation, this leads to a situation where a mode-collapsing G that produces the same one sentence from the corpus gets a score of 100%. 2) It penalizes the generation of grammatically coherent sentences with novel n-grams, just because they are absent from the original corpus. Despite these problems, we use BLEU to be consistent with other GANs for text papers. We also present generated samples for the sake of qualitative evaluation by the reader.

6.2 Self-BLEU

Self-BLEU is introduced as a metric to measure the diversity of the generated sentences. It does a corpus-level BLEU on a set of generated sentences, and reports the average BLEU as a metric for a given model. A lower self-BLEU implies a higher diversity in the generated sentences, and accordingly a lower chance that the model has mode collapsed.

It is not clear from (Zhu et al., 2018)'s work on how many sentences *Texygen* generates to calculate Self-BLEU. For purposes of GAN2vec's results, we produce 1000 sentences, and for every sentence do a corpus-level BLEU on remaining 999 sentences. Our results report the average BLEU across all the outputs.

7 Chinese Poetry Dataset

The Chinese Poetry dataset, introduced by (Zhang and Lapata, 2014) presents simple 4-line poems in Chinese with a length of 5 or 7 tokens (henceforth referred to Poem 5 and Poem 7 respectively). Following previous work by (Rajeswar et al., 2017) and (Yu et al., 2017), we treat every line as a separate data point. We modify the Poem 5 dataset to add start and end of tokens, to ensure the model captures (at least) that pattern through the corpus (given our lack of Chinese knowledge). This setup allows us to use identical architectures for both the Poem 5 and Poem 7 datasets. We also modify the GAN2vec loss function with the objective in Eq. 2, and report the results below.

	Rajeswar et al.	GAN2vec	GAN2vec (wGAN)
Poem 5	– (train)	37.90% (train)	**53.5%** (train)
	87.80% (test)	22.50% (test)	**25.78%** (test)
Poem 7	– (train)	30.14% (train)	**66.45%** (train)
	65.60% (test)	10.20% (test)	**22.07%** (test)

Table 1: Chinese Poetry BLEU-2 scores.

The better performance of the GAN2vec model with the wGAN objective is in-line with the im-

age results in Gulrajani et al. (2017)'s work. We were not able to replicate (Rajeswar et al., 2017)'s model on the Chinese Poetry dataset to get the reported results on the test set. This conclusion is in-line with our expectation of lower performance on the test set, given the small overlap in the bigram coverage between the provided train and test sets. (Lu et al., 2018) also point out that this work is unreliable, and that their replicated model suffered from severe mode-collapse. On 1000 generated sentences of the Poem-5 dataset, our model has a self BLEU-2 of **66.08%** and self BLEU-3 of **35.29%**, thereby showing that our model does not mode collapse.

8 CMU-SE Dataset

CMU-SE[3] is a pre-processed collections of simple English sentences, consisting of 44,016 sentences and a vocabulary of 3,122-word types. For purposes of our experiments here, we limit the number of sentences to 7, chosen empirically to capture a significant share of the examples. For the sake of simplicity in these experiments, for the *real* corpus, sentences with fewer than seven words are ignored, and those with more than seven words are cut-off at the seventh word.

Table 1 presents sentences generated by the original GAN2vec model. Appendix A.2 includes additional examples. While this is a small subset of randomly sampled examples, on a relatively simple dataset, the text quality appears competitive to the work of (Rajeswar et al., 2017) on this corpus.

Rajeswar et al. (2017)
<s> will you have two moment ? </s>
<s> how is the another headache ? </s>
<s> what s in the friday food ? ? </s>
<s> i d like to fax a newspaper . </s>
GAN2vec
<s> i dropped my camera . </s>
<s> i 'd like to transfer it
<s> i 'll take that car ,
<s> prepare whisky and coffee , please

Table 2: Example sentences generated by the original GAN2vec. We report example sentences from Rajeswar et al. (2017) and from our GAN2vec model on CMU-SE.

---

[3] https://github.com/clab/sp2016. 11-731/tree/master/hw4/data

8.1 Conditional GAN2vec

We split the CMU-SE dataset into *questions* and *sentences*, checking for the presence of a question mark. We modify the original GAN2vec, as seen in Section A.1, to now include these labels. Our conditional GANs learn to generate mainly coherent sentences on the CMU-SE dataset, as seen in Table 3.

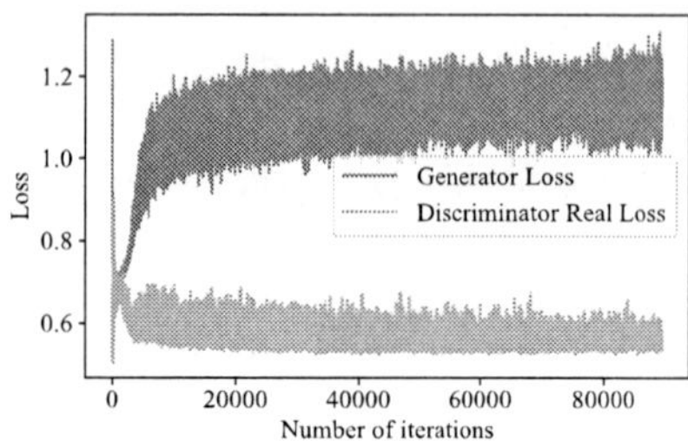

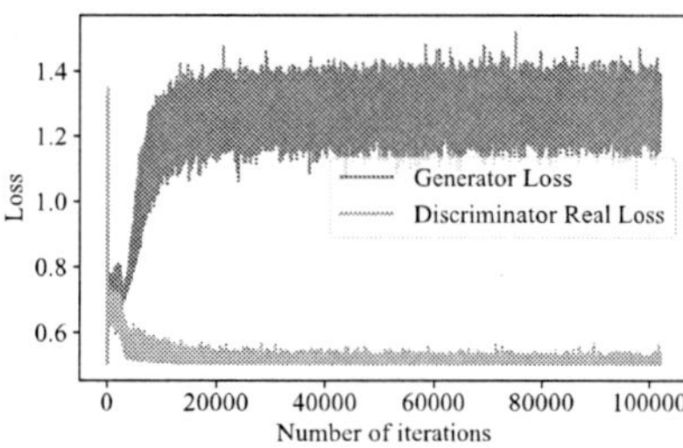

Figure 2: The minimax loss of D and G, with increasing iterations for the GAN2vec model (top) and the conditional GAN2vec (bottom).

Figure 2 shows the loss graphs for our GAN2vec and conditional GAN2vec trained for ~300 epochs. As seen above, the conditional GAN2vec model generates relatively atypical sentences. This is supported by the second loss curve in Figure 2. The G loss follows a progression similar to the normal GAN2vec case, but the loss is about 16% more through the 100 epochs.

8.2 Hyperparameter Variation Study

We study the effects of different initial hyperparameters for GAN2vec by reporting the results in Table 4. All the experiments were run ten times, and we report the best scores for every configuration. It must be noted that for conditional GAN2vec training for this experiment, we randomly sample points from the CMU-SE corpus to enforce a 50-50 split across the two labels (question and sentence).

The overall performance of most of the models is respectable, with all models generating gram-

matically coherent sentences. GAN2vec with wGAN objective outperforms original GAN2vec, and is inline with the results of (Gulrajani et al., 2017) and our results in Section 7. Sense2vec does not have a significant improvement over the original word2vec representations. In agreement with (Goodfellow, 2016), providing labels in the conditional variant leads to better performance.

8.3 Word2vec cosine similarity

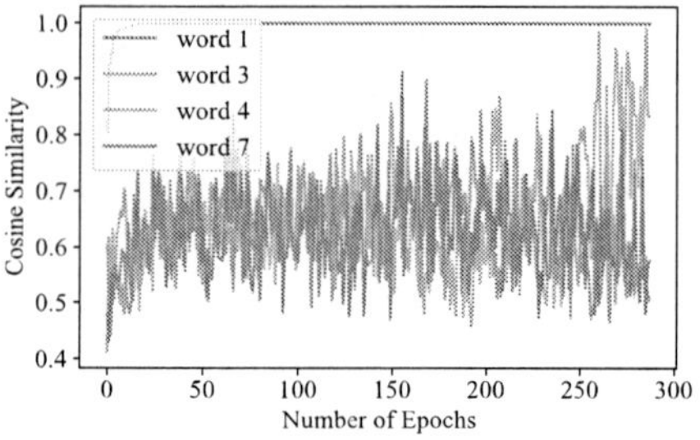

Figure 3: Cosine similarities of the first, third, fourth, and seventh words to the closest words from sentences generated by GAN2vec trained on the CMU-SE dataset.

During training, we map our generated word2vec vectors to the closest words in the embedding space and measure the point-wise cosine similarity of the generated vector and the closest neighbour's vector. Figure 3 shows these scores for the first, third, fourth and seventh word of the 7-word generated sentences on the CMU-SE dataset for about 300 epochs. The model immediately learns that it needs to start a sentence with <s> and gets a cosine similarity of around 1. For the other words in that sentence, the model tends to get better at generating word vectors that are close to their real-valued counterparts of the nearest neighbours. It seems as if the words close to the start of the sentence follow this trend more strongly (as seen with words 1 and 3) and it is relatively weaker for the last word of the sentence.

9 Coco Image Captions Dataset

The Coco Dataset is used to train and generate synthetic data as a common dataset for all the best-performing models over the last two years. In *Texygen*, the authors set the sentence length to 20. They train an oracle that generates 20,000 sentences, with one half used as the training set and the rest as the test set. All the models in this benchmark are trained for 180 epochs.

Questions	Sentences
<s> can i get you want him	<s> i bring your sweet inexpensive beer
<s> where 's the hotel ?	<s> they will stop your ship at
<s> what is the fare ? </s>	<s> i had a pocket . </s>
<s> could you buy the timetable ?	<s> it 's ten at detroit western

Table 3: Examples of sentences generated by the conditional GAN. We report examples of sentences with our model conditioned on sentence type, i.e., question or sentence.

Architecture	Conditional	Vector Type	Loss function	BLEU-2	BLEU-3
R.1	No	Sense2vec	Original	0.743	0.41
R.1	No	Sense2vec	wgan	0.7933	0.4728
R.1	No	Word2Vec	wgan	0.74	0.43
C.1	Yes	word2vec	Original (Real)	0.717	0.412
C.1	Yes	word2vec	Original	0.743	0.4927
C.1	Yes	word2vec	wgan	**0.7995**	**0.5168**
C.1	Yes	word2vec	wgan	**0.821**	**0.51**
C.2	Yes	word2vec	wgan	**0.8053**	**0.499**

Table 4: Performance of different models on the CMU-SE train dataset. $R.1$ is the original GAN2vec, $C.1$ is $R.1$ modified with addition of labels, $C.2$ adds batch normalization on the CNN layer of G. Original (Real) sets the real label to 0.9, the rest use 1.

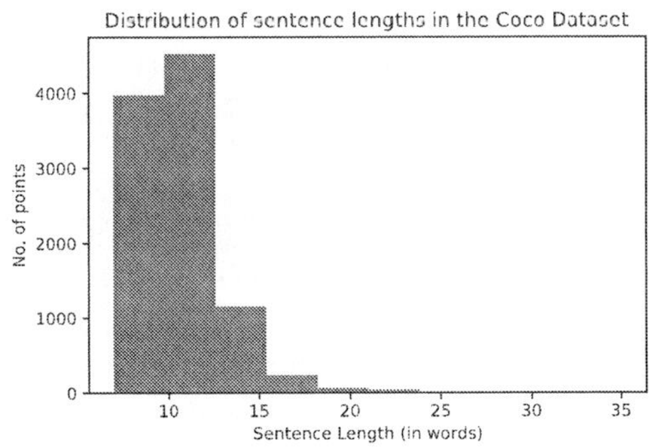

Figure 4: Distribution of sentence lengths in the Coco dataset. Most of the captions have less than 20 words, the cut-off set by *Texygen*.

Figure 4 shows the distribution of the sentence lengths in this corpus. For purposes of studying the effects of longer training sentences on GAN2vec, we set the sentence lengths to 7, 10 and 20 (with the respective models labeled as GAN2vec-7, GAN2vec-10, GAN2vec-20 going forward). Any sentence longer than the predefined sentence length is cut off to include only the initial words. Sentences shorter than this length are padded with an end of sentence character to fill up the remaining words (we use a comma (,) for purposes of our experiments as all the sentences in the corpus end with either a full stop or a word). We tokenize the sentences us-

ing NLTK's word tokenizer[4] which uses regular expressions to tokenize text as in the Penn Treebank corpus[5]. We also report the results of a naive *split at space* approach for the GAN2vec-20 architecture (GAN2vec-20-a), to compare different ways of tokenizing the corpus. We only use the objective from Equation 2, given its superior performance to original GAN2vec, as seen in the previous sections.

The results are summarized in the tables below:

Model	BLEU-2	BLEU-3
LeakGAN	0.926	0.816
SeqGAN	0.917	0.747
MLE	0.731	0.497
TextGAN	0.65	0.645
GAN2vec-7	0.548	0.271
GAN2vec-10	0.641	**0.342**
GAN2vec-20-a	0.618	0.294
GAN2vec-20	**0.661**	0.335

Table 5: Model BLEU scores on Train Set of the Coco Dataset (higher is better).

On the train set (Table 5), GAN2vec models have BLEU-2 scores comparable to its SOTA

---

[4] https://www.nltk.org/api/nltk.tokenize.html#nltk.tokenize.word_tokenize

[5] https://catalog.ldc.upenn.edu/docs/LDC95T7/cl93.html

counterparts, with the GAN2vec-20 model having better bigram coverage that TextGAN. The BLEU-3 scores, even though commendable, do not match up as well, possibly signaling that our models cannot keep coherence through longer sentences. The increase in the cut-off sentence length, surprisingly, does not degrade performance. As expected, a trained word tokenizer outperforms its *space-split* counterpart. The performance of the GAN2vec models on the test set (Table 6) follows the same trends as that on the train set.

Model	BLEU-2	BLEU-3
LeakGAN	0.746	0.816
SeqGAN	0.745	0.53
MLE	0.731	0.497
TextGAN	0.593	0.645
GAN2vec-7	0.429	0.196
GAN2vec-10	0.527	**0.245**
GAN2vec-20-a	0.484	0.206
GAN2vec-20	**0.551**	0.232

Table 6: Model BLEU scores on Test Set of the Coco Dataset (higher is better).

Model	BLEU-2	BLEU-3
LeakGAN	0.966	0.913
SeqGAN	0.95	0.84
MLE	0.916	0.769
TextGAN	0.942	0.931
GAN2vec-7	**0.537**	**0.254**
GAN2vec-10	0.657	0.394
GAN2vec-20-a	0.709	0.394
GAN2vec-20	0.762	0.518

Table 7: Self BLEU scores of the models trained on the Coco dataset (lower is better).

Table 7 reports the self-BLEU scores, and all the GAN2vec models significantly outperform the SOTA models, including MLE. This implies that GAN2vec leads to more diverse sentence generations and is less susceptible to mode collapse.

10   Discussions

Overall, GAN2vec can generate grammatically coherent sentences, with a good bi-gram and tri-gram coverage from the chosen corpus. BLEU does not reward the generation of semantically and syntactically correct sentences if the associated n-grams are not present in the corpus, and

coming up with a new standard evaluation metric is part of on-going work. GAN2vec seems to have comparable, if not better, performance compared to Rajeswar et al. (2017)'s work on two distinct datasets. It depicts the ability to capture the critical nuances when trained on a conditional corpus. While GAN2vec performs slightly worse than most of the SOTA models using the *Texygen* benchmark, it can generate a wide variety of sentences, possibly given the inherent nature of word vectors, and is less susceptible to mode collapse compared to each of the models. GAN2vec provides a simple framework, with almost no overhead, to transfer state of the art GAN research in computer vision to natural language generation.

We observe that the performance of GAN2vec gets better with an increase in the cut-off length of the sentences. This improvement could be because of *extra* training points for the model. The drop from BLEU-2 to BLEU-3 scores is more extreme than the other SOTA models, indicating that GAN2vec may lack the ability to generate *long* coherent sentences. This behavior could be a manifestation of the chosen D and G architectures, specifically the filter dimensions of the convolution neural networks. Exploration of other structures, including RNN-based models with their ability to remember long term dependencies, might be good alternatives to these initial architecture choices. Throughout all the models in the *Texygen* benchmark, there seems to be a mild negative correlation between diversity and performance. GAN2vec in its original setup leans more towards the generation of new and diverse sentences, and modification of its loss function could allow for tilting the model more towards accurate NLG.

11   Conclusion

While various research has extended GANs to operate on discrete data, most approaches have approximated the gradient in order to keep the model end-to-end differentiable. We instead explore a different approach, and work in the continuous domain using word embedding representations. The performance of our model is encouraging in terms of BLEU scores, and the outputs suggest that it is successfully utilizing the semantic information encoded in the word vectors to produce new, coherent and diverse sentences.

Acknowledgements

This study was partially funded by the Vector Institute for Artificial Intelligence. Rudzicz is an Inaugural CIFAR Chair in artificial intelligence.

References

Martin Arjovsky, Soumith Chintala, and Léon Bottou. 2017. Wasserstein GAN. *arXiv preprint arXiv:1701.07875*.

Andrew Brock, Jeff Donahue, and Karen Simonyan. 2018. Large scale gan training for high fidelity natural image synthesis. *arXiv preprint arXiv:1809.11096*.

Tong Che, Yanran Li, Ruixiang Zhang, R Devon Hjelm, Wenjie Li, Yangqiu Song, and Yoshua Bengio. 2017. Maximum-likelihood augmented discrete generative adversarial networks. *arXiv preprint arXiv:1702.07983*.

Soumith Chintala, Emily Denton, Martin Arjovsky, and Michael Mathieu. 2016. How to train a gan? tips and tricks to make gans work.

Kawin Ethayarajh, David Duvenaud, and Graeme Hirst. 2018. Towards understanding linear word analogies. *arXiv preprint arXiv:1810.04882*.

William Fedus, Ian Goodfellow, and Andrew M Dai. 2018. MaskGAN: Better Text Generation via Filling in the _. *arXiv preprint arXiv:1801.07736*.

Ian Goodfellow. 2016. NIPS 2016 tutorial: Generative adversarial networks. *arXiv preprint arXiv:1701.00160*.

Ian Goodfellow, Jean Pouget-Abadie, Mehdi Mirza, Bing Xu, David Warde-Farley, Sherjil Ozair, Aaron Courville, and Yoshua Bengio. 2014. Generative adversarial nets. In *Advances in neural information processing systems*, pages 2672–2680.

Ishaan Gulrajani, Faruk Ahmed, Martin Arjovsky, Vincent Dumoulin, and Aaron C Courville. 2017. Improved training of wasserstein gans. In *Advances in Neural Information Processing Systems*, pages 5767–5777.

Jiaxian Guo, Sidi Lu, Han Cai, Weinan Zhang, Yong Yu, and Jun Wang. 2018. Long text generation via adversarial training with leaked information. In *Thirty-Second AAAI Conference on Artificial Intelligence*.

Eric Jang, Shixiang Gu, and Ben Poole. 2016. Categorical reparameterization with Gumbel-softmax. *arXiv preprint arXiv:1611.01144*.

Sachin Kumar and Yulia Tsvetkov. 2018. Von mises-fisher loss for training sequence to sequence models with continuous outputs. *arXiv preprint arXiv:1812.04616*.

Matt J Kusner and José Miguel Hernández-Lobato. 2016. GANs for sequences of discrete elements with the Gumbel-softmax distribution. *arXiv preprint arXiv:1611.04051*.

Kevin Lin, Dianqi Li, Xiaodong He, Zhengyou Zhang, and Ming-Ting Sun. 2017. Adversarial ranking for language generation. In *Advances in Neural Information Processing Systems*, pages 3155–3165.

Sidi Lu, Yaoming Zhu, Weinan Zhang, Jun Wang, and Yong Yu. 2018. Neural text generation: Past, present and beyond. *arXiv preprint arXiv:1803.07133*.

Tomas Mikolov, Ilya Sutskever, Kai Chen, Greg S Corrado, and Jeff Dean. 2013. Distributed representations of words and phrases and their compositionality. In *Advances in neural information processing systems*, pages 3111–3119.

Mehdi Mirza and Simon Osindero. 2014. Conditional generative adversarial nets. *arXiv preprint arXiv:1411.1784*.

Katta G Murty and Santosh N Kabadi. 1987. Some np-complete problems in quadratic and nonlinear programming. *Mathematical programming*, 39(2):117–129.

Kishore Papineni, Salim Roukos, Todd Ward, and Wei-Jing Zhu. 2002. Bleu: a method for automatic evaluation of machine translation. In *Proceedings of the 40th annual meeting on association for computational linguistics*, pages 311–318. Association for Computational Linguistics.

Adam Paszke, Sam Gross, Soumith Chintala, and Gregory Chanan. 2017. Pytorch.

Alec Radford, Luke Metz, and Soumith Chintala. 2015. Unsupervised representation learning with deep convolutional generative adversarial networks. *arXiv preprint arXiv:1511.06434*.

Sai Rajeswar, Sandeep Subramanian, Francis Dutil, Christopher Pal, and Aaron Courville. 2017. Adversarial generation of natural language. *arXiv preprint arXiv:1705.10929*.

Radim Řehůřek and Petr Sojka. 2010. Software Framework for Topic Modelling with Large Corpora. In *Proceedings of the LREC 2010 Workshop on New Challenges for NLP Frameworks*, pages 45–50, Valletta, Malta. ELRA. http://is.muni.cz/publication/884893/en.

SS Vallender. 1974. Calculation of the wasserstein distance between probability distributions on the line. *Theory of Probability & Its Applications*, 18(4):784–786.

Ronald J Williams. 1992. Simple statistical gradient-following algorithms for connectionist reinforcement learning. In *Reinforcement Learning*, pages 5–32. Springer.

Lantao Yu, Weinan Zhang, Jun Wang, and Yong Yu. 2017. SeqGAN: Sequence Generative Adversarial Nets with Policy Gradient. In *AAAI*, pages 2852–2858.

Xingxing Zhang and Mirella Lapata. 2014. Chinese poetry generation with recurrent neural networks. In *Proceedings of the 2014 Conference on Empirical Methods in Natural Language Processing (EMNLP)*, pages 670–680, Doha, Qatar. Association for Computational Linguistics.

Yizhe Zhang, Zhe Gan, Kai Fan, Zhi Chen, Ricardo Henao, Dinghan Shen, and Lawrence Carin. 2017. Adversarial feature matching for text generation. *arXiv preprint arXiv:1706.03850*.

Yaoming Zhu, Sidi Lu, Lei Zheng, Jiaxian Guo, Weinan Zhang, Jun Wang, and Yong Yu. 2018. Texygen: A benchmarking platform for text generation models. *arXiv preprint arXiv:1802.01886*.

A CMU-SE

A.1 Conditional Architecture

While designing GAN2vec to support conditional labels, as presented in Mirza and Osindero (2014), we used the architecture in Figure 5 for our G. The label is sent as an input to both the fully connected and the de-convolution neural layers. The same change is followed while updating D to support document labels.

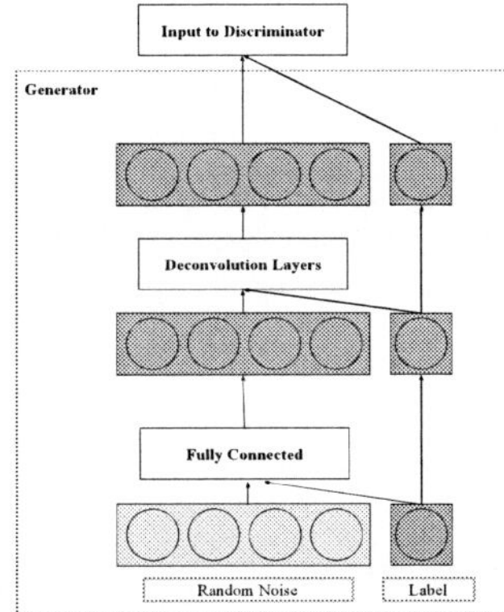

Figure 5: Generator Architecture for Conditional GAN2vec.

A.2 Examples of Generated Sentences

Table 8: Sentences Generated with GAN2vec on CMU-SE

Generated Sentences
<s> can you have a home </s>
<s> i 'd like to leave the
<s> this is the baggage . </s>
<s> i 'd like a driver ?
<s> do you draw well . </s>
<s> i 'd like to transfer it
<s> please explain it <unk>. </s>
<s> can i book a table .
<s> i 'll take that car ,
<s> would i like a stay ?
<s> will you check it . </s>
<s> do you find it ? </s>
<s> i want some lovely cream .
<s> could you recommend a hotel with
<s> can you get this one in
<s> where 's the petrol station ?
<s> what 's the problem ? </s>
<s> i have a hangover dark .
<s> i come on the monday .
<s> i appreciate having a sushi .
<s> the bus is busy , please
<s> i dropped my camera . </s>
<s> i want to wash something .
<s> it 's too great for <unk>
<s> i have a driver in the
<s> it is delicious and <unk><unk>
<s> please leave your luggage . .
<s> i had alcohol wow , </s>
<s> it is very true . </s>
<s> where 's the hotel ? </s>
<s> will you see the cat ? </s>
<s> where is this bus ? </s>
<s> how was the spirits airline warranty
<s> i would n't sunburn you
<s> prepare whisky and coffee , please

An Evaluation of Language-Agnostic Inner-Attention-Based Representations in Machine Translation

Alessandro Raganato,[*][†] **Raúl Vázquez,**[*] **Mathias Creutz**[*] **and Jörg Tiedemann**[*]
[*]University of Helsinki, Department of Digital Humanities
[†]Basement AI
`{name.surname}@helsinki.fi`

Abstract

In this paper, we explore a multilingual translation model with a cross-lingually shared layer that can be used as fixed-size sentence representation in different downstream tasks. We systematically study the impact of the size of the shared layer and the effect of including additional languages in the model. In contrast to related previous work, we demonstrate that the performance in translation does correlate with trainable downstream tasks. In particular, we show that larger intermediate layers not only improve translation quality, especially for long sentences, but also push the accuracy of trainable classification tasks. On the other hand, shorter representations lead to increased compression that is beneficial in non-trainable similarity tasks. We hypothesize that the training procedure on the downstream task enables the model to identify the encoded information that is useful for the specific task whereas non-trainable benchmarks can be confused by other types of information also encoded in the representation of a sentence.

1 Introduction

Neural Machine Translation (NMT) has rapidly become the new Machine Translation (MT) paradigm, significantly improving over the traditional statistical machine translation procedure (Bojar et al., 2018). Recently, several models and variants have been proposed with increased research efforts towards multilingual machine translation (Firat et al., 2016; Lakew et al., 2018; Wang et al., 2018; Blackwood et al., 2018; Lu et al., 2018). The main motivation of multilingual models is the effect of transfer learning that enables machine translation systems to benefit from relationships between languages and training signals that come from different datasets (Ha et al., 2016; Johnson et al., 2017; Gu et al., 2018). Another aspect that draws interest in translation models is the

effective computation of sentence representations using the translation task as an auxiliary semantic signal (Hill et al., 2016; McCann et al., 2017; Schwenk and Douze, 2017; Subramanian et al., 2018). An important feature that enables an immediate use of the MT-based representations in other downstream tasks is the creation of fixed-sized sentence embeddings (Cífka and Bojar, 2018).

However, the effects of the size of sentence embeddings and the relation between translation performance and meaning representation quality are not entirely clear. Recent studies based on NMT either focus entirely on the use of MT-based sentence embeddings in other tasks (Schwenk, 2018), on translation quality (Lu et al., 2018), on speed comparison (Britz et al., 2017), or only exploring a bilingual scenario (Cífka and Bojar, 2018).

In this paper, we are interested in exploring a cross-lingual intermediate shared layer (called *attention bridge*) in an attentive encoder-decoder MT model. This shared layer serves as a fixed-size sentence representation that can be straightforwardly applied to downstream tasks. We examine this model with a systematic evaluation on different sizes of the attention bridge and extensive experiments to study the abstractions it learns from multiple translation tasks. In contrast to previous work (Cífka and Bojar, 2018), we demonstrate that there is a correlation between translation performance and trainable downstream tasks when adjusting the size of the intermediate layer. The trend is different for non-trainable tasks that benefit from the increased compression that denser representations achieve, which typically hurts the translation performance because of the decreased capacity of the model. We also show that multilingual models improve trainable downstream tasks even further, demonstrating the additional abstraction that is pushed into the representations through additional translation tasks involved in training.

Proceedings of the 4th Workshop on Representation Learning for NLP (RepL4NLP-2019), pages 27–32
Florence, Italy, August 2, 2019. ©2019 Association for Computational Linguistics

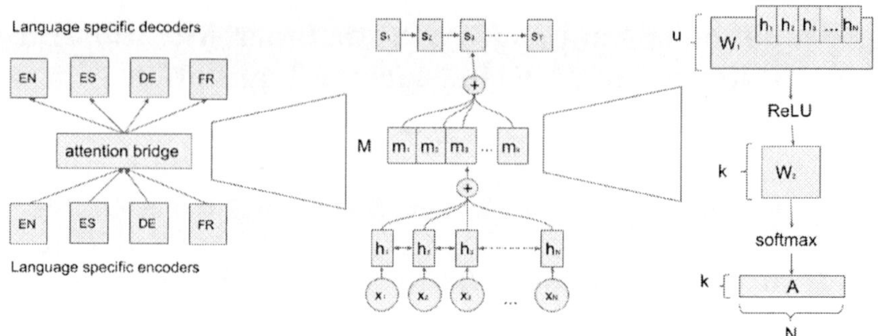

Figure 1: Architecture of our multilingual NMT system: (left) the attention bridge connects the language-specific encoders and decoders; (center) input $x_1 \ldots x_n$ is translated into the decoder states $s_1 \ldots s_t$ via the encoder states $H = h_1 \ldots h_n$ and the attention bridge $m_1 \ldots m_k$; (right) Computation of the hidden representation matrix A, needed to obtain the fixed-size attentive matrix $M = AH^T$.

2   Architecture

Our architecture follows the standard setup of an encoder-decoder model in machine translation with a traditional attention mechanism (Luong et al., 2015). However, we augment the network with language specific encoders and decoders to enable multilingual training as in Lu et al. (2018), plus we introduce an inner-attention layer (Liu et al., 2016; Lin et al., 2017) that summarizes the encoder information in a fixed-size vector representation that can easily be shared among different translation tasks with the language-specific encoders and decoders connecting to it. The overall architecture is illustrated in Figure 1 (see also Vázquez et al., 2019). Due to the attentive connection between encoders and decoders we call this layer *attention bridge*, and its architecture is an adaptation from the model proposed by Cífka and Bojar (2018). Finally, each decoder follows a common attention mechanism in NMT, with the only exception that the context vector is computed on the *attention bridge*, and the initialization is performed by a mean pooling over it. Hence, the decoder receives the information only through the shared attention bridge.

The fixed-sized representation coming out of the shared layer can immediately be applied to downstream tasks.[1] However, selecting a reasonable size of the attention bridge in terms of *attention heads* (m_i in Figure 1) is crucial for the performance both in a bilingual and multilingual sce-

nario as we will see in the experiments below.

3   Experimental setup

All models are implemented using the OpenNMT framework (Klein et al., 2017) trained using the same set of hyper-parameters.[2] We use embedding layers of 512 dimensions, two stacked bidirectional LSTM layers with 512 hidden units (256 per direction) and an attentive decoder composed of two unidirectional LSTM layers with 512 units. Regarding the attention bridge, we experimented with four different configurations: 1, 10, 25 and 50 *attention heads* with 1024 hidden units each. For multilingual models, we used a language-rotating scheduler, in which each mini-batch contains sentences from a different language pair, cycling through all the language pairs uniformly. We selected the best model according to the BLEU score on the validation set. We train all the models using the Europarl Corpus v7 (Koehn, 2005), focusing on 4 languages: English (EN), French (FR), German (DE) and Spanish (ES). First we train bilingual models for EN→DE; then we train multilingual models {DE,ES,FR}↔EN; lastly we train a final Many-to-Many model using the biggest size, i.e., 50 *attention heads*, involving all translation directions between the three languages, i.e., we also include DE–ES, DE–FR and ES–FR.

To evaluate the sentence representations we utilize the SentEval toolkit (Conneau and Kiela, 2018) that combines various established downstream tasks for testing representations of English

---

[1] As in Lu et al. (2018), we note that the attention bridge is independent of the underlying encoder and decoder. While we use LSTM, it could be easily replaced with a transformer type network (Vaswani et al., 2017) or with a CNN (Gehring et al., 2017).

[2] Our fork implementation is available at `https://github.com/Helsinki-NLP/OpenNMT-py/tree/att-brg`.

		SNLI	SICK-E	AVG
en→de	k=1	63.86	77.09	71.46
en→de	k=10	**65.30**	78.77	72.02
en→de	k=25	65.13	79.34	**72.68**
en→de	k=50	**65.30**	**79.36**	72.60
Multilingual	k=1	65.56	77.96	72.67
Multilingual	k=10	67.01	79.48	72.89
Multilingual	k=25	66.94	79.85	**73.67**
Multilingual	k=50	**67.38**	**80.54**	73.39
Many-to-Many	k=50	**67.73**	**81.12**	**74.33**
Most frequent baseline[†]		34.30	56.70	48.19
GloVe-BOW[†]		66.00	78.20	75.81
Cífka and Bojar (2018) en→cs[†]		69.30	80.80	73.40

Table 1: Accuracy of different models on two SentEval tasks as well as the overall average accuracy on all of them. The general trend is that a higher number of attention heads and multilingual models are beneficial. Results with † taken from Cífka and Bojar (2018).

		SICK-R	STSB	AVG
en→de	k=1	0.74 / 0.67	**0.69 / 0.69**	**0.57**
en→de	k=10	0.76 / 0.71	**0.69 / 0.69**	0.52
en→de	k=25	**0.78 / 0.73**	0.67 / 0.66	0.49
en→de	k=50	0.78 / 0.72	0.65 / 0.64	0.46
Multilingual	k=1	0.76 / 0.71	0.69 / 0.68	**0.50**
Multilingual	k=10	0.78 / 0.74	**0.69 / 0.69**	0.48
Multilingual	k=25	0.78 / 0.74	0.68 / 0.67	0.43
Multilingual	k=50	**0.79 / 0.74**	0.66 / 0.64	0.40
Many-to-Many	k=50	**0.79 / 0.74**	**0.69 / 0.68**	0.40
InferSent[†]		0.88 / 0.83	0.76 / 0.75	0.66
GloVe-BOW[†]		0.80 / 0.72	0.64 / 0.62	0.53
Cífka and Bojar (2018) en→cs[†]		0.81 / 0.76	0.73 / 0.73	0.45

Table 2: Results from supervised similarity tasks (SICK-R and STSB), measured using Pearson's (r) and Spearman's (ρ) correlation coefficients (r/ρ). The average across unsupervised similarity tasks on Pearson's measures are displayed in the right-most column. Results with † taken from Cífka and Bojar (2018).

sentences.[3] In order to obtain a sentence vector out of multiple attention heads we apply mean pooling over the *attention bridge*.

We are also interested in the translation quality to verify the appropriateness of our models with respect to the main objective they are trained for. For this, we adopt the in-domain development and evaluation dataset from the ACL-WMT07 shared task. Sentences are encoded using Byte-Pair Encoding (Sennrich et al., 2016), with 32,000 merge operations for each language.

4 SentEval: Classification tasks

Table 1 shows the performance of our models on two popular tasks (SNLI and SICK-E) as in Cífka and Bojar (2018) as well as the average of all 10 SentEval downstream tasks. The experiments reveal two important findings:

(1) In contrast with the results from Cífka and Bojar (2018), our scores demonstrate that an increasing number of attention heads is beneficial for classification-based downstream tasks. All models perform best with more than one attention head and the general trend is that the accuracies improve with larger representations. The previous claim was that there is the opposite effect and lower numbers of attention heads lead to higher performances in downstream tasks, but we do not see that effect in our setup, at least not in the classification tasks.

(2) The second outcome is the positive effect of multilingual training. We can see that multilingual training objectives are generally helpful for the trainable downstream tasks.

Particularly interesting is the fact that the Many-to-Many model performs best on average even though it does not add any further training examples for English (compared to the other multilingual models), which is the target language of the downstream tasks. This suggests that the model is able to improve generalizations even from other language pairs (DE–ES, FR–ES, FR–DE) that are not directly involved in training the representations of English sentences.

Comparing against benchmarks, our results are in line with competitive baselines (Arora et al., 2017). While our aim is not to beat the state of the art trained on different data, but rather to understand the impact of various sizes of attention heads in a bi- and multilingual scenario, we argue that a larger attention bridge and multilinguality constitute a preferable starting point to learn more meaningful sentence representations.

5 SentEval: Similarity tasks

Table 2 summarizes the results using Pearson's and Spearman's coefficient on the two SentEval supervised textual similarity tasks, SICK-R and STSB, and the average Pearson's measure on the remaining unsupervised similarity tasks.

Two different trends become visible: i) On the unsupervised textual similarity tasks, having fewer attention heads is beneficial. Contrary to the results in the classification tasks, the best overall

---

[3]Due to the large number of SentEval tasks, we report results on natural language inference (SNLI, SICK-E/SICK-R) and the average of all tasks.

		k=1	k=10	k=25	k=50	M-to-M	att.
en	de	14.66	19.87	20.61	20.83	20.47	22.72
	es	21.82	27.55	28.41	28.13	27.6	30.28
	fr	17.8	23.35	24.36	23.79	24.15	25.88
de		16.97	21.39	23.42	24	24.4	24.28
es	en	18.38	25.39	27.01	27.12	26.98	28.16
fr		17.52	21.93	24.4	23.9	24.47	25.39

Table 3: BLEU scores for multilingual models. Baseline system in the right-most column.

model is provided by a bilingual setting with only one attention head. This is in line with the findings of Cífka and Bojar (2018) and could also be expected as the model is more strongly pushed into a dense semantic abstraction that is beneficial for measuring similarities without further training. More surprising is the negative effect of the multilingual models. We believe that the multilingual information encoded jointly in the attention bridge hampers the results for the monolingual semantic similarity measured with the cosine distance, while it becomes easier in a bilingual scenario where the vector encodes only one source language, English in this case.

ii) On the supervised textual similarity tasks, we find a similar trend as in the previous section for SICK: both a higher number of attention heads and multilinguality contribute to better scores, while for STSB, we notice a different pattern.

This general discrepancy between results in supervised and unsupervised tasks is not new in the literature (Hill et al., 2016). We hypothesize that the training procedure is able to pick up the information needed for the task, while in the unsupervised case a more dense representation is essential.

6 Translation quality

Finally, we also look at the translation performance of the multilingual models we have introduced above compared with a baseline, an standard encoder-decoder model with attention (Luong et al., 2015). In this section, we verify that the attention bridge model is stable and successfully learns to translate in the multilingual case.

Table 3 shows the comparison between the multilingual models. In general, we observe the same trend as in the bilingual evaluation concerning the size of the attention bridge. Namely, more attention heads lead to a higher BLEU score. The model with 50 heads achieves the best results among our models. It obtains scores that range in the same ballpark as the baseline, only in a few

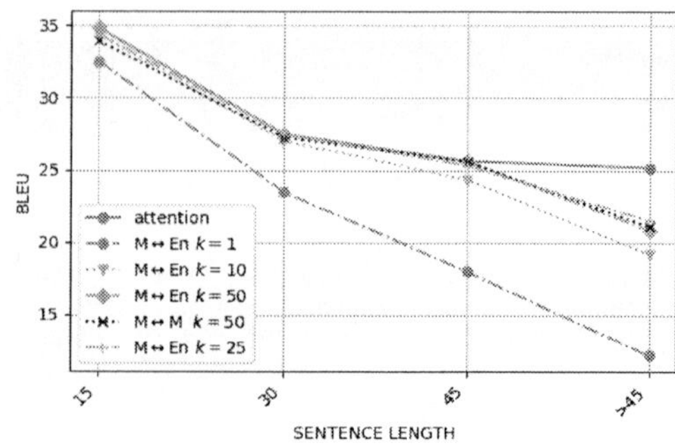

Figure 2: The BLEU scores obtained by the multilingual models and baseline system with respect to different sentence length.

cases there is a degradation of few BLEU points. Notably, we do not see any increase in translation quality from the {DE,ES,FR}↔EN model to the Many-to-Many model; the BLEU scores are statistically equivalent for all six translation directions.

One of the main motivations for having more attention heads lies in the better support of longer sentences. To study the effect, we group sentences of similar length and compute the BLEU score for each group. As we can see from Figure 2 a larger number of attention heads has, indeed, a positive impact when translating longer sentences. Interestingly enough, on sentences with up to 45 words, there is no real gap between the results of the baseline model and our bridge models with a high number of attention heads. It looks like the performance drop of the attention bridge models is entirely due to sentences longer than 45 words.

We hypothesize that this might be due to the increasing syntactic divergences between the languages that have to be encoded. The shared self-attention layer needs to learn to focus on different parts of a sentence depending on the language it reads and, with increasing lengths of a sentence, this ability becomes harder and more difficult to pick up from the data alone.

7 Conclusion

We have shown that fixed-size sentence representations can effectively be learned with multilingual machine translation using a inner-attention layer and scheduled training with multiple translation tasks. The performance of the model heavily depends on the size of the intermediate representation layer and we show that a higher number of attention heads leads to improved translation and stronger representations in supervised downstream tasks (contradicting earlier findings) and multilinguality also helps in the same downstream tasks. Our analysis reveals that the attention bridge model mainly suffers on long sentences. The next steps will include a deeper linguistic analysis of the translation model and the extension to multilingual models with more languages with greater linguistic diversity.

Acknowledgments

This work is part of the FoTran project, funded by the European Research Council (ERC) under the European Union's Horizon 2020 research and innovation programme (grant agreement No 771113).

The authors gratefully acknowledge the support of the Academy of Finland through project 314062 from the ICT 2023 call on Computation, Machine Learning and Artificial Intelligence and project 270354/273457. Finally, We would also like to acknowledge NVIDIA and their GPU grant.

References

Sanjeev Arora, Yingyu Liang, and Tengyu Ma. 2017. A simple but tough-to-beat baseline for sentence embeddings. *ICLR*.

Graeme Blackwood, Miguel Ballesteros, and Todd Ward. 2018. Multilingual neural machine translation with task-specific attention. In *Proceedings of the 27th International Conference on Computational Linguistics*, pages 3112–3122. Association for Computational Linguistics.

Ondej Bojar, Rajen Chatterjee, Christian Federmann, Mark Fishel, Yvette Graham, Barry Haddow, Matthias Huck, Antonio Jimeno Yepes, Philipp Koehn, Christof Monz, Matteo Negri, Aurlie Nvol, Mariana Neves, Matt Post, Lucia Specia, Marco Turchi, and Karin Verspoor, editors. 2018. *Proceedings of the Third Conference on Machine Translation*. Association for Computational Linguistics, Belgium, Brussels.

Denny Britz, Melody Guan, and Minh-Thang Luong. 2017. Efficient attention using a fixed-size memory representation. In *Proceedings of the 2017 Conference on Empirical Methods in Natural Language Processing*, pages 392–400.

Ondřej Cífka and Ondřej Bojar. 2018. Are bleu and meaning representation in opposition? In *Proceedings of the 56th Annual Meeting of the Association for Computational Linguistics (Volume 1: Long Papers)*, pages 1362–1371. Association for Computational Linguistics.

Alexis Conneau and Douwe Kiela. 2018. SentEval: An Evaluation Toolkit for Universal Sentence Representations. In *Proceedings of the Eleventh International Conference on Language Resources and Evaluation (LREC 2018)*, Miyazaki, Japan. European Language Resources Association (ELRA).

Orhan Firat, Baskaran Sankaran, Yaser Al-Onaizan, Fatos T. Yarman Vural, and Kyunghyun Cho. 2016. Zero-resource translation with multi-lingual neural machine translation. In *Proceedings of the 2016 Conference on Empirical Methods in Natural Language Processing*, pages 268–277. Association for Computational Linguistics.

Jonas Gehring, Michael Auli, David Grangier, Denis Yarats, and Yann N Dauphin. 2017. Convolutional Sequence to Sequence Learning. In *Proc. of ICML*.

Jiatao Gu, Hany Hassan, Jacob Devlin, and Victor OK Li. 2018. Universal neural machine translation for extremely low resource languages. In *Proceedings of the 2018 Conference of the North American Chapter of the Association for Computational Linguistics: Human Language Technologies, Volume 1 (Long Papers)*, volume 1, pages 344–354.

Thanh-Le Ha, Jan Niehues, and Alexander Waibel. 2016. Toward multilingual neural machine translation with universal encoder and decoder. *arXiv preprint arXiv:1611.04798*.

Felix Hill, Kyunghyun Cho, and Anna Korhonen. 2016. Learning distributed representations of sentences from unlabelled data. In *Proceedings of the 2016 Conference of the North American Chapter of the Association for Computational Linguistics: Human Language Technologies*, pages 1367–1377.

Melvin Johnson, Mike Schuster, Quoc V Le, Maxim Krikun, Yonghui Wu, Zhifeng Chen, Nikhil Thorat, Fernanda Viégas, Martin Wattenberg, Greg Corrado, et al. 2017. Google's multilingual neural machine translation system: Enabling zero-shot translation. *Transactions of the Association of Computational Linguistics*, 5(1):339–351.

Guillaume Klein, Yoon Kim, Yuntian Deng, Jean Senellart, and Alexander Rush. 2017. Opennmt: Open-source toolkit for neural machine translation. *Proceedings of ACL 2017, System Demonstrations*, pages 67–72.

Philipp Koehn. 2005. Europarl: A parallel corpus for statistical machine translation. In *MT summit*, volume 5, pages 79–86.

Surafel Melaku Lakew, Mauro Cettolo, and Marcello Federico. 2018. A comparison of transformer and recurrent neural networks on multilingual neural machine translation. In *Proceedings of the 27th International Conference on Computational Linguistics*, pages 641–652. Association for Computational Linguistics.

Zhouhan Lin, Minwei Feng, Cicero Nogueira dos Santos, Mo Yu, Bing Xiang, Bowen Zhou, and Yoshua Bengio. 2017. A structured self-attentive sentence embedding. *ICLR*.

Yang Liu, Chengjie Sun, Lei Lin, and Xiaolong Wang. 2016. Learning natural language inference using bidirectional lstm model and inner-attention. *arXiv preprint arXiv:1605.09090*.

Yichao Lu, Phillip Keung, Faisal Ladhak, Vikas Bhardwaj, Shaonan Zhang, and Jason Sun. 2018. A neural interlingua for multilingual machine translation. In *Proceedings of the Third Conference on Machine Translation: Research Papers*, pages 84–92. Association for Computational Linguistics.

Thang Luong, Hieu Pham, and Christopher D Manning. 2015. Effective approaches to attention-based neural machine translation. In *Proceedings of the 2015 Conference on Empirical Methods in Natural Language Processing*, pages 1412–1421.

Bryan McCann, James Bradbury, Caiming Xiong, and Richard Socher. 2017. Learned in translation: Contextualized word vectors. In *Advances in Neural Information Processing Systems*, pages 6294–6305.

Holger Schwenk. 2018. Filtering and mining parallel data in a joint multilingual space. In *Proceedings of the 56th Annual Meeting of the Association for Computational Linguistics (Volume 2: Short Papers)*, volume 2, pages 228–234.

Holger Schwenk and Matthijs Douze. 2017. Learning joint multilingual sentence representations with neural machine translation. In *ACL workshop on Representation Learning for NLP*.

Rico Sennrich, Barry Haddow, and Alexandra Birch. 2016. Neural machine translation of rare words with subword units. In *Proceedings of the 54th Annual Meeting of the Association for Computational Linguistics (Volume 1: Long Papers)*, volume 1, pages 1715–1725.

Sandeep Subramanian, Adam Trischler, Yoshua Bengio, and Christopher J Pal. 2018. Learning general purpose distributed sentence representations via large scale multi-task learning. *ICLR*.

Ashish Vaswani, Noam Shazeer, Niki Parmar, Jakob Uszkoreit, Llion Jones, Aidan N Gomez, Łukasz Kaiser, and Illia Polosukhin. 2017. Attention is all you need. In *Advances in Neural Information Processing Systems*, pages 5998–6008.

Raúl Vázquez, Alessandro Raganato, Jörg Tiedemann, and Mathias Creutz. 2019. Multilingual NMT with a language-independent attention bridge. In *Proceedings of The Fourth Workshop on Representation Learning for NLP (RepL4NLP)*. Association for Computational Linguistics.

Yining Wang, Jiajun Zhang, Feifei Zhai, Jingfang Xu, and Chengqing Zong. 2018. Three strategies to improve one-to-many multilingual translation. In *Proceedings of the 2018 Conference on Empirical Methods in Natural Language Processing*, pages 2955–2960. Association for Computational Linguistics.

Multilingual NMT with a language-independent attention bridge

Raúl Vázquez,* Alessandro Raganato,*† Jörg Tiedemann* and Mathias Creutz*
*University of Helsinki, Department of Digital Humanities
†Basement AI
{name.surname}@helsinki.fi

Abstract

In this paper, we propose an architecture for machine translation (MT) capable of obtaining multilingual sentence representations by incorporating an intermediate *attention bridge* that is shared across all languages. We train the model with language-specific encoders and decoders that are connected through an inner-attention layer on the encoder side. The attention bridge exploits the semantics from each language for translation and develops into a language-agnostic meaning representation that can efficiently be used for transfer learning. We present a new framework for the efficient development of multilingual neural machine translation (NMT) using this model and scheduled training. We have tested the approach in a systematic way with a multi-parallel data set. The model achieves substantial improvements over strong bilingual models and performs well for zero-shot translation, which demonstrates its ability of abstraction and transfer learning.

1 Introduction

Neural machine translation (NMT) provides an ideal setting for multilingual MT because it can efficiently share model parameters and take advantage of the various similarities found by the model in the hidden layers and word embeddings (Firat et al., 2016a; Johnson et al., 2017; Blackwood et al., 2018). Furthermore, multilingual NMT has the potential of considerably improving the performance of neural translation systems for low-resource languages (Lakew et al., 2017) and enables zero-shot translation, i.e., translating between language pairs that were not seen during training (Firat et al., 2016b; Johnson et al., 2017).

For this study we focus on models for multilingual translation that learn language-agnostic representations, where we outline the development of a language-independent representation based on an *attention bridge* shared across all languages. For this, we apply an architecture based on shared self-attention with language-specific encoders and decoders that can easily scale to a large number of languages while addressing the task of obtaining language-independent sentence embeddings (Cífka and Bojar, 2018; Lu et al., 2018; Lin et al., 2017). Those embeddings are created from the encoder's self-attention and connect to the language-specific decoders that attend to them, hence the name 'bridge'. Additionally, we add a penalty term to avoid redundancy in the shared layer. More details of the architecture are given in section 2.

To summarise our contributions, we **i)** present a multilingual translation system that efficiently tackles the task of learning language-agnostic sentence representations; **ii)** verify that this model enables effective transfer learning and zero-shot translation through the shared representation layer; and **iii)** show that multilingually trained embeddings improve the majority of downstream and sentence probing tasks demonstrating the abstractions learned from the combined translation tasks.

2 Model Architecture

Our architecture follows the standard setup of an encoder-decoder model of machine translation with a traditional attention mechanism (Bahdanau et al., 2015; Luong et al., 2015). However, to enable multilingual training we augment the network with language-specific encoders and decoders trainable with a language-rotating scheduler (Dong et al., 2015; Schwenk and Douze, 2017). We also incorporate a self-attention layer (attention bridge), shared among all language pairs, to serve as a language-agnostic layer (Cífka and Bojar, 2018; Lu et al., 2018)

Attention bridge: Each encoder takes as input

Proceedings of the 4th Workshop on Representation Learning for NLP (RepL4NLP-2019), pages 33–39
Florence, Italy, August 2, 2019. ©2019 Association for Computational Linguistics

a sequence of tokens $(x_1, \ldots, x_n)$ and produces n d_h–dimensional hidden states, $H = (h_1, \ldots, h_n)$ with $h_i \in \mathbb{R}^{d_h}$, in our case using a bidirectional long short-term memory (LSTM) (Graves and Schmidhuber, 2005)[1]. Next, we encode this variable length sentence-embedding matrix H into a fixed size $M \in \mathbb{R}^{d_h \times k}$ capable of focusing on k different components of the sentence (Lin et al., 2017; Chen et al., 2018; Cífka and Bojar, 2018), using self-attention as follows:

$$A = softmax\left(W_2 \text{ReLU}(W_1 H^T)\right) \quad (1)$$
$$M = AH \quad (2)$$

where $W_1 \in \mathbb{R}^{d_w \times d_h}$ and $W_2 \in \mathbb{R}^{k \times d_w}$ are weight matrices, with d_w a hyper-parameter set arbitrarily, and k is the number of *attention heads* in the attention bridge.

Each decoder follows a common attention mechanism in NMT (Luong et al., 2015), with an initial state computed by mean pooling over M, and using M instead of the hidden states of the encoder for computing the context vector.

Penalty term: The attention bridge matrix M from Eq. (2) could learn repetitive information for different attention heads. To address this issue, we add a penalty term to the loss function, proven effective in related work (Lin et al., 2017; Chen et al., 2018; Tao et al., 2018), which forces each vector to focus on different aspects of the sentence by making the columns of A to be approximately orthogonal in the Frobenius norm:

$$\mathcal{L} = -\log\left(p\left(Y|X\right)\right) + \left\|AA^T - I\right\|_F^2, \quad (3)$$

where the Frobenius norm of a matrix A can be defined as the sum of the squared singular values of A. By incorporating this term into the loss function we force matrix AA^T to be similar to the identity matrix, that is, $\sum_j a_{ij} a_{ji} \approx 1$. Additionally, considering the fact that the rows of A sum to 1, with entries in $[0, 1]$, it follows that the columns of A will be forced to be approximately orthogonal, and hence penalize redundancy, similar to the double stochastic attention in Xu et al. (2015).

3 Experimental Setup

We conducted four translation experiments and tested the learned sentence representations via downstream tasks. We used the multi30k dataset (Elliott et al., 2016) for training and validation in all available languages: Czech, German, French and English, and tested the trained model with the flickr 2016 test data of the same dataset and obtained BLEU scores using the sacreBLEU script[2] (Post, 2018). We lowercased, normalized and tokenized using the Moses toolkit (Koehn et al., 2007), and applied a 10K-operations Byte Pair Encoding (BPE) model per language (Sennrich et al., 2016).

Each encoder consists of 2 stacked BiLSTMs of size $d_h = 512$, i.e., the hidden states per direction are of size 256. Each decoder includes 2 stacked unidirectional LSTMs with hidden states of size 512. For the model input and output, the word embeddings have dimension $d_x = d_y = 512$. We used an attention bridge layer with 10 attention heads with $d_w = 1024$, the dimensions of W_1 and W_2 from Eq. (1). We chose $k = 10$ because the mean length of a preprocessed sentence in the training data is 13.2 tokens in our case. Choosing a much smaller k would create a bottleneck in the flow of information, and a bigger one would make the model slower and prone to overfitting (Raganato et al., 2019).

We used a Stochastic Gradient Descent (SGD) optimizer with a learning rate of 1.0 and batch size 64, and selected the best model on the development set for each experiment. We implemented our model on top of an OpenNMT-py (Klein et al., 2017) fork, which we make available for reproducibility purposes.[3]

4 Results

First, we verify the correct functionality of the architecture in a bilingual setting, which will become our baseline for comparison to the multilingual models - both with and without an attention bridge.

On the *left* side of Table 1, we can see that the attention bridge model is almost on par with the standard bilingual model for all language pairs in our data set. A decrease in performance is to be

---

[1]Note that the attention bridge is independent of the underlying encoder and decoder (Lu et al., 2018). While we use a biLSTM, it could be replaced with a gated recurrent unit (GRU) (Cho et al., 2014), a transformer type network (Vaswani et al., 2017) or with a convolutional neural network (CNN) (Gehring et al., 2017).

[2]with signature BLEU+case.lc+numrefs.1+smooth.exp+tok.13a+version.1.2.11
[3]`https://github.com/Helsinki-NLP/OpenNMT-py/tree/att-brg`.

src/tgt	BILINGUAL				{DE,FR,CS} ↔ EN				M-2-M			
	EN	DE	CS	FR	EN	DE	CS	FR	EN	DE	CS	FR
EN	-	36.78	28.00	55.96	-	37.85	29.51	57.87	-	37.70	29.67	55.78
DE	39.00	-	23.44	38.22	39.39	-	*0.35*	*0.83*	40.68	-	26.78	41.07
CS	35.89	28.98	-	36.44	37.20	*0.65*	-	*1.02*	38.42	31.07	-	40.27
FR	49.54	32.92	25.98	-	48.49	*0.60*	*0.30*	-	49.92	34.63	26.92	-

src/tgt	BILINGUAL + ATT BRIDGE				{DE,FR,CS} ↔ EN + MONOLING				M-2-M + MONOLINGUAL			
	EN	DE	CS	FR	EN	DE	CS	FR	EN	DE	CS	FR
EN	-	35.85	27.10	53.03	-	38.92	30.27	57.87	-	38.48	30.47	57.35
DE	38.19	-	23.97	37.40	40.17	-	*19.50*	*26.46*	41.82	-	26.90	41.49
CS	36.41	27.28	-	36.41	37.30	*22.13*	-	*22.80*	39.58	31.51	-	40.87
FR	48.93	31.70	25.96	-	50.41	*25.96*	*20.09*	-	50.94	35.25	28.80	-

Table 1: BLEU scores obtained in the experiments. *Left:* Bilingual models, our baselines. *Center:* Models trained on {De,Fr,Cs}↔En, with zero-shot translations in italics. *Right:* Many-to-many model. Both zero-shot and M-2-M translations improve significantly when including monolingual data. (Best results in green cells.)

expected since we pass the information through a fixed size representation made out of 10 self-attention heads without including multilingual information. However, the drop is less than one BLEU point except for English to French, which seems to be an exceptional outlier.

With this result we can justify the validity of the architecture assuring that the additional bottleneck does not create significant deterioration and we can move on with the multilingual models.

4.1 Many-To-One and One-To-Many Models

The power of the attention bridge comes from its ability to share information across various language pairs. We now assess the effects of multilingual information on the translation of individual language pairs, by training many-to-one and one-to-many models. This setup allows us to test the abstraction potential of the attention bridge and its effectiveness to encode multilingual information in zero-shot translation.

First we trained a {De,Fr,Cs}↔En model (Table 1 *(center-top)*), which resulted in substantial improvements for the language pairs seen during training, exceeding both bilingual baselines. However, this model is entirely incapable of performing zero-shot translations. We believe that the inability of the model to generalize to unseen language-pairs arises from the fact that every non-English encoder (or decoder) only learned to process information that was to be decoded into English (or encoded from English input), a finding consistent with Lu et al. (2018). To address this problem, we incorporate monolingual data during training, that is, for each available language A, we included pairs of identical copies of each sentence in A in the training data. All examples come from

the same parallel corpus as before and no additional data is used.

As a consequence, we see a remarkable increase in the BLEU scores, including a substantial boost for the language pairs not seen during training (Table 1 *(center-bottom)*). It seems that the monolingual data informs the model that English is not the unique source/target language. Additionally, there is a positive effect on the seen language pairs (up to almost 2 BLEU points for French to English), the cause of which is not immediately evident. It is possible that the shared layer acquires additional information that can be included in the abstraction process yet not available to the other models.

4.2 Many-to-Many Models

We also tested the architecture in a many-to-many setting with all language pairs included, and summarize our results in Table 1 *(right)*. As in the previous case, we compare settings with and without monolingual training data.

The inclusion of language pairs results in an improved performance when compared to the bilingual baselines, as well as the Many↔En cases, except for the En→Fr and En→De tasks. Moreover, the addition of monolingual data leads to even higher scores, producing the overall best model. The improvements in BLEU range from 1.40 to a remarkable 4.43 when compared to the standard bilingual model.

The zero-shot translation capabilities also deserve a closer look. Figure 1 summarizes a systematic evaluation in which we trained six different models where we include all but one of the available language pairs in training. The cyan bars illustrate the performance of the model on the unseen language pairs compared to our best multilingual model (in red) and the bilingual, fully supervised model (in dark blue). Note, that those zero-shot models are generally better than the ones from the previously discussed {De,Fr,Cs,En}↔En model in Table 1. In most cases, they come very close to the supervised model and even fare well against the multilingual ones.

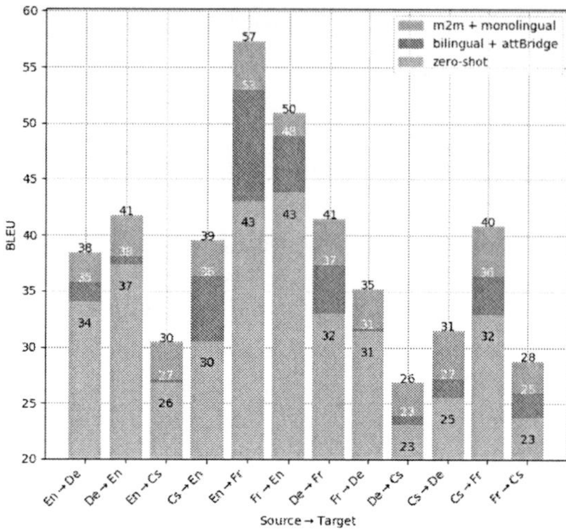

Figure 1: For every language pair, we compare the BLEU scores between our best model (M-2-M with monolingual data), the zero-shot of the model trained without that specific language pair and the bilingual model of that language pair.

5 Downstream Tasks

We apply the sentence representations learned by our model to downstream tasks collected in the SentEval toolkit (Conneau and Kiela, 2018) to evaluate the quality of our language-agnostic sentence embeddings. We run each experiment with five different seeds, and present the average of these scores in Table 2, where we compare our bilingual models against a baseline consisting of the best score achieved by the bilingual models with attention bridge. Since our models were trained on limited data and are not directly comparable to models trained on large-scale data sets, for comparison purposes we present results obtained with GloVe-BoW vectors (Pennington et al., 2014) trained with the same BPE-encoded data as the models.

The sentence embeddings produced by the multilingual models show consistent improvements, for the classification tasks of the SentEval collection, with only two exceptions. Moreover, our many-to-many model obtains better results in the

SICK Relatedness (SICKR) and STS-Benchmark (STS-B); that is, the trainable semantic similarity tasks. [2]

For the SentEval probing tasks (Conneau et al., 2018) we use the default recommended settings, i.e., a multilayer perceptron classifier with sigmoid nonlinearity, 200 hidden units, and 0.1 dropout rate. Again, we can observe improvements in the majority of cases when adding multiple languages to the training procedure. Remarkably, we observe a significant increment on the accuracy for the specific tasks of Length (superficial property), Top Constituents (syntactic property) and Object Number (semantic information) when training the encoders with multilingual data. Multilingual models outperform the bilingual models in all but one test.

	DOWNSTREAM TASKS			
TASK	BASELINE	M ↔ EN	M-2-M	GloVe-BoW
CR	68.52	68.32	69.01	63.97
MR	60.08	60.40	61.80	52.32
MPQA	73.51	72.98	73.28	68.76
SUBJ	77.25	78.64	80.88	58.75
SST2	61.92	62.02	62.24	54.68
SST5	31.15	32.10	31.83	28.20
TREC	67.75	69.84	66.40	21.16
MRPC	70.96	68.83	70.43	64.87
SNLI	61.75	64.52	65.12	35.05
SICKE	74.85	75.46	76.92	56.62
SICKR	*0.652*	*0.659*	*0.677*	*0.174*
STS-B	*0.616*	*0.618*	*0.630*	*0.163*
	PROBING TASKS			
Length	80.76	84.76	85.41	30.90
WC	10.02	9.56	9.13	0.22
Depth	32.14	33.05	31.60	20.66
TopConst	40.12	44.04	39.76	11.48
BShift	57.41	58.35	59.76	50.08
Tense	67.61	69.36	68.27	54.72
SubjNum	68.55	69.67	69.89	54.32
ObjNum	70.01	72.19	73.29	60.58
SOMO	49.90	49.46	50.12	50.03
CoordInv	61.38	60.57	62.21	49.88

Table 2: Scores obtained in the SentEval tasks. The BASELINE column reports the best score among the bilingual models + att bridge. Green cells indicate the highest score. All tasks show the accuracy of the model except for SICKR and STS-B tasks, which include Pearson mean values.

---

[2] However, the non-trainable semantic similarity tasks exhibited decreasing scores for multilingual models (not shown here due to space limitations). This can be explained by the fact that the additional information encoded in our multilingual embeddings cannot effectively be separated from the information that is necessary for monolingual similarity measures, without further training.

6 Effect of the Penalty Term

In order to study the effect of the penalty term, we train additional bilingual models, without using the penalty term (Eq. 3) in the training. We then compare BLEU scores, where the penalty term is present and absent, as shown in Table 3. Overall, both types of models show performance in the same ballpark yielding similar results. As discussed in Lin et al. (2017), the quantitative effect of the penalty term might not be obvious for some tasks, while keeping the positive effect of encouraging the attentive matrix to be focused on different aspects of the sentence.

	WITH PENALTY TERM			
	EN	DE	CS	FR
EN	-	35.85	27.10	53.03
DE	38.19	-	23.97	37.40
CS	36.41	27.28	-	36.41
FR	48.93	31.70	25.96	-

	WITHOUT PENALTY TERM			
	EN	DE	CS	FR
EN	-	34.67	27.22	54.39
DE	38.70	-	23.44	38.2
CS	35.76	28.50	-	36.4
FR	48.76	31.60	25.55	-

Table 3: BLEU scores obtained with the BILINGUAL + ATT BRIDGE models in the experiments with and without penalty term.

While the effect of the penalty term might not be very significant in this case, we note that adding the penalty term does not hurt the performance while helping the model not to learn potential redundant information.

7 Conclusion

We propose a multilingual NMT architecture with three modifications to the common attentive encoder-decoder architecture: language-specific encoders and decoders, a shared language-independent attention bridge and a penalty term that forces this layer to attend different parts of the input sentence. This constitutes a multilingual translation system that efficiently incorporates transfer learning and can also tackle the task of learning multilingual sentence representations. The results suggest that the attention bridge layer can efficiently share parameters in a multilingual setting, increasing up to 4.4 BLEU points compared to the baselines. Additionally, we make use of the sentence representations produced by the shared attention bridge of the trained models for downstream-testing, which helped us to verify the generalization capabilities of the model. The results suggest that sentence embeddings improve with additional languages involved in training the underlying machine translation model.

Acknowledgments

 This work is part of the FoTran project, funded by the European Research Council (ERC) under the European Union's Horizon 2020 research and innovation programme (grant agreement No 771113).

The authors gratefully acknowledge the support of the Academy of Finland through project 314062 from the ICT 2023 call on Computation, Machine Learning and Artificial Intelligence. We thank the participants that contributed to the project we lead during the 13th MT Marathon in Prague. We are particularly grateful with Chris Hokamp, whose help was crucial during that time. Finally, We would also like to acknowledge NVIDIA and their GPU grant.

References

Dzimitry Bahdanau, Kyunghyun Cho, and Yoshua Bengio. 2015. Neural machine translation by jointly learning to align and translate. *ICLR 2015*.

Graeme Blackwood, Miguel Ballesteros, and Todd Ward. 2018. Multilingual Neural Machine Translation with Task-Specific Attention. *Proceedings of the 27th Conference on Computational Linguistics*, pages 3112–3122.

Qian Chen, Zhen-Hua Ling, and Xiaodan Zhu. 2018. Enhancing sentence embedding with generalized pooling. In *Proceedings of the 27th International Conference on Computational Linguistics*, pages 1815–1826.

Kyunghyun Cho, Bart van Merrienboer, Caglar Gulcehre, Dzmitry Bahdanau, Fethi Bougares, Holger Schwenk, and Yoshua Bengio. 2014. Learning phrase representations using rnn encoder–decoder for statistical machine translation. In *Proceedings of the 2014 Conference on Empirical Methods in Natural Language Processing (EMNLP)*, pages 1724–1734.

Ondřej Cífka and Ondřej Bojar. 2018. Are bleu and meaning representation in opposition? In *Proceedings of the 56th Annual Meeting of the Association for Computational Linguistics (Volume 1: Long Papers)*, pages 1362–1371.

Alexis Conneau and Douwe Kiela. 2018. Senteval: An evaluation toolkit for universal sentence representations. In *Proceedings of the Eleventh International Conference on Language Resources and Evaluation (LREC-2018)*.

Alexis Conneau, Germán Kruszewski, Guillaume Lample, Loïc Barrault, and Marco Baroni. 2018. What you can cram into a single vector: Probing sentence embeddings for linguistic properties. In *Proceedings of the 56th Annual Meeting of the Association for Computational Linguistics (Volume 1: Long Papers)*, pages 2126–2136.

Daxiang Dong, Hua Wu, Wei He, Dianhai Yu, and Haifeng Wang. 2015. Multi-Task Learning for Multiple Language Translation. In *Proceedings of the 53rd Annual Meeting of the Association for Computational Linguistics and the 7th International Joint Conference on Natural Language Processing (Volume 1: Long Papers)*, pages 1723–1732, Beijing, China. Association for Computational Linguistics.

D. Elliott, S. Frank, K. Sima'an, and L. Specia. 2016. Multi30k: Multilingual english-german image descriptions. In *Proceedings of the 5th Workshop on Vision and Language*, pages 70–74.

Orhan Firat, Kyunghyun Cho, and Yoshua Bengio. 2016a. Multi-Way, Multilingual Neural Machine Translation with a Shared Attention Mechanism. In *Proceedings of the 2016 Conference of the North American Chapter of the Association for Computational Linguistics: Human Language Technologies*, pages 866–875, San Diego, California. Association for Computational Linguistics.

Orhan Firat, Baskaran Sankaran, Yaser Al-Onaizan, Fatos T. Yarman Vural, and Kyunghyun Cho. 2016b. Zero-Resource Translation with Multi-Lingual Neural Machine Translation. In *Proceedings of the 2016 Conference on Empirical Methods in Natural Language Processing*, pages 268–277, Austin, Texas. Association for Computational Linguistics.

Jonas Gehring, Michael Auli, David Grangier, Denis Yarats, and Yann N Dauphin. 2017. Convolutional Sequence to Sequence Learning. In *Proc. of ICML*.

Alex Graves and Jürgen Schmidhuber. 2005. Framewise phoneme classification with bidirectional lstm and other neural network architectures. *Neural Networks*, 18(5-6):602–610.

Melvin Johnson, Mike Schuster, Quoc V Le, Maxim Krikun, Yonghui Wu, Zhifeng Chen, Nikhil Thorat, Fernanda Viégas, Martin Wattenberg, Greg Corrado, et al. 2017. Googles multilingual neural machine translation system: Enabling zero-shot translation. *Transactions of the Association for Computational Linguistics*, 5:339–351.

Guillaume Klein, Yoon Kim, Yuntian Deng, Jean Senellart, and Alexander Rush. 2017. Opennmt: Open-source toolkit for neural machine translation.

Proceedings of ACL 2017, System Demonstrations, pages 67–72.

Philipp Koehn, Hieu Hoang, Alexandra Birch, Chris Callison-Burch, Marcello Federico, Nicola Bertoldi, Brooke Cowan, Wade Shen, Christine Moran, Richard Zens, Chris Dyer, Ondrej Bojar, and Alexandra Constantinand Evan Herbst. 2007. Moses: Open source toolkit for statistical machine translation. *Annual Meeting of the Association for Computational Linguistics (ACL)*, Demo and Poster Sessions.

Surafel M Lakew, Quintino F Lotito, Matteo Negri, Marco Turchi, and Marcello Federico. 2017. Improving Zero-Shot Translation of Low-Resource Languages. *Proceedings of the 14th International Workshop on Spoken Language Translation*, pages 113–119.

Zhouhan Lin, Minwei Feng, Cícero Nogueira dos Santos, Mo Yu, Bing Xiang, Bowen Zhou, and Yoshua Bengio. 2017. A structured self-attentive sentence embedding. *5th International Conference on Learning Representations (ICLR 2017)*.

Yichao Lu, Phillip Keung, Faisal Ladhak, Vikas Bhardwaj, Shaonan Zhang, and Jason Sun. 2018. A neural interlingua for multilingual machine translation. In *Proceedings of the Third Conference on Machine Translation: Research Papers*, pages 84–92.

Thang Luong, Hieu Pham, and Christopher D Manning. 2015. Effective approaches to attention-based neural machine translation. In *Proceedings of the 2015 Conference on Empirical Methods in Natural Language Processing*, pages 1412–1421.

Jeffrey Pennington, Richard Socher, and Christopher D. Manning. 2014. Glove: Global vectors for word representation. *Proceedings of the 2014 Conference on Empirical Methods in Natural Language Processing (EMNLP)*, pages 1532–1543.

Matt Post. 2018. A call for clarity in reporting bleu scores. In *Proceedings of the Third Conference on Machine Translation: Research Papers*, pages 186–191.

Alessandro Raganato, Raúl Vázquez, Mathias Creutz, and Jörg Tiedemann. 2019. An evaluation of language-agnostic inner-attention-based representations in machine translation. In *Proceedings of The Fourth Workshop on Representation Learning for NLP (RepL4NLP)*. Association for Computational Linguistics.

Holger Schwenk and Matthijs Douze. 2017. Learning Multilingual Sentence Representations with Neural Machine Translation. In *2nd Workshop on Representation Learning for NLP*, pages 157–167. Association for Computational Linguistics.

Rico Sennrich, Barry Haddow, and Alexandra Birch. 2016. Neural machine translation of rare words with subword units. *Proceedings of the 54th Annual Meeting of the Association for Computational Linguistics (Volume 1: Long Papers)*, pages 1715–1725.

Chongyang Tao, Shen Gao, Mingyue Shang, Wei Wu, Dongyan Zhao, and Rui Yan. 2018. Get The Point of My Utterance! Learning Towards Effective Responses with Multi-Head Attention Mechanism. In *Proceedings of the Twenty-Seventh International Joint Conference on Artificial Intelligence*, pages 4418–4424, Stockholm, Sweden. International Joint Conferences on Artificial Intelligence Organization.

Ashish Vaswani, Noam Shazeer, Niki Parmar, Jakob Uszkoreit, Llion Jones, Aidan N Gomez, Ł ukasz Kaiser, and Illia Polosukhin. 2017. Attention is all you need. In I. Guyon, U. V. Luxburg, S. Bengio, H. Wallach, R. Fergus, S. Vishwanathan, and R. Garnett, editors, *Advances in Neural Information Processing Systems 30*, pages 5998–6008. Curran Associates, Inc.

Kelvin Xu, Jimmy Lei Ba, Ryan Kiros, Kyunghyun Cho, Aaron Courville, Ruslan Salakhutdinov, Richard S. Zemel, and Yoshua Bengio. 2015. Show, attend and tell: Neural image captiongeneration with visual attention. *Proceedings of the 32nd International Conference on Machine Learning*, pages 1532–1543.

Efficient Language Modeling with Automatic Relevance Determination in Recurrent Neural Networks

Maxim Kodryan[*]
Moscow State University
Moscow, Russia
maxkordn54@gmail.com

Artem Grachev[*]
Samsung R&D Institute,
National Research University
Higher School of Economics
Moscow, Russia
grachev.art@gmail.com

Dmitry Ignatov
National Research University
Higher School of Economics
Moscow, Russia

Dmitry Vetrov
Samsung AI Center,
National Research University
Higher School of Economics
Moscow, Russia

Abstract

Reduction of the number of parameters is one of the most important goals in Deep Learning. In this article we propose an adaptation of Doubly Stochastic Variational Inference for Automatic Relevance Determination (DSVI-ARD) for neural networks compression. We find this method to be especially useful in language modeling tasks, where large number of parameters in the input and output layers is often excessive. We also show that DSVI-ARD can be applied together with encoder-decoder weight tying allowing to achieve even better sparsity and performance. Our experiments demonstrate that more than 90% of the weights in both encoder and decoder layers can be removed with a minimal quality loss.

1 Introduction

The problem of neural networks compression has recently gained more interest as the number of parameters (and hence memory size) of modern neural networks increased drastically. Moreover, only a few weights prove to be relevant for prediction while the majority are de facto redundant (Han et al., 2015).

In this paper we suggest an adaptation of a Bayesian approach called *Automatic Relevance Determination* (ARD) for neural networks compression in language modeling tasks, where the first and the last linear layers often have enormous size. We derive the *Doubly Stochastic Variational Inference* (DSVI) algorithm for non-iid (not independent and identically distributed) objects, a common case in language modeling, and use it to perform optimization of our models.

Furthermore, we extend this approach so that it could be applied together with the weight tying technique (Press and Wolf, 2017; Inan et al., 2016), i.e., using the same set of parameters for both weight matrices of the first and the last layers, which has been proved highly efficient.

2 Related works

Most of the works on neural networks compression can be roughly divided into two categories: those dealing with matrix decomposition approaches (Lu et al., 2016; Arjovsky et al., 2016; Tjandra et al., 2017; Grachev et al., 2019) and those that leverage pruning techniques (Han et al., 2015; Narang et al., 2017). From this point of view methods based on Bayesian techniques (Louizos et al., 2017; Molchanov et al., 2017) can be considered as a more mathematically justified version of pruning.

We have focused on the pruning in application to word-level language modeling as this task usually involves a large vocabulary, hence, causing weight matrices of the first and the last layers to be huge. Chirkova et al. (2018) also consider Bayesian pruning in language modeling, though their approach is based on the Variational Dropout (VD) technique, which has been proved to be

---

[*] These two authors contributed equally; the ordering of their names was chosen arbitrarily. The work was done when the first author was an intern at the Samsung R&D Institute.

Proceedings of the 4th Workshop on Representation Learning for NLP (RepL4NLP-2019), pages 40–48
Florence, Italy, August 2, 2019. ©2019 Association for Computational Linguistics

poorly theoretically justified (Hron et al., 2018), whereas ARD does not encounter these issues while maintaining similar efficacy (Kharitonov et al., 2018).

At last, as far as we are concerned, combining DSVI-ARD (or other Bayesian prunning techniques) with weight tying has not been considered previously.

3 Language modeling with neural networks

The language modeling problem is one of the important classical NLP problems and has various applications such as machine translation and text classification.

This problem is usually formulated as probabilistic prediction of a word sequence $(w_1, \ldots, w_T) = (w_i)_{i=1}^{T}$ as follows:

$$\mathsf{P}\left((w_i)_{i=1}^{T}\right) = \mathsf{P}\left(w_T \mid (w_i)_{i=1}^{T-1}\right)\mathsf{P}\left((w_i)_{i=1}^{T-1}\right) =$$
$$= \prod_{t=1}^{T}\mathsf{P}\left(w_t \mid (w_i)_{i=1}^{t-1}\right) \approx \prod_{t=1}^{T}\mathsf{P}\left(w_t \mid (w_i)_{i=t-T_0}^{t-1}\right) \tag{1}$$

The last equation in (1) is approximated as it is almost always impossible to calculate this expression exactly for a sequence of words of arbitrary length. Therefore, the calculation is performed only within a context of a fixed size T_0.

Nowadays, approaches that perform the approximation for whole words involve different variations of RNNs (Bengio et al., 2003; Mikolov, 2012) such as LSTM or GRU (Hochreiter and Schmidhuber, 1997; Cho et al., 2014). In word-level models the input layer maps words from the vocabulary $\mathbb{V}$ to some vector representation, and vice versa for the output layer: from a vector to a distribution over words in the vocabulary. It leads to sizes of these layers being proportional to the vocabulary size $|\mathbb{V}|$ which is tens of thousands in a typical use case.

Assume using LSTM cells as recurrent units. We can compute the total number of parameters in a network via the following formula:

$$n_{total} = 8LD^2 + 2|\mathbb{V}|D, \tag{2}$$

where L is the number of recurrent hidden layers, and D is the hidden layers size (for simplicity we let all hidden layers be of the same size). Various designs (Bengio and Senecal, 2003; Chen et al., 2016) have been proposed to reduce it, but still in word-level language modeling tasks with a significantly large vocabulary size the second term in the sum (2) makes the largest contribution. Sometimes the softmax (decoder) layer can solely occupy up to a third of the whole network memory space.

The following section describes the technique that performs efficient reduction of parameters in linear layers. This technique can be applied to the decoder layer of RNN (or to both decoder and encoder layers in tied-weight setting) providing the overall network compression with a negligible drop in quality.

4 DSVI-ARD

In this section we describe how the Doubly Stochastic Variational Inference algorithm for Automatic Relevance Determination (DSVI-ARD) originally proposed in (Titsias and Lázaro-Gredilla, 2014) can be adopted for solving multiclass classification task and, thus, leveraged in neural networks training for compressing their dense layers (in particular, decoder layers in RNNs).

4.1 Automatic Relevance Determination

We formulate the multiclass classification problem in a Bayesian framework that can provide a useful tool for feature selection — the so-called Automatic Relevance Determination (ARD).[1]

Consider a discriminative probabilistic model given a training dataset $(X, Y) = \{(\boldsymbol{x}_n, y_n)\}_{n=1}^{N}$ of N independent objects:

$$p(W, Y \mid X, \Lambda) = p(W \mid \Lambda) \prod_{n=1}^{N} p(y_n \mid W, \boldsymbol{x}_n) =$$
$$= \prod_{i=1}^{K}\prod_{j=1}^{D} \mathcal{N}\left(w_{ij} \mid 0, \lambda_{ij}\right) \prod_{n=1}^{N} \mathrm{Softmax}\left(W\boldsymbol{x}_n\right)_{y_n} \tag{3}$$

Here $\boldsymbol{x}_n \in \mathbb{R}^D$ is the feature vector of the n-th object, $y_n \in \{1, \ldots, K\}$ is the label of the n-th object's class, $W \in \mathbb{R}^{K \times D}$ is the matrix of model parameters and $\Lambda \in \mathbb{R}^{K \times D}$ is the matrix of hyperparameters defining the prior distribution $p(W \mid \Lambda)$ over parameters W.

---

[1] Here we consider linear classification for simplicity, although the same model is applicable to neural networks, see subsection 4.3.

The prior distribution $p(W \mid \Lambda)$ is considered to be element-wise factorized Gaussian over each element w_{ij} (zero mean and tunable variance λ_{ij}). The likelihood function $p(y_n \mid W, \boldsymbol{x}_n)$ is the y_n-th element of the softmax vector of linear logits $W\boldsymbol{x}_n$. Such a likelihood function is quite typical in classification tasks and can be encountered in multivariate Logistic Regression.

The two goals of the subsequent Bayesian inference are, first, obtaining posterior distribution over the model parameters conditioned on the training dataset $p(W \mid X, Y, \Lambda)$, which can be leveraged in prediction on the test set, and, second, optimal model selection, i.e., hyperparameters tuning. Both problems can be solved simultaneously by maximizing the Evidence Lower Bound (ELBO):

$$\mathcal{L}(q, \Lambda) = \mathbb{E}_{W \sim q(W)}\left[\log p(Y \mid W, X)\right] - \\ - KL\left(q(W) \| p(W \mid \Lambda)\right). \tag{4}$$

ELBO is a function of two variables: an arbitrary *variational distribution* over parameters $q(W)$ and model hyperparameters Λ, and can be decomposed into two parts: the data term $\mathbb{E}_{W \sim q(W)}\left[\log p(Y \mid W, X)\right]$ and the negative KL-divergence between the variational approximation $q(W)$ and the prior distribution $p(W \mid \Lambda)$ (KL-term) $-KL\left(q(W) \| p(W \mid \Lambda)\right)$. We further show that maximization of ELBO with respect to both q and Λ solves the model selection problem while also fitting q to the posterior.

ELBO has several useful properties such as $\mathcal{L}(q, \Lambda) \leq \log p(Y \mid X, \Lambda), \forall q, \Lambda$ (bounds the evidence logarithm $\log p(Y \mid X, \Lambda)$ from below) and $\mathcal{L}(q, \Lambda) = \log p(Y \mid X, \Lambda)$ if and only if $q(W) = p(W \mid X, Y, \Lambda)$, so maximization of ELBO with respect to q for fixed Λ is equivalent to fitting q to the posterior $p(W \mid X, Y, \Lambda)$, hence solving the first of the mentioned Bayesian inference problems.

Maximization of the evidence $p(Y \mid X, \Lambda)$ with respect to hyperparameters Λ is a well-known Bayesian model selection method, also known as empirical Bayes estimation (Carlin and Louis, 1997). A model with the highest evidence is considered to be "the best" in terms of both data fit and model complexity. Evidence maximization can be performed via ELBO maximization as

$$\max_{\Lambda} \log p(Y \mid X, \Lambda) = \max_{q, \Lambda} \mathcal{L}(q, \Lambda). \tag{5}$$

Finally, this double maximization procedure, as we have shown above, handles the model selection problem while also fitting q to the posterior.

From the view of the ELBO functional it is clear that only the KL-term $KL\left(q(W) \| p(W \mid \Lambda)\right)$ depends on Λ, hence maximization of ELBO with respect to Λ is equivalent to minimization of the KL-term with respect to Λ.

Now we restrict the variational distribution q to the factorized Gaussian:

$$q(W \mid \boldsymbol{\mu}, \boldsymbol{\sigma}) = \prod_{i=1}^{K}\prod_{j=1}^{D} \mathcal{N}(w_{ij} \mid \mu_{ij}, \sigma_{ij}^2), \tag{6}$$

where $\boldsymbol{\mu}, \boldsymbol{\sigma} \in \mathbb{R}^{K \times D}$ are the *variational parameters*.

This way ELBO maximization (or equivalently, KL-term minimization) with respect to Λ can be performed analytically with the solution at

$$\lambda_{ij}^* = \mu_{ij}^2 + \sigma_{ij}^2. \tag{7}$$

After substituting Λ^* from (7) into the ELBO equation (4) and taking into account the variational family restriction (6) we can rewrite the maximization problem (5) as follows:

$$\mathbb{E}_{W \sim q(W \mid \boldsymbol{\mu}, \boldsymbol{\sigma})}\left[\log p(Y \mid W, X)\right] + \\ + \frac{1}{2}\sum_{i=1}^{K}\sum_{j=1}^{D} \log \frac{\sigma_{ij}^2}{\mu_{ij}^2 + \sigma_{ij}^2} \longrightarrow \max_{\boldsymbol{\mu}, \boldsymbol{\sigma}} \tag{8}$$

This equation (8) is the final form of the ARD ELBO maximization problem. We can see that the first term (data term) induces the variational parameters to describe the observed data well by sharpening the variational distribution at the maximum likelihood point, while the second term (KL-term) makes irrelevant parameters shrink. The mutual maximization of both terms leads to a sparse solution (in the limit), at which all redundant features are zeroed. The following subsections describe how it can be performed in practice, especially in application to recurrent neural networks.

4.2 DSVI

The Doubly Stochastic Variational Inference (DSVI) is a method of stochastic gradient maximization of ELBO with respect to the variational parameters. We provide the standard DSVI-ARD description in Algorithm 1. At each iteration two types of random variables are sampled: a mini-batch of objects $\{\boldsymbol{x}_m, y_m\}_{m=1}^{M} \subseteq (X, Y)$

and a set of "proto-weights" for each object in the mini-batch $\epsilon_m \sim \mathcal{N}(\mathbf{0}, I), \epsilon_m \in \mathbb{R}^{K \times D}$, which are used to obtain stochastic gradients of the log-likelihood with respect to the variational parameters via the reparametrization trick (RT) (Kingma et al., 2015). DSVI does not depend on a specific form of the log-likelihood function $\log p(y \mid W, x)$, but only requires its gradient $\nabla_W \log p(y \mid W, x)$, so the same procedure is applicable for different models with differentiable log-likelihoods. DSVI can also be regarded as efficient SGD minimization of the negative ELBO loss functional (8), which consists of the data term and the KL-regularizer.

Algorithm 1 Doubly stochastic variational inference

Input: log-likelihood $\log p(y \mid W, \mathbf{x})$, training dataset (X, Y) of size N, learning rates $\{\rho_k\}$, mini-batch size M

Initialize the variational parameters $\boldsymbol{\mu}^{(0)}, \boldsymbol{\sigma}^{(0)}$, $k = 0$

repeat

    $k = k + 1$

    Sample a mini-batch

    $\{\boldsymbol{x}_m, y_m\}_{m=1}^M \subseteq (X, Y)$

    for all objects $(\boldsymbol{x}_m, y_m)$ in the mini-batch **do**

        Sample $\epsilon_m \sim \mathcal{N}(\mathbf{0}, I), \epsilon_m \in \mathbb{R}^{K \times D}$

        $W_m := \boldsymbol{\mu}^{(k-1)} + \boldsymbol{\sigma}^{(k-1)} \odot \epsilon_m$

    end for

$$g_{\boldsymbol{\mu}}^{Data} := \frac{N}{M} \sum_{m=1}^M \nabla_{\boldsymbol{\mu}} \log p(y_m \mid W_m, \boldsymbol{x}_m)$$

$$g_{\boldsymbol{\sigma}}^{Data} := \frac{N}{M} \sum_{m=1}^M \nabla_{\boldsymbol{\sigma}} \log p(y_m \mid W_m, \boldsymbol{x}_m)$$

$$g_{\boldsymbol{\mu}}^{KL} := \nabla_{\boldsymbol{\mu}} \left[\frac{1}{2} \sum_{i=1}^K \sum_{j=1}^D \log \frac{\sigma_{ij}^2}{\mu_{ij}^2 + \sigma_{ij}^2} \right] \Big|_{\substack{\boldsymbol{\mu} = \boldsymbol{\mu}^{(k-1)} \\ \boldsymbol{\sigma} = \boldsymbol{\sigma}^{(k-1)}}}$$

$$g_{\boldsymbol{\sigma}}^{KL} := \nabla_{\boldsymbol{\sigma}} \left[\frac{1}{2} \sum_{i=1}^K \sum_{j=1}^D \log \frac{\sigma_{ij}^2}{\mu_{ij}^2 + \sigma_{ij}^2} \right] \Big|_{\substack{\boldsymbol{\mu} = \boldsymbol{\mu}^{(k-1)} \\ \boldsymbol{\sigma} = \boldsymbol{\sigma}^{(k-1)}}}$$

$$g_{\boldsymbol{\mu}} := g_{\boldsymbol{\mu}}^{Data} + g_{\boldsymbol{\mu}}^{KL}$$

$$g_{\boldsymbol{\sigma}} := g_{\boldsymbol{\sigma}}^{Data} + g_{\boldsymbol{\sigma}}^{KL}$$

$$\boldsymbol{\mu}^{(k)} = \boldsymbol{\mu}^{(k-1)} + \rho_k g_{\boldsymbol{\mu}}$$

$$\boldsymbol{\sigma}^{(k)} = \boldsymbol{\sigma}^{(k-1)} + \rho_k g_{\boldsymbol{\sigma}}$$

until convergence criterion is met

4.3 DSVI-ARD in Recurrent Neural Networks

As was noted above, DSVI can be applied to any probabilistic ARD model with differentiable likelihood. A neural network with a softmax layer in-

---

Algorithm 2 Doubly stochastic variational inference for non-independent data

---

Input: log-likelihood $\log p(y \mid W, \mathbf{x})$, training dataset (X, Y) of size N, learning rates $\{\rho_k\}$, mini-batch size M

Initialize the variational parameters $\boldsymbol{\mu}^{(0)}, \boldsymbol{\sigma}^{(0)}$, $k = 0$

repeat

    $k = k + 1$

    Sample a mini-batch

    $\{\boldsymbol{x}_m, y_m\}_{m=1}^M \subseteq (X, Y)$ of non-iid objects

    Sample one $\epsilon \sim \mathcal{N}(\mathbf{0}, I), \epsilon \in \mathbb{R}^{K \times D}$

    $W := \boldsymbol{\mu}^{(k-1)} + \boldsymbol{\sigma}^{(k-1)} \odot \epsilon$

$$g_{\boldsymbol{\mu}}^{Data} := \frac{N}{M} \sum_{m=1}^M \nabla_{\boldsymbol{\mu}} \log p(y_m \mid W, \boldsymbol{x}_m)$$

$$g_{\boldsymbol{\sigma}}^{Data} := \frac{N}{M} \sum_{m=1}^M \nabla_{\boldsymbol{\sigma}} \log p(y_m \mid W, \boldsymbol{x}_m)$$

$$g_{\boldsymbol{\mu}}^{KL} := \nabla_{\boldsymbol{\mu}} \left[\frac{1}{2} \sum_{i=1}^K \sum_{j=1}^D \log \frac{\sigma_{ij}^2}{\mu_{ij}^2 + \sigma_{ij}^2} \right] \Big|_{\substack{\boldsymbol{\mu} = \boldsymbol{\mu}^{(k-1)} \\ \boldsymbol{\sigma} = \boldsymbol{\sigma}^{(k-1)}}}$$

$$g_{\boldsymbol{\sigma}}^{KL} := \nabla_{\boldsymbol{\sigma}} \left[\frac{1}{2} \sum_{i=1}^K \sum_{j=1}^D \log \frac{\sigma_{ij}^2}{\mu_{ij}^2 + \sigma_{ij}^2} \right] \Big|_{\substack{\boldsymbol{\mu} = \boldsymbol{\mu}^{(k-1)} \\ \boldsymbol{\sigma} = \boldsymbol{\sigma}^{(k-1)}}}$$

$$g_{\boldsymbol{\mu}} := g_{\boldsymbol{\mu}}^{Data} + g_{\boldsymbol{\mu}}^{KL}$$

$$g_{\boldsymbol{\sigma}} := g_{\boldsymbol{\sigma}}^{Data} + g_{\boldsymbol{\sigma}}^{KL}$$

$$\boldsymbol{\mu}^{(k)} = \boldsymbol{\mu}^{(k-1)} + \rho_k g_{\boldsymbol{\mu}}$$

$$\boldsymbol{\sigma}^{(k)} = \boldsymbol{\sigma}^{(k-1)} + \rho_k g_{\boldsymbol{\sigma}}$$

until convergence criterion is met

---

troduces a likelihood function similar to the one considered in (3). Hence, we suggest replacing the softmax output layer with the ARD layer for multiclass classification and train it with the DSVI algorithm computing its log-likelihood gradients via backpropagation due to the usage of the RT.

When training RNN with a DSVI-ARD layer as a decoder (softmax layer in this case) we encounter the question of sampling strategy for parameters: one sample per object or once for the whole mini-batch of objects. The first strategy is typical for standard classification tasks and is implemented in the classical DSVI algorithm 1. The second one is more justified in the RNN case because objects in one sequence (mini-batch) are not independent and should better be processed with the same weights. We propose Algorithm 2, which is applicable in the case of non-iid objects in a mini-batch. Summing it up, it differs from the standard DSVI only in that the "proto-weights" $\epsilon \in \mathbb{R}^{K \times D}$ are sampled once for the whole mini-batch at each iteration.

We also consider applying DSVI-ARD in a tied-weight setting. For that we slightly change the model so that both the encoder and decoder layers contribute into the likelihood via the same set of weights. Now (in the non-iid DSVI algorithm 2) the same set of parameters (weight matrix) is sampled for both layers, and their gradients with respect to the variational parameters are summed to obtain the mutual gradient of $\log p(y \mid W, \boldsymbol{x})$ for the data term update g^{Data}. The KL-term remains the same as neither new random variables are added to the model nor its prior distribution or variational approximation changes. The only thing that varies is the likelihood of the model, i.e., the data term: now the encoder is also conditioned on the variational parameters $\boldsymbol{\mu}$ and $\boldsymbol{\sigma}$. This basically means that the gradients w.r.t. the encoder's weights are propagated back to the variational parameters.

5 Experiments

We have conducted several experiments to test the DSVI-ARD compression approach in language modeling. We used LSTM and LSTM with tied weights models from (Zaremba et al., 2014; Inan et al., 2016) respectively as our baselines: the experiments involved the same LSTM architecture with two hidden layers of size 650 and two datasets: PTB (Mikolov et al., 2010) and Wikitext2 (Merity et al., 2016); also each mini-batch of objects was constructed from bs word sequences ($bs = 10$ and $bs = 20$ for evaluation and training respectively) of length $bptt = 35$.

We applied dropout after the embedding (except for the tied-weight ARD models because ARD can be regarded as a special form of regularization by itself) and hidden layers, with a dropout rate as a hyperparameter. We used stochastic gradient descent (SGD) as an optimization procedure, with adaptive learning rate decreasing from the starting value by a multiplicative factor (both are hyperparameters) each time validation perplexity has stopped improving.

We also compared our approach to other compression techniques: matrix decomposition-based (Grachev et al., 2019) and VD-based (Chirkova et al., 2018). For the last one we used a similar model: a network with one LSTM layer of 256 hidden units.

5.1 Training and evaluation

The whole set of parameters of a model with DSVI-ARD layers can be divided into the varia-

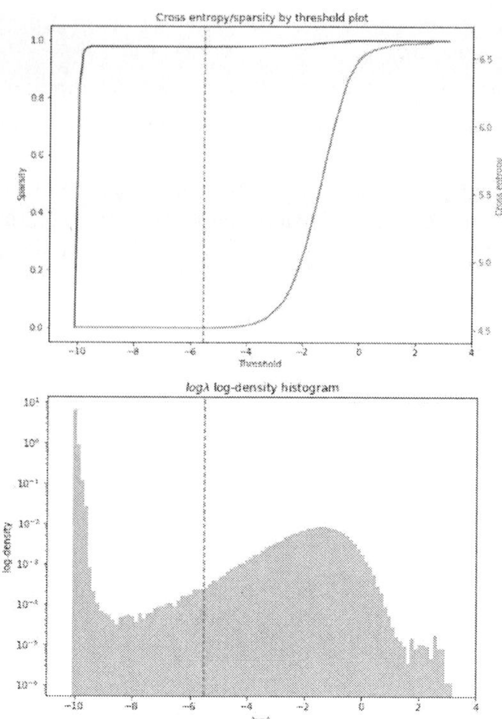

Figure 1: Plots of validation cross-entropy (red line) of a LSTM model with a DSVI-ARD softmax layer on the PTB dataset and its corresponding sparsity (blue line) for different possible threshold $\log \lambda_{thresh}$ values (**top**) and the distribution histogram of its prior log-variances $\log \lambda_{ij}$ (**bottom**). We display the density on a **log scale** due to a very sparse distribution. The threshold chosen for further model evaluation (the best in terms of perplexity on the validation set) $\log \lambda_{thresh}^{opt}$ is marked with a green dashed line.

tional parameters $\boldsymbol{\mu}, \boldsymbol{\sigma}$ and all the other network parameters (including biases of the DSVI-ARD layers). Variational optimization is performed with the DSVI-ARD algorithm, which, in turn, only requires gradients of the log-likelihood and KL-divergence. Therefore, overall model training is a standard gradient optimization of parameters based on backpropagation (specifically, BPTT in the RNN case) with negative ELBO as the loss function.

For more efficient training we applied the KL-cost annealing technique (Sønderby et al., 2016). The idea is to multiply the KL-term in ELBO by a variable weight, called the KL-weight, at training time. The weight gradually increases from zero to one during the first several epochs of training. This technique allows achieving better final performance of the model because such a train-

Original model	Dataset	Architecture	Number of parameters, M (Full / Softmax)	Removed parameters, % (Full / Softmax)	Perplexity	Accuracy, %
LSTM, (Zaremba et al., 2014)	PTB	*Original*	19.8 / 6.5	No compression	80.85	27.4%
		DSVI-ARD (ours)	**13.4 / 0.14**	**32.1% / 97.8%**	91.84	27.2%
		LR for Softmax, (Grachev et al., 2019)	14.5 / 1.19	26.8 % / 81.7 %	84.12	N/A
		TT for Softmax, (Grachev et al., 2019)	14.3 / 1.03	27.8 % / 84.2 %	88.55	N/A
	Wikitext2	*Original*	50.1 / 21.6	No compression	94.27	27.5%
		DSVI-ARD (ours)	**28.9 / 0.43**	**42.3% / 98.0%**	103.54	**27.6%**
LSTM + tied weights, (Inan et al., 2016)	PTB	*Original*	13.3 / 6.5	No compression	75.68	27.7%
		DSVI-ARD (ours)	**7.4 / 0.66**	**44.0% / 89.9%**	82.27	27.3%
	Wikitext2	*Original*	28.4 / 21.6	No compression	86.62	27.9%
		DSVI-ARD (ours)	**8.7 / 1.94**	**69.3% / 91.0%**	87.36	**28.1%**
LSTM, (Chirkova et al., 2018)	PTB	*Original*	5.64 / 2.56	No compression	129.3	N/A
		VD, (Chirkova et al., 2018)	3.2 / 0.12	43.3 % / 95.5 %	109.2	N/A
		DSVI-ARD (Ours)	**3.18 / 0.1**	**43.6 % / 96.1 %**	**106.2**	25.9 %

Table 1: Language modeling experiments results. We provide the number of parameters left after pruning (in millions) and the achieved compression ratios (in percents) of the whole network and the softmax layer alone along with the final quality (perplexity and accuracy) on the test set for each evaluated model. The original (uncompressed) models quality is provided for comparison.

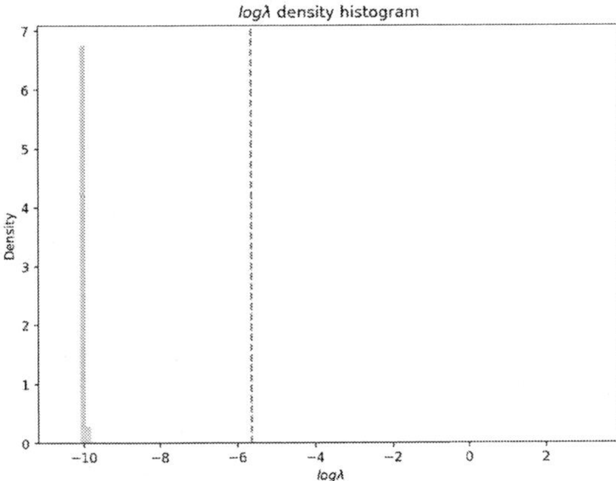

Figure 2: Distribution histogram of the prior log-variances $\log \lambda_{ij}$ obtained for a LSTM model with a DSVI-ARD softmax layer on the PTB dataset. We provide the standard-scaled density to justify the usage of a log scale in Fig. 1 (**bottom**).

ing procedure can be considered as pre-training on data (when the data term in ELBO dominates) and then starting fair optimization of the true ELBO (when the KL-weight reaches one). We used a simple linear KL-weight increasing strategy with a step selected as a hyperparameter.

During the evaluation of our models we do not sample parameters as we do in the training phase but instead set the approximated posterior mean μ as DSVI-ARD layers weights. Then we zero out the weights with the corresponding logarithms of prior variances lower than a certain threshold $\log \lambda_{thresh}$ (a hyperparameter selected on valida-

tion):

$$\log \lambda_{ij}^* < \log \lambda_{thresh} \Rightarrow \mu_{ij} := 0. \qquad (9)$$

This procedure essentially provides the desired sparsity as redundant weights are being literally removed from the network.

Each experiment was conducted as follows. We trained several models for some number of epochs with different hyperparameter initialization (such as dropout rate, learning rate, etc.). Then we picked the best model in terms of cross-entropy (log-perplexity) on the validation set at the last training epoch. We did not zero weights during evaluation at this phase, in other words, $\log \lambda_{thresh} = -\infty$ in equation (9). After that, we started threshold selection for the picked model: we iterated over possible values of $\log \lambda_{thresh}$ from the "leave-all" to the "remove-all" extreme values and chose the one (denoted by $\log \lambda_{thresh}^{opt}$) at which the best validation perplexity was obtained. Finally, we evaluated the model on the test set using the chosen optimal threshold $\log \lambda_{thresh}^{opt}$.

In our results we report the achieved compression ratio $cr = \frac{\sum_{i=1}^{K} \sum_{j=1}^{D} \mathbb{1}[\log \lambda_{ij}^* < \log \lambda_{thresh}^{opt}]}{KD}$, perplexity and accuracy[2] on the test set.

5.2 Results

Table 1 concludes all the results obtained during our experiments.

The comparison of DSVI-ARD with other dense layers compression approaches revealed

---

[2]By accuracy, we mean the fraction of correctly predicted words. The prediction is performed by taking the argmax of the softmax distribution over vocabulary words.

that our models can exhibit comparable perplexity quality while achieving much higher compression (in Grachev et al. (2019) case) and even surpass models based on similar Bayesian compression techniques (in Chirkova et al. (2018) case).

Also it can be seen that encoder-decoder weight tying helps to obtain higher overall compression (from almost 45% to 70% reduction of all model weights), due to a smaller number of parameters in the whole network, and even better results in both perplexity and accuracy on both datasets. Quality improvement after weight tying is a common case, however, we see that it helps to especially enhance the performance of our models (perplexity drops by almost 10 points in PTB case and more than 16 points in Wikitext2 case), which gives grounds for the proposed combination of DSVI-ARD and weight tying.

One can argue that DSVI-ARD may lead to overpruning (Trippe and Turner, 2018) because in all our experiments (except the last one, comparing with Chirkova et al. (2018) results) a slight quality drop in terms of perplexity can be observed. However, we specifically provide the test accuracy as well, in terms of which we achieve comparable or even better results than original models. We suggest that this effect might be caused by prediction uncertainty (or entropy) increase rather than model quality deterioration.

Fig. 1 demonstrates plots of cross-entropy (log-perplexity) and sparsity for different thresholds $\log \lambda_{thresh}$ — essentially the compression-quality trade-off plot — and the log-scaled distribution histogram of the decoder layer's prior log-variances $\log \lambda_{ij}^*$ obtained for a DSVI-ARD LSTM model trained on the PTB dataset. We also provide the same distribution on the standard scale (Fig. 2) for comparison. The dashed green line denotes the value of the chosen threshold $\log \lambda_{thresh}^{opt}$ which provides the best validation perplexity. We can observe that the overwhelming majority of weights in the last layer are indeed redundant, i.e., have small prior variances, do not contribute to the inference, and can be removed without harming much model performance. We argue that DSVI-ARD eliminates weights that obstruct generalization while leaving only those actually necessary for correct prediction.

6 Conclusion

In this paper we adopted the DSVI-ARD algorithm for compressing recurrent neural networks. Our main contributions are extending DSVI-ARD to the case of non-iid objects and combining it with the weight tying technique. In our experiments involving LSTM networks in language modeling tasks, we have managed to obtain substantially high compression ratios at an acceptable quality loss. The proposed method turned out to be comparable to or even surpassing other compression techniques like matrix decomposition and variational dropout.

There are several possible avenues for future work. An intriguing application of the proposed DSVI-ARD method for RNNs is the compression of current state-of-the-art models (Yang et al., 2017; Dai et al., 2019), which require enormous amounts of memory and computational resources. At the same time, one of the drawbacks of the current Bayesian compression approaches is a lack of their expressive ability, i.e., most of them are based on oversimplified posterior approximations and prior distributions (e.g., factorized Gaussian), which may lead to overly rough estimates and overall model inefficiency. A rigorous study of this problem is required. Another possible direction is bringing Bayesian framework into matrix decomposition-based methods as well. This fusion may lead to more effective and justified compression techniques.

Acknowledgments

The article was prepared within the framework of the HSE University Basic Research Program and funded by the Russian Academic Excellence Project '5-100'.

References

Martín Arjovsky, Amar Shah, and Yoshua Bengio. 2016. Unitary evolution recurrent neural networks. In *Proceedings of the 33nd International Conference on Machine Learning, ICML 2016, New York City, NY, USA, June 19-24, 2016*, pages 1120–1128.

Yoshua Bengio, Réjean Ducharme, Pascal Vincent, and Christian Janvin. 2003. A neural probabilistic language model. *Journal of Machine Learning Research*, 3:1137–1155.

Yoshua Bengio and Jean-Sébastien Senecal. 2003. Quick training of probabilistic neural nets by importance sampling. In *Proceedings of the Ninth In-*

ternational Workshop on Artificial Intelligence and Statistics, AISTATS 2003, Key West, Florida, USA, January 3-6, 2003.

Bradley P. Carlin and Thomas A. Louis. 1997. BAYES AND EMPIRICAL BAYES METHODS FOR DATA ANALYSIS. *Statistics and Computing*, 7(2):153–154.

Wenlin Chen, David Grangier, and Michael Auli. 2016. Strategies for training large vocabulary neural language models. In *Proceedings of the 54th Annual Meeting of the Association for Computational Linguistics, ACL 2016, August 7-12, 2016, Berlin, Germany, Volume 1: Long Papers.*

Nadezhda Chirkova, Ekaterina Lobacheva, and Dmitry P. Vetrov. 2018. Bayesian compression for natural language processing. In *Proceedings of the 2018 Conference on Empirical Methods in Natural Language Processing, Brussels, Belgium, October 31 - November 4, 2018*, pages 2910–2915.

Kyunghyun Cho, Bart van Merrienboer, Dzmitry Bahdanau, and Yoshua Bengio. 2014. On the properties of neural machine translation: Encoder-decoder approaches. In *Proceedings of SSST@EMNLP 2014, Eighth Workshop on Syntax, Semantics and Structure in Statistical Translation, Doha, Qatar, 25 October 2014*, pages 103–111.

Zihang Dai, Zhilin Yang, Yiming Yang, Jaime G. Carbonell, Quoc V. Le, and Ruslan Salakhutdinov. 2019. Transformer-xl: Attentive language models beyond a fixed-length context. *CoRR*, abs/1901.02860.

Artem M. Grachev, Dmitry I. Ignatov, and Andrey V. Savchenko. 2019. Compression of recurrent neural networks for efficient language modeling. *Applied Soft Computing*, 79:354 – 362.

Song Han, Huizi Mao, and William J. Dally. 2015. Deep compression: Compressing deep neural network with pruning, trained quantization and huffman coding. *CoRR*, abs/1510.00149.

Sepp Hochreiter and Jürgen Schmidhuber. 1997. Long short-term memory. *Neural Computation*, 9(8):1735–1780.

Jiri Hron, Alexander G. de G. Matthews, and Zoubin Ghahramani. 2018. Variational bayesian dropout: pitfalls and fixes. *CoRR*, abs/1807.01969.

Hakan Inan, Khashayar Khosravi, and Richard Socher. 2016. Tying word vectors and word classifiers: A loss framework for language modeling. *arXiv preprint arXiv:1611.01462.*

Valery Kharitonov, Dmitry Molchanov, and Dmitry Vetrov. 2018. Variational dropout via empirical bayes. *CoRR*, abs/1811.00596.

Diederik P. Kingma, Tim Salimans, and Max Welling. 2015. Variational dropout and the local reparameterization trick. *CoRR*, abs/1506.02557.

Christos Louizos, Karen Ullrich, and Max Welling. 2017. Bayesian compression for deep learning. In *Advances in Neural Information Processing Systems*, pages 3288–3298.

Zhiyun Lu, Vikas Sindhwani, and Tara N. Sainath. 2016. Learning compact recurrent neural networks. In *2016 IEEE International Conference on Acoustics, Speech and Signal Processing, ICASSP 2016, Shanghai, China, March 20-25, 2016*, pages 5960–5964.

Stephen Merity, Caiming Xiong, James Bradbury, and Richard Socher. 2016. Pointer sentinel mixture models. *CoRR*, abs/1609.07843.

Tomáš Mikolov. 2012. *Statistical Language Models Based on Neural Networks*. Ph.D. thesis, Brno University of Technology.

Tomas Mikolov, Martin Karafiát, Lukás Burget, Jan Cernocký, and Sanjeev Khudanpur. 2010. Recurrent neural network based language model. In *INTERSPEECH 2010, 11th Annual Conference of the International Speech Communication Association, Makuhari, Chiba, Japan, September 26-30, 2010*, pages 1045–1048.

Dmitry Molchanov, Arsenii Ashukha, and Dmitry P. Vetrov. 2017. Variational dropout sparsifies deep neural networks. In *Proceedings of the 34th International Conference on Machine Learning, ICML 2017, Sydney, NSW, Australia, 6-11 August 2017*, pages 2498–2507.

Sharan Narang, Erich Elsen, Gregory Diamos, and Shubho Sengupta. 2017. Exploring sparsity in recurrent neural networks. *arXiv preprint arXiv:1704.05119.*

Ofir Press and Lior Wolf. 2017. Using the output embedding to improve language models. In *Proceedings of the 15th Conference of the European Chapter of the Association for Computational Linguistics, EACL 2017, Valencia, Spain, April 3-7, 2017, Volume 2: Short Papers*, pages 157–163.

Casper Kaae Sønderby, Tapani Raiko, Lars Maaløe, Søren Kaae Sønderby, and Ole Winther. 2016. How to train deep variational autoencoders and probabilistic ladder networks. *CoRR*, abs/1602.02282.

Michalis K. Titsias and Miguel Lázaro-Gredilla. 2014. Doubly stochastic variational bayes for nonconjugate inference. In *Proceedings of the 31th International Conference on Machine Learning, ICML 2014, Beijing, China, 21-26 June 2014*, pages 1971–1979.

Andros Tjandra, Sakriani Sakti, and Satoshi Nakamura. 2017. Compressing recurrent neural network with tensor train. In *2017 International Joint Conference on Neural Networks, IJCNN 2017, Anchorage, AK, USA, May 14-19, 2017*, pages 4451–4458.

Brian Trippe and Richard Turner. 2018. Overpruning in variational bayesian neural networks. *arXiv preprint arXiv:1801.06230*.

Zhilin Yang, Zihang Dai, Ruslan Salakhutdinov, and William W. Cohen. 2017. Breaking the softmax bottleneck: A high-rank RNN language model. *CoRR*, abs/1711.03953.

Wojciech Zaremba, Ilya Sutskever, and Oriol Vinyals. 2014. Recurrent neural network regularization. *CoRR*, abs/1409.2329.

MoRTy: Unsupervised Learning of Task-specialized Word Embeddings by Autoencoding

Nils Rethmeier
German Research Center for AI (DFKI)
Alt-Moabit 91c
10559 Berlin. Germany
`nils.rethmeier@dfki.de`

Barbara Plank
Department of Computer Science
IT University of Copenhagen
Rued Langgaards Vej 7
2300 Copenhagen S, Denmark
`bplank@itu.dk`

Abstract

Word embeddings have undoubtedly revolutionized NLP. However, pre-trained embeddings do not always work for a specific task (or set of tasks), particularly in limited resource setups. We introduce a simple yet effective, self-supervised post-processing method that constructs task-specialized word representations by picking from a menu of reconstructing transformations to yield improved end-task performance (MoRTy). The method is complementary to recent state-of-the-art approaches to inductive transfer via fine-tuning, and forgoes costly model architectures and annotation. We evaluate MoRTy on a broad range of setups, including different word embedding methods, corpus sizes and end-task semantics. Finally, we provide a surprisingly simple recipe to obtain specialized embeddings that better fit end-tasks.

1 Introduction

Word embeddings are ubiquitous in Natural Language Processing. They provide a low-effort, high pay-off way to improve the performance of a specific supervised end-task by transferring knowledge. However, recent works indicate that universally best embeddings are not yet possible (Bollegala and Bao, 2018; Kiela et al., 2018a; Dingwall and Potts, 2018), and that they instead need to be tuned to fit specific end-tasks using inductive bias – i.e., semantic supervision for the unsupervised embedding learning process (Conneau et al., 2018; Perone et al., 2018). This way, embeddings can be tuned to fit a specific single-task (ST) or multi-task (MT: set of tasks) semantic (Xiong et al., 2018).

Fine-tuning requires labeled data, which is often either too small, not available or of low quality and creating or extending labeled data is costly and slow. Word embeddings are typically induced from huge unlabeled corpora with billions of tokens, but for limited-resource domains like biology or medicine, it becomes less clear whether there is still transfer. We set out to create task-specified embeddings cheaply, with self-supervision, that are able to provide consistent improvements, even in limited resource settings.

We evaluate the impact of our method, named MoRTy, on 18 publicly available benchmark tasks developed by Jastrzebski et al. (2017)[1] using two ways to induce embeddings, Fasttext and GloVe. We test them in two setups corresponding to two different overall aims: (a) to specialize embeddings to better fit a *single* supervised task or, (b) to generalize embeddings for *multiple* supervised end-tasks, i.e., to optimize MoRTys for *single* or *multi-task* settings. Since most embeddings are pre-trained on large corpora, we also investigate whether our method further improves embeddings trained on small corpus setups.

Hence, we demonstrate the method's application for single-task, multi-task, small, medium and web-scale (common crawl) corpus-size settings (Section 4). *Learning to scale-up* by pre-training on more (un-)labeled data is both: (a) not always possible in low-resource domains due to lack of such data, and (b) heavily increases the compute requirements of comparatively small supervised down-stream task. This not only leads to high per model-instance costs but also limits *learning to scale-out*, i.e., when combining many smaller models into a larger dynamic model as is desirable in continual learning settings, where models, inputs and objectives may emerge or disappear over time. To provide an alternative in such settings we design MoRTy as a *learning-to-scale-down* approach, that uses less data and compute to achieve a performance improvement despite *forgoing (un-)supervised fine tuning* on target domain data. Consequently, MoRTy uses

---

[1] `https://github.com/kudkudak/word-embeddings-benchmarks`

Proceedings of the 4th Workshop on Representation Learning for NLP (RepL4NLP-2019), pages 49–54
Florence, Italy, August 2, 2019. ©2019 Association for Computational Linguistics

very little resources,[2] producing a low carbon footprint, especially regarding recent, compute intensive, *scale-up* approaches like ELMo or BERT (Peters et al., 2018; Devlin et al., 2018) which have high hardware and training time requirements and a large carbon footprint as recently demonstrated by Strubell et al. (2019). As a result, we demonstrate a simple, unsupervised scale-down method, that allows further pretraining exploitation, while requiring minimum extra effort, time and compute resources. As in standard methodology, optimal post-processed embeddings can be selected according to multiple proxy-tasks for overall improvement or using a single end-task's development split—e.g., on a fast baseline model for further time reduction.

2 MoRTy embeddings

Our proposed post-processing method provides a **Menu** of **R**econstructing **T**ransformations to **y**ield improved end-task performance (MoRTy).

Approach: The key idea of MoRTy is to create a family of embeddings by learning to reconstruct the original pre-trained embeddings space via autoencoders.

The resulting family or representations (post-processed embeddings) gives a "menu" which can be picked from in two ways: (a) standard development set tuning, to gain performance at a *single* supervised task (ST), or (b) via benchmark tasks, to boost performance of *multiple tasks* (MT). The first is geared towards optimizing embeddings for a single specific task (specialization), the latter aims at embedding generalization, that works well across tasks.

In more details, the overall MoRTy recipe is: **(1) Train (or take):** an original (pre-trained) embedding space E_{org} using embedding method f. **(2) Reconstruct** E_{org}: compute multiple randomly initialized representations of E_{org} using a reconstruction loss (mean square error, cf. below). **(3) Pick:** performance-optimal representation for the end-task(s) via a task's development split(s) or proxy tasks, depending on the end-goal, i.e., specialization or generalization. **(4) Gain:** use optimal MoRTy (E_{post}) to push relative performance on end task(s).

Which autoencoder variant? For step (2), we found the following autoencoder recipe to work best: A linear autoencoder with one hidden layer, trained via bRMSE (batch-wise root mean squared error), the same hidden layer size as the original embedding model and half of its learning rate[3]— i.e., *a linear, complete autoencoder*, trained for a single epoch (cf. end of Section 3).

We experimented with alternative autoencoders: sparse (Ranzato et al., 2007), denoising, discrete (Subramanian et al., 2018), and undercomplete autoencoders, but found the simple recipe to work best. In the remainder of the paper, we test this 'imitation-scheme' setup recipe.

3 Experiments

With the aim of deriving a simple yet effective 'best practice' usage recipe, we evaluate MoRTy as follows: a) using two word embedding methods f; b) corpora of different sizes to induce E_{org}, i.e., small, medium and web-scale; c) evaluation across 18 semantic benchmark tasks spanning three semantic categories to broadly examine MoRTy's impact, while assessing both single and multi-task end goals; and finally e) evaluate 1-epoch setups in relation to different corpus sizes.

Embeddings and Corpus Size: We evaluate embeddings trained on small, medium (millions of tokens) and large (billions of tokens) corpus sizes. In particular, we train 100-dimensional embeddings with Fasttext (Bojanowski et al., 2016)[4] and GloVe (Pennington et al., 2014)[5] on the 2M and 103M WikiText created by Merity et al. (2016). We complement them with off-the-shelf webscale Fasttext and GloVe embeddings (trained on 600B and 840B tokens, respectively). This results in the following vocabulary sizes for Fasttext and GloVe embeddings, respectively: on 2M 25,249 and 33,237 word types. For 103M we get 197,256 and 267,633 vocabulary words. Public, off-the-shelf – common-crawl trained – Fasttext and GloVe embeddings have very large vocabularies of 1,999,995 and 2,196,008 words.

To account for variation in results, we train both embedding methods *five times each*[6] on the two WikiText corpus sizes. We observed only minor

---

[2] $<$ 1GB memory including the whole dataset, computes fast on GPU and CPU and inherits FastText's dynamic out-of-vocabulary token embedding generation, which is useful in handling unforeseen words in down-stream tasks.

[3] Original Fasttext and GloVe used $lr = 0.05$, so $lr \approx$ 0.025 is a 'careful' rate and used throughout the experiments in this paper.

[4] To train Fasttext we used `https://fasttext.cc`

[5] To train GloVe we used the python glove_python wheel

[6] Fasttext was trained using the implementation's

50

variations, $< 0.5\%$ between runs for both Fasttext and GloVe, in overall performance Σ – i.e., when summing the scores of all benchmark tasks.

Semantic benchmark tasks: We use a publicly available word embedding benchmark implementation developed by Jastrzebski et al. (2017) – chosen for reproducibility and breadth. The 18 tasks span three semantic categories: (a) word similarity (6 tasks), (b) word analogy (3 tasks), and (c) word and sentence categorization (9 tasks).[7]

Evaluation and Experimental Details For the single-task setup we show MORTY'S relative, percentual performance change (ST % change) produced by choosing the best MORTY embedding per task – 18 MORTYs. Correspondingly, for multi-task results we show MT % change obtained by choosing the MORTY embedding with the best score over all tasks Σ – i.e., one MORTY for all tasks. Performances in Table 1 are averaged over 5 runs each of Fasttext and GloVe per corpus size. To maximize MORTY'S usability we evaluate a **1-epoch** training scheme. We test its robustness – *particularly for limited resource use* – by training 1 epoch on three corpus sizes (small to web-scale), using the best multi-task (MT/ Σ) base embedder – see Fasttext Table 1. We again account for variation by using 3 randomly initialized MORTY runs, each over the 5 respective runs per corpus size. In this experiment, a single epoch yielded very stable boosts, that are comparable to multi-epoch training.

4 Results

The main results are provided in Table 1 and Figure 1. There are several take-aways.

f: **Fasttext and GloVe:** First, regarding the base embeddings (cf. per-category base performance scores in Table 1): i) we notice that Fasttext performs overall better than GloVe; ii) classification and similarity results improve the larger the corpus; consistently over f; and iii) GloVe is better for the analogy tasks on web-scale data.[8]

MORTY for multi-task application: Second, the MT % change columns show that a single best MORTY improves overall performance Σ (black row)[9] – the sum of 18 tasks – by 8.9, 5.8 and 3.4 percent compared to Fasttext base. As corpus size increases, there is less space for MORTY to improve Σ scores. What is interesting to note is that MORTY is able to recover analogy performance on 103M (to more than 2M level). This is also reflected in the Google and MSR analogy scores doubling and tripling (middle column). On 2M we also see a modest improvement (6.2) for similarity tasks, while classification on 2M slightly dropped. Regarding GloVe (3 rightmost columns) we notice lower overall performance (black column), which is consistent with findings by Levy et al. (2015). MORTY on GloVe produces lower but more stable improvements for the MT setting (middle column), with analogy and similarity performance noticeably increasing for the small 2M dataset. Generally, we see both performance increases and drops for individual task, especially on 2M and Fasttext, indicating that, a single overall best MORTY specializes the base Fasttext embedding to better fit a specific subset of the 18 tasks, while still beating the base embedders f in overall score (Σ).

MORTY for single-task application: In the ST % change columns we see best single task (ST) results for task-specific optimal MORTY embeddings. Both embedders get consistent boosts, with Fasttext exhibiting significantly higher improvement from MORTY on 2M and 103M, despite already starting out at a higher base performance.

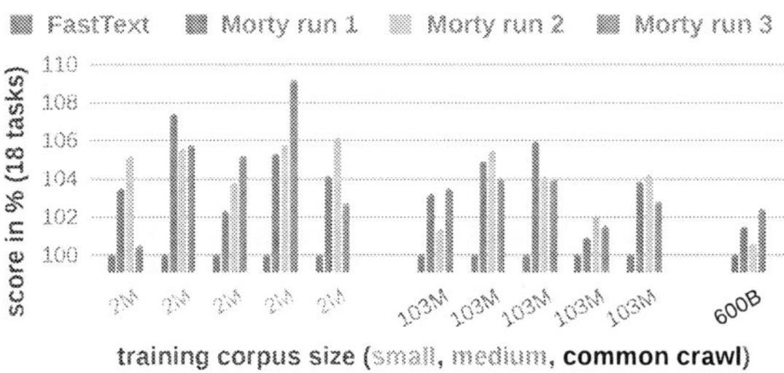

Figure 1: **1-epoch MORTY (MT %) performance change over Fasttext:** Blue bars show Fasttext baseline performance (100%). 3 Morty runs: trained on Fasttext for **1 epoch** (2x5 Fasttext for corpus sizes 2M and 103M and 1x for 600B). Detailed description on next page.

(fasttext.cc) default parameters. GloVe was trained with the same parameters as in (Pennington et al., 2014) – Figure 4b. Though, 4a gave the same results.

[7]Jastrzebski et al. (2017) use measures form the dataset literature: Spearman correlation for similarity, 3CosAdd for analogy and accuracy and cluster purity for categorization.

[8]GloVe 3CosAdd matches (Levy and Goldberg, 2014).

---

[9]Note that, % change for Σ is not the average of the individual task changes, but the % change of the sum of 18 individual scores.

embedder model	Fasttext base performance			MT % change by 1 overall Morty			ST % change by 18 single Mortys			GloVe base performance			MT % change by 1 overall Morty			ST % change by 18 single Mortys		
train size	2M	103M	600B	2M	103M	600B	2M	103M	600B	2M	103M	840B	2M	103M	840B	2M	103M	840B
AP	0.31	0.59	0.68	-6.1	-0.9	-1.5	8.2	5.2	4	0.2	0.43	0.61	2.7	5.6	9.3	13.2	9.2	12.2
BLESS	0.3	0.73	0.84	-2.2	3.8	-3	13	9.7	5.4	0.27	0.51	0.85	1.6	-1.6	-1.8	7.9	7.9	4.7
Battig	0.14	0.32	0.48	-3.6	0.1	-3.7	7	4	0.5	0.1	0.19	0.46	3.5	2	1.9	7.4	5.4	8.5
ESSLI 1a	0.48	0.76	0.77	2.2	4.3	17.6	27.5	10.2	17.6	0.46	0.63	0.75	0	3.1	9.1	8	8.9	12.1
ESSLI 2b	0.63	0.75	0.78	9.2	2.7	0	26.5	11.3	12.9	0.51	0.74	0.75	19.9	-0.5	6.7	23.7	11.7	16.7
ESSLI 2c	0.54	0.54	0.62	-3.7	10.7	-10.7	11	19.7	10.7	0.46	0.54	0.62	2.1	2.7	0	16.9	16.7	10.7
Google	0.06	0.04	0.12	33.6	293.8	187.3	45.3	319.3	217.2	0	0.05	0.58	42.7	13.8	2.8	60.4	18.6	5.9
SEval 12 2	0.11	0.16	0.24	1.6	4.3	-2.8	18.1	14.1	4.8	0.11	0.15	0.2	6.5	2.2	1	11.4	5	2.4
MSR	0.28	0.08	0.18	18.8	246.2	117.1	27.5	267.3	137	0	0.09	0.57	45.6	30.9	-2.4	100.7	38.1	10.1
MTurk	0.24	0.52	0.73	65.6	5.1	1.1	98	12.6	1.5	0.3	0.46	0.69	-22.4	2.6	0.5	1.6	4.2	2.6
RG65	0.29	0.71	0.86	65.2	0.7	2.1	104.7	5.3	5.6	0.15	0.44	0.77	11.6	3.9	-1.3	30.8	10	4
RW	0.21	0.38	0.59	-17.1	-0.8	-2	4.1	2.4	0.9	0.2	0.21	0.46	-2.1	11.8	2	4	19.8	10.3
MEN	0.36	0.71	0.84	13	0.4	-0.4	22	2.3	0.3	0.16	0.51	0.8	3.6	5.6	0.5	15.1	7	7.7
SimLex999	0.18	0.31	0.5	-23.2	3.7	-1.2	7.3	9	3.1	0.03	0.22	0.41	147.8	7.3	3.1	228.3	11.7	9.3
TR9856	0.1	0.13	0.18	2.8	-4.1	-37.1	20.5	17.3	-2.5	0.09	0.08	0.1	13.9	8.9	-4.7	19.8	47.3	36.7
WS353	0.46	0.69	0.79	3.9	1	-1.7	10	2.9	0.6	0.16	0.45	0.74	31.5	7.2	0.7	36.8	8.2	5.6
WS353R	0.35	0.63	0.74	16.4	1.7	-2.8	24.3	4.1	1.6	0.08	0.4	0.69	53.1	6.5	1.1	62	8.2	2.7
WS353S	0.52	0.77	0.84	3.2	0.4	0.6	13.3	3	1.9	0.27	0.58	0.8	15.1	6.5	0.3	20.2	7.6	5.9
Σ tasks	5.55	8.83	10.79	8.9	5.8	3.4	8.9	5.8	3.6	3.56	6.68	10.84	7.8	4.3	1.9	7.8	4.3	1.9
category	2.39	3.7	4.17	-2.1	-0.2	1.8	11.4	4.5	3.1	2	3.04	4.05	3.5	-0.8	2.4	7.3	3.3	5.5
analogy	0.45	0.28	0.55	15.5	115	72.2	24.6	125.2	92.7	0.11	0.29	1.34	7.4	4.2	1.3	12.3	15.8	6.5
similarity	2.71	4.85	6.07	6.2	-0.6	-4.7	17.3	2.2	-0.3	1.45	3.35	5.45	9.2	1.8	0	11	6.3	2.9
legend	<50%	50%	>50%	< -10%	no change	> +10%				<50%	50%	>50%	< -10%	no change	> +10%			

Table 1: **MoRTy on Fasttext and GloVe**: Above are scores for: 18 individual tasks (AP-WS353S), the sum of 18 scores Σ, and scores grouped by semantic: similarity (AP-ESSLI2c), analogy (Google-MSR), classification (MTurk-WS253S). **Left column:** shows absolute scores of the original embedder. **Middle column:** shows % score change after fine-tuning with the MoRTy that has the *highest overall score* Σ – i.e., 1 MoRTy for all tasks (`multi-task`). **Right column:** shows % score change after applying 18 individually best MoRTys per `single-task` – i.e., 18 MoRTys . Each column is further split by corpus size – 2M, 103M(illion) and 600/840B(illion) tokens. All scores are averages over 5 original embedder scores and respective MoRTy changes.

Applying the MoRTy 1-epoch recipe So far, we saw MoRTys potential for overall (ST/MT/Σ) performance improvements, but will we observe the same *in the wild*? To answer this question for the MT use-case, we apply a *1-epoch* training only recipe. That is, we train *1-epoch* using a linear, complete autoencoder using *half of the base embedders learning rate* on three randomly initialized MoRTys, and then test them on the 18 task (MT) setup. Figure 1 shows consistent MT/Σ score improvements for each of the 3 MoRTy-over-Fasttext runs (red, yellow, green) on 2M, 103M, and 600B vs. base Fasttext (blue 100).

We see that, for practical application, this allows MoRTy to boost supervised MT performance even without using a supervised development split or proxy task(s), while also *eliminating multi-epoch tuning*. Both Figure 1 and Table 1 show similar overall (MT) improvements per corpus size, which suggests that 1-epoch training is sufficient and that **MoRTy is especially beneficial on smaller corpora** – i.e., in limited resource settings.

5 Related Work

There is a large body of work on information transfer between supervised and unsupervised tasks. First and foremost **unsupervised-to-supervised** transfer includes using embeddings for supervised tasks. However, transfer also works vice versa, in a **supervised-to-unsupervised** setup to (learn to) specialize embeddings to better fit a specific supervised signal (Ruder and Plank, 2017; Ye et al., 2018). This includes injecting generally relevant semantics via retrofitting or auxiliary multi-task supervision (Faruqui et al., 2015; Kiela et al., 2018b). **Supervised-to-supervised** methods provide knowledge transfer between supervised tasks which is exploited successively (Kirkpatrick et al., 2017), jointly (Kiela et al., 2018b) and in joint-succession (Hashimoto et al., 2017).

Unsupervised-to-unsupervised transfer is less studied. Dingwall and Potts (2018) proposed a GloVe *model-modification* that retrofits publicly available GloVe embeddings to produce specialized domain embeddings, while Bollegala and

Bao (2018) propose *meta-embeddings* via denoising autoencoders to *merge* diverse (Fasttext and GloVe) embeddings spaces. The later, is also a low-effort approach and closest to ours. However, it focuses on embedding merging that they *tuned on a single* semantic similarity task, while MORTY provides an overview of *tuning for 19 different settings*. Furthermore, MORTY requires only a single embedding space, which contributes to the literature by outlining that meta-embedding improvements may partly stem from re-encoding rather than only from semantic merging.

6 Conclusion

We demonstrated a low-effort, self-supervised, *learning scale-down* method to *construct task-optimized* word embeddings from existing ones to gain performance on a (set of) supervised end-task(s) without direct domain adaptation. Despite its simplicity, MORTY is able to produce significant performance improvements for *single* and *multi-task* supervision settings as well as for a variety of desirable word encoding properties while forgoing building and tuning complex model architectures and labeling.[10] Perhaps most importantly, MORTY shows considerable benefits for low-resource settings and thus provides a *learning-to-scale-down* alternative to recent *scale-up* approaches.

7 Acknowledgements

This work was supported by the German Federal Ministry of Education and Research (BMBF) through the project DEEPLEE (01IW17001) and by the European Unions Horizon 2020 research and innovation programme under grant agreement No 780495 (BigMedilytics). We also thank Philippe Thomas and Isabelle Augenstein for helpful discussions.

References

Piotr Bojanowski, Edouard Grave, Armand Joulin, and Tomas Mikolov. 2016. Enriching word vectors with subword information. *CoRR*, abs/1607.04606.

Danushka Bollegala and Cong Bao. 2018. Learning word meta-embeddings by autoencoding. In *Proceedings of the 27th International Conference on Computational Linguistics*, pages 1650–1661. Association for Computational Linguistics.

Alexis Conneau, Germán Kruszewski, Guillaume Lample, Loïc Barrault, and Marco" Baroni. 2018. What you can cram into a single $&!#* vector: Probing sentence embeddings for linguistic properties. In *Proceedings of the 56th Annual Meeting of the Association for Computational Linguistics (Volume 1: Long Papers)*, pages 2126–2136. Association for Computational Linguistics.

Jacob Devlin, Ming-Wei Chang, Kenton Lee, and Kristina Toutanova. 2018. Bert: Pre-training of deep bidirectional transformers for language understanding. *arXiv preprint arXiv:1810.04805*.

Nicholas Dingwall and Christopher Potts. 2018. Mittens: an extension of glove for learning domain-specialized representations. In *Proceedings of the 2018 Conference of the North American Chapter of the Association for Computational Linguistics: Human Language Technologies, Volume 2 (Short Papers)*, pages 212–217. Association for Computational Linguistics.

Manaal Faruqui, Jesse Dodge, Sujay Kumar Jauhar, Chris Dyer, Eduard Hovy, and Noah A Smith. 2015. Retrofitting word vectors to semantic lexicons. In *Proceedings of the 2015 Conference of the North American Chapter of the Association for Computational Linguistics: Human Language Technologies*, pages 1606–1615. Association for Computational Linguistics.

Kazuma Hashimoto, caiming xiong, Yoshimasa Tsuruoka, and Richard Socher. 2017. A joint many-task model: Growing a neural network for multiple nlp tasks. In *Proceedings of the 2017 Conference on Empirical Methods in Natural Language Processing*, pages 1923–1933. Association for Computational Linguistics.

Stanislaw Jastrzebski, Damian Lesniak, and Wojciech Marian Czarnecki. 2017. How to evaluate word embeddings? on importance of data efficiency and simple supervised tasks. *CoRR*, abs/1702.02170.

Douwe Kiela, Changhan Wang, and Kyunghyun Cho. 2018a. Context-attentive embeddings for improved sentence representations. *CoRR*, abs/1804.07983.

Douwe Kiela, Changhan Wang, and Kyunghyun Cho. 2018b. Dynamic meta-embeddings for improved sentence representations. In *Proceedings of the 2018 Conference on Empirical Methods in Natural Language Processing*, pages 1466–1477. Association for Computational Linguistics.

James Kirkpatrick, Razvan Pascanu, Neil Rabinowitz, Joel Veness, Guillaume Desjardins, Andrei A Rusu, Kieran Milan, John Quan, Tiago Ramalho, Agnieszka Grabska-Barwinska, et al. 2017. Overcoming catastrophic forgetting in neural networks. *Proceedings of the National Academy of Sciences*, 114(13):3521–3526.

---

[10]Source code at `https://github.com/NilsRethmeier/MoRTy`

Omer Levy and Yoav Goldberg. 2014. Linguistic regularities in sparse and explicit word representations. In *Proceedings of the Eighteenth Conference on Computational Natural Language Learning*, pages 171–180. Association for Computational Linguistics.

Omer Levy, Yoav Goldberg, and Ido Dagan. 2015. Improving distributional similarity with lessons learned from word embeddings. *Transactions of the Association for Computational Linguistics*, 3:211–225.

Stephen Merity, Caiming Xiong, James Bradbury, and Richard Socher. 2016. Pointer sentinel mixture models. *CoRR*, abs/1609.07843.

Jeffrey Pennington, Richard Socher, and Christopher Manning. 2014. Glove: Global vectors for word representation. In *Proceedings of the 2014 Conference on Empirical Methods in Natural Language Processing (EMNLP)*, pages 1532–1543. Association for Computational Linguistics.

Christian S. Perone, Roberto Silveira, and Thomas S. Paula. 2018. Evaluation of sentence embeddings in downstream and linguistic probing tasks.

Matthew E. Peters, Mark Neumann, Mohit Iyyer, Matt Gardner, Christopher Clark, Kenton Lee, and Luke Zettlemoyer. 2018. Deep contextualized word representations. *CoRR*, abs/1802.05365.

Marc' Aurelio Ranzato, Y-Lan Boureau, and Yann LeCun. 2007. Sparse feature learning for deep belief networks. In *Proceedings of the 20th International Conference on Neural Information Processing Systems*, NIPS'07, pages 1185–1192, USA. Curran Associates Inc.

Sebastian Ruder and Barbara Plank. 2017. Learning to select data for transfer learning with bayesian optimization. In *Proceedings of the 2017 Conference on Empirical Methods in Natural Language Processing*, pages 372–382. Association for Computational Linguistics.

Emma Strubell, Ananya Ganesh, and Andrew McCallum. 2019. Energy and policy considerations for deep learning in nlp. In *Proceedings of ACL 2019, Florence, Italy, July 28 - August 2, 2019*. Association for Computational Linguistics.

Anant Subramanian, Danish Pruthi, Harsh Jhamtani, Taylor Berg-Kirkpatrick, and Eduard Hovy. 2018. Spine: Sparse interpretable neural embeddings. In *Thirty-Second AAAI Conference on Artificial Intelligence*.

Shufeng Xiong, Hailian Lv, Weiting Zhao, and Donghong Ji. 2018. Towards twitter sentiment classification by multi-level sentiment-enriched word embeddings. *Neurocomputing*, 275:2459–2466.

Zhe Ye, Fang Li, and Timothy Baldwin. 2018. Encoding sentiment information into word vectors for sentiment analysis. In *Proceedings of the 27th International Conference on Computational Linguistics*, pages 997–1007. Association for Computational Linguistics.

Pitfalls in the Evaluation of Sentence Embeddings

Steffen Eger[†‡], **Andreas Rücklé**[†], **Iryna Gurevych**[†‡]
[†]Ubiquitous Knowledge Processing Lab (UKP-TUDA)
[‡]Research Training Group AIPHES
Department of Computer Science, Technische Universität Darmstadt
[†]www.ukp.tu-darmstadt.de
[‡]www.aiphes.tu-darmstadt.de

Abstract

Deep learning models continuously break new records across different NLP tasks. At the same time, their success exposes weaknesses of model evaluation. Here, we compile several key pitfalls of evaluation of sentence embeddings, a currently very popular NLP paradigm. These pitfalls include the comparison of embeddings of different sizes, normalization of embeddings, and the low (and diverging) correlations between transfer and probing tasks. Our motivation is to challenge the current evaluation of sentence embeddings and to provide an easy-to-access reference for future research. Based on our insights, we also recommend better practices for better future evaluations of sentence embeddings.

1 Introduction

The field of natural language processing (NLP) is currently in upheaval. A reason for this is the success story of deep learning, which has led to ever better reported performances across many different NLP tasks, sometimes exceeding the scores achieved by humans. These fanfares of victory are echoed by isolated voices raising concern about the trustworthiness of some of the reported results. For instance, Melis et al. (2017) find that neural language models have been misleadingly evaluated and that, under fair conditions, standard LSTMs outperform more recent innovations. Reimers and Gurevych (2017) find that reporting single performance scores is insufficient for comparing non-deterministic approaches such as neural networks. Post (2018) holds that neural MT systems are unfairly compared in the literature using different variants of the BLEU score metric. In an even more general context, Lipton and Steinhardt (2018) detect several current "troubling trends" in machine learning scholarship, some of which refer to evaluation.

Sentence encoders (Kiros et al., 2015; Conneau et al., 2017; Pagliardini et al., 2018) are one particularly hot deep learning topic. Generalizing the popular word-level representations (Mikolov et al., 2013; Pennington et al., 2014) to the sentence level, they are valuable in a variety of contexts: (i) clustering of sentences and short texts; (ii) retrieval tasks, e.g., retrieving answer passages for a question; and (iii) when task-specific training data is scarce—i.e., when the full potential of task-specific word-level representation approaches cannot be leveraged (Subramanian et al., 2018).

The popularity of sentence encoders has led to a large variety of proposed techniques. These range from 'complex' unsupervised RNN models predicting context sentences (Kiros et al., 2015) to supervised RNN models predicting semantic relationships between sentence pairs (Conneau et al., 2017). Even more complex models learn sentence embeddings in a multi-task setup (Subramanian et al., 2018). In contrast, 'simple' encoders compute sentence embeddings as an elementary function of word embeddings. They compute a weighted average of word embeddings and then modify these representations via principal component analysis (SIF) (Arora et al., 2017); average n-gram embeddings (Sent2Vec) (Pagliardini et al., 2018); consider generalized pooling mechanisms (Shen et al., 2018; Rücklé et al., 2018); or combine word embeddings via randomly initialized projection matrices (Wieting and Kiela, 2019).

The embeddings of different encoders vary across various dimensions, the most obvious being their size. E.g., the literature has proposed embeddings ranging from 300d average word embeddings to 700d n-gram embeddings, to 4096d InferSent embeddings, to 24k dimensional random embeddings (Wieting and Kiela, 2019). Unsurprisingly, comparing embeddings of different sizes is unfair when size itself is crucially related to performances

55

Proceedings of the 4th Workshop on Representation Learning for NLP (RepL4NLP-2019), pages 55–60
Florence, Italy, August 2, 2019. ©2019 Association for Computational Linguistics

in downstream tasks, as has been highlighted before (Rücklé et al., 2018; Wieting and Kiela, 2019).

We compile several pitfalls when evaluating and comparing sentence encoders. These relate to (i) the embedding sizes, (ii) normalization of embeddings before feeding them to classifiers, and (iii) unsupervised semantic similarity evaluation. We also discuss (iv) the choice of classifier used on top of sentence embeddings and (v) divergence in performance results which compare downstream tasks and so-called probing tasks (Conneau et al., 2018).

Our motivation is to assemble diverse observations from different published works regarding problematic aspects of the emerging field of sentence encoders. We do so in order to provide future research with an easy-to-access reference about issues that may not (yet) be widely known. We also want to provide the newcomer to sentence encoders a guide for avoiding pitfalls that even experienced researchers have fallen prey to. We also recommend best practices, from our viewpoint.

2 Setup

We compare several freely available sentence encoders (listed in Table 1) with SentEval (Conneau and Kiela, 2018), using its default settings. SentEval trains a logistic regression classifier for specific downstream tasks with the sentence embeddings as the input. We compare 6 downstream tasks from the fields of sentiment analysis (MR, SST), product reviews (CR), subjectivity (SUBJ), opinion polarity (MPQA), and question-type classification (TREC). In these tasks, the goal is to label a single sentence with one of several classes. We also evaluate on the STSBenchmark (Cer et al., 2017), which evaluates semantic similarity of *pairs* of sentences.

Sentence Encoder	Emb. Size
InferSent (Conneau et al., 2017)	4096
Sent2Vec (Pagliardini et al., 2018)	700
PMeans (Rücklé et al., 2018)	3600
USE (Cer et al., 2018)	512
Avg. Glove (Pennington et al., 2014)	300
Avg. Word2Vec (Mikolov et al., 2013)	variable
SIF-Glove (Arora et al., 2017)	300

Table 1: Sentence encoders used in this work, together with the sizes of the resulting sentence embeddings.

3 Problems

Size matters. Currently, there is no standard size for sentence embeddings and different encoders induce embeddings of vastly different sizes.

For example, the sentence encoders of Conneau et al. (2017), Pagliardini et al. (2018), Rücklé et al. (2018), Cer et al. (2018), Kiros et al. (2015), Subramanian et al. (2018) are 4096, 700, 3600, 512, 4800, 1500/2048 dimensional, respectively. However, Conneau et al. (2017) show that their own model performs better when dimensionality of the embeddings is larger. They hypothesize that the linear model they use for evaluation (logistic regression) performs better with higher dimensional embeddings because these are more likely to be linearly separable. Rücklé et al. (2018) then argued that a comparison to low-dimensional baselines is unfair under this finding and increase the size of the baselines by concatenating different word embedding types or by concatenating different pooling operations (min, max, average). Wieting and Kiela (2019) further extend this idea by enlarging the word embedding size with randomly initialized matrices before averaging. All three works show that performance increases as a concave function of embedding size, when a linear model is used on top of embeddings for evaluation.

We also observe this trend when we merely train higher-dimensional word2vec word embeddings (on Wikipedia) and then average them, see Figure 1. At *equal* embedding size, some models such as USE and Sent2Vec, have no or very little advantage over average word embeddings. Therefore, we strongly encourage future research to compare embeddings of the same sizes to provide a fair evaluation (or at least similar sizes).

Cosine similarity and Pearson correlation may give misleading results. The following evaluation scenario is common when testing for *semantic similarity*: given two inputs (words or sentences), embed each of them, (i) compute the cosine similarity of the pairs of vectors, and then (ii) calculate the Pearson (or Spearman) correlation with human judgments for the same pairs. Both steps are problematic: (i) it is unclear whether cosine similarity is better suited to measure semantic similarity than other similarity functions; (ii) Pearson correlation is known for its deficiencies—e.g., it only measures linear correlation and it is sensitive to outliers. A popular example for failure of Pearson correlation

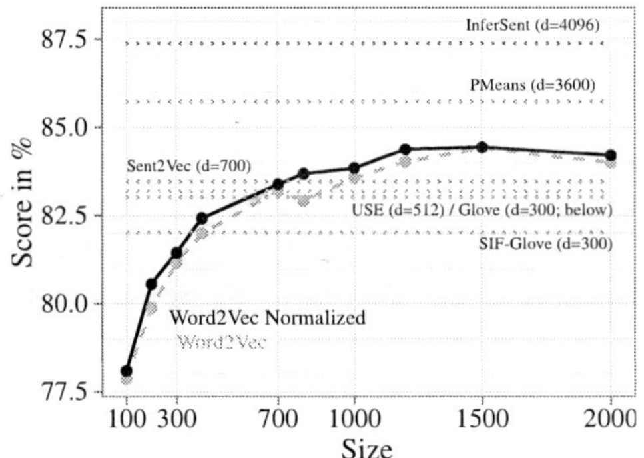

Figure 1: Avg. score across 6 transfer tasks for different sizes of Word2Vec embeddings vs. scores of other encoders (with constant embedding sizes as given in Table 1). 'Word2Vec Normalized' is discussed below.

is Anscombe's quartet (Anscombe, 1973).

Indeed, using such *unsupervised* evaluations based on cosine similarity and Pearson correlation (which we denote UCP) may be misleading, as pointed out by Lu et al. (2015). When they normalized word embeddings, their WS353 semantic similarity (Finkelstein et al., 2001) scores using UCP increased by almost 20 percentage points (pp). Since normalization is a simple operation that could easily be *learned* by a machine learning model, this indicates that UCP scores may yield unreliable conclusions regarding the quality of the underlying embeddings.

We wanted to verify if this was also true when comparing different sentence encoders, and therefore used the popular STSBenchmark dataset in the UCP setup. The results in Table 2 show that the outcomes vary strongly, with Glove-300d embeddings performing worst (0.41 correlation) and USE-512d embeddings best (0.70 correlation). We then normalized all sentence embeddings with z-norm[1], which is given as a recommendation in LeCun et al. (1998) to process inputs for deep learning systems.

With normalization, we observe a reduction in the range of the distribution of UCP scores across the nine systems from 29% to 9%; similarly, the standard deviation decreases from 8.6% to 2.4%. In particular, the worst sentence encoders catch up substantially: e.g., average Glove embeddings improve from 0.41 Pearson to 0.62 Pearson and the improvement of more complex systems over simple

---

¹

	Standard	Normalized	Δ
Glove-300d	0.41	0.62	+21
Word2Vec-300d	0.56	0.65	+9
Word2Vec-800d	0.56	0.67	+11
InferSent-4096d	0.67	0.67	+0
SIF-Glove-300d	0.66	0.67	+1
SIF-Word2Vec-300d	0.67	0.67	+0
USE-512d	0.70	0.70	+0
Sent2Vec-700d	0.67	0.71	+4
PMean-3600d	0.64	0.66	+2

Table 2: Unsupervised cosine similarity + Pearson correlation (UCP) on STSBench (test data). Δ in pp.

averaging baselines appears much less pronounced than before the normalization.

When replacing Pearson by Spearman correlation, we observed very similar trends: e.g., Glove-300d had 0.44 before and 0.58 after normalization.

This shows that that UCP requires specific normalization of the inputs for a fair comparison. Parallel to the suggestion of Lu et al. (2015), we recommend considering to use *learned* similarity functions and mean-square error (MSE) as an alternative to UCP.

Normalization. Indeed, we also evaluated the effect of normalization for *supervised* transfer tasks, i.e., with learned similarity function. To this end, we compared the 9 sentence encoders from Table 2 across 6 transfer tasks (averaged results) and STSBench (learned similarity function on training data instead of cosine similarity).[2]

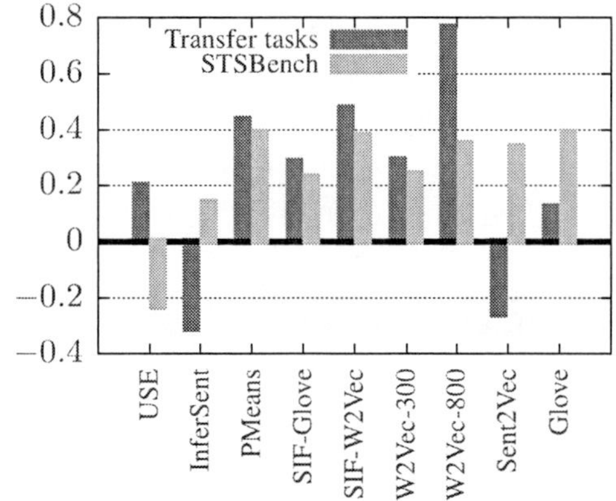

Figure 2: Δ in pp of normalization and no normalization. Average across transfer tasks. STSBench differences are scaled down by factor of 10.

---

¹Subtracting the mean from each column of the embedding matrix of the whole data ($2N$ rows, one for each of N pairs, and d columns, where d is the embedding size) and dividing by the standard deviation; after that we normalized each row to have unit length (ℓ_2 norm).

²We estimated normalization vectors for mean and standard deviation on the training data and used these fixed values to normalize the test data.

Figure 2 shows that most techniques profit from normalization (on average), both on the transfer tasks and STSBench, even though gains are often substantially smaller than in the UCP setting. Since the normalization can lead to rank changes (which we, e.g., observe between W2Vec-800, USE, and Sent2Vec) we thus recommend introducing normalization as a binary hyperparameter that is tuned for each sentence encoder and downstream task also in supervised settings with learned similarity function.

Different classifiers for evaluation. The popular SentEval evaluation tool feeds sentence embeddings into a logistic regression classifier. The underlying assumption is that in order to evaluate the embeddings *themselves* the classifier used on top of embeddings should be as simple as possible. While the argument has some appeal, one wonders how relevant such an evaluation is when in practice more powerful classifiers would probably be used, e.g., deeper networks (current versions of SentEval also offer evaluating with a multi-layer perceptron (MLP)). In particular, we note here an asymmetry between the extrinsic evaluation of word and sentence embeddings: word embeddings have traditionally been compared extrinsically by feeding them into different powerful architectures, such as BiLSTMs, while sentence embeddings are compared using the simplest possible architecture, logistic regression. While this is cheaper and focuses more on the embeddings themselves, it is less practically relevant, as discussed, and may have undesirable side effects, such as the preference for embeddings of larger size.

A main problem arises when the ranking of systems is not stable across different classifiers. To our knowledge, this is an open issue. We are only aware of Subramanian et al. (2018), who evaluate a few setups both with logistic regression and using an MLP, and their results indicate that their own approach profits much more from the MLP than the InferSent embeddings they compare to (+3.4pp vs. +2.2pp).

Thus, it is not sufficient to only report results with logistic regression, and evaluations with better-performing approaches would provide a more realistic comparison for actual use-case scenarios. We suggest reporting results for at least logistic regression and MLP.

Correlation of transfer tasks and probing tasks. Besides transfer tasks, the literature has recently suggested evaluating sentence encoders with probing tasks (Conneau et al., 2018) that query embeddings for certain linguistic features, such as to detect whether a sentence contains certain words (WC) or to determine the sentence length (SentLen). Perone et al. (2018) evaluate 11 different sentence encoders on 9 transfer tasks and 10 probing tasks. We plot the Spearman correlation between their transfer task results and their probing task results in Figure 3. The average Spearman correlation is 0.64. The highest average correlation to transfer tasks has SentLen (0.83), and the lowest score has WC (0.04). Taken at face value, this may mean that current transfer tasks query more for superficial sentence features (knowing that embedding A can better predict sentence length than embedding B is indicative that A outperforms B on the transfer tasks) than for actual semantic content, as the embeddings were originally designed for.

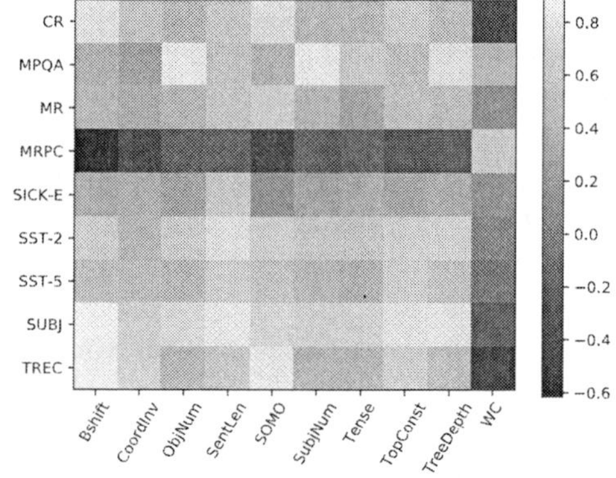

Figure 3: Correlation of 11 sentence encoders on transfer tasks (y-axis) and probing tasks (x-axis) in Perone et al. (2018).

Thus, future research might focus on more suitable (difficult) datasets and sentence classification tasks for the evaluation of sentence embeddings, a lesson already learned in other fields (Läubli et al., 2018; Yu et al., 2018).

Importantly, depending on the set of evaluated sentence encoders, such correlations can yield contradictory outcomes. For example, Conneau et al. (2018) evaluate more than 40 combinations of *similar* sentence encoder architectures and observe the strongest correlation with downstream task performances for WC (cf. their figure 2). This is in contrast to the correlations from the results of Perone et al. (2018), where WC had the *lowest* correlation. Thus, it remains unclear to which extent downstram tasks benefit from the different properties that are defined by many probing tasks.

4 Conclusion

Others have laid out problems with the evaluation of *word* embeddings (Faruqui et al., 2016) using word similarity tasks. They referred to the vagueness of the data underlying the tasks (as well as its annotations), the low correlations between extrinsic and intrinsic evaluations, and the lack of statistical tests. Our critique differs (in part) from this in that we also address extrinsic evaluation and the evaluation techniques themselves,[3] and in that we believe that the comparison between sentence embeddings is not always fair, especially given the current evaluations using logistic regression. This implicitly favors larger embeddings, and may therefore result in misleading conclusions regarding the superiority of different encoders.

As practical recommendations, we encourage future research in sentence embeddings to (1) compare embeddings of the same size; (2) treat normalization as a further hyperparameter; and (3) use multiple classifiers during evaluation, i.e., at least logistic regression and an MLP. We recommend against using unsupervised cosine+Pearson evaluations but instead to use a learned similarity function, and to report MSE as an alternative to Pearson/Spearman correlations. If unsupervised evaluation is unavoidable, normalization is even more important. Finally, we think that current transfer tasks for sentence embeddings should be complemented by more challenging ones for which bag-of-words models or random projection models cannot as easily compete.

Acknowledgments

We thank the reviewers for their helpful feedback. This work has been supported by the German Research Foundation (DFG) funded research training group "Adaptive Preparation of Information form Heterogeneous Sources" (AIPHES, GRK 1994/1) and the DFG-funded project QA-EduInf (GU 798/18-1, RI 803/12-1). Some calculations of this research were conducted on the Lichtenberg high performance cluster of the TU Darmstadt.

---

[3]Faruqui et al. (2016) also discuss some short-comings of cosine similarity.

References

Frank J. Anscombe. 1973. Graphs in Statistical Analysis. *The American Statistician*, 27(1):17–21.

Sanjeev Arora, Yingyu Liang, and Tengyu Ma. 2017. A Simple but Tough-to-Beat Baseline for Sentence Embeddings. In *International Conference on Learning Representations (ICLR 2017)*.

Daniel Cer, Yinfei Yang, Sheng-yi Kong, Nan Hua, Nicole Limtiaco, Rhomni St. John, Noah Constant, Mario Guajardo-Cespedes, Steve Yuan, Chris Tar, Yun-Hsuan Sung, Brian Strope, and Ray Kurzweil. 2018. Universal Sentence Encoder. *CoRR*, abs/1803.11175.

Daniel M. Cer, Mona T. Diab, Eneko Agirre, Iñigo Lopez-Gazpio, and Lucia Specia. 2017. SemEval-2017 Task 1: Semantic Textual Similarity Multilingual and Crosslingual Focused Evaluation. In *SemEval@ACL*, pages 1–14. Association for Computational Linguistics.

Alexis Conneau and Douwe Kiela. 2018. Senteval: An evaluation toolkit for universal sentence representations. In *Proceedings of the Eleventh International Conference on Language Resources and Evaluation (LREC 2018)*. European Language Resource Association.

Alexis Conneau, Douwe Kiela, Holger Schwenk, Loic Barrault, and Antoine Bordes. 2017. Supervised Learning of Universal Sentence Representations from Natural Language Inference Data. In *Proceedings of the 2017 Conference on Empirical Methods in Natural Language Processing (EMNLP 2017)*, pages 681–691. Association for Computational Linguistics.

Alexis Conneau, Germán Kruszewski, Guillaume Lample, Loïc Barrault, and Marco Baroni. 2018. What you can cram into a single $&!#* vector: Probing sentence embeddings for linguistic properties. In *Proceedings of the 56th Annual Meeting of the Association for Computational Linguistics (ACL 2018)*, pages 2126–2136. Association for Computational Linguistics.

Manaal Faruqui, Yulia Tsvetkov, Pushpendre Rastogi, and Chris Dyer. 2016. Problems With Evaluation of Word Embeddings Using Word Similarity Tasks. In *Proceedings of the 1st Workshop on Evaluating Vector-Space Representations for NLP*, pages 30–35. Association for Computational Linguistics.

Lev Finkelstein, Evgeniy Gabrilovich, Yossi Matias, Ehud Rivlin, Zach Solan, Gadi Wolfman, and Eytan Ruppin. 2001. Placing search in context: The concept revisited. In *Proceedings of the 10th International Conference on World Wide Web (WWW '01)*, pages 406–414. ACM.

Ryan Kiros, Yukun Zhu, Ruslan Salakhutdinov, Richard S. Zemel, Antonio Torralba, Raquel Urtasun, and Sanja Fidler. 2015. Skip-thought Vectors.

In *Proceedings of the 28th International Conference on Neural Information Processing Systems (NIPS 2015)*, pages 3294–3302.

Samuel Läubli, Rico Sennrich, and Martin Volk. 2018. Has machine translation achieved human parity? a case for document-level evaluation. In *Proceedings of the 2018 Conference on Empirical Methods in Natural Language Processing (EMNLP 2018)*, pages 4791–4796. Association for Computational Linguistics.

Yann LeCun, Leon Bottou, Genevieve B. Orr, and Klaus Robert Müller. 1998. *Efficient BackProp*. Springer Berlin Heidelberg, Berlin, Heidelberg.

Zachary C. Lipton and Jacob Steinhardt. 2018. Troubling Trends in Machine Learning Scholarship. *CoRR*, abs/1807.03341.

Ang Lu, Weiran Wang, Mohit Bansal, Kevin Gimpel, and Karen Livescu. 2015. Deep Multilingual Correlation for Improved Word Embeddings. In *Proceedings of the 2015 Conference of the North American Chapter of the Association for Computational Linguistics: Human Language Technologies (NAACL-HLT 2015)*, pages 250–256, Denver, Colorado. Association for Computational Linguistics.

Gábor Melis, Chris Dyer, and Phil Blunsom. 2017. On the state of the art of evaluation in neural language models. *CoRR*, abs/1707.05589.

Tomas Mikolov, Ilya Sutskever, Kai Chen, Greg S Corrado, and Jeff Dean. 2013. Distributed Representations of Words and Phrases and their Compositionality. In *Advances in neural information processing systems (NIPS 2013)*, pages 3111–3119.

Matteo Pagliardini, Prakhar Gupta, and Martin Jaggi. 2018. Unsupervised Learning of Sentence Embeddings Using Compositional n-Gram Features. In *Proceedings of the 2018 Conference of the North American Chapter of the Association for Computational Linguistics: Human Language Technologies (NAACL-HLT 2018)*, pages 528–540, New Orleans, Louisiana. Association for Computational Linguistics.

Jeffrey Pennington, Richard Socher, and Christopher Manning. 2014. Glove: Global Vectors for Word Representation. In *Proceedings of the 2014 Conference on Empirical Methods in Natural Language Processing (EMNLP 2014)*, pages 1532–1543. Association for Computational Linguistics.

Christian S. Perone, Roberto Silveira, and Thomas S. Paula. 2018. Evaluation of sentence embeddings in downstream and linguistic probing tasks. *CoRR*, abs/1806.06259.

Matt Post. 2018. A Call for Clarity in Reporting BLEU Scores. In *Proceedings of the Third Conference on Machine Translation: Research Papers*, pages 186–191. Association for Computational Linguistics.

Nils Reimers and Iryna Gurevych. 2017. Reporting Score Distributions Makes a Difference: Performance Study of LSTM-networks for Sequence Tagging. In *Proceedings of the 2017 Conference on Empirical Methods in Natural Language Processing (EMNLP 2017)*, pages 338–348.

Andreas Rücklé, Steffen Eger, Maxime Peyrard, and Iryna Gurevych. 2018. Concatenated power mean embeddings as universal cross-lingual sentence representations. *CoRR*, abs/1803.01400.

Dinghan Shen, Guoyin Wang, Wenlin Wang, Martin Renqiang Min, Qinliang Su, Yizhe Zhang, Chunyuan Li, Ricardo Henao, and Lawrence Carin. 2018. Baseline Needs More Love: On Simple Word-Embedding-Based Models and Associated Pooling Mechanisms. In *Proceedings of the 56th Annual Meeting of the Association for Computational Linguistics (ACL 2018)*, pages 440–450. Association for Computational Linguistics.

Sandeep Subramanian, Adam Trischler, Yoshua Bengio, and Christopher J Pal. 2018. Learning general purpose distributed sentence representations via large scale multi-task learning. In *International Conference on Learning Representations (ICLR 2018)*.

John Wieting and Douwe Kiela. 2019. No Training Required: Exploring Random Encoders for Sentence Classification. In *International Conference on Learning Representations (ICLR 2019)*.

Tao Yu, Rui Zhang, Kai Yang, Michihiro Yasunaga, Dongxu Wang, Zifan Li, James Ma, Irene Li, Qingning Yao, Shanelle Roman, Zilin Zhang, and Dragomir Radev. 2018. Spider: A Large-Scale Human-Labeled Dataset for Complex and Cross-Domain Semantic Parsing and Text-to-SQL Task. In *Proceedings of the 2018 Conference on Empirical Methods in Natural Language Processing (EMNLP 2018)*, pages 3911–3921. Association for Computational Linguistics.

Learning Bilingual Sentence Embeddings via Autoencoding and Computing Similarities with a Multilayer Perceptron

Yunsu Kim[2]   Hendrik Rosendahl[1,2]   Nick Rossenbach[2]
Jan Rosendahl[2]   Shahram Khadivi[1]   Hermann Ney[2]

[1]eBay, Inc., Aachen, Germany
{hrosendahl,skhadivi}@ebay.com
[2]RWTH Aachen University, Aachen, Germany
{surname}@cs.rwth-aachen.de

Abstract

We propose a novel model architecture and training algorithm to learn bilingual sentence embeddings from a combination of parallel and monolingual data. Our method connects autoencoding and neural machine translation to force the source and target sentence embeddings to share the same space without the help of a pivot language or an additional transformation. We train a multilayer perceptron on top of the sentence embeddings to extract good bilingual sentence pairs from nonparallel or noisy parallel data. Our approach shows promising performance on sentence alignment recovery and the WMT 2018 parallel corpus filtering tasks with only a single model.

1 Introduction

Data crawling is increasingly important in machine translation (MT), especially for neural network models. Without sufficient bilingual data, neural machine translation (NMT) fails to learn meaningful translation parameters (Koehn and Knowles, 2017). Even for high-resource language pairs, it is common to augment the training data with web-crawled bilingual sentences to improve the translation performance (Bojar et al., 2018).

Using crawled data in MT typically involves two core steps: mining and filtering. Mining parallel sentences, i.e. aligning source and target sentences, is usually done with lots of heuristics and features: document/URL meta information (Resnik and Smith, 2003; Esplá-Gomis and Forcada, 2009), sentence lengths with self-induced lexicon (Moore, 2002; Varga et al., 2005; Etchegoyhen and Azpeitia, 2016), word alignment statistics and linguistic tags (Ştefănescu et al., 2012; Kaufmann, 2012).

Filtering aligned sentence pairs also often involves heavy feature engineering (Taghipour et al.,

2011; Xu and Koehn, 2017). Most of the participants in the WMT 2018 parallel corpus filtering task use large-scale neural MT models and language models as the features (Koehn et al., 2018).

Bilingual sentence embeddings can be an elegant and unified solution for parallel corpus mining and filtering. They compress the information of each sentence into a single vector, which lies in a shared space between source and target languages. Scoring a source-target sentence pair is done by computing similarity between the source embedding vector and the target embedding vector. It is much more efficient than scoring by decoding, e.g. with a translation model.

Bilingual sentence embeddings have been studied primarily for transfer learning of monolingual downstream tasks across languages (Hermann and Blunsom, 2014; Pham et al., 2015; Zhou et al., 2016). However, few papers apply it to bilingual corpus mining; many of them require parallel training data with additional pivot languages (Espana-Bonet et al., 2017; Schwenk, 2018) or lack an investigation into similarity between the embeddings (Guo et al., 2018).

This work solves these issues as follows:

- We propose a simple end-to-end training approach of bilingual sentence embeddings with parallel and monolingual data only of the corresponding language pair.

- We use a multilayer perceptron (MLP) as a trainable similarity measure to match source and target sentence embeddings.

- We compare various similarity measures for embeddings in terms of score distribution, geometric interpretation, and performance in downstream tasks.

- We demonstrate competitive performance in sentence alignment recovery and parallel cor-

Proceedings of the 4th Workshop on Representation Learning for NLP (RepL4NLP-2019), pages 61–71
Florence, Italy, August 2, 2019. ©2019 Association for Computational Linguistics

pus filtering tasks without a complex combination of translation/language models.

- We analyze the effect of negative examples on training an MLP similarity, using different levels of negativity.

2 Related Work

Bilingual representation of a sentence was at first built by averaging pre-trained bilingual word embeddings (Huang et al., 2012; Klementiev et al., 2012). The compositionality from words to sentences is integrated into end-to-end training in Hermann and Blunsom (2014).

Explicit modeling of a sentence-level bilingual embedding was first discussed in Chandar et al. (2013), training an autoencoder on monolingual sentence embeddings of two languages. Pham et al. (2015) jointly learn bilingual sentence and word embeddings by feeding a shared sentence embedding to n-gram models. Zhou et al. (2016) add document-level alignment information to this model as a constraint in training.

Recently, sequence-to-sequence NMT models were adapted to learn cross-lingual sentence embeddings. Schwenk and Douze (2017) connect multiple source encoders to a shared decoder of a pivot target language, forcing the consistency of encoder representations. Schwenk (2018) extend this work to use a single encoder for many source languages. Both methods rely on N-way parallel training data, which are seriously limited to certain languages and domains. Artetxe and Schwenk (2018b) relax this data condition to pairwise parallel data including the pivot language, but it is still unrealistic for many scenarios (see Section 4.2). In contrast, our method needs only parallel and monolingual data for source and target languages of concern without any pivot languages.

Hassan et al. (2018) train a bidirectional NMT model with a single encoder-decoder, taking the average of top-layer encoder states as the sentence embedding. They do not include any details on the data or translation performance before/after the filtering with this embedding. Junczys-Dowmunt (2018) apply this method to WMT 2018 parallel corpus filtering task, yet showing significantly worse performance than a combination of translation/language models. Our method shows comparable results to such model combinations in the same task.

Guo et al. (2018) replace the decoder with a feedforward network and use the parallel sentences as input to the two encoders. Similarly to our work, the feedforward network measures the similarity of sentence pairs, except that the source and target sentence embeddings are combined via dot product instead of concatenation. Their model, however, is not directly optimizing the source and target sentences to be translations of each other; it only attaches two encoders in the output level without a decoder.

Based on the model of Artetxe and Schwenk (2018b), Artetxe and Schwenk (2018a) scale cosine similarity between sentence embeddings with average similarity of the nearest neighbors. Searching for the nearest neighbors among hundreds of millions of sentences may cause a huge computational problem. On the other hand, our similarity calculation is much quicker and support batch computation while preserving strong performance in parallel corpus filtering.

Neither of the above-mentioned methods utilize monolingual data. We integrate autoencoding into NMT to maximize the usage of parallel and monolingual data together in learning bilingual sentence embeddings.

3 Bilingual Sentence Embeddings

A bilingual sentence embedding function maps sentences from both the source and target language into a single joint vector space. Once we obtain such a space, we can search for a similar target sentence embedding given a source sentence embedding, or vice versa.

3.1 Model

In this work, we learn bilingual sentence embeddings via NMT and autoencoding given parallel and monolingual corpora. Since our purpose is to pair source and target sentences, translation is a natural base task to connect sentences in two different languages. We adopt a basic encoder-decoder approach from Sutskever et al. (2014). The encoder produces a fixed-length embedding of a source sentence, which is used by the decoder to generate the target hypothesis.

First, the encoder takes a source sentence $f_1^J = f_1, ..., f_j, ..., f_J$ (length J) as input, where each f_j is a source word. It computes hidden representations $\mathbf{h}_j \in \mathbb{R}^D$ for all source positions j:

$$\mathbf{h}_1^J = \mathrm{enc}_{\mathrm{src}}(f_1^J) \tag{1}$$

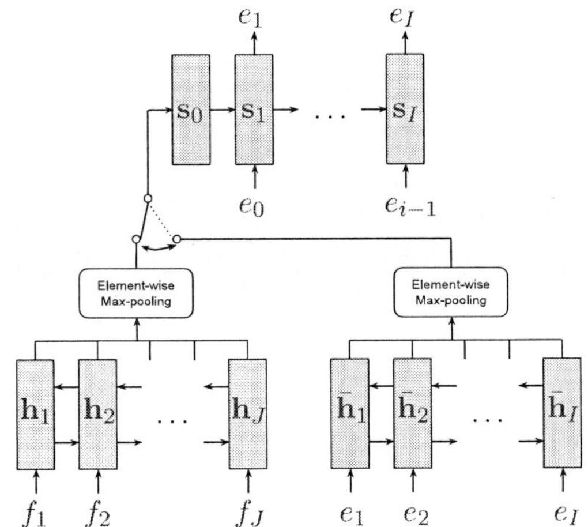

Figure 1: Our proposed model for learning bilingual sentence embeddings. A decoder (above) is shared over two encoders (below). The decoder accepts a max-pooled representation from either one of the encoders as its first state $\mathbf{s}_0$, depending on the training objective (Equation 7 and 8).

$\mathrm{enc}_{\mathrm{src}}$ is implemented as a bidirectional recurrent neural network (RNN). We denote a target output sentence by $e_1^I = e_1, ..., e_i, ..., e_I$ (length I). The decoder is an unidirectional RNN whose internal state for a target position i is:

$$\mathbf{s}_i = \mathrm{dec}(\mathbf{s}_{i-1}, e_{i-1}) \qquad (2)$$

where its initial state is element-wise max-pooling of the encoder representations $\mathbf{h}_1^J$:

$$\mathbf{s}_0 = \mathrm{maxpool}(\mathbf{h}_1^J)$$
$$= \left[\max_{j=1,...,J} \mathbf{h}_{j1}, \ ..., \ \max_{j=1,...,J} \mathbf{h}_{jD} \right]^\top \qquad (3)$$

We empirically found that the max-pooling performs much better than averaging or choosing the first ($\mathbf{h}_1$) or last ($\mathbf{h}_J$) representation. Finally, an output layer predicts a target word e_i:

$$p_\theta(e_i|e_1^{i-1}, f_1^J) = \mathrm{softmax}(\mathrm{linear}(\mathbf{s}_i)) \qquad (4)$$

where θ denotes a set of model parameters.

Note that the decoder has access to the source sentence only through $\mathbf{s}_0$, which we take as the sentence embedding of f_1^J. This assumes that the source sentence embedding contains sufficient information for translating to a target sentence, which is desired for a bilingual embedding space.

However, this plain NMT model can generate only source sentence embeddings through the encoder. The decoder cannot process a new target sentence without a proper source language input. We can perform decoding with an empty source input and take the last decoder state $\mathbf{s}_I$ as the sentence embedding of e_1^I, but it is not compatible with the source embedding and contradicts the way in which the model is trained.

Therefore, we attach another encoder of the target language to the same (target) decoder:

$$\bar{\mathbf{h}}_1^I = \mathrm{enc}_{\mathrm{tgt}}(e_1^I) \qquad (5)$$
$$\mathbf{s}_0 = \left[\max_{i=1,...,I} \bar{\mathbf{h}}_{i1}, \ ..., \ \max_{i=1,...,I} \bar{\mathbf{h}}_{iD} \right]^\top \qquad (6)$$

$\mathrm{enc}_{\mathrm{tgt}}$ has the same architecture as $\mathrm{enc}_{\mathrm{src}}$. The model has now an additional information flow from a target input sentence to the same target (output) sentence, also known as sequential autoencoder (Li et al., 2015).

Figure 1 is a diagram of our model. A decoder is shared between NMT and autoencoding parts; it takes either source or target sentence embedding and does not differentiate between the two when producing an output. The two encoders are constrained to provide mathematically consistent representations over the languages (to the decoder).

Note that our model does not have any attention component (Bahdanau et al., 2014). The attention mechanism in NMT makes the decoder attend to encoder representations at all source positions. This is counterintuitive for our purpose; we need to optimize the encoder to produce a single representation vector, but the attention model allows the encoder to distribute information over many different positions. In our initial experiments, the same model with the attention mechanism showed exorbitantly bad performance, so we removed it in the main experiments of Section 4.

3.2 Training and Inference

Let $\theta_{\mathrm{enc}_{\mathrm{src}}}$, $\theta_{\mathrm{enc}_{\mathrm{tgt}}}$, and θ_{dec} the parameters of the source encoder, the target encoder, and the (shared) decoder, respectively. Given a parallel corpus $\mathcal{P}$ and a target monolingual corpus $\mathcal{M}_{\mathrm{tgt}}$, the training criterion of our model is the cross-entropy on two input-output paths. The NMT objective (Equation 7) is for training $\theta_1 = \{\theta_{\mathrm{enc}_{\mathrm{src}}}, \theta_{\mathrm{dec}}\}$, and the autoencoding objective (Equation 8) is for training $\theta_2 = \{\theta_{\mathrm{enc}_{\mathrm{tgt}}}, \theta_{\mathrm{dec}}\}$:

$$L_{\mathrm{emb}}(\theta) = -\sum_{(f_1^J, e_1^I) \in \mathcal{P}} \log p_{\theta_1}(e_1^I | f_1^J) \qquad (7)$$

$$- \sum_{e_1^I \in \mathcal{M}_{\text{tgt}}} \log p_{\theta_2}(e_1^I | e_1^I) \tag{8}$$

where $\theta = \{\theta_1, \theta_2\}$. During the training, each mini-batch contains examples of the both objectives with a 1:1 ratio. In this way, we prevent one encoder from being optimized more than the other, forcing the two encoders produce balanced sentence embeddings that fit to the same decoder.

The autoencoding part can be trained with a separate target monolingual corpus. To provide a stronger training signal for the shared embedding space, we use also the target side of $\mathcal{P}$; the model learns to produce the same target sentence from the corresponding source and target inputs.

In order to guide the training to bilingual representations, we initialize the word embedding layers with a pre-trained bilingual word embedding. The word embedding for each language is trained with a skip-gram algorithm (Mikolov et al., 2013), later mapped across the languages with adversarial training (Conneau et al., 2018) and self-dictionary refinements (Artetxe et al., 2017).

Our model can be built also in the opposite direction, i.e. with a target-to-source NMT model and a source autoencoder:

$$L_{\text{emb}}(\theta) = - \sum_{(f_1^J, e_1^I) \in \mathcal{P}} \log p_{\theta_2}(f_1^J | e_1^I) \tag{9}$$

$$- \sum_{f_1^J \in \mathcal{M}_{\text{src}}} \log p_{\theta_1}(f_1^J | f_1^J) \tag{10}$$

Once the model is trained, we need only the encoders to query sentence embeddings. Let $\mathbf{a}$ and $\mathbf{b}$ be embeddings of a source sentence f_1^J and a target sentence e_1^I, respectively:

$$\mathbf{a} = \text{maxpool}(\text{enc}_{\text{src}}(f_1^J)) \tag{11}$$

$$\mathbf{b} = \text{maxpool}(\text{enc}_{\text{tgt}}(e_1^I)) \tag{12}$$

3.3 Computing Similarities

The next step is to evaluate how close the two embeddings are to each other, i.e. to compute a similarity measure between them. In this paper, we consider two types of similarity measures.

Predefined mathematical functions Cosine similarity is a conventional choice for measuring the similarity in vector space modeling of information retrieval or text mining (Singhal, 2001). It computes the angle between two vectors (rotation) and ignore the lengths:

$$\cos(\mathbf{a}, \mathbf{b}) = \frac{\mathbf{a} \cdot \mathbf{b}}{\|\mathbf{a}\| \|\mathbf{b}\|} \tag{13}$$

Euclidean distance indicates how much distance must be traveled to move from the end of a vector to that of the other (transition). We reverse this distance to use it as a similarity measure:

$$\text{Euclidean}(\mathbf{a}, \mathbf{b}) = -\|\mathbf{a} - \mathbf{b}\| \tag{14}$$

However, these simple measures, i.e. a single rotation or transition, might not be sufficient to define the similarity of complex natural language sentences across different languages. Also, the learned joint embedding space is not necessarily perfect in the sense of vector space geometry; even if we train it with a decent algorithm, the structure and quality of the embedding space are highly dependent on the amount of parallel training data and its domain. This might hinder the simple functions from working well for our purpose.

Trainable multilayer perceptron To model relations of sentence embeddings by combining rotation, shift, and even nonlinear transformations, We train a small multilayer perceptron (MLP) (Bishop et al., 1995) and use it as a similarity measure. We design the MLP network $q(\mathbf{a}, \mathbf{b})$ as a simple binary classifier whose input is a concatenation of source and target sentence embeddings: $[\mathbf{a}; \mathbf{b}]^\top$. It is passed through feedforward hidden layers with nonlinear activations. The output layer has a single node with sigmoid activation, representing how probable the source and target sentences are translations of each other.

To train this model, we must have positive examples (real parallel sentence pairs, $\mathcal{P}_{\text{pos}}$) and negative examples (nonparallel or noisy sentence pairs, $\mathcal{P}_{\text{neg}}$). The training criterion is:

$$L_{\text{sim}} = - \sum_{(\mathbf{a}, \mathbf{b}) \in \mathcal{P}_{\text{pos}}} \log q(\mathbf{a}, \mathbf{b})$$

$$- \sum_{(\mathbf{a}, \mathbf{b}) \in \mathcal{P}_{\text{neg}}} (1 - \log q(\mathbf{a}, \mathbf{b})) \tag{15}$$

which naturally fits to the main task of interest: parallel corpus filtering (Section 4.2). Note that the output of the MLP can be quite biased to the extremes (0 or 1) in order to clearly distinguish good and bad examples. This has both advantages and disadvantages as explained in Section 5.1.

Our MLP similarity can be optimized differently for each embedding space. Furthermore, the user can inject domain-specific knowledge into the MLP similarity by training only with in-domain parallel data. The resulting MLP would devalue not only nonparallel sentence pairs but also out-of-domain instances.

4 Evaluation

We evaluated our bilingual sentence embedding and the MLP similarity on two tasks: sentence alignment recovery and parallel corpus filtering. The sentence embedding was trained with WMT 2018 English-German parallel data and 100M German sentences from the News Crawl mono-lingual data[1], where we use German as the auto-encoded language. All sentences were lower-cased and limited to the length of 60. We learned the byte pair encoding (Sennrich et al., 2016) jointly for the two languages with 20k merge oper-ations. We pre-trained bilingual word embeddings on 100M sentences from the News Crawl data for each language using FASTTEXT (Bojanowski et al., 2017) and MUSE (Conneau et al., 2018).

Our sentence embedding model has 1-layer RNN encoder/decoder, where the word embed-ding and hidden layers have a size of 512. The training was done with stochastic gradient descent with initial learning rate of 1.0, batch size of 120 sentences, and maximum 800k updates. After 100k updates, we reduced the learning rate by a factor of 0.9 for every 50k updates.

Our MLP similarity model has 2 hidden lay-ers of size 512 with ReLU (Nair and Hinton, 2010), trained with SCIKIT-LEARN (Pedregosa et al., 2011) with maximum 1,000 updates. For a positive training set, we used newstest2007-2015 from WMT (around 21k sentences). Unless other-wise noted, we took a comparable size of negative examples from the worst-scored sentence pairs of ParaCrawl[2] English-German corpus. The scoring was done with our bilingual sentence embedding and cosine similarity.

Note that the negative examples are selected via cosine similarity but the similarity values are not used in the MLP training (Equation 15). Thus it does not learn to mimic the cosine similarity function again, but has a new sorting of sentence pairs—also encoding the domain information.

4.1 Sentence Alignment Recovery

In this task, we corrupt the sentence alignments of a parallel test set by shuffling one side, and find

the original alignments; also known as corpus re-construction (Schwenk and Douze, 2017).

Given a source sentence, we compute a simi-larity score with every possible target sentence in the data and take the top-scored one as the align-ment. The error rate is the number of incorrect sentence alignments divided by the total number of sentences. We compute this also in the oppo-site direction and take an average of the two error rates. It is an intrinsic evaluation for parallel cor-pus mining. We choose two test sets: WMT new-stest2018 (2998 lines) and IWSLT tst2015 (1080 lines).

As baselines, we used character-level Leven-shtein distance and length-normalized posterior scores of German$\rightarrow$English/English$\rightarrow$German NMT models. Each NMT model is a 3-layer base Transformer (Vaswani et al., 2017) trained on the same training data as the sentence embedding.

Method	Error [%]	
	WMT	IWSLT
Levenshtein distance	37.4	54.6
NMT de-en + en-de	**1.7**	**13.3**
Our method (Cosine similarity)	**4.3**	**13.8**
Our method (MLP similarity)	89.9	72.6

Table 1: Sentence alignment recovery results. Our method results use cosine similarity except the last row.

Table 1 shows the results. The Levenshtein dis-tance gives a poor performance. NMT models are better than the other methods, but takes too long to compute posteriors for all possible pairs of source and target sentences (about 12 hours for the WMT test set). This is absolutely not feasible for a real mining task with hundreds of millions of sentences.

Our bilingual sentence embeddings (with us-ing cosine similarity) show error rates close to the NMT models, especially in the IWSLT test set. Computing similarities between embeddings is ex-tremely fast (about 3 minutes for the WMT test set), which perfectly fits to mining scenarios.

However, the MLP similarity performs bad in aligning sentence pairs. Given a source sentence, it puts all reasonably similar target sentences to the score 1 and does not precisely distinguish between them. Detailed investigation of this behavior is in Section 5.1. As we will find out, this is ironically very effective in parallel corpus filtering.

---

[1]http://www.statmt.org/wmt18/translation-task.html
[2]https://www.paracrawl.eu/

| Method | BLEU [%] | | | |
| | 10M words | | 100M words | |
	test2017	test2018	test2017	test2018
Random sampling	19.1	23.1	23.2	29.3
Pivot-based embedding (Schwenk and Douze, 2017)	26.1	32.4	30.0	37.5
NMT + LM, 4 models (Rossenbach et al., 2018)	29.1	35.2	**31.3**	**38.2**
Our method (cosine similarity)	23.0	28.4	27.9	34.4
Our method (MLP similarity)	**29.2**	**35.4**	30.6	37.5

Table 2: Parallel corpus filtering results (German→English).

4.2 Parallel Corpus Filtering

We also test our methods in the WMT 2018 parallel corpus filtering task (Koehn et al., 2018).

Data The task is to score each line of a very noisy, web-crawled corpus of 104M parallel lines (ParaCrawl English-German). We pre-filtered the given raw corpus with the heuristics of Rossenbach et al. (2018). Only the data for WMT 2018 English-German news translation task is allowed to train scoring models. The evaluation procedure is: subsample top-scored lines which amounts to 10M/100M words, train a small NMT model with the subsampled data, and check its translation performance. We follow the official pipeline except that we train 3-layer Transformer NMT model using Sockeye (Hieber et al., 2017) for evaluation.

Baselines We have three comparative baselines: 1) random sampling, 2) bilingual sentence embedding learned with a third pivot target language (Schwenk and Douze, 2017), 3) combination of source-to-target/target-to-source NMT and source/target LM (Rossenbach et al., 2018), a top-ranked system in the official evaluation.

Note that the second method violates the official data condition of the task since it requires parallel data in German-Pivot and English-Pivot. This method is not practical when learning multilingual embeddings for English and other languages, since it is hard to collect pairwise parallel data involving a non-English pivot language (except among European languages). We trained this method with N-way parallel UN corpus (Ziemski et al., 2016) with French as the pivot language. The size of this model is the same as that of our autoencoding-based model except the word embedding layers.

The results are shown in Table 2, where cosine similarity was used by default for sentence embedding methods except the last row. Pivot-based sentence embedding (Schwenk and Douze, 2017) improves upon the random sampling, but it has an impractical data condition. The four-model combination of NMT models and LMs (Rossenbach et al., 2018) provide 1-3% more BLEU improvement. Note that, for the third method, each model costs 1-2 weeks to train.

Our bilingual sentence embedding method greatly improves over the random sampling baseline up to 5.3% BLEU in the 10M-word case and 5.1% BLEU in the 100M-word case. With our MLP similarity, the improvement in BLEU is up to 12.3% and 8.2% in the 10M-word case and the 100M-word case, respectively. It outperforms the pivot-based embedding method significantly and gets close to the performance of the four-model combination. Note that we use only a single model trained with only given parallel/monolingual data for the corresponding language pair, i.e. English-German. In contrast to sentence alignment recovery experiments, the MLP similarity boosts the filtering performance by a large margin.

5 Analysis

In this section, we provide more in-depth analyses to compare 1) various similarity measures and 2) different choices of the negative training set for the MLP similarity model.

5.1 Similarity Measures

In Table 3, we compare sentence alignment recovery performance with different similarity measures.

Euclidean distance shows a worse performance than cosine similarity. This means that in a sentence embedding space, we should consider rotation more than transition when comparing two

	Error [%]		
Similarity	de-en	en-de	Average
Euclidean	7.9	99.8	53.8
Cosine	4.3	4.2	4.3
CSLS	1.9	2.2	2.1
MLP	85.0	94.8	89.9

Table 3: Sentence alignment recovery results with different similarity measures (newstest2018).

vectors. Particularly, the English→German direction has a peculiarly bad result with Euclidean distance. This is due to a hubness problem in a high-dimensional space, where some vectors are highly likely to be nearest neighbors of many others.

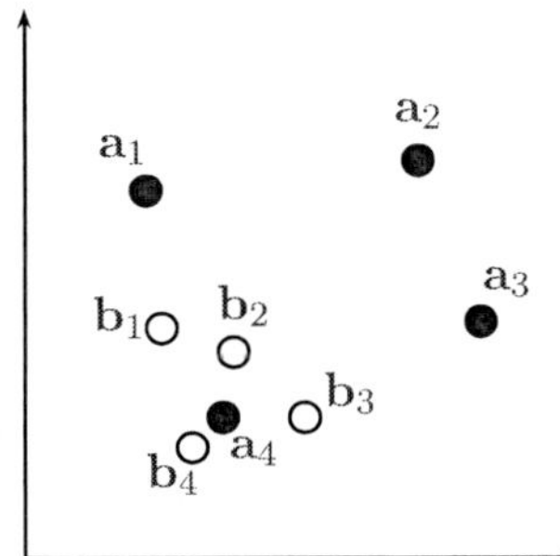

Figure 2: Schematic diagram of the hubness problem. Filled circles indicate German sentence embeddings, while empty circles denote English sentence embeddings. All embeddings are assumed to be normalized.

Figure 2 illustrates that Euclidean distance is more prone to the hubs than cosine similarity. Assume that German sentence embeddings $\mathbf{a}_n$ and English sentence embeddings $\mathbf{b}_n$ should match to each other with the same index n, e.g. $(\mathbf{a}_1, \mathbf{b}_1)$ is a correct match. With cosine similarity, the nearest neighbor of $\mathbf{a}_n$ is always $\mathbf{b}_n$ for all $n = 1, ..., 4$ and vice versa, considering only the angles between the vectors. However, when using Euclidean distance, there is a discrepancy between German→English and English→German directions: The nearest neighbor of each $\mathbf{a}_n$ is $\mathbf{b}_n$, but the nearest neighbor of all $\mathbf{b}_n$ is always $\mathbf{a}_4$. This leads to a serious performance drop only in English→German. The figure is depicted in a two-dimensional space for simplicity, but the hubness problem becomes worse for an actual high-dimensional space of sentence embeddings.

Cross-domain similarity local scaling (CSLS) is developed to counteract the hubness problem by

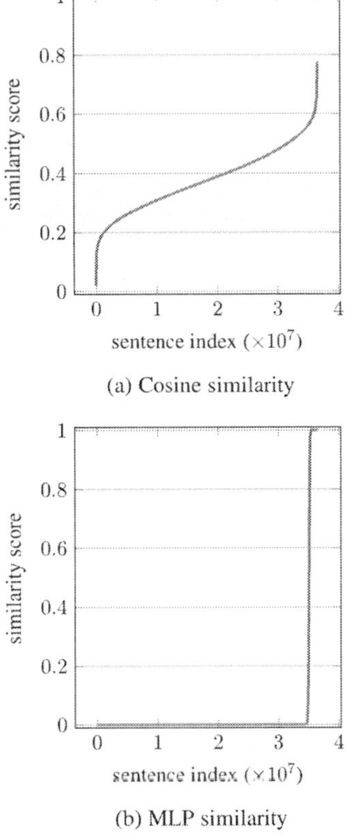

(a) Cosine similarity

(b) MLP similarity

Figure 3: The score distribution of similarity measures. The sentences are sorted by their similarity scores. Cosine similarity values are linearly rescaled to $[0, 1]$.

penalizing similarity values in dense areas of the embedding distribution (Conneau et al., 2018):

$$\text{CSLS}(\mathbf{a}, \mathbf{b}) = 2 \cdot \cos(\mathbf{a}, \mathbf{b}) \tag{16}$$

$$- \frac{1}{K} \sum_{\mathbf{b}' \in \text{NN}(\mathbf{a})} \cos(\mathbf{a}, \mathbf{b}') \tag{17}$$

$$- \frac{1}{K} \sum_{\mathbf{a}' \in \text{NN}(\mathbf{b})} \cos(\mathbf{a}', \mathbf{b}) \tag{18}$$

where K is the number of nearest neighbors. CSLS outperforms cosine similarity in our experiments. For a large-scale mining scenario, however, the measure requires heavy computations for the penalty terms (Equation 17 and 18), i.e. nearest neighbor search in all combinations of source and target sentences and sorting the scores over e.g. a few hundred million instances.

The MLP similarity is not performing well as opposed to its results in parallel corpus filtering. To explain this, we depict score distributions of cosine and MLP similarity over the ParaCrawl corpus in Figure 3. As for cosine similarity, only

German sentence	English sentence	Similarity	
		Cosine	MLP
the requested URL / dictionary / m / _ mar _ eisimpleir.htm was not found on this server.	additionally, a 404 Not Found error was encountered while trying to use an ErrorDocument to handle the request.	0.185	0.000
becoming Prestigious In The Right Way	how I Feel About School	0.199	0.000
nach dieser Aussage sollte die türkische Armee somit eine internationale Intervention gegen Syrien provozieren .	according to his report, the Turkish army was aiming to provoke an international intervention against Syria.	0.563	1.000
allen Menschen und Beschäftigten, die um Freiheit kämpfen oder bei Kundgebungen ums Leben kamen, Achtung zu bezeugen und die unverzügliche Freilassung aller Inhaftierten zu fordern	to pay tribute to all people and workers who have been fighting for freedom or fallen in demonstrations and demand the immediate release of all detainees	0.427	0.999

Table 4: Example sentence pairs in the ParaCrawl corpus (Section 4.2) with their similarity values.

a small fraction of the corpus is given low- or high-range scores (smaller than 0.2 or larger than 0.6). The remaining sentences are distributed almost uniformly within the score range inbetween.

The distribution curve of the MLP similarity has a completely different shape. It has a strong tendency to classify a sentence pair to be extremely bad or extremely good: nearly 80% of the corpus is scored with zero and only 3.25% gets scores between 0.99 and 1.0. Table 4 shows some example sentence pairs with extreme MLP similarity values.

This is the reason why the MLP similarity does a good job in filtering, especially in selecting a small portion (10M-word) of good parallel sentences. Table 4 compares cosine similarities and the MLP scores for some sentence pairs in the raw corpus for our filtering task (Section 4.2). The first two sentence pairs are absolutely nonparallel; both similarity measures give low scores, while the MLP similarity emphasizes the bad quality with zero scores. The third example is a decent parallel sentence pair with a minor ambiguity, i.e. *his* in English can be a translation of *dieser* in German or not, depending on the document-level context. Both measures see this sentence pair as a positive example.

The last example is parallel but the translation involves severe reordering: long-distance changes in verb positions, switching the order of relative clauses, etc. Here, cosine similarity has trouble in rating this case highly even if it is perfectly parallel, eventually filtering it out from the training data. On the other hand, our MLP similarity correctly evaluates this difficult case by giving a nearly perfect score.

However, the MLP is not optimized for precise differentiation among the good parallel matches. It is thus not appropriate for sentence alignment recovery that requires exact 1-1 matching of potential source-target pairs. A steep drop in the curve of Figure 3b also explains why it performs slightly inferior to the best system in the 100M-word filtering task (Table 2). The subsampling exceeds the dropping region and includes many zero-scored sentence pairs, where the MLP similarity cannot measure the quality well.

5.2 Negative Training Examples

In the MLP similarity training, we can use publicly available parallel corpora as the positive sets. For the negative sets, however, it is not clear which dataset we should use: entirely nonparallel sentences, partly parallel sentences, or sentence pairs of quality inbetween. We experimented with negative examples of different quality in Table 5. Here is how we vary the negativity:

1. Score the sentence pairs of the ParaCrawl corpus with our bilingual sentence embedding using cosine similarity.

2. Sort the sentence pairs by the scores.

3. Divide the sorted corpus into five portions by top-scored cut of 20%, 40%, 60%, 80%, and

Negative examples	BLEU [%]
Random sampling	33.3
20% worst	29.9
40% worst	33.3
60% worst	**33.7**
80% worst	32.1
100% worst	25.7

Table 5: Parallel corpus filtering results (10M-word task) with different negative sets for training MLP similarity (newstest2016, i.e. the validation set).

100%.

4. Take the last 100k lines for each portion.

A negative set from the 20%-worst part stands for relatively less problematic sentence pairs, intending for elaborate classification among perfect parallel sentences (positive set) and almost perfect ones. With the 100%-worst examples, we focus on removing absolutely nonsense pairing of sentences. As a simple baseline, we also take 100k sentences randomly without scoring, representing mixed levels of negativity.

The results in Table 5 show that a moderate level of negativity (60%-worst) is most suitable for training an MLP similarity model. If the negative set contains too many excellent examples, the model may mark acceptable parallel sentence pairs with zero scores. If the negative set consists only of certainly nonparallel sentence pairs, the model is weak in discriminating mid-quality instances, some of which are crucial to improve the translation system.

Random selection of sentence pairs also works surprisingly well compared to carefully tailored negative sets. It does not require us to score and sort the raw corpus, so it is very efficient, sacrificing performance slightly. We hypothesize that the average negative level of this random set is also moderate and similar to that of the 60%-worst.

6   Conclusion

In this work, we present a simple method to train bilingual sentence embeddings by combining vanilla RNN NMT (without attention component) and sequential autoencoder. By optimizing a shared decoder with combined training objectives, we force the source and target sentence embeddings to share their space. Our model is trained with parallel and monolingual data of the corresponding language pair, with neither pivot languages nor N-way parallel data. We also propose to use a binary classification MLP as a similarity measure for matching source and target sentence embeddings.

Our bilingual sentence embeddings show consistently strong performance in both sentence alignment recovery and the WMT 2018 parallel corpus filtering tasks with only a single model. We compare various similarity measures for bilingual sentence matching, verifying that cosine similarity is preferred for a mining task and our MLP similarity is very effective in a filtering task. We also show that a moderate level of negativity is appropriate for training the MLP similarity, using either random examples or mid-range scored examples from a noisy parallel corpus.

Future work would be regularizing the MLP training to obtain a smoother distribution of the similarity scores, which could supplement the weakness of the MLP similarity (Section 5.1). Furthermore, we plan to adjust our learning procedure towards the downstream tasks, e.g. with an additional training objective to maximize the cosine similarity between the source and target encoders (Arivazhagan et al., 2019). Our method should be tested also on many other language pairs which do not have parallel data involving a pivot language.

Acknowledgments

This work has received funding from the European Research Council (ERC) (under the European Union's Horizon 2020 research and innovation programme, grant agreement No 694537, project "SEQCLAS"), the Deutsche Forschungsgemeinschaft (DFG; grant agreement NE 572/8-1, project "CoreTec"), and eBay Inc. The GPU cluster used for the experiments was partially funded by DFG Grant INST 222/1168-1. The work reflects only the authors' views and none of the funding agencies is responsible for any use that may be made of the information it contains.

References

Naveen Arivazhagan, Ankur Bapna, Orhan Firat, Roee Aharoni, Melvin Johnson, and Wolfgang Macherey. 2019. The missing ingredient in zero-shot neural machine translation. *arXiv:1903.07091*.

Mikel Artetxe, Gorka Labaka, and Eneko Agirre. 2017. Learning bilingual word embeddings with (almost) no bilingual data. In *Proceedings of the 55th Annual Meeting of the Association for Computational Linguistics (ACL 2017)*, volume 1, pages 451–462.

Mikel Artetxe and Holger Schwenk. 2018a. Margin-based parallel corpus mining with multilingual sentence embeddings. *arXiv:1811.01136*.

Mikel Artetxe and Holger Schwenk. 2018b. Massively multilingual sentence embeddings for zero-shot cross-lingual transfer and beyond. *arXiv:1812.10464*.

Dzmitry Bahdanau, Kyunghyun Cho, and Yoshua Bengio. 2014. Neural machine translation by jointly learning to align and translate. *arXiv*, pages arXiv–1409.

Christopher M Bishop et al. 1995. *Neural networks for pattern recognition*. Oxford university press.

Piotr Bojanowski, Edouard Grave, Armand Joulin, and Tomas Mikolov. 2017. Enriching word vectors with subword information. *Transactions of the Association for Computational Linguistics*, 5:135–146.

Ondřej Bojar, Christian Federmann, Mark Fishel, Yvette Graham, Barry Haddow, Matthias Huck, Philipp Koehn, and Christof Monz. 2018. Findings of the 2018 conference on machine translation (wmt18). In *Proceedings of the Third Conference on Machine Translation, Volume 2: Shared Task Papers*, pages 272–307, Belgium, Brussels.

AP Sarath Chandar, Mitesh M Khapra, Balaraman Ravindran, Vikas Raykar, and Amrita Saha. 2013. Multilingual deep learning. In *Deep Learning Workshop at NIPS*.

Alexis Conneau, Guillaume Lample, Marc'Aurelio Ranzato, Ludovic Denoyer, and Hervé Jégou. 2018. Word translation without parallel data. In *Proceedings of 6th International Conference on Learning Representations (ICLR 2018)*.

Dan Ştefănescu, Radu Ion, and Sabine Hunsicker. 2012. Hybrid parallel sentence mining from comparable corpora. In *Proceedings of the 16th Conference of the European Association for Machine Translation*, pages 137–144.

Cristina Espana-Bonet, Adám Csaba Varga, Alberto Barrón-Cedeño, and Josef van Genabith. 2017. An empirical analysis of nmt-derived interlingual embeddings and their use in parallel sentence identification. *IEEE Journal of Selected Topics in Signal Processing*, 11(8):1340–1350.

Miquel Esplá-Gomis and Mikel L. Forcada. 2009. Bitextor, a free/open-source software to harvest translation memories from multilingual websites. In *Proceedings of MT Summit XII*, Ottawa, Canada.

Thierry Etchegoyhen and Andoni Azpeitia. 2016. Set-theoretic alignment for comparable corpora. In *Proceedings of the 54th Annual Meeting of the Association for Computational Linguistics (Volume 1: Long Papers)*, volume 1, pages 2009–2018.

Mandy Guo, Qinlan Shen, Yinfei Yang, Heming Ge, Daniel Cer, Gustavo Hernandez Abrego, Keith Stevens, Noah Constant, Yun-hsuan Sung, Brian Strope, et al. 2018. Effective parallel corpus mining using bilingual sentence embeddings. In *Proceedings of the Third Conference on Machine Translation: Research Papers*, pages 165–176.

Hany Hassan, Anthony Aue, Chang Chen, Vishal Chowdhary, Jonathan Clark, Christian Federmann, Xuedong Huang, Marcin Junczys-Downmunt, William Lewis, Mu Li, et al. 2018. Achieving human parity on automatic chinese to english news translation. *arXiv preprint arXiv:1803.05567*.

Karl Moritz Hermann and Phil Blunsom. 2014. Multilingual models for compositional distributed semantics. In *Proceedings of the 52nd Annual Meeting of the Association for Computational Linguistics (Volume 1: Long Papers)*, volume 1, pages 58–68.

Felix Hieber, Tobias Domhan, Michael Denkowski, David Vilar, Artem Sokolov, Ann Clifton, and Matt Post. 2017. Sockeye: A toolkit for neural machine translation. *arXiv preprint arXiv:1712.05690*.

Eric H Huang, Richard Socher, Christopher D Manning, and Andrew Y Ng. 2012. Improving word representations via global context and multiple word prototypes. In *Proceedings of the 50th Annual Meeting of the Association for Computational Linguistics: Long Papers-Volume 1*, pages 873–882. Association for Computational Linguistics.

Marcin Junczys-Downmunt. 2018. Dual conditional cross-entropy filtering of noisy parallel corpora. In *Proceedings of the Third Conference on Machine Translation: Shared Task Papers*, pages 888–895.

Max Kaufmann. 2012. Jmaxalign: A maximum entropy parallel sentence alignment tool. *Proceedings of COLING 2012: Demonstration Papers*, pages 277–288.

Alexandre Klementiev, Ivan Titov, and Binod Bhattarai. 2012. Inducing crosslingual distributed representations of words. In *Proceedings of COLING 2012*, pages 1459–1474.

Philipp Koehn, Huda Khayrallah, Kenneth Heafield, and Mikel L Forcada. 2018. Findings of the wmt 2018 shared task on parallel corpus filtering. In *Proceedings of the Third Conference on Machine Translation: Shared Task Papers*, pages 726–739.

Philipp Koehn and Rebecca Knowles. 2017. Six challenges for neural machine translation. In *Proceedings of the 1st ACL Workshop on Neural Machine Translation (WNMT 2017)*, pages 28–39.

Jiwei Li, Thang Luong, and Dan Jurafsky. 2015. A hierarchical neural autoencoder for paragraphs and documents. In *Proceedings of the 53rd Annual Meeting of the Association for Computational Linguistics and the 7th International Joint Conference on Natural Language Processing (Volume 1: Long Papers)*, volume 1, pages 1106–1115.

Tomas Mikolov, Kai Chen, Greg Corrado, and Jeffrey Dean. 2013. Efficient estimation of word representations in vector space. *arXiv preprint arXiv:1301.3781*.

Robert C Moore. 2002. Fast and accurate sentence alignment of bilingual corpora. In *Conference of the Association for Machine Translation in the Americas*, pages 135–144. Springer.

Vinod Nair and Geoffrey E Hinton. 2010. Rectified linear units improve restricted boltzmann machines. In *Proceedings of the 27th international conference on machine learning (ICML-10)*, pages 807–814.

F. Pedregosa, G. Varoquaux, A. Gramfort, V. Michel, B. Thirion, O. Grisel, M. Blondel, P. Prettenhofer, R. Weiss, V. Dubourg, J. Vanderplas, A. Passos, D. Cournapeau, M. Brucher, M. Perrot, and E. Duchesnay. 2011. Scikit-learn: Machine learning in Python. *Journal of Machine Learning Research*, 12:2825–2830.

Hieu Pham, Thang Luong, and Christopher Manning. 2015. Learning distributed representations for multilingual text sequences. In *Proceedings of the 1st Workshop on Vector Space Modeling for Natural Language Processing*, pages 88–94.

Philip Resnik and Noah A Smith. 2003. The web as a parallel corpus. *Computational Linguistics*, 29(3).

Nick Rossenbach, Jan Rosendahl, Yunsu Kim, Miguel Graça, Aman Gokrani, and Hermann Ney. 2018. The rwth aachen university filtering system for the wmt 2018 parallel corpus filtering task. In *Proceedings of the Third Conference on Machine Translation: Shared Task Papers*, pages 946–954.

Holger Schwenk. 2018. Filtering and mining parallel data in a joint multilingual space. In *Proceedings of the 56th Annual Meeting of the Association for Computational Linguistics (Volume 2: Short Papers)*, pages 228–234.

Holger Schwenk and Matthijs Douze. 2017. Learning joint multilingual sentence representations with neural machine translation. In *Proceedings of the 2nd Workshop on Representation Learning for NLP*, pages 157–167.

Rico Sennrich, Barry Haddow, and Alexandra Birch. 2016. Neural machine translation of rare words with subword units. In *Proceedings of the 54th Annual Meeting of the Association for Computational Linguistics (Volume 1: Long Papers)*, volume 1, pages 1715–1725.

Amit Singhal. 2001. Modern information retrieval: A brief overview. *Bulletin of the Technical Committee on*, page 35.

Ilya Sutskever, Oriol Vinyals, and Quoc V Le. 2014. Sequence to sequence learning with neural networks. In *Proceedings of the 27th International Conference on Neural Information Processing Systems-Volume 2*, pages 3104–3112. MIT Press.

Kaveh Taghipour, Shahram Khadivi, and Jia Xu. 2011. Parallel corpus refinement as an outlier detection algorithm. In *Proceedings of the 13th Machine Translation Summit (MT Summit XIII)*, pages 414–421.

Dániel Varga, András Kornai, Viktor Nagy, László Németh, and Viktor Trón. 2005. Parallel corpora for medium density languages. In *Proceedings of RANLP 2005*, pages 590–596.

Ashish Vaswani, Noam Shazeer, Niki Parmar, Jakob Uszkoreit, Llion Jones, Aidan N Gomez, Łukasz Kaiser, and Illia Polosukhin. 2017. Attention is all you need. In *Advances in Neural Information Processing Systems*, pages 5998–6008.

Hainan Xu and Philipp Koehn. 2017. Zipporah: a fast and scalable data cleaning system for noisy webcrawled parallel corpora. In *Proceedings of the 2017 Conference on Empirical Methods in Natural Language Processing*, pages 2945–2950.

Xinjie Zhou, Xiaojun Wan, and Jianguo Xiao. 2016. Cross-lingual sentiment classification with bilingual document representation learning. In *Proceedings of the 54th Annual Meeting of the Association for Computational Linguistics (Volume 1: Long Papers)*, volume 1, pages 1403–1412.

Michal Ziemski, Marcin Junczys-Dowmunt, and Bruno Pouliquen. 2016. The united nations parallel corpus v1.0. In *Proceedings of Language Resources and Evaluation (LREC 2016)*, Portorož, Slovenia.

Specializing Distributional Vectors of All Words for Lexical Entailment

Aishwarya Kamath[1*], **Jonas Pfeiffer**[2*], **Edoardo M. Ponti**[3], **Goran Glavaš**[4], **Ivan Vulić**[3]

[1]Oracle Labs
[2]Ubiquitous Knowledge Processing Lab (UKP-TUDA), TU Darmstadt
[3]Language Technology Lab, TAL, University of Cambridge
[4]Data and Web Science Group, University of Mannheim

[1]aishwarya.kamath@oracle.com
[2]pfeiffer@ukp.informatik.tu-darmstadt.de
[3]{ep490,iv250}@cam.ac.uk
[4]goran@informatik.uni-mannheim.de

Abstract

Semantic specialization methods fine-tune distributional word vectors using lexical knowledge from external resources (e.g., WordNet) to accentuate a particular relation between words. However, such post-processing methods suffer from limited coverage as they affect only vectors of words *seen* in the external resources. We present the first post-processing method that specializes vectors of *all vocabulary words* – including those *unseen* in the resources – for the *asymmetric* relation of lexical entailment (LE) (i.e., hyponymy-hypernymy relation). Leveraging a partially LE-specialized distributional space, our POS-TLE (i.e., *post-specialization* for LE) model learns an explicit global specialization function, allowing for specialization of vectors of unseen words, as well as word vectors from other languages via cross-lingual transfer. We capture the function as a deep feedforward neural network: its objective re-scales vector norms to reflect the concept hierarchy while simultaneously attracting hyponymy-hypernymy pairs to better reflect semantic similarity. An extended model variant augments the basic architecture with an adversarial discriminator. We demonstrate the usefulness and versatility of POSTLE models with different input distributional spaces in different scenarios (monolingual LE and zero-shot cross-lingual LE transfer) and tasks (binary and graded LE). We report consistent gains over state-of-the-art LE-specialization methods, and successfully LE-specialize word vectors for languages without any external lexical knowledge.

1 Introduction

Word-level lexical entailment (LE), also known as the TYPE-OF or hyponymy-hypernymy relation, is a fundamental *asymmetric* lexico-semantic relation (Collins and Quillian, 1972; Beckwith et al., 1991).

The set of these relations constitutes a hierarchical structure that forms the backbone of semantic networks such as WordNet (Fellbaum, 1998). Automatic reasoning about word-level LE benefits a plethora of tasks such as natural language inference (Dagan et al., 2013; Bowman et al., 2015; Williams et al., 2018), text generation (Biran and McKeown, 2013), metaphor detection (Mohler et al., 2013), and automatic taxonomy creation (Snow et al., 2006; Navigli et al., 2011; Gupta et al., 2017).

However, standard techniques for inducing word embeddings (Mikolov et al., 2013; Pennington et al., 2014; Melamud et al., 2016; Bojanowski et al., 2017; Peters et al., 2018, *inter alia*) are unable to effectively capture LE. Due to their crucial dependence on contextual information and the distributional hypothesis (Harris, 1954), they display a clear tendency towards conflating different relationships such as synonymy, antonymy, meronymy and LE and broader topical relatedness (Schwartz et al., 2015; Mrkšić et al., 2017).

To mitigate this deficiency, a standard solution is a *post-processing* step: distributional vectors are gradually refined to satisfy linguistic constraints extracted from external resources such as Word-Net (Fellbaum, 1998) or BabelNet (Navigli and Ponzetto, 2012). This process, termed *retrofitting* or *semantic specialization*, is beneficial to language understanding tasks (Faruqui, 2016; Glavaš and Vulić, 2018) and is extremely versatile as it can be applied on top of any input distributional space.

Retrofitting methods, however, have a major weakness: they only *locally* update vectors of words *seen* in the external resources, while leaving vectors of all other *unseen* words unchanged, as illustrated in Figure 1. Recent work (Glavaš and Vulić, 2018; Ponti et al., 2018) has demonstrated how to specialize the *full* distributional space for the *symmetric* relation of semantic (dis)similarity. The so-called *post-specialization* model learns a

---

[*]Both authors contributed equally to this work.

Proceedings of the 4th Workshop on Representation Learning for NLP (RepL4NLP-2019), pages 72–83
Florence, Italy, August 2, 2019. ©2019 Association for Computational Linguistics

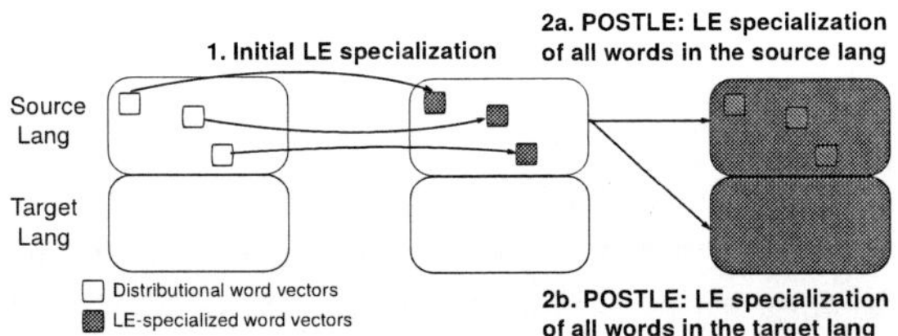

Figure 1: High-level overview of a) the POSTLE full vocabulary specialization process; and b) zero-shot cross-lingual specialization for LE. This relies on an initial shared cross-lingual word embedding space (see §2).

global and *explicit* specialization function that imitates the transformation from the distributional space to the retrofitted space, and applies it to the large subspace of unseen words' vectors.

In this work, we present POSTLE, an all-words post-specialization model for the asymmetric LE relation. This model propagates the signal on the hierarchical organization of concepts to the ones unseen in external resources, resulting in a word vector space which is fully specialized for the LE relation. Previous LE specialization methods simply integrated available LE knowledge into the input distributional space (Vulić and Mrkšić, 2018), or provided means to learn dense word embeddings of the external resource only (Nickel and Kiela, 2017, 2018; Ganea et al., 2018; Sala et al., 2018). In contrast, we show that our POSTLE method can combine distributional and external lexical knowledge and generalize over unseen concepts.

The main contribution of POSTLE is a novel global transformation function that re-scales vector norms to reflect the concept hierarchy while simultaneously attracting hyponymy-hypernymy word pairs to reflect their semantic similarity in the specialized space. We propose and evaluate two variants of this idea. The first variant learns the global function through a deep non-linear feed-forward network. The extended variant leverages the deep feed-forward net as the generator component of an adversarial model. The role of the accompanying discriminator is then to distinguish between original LE-specialized vectors (produced by any initial post-processor) from vectors produced by transforming distributional vectors with the generator.

We demonstrate that the proposed POSTLE methods yield considerable gains over state-of-the-art LE-specialization models (Nickel and Kiela, 2017; Vulić and Mrkšić, 2018), with the adversarial variant having an edge over the other. The gains are

observed with different input distributional spaces in several LE-related tasks such as hypernymy detection and directionality, and graded lexical entailment. What is more, the highest gains are reported for resource-lean data scenarios where a high percentage of words in the datasets is unseen.

Finally, we show how to LE-specialize distributional spaces for target languages that lack external lexical knowledge. POSTLE can be coupled with any model for inducing cross-lingual embedding spaces (Conneau et al., 2018; Artetxe et al., 2018; Smith et al., 2017). If this model is unsupervised, the procedure effectively yields a zero-shot LE specialization transfer, and holds promise to support the construction of hierarchical semantic networks for resource-lean languages in future work.

2 Post-Specialization for LE

Our post-specialization starts with the Lexical Entailment Attract-Repel (LEAR) model (Vulić and Mrkšić, 2018), a state-of-the-art retrofitting model for LE, summarized in §2.1. While we opt for LEAR because of its strong performance and ease of use, it is important to note that our POSTLE models (§2.2 and §2.3) are not in any way bound to LEAR and can be applied on top of any LE retrofitting model.

2.1 Initial LE Specialization: LEAR

LEAR fine-tunes the vectors of words observed in a set of external linguistic constraints $C = S \cup A \cup L$, consisting of synonymy pairs S such as *(clever, intelligent)*, antonymy pairs A such as *(war, peace)*, and lexical entailment (i.e., hyponymy-hypernymy) pairs L such as *(dog, animal)*. For the L pairs, the order of words is important: we assume that the left word always refers to the hyponym.

Extending the ATTRACT-REPEL model for symmetric similarity specialization (Mrkšić et al., 2017), LEAR defines two types of objectives: 1) the ATTRACT (*Att*) objective aims to bring closer together in the vector space words that are semantically similar (i.e., synonyms and hyponym-hypernym pairs); 2) the REPEL (*Rep*) objective pushes further apart vectors of dissimilar words (i.e., antonyms). Let $\mathcal{B} = \{(\mathbf{x}_l^{(k)}, \mathbf{x}_r^{(k)})\}_{k=1}^K$ be the set of K word pairs for which the *Att* or *Rep* score is to be computed – these are the *positive examples*. The set of corresponding negative examples T is created by coupling each positive ATTRACT example $(\mathbf{x}_l, \mathbf{x}_r)$ with a negative example pair $(\mathbf{t}_l, \mathbf{t}_r)$, where $\mathbf{t}_l$ is the vector closest (in terms of cosine similarity, within the batch) to $\mathbf{x}_l$ and $\mathbf{t}_r$ vector closest to $\mathbf{x}_r$. The *Att* objective for a batch of ATTRACT constraints $\mathcal{B}_A$ is then given as:

$$Att(\mathcal{B}_A, T_A) =$$
$$\sum_{k=1}^{K} \left[\tau \left(\delta_{att} + \cos\left(\mathbf{x}_l^{(k)}, \mathbf{t}_l^{(k)}\right) - \cos\left(\mathbf{x}_l^{(k)}, \mathbf{x}_r^{(k)}\right)\right) \right.$$
$$\left. + \tau \left(\delta_{att} + \cos\left(\mathbf{x}_r^{(k)}, \mathbf{t}_r^{(k)}\right) - \cos\left(\mathbf{x}_l^{(k)}, \mathbf{x}_r^{(k)}\right)\right) \right]. \quad (1)$$

$\tau(x) = max(0, x)$ is the hinge loss and δ_{att} is the similarity margin imposed between the negative and positive vector pairs. In contrast, for each positive REPEL example, the negative example $(\mathbf{t}_l, \mathbf{t}_r)$ couples the vector $\mathbf{t}_l$ that is most distant from $\mathbf{x}_l$ and $\mathbf{t}_r$, most distant from $\mathbf{x}_r$. The *Rep* objective for a batch of REPEL word pairs $\mathcal{B}_R$ is then:

$$Rep(\mathcal{B}_R, T_R) =$$
$$\sum_{k=1}^{K} \left[\tau \left(\delta_{rep} + \cos\left(\mathbf{x}_l^{(k)}, \mathbf{x}_r^{(k)}\right) - \cos\left(\mathbf{x}_l^{(k)}, \mathbf{t}_l^{(k)}\right)\right) \right.$$
$$\left. + \tau \left(\delta_{rep} + \cos\left(\mathbf{x}_l^{(k)}, \mathbf{x}_r^{(k)}\right) - \cos\left(\mathbf{x}_r^{(k)}, \mathbf{t}_r^{(k)}\right)\right) \right]. \quad (2)$$

LEAR additionally defines a regularization term in order to preserve the useful semantic information from the original distributional space. With $V(\mathcal{B})$ as the set of distinct words in a constraint batch $\mathcal{B}$, the regularization term is: $Reg(\mathcal{B}) = \lambda_{reg} \sum_{\mathbf{x} \in V(\mathcal{B})} \|\mathbf{y} - \mathbf{x}\|_2$, where $\mathbf{y}$ is the LEAR-specialization of the distributional vector $\mathbf{x}$, and λ_{reg} is the regularization factor.

Crucially, LEAR forces specialized vectors to reflect the asymmetry of the LE relation with an asymmetric distance-based objective. The goal is to preserve the cosine distances in the specialized space while steering vectors of more general concepts (those found higher in the concept hierarchy) to take larger norms.[1] Vulić and Mrkšić (2018) test several asymmetric objectives, and we adopt the one reported to be the most robust:

$$LE(\mathcal{B}_L) = \sum_{k=1}^{K} \frac{\|\mathbf{x}_l^{(k)}\| - \|\mathbf{x}_r^{(k)}\|}{\|\mathbf{x}_l^{(k)}\| + \|\mathbf{x}_r^{(k)}\|}. \quad (3)$$

$\mathcal{B}_L$ denotes a batch of LE constraints. The full LEAR objective is then defined as:

$$J = Att(\mathcal{B}_S, T_S) + Rep(\mathcal{B}_A, T_A)$$
$$+ Att(\mathcal{B}_L, T_L) + LE(\mathcal{B}_L) + Reg(\mathcal{B}_S, \mathcal{B}_A, \mathcal{B}_L) \quad (4)$$

---

[1] E.g., while *dog* and *animal* should be close in the LE-specialized space in terms of cosine distance, the vector norm of *animal* should be larger than that of *dog*.

In summary, LEAR pulls words from synonymy and LE pairs closer together ($Att(\mathcal{B}_S, T_S)$ and $Att(\mathcal{B}_L, T_L)$), while simultaneously pushing vectors of antonyms further apart ($Rep(\mathcal{B}_A, T_A)$) and enforcing asymmetric distances for hyponymy-hypernymy pairs ($LE(\mathcal{B}_L)$).

2.2 Post-Specialization Model

The retrofitting model (LEAR) specializes vectors only for a subset of the full vocabulary: the words it has *seen* in the external lexical resource. Such resources are still fairly incomplete, even for major languages (e.g., WordNet for English), and fail to cover a large portion of the distributional vocabulary (referred to as *unseen* words). The transformation of the seen subspace, however, provides evidence on the desired effects of LE-specialization. We seek a post-specialization procedure for LE (termed POSTLE) that propagates this useful signal to the subspace of unseen words and LE-specializes the entire distributional space (see Figure 1).

Let $\mathbf{X}_s$ be the subset of the distributional space containing vectors of words seen in lexical constraints and let $\mathbf{Y}_s$ denote LE-specialized vectors of those words produced by the initial LE specialization model. For seen words, we pair their original distributional vectors $\mathbf{x}_s \in \mathbf{X}_s$ with corresponding LEAR-specialized vectors $\mathbf{y}_s$: post-specialization then directly uses pairs $(\mathbf{x}_s, \mathbf{y}_s)$ as training instances for learning a global specialization function, which is then applied to LE-specialize the remainder of the distributional space, i.e., the specialization function learned from $(\mathbf{X}_s, \mathbf{Y}_s)$ is applied to the subspace of unseen words' vectors $\mathbf{X}_u$.

Let $G(\mathbf{x}_i; \theta_G) : \mathbb{R}^d \to \mathbb{R}^d$ (with d as the dimensionality of the vector space) be the specialization function we are trying to learn using pairs of distributional and LEAR-specialized vectors as training instances. We first instantiate the post-specialization model $G(\mathbf{x}_i; \theta_G)$ as a deep fully-connected feed-forward network (DFFN) with H hidden layers and m units per layer. The mapping of the j-th hidden layer is given as:

$$\mathbf{x}^{(j)} = activ\left(\mathbf{x}^{(j-1)}\mathbf{W}^j + \mathbf{b}^{(j)}\right). \quad (5)$$

activ refers to a non-linear activation function,[2]

---

[2] As discussed by Vulić et al. (2018); Ponti et al. (2018), non-linear transformations yield better results: linear transformations cannot fully capture the subtle fine-tuning done by the retrofitting process, guided by millions of pairwise constraints. We also verify that linear transformations yield poorer performance, but we do not report these results for brevity.

$\mathbf{x}^{(j-1)}$ is the output of the previous layer ($\mathbf{x}^{(0)}$ is the input distributional vector), and $(\mathbf{W}^{(j)}, \mathbf{b}^{(j)})$, $j \in \{1, \ldots, H\}$ are the model's parameters θ_G.

The aim is to obtain predictions $G(\mathbf{x}_s; \theta_G)$ that are as close as possible to the corresponding LEAR-specializations $\mathbf{y}_s$. For symmetric similarity-based post-specialization prior work relied on cosine distance to measure discrepancy between the predicted and expected specialization (Vulić et al., 2018). Since we are specializing vectors for the asymmetric LE relation, the predicted vector $G(\mathbf{x}_s; \theta_G)$ has to match $\mathbf{y}_s$ not only in direction (as captured by cosine distance) but also in size (i.e., the vector norm). Therefore, the POSTLE objective augments cosine distance $dcos$ with the absolute difference of $G(\mathbf{x}_s; \theta_G)$ and $\mathbf{y}_s$ norms:[3]

$$\mathcal{L}_S = dcos\left(G(\mathbf{x}_s; \theta_G), \mathbf{y}_s\right) \\ + \delta_n \left| \|G(\mathbf{x}_s; \theta_G)\| - \|\mathbf{y}_s\| \right|. \tag{6}$$

The hyperparameter δ_n determines the contribution of the norm difference to the overall loss.

2.3 Adversarial LE Post-Specialization

We next extend the DFFN post-specialization model with an adversarial architecture (ADV), following Ponti et al. (2018) who demonstrated its usefulness for similarity-based specialization. The intuition behind the adversarial extension is as follows: the specialization function $G(\mathbf{x}_s; \theta_G)$ should not only produce vectors that have high cosine similarity and similar norms with corresponding LEAR-specialized vectors $\mathbf{y}_s$, but should also ensure that these vectors seem "natural", that is, as if they were indeed sampled from $\mathbf{Y}_s$. We can force the post-specialized vectors $G(\mathbf{x}_s; \theta_G)$ to be legitimate samples from the $\mathbf{Y}_s$ distribution by introducing an adversary that learns to discriminate whether a given vector has been generated by the specialization function or directly sampled from $\mathbf{Y}_s$. Such adversaries prevent the generation of unrealistic outputs, as demonstrated in computer vision (Pathak et al., 2016; Ledig et al., 2017; Odena et al., 2017).

The DFFN function $G(\mathbf{x}; \theta_G)$ from §2.2 can be seen as the generator component. We couple the generator with the discriminator $D(\mathbf{x}; \theta_D)$, also instantiated as a DFFN. The discriminator performs binary classification: presented with a word vector, it predicts whether it has been produced by G or

---

[3] Simply minimizing Euclidean distance also aligns vectors in terms of both direction and size. However, we consistently obtained better results by the objective function from Eq. (6).

sampled from the LEAR-specialized subspace $\mathbf{Y}_s$. On the other hand, the generator tries to produce vectors which the discriminator would misclassify as sampled from $\mathbf{Y}_s$. The discriminator's loss is defined via negative log-likelihood over two sets of inputs; generator produced vectors $G(\mathbf{x}_s; \theta_G)$ and LEAR specializations $\mathbf{y}_s$:

$$\mathcal{L}_D = - \sum_{s=1}^{N} \log P(\text{spec} = 0 | G(\mathbf{x}_s; \theta_G); \theta_D) \\ - \sum_{s=1}^{M} \log P(\text{spec} = 1 | \mathbf{y}_s; \theta_D) \tag{7}$$

Besides minimizing the similarity-based loss $\mathcal{L}_S$, the generator has the additional task of confusing the discriminator: it thus perceives the discriminator's correct predictions as its additional loss $\mathcal{L}_G$:

$$\mathcal{L}_G = - \sum_{s=1}^{N} \log P(\text{spec} = 1 | G(\mathbf{x}_s; \theta_G); \theta_D) \\ - \sum_{s=1}^{M} \log P(\text{spec} - 0 | \mathbf{y}_s, \theta_D) \tag{8}$$

We learn G's and D's parameters with stochastic gradient descent – to reduce the co-variance shift and make training more robust, each batch contains examples of the same class (either only predicted vectors or only LEAR vectors). Moreover, for each update step of $\mathcal{L}_G$ we alternate between s_D update steps for $\mathcal{L}_D$ and s_S update steps for $\mathcal{L}_S$.

2.4 Cross-Lingual LE Specialization Transfer

The POSTLE models enable LE specialization of vectors of words unseen in lexical constraints. Conceptually, this also allows for a LE-specialization of a distributional space of another language (possibly without any external constraints), provided a shared bilingual distributional word vector space. To this end, we can resort to any of the methods for inducing shared cross-lingual vector spaces (Ruder et al., 2018). What is more, most recent methods successfully learn the shared space without any bilingual signal (Conneau et al., 2018; Artetxe et al., 2018; Chen and Cardie, 2018; Hoshen and Wolf, 2018).

Let $\mathbf{X}_t$ be the distributional space of some target language for which we have no external lexical constraints and let $P(\mathbf{x}; \theta_P) : \mathbb{R}^{d_t} \mapsto \mathbb{R}^{d_s}$ be the (linear) function projecting vectors $\mathbf{x}_t \in \mathbf{X}_t$ to the distributional space $\mathbf{X}_{ds}$ of the source language with available lexical constraints for which we trained the post-specialization model. We then simply obtain the LE-specialized space $\mathbf{Y}_t$ of the target language by composing the projection P with the post-specialization G (see Figure 1):

$$\mathbf{Y}_t = G(P(\mathbf{X}_t; \theta_P); \theta_G) \tag{9}$$

In §4.3 we report on language transfer experiments with three different linear projection models P in order to verify the robustness of the cross-lingual LE-specialization transfer.[4]

3 Experimental Setup

Distributional Vectors. To test the robustness of the POSTLE approach, we experiment with two pre-trained English word vector spaces: (1) vectors trained by Levy and Goldberg (2014) on the Polyglot Wikipedia (Al-Rfou et al., 2013) using Skip-Gram with Negative Sampling (SGNS-BOW2) (Mikolov et al., 2013) and (2) GLOVE embeddings trained on the Common Crawl (Pennington et al., 2014). In the cross-lingual transfer experiments (§4.3), we use English, Spanish, and French FASTTEXT embeddings trained on respective Wikipedias (Bojanowski et al., 2017).

Linguistic Constraints. We use the same set of constraints as LEAR in prior work (Vulić and Mrkšić, 2018): synonymy and antonymy constraints from (Zhang et al., 2014; Ono et al., 2015) are extracted from WordNet and Roget's Thesaurus (Kipfer, 2009). As in other work on LE specialization (Nguyen et al., 2017; Nickel and Kiela, 2017), asymmetric LE constraints are extracted from Word-Net, and we collect both direct and indirect LE pairs (i.e., *(parrot, bird)*, *(bird, animal)*, and *(parrot, animal)* are in the LE set) In total, we work with 1,023,082 pairs of synonyms, 380,873 pairs of antonyms, and 1,545,630 LE pairs.

Training Configurations. For LEAR, we adopt the hyperparameter setting reported in the original paper: $\delta_{att} = 0.6$, $\delta_{rep} = 0$, $\lambda_{reg} = 10^{-9}$. For POS-TLE, we fine-tune the hyperparameters via random search on the validation set: 1) DFFN uses $H = 4$ hidden layers, each with $1,536$ units and Swish as the activation function (Ramachandran et al., 2018); 2) ADV relies on $H = 4$ hidden layers, each

with $m = 2,048$ units and Leaky ReLU (slope 0.2) (Maas et al., 2014) for the generator. The discriminator uses $H = 2$ layers with $1,024$ units and Leaky ReLU. For each update based on the generator loss ($\mathcal{L}_G$), we perform $s_S = 3$ updates based on the similarity loss ($\mathcal{L}_S$) and $s_D = 5$ updates based on the discriminator loss ($\mathcal{L}_D$). The value for the norm difference contribution in $\mathcal{L}_S$ is set to to $\delta_n = 0.1$ (see Eq. (6)) for both POSTLE variants. We train POSTLE models using SGD with the batch size 32, the initial learning rate 0.1, and a decay rate of 0.98 applied every 1M examples.

Asymmetric LE Distance. The distance that measures the strength of the LE relation in the specialized space reflects both the cosine distance between the vectors as well as the asymmetric difference between their norms (Vulić and Mrkšić, 2018):

$$I_{LE}(\mathbf{x}, \mathbf{y}) = dcos(\mathbf{x}, \mathbf{y}) + \frac{\|\mathbf{x}\| - \|\mathbf{y}\|}{\|\mathbf{x}\| + \|\mathbf{y}\|} \tag{10}$$

LE-specialized vectors of general concepts obtain larger norms than vectors of specific concepts. True LE pairs should display both a small cosine distance and a negative norm difference. Therefore, in different LE tasks we can rank the candidate pairs in the ascending order of their asymmetric LE distance I_{LE}. The LE distances are trivially transformed into binary LE predictions, using a binarization threshold t: if $I_{LE}(\mathbf{x}, \mathbf{y}) < t$, we predict that LE holds between words x and y with vectors $\mathbf{x}$ and $\mathbf{y}$.

4 Evaluation and Results

We extensively evaluate the proposed POSTLE models on two fundamental LE tasks: 1) predicting graded LE and 2) LE detection (and directionality), in monolingual and cross-lingual transfer settings.

4.1 Predicting Graded LE

The asymmetric distance I_{LE} can be directly used to make fine-grained graded assertions about the hierarchical relationships between concepts. Following previous work (Nickel and Kiela, 2017; Vulić and Mrkšić, 2018), we evaluate graded LE on the standard HyperLex dataset (Vulić et al., 2017).[5] HyperLex contains 2,616 word pairs (2,163 noun pairs, the rest are verb pairs) rated by humans by

---

[4]We experiment with unsupervised and weakly supervised models for inducing cross-lingual embedding spaces. However, we stress that the POSTLE specialization transfer is equally applicable on top of any method for inducing cross-lingual word vectors, some of which may require more bilingual supervision (Upadhyay et al., 2016; Ruder et al., 2018).

[5]Graded LE is a phenomenon deeply rooted in cognitive science and linguistics: it captures the notions of *concept prototypicality* (Rosch, 1973; Medin et al., 1984) and *category vagueness* (Kamp and Partee, 1995; Hampton, 2007). We refer the reader to the original paper for a more detailed discussion.

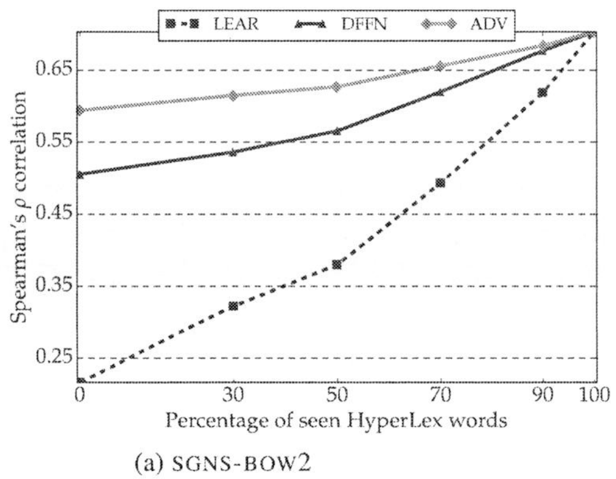

(a) SGNS-BOW2

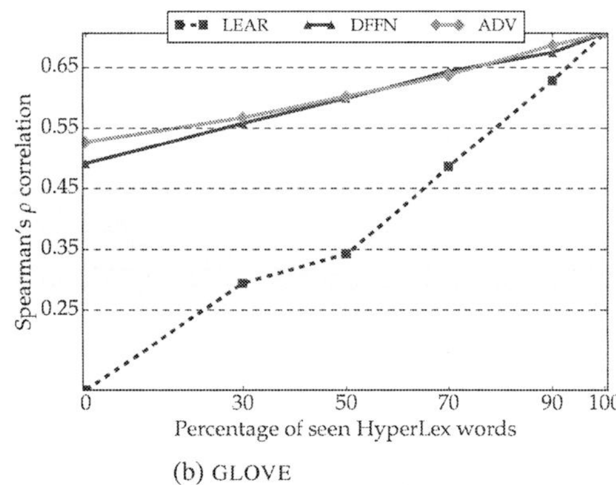

(b) GLOVE

Figure 2: Spearman's ρ correlation scores for two input distributional spaces on the noun portion of HyperLex (2,163 concept pairs) conditioned on the number of test words covered (i.e., *seen*) in the external lexical resource. Similar patterns are observed on the full HyperLex dataset. Two other baseline models report the following scores on the noun portion of HyperLex in the 100% setting: 0.512 (Nickel and Kiela, 2017); 0.540 (Nguyen et al., 2017).

estimating on a [0, 6] scale the *degree* to which the first concept is *a type of* the second concept.

Results and Discussion. We evaluate the performance of LE specialization models in a deliberately controlled setup: we (randomly) select a percentage of HyperLex words (0%, 30%, 50%, 70%, 90% and 100%) which are allowed to be *seen* in the external constraints, and discard the constraints containing other HyperLex words, making them effectively unseen by the initial LEAR model. In the 0% setting all constraints containing any of the HyperLex words have been removed, whereas in the 100% setting, all available constraints are used. The scores are summarized in Figure 2.

The 0% setting is especially indicative of POSTLE performance: we notice large gains in performance without seeing a single word from HyperLex in the external resource. This result verifies that the POSTLE models can generalize well to words unseen in the resources. Intuitively, the gap between POSTLE and LEAR is reduced in the settings where LEAR "sees" more words. In the 100% setting we report the same scores for LEAR and POSTLE: this is an artefact of the HyperLex dataset construction as all HyperLex word pairs were sampled from WordNet (i.e., the coverage of test words is 100%). Another finding is that in the resource-leaner 0% and 30% settings POSTLE outperforms two other baselines (Nguyen et al., 2017; Nickel and Kiela, 2017), despite the fact that the two baselines have "seen" all HyperLex words. The results further indicate that POSTLE yields gains on top of different initial distributional spaces. As expected, the scores are higher with the more sophisticated ADV variant.

4.2 LE Detection

Detection and Directionality Tasks. We now evaluate POSTLE models on three binary classification datasets commonly used for evaluating LE models (Roller et al., 2014; Shwartz et al., 2017; Nguyen et al., 2017), compiled into an integrated benchmark by Kiela et al. (2015).[6]

The first task, LE directionality, is evaluated on 1,337 true LE pairs (DBLESS) extracted from BLESS (Baroni and Lenci, 2011). The task tests the models' ability to predict which word in the LE pair is the hypernym. This is simply achieved by taking the word with a larger word vector norm as the hypernym. The second task, LE detection, is evaluated on the WBLESS dataset (Weeds et al., 2014), comprising 1,668 word pairs standing in one of several lexical relations (LE, meronymy-holonymy, co-hyponymy, reverse LE, and no relation). The models have to distinguish true LE pairs from pairs that stand in other relations (including the reverse LE). We score all pairs using the I_{LE} distance. Following Nguyen et al. (2017), we find the threshold t via cross-validation.[7] Finally, we evaluate LE detection and directionality simultaneously on BIBLESS, a relabeled variant of WBLESS. The task is to detect true LE pairs (including the reverse LE pairs), and also to determine the relation directionality. We again use I_{LE} to detect LE pairs, and then compare the vector norms to select the hypernym.

For all three tasks, we consider two evaluation

---

[6]http://www.cl.cam.ac.uk/~dk427/generality.html

[7]In each of the 1,000 iterations, 2% of the pairs are sampled for threshold tuning, and the remaining 98% are used for testing. The reported numbers are therefore averaged scores.

| | Setup: FULL | | | | | | Setup: DISJOINT | | | | | |
| | DBLESS | | WBLESS | | BIBLESS | | DBLESS | | WBLESS | | BIBLESS | |
	SG	GL	SG	GL	SG	GL	SG	GL	SG	GL	SG	GL
LEAR (Vulić et al., 2018)	.957	.955	.905	.910	.872	.875	.528	.531	.555	.529	.381	.389
POSTLE DFFN	.957	.955	.905	.910	.872	.875	.898	.825	.754	.746	.696	.677
POSTLE ADV	.957	.955	.905	.910	.872	.875	**.942**	**.888**	**.832**	**.766**	**.757**	**.690**

Table 1: Accuracy of POSTLE models on *BLESS datasets, for two different sets of English distributional vectors: Skip-Gram (SG) and GloVe (GL). LEAR reports highest scores on *BLESS datasets in the literature.

	Target: SPANISH			Target: FRENCH		
Random		.498			.515	
Distributional		.362			.387	
	Ar	Co	Sm	Ar	Co	Sm
POSTLE DFFN	**.798**	.740	.728	.688	.735	.742
POSTLE ADV	.768	**.790**	**.782**	**.746**	**.770**	**.786**

Table 2: Average precision (AP) of POSTLE models in cross-lingual transfer. Results are shown for both POSTLE models (DFFN and ADV), two target languages (Spanish and French) and three methods for inducing bilingual vector spaces: *Ar* (Artetxe et al., 2018), *Co* (Conneau et al., 2018), and *Sm* (Smith et al., 2017).

settings: 1) in the FULL setting we use all available lexical constraints (see §3) for the initial LEAR specialization; 2) in the DISJOINT setting, we remove all constraints that contain any of the test words, making all test words effectively unseen by LEAR.

Results and Discussion. The accuracy scores on *BLESS test sets are provided in Table 1.[8] Our POSTLE models display exactly the same performance as LEAR in the FULL setting: this is simply because *all* words found in *BLESS datasets are covered by the lexical constraints, and POSTLE does not generalize the initial LEAR transformation to unseen test words. In the DISJOINT setting, however, LEAR is left "blind" as it has not seen a single test word in the constraints: it leaves distributional vectors of *BLESS test words identical. In this setting, LEAR performance is equivalent to the original distributional space. In contrast, learning to generalize the LE specialization function from LEAR-specializations of other words, POSTLE models are able to successfully LE-specialize vectors of test *BLESS words. As in the graded LE, the adversarial POSTLE architecture outperforms the simpler DFFN model.

---

[8]We have evaluated the prediction performance also in terms of F_1 and, in the ranking formulation, in terms of *average precision* (AP) and observed the same trends in results.

4.3 Cross-Lingual Transfer

Finally, we evaluate cross-lingual transfer of LE specialization. We train POSTLE models using distributional (FASTTEXT) English (EN) vectors as input. Afterwards, we apply those models to the distributional vector spaces of two other languages, French (FR) and Spanish (ES), after mapping them into the same space as English as described in §2.4.

We experiment with several methods to induce cross-lingual word embeddings: 1) MUSE, an adversarial unsupervised model fine-tuned with the closed-form Procustes solution (Conneau et al., 2018); 2) an unsupervised self-learning algorithm that iteratively bootstraps new bilingual seeds, initialized according to structural similarities of the monolingual spaces (Artetxe et al., 2018); 3) an orthogonal linear mapping with inverse softmax, supervised by 5K bilingual seeds (Smith et al., 2017).

We test POSTLE-specialized Spanish and French word vectors on WN-Hy-ES and WN-Hy-FR, two equally sized datasets (148K word pairs) created by Glavaš and Ponzetto (2017) using the ES WordNet (Gonzalez-Agirre et al., 2012) and the FR WordNet (Sagot and Fišer, 2008). We perform a ranking evaluation: the aim is to rank LE pairs above pairs standing in other relations (meronyms, synonyms, antonyms, and reverse LE). We rank word pairs in the ascending order based on I_{LE}, see Eq. (10).

Results and Discussion. The average precision (AP) ranking scores achieved via cross-lingual transfer of POSTLE are shown in Table 2. We report AP scores using three methods for cross-lingual word embedding induction, and compare their performance to two baselines: 1) random word pair scoring, and 2) the original (FASTTEXT) vectors.

The results uncover the inability of distributional vectors to capture LE – they yield lower performance than the random baseline, which strongly emphasizes the need for the LE-specialization. The transferred POSTLE yields an immense improvement over the distributional baselines (up to +0.428, i.e. +118%). Again, the adversarial architecture surpasses DFFN across the board, with the single exception of EN-ES transfer coupled with Artetxe et al. (2018)'s cross-lingual model. Furthermore, transfers with unsupervised (Ar, Co) and supervised bilingual mapping (Sm) yield comparable performance. This implies that a robust LE-specialization of distributional vectors for languages with no lexico-semantic resources is possible even without any bilingual signal or translation effort.

5   Related Work

Vector Space Specialization. In general, lexical specialization models fall into two categories: 1) joint optimization models and 2) post-processing or retrofitting models. Joint models integrate external constraints directly into the distributional objective of embedding algorithms such as Skip-Gram and CBOW (Mikolov et al., 2013), or Canonical Correlation Analysis (Dhillon et al., 2015). They either modify the prior or regularization of the objective (Yu and Dredze, 2014; Xu et al., 2014; Kiela et al., 2015) or augment it with factors reflecting external lexical knowledge (Liu et al., 2015; Ono et al., 2015; Osborne et al., 2016; Nguyen et al., 2017). Each joint model is tightly coupled to a specific distributional objective: any change to the underlying distributional model requires a modification of the whole joint model and expensive retraining.

In contrast, retrofitting models (Faruqui et al., 2015; Rothe and Schütze, 2015; Wieting et al., 2015; Jauhar et al., 2015; Nguyen et al., 2016; Mrkšić et al., 2016; Mrkšić et al., 2017; Vulić and Mrkšić, 2018) use external constraints to post-hoc fine-tune distributional spaces. Effectively, this makes them applicable to any input distributional space, but they modify only vectors of words seen in the external resource. Nonetheless, retrofitting models tend to outperform joint models in the context of both similarity-based (Mrkšić et al., 2016) and LE specialization (Vulić and Mrkšić, 2018).

The recent post-specialization paradigm has been so far applied only to the symmetric semantic similarity relation. Vulić et al. (2018) generalize over the retrofitting ATTRACT-REPEL (AR) model (Mrkšić et al., 2017) by learning a global similarity-focused specialization function implemented as a DFFN. Ponti et al. (2018) further propose an adversarial post-specialization architecture. In this work, we show that post-specialization represents a viable methodology for specializing all distributional word vectors for the LE relation as well.

Modeling Lexical Entailment. Extensive research effort in lexical semantics has been dedicated to automatic detection of the fundamental taxonomic LE relation. Early approaches (Weeds et al., 2004; Clarke, 2009; Kotlerman et al., 2010; Lenci and Benotto, 2012, *inter alia*) detected LE word pairs by means of asymmetric direction-aware mechanisms such as distributional inclusion hypothesis (Geffet and Dagan, 2005), and concept informativeness and generality (Herbelot and Ganesalingam, 2013; Santus et al., 2014; Shwartz et al., 2017), but were surpassed by more recent methods that leverage word embeddings.

Embedding-based methods either 1) induce LE-oriented vector spaces using text (Vilnis and McCallum, 2015; Yu et al., 2015; Vendrov et al., 2016; Henderson and Popa, 2016; Nguyen et al., 2017; Chang et al., 2018; Vulić and Mrkšić, 2018) and/or external hierarchies (Nickel and Kiela, 2017, 2018; Sala et al., 2018) or 2) use distributional vectors as features for supervised LE detection models (Baroni et al., 2012; Tuan et al., 2016; Shwartz et al., 2016; Glavaš and Ponzetto, 2017; Rei et al., 2018). Our POSTLE method belongs to the first group.

Vulić and Mrkšić (2018) proposed LEAR, a retrofitting LE model which displays performance gains on a spectrum of graded and ungraded LE evaluations compared to joint specialization models (Nguyen et al., 2017). However, LEAR still specializes only the vectors of words seen in external resources. The same limitation holds for a family of recent models that embed concept hierarchies (i.e., trees or directed acyclic graphs) in hyperbolic spaces (Nickel and Kiela, 2017; Chamberlain et al., 2017; Nickel and Kiela, 2018; Sala et al., 2018; Ganea et al., 2018). Although hyperbolic spaces are arguably more suitable for embedding hierarchies than the Euclidean space, the "Euclidean-based" LEAR has been proven to outperform the hyperbolic embedding of the WordNet hierarchy across a range of LE tasks (Vulić and Mrkšić, 2018).

The proposed POSTLE framework 1) mitigates the limited coverage issue of retrofitting LE-specialization models, and 2) removes the problem of dependence on distributional objective in joint models. Unlike retrofitting models, POSTLE LE-specializes vectors of *all* vocabulary words, and unlike joint models, it is computationally inexpensive and applicable to any distributional vector space.

6 Conclusion

We have presented POSTLE, a novel neural post-specialization framework that specializes distributional vectors of all words – including the ones unseen in external lexical resources – to accentuate the hierarchical asymmetric lexical entailment (LE or hyponymy-hypernymy) relation. The benefits of our two all-words POSTLE model variants have been shown across a range of graded and binary LE detection tasks on standard benchmarks. What is more, we have indicated the usefulness of the POSTLE paradigm for zero-shot cross-lingual LE specialization of word vectors in target languages, even without having any external lexical knowledge in the target. In future work, we will experiment with more sophisticated neural architectures, other resource-lean languages, and bootstrapping approaches to LE specialization. Code and POSTLE-specialized vectors are available at: [https://github.com/ashkamath/POSTLE].

Acknowledgments

EMP and IV are supported by the ERC Consolidator Grant LEXICAL (648909). The authors would like to thank the anonymous reviewers for their helpful suggestions.

References

Rami Al-Rfou, Bryan Perozzi, and Steven Skiena. 2013. Polyglot: Distributed word representations for multilingual NLP. In *Proceedings of CoNLL*, pages 183–192.

Mikel Artetxe, Gorka Labaka, and Eneko Agirre. 2018. A robust self-learning method for fully unsupervised cross-lingual mappings of word embeddings. In *Proceedings of ACL*, pages 789–798.

Marco Baroni, Raffaella Bernardi, Ngoc-Quynh Do, and Chung-chieh Shan. 2012. Entailment above the word level in distributional semantics. In *Proceedings of EACL*, pages 23–32.

Marco Baroni and Alessandro Lenci. 2011. How we BLESSed distributional semantic evaluation. In *Proceedings of the GEMS 2011 Workshop*, pages 1–10.

Richard Beckwith, Christiane Fellbaum, Derek Gross, and George A. Miller. 1991. WordNet: A lexical database organized on psycholinguistic principles. *Lexical acquisition: Exploiting on-line resources to build a lexicon*, pages 211–231.

Or Biran and Kathleen McKeown. 2013. Classifying taxonomic relations between pairs of Wikipedia articles. In *Proceedings of IJCNLP*, pages 788–794.

Piotr Bojanowski, Edouard Grave, Armand Joulin, and Tomas Mikolov. 2017. Enriching word vectors with subword information. *Transactions of the ACL*, 5:135–146.

Samuel R. Bowman, Gabor Angeli, Christopher Potts, and Christopher D. Manning. 2015. A large annotated corpus for learning natural language inference. In *Proceedings of EMNLP*, pages 632–642.

Benjamin Paul Chamberlain, James Clough, and Marc Peter Deisenroth. 2017. Neural embeddings of graphs in hyperbolic space. *CoRR*, abs/1705.10359.

Haw-Shiuan Chang, Ziyun Wang, Luke Vilnis, and Andrew McCallum. 2018. Distributional inclusion vector embedding for unsupervised hypernymy detection. In *Proceedings of NAACL-HLT*, pages 485–495.

Xilun Chen and Claire Cardie. 2018. Unsupervised multilingual word embeddings. In *Proceedings of EMNLP*, pages 261–270.

Daoud Clarke. 2009. Context-theoretic semantics for natural language: An overview. In *Proceedings of the Workshop on Geometrical Models of Natural Language Semantics (GEMS)*, pages 112–119.

Allan M. Collins and Ross M. Quillian. 1972. Experiments on semantic memory and language comprehension. *Cognition in Learning and Memory*.

Alexis Conneau, Guillaume Lample, Marc'Aurelio Ranzato, Ludovic Denoyer, and Hervé Jégou. 2018. Word translation without parallel data. In *Proceedings of ICLR (Conference Track)*.

Ido Dagan, Dan Roth, Mark Sammons, and Fabio Massimo Zanzotto. 2013. Recognizing textual entailment: Models and applications. *Synthesis Lectures on Human Language Technologies*, 6(4):1–220.

Paramveer S. Dhillon, Dean P. Foster, and Lyle H. Ungar. 2015. Eigenwords: Spectral word embeddings. *Journal of Machine Learning Research*, 16:3035–3078.

Manaal Faruqui. 2016. *Diverse Context for Learning Word Representations*. Ph.D. thesis, Carnegie Mellon University.

Manaal Faruqui, Jesse Dodge, Sujay Kumar Jauhar, Chris Dyer, Eduard Hovy, and Noah A. Smith. 2015. Retrofitting word vectors to semantic lexicons. In *Proceedings of NAACL-HLT*, pages 1606–1615.

Christiane Fellbaum. 1998. *WordNet*. MIT Press.

Octavian-Eugen Ganea, Gary Bécigneul, and Thomas Hofmann. 2018. Hyperbolic entailment cones for learning hierarchical embeddings. In *Proceedings of ICML*, pages 1632–1641.

Maayan Geffet and Ido Dagan. 2005. The distributional inclusion hypotheses and lexical entailment. In *Proceedings of ACL*, pages 107–114.

Goran Glavaš and Ivan Vulić. 2018. Explicit retrofitting of distributional word vectors. In *Proceedings of ACL*, pages 34–45.

Goran Glavaš and Simone Paolo Ponzetto. 2017. Dual tensor model for detecting asymmetric lexico-semantic relations. In *Proceedings of EMNLP*, pages 1758–1768.

Aitor Gonzalez-Agirre, Egoitz Laparra, and German Rigau. 2012. Multilingual central repository version 3.0. In *LREC*, pages 2525–2529.

Amit Gupta, Rémi Lebret, Hamza Harkous, and Karl Aberer. 2017. Taxonomy induction using hypernym subsequences. In *Proceedings of CIKM*, pages 1329–1338.

James A. Hampton. 2007. Typicality, graded membership, and vagueness. *Cognitive Science*, 31(3):355–384.

Zellig S. Harris. 1954. Distributional structure. *Word*, 10(23):146–162.

James Henderson and Diana Popa. 2016. A vector space for distributional semantics for entailment. In *Proceedings of ACL*, pages 2052–2062.

Aurélie Herbelot and Mohan Ganesalingam. 2013. Measuring semantic content in distributional vectors. In *Proceedings of ACL*, pages 440–445.

Yedid Hoshen and Lior Wolf. 2018. Non-adversarial unsupervised word translation. In *Proceedings of EMNLP*, pages 469–478.

Sujay Kumar Jauhar, Chris Dyer, and Eduard H. Hovy. 2015. Ontologically grounded multi-sense representation learning for semantic vector space models. In *Proceedings of NAACL*, pages 683–693.

Hans Kamp and Barbara Partee. 1995. Prototype theory and compositionality. *Cognition*, 57(2):129–191.

Douwe Kiela, Laura Rimell, Ivan Vulić, and Stephen Clark. 2015. Exploiting image generality for lexical entailment detection. In *Proceedings of ACL*, pages 119–124.

Barbara Ann Kipfer. 2009. *Roget's 21st Century Thesaurus (3rd Edition)*. Philip Lief Group.

Lili Kotlerman, Ido Dagan, Idan Szpektor, and Maayan Zhitomirsky-Geffet. 2010. Directional distributional similarity for lexical inference. *Natural Language Engineering*, 16(4):359–389.

Christian Ledig, Lucas Theis, Ferenc Huszar, Jose Caballero, Andrew Cunningham, Alejandro Acosta, Andrew Aitken, Alykhan Tejani, Johannes Totz, Zehan Wang, et al. 2017. Photo-realistic single image super-resolution using a generative adversarial network. In *Proceedings of CVPR*, pages 4681–4690.

Alessandro Lenci and Giulia Benotto. 2012. Identifying hypernyms in distributional semantic spaces. In *Proceedings of *SEM*, pages 75–79.

Omer Levy and Yoav Goldberg. 2014. Dependency-based word embeddings. In *Proceedings of ACL*, pages 302–308.

Quan Liu, Hui Jiang, Si Wei, Zhen-Hua Ling, and Yu Hu. 2015. Learning semantic word embeddings based on ordinal knowledge constraints. In *Proceedings of ACL*, pages 1501–1511.

Andrew L. Maas, Awni Y. Hannun, and Andrew Y. Ng. 2014. Rectifier nonlinearities improve neural network acoustic models. In *Proceedings of ICML*.

Douglas L. Medin, Mark W. Altom, and Timothy D. Murphy. 1984. Given versus induced category representations: Use of prototype and exemplar information in classification. *Journal of Experimental Psychology*, 10(3):333–352.

Oren Melamud, Jacob Goldberger, and Ido Dagan. 2016. Context2vec: Learning generic context embedding with bidirectional LSTM. In *Proceedings of CoNLL*, pages 51–61.

Tomas Mikolov, Ilya Sutskever, Kai Chen, Gregory S. Corrado, and Jeffrey Dean. 2013. Distributed representations of words and phrases and their compositionality. In *Proceedings of NIPS*, pages 3111–3119.

Michael Mohler, David Bracewell, Marc Tomlinson, and David Hinote. 2013. Semantic signatures for example-based linguistic metaphor detection. In *Proceedings of the First Workshop on Metaphor in NLP*, pages 27–35.

Nikola Mrkšić, Diarmuid Ó Séaghdha, Blaise Thomson, Milica Gašić, Lina Maria Rojas-Barahona, Pei-Hao Su, David Vandyke, Tsung-Hsien Wen, and Steve Young. 2016. Counter-fitting word vectors to linguistic constraints. In *Proceedings of NAACL-HLT*, pages 142–148.

Nikola Mrkšić, Ivan Vulić, Diarmuid Ó Séaghdha, Ira Leviant, Roi Reichart, Milica Gašić, Anna Korhonen, and Steve Young. 2017. Semantic specialisation of distributional word vector spaces using monolingual and cross-lingual constraints. *Transactions of the ACL*, 5:309–324.

Roberto Navigli and Simone Paolo Ponzetto. 2012. BabelNet: The automatic construction, evaluation and application of a wide-coverage multilingual semantic network. *Artificial Intelligence*, 193:217–250.

Roberto Navigli, Paola Velardi, and Stefano Faralli. 2011. A graph-based algorithm for inducing lexical taxonomies from scratch. In *Proceedings of IJCAI*, pages 1872–1877.

Kim Anh Nguyen, Maximilian Köper, Sabine Schulte im Walde, and Ngoc Thang Vu. 2017. Hierarchical embeddings for hypernymy detection and directionality. In *Proceedings of EMNLP*, pages 233–243.

Kim Anh Nguyen, Sabine Schulte im Walde, and Ngoc Thang Vu. 2016. Integrating distributional lexical contrast into word embeddings for antonym-synonym distinction. In *Proceedings of ACL*, pages 454–459.

Maximilian Nickel and Douwe Kiela. 2017. Poincaré embeddings for learning hierarchical representations. In *Proceedings of NIPS*, pages 6341–6350.

Maximilian Nickel and Douwe Kiela. 2018. Learning continuous hierarchies in the Lorentz model of hyperbolic geometry. In *Proceedings of ICML*, pages 3776–3785.

Augustus Odena, Christopher Olah, and Jonathon Shlens. 2017. Conditional image synthesis with auxiliary classifier gans. In *Proceedings of ICML*, pages 2642–2651.

Masataka Ono, Makoto Miwa, and Yutaka Sasaki. 2015. Word Embedding-based Antonym Detection using Thesauri and Distributional Information. In *Proceedings of NAACL*, pages 984–989.

Dominique Osborne, Shashi Narayan, and Shay Cohen. 2016. Encoding prior knowledge with eigenword embeddings. *Transactions of the ACL*, 4:417–430.

Deepak Pathak, Philipp Krähenbühl, Jeff Donahue, Trevor Darrell, and Alexei A. Efros. 2016. Context encoders: Feature learning by inpainting. In *Proceedings of CVPR*, pages 2536–2544.

Jeffrey Pennington, Richard Socher, and Christopher Manning. 2014. Glove: Global vectors for word representation. In *Proceedings of EMNLP*, pages 1532–1543.

Matthew Peters, Mark Neumann, Mohit Iyyer, Matt Gardner, Christopher Clark, Kenton Lee, and Luke Zettlemoyer. 2018. Deep contextualized word representations. In *Proceedings of NAACL-HLT*, pages 2227–2237.

Edoardo Maria Ponti, Ivan Vulić, Goran Glavaš, Nikola Mrkšić, and Anna Korhonen. 2018. Adversarial propagation and zero-shot cross-lingual transfer of word vector specialization. In *Proceedings of EMNLP*, pages 282–293.

Prajit Ramachandran, Barret Zoph, and Quoc V Le. 2018. Searching for activation functions. In *Proceedings of ICML*.

Marek Rei, Daniela Gerz, and Ivan Vulić. 2018. Scoring lexical entailment with a supervised directional similarity network. In *Proceedings of ACL*, pages 638–643.

Stephen Roller, Katrin Erk, and Gemma Boleda. 2014. Inclusive yet selective: Supervised distributional hypernymy detection. In *Proceedings of COLING*, pages 1025–1036.

Eleanor H. Rosch. 1973. Natural categories. *Cognitive Psychology*, 4(3):328–350.

Sascha Rothe and Hinrich Schütze. 2015. AutoExtend: Extending word embeddings to embeddings for synsets and lexemes. In *Proceedings of ACL*, pages 1793–1803.

Sebastian Ruder, Ivan Vulić, and Anders Søgaard. 2018. A survey of cross-lingual embedding models. *Journal of Artificial Intelligence Research*.

Benoît Sagot and Darja Fišer. 2008. Building a free french wordnet from multilingual resources. In *Proccedings of the OntoLex Workshop*.

Frederic Sala, Christopher De Sa, Albert Gu, and Christopher Ré. 2018. Representation tradeoffs for hyperbolic embeddings. In *Proceedings of ICML*, pages 4457–4466.

Enrico Santus, Alessandro Lenci, Qin Lu, and Sabine Schulte im Walde. 2014. Chasing hypernyms in vector spaces with entropy. In *Proceedings of EACL*, pages 38–42.

Roy Schwartz, Roi Reichart, and Ari Rappoport. 2015. Symmetric pattern based word embeddings for improved word similarity prediction. In *Proceedings of CoNLL*, pages 258–267.

Vered Shwartz, Yoav Goldberg, and Ido Dagan. 2016. Improving hypernymy detection with an integrated path-based and distributional method. In *Proceedings of ACL*, pages 2389–2398.

Vered Shwartz, Enrico Santus, and Dominik Schlechtweg. 2017. Hypernyms under siege: Linguistically-motivated artillery for hypernymy detection. In *Proceedings of EACL*, pages 65–75.

Samuel L. Smith, David H.P. Turban, Steven Hamblin, and Nils Y. Hammerla. 2017. Offline bilingual word vectors, orthogonal transformations and the inverted softmax. In *Proceedings of ICLR (Conference Track)*.

Rion Snow, Daniel Jurafsky, and Andrew Y. Ng. 2006. Semantic taxonomy induction from heterogenous evidence. In *Proceedings of ACL*, pages 801–808.

Luu Anh Tuan, Yi Tay, Siu Cheung Hui, and See Kiong Ng. 2016. Learning term embeddings for taxonomic relation identification using dynamic weighting neural network. In *Proceedings of EMNLP*, pages 403–413.

Shyam Upadhyay, Manaal Faruqui, Chris Dyer, and Dan Roth. 2016. Cross-lingual models of word embeddings: An empirical comparison. In *Proceedings of ACL*, pages 1661–1670.

Ivan Vendrov, Ryan Kiros, Sanja Fidler, and Raquel Urtasun. 2016. Order-embeddings of images and language. In *Proceedings of ICLR (Conference Track)*.

Luke Vilnis and Andrew McCallum. 2015. Word representations via Gaussian embedding. In *Proceedings of ICLR (Conference Track)*.

Ivan Vulić, Daniela Gerz, Douwe Kiela, Felix Hill, and Anna Korhonen. 2017. Hyperlex: A large-scale evaluation of graded lexical entailment. *Computational Linguistics*, 43(4):781–835.

Ivan Vulić, Goran Glavaš, Nikola Mrkšić, and Anna Korhonen. 2018. Post-specialisation: Retrofitting vectors of words unseen in lexical resources. In *Proceedings of NAACL-HLT*, pages 516–527.

Ivan Vulić and Nikola Mrkšić. 2018. Specialising word vectors for lexical entailment. In *Proceedings of NAACL-HLT*, pages 1134–1145.

Julie Weeds, Daoud Clarke, Jeremy Reffin, David Weir, and Bill Keller. 2014. Learning to distinguish hypernyms and co-hyponyms. In *Proceedings of COLING*, pages 2249–2259.

Julie Weeds, David Weir, and Diana McCarthy. 2004. Characterising measures of lexical distributional similarity. In *Proceedings of COLING*, pages 1015–1021.

John Wieting, Mohit Bansal, Kevin Gimpel, and Karen Livescu. 2015. From paraphrase database to compositional paraphrase model and back. *Transactions of the ACL*, 3:345–358.

Adina Williams, Nikita Nangia, and Samuel Bowman. 2018. A broad-coverage challenge corpus for sentence understanding through inference. In *Proceedings of NAACL-HLT*, pages 1112–1122.

Chang Xu, Yalong Bai, Jiang Bian, Bin Gao, Gang Wang, Xiaoguang Liu, and Tie-Yan Liu. 2014. RC-NET: A general framework for incorporating knowledge into word representations. In *Proceedings of CIKM*, pages 1219–1228.

Mo Yu and Mark Dredze. 2014. Improving lexical embeddings with semantic knowledge. In *Proceedings of ACL*, pages 545–550.

Zheng Yu, Haixun Wang, Xuemin Lin, and Min Wang. 2015. Learning term embeddings for hypernymy identification. In *Proceedings of IJCAI*, pages 1390–1397.

Jingwei Zhang, Jeremy Salwen, Michael Glass, and Alfio Gliozzo. 2014. Word semantic representations using bayesian probabilistic tensor factorization. In *Proceedings of EMNLP*, pages 1522–1531.

Composing noun phrase vector representations

Aikaterini-Lida Kalouli
University of Konstanz
aikaterini-lida.kalouli@uni-konstanz.de

Valeria de Paiva
University of Birmingham

Richard Crouch
Chegg

{valeria.depaiva,dick.crouch}@gmail.com

Abstract

Vector representations of words have seen an increasing success over the past years in a variety of NLP tasks. While there seems to be a consensus about the usefulness of word embeddings and how to learn them, it is still unclear which representations can capture the meaning of phrases or even whole sentences. Recent work has shown that simple operations outperform more complex deep architectures. In this work, we propose two novel constraints for computing noun phrase vector representations. First, we propose that the semantic and not the syntactic contribution of each component of a noun phrase should be considered, so that the resulting composed vectors express more of the phrase meaning. Second, the composition process of the two phrase vectors should apply suitable dimensions' selection in a way that specific semantic features captured by the phrase's meaning become more salient. Our proposed methods are compared to 11 other approaches, including popular baselines and a neural net architecture, and are evaluated across 6 tasks and 2 datasets. Our results show that these constraints lead to more expressive phrase representations and can be applied to other state-of-the-art methods to improve their performance.

1 Introduction

Vector representations of words date back to the 1990's (Landauer and Dumais, 1997) and have seen an increasing success over the past years (Mikolov et al., 2013; Pennington et al., 2014; Devlin et al., 2018). While there seems to be a consensus about the usefulness of word embeddings and how to learn them, it is still controversial how to learn representations that capture the meaning of phrases or even whole sentences (Zhu et al., 2018). Generally, two main approaches are used to compute phrase representations: non-compositional and compositional. The former treats phrases as single units and attempts to learn their representations directly from corpora, much as it is done for words (Socher et al., 2010; Mikolov et al., 2013; Yin and Schütze, 2014). These approaches ignore the components of the phrase and are not scalable to all possible phrases of a language. On the other hand, the compositional approach derives a phrase or sentence representation from the embeddings of its component words in various ways, from simple addition and average operations, e.g., Mitchell and Lapata (2010); Turney (2012), to more complex neural net architectures, e.g., Pagliardini et al. (2018); Conneau et al. (2017). However, such approaches often ignore word order and other linguistic intuitions and lead to representations that cannot truly express the meaning of the sentence, as recently discussed by Zhu et al. (2018).

We concentrate on efficient *phrase* representations which capture meaning and can be handled as sentence components. We believe that from such representations the meaning of a full sentence can be *compositionally* computed, much as in more traditional semantic theories, e.g. in the Fregean functional application. For example, if we can compute efficient representations for all possible phrases contained in constituency parsing, say NP, VP, PP, etc., we can then derive the meaning of the whole sentence by functionally applying the constituents' representations on each other. To this end, we believe that for compositional phrases there should be compositional phrase representations, while for non-compositional ones, e.g., idioms, learning direct representations from corpora might be more effective. In this paper, we focus on *bigram compositional* nominal phrase vectors of adjective-noun and noun-noun (compounds) combinations. By starting from this linguistic category, we can reliably evaluate the two constraints we propose on one of the most common con-

Proceedings of the 4th Workshop on Representation Learning for NLP (RepL4NLP-2019), pages 84–95
Florence, Italy, August 2, 2019. ©2019 Association for Computational Linguistics

stituent types, namely the NP phrase. Specifically, in this work we propose two novel constraints for computing such phrase vectors that are *linguistically informed* and *intuitively explainable*. First, we propose to focus on the *semantic* – and not the syntactic – contribution of each phrase component and decide whether the syntactic head or the syntactic modifier (Marneffe et al., 2006; McDonald et al., 2013) is semantically more *significant* for the meaning of the phrase. The phrase component with the most clear contribution to the meaning of the phrase might actually be the syntactic modifier and not the syntactic head and then this word is to be treated as the semantic head for the composition. Second, we propose that for two given word embeddings that need to be composed, we should select for the composition only those dimensions of the semantic modifier embedding that are more relevant to the semantic head of the phrase. In order words, we need to pick from the semantic modifier these attributes that are more relevant to the semantic head phrase. For example, for the compositional phrase *black magic*, intuitively we want to select all dimensions of *black* that have to do something with *magic* and not others that have to do with, e.g. *t-shirt*. In this way, we can compose the representation *black magic* by combining the attributes of *magic* with the "magic-like" attributes of *black*.

The contributions of this paper are three-fold: Firstly, we propose two novel constraints for composing *linguistically informed* and *intuitively explainable* noun phrase representations and show how these approaches could benefit future composition methods. Secondly, we provide a thorough evaluation of our methods over 6 evaluation tasks, 2 datasets and 11 other methods. Thirdly, we create an evaluation dataset of nomimal phrase-unigram paraphrase pairs, which we make openly available.

2   Relevant work

Early work on representing word sequences focused on bigram compositionality and considered various simple functions, such as vector addition and averaging (Mitchell and Lapata, 2010; Blacoe and Lapata, 2012), while already Turney (2012) integrated features for more meaningful relations. This early work focused on the representation of specific syntactic constructions and specific number of words and continues to be an ongoing research topic: representations of verb phrases (Hashimoto and Tsuruoka, 2016), noun phrases (Baroni and Zamparelli, 2010; Boleda et al., 2013; Dima, 2016), a combination of the two (Zanzotto et al., 2010; Wieting et al., 2015), noun-noun compositionality (Reddy et al., 2011; Hermann et al., 2012; Cordeiro et al., 2018), noun phrases attribute meaning (Hartung et al., 2017; Shwartz and Waterson, 2018), etc. This strand of research covers a variety of approaches ranging from the simple vector arithmetics mentioned to vector-matrix composition operations (Zanzotto et al., 2010; Guevara, 2010; Baroni and Zamparelli, 2010; Boleda et al., 2013), to the functional application of word vectors (Coecke et al., 2010; Grefenstette et al., 2014) to RNNs (Wieting et al., 2015) and other supervised (Hartung et al., 2017; Shwartz and Waterson, 2018) or unsupervised approaches (Hermann et al., 2012). Particularly, recent research producing context-aware representations of words (Peters et al., 2018; Devlin et al., 2018) has already had a great impact on the performance of many of these composition functions. At the same time, another strand of research concentrates on representing arbitrarily long phrases and sentences and mainly employs neural nets architectures: bag-of-words models (Kalchbrenner et al., 2014), feature-weighted average (Yu and Dredze, 2015) models, deep averaging networks (Iyyer et al., 2015), recursive (Socher et al., 2013; Conneau et al., 2017) and convolutional NNs (Yin and Schütze, 2015), encoding-decoding architectures (Kiros et al., 2015), to name only a few. Despite the large number of such approaches, it is still not clear that the composed phrase or sentence embeddings express the intended meaning, as recently shown by Shwartz and Dagan (2019), Zhu et al. (2018) and Dasgupta et al. (2018). Even more interesting is the fact that averaging and weighted averaging approaches have been shown to outperform complex deep learning methods (White et al., 2015; Wieting et al., 2016; Arora et al., 2017). This shows potential in exploiting the merits of simpler approaches but boosting them up with more powerful intuitive and linguistic constraints, as the ones proposed in this work.

3   Proposed Constraints

3.1   Constraint One: Semantic Contribution

The (dependency) syntax informs us that in an English bigram compositional, nominal phrase, the first word is the modifier and the second the head. However, we observe that this syntactic decision does not always coincide with the role that each word plays in the meaning of the phrase. It can be the case that the modifier is more "meaningful" for the phrase. For example, if someone says *space ship*, we would be inclined to first think of *space* than of a prototypical ship. In that sense, *space* has a more significant contribution to the meaning of the phrase than *ship* has. By contrast, in the phrase *black magic* the notion of *magic* is more prototypical for the meaning of the phrase.

Current work that aims at compositionally constructing phrase representations takes the asymmetric contribution of the phrase components into account, e.g. by assigning different weights to the modifier and the head. However, all of this work bases the contribution decision on the syntax, i.e. on the syntactic head and modifier. However, as it has already been observed for English noun-noun compositionality (Bannard et al., 2003; Reddy et al., 2011; Cordeiro et al., 2018), the first component of a noun-noun phrase, i.e. the (syntactic) modifier, might have a greater contribution to the meaning of the phrase. Similar is the literature for other linguistic phenomena, e.g., light verbs (e.g., take a shower, give a kiss) or auxiliaries where the syntactic head does not coincide with the semantic, (see, e.g., Butt, 2010), but also in traditional semantic composition (e.g., lambda calculus) the quantifier of a sentence serves as the head, although the verb is considered the syntactic head of the sentence. Although this asymmetry has been observed for nominal phrases as well, e.g. by Hartung et al. (2017) who find that adjective representations capture more of the compositional semantics of an adjective-noun phrase than nouns do and implicitly also by Mitchell and Lapata (2010), whose composition functions give more weight to the adjectives than to the nouns, to our knowledge this is the first work that actively proposes and integrates this constraint into the composition process.

To compose meaningful phrase representations, we propose to consider the semantic contribution of the syntactic head and modifier of a phrase. In other words, we need to consider which is the *semantic* head and which is the *semantic* modifier. To this end, we can use word embeddings to decide whether a phrase is *heady*, i.e. the syntactic head has a stronger semantic contribution than the syntactic modifier, *mody*, i.e. the syntactic modifier has a stronger semantic contribution than the syntactic head, or *equal*, i.e. the syntactic head and modifier have both the same contribution to the meaning of the phrase. For bigram phrases that can be paraphrased by a single synonym –called *target* from now on – (e.g. black magic = sorcery), we find that the embeddings of some targets are more similar to the syntactic modifier embedding and of some others more similar to the syntactic head embedding of the phrase. We implement this observation: we compute the cosine similarity of the syntactic head to the target and of the syntactic modifier to the target and calculate their Δ. If the Δ is more than one standard deviation under the mean of all Δs (z-score computation), then the label *equal* is given, to account for cases where both words have an equal contribution to the meaning. Otherwise, the phrase is labeled based on whether the similarity of the syntactic head to the target or the syntactic modifier to the target is greater.

Since this approach for deciding on the semantic contribution of the syntactic head and modifier relies on the similarity of each of those components to a target, it is not available for all possible phrases because there is not one suitable unigram paraphrase/synonym for each phrase. Therefore, we want to test if the semantic contribution constraint is indeed a quantifiable, inherent property of the phrases that can be learned and can thus still be applied to phrases without targets. We did initial experimenting to train a classifier with a balanced set of 1000 *headys* and 1000 *modys*.[1] The collection of this set will be described in Section 4.2. For the classifier, we used 80% of the instances for training and 20% for testing. The classifier had to learn the *mody-heady* label solely based on the embeddings of the phrase components and *without* seeing any target embedding. The best trained model so far has been a MultiLayer Perceptron (MLP) with 3 hidden layers, 70 neurons per layer, 200 iterations and random weight initialization, delivering an accuracy of 74.8%. This shows that the semantic contribution constraint is indeed an inherent property of the embeddings that can be learnt from phrases having synonym-targets and be used for labeling phrases without such targets. Further experimenting and more training data can potentially improve

---

[1] We left out the *equal* label for this experiment due to the low number of such training samples.

this performance further.

3.2 Constraint Two: Dimensions' selection

The first constraint allows us to formulate a further one that directly shapes the composition process of phrase representations. Precisely, we propose that a composed representation of a bigram phrase should contain attributes of the semantic head embedding and only those attributes of the semantic modifier that are more relevant to the semantic head. This means that we need to select only those dimensions of the embedding of the semantic modifier that are related to the semantic head. Let's look at an example: *black magic* is a *heady* phrase, i.e. the contribution of the syntactic head *magic* is more significant for the overall meaning of the phrase than the contribution of *black*. This becomes even clearer if we think of a target synonym such as *sorcery*: for the meaning of the word *sorcery*, *magic* has a stronger correlation than *black* has. Thus, in this example, the composed vector should include the dimensions of *magic* and only those dimensions of *black* that are relevant to *magic*. "More relevant" dimensions are formalized as dimensions that are closer together. Even in embeddings, where the vectors do not mirror the frequency co-occurrences of the given word to other words of the vocabulary in a one-to-one fashion and no matter the dimensionality reduction approach, the same dimension should be capturing similar properties across different words, since each dimension corresponds to the same neuron having produced it. Thus, the same dimensions of the two phrase components embeddings that are closer together should correspond to similar notions and closer points in the vector space.

Intuitively, this dimensions' selection implements the idea that the composition of two words results in specific semantic aspects becoming more salient. This intuition is close to the dilation model of Mitchell and Lapata (2010), which attempts to stretch a vector v to the direction of a vector u in order to compute their composed vector. It is also similar to the more traditional idea of functional application: one tensor or vector is applied to another, resulting into their compositional representation (Coecke et al., 2010; Grefenstette et al., 2014). This has also been proposed by Baroni and Zamparelli (2010) for adjective-noun composition: the nouns are vectors and corpus-learned adjective matrices apply to these vectors producing other vectors. However, this only works for adjective-noun phrases where the adjectives can be clearly defined as the functions. For handling noun-noun phrases (and potentially other phrases), both phrase constituents have to be seen as *terms* (similar to λ calculus-like *terms*) and thus as vectors that can be applied in any direction. This allows us to formulate the following functions, which perform a kind of functional application, by taking the semantic modifiers as the functions and the semantic heads as the terms applied on them.

Compositional Function 1 SD

```
1: function ComposeSelectedDimsVec
2:     selected_dims ← []
3:     for i = 0 to headEmbed.length do
4:         headDim ← headEmbed[i]
5:         modDim ← modEmbed[i]
6:         if headDim − modDim < τ then
7:             selected_dims.append(modDim)
8:         else
9:             selected_dims.append(headDim)
    return selected_dims
```

Compositional Function 2 MOD-SD

```
1: function ComposeModAndSelectedDimsVec
2:     mod_selected_dims ← α · modEmbed + β · SD
```

In the first compositional function 1 (*SD*) we compare each dimension of the embedding of the semantic head of the phrase with the corresponding dimension of the semantic modifier of the phrase. If their Δ is under a threshold τ, then the dimensions are taken to be close enough and thus relevant and the dimension of the semantic modifier embedding is inserted unchanged into the new vector *selected_dims*. If the Δ is greater than τ, then the dimensions are taken to be distant and thus irrelevant to each other other and the dimension of the head is inserted into *selected_dims*. The final vector is a mixed vector consisting of a combination of the original modifier and head dimensions. Based on a grid search in steps of 10% from 0 to 1, we find $\tau = 0.3$ as the best parameter for the required threshold. Note that this is different than the elementwise max operation, as we do not select the dimension with the highest value among the two but instead we always select the semantic modifier dimension as long as its difference to the semantic head dimension is smaller than τ, no matter if the semantic modifier's dimension is greater or smaller than the head's. In our second proposed composition function (*MOD-SD*) we make use of the vector produced by function 1: we weight the entire vector *SD* by β and add it to the original embedding of the semantic modifier which is also weighted by α. This function is inspired by the well-performing weighted addition operation but instead of the original semantic head vector, it uses the constructed functional vector of 1, which captures only the semantic head-relevant attributes of the semantic modifier and the semantic head attributes. Suitable grid search in steps of 0.02 shows $\alpha = 0.32$ and $\beta = 0.68$ as the best parameters. All tuning was performed on a held-out set, consisting of the 50% of the created dataset, described in Section 4.2.

As it is clear, these two composition functions heavily depend on the head and modifier roles of the phrase and are therefore inseparably connected with the constraint of the semantic contribution proposed in Section 3.1.

4 Evaluation of the constraints

4.1 Compared Approaches

For evaluation we include baseline approaches of vector arithmetics, the popular matrix-vector composition approach and an own trained neural network. If the injection of our first constraint into those approaches boosts their performance, the semantic contribution constraint can be considered for future composition approaches, especially those aiming at simple but linguistically informed operations. On the other hand, if the composition process described in our second constraint outperforms the compared approaches, we can be confident that the dimensions' selection as proposed in the previous section is a useful intuition capturing compositionality and can be safely integrated in future composition tasks.

Baseline approaches We include baseline operations from the literature that were recently shown to outperform complex deep architectures (White et al., 2015; Wieting et al., 2016; Arora et al., 2017). We use weighted elementwise vector addition (1) and multiplication (2) (Mitchell and Lapata, 2010; Turney, 2012; White et al., 2015; Hartung et al., 2017; Arora et al., 2017) and weighted elementwise average (3) (Mikolov et al., 2013; Wieting et al., 2016). Since addition and multiplication have been shown to perform so strongly and since multiplicative models have the drawback

that the presence of zeroes in either of the vectors leads to information essentially being lost, we follow Mitchell and Lapata (2010) and also include a fourth equation, combining the addition and multiplication operations (4). For the weighting we do our own fine-tuning which is specific to the dataset we use.[2] This fine-tuning also showed that for our set the distinction between weights for adjective-noun and noun-noun phrases is not beneficial, contrary to Mitchell and Lapata (2010), who set the weights based on the part-of-speech. After tuning, the parameters are set to $\alpha = \beta = 1.0$, which in practice means that the unweighted variants perform better than their weighted counterparts. We also include "easy" baselines involving only the syntactic head or the syntactic modifier of the phrase and check whether the proposed compositional functions are better than those variants with no composition at all.

(1) $\quad wei\_add_j : r_j = \alpha m_j + \beta h_j$

(2) $\quad wei\_mult_j : r_j = \alpha m_j \cdot \beta h_j$

(3) $\quad wei\_aver_j : r_j = \frac{\alpha m_j + \beta h_j}{2}$

(4) $\quad wei\_comb_j : r_j = \alpha m_j + \beta h_j + \alpha m_j \cdot \beta h_j$

Matrix-vector approaches As already discussed before, popular approaches for computing phrases representations are the various matrix-vector composition operations. Already explored by Guevara (2010), Baroni and Zamparelli (2010) and Zanzotto et al. (2010) these approaches have since been used by various researchers, e.g. Boleda et al. (2013); Dima (2016). In these approaches the two constituent vectors of a phrase u and $v \in \mathbb{R}^n$ are composed by multiplying them via two matrices $A, B \in \mathbb{R}^{n \times n}$. For Zanzotto et al. (2010) and Guevara (2010), A and B are the same for every u and v and are calculated with partial least squares regression, while for the adjective-noun composition of Baroni and Zamparelli (2010), A is set to 0 and the weight matrix B is specifically learned for each single adjective. The mathematical formulation of this approach is: $r = Au + Bv$. Given the effectiveness of this approach (see e.g. Boleda et al. (2013)), we compare our proposed functions to it. From the three works mentioned above implementing this approach, only Zanzotto et al.'s is suitable for our purposes because a) it can handle both adjective-noun and noun-noun combinations and b) its dataset is openly available.

---

[2] In fact, we did test with the original parameters and found out that they deliver worse performance.

Deep Learning approach Although White et al. (2015), Wieting et al. (2016) and Arora et al. (2017) found that simple operations outperform complex deep architectures, there is still value in comparing the performance of a trained neural net to the performance of the other methods. For this purpose we experimented with multiple architectures, including feedforward nets, RNNs and LSTMs, attempting to find the best that fits our data. The training (80% of the set) and testing data (20% of the set) we used will be analyzed in more detail in the next section. Briefly, the datasets consisted of pairs of embeddings of the phrase components and their unigram synonym/paraphrase. For example, the embeddings of *dog* and *house* were paired with the embedding of the synonymous *kennel*. The neural net had to learn the synonym embedding by considering the two word embeddings as input. The best performing model was a feedforward neural net with 2 hidden dense layers. We used Xavier weight initialization (Glorot and Bengio, 2010) and the ELU (Clevert et al., 2015) activation function for all layers. Our updater was ADADELTA (Zeiler, 2012) and our learning rate 0.1. The training run for 200 epochs with 0.5 global dropout.

The left-most column of Table 1 gives a better overview of all compared methods.

4.2 Data

Data collection To tune and evaluate our proposals we needed a set that contains bigram noun phrases matched to unigram paraphrase/synonym targets, so that we have a "stable, uncontroversial" representation to compare our composed representations to (see also Zanzotto et al. (2010) and Turney (2012)). In this way, we can compose the representation of each phrase of the set with each of the methods under comparison and ideally, the composed representations are very similar to the embedding of the target of the pair since phrase and target have a synonymy/paraphrase relation. This is a harder task than comparing the composed representation to a corpus-learned representation of the phrase because the target representation is "independent", i.e. it does not capture cooccurrence effects of the components of the phrase, as the corpus-learned representation does. To this end, we created a new dataset which we

make openly available.[3] The creation process of the set is similar to that of Turney (2012): we extract the nouns of WordNet (Fellbaum, 1998) that have a bigram phrase synonym in their synset and pair them together, e.g., from the entry *kennel, doghouse, dog house (outbuilding that serves as a shelter for a dog)* we extract the pair *dog house - kennel* . The pairs were cleaned to exclude all proper names and were further expanded by Turney's (2012) set which has the same format.[4] This process resulted in 6109 pairs of this format. However, not all pairs are compositional; since we are interested in creating *compositional* phrase representations, we wanted to ensure that we are only evaluating on suitable pairs, as a *hot dog* can never be a composition of *hot* and *dog*. To this end, we attempted to automatically exclude non-compositional pairs by following Turney (2012), who proposes two WordNet-based approaches: the phrase is most likely compositional if a) one of the words of the phrase is also present in the gloss of this phrase (cf. the *dog house* entry) or b) the (syntactic) head noun of the phrase is also a hypernym of the phrase (e.g., *brain surgery* has *surgery* as its hypernym and it is thus compositional). We are aware that these methods cannot eliminate all unsuitable pairs, but the data is much less noisy now. Future work may attempt to do a better filtering of non-compositional pairs. 4475 pairs are left, from which we further exclude the ones where one of the words of the phrase is also the target (e.g. *abdominal muscle - abdominal*) and we get 1914 final pairs. 50% of that set forms the held-out set used for tuning purposes (Section 3) and the rest of the dataset is used for the evaluation of the methods.

We also evaluate our methods on a second dataset, the only other dataset we could find fulfilling the requirements of our task[5]: the noun-noun set created by Zanzotto et al. (2010) (ZZ from now on). This set contains the same data format (bigram phrases-unigram paraphrase) and includes 1066 positive examples, i.e. examples where the

---

[3] https://github.com/kkalouli/compositional_phrase_vectors

[4] The Turney (2012) set was also scraped from WordNet but we observed that this set and our scraped set were not subsets, probably due to changes on WordNet over the years or differences in the scraping process.

[5] The probably most popular dataset of Mitchell and Lapata (2010) was not suitable due to its format (no unigram as comparison element) and the nature of the data, i.e. no truly synonymous/paraphrastic phrases-targets, merely *similar* pairs; also observed by Wieting et al. (2015)

paraphrase is a valid one for this phrase, and 379 negative ones, where the unigram is not a paraphrase of the bigram.[6]

Data preprocessing   Since the goal of this work is to examine the efficiency of the proposed constraints for the compositionality of the vectors, we use pretrained embeddings; however training more specific embeddings or using state-of-the-art context-aware embeddings (e.g. Devlin et al. (2018); Peters et al. (2018)) could be even more beneficial for the approaches. In fact, by using such contextualized embeddings, our constraints could better handle polysemous words as the base embeddings would be partly disambiguated from the context. For now, the two datasets are first matched to the pretrained GloVe (Pennington et al., 2014) embeddings,[7] so that each phrase component and target word are mapped to their embedding. Then, a module determines whether the phrase is *mody*, *heady* or *equal*, based on the procedure described in Section 3.1. This procedure results into 895/515 *heady*, 792/190 *mody* and 227/119 *equal* for our set and the ZZ set, respectively. So, pairs like *black magic - sorcery* and *body armor - cataphract* become "heady", *archeological site - dig* and *baseball player - ballplayer* "mody", and *dramatic art - dramaturgy* and *female parent - mother* "equal".

4.3   Evaluation Tasks

To compare the approaches, we employed 6 evaluations tasks, aiming at testing different semantic aspects of the phrases. Our goal is to see which of the 13 methods perform best in each of the tasks. We include popular tasks, like synonymy detection and concept clustering (see, e.g., Baroni et al., 2014; Schnabel et al., 2015), but we do not employ the human similarity judgments task. We are not convinced that semantic similarity can be scaled in a range of 1 to 7 as we are not sure how one should decide, e.g., between a 3 and a 4. Such criticisms were also discussed by Faruqui et al. (2016).

Plain similarity   One of the most common intrinsic evaluation tasks is the semantic similarity between an item and a target. Since targets are part of our dataset, the simplest task is to calculate the cosine similarity between the composed vector of a phrase and the embedding of its target.

Precision   This task is a modification of the analogy task of Mikolov et al. (2013). Given a phrase vector and its neighbors in the semantic space, we check if the target word is its closest neighbor (cf. Baroni and Zamparelli (2010); Mikolov et al. (2013)). The task is also undertaken for the next two closest neighbors of the phrase. Ultimately, we measure Precision@1, Precision@2 and Precision@3, respectively, for how many items of our set had their targets as neighbors at the corresponding positions.

Overlapping neighbors   Here we measure how many neighbors of the phrase representation are also neighbors of the target embedding. Since embeddings capture the relational co-occurrences of words, it should be the case that the phrase and the target vectors share neighbors. This would mean that they are closer in the semantic space than items not sharing any neighbors, even if the target word itself is not a neighbor of the phrase embedding.

Synonymy detection   This popular task, first applied on the TOEFL examples for word embeddings (Landauer and Dumais, 1997), is to select out of some candidate targets, the one with the highest similarity to the given word. Similarly, (cf. Turney, 2012) we create a set of 7 candidate unigrams for each given phrase: its syntactic modifier, its syntactic head, its target, a synonym of its syntactic modifier and of its syntactic head[8] and two random words. We compute the similarity of the phrase representation to each of those and create a ranked list of the 7 candidates. Targets that are lower in the ranked list are penalized and targets that are higher up are boosted; conversely for the random words. Ultimately, we obtain a score between -1 and 1, with -1 being the worst with a random word at rank 1 and the target at the last rank and 1 standing for the best case where the target is at rank 1 and the randoms last.

Clustering   A popular task is concept categorization or clustering. Given a set of concepts, the task is to group them into categories. We adjust this task to measure how many of the phrase representations are clustered together with their target embedding. If the phrase vector truly expresses

---

[6]For our purposes, we excluded pairs containing proper names in capital due to the lack of pretrained embeddings for those, resulting in a set of 824 pairs.

[7]Trained on Wikipedia 2014 and Gigaword 5, 300 dim.

[8]Extracted from WordNet.

Method	Created dataset							ZZ dataset
	Sim	**Pr@1**	**Pr@2**	**Pr@3**	**OveNei**	**Syn**	**Clus**	**DistSim**
only_head	21.6	1.3	2.3	3.3	0.92	0.17	5.2	2.82E-31
only_mod	20.6	4.5	6.8	8.3	1.08	0.16	3.5	6.68E-52
sd (Const1 + Const2)	**28.5**	**5.6**	**8.4**	**10.3**	**1.80**	**0.23**	**6.7**	1.09E-41
mod-sd (Const1 + Const2)	**28.0**	**6.0**	**8.3**	**10.1**	**1.75**	0.17	**6.8**	**6.71E-47**
add	26.3	4.1	**7.6**	9.2	1.54	0.16	4.9	**9.43E-49**
mult	-0.5	0.0	0.0	0.0	0.01	-0.37	1.7	0.0801
aver	26.3	4.1	**7.6**	9.2	1.54	0.16	5.9	**9.43E-49**
comb	25.9	4.4	**7.6**	**10.0**	1.65	0.17	4.9	3.58E-44
add+Const1	**29.0**	**5.7**	**8.9**	**10.4**	**1.80**	0.18	**7.0**	**8.58E-47**
aver+Const1	**29.0**	**5.7**	**8.9**	**10.4**	**1.80**	0.18	4.1	**8.58E-47**
comb+Const1	**29.2**	**5.7**	**8.5**	**11.0**	**1.85**	0.19	**7.0**	6.27E-46
feedforward NN	24.0	0.2	0.2	0.2	0.36	**0.24**	0.5	-
matr-vec (Zanzotto et al., 2010)	-	-	-	-	-	-	-	1.00E-10

Table 1: Overview of all compared methods across the 6 evaluation tasks. The notation +*Const1* is added to the methods containing the semantic contribution constraint (Constraint One). The metric given for each task is the average metric across the entire dataset. Numbers in boldface mark the best performance per task. Multiple numbers may be in boldface in the same task, if there is no statistically significant difference between them.

meaning, the two should be clustered together. We use k-means clustering with 1914 clusters (as many as the pairs of our set) and 99 iterations.

Positive-Negative Similarity Distribution This task is the original used by Zanzotto et al. (2010), so we only apply it on the ZZ set. Here, we test if the distribution of the cosine similarities of the positive pairs is statistically different from the distribution of the similarities of the negative pairs: if it is, it means that the corresponding functions perform well because they can keep the two categories apart (see Zanzotto et al. (2010) for more details). As in the original experiment, the results show p-values, calculated with the Students t-test for two independent samples of different sizes: lower values characterize better models.

4.4 Results

In Table 1 we list all 13 methods compared in this work and their performance across all evaluation tasks. To test for statistical significance, the results were first grouped into categories and were analyzed using linear mixed effects regression models with the corresponding conditions (Method and Constraint) as fixed factors and random intercepts for the phrases of the dataset.[9] P-values were calculated using the Satterthwaite approximation of degrees-of-freedom in the R-package lmerTest

(Kuznetsova et al., 2017). The above process was done separately for each of the evaluation tasks.

Within the separate categories, the models showed main effects and interactions of both Method and Constraint across all tasks. The proposed *sd* and *mod − sd* functions (lines 3-4 of Table 1) perform statistically the same across tasks: *sd* does outperform *mod − sd* in the *Syn* task but the latter outperforms the former in the *DistSim* task, so that they exhibit an equal behavior. Concerning the baselines, the methods of addition, average and combined addition-multiplication (lines 5-8) perform statistically the same across tasks but heavily outperform the multiplication approach (contrary to Mitchell and Lapata (2010) but similar to Boleda et al. (2013)). The same operations but with our semantic contribution constraint (*baselines*+*Const1*, lines 9-11) also perform statistically the same across tasks.

More interesting are the overall results across categories: here, there is a main effect of *Method*. In the *Sim* task, in all three precision tasks, in *OveNei* and in *Clus*, the proposed *sd* and *mod − sd* together with the *baselines*+*Const1* are statistically best without any difference between them. In the *Syn* task, the *sd* and the NN[10] provide the statistically best results, with the *addition-*

---

[9] The models further included random slopes for the within-group factors when this improved the fit of the model, as determined by LogLikelihood comparisons, using the R-function anova().

[10] It is not surprising that the NN performs that well in this task. Since the NN is trained to learn/resemble the target embedding, its similarity to this specific target is higher than to other words on which it has not been trained. Thus, here it achieves better accuracy than in other tasks as it's the relative similarity to the target vs. to the other words that is measured.

multiplication+Const1 operation following. For the *DistSim* task, $mod - sd$, the *addition+Const1* and *average+Const1* as well as the simple baselines perform best and all methods outperform what is reported by Zanzotto et al. (2010).

5 Discussion

The first proposed constraint of this paper, the semantic contribution of heads and modifiers, proves powerful: the *+Const1* addition, average and combined addition-multiplication operations heavily outperform their counterparts without the constraint and come to be the statistically best in 5 of the 6 tasks, also outperforming the NN and Zanzotto et al.'s approach. This confirms that the semantic contribution constraint is indeed beneficial: it's the *semantic* contribution of the phrase components that should be considered for the weighting and not the syntactic role. The fact that this constraint boosts simple baselines like the ones presented here shows the potential in exploring how it could also boost other existing (deep) models.

On the other hand, the dimensions' selection constraint proposed in sd and $mod - sd$ performs statistically best in 5 of the 6 tasks. They outperform the non-compositional baselines (*only_head* and *only_mod*), showing that they indeed capture compositionality. They also outperform the standard baselines, the NN and Zanzotto et al.'s approach. This result shows the benefits of our proposed functions: selecting only those dimensions of the semantic modifier that are relevant to the head, i.e. implementing the intuition of functional application of one vector onto the other, but relying on semantic heads and modifiers as opposed to syntactic ones. Both functions have a heavier presence of semantic head dimensions than semantic modifier dimensions due to their composition process (see Section 3.2). From this we can conclude that compositional vectors are more efficient when more semantic head attributes than semantic modifier attributes are present. Between the two approaches there is no apparent difference: sd is better in the *Syn* task and $mod - sd$ in *DistSim*. Further evaluation tasks will have to determine any performance differences. $mod - sd$ might be able to capture more information because it combines the semantic modifier dimensions with the dimensions of the constructed functional vector which contains the semantic head attributes "dilated" in the direction of the semantic modifier.

The tasks included in the current evaluation show no real differences between the proposed methods sd and $mod - sd$ and the *baselines+Const1*, which might raise some doubt on the real value and powerfulness of the dimensions' selection constraint. However, the goal of this work was to test the intuition behind this approach and see whether it can compete with other state-of-the-art results. In that respect, the results are promising. Particularly, we expect that the proposed functions can be improved with further fine-tuning of the dimensions' selection process to outperform the standard baselines. On the contrary, the baseline operations have less room for improvement. We hope that future tasks can show more clearly the weaknesses and strengths of each approach. We are particularly interested in testing this approach on other types of phrases, e.g. verb phrases (VP), to see how our two constraints generalize. For example, concerning our first constraint, for English VPs containing a verb and an object, we expect all verbs to behave as semantic heads (and the objects as semantic modifiers) except for light verbs, where the objects should be the semantic heads. In fact, preliminary experimenting with VPs shows that both constraints can be extended to them with promising results.

6 Conclusion

In this paper, we proposed two novel constraints for composing linguistically-informed and intuitively-explainable nominal phrase vectors. After a thorough evaluation, we showed that these constraints lead to more expressive phrase vectors, outperforming popular baselines. Other evaluation tasks might prove more suitable for showing specific strengths and weaknesses of the proposed constraints. In the future, we wish to apply our approach to other kinds of phrases, e.g., verb phrases, and try to derive a representation for a whole sentence by iteratively combining the different constituent phrases of the sentence through the proposed constraints. Additionally, we would like to train a better semantic contribution classifier and make it openly available for use.

Acknowledgments

We would like to thank Bettina Braun und Katharina Zahner for useful feedback on the statistics, as well as Miriam Butt and the anonymous reviewers for constructive comments.

References

Sanjeev Arora, Yingyu Liang, and Tengyu Ma. 2017. A simple but tough-to-beat baseline for sentence embeddings. In *International Conference on Learning Representations (ICLR)*.

Colin Bannard, Timothy Baldwin, and Alex Lascarides. 2003. A Statistical Approach to the Semantics of Verb-particles. In *Proceedings of the ACL 2003 Workshop on Multiword Expressions: Analysis, Acquisition and Treatment - Volume 18*, MWE '03, pages 65–72, Stroudsburg, PA, USA. Association for Computational Linguistics.

Marco Baroni, Georgiana Dinu, and Germán Kruszewski. 2014. Don't count, predict! A systematic comparison of context-counting vs. context-predicting semantic vectors. In *Proceedings of the 52nd Annual Meeting of the Association for Computational Linguistics (Volume 1: Long Papers)*, pages 238–247. Association for Computational Linguistics.

Marco Baroni and Roberto Zamparelli. 2010. Nouns are vectors, adjectives are matrices: Representing adjective-noun constructions in semantic space. In *Proceedings of the 2010 Conference on Empirical Methods in Natural Language Processing*, pages 1183–1193. Association for Computational Linguistics.

William Blacoe and Mirella Lapata. 2012. A comparison of vector-based representations for semantic composition. In *Proceedings of the 2012 Joint Conference on Empirical Methods in Natural Language Processing and Computational Natural Language Learning*, EMNLP-CoNLL '12, pages 546–556, Stroudsburg, PA, USA. Association for Computational Linguistics.

Gemma Boleda, Marco Baroni, The Nghia Pham, and Louise McNally. 2013. Intensionality was only alleged: On adjective-noun composition in distributional semantics. In *Proceedings of the 10th International Conference on Computational Semantics (IWCS 2013) – Long Papers*, pages 35–46, Potsdam, Germany. Association for Computational Linguistics.

Miriam Butt. 2010. The light verb jungle : still hacking away. In Mengistu Amberber, Brett Baker, and Mark Harvey, editors, *Complex predicates : cross-linguistic perspectives on event structure*, pages 48–78. Cambridge University Press, Cambridge.

Djork-Arné Clevert, Thomas Unterthiner, and Sepp Hochreiter. 2015. Fast and Accurate Deep Network Learning by Exponential Linear Units (ELUs). *CoRR*, abs/1511.07289.

Bob Coecke, Mehrnoosh Sadrzadeh, and Stephen Clark. 2010. Mathematical Foundations for a Compositional Distributional Model of Meaning. *Lambek Festschrift Linguistic Analysis*, 36.

Alexis Conneau, Douwe Kiela, Holger Schwenk, Loïc Barrault, and Antoine Bordes. 2017. Supervised Learning of Universal Sentence Representations from Natural Language Inference Data. In *Proceedings of the 2017 Conference on Empirical Methods in Natural Language Processing*, pages 670–680, Copenhagen, Denmark. Association for Computational Linguistics.

Silvio Cordeiro, Aline Villavicencio, Marco Idiart, and Carlos Ramisch. 2018. Unsupervised Compositionality Prediction of Nominal Compounds. *Computational Linguistics*, pages 1–80.

Ishita Dasgupta, Demi Guo, Andreas Stuhlmüller, Samuel J. Gershman, and Noah D. Goodman. 2018. Evaluating Compositionality in Sentence Embeddings. *CoRR*, abs/1802.04302.

Jacob Devlin, Ming-Wei Chang, Kenton Lee, and Kristina Toutanova. 2018. BERT: Pre-training of Deep Bidirectional Transformers for Language Understanding. *CoRR*, abs/1810.04805.

Corina Dima. 2016. On the Compositionality and Semantic Interpretation of English Noun Compounds. In *Proceedings of the 1st Workshop on Representation Learning for NLP*, pages 27–39. Association for Computational Linguistics.

Manaal Faruqui, Yulia Tsvetkov, Pushpendre Rastogi, and Chris Dyer. 2016. Problems with Evaluation of Word Embeddings Using Word Similarity Tasks. In *Proceedings of the 1st Workshop on Evaluating Vector-Space Representations for NLP*, pages 30–35. Association for Computational Linguistics.

Christiane Fellbaum. 1998. *WordNet: An Electronic Lexical Database (Language, Speech, and Communication)*. The MIT Press.

Xavier Glorot and Yoshua Bengio. 2010. Understanding the difficulty of training deep feedforward neural networks. In *Proceedings of the Thirteenth International Conference on Artificial Intelligence and Statistics*, volume 9 of *Proceedings of Machine Learning Research*, pages 249–256, Chia Laguna Resort, Sardinia, Italy. PMLR.

Edward Grefenstette, Mehrnoosh Sadrzadeh, Stephen Clark, Bob Coecke, and Stephen Pulman. 2014. Concrete Sentence Spaces for Compositional Distributional Models of Meaning. *Computing Meaning*, 4:71–86.

Emiliano Guevara. 2010. A Regression Model of Adjective-Noun Compositionality in Distributional Semantics. In *Proceedings of the 2010 Workshop on GEometrical Models of Natural Language Semantics*, pages 33–37. Association for Computational Linguistics.

Matthias Hartung, Fabian Kaupmann, Soufian Jebbara, and Philipp Cimiano. 2017. Learning Compositionality Functions on Word Embeddings for Modelling Attribute Meaning in Adjective-Noun Phrases. In

Proceedings of the 15th Conference of the European Chapter of the Association for Computational Linguistics: Volume 1, Long Papers, pages 54–64. Association for Computational Linguistics.

Kazuma Hashimoto and Yoshimasa Tsuruoka. 2016. Adaptive Joint Learning of Compositional and Non-Compositional Phrase Embeddings. In *Proceedings of the 54th Annual Meeting of the Association for Computational Linguistics (Volume 1: Long Papers)*, pages 205–215. Association for Computational Linguistics.

Karl Moritz Hermann, Phil Blunsom, and Stephen Pulman. 2012. An Unsupervised Ranking Model for Noun-noun Compositionality. In *Proceedings of the First Joint Conference on Lexical and Computational Semantics*, SemEval '12, pages 132–141, Stroudsburg, PA, USA. Association for Computational Linguistics.

Mohit Iyyer, Varun Manjunatha, Jordan Boyd-Graber, and Hal Daumé III. 2015. Deep unordered composition rivals syntactic methods for text classification. In *Proceedings of the 53rd Annual Meeting of the Association for Computational Linguistics and the 7th International Joint Conference on Natural Language Processing (Volume 1: Long Papers)*, pages 1681–1691. Association for Computational Linguistics.

Nal Kalchbrenner, Edward Grefenstette, and Phil Blunsom. 2014. A Convolutional Neural Network for Modelling Sentences. In *Proceedings of the 52nd Annual Meeting of the Association for Computational Linguistics (Volume 1: Long Papers)*, pages 655–665, Baltimore, Maryland. Association for Computational Linguistics.

Ryan Kiros, Yukun Zhu, Ruslan Salakhutdinov, Richard S. Zemel, Antonio Torralba, Raquel Urtasun, and Sanja Fidler. 2015. Skip-Thought Vectors. *CoRR*, abs/1506.06726.

Alexandra Kuznetsova, Per Brockhoff, and Rune Christensen. 2017. lmerTest Package: Tests in Linear Mixed Effects Models. *Journal of Statistical Software, Articles*, 82(13):1–26.

Thomas Landauer and Susan Dumais. 1997. A solution to Plato's problem: The latent semantic analysis theory of acquisition, induction, and representation of knowledge. *Psychological Review*, 104:211–240.

M. Marneffe, B. Maccartney, and C. Manning. 2006. Generating Typed Dependency Parses from Phrase Structure Parses. In *Proceedings of the Fifth International Conference on Language Resources and Evaluation (LREC'06)*. European Language Resources Association (ELRA).

Ryan McDonald, Joakim Nivre, Yvonne Quirmbach-Brundage, Yoav Goldberg, Dipanjan Das, Kuzman Ganchev, Keith Hall, Slav Petrov, Hao Zhang, Oscar Täckström, Claudia Bedini, Núria Bertomeu Castelló, and Jungmee Lee. 2013. Universal dependency annotation for multilingual parsing. In *Proceedings of the 51st Annual Meeting of the Association for Computational Linguistics (Volume 2: Short Papers)*, pages 92–97. Association for Computational Linguistics.

Tomas Mikolov, Kai Chen, G.s Corrado, and Jeffrey Dean. 2013. Efficient Estimation of Word Representations in Vector Space. *Proceedings of Workshop at ICLR*, 2013.

Jeff Mitchell and Mirella Lapata. 2010. Composition in Distributional Models of Semantics. *Cognitive Science*, 34(8):1388–1429.

Matteo Pagliardini, Prakhar Gupta, and Martin Jaggi. 2018. Unsupervised Learning of Sentence Embeddings Using Compositional n-Gram Features. In *Proceedings of the 2018 Conference of the North American Chapter of the Association for Computational Linguistics: Human Language Technologies, Volume 1 (Long Papers)*, pages 528–540, New Orleans, Louisiana. Association for Computational Linguistics.

Jeffrey Pennington, Richard Socher, and Christopher D. Manning. 2014. Glove: Global Vectors for Word Representation. In *Proceedings of the 2014 Conference on Empirical Methods in Natural Language Processing (EMNLP)*, pages 1532–1543.

Matthew Peters, Mark Neumann, Mohit Iyyer, Matt Gardner, Christopher Clark, Kenton Lee, and Luke Zettlemoyer. 2018. Deep Contextualized Word Representations. In *Proceedings of the 2018 Conference of the North American Chapter of the Association for Computational Linguistics: Human Language Technologies, Volume 1 (Long Papers)*, pages 2227–2237, New Orleans, Louisiana. Association for Computational Linguistics.

Siva Reddy, Diana McCarthy, and Suresh Manandhar. 2011. An Empirical Study on Compositionality in Compound Nouns. In *Proceedings of 5th International Joint Conference on Natural Language Processing*, pages 210–218. Asian Federation of Natural Language Processing.

Tobias Schnabel, Igor Labutov, David Mimno, and Thorsten Joachims. 2015. Evaluation methods for unsupervised word embeddings. In *Proceedings of the 2015 Conference on Empirical Methods in Natural Language Processing*, pages 298–307. Association for Computational Linguistics.

Vered Shwartz and Ido Dagan. 2019. Still a pain in the neck: Evaluating text representations on lexical composition.

Vered Shwartz and Chris Waterson. 2018. Olive Oil is Made *of* Olives, Baby Oil is Made *for* Babies: Interpreting Noun Compounds Using Paraphrases in a

Neural Model. In *Proceedings of the 2018 Conference of the North American Chapter of the Association for Computational Linguistics: Human Language Technologies, Volume 2 (Short Papers)*, pages 218–224, New Orleans, Louisiana. Association for Computational Linguistics.

Richard Socher, Christopher D. Manning, and Andrew Y. Ng. 2010. Learning continuous phrase representations and syntactic parsing with recursive neural networks. In *Proceedings of the NIPS-2010 Deep Learning and Unsupervised Feature Learning Workshop*.

Richard Socher, Alex Perelygin, Jean Wu, Jason Chuang, Christopher D. Manning, Andrew Ng, and Christopher Potts. 2013. Recursive Deep Models for Semantic Compositionality Over a Sentiment Treebank. In *Proceedings of the 2013 Conference on Empirical Methods in Natural Language Processing (EMNLP)*, pages 1631–1642. Association for Computational Linguistics.

Peter D. Turney. 2012. Domain and Function: A Dual-Space Model of Semantic Relations and Compositions. *Journal of Artificial Intelligence Research*, 44:533–585.

Lyndon White, Roberto Togneri, Wei Liu, and Mohammed Bennamoun. 2015. How Well Sentence Embeddings Capture Meaning. In *Proceedings of the 20th Australasian Document Computing Symposium*, ADCS '15, pages 9:1–9:8, New York, NY, USA. ACM.

John Wieting, Mohit Bansal, Kevin Gimpel, and Karen Livescu. 2015. From Paraphrase Database to Compositional Paraphrase Model and Back. *Transactions of the Association for Computational Linguistics*, 3:345–358.

John Wieting, Mohit Bansal, Kevin Gimpel, and Karen Livescu. 2016. Towards Universal Paraphrastic Sentence Embeddings. *CoRR*, abs/1511.08198.

Wenpeng Yin and Hinrich Schütze. 2014. An Exploration of Embeddings for Generalized Phrases. In *Proceedings of the ACL 2014 Student Research Workshop*, pages 41–47. Association for Computational Linguistics.

Wenpeng Yin and Hinrich Schütze. 2015. Convolutional Neural Network for Paraphrase Identification. In *Proceedings of the 2015 Conference of the North American Chapter of the Association for Computational Linguistics: Human Language Technologies*, pages 901–911, Denver, Colorado. Association for Computational Linguistics.

Mo Yu and Mark Dredze. 2015. Learning Composition Models for Phrase Embeddings. *Transactions of the Association for Computational Linguistics*, 3:227–242.

Fabio Massimo Zanzotto, Ioannis Korkontzelos, Francesca Fallucchi, and Suresh Manandhar. 2010. Estimating Linear Models for Compositional Distributional Semantics. In *Proceedings of the 23rd International Conference on Computational Linguistics*, COLING '10, pages 1263–1271, Stroudsburg, PA, USA. Association for Computational Linguistics.

Matthew D. Zeiler. 2012. ADADELTA: An Adaptive Learning Rate Method. *CoRR*, abs/1212.5701.

Xunjie Zhu, Tingfeng Li, and Gerard de Melo. 2018. Exploring Semantic Properties of Sentence Embeddings. In *Proceedings of the 56th Annual Meeting of the Association for Computational Linguistics (Volume 2: Short Papers)*, pages 632–637, Melbourne, Australia. Association for Computational Linguistics.

Towards Robust Named Entity Recognition for Historic German

Stefan Schweter and Johannes Baiter
Bayerische Staatsbibliothek München
Digital Library/Munich Digitization Center
80539 Munich, Germany
{stefan.schweter, johannes.baiter}@bsb-muenchen.de

Abstract

Recent advances in language modeling using deep neural networks have shown that these models learn representations, that vary with the network depth from morphology to semantic relationships like co-reference. We apply pre-trained language models to low-resource named entity recognition for Historic German. We show on a series of experiments that character-based pre-trained language models do not run into trouble when faced with low-resource datasets. Our pre-trained character-based language models improve upon classical CRF-based methods and previous work on Bi-LSTMs by boosting F1 score performance by up to 6%. Our pre-trained language and NER models are publicly available[1].

1   Introduction

Named entity recognition (NER) is a central component in natural language processing tasks. Identifying named entities is a key part in systems e.g. for question answering or entity linking. Traditionally, NER systems are built using conditional random fields (CRFs). Recent systems are using neural network architectures like bidirectional LSTM with a CRF-layer ontop and pre-trained word embeddings (Ma and Hovy, 2016; Lample et al., 2016a; Reimers and Gurevych, 2017; Lin et al., 2017).

Pre-trained word embeddings have been shown to be of great use for downstream NLP tasks (Mikolov et al., 2013; Pennington et al., 2014). Many recently proposed approaches go beyond these pre-trained embeddings. Recent works have proposed methods that produce different representations for the same word depending on its contextual usage (Peters et al., 2017, 2018a; Akbik et al., 2018; Devlin et al., 2018). These methods have

shown to be very powerful in the fields of named entity recognition, coreference resolution, part-of-speech tagging and question answering, especially in combination with classic word embeddings.

Our paper is based on the work of Riedl and Padó (2018). They showed how to build a model for German named entity recognition (NER) that performs at the state of the art for both contemporary and historical texts. Labeled historical texts for German named entity recognition are a low-resource domain. In order to achieve robust state-of-the-art results for historical texts they used transfer-learning with labeled data from other high-resource domains like CoNLL-2003 (Tjong Kim Sang and De Meulder, 2003) or GermEval (Benikova et al., 2014). They showed that using Bi-LSTM with a CRF as the top layer and word embeddings outperforms CRFs with hand-coded features in a big-data situation.

We build up upon their work and use the same low-resource datasets for Historic German. Furthermore, we show how to achieve new state-of-the-art results for Historic German named entity recognition by using only unlabeled data via pre-trained language models and word embeddings. We also introduce a novel language model pre-training objective, that uses only contemporary texts for training to achieve comparable state-of-the-art results on historical texts.

2   Model

In this paper, we use contextualized string embeddings as proposed by Akbik et al. (2018), as they have shown to be very effective in named entity recognition. We use the FLAIR[2] (Akbik et al., 2018) library to train all NER and pre-trained language models. We use FastText (Wikipedia and

---

[1] https://github.com/stefan-it/historic-ner

[2] https://github.com/zalandoresearch/flair

Proceedings of the 4th Workshop on Representation Learning for NLP (RepL4NLP-2019), pages 96–103
Florence, Italy, August 2, 2019. ©2019 Association for Computational Linguistics

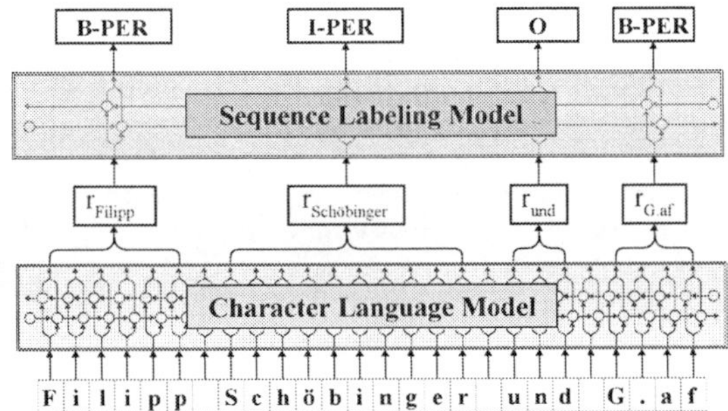

Figure 1: High level overview of our used model. A sentence is input as a character sequence into a pre-trained bidirectional character language model. From this LM, we retrieve for each word a contextual embedding that we pass into a vanilla Bi-LSTM-CRF.

Crawl) as word embeddings. FLAIR allows us to easily combine ("stacking") different embeddings types. For instance, Lample et al. (2016b) combine word embeddings with character features. In our experiments we combined several embedding types and language models. Contextualized string embeddings were trained with a forward and backward character-based language model (LSTM) on two historic datasets. This process is further called "pre-training". We use a Bi-LSTM with CRF on top as proposed by Huang et al. (2015). A high level system overview of our used model is shown in figure 1.

3 Datasets

We use the same two datasets for Historic German as used by Riedl and Padó (2018). These datasets are based on historical texts that were extracted (Neudecker, 2016) from the Europeana collection of historical newspapers[3]. The first corpus is the collection of Tyrolean periodicals and newspapers from the Dr Friedrich Temann Library (LFT). The LFT corpus consists of approximately 87,000 tokens from 1926. The second corpus is a collection of Austrian newspaper texts from the Austrian National Library (ONB). The ONB corpus consists of approximately 35,000 tokens from texts created between 1710 and 1873.

The tagset includes locations (LOC), organizations (ORG), persons (PER) and the remaining entities as miscellaneous (MISC). Figures 1-2 contain an overview of the number of named entities of the two datasets. No miscellaneous entities (MISC) are found in the ONB dataset and only

a few are annotated in the LFT dataset. The two corpora pose three challenging problems: they are relatively small compared to contemporary corpora like CoNLL-2003 or GermEval. They also have a different language variety (German and Austrian) and they include a high rate of OCR errors[4] since they were originally printed in Gothic type-face (Fraktur), a low resource font, which has not been the main focus of recent OCR research.

Dataset	LOC	MISC	ORG	PER
Training	1,605	0	182	2,674
Development	207	0	10	447
Test	221	0	16	355

Table 1: Number of named entities in ONB dataset.

Dataset	LOC	MISC	ORG	PER
Training	3,998	2	2,293	4,009
Development	406	0	264	558
Test	441	1	324	506

Table 2: Number of named entities in LFT dataset.

4 Experiments

4.1 Experiment 1: Different Word Embeddings

In the first experiment we use different types of embeddings on the two datasets: (a) FastText embeddings trained on German Wikipedia articles, (b) FastText embeddings trained on Common Crawl and (c) character embeddings, as proposed by Lample et al. (2016b). We use pre-trained Fast-Text embeddings[5] without subword information, as we found out that subword information could harm performance (0.8 to 1.5%) of our system in some cases.

Table 3 shows, that combining pre-trained Fast-Text for Wikipedia and Common Crawl leads to a F1 score of 72.50% on the LFT dataset. Adding character embeddings has a positive impact of 2% and yields 74.50%. This result is higher than the reported one by Riedl and Padó (2018)

---

[3] https://www.europeana.eu/portal/de

[4] Typical OCR errors would be segmentation and hyphenation errors or misrecognition of characters (e.g. $Bifmarck$ instead of $Bifmarck$).

[5] https://fasttext.cc/docs/en/crawl-vectors.html

Configuration		F-Score
	Wikipedia	69.59%
	Common Crawl	68.97%
LFT	Wikipedia + Common Crawl	72.00%
	Wikipedia + Common Crawl + Character	**74.50%**
	Riedl and Padó (2018) (no transfer-learning)	69.62%
	Riedl and Padó (2018) (with transfer-learning)	74.33%
	Wikipedia	75.80%
	CommonCrawl	78.70%
ONB	Wikipedia + CommonCrawl	79.46%
	Wikipedia + CommonCrawl + Character	**80.48%**
	Riedl and Padó (2018) (no transfer-learning)	73.31%
	Riedl and Padó (2018) (with transfer-learning)	78.56%

Table 3: Results on LFT and ONB dataset with different configurations. Wikipedia and Common Crawl are pre-trained FastText word embeddings. The best configurations reported by Riedl and Padó (2018) used Wikipedia or Europeana word embeddings with subword information and character embeddings.

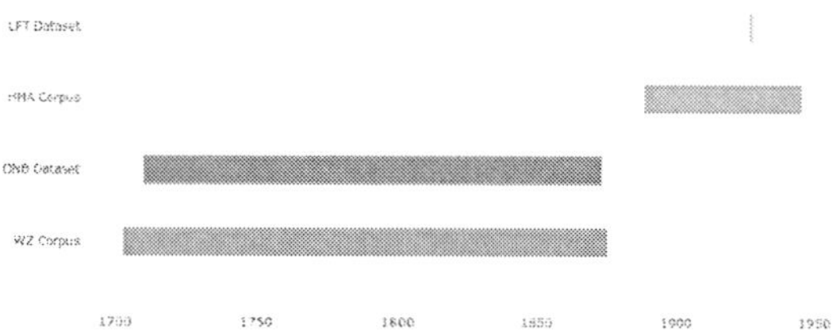

Figure 2: Temporal overlap for language model corpora and historic datasets.

(74.33%), who used transfer-learning with more labeled data. Table 3 also shows the same effect for ONB: combining Wikipedia and Common Crawl embeddings leads to 79.46% and adding character embeddings marginally improves the result to 80.48%. This result is also higher than the reported one by Riedl and Padó (2018) (78.56%).

4.2 Experiment 2: Language model pre-training

For the next experiments we train contextualized string embeddings as proposed by Akbik et al. (2018). We train language models on two datasets from the Europeana collection of historical newspapers. The first corpus consists of articles from the Hamburger Anzeiger newspaper (HHA) covering 741,575,357 tokens from 1888 - 1945. The second corpus consists of articles from the Wiener Zeitung newspaper (WZ) covering 801,543,845 tokens from 1703 - 1875. We choose the two corpora, because they have a temporal overlap with the LFT corpus (1926) and the ONB corpus (1710

- 1873). Figure 2 shows the temporal overlap for the language model corpora and the datasets used in the downstream task. There is a huge temporal overlap between the ONB dataset and the WZ corpus, whereas the overlap between the LFT dataset and the HHA corpus is relatively small.

Additionally we use the BERT model, that was trained on Wikipedia for 104 languages[6] for comparison. We perform a per-layer analysis of the multi-lingual BERT model on the development set to find the best layer for our task. For the German language model, we use the same pre-trained language model for German as used in Akbik et al. (2018). This model was trained on various sources (Wikipedia, OPUS) with a training data set size of half a billion tokens.

Table 4 shows that the temporal aspect of training data for the language models has deep impact on the performance. On LFT (1926) the language model trained on the HHA corpus (1888 - 1945) leads to a F1 score of 77.51%, which is a new state-of-the art result on this dataset. The result is 3.18% better than the result reported by Riedl and Padó (2018), which uses transfer-learning with more labeled training data. The language model trained on the WZ corpus (1703-1875) only achieves a F1 score of 75.60%, likely because the time period of the data used for pre-training (19th century) is too far removed from

---

[6]`https://github.com/google-research/bert/blob/f39e881b169b9d53bea03d2d341b31707a6c052b/multilingual.md`

	Configuration	Pre-trained LM	Pre-training data	**F-Score**
LFT (1926)	German	✓	Wikipedia, OPUS	76.04%
	Hamburger Anzeiger (HHA)	✓	Newspaper (1888 - 1945)	**77.51%**
	Wiener Zeitung (WZ)	✓	Newspaper (1703 - 1875)	75.60%
	Multi-lingual BERT	✓	Wikipedia	74.39%
	SMLM (synthetic corpus)	✓	Wikipedia	77.16%
	Riedl and Padó (2018)	-	-	69.62%
	Riedl and Padó (2018)†	-	-	74.33%
ONB (1710-1873)	German	✓	Wikipedia, OPUS	80.06%
	Hamburger Anzeiger (HHA)	✓	Newspaper (1888 - 1945)	83.28%
	Wiener Zeitung (WZ)	✓	Newspaper (1703 - 1875)	**85.31%**
	Multi-lingual BERT	✓	Wikipedia	77.19%
	SMLM (synthetic corpus)	✓	Wikipedia	82.15%
	Riedl and Padó (2018)	-	-	73.31%
	Riedl and Padó (2018)†	-	-	78.56%

Table 4: Results on LFT and ONB with different language models. The German language model refers to the model used in Akbik et al. (2018). We perform a per-layer analysis for BERT on the development set and use the best layer. For all experiments we also use pre-trained FastText embeddings on Wikipedia and Common Crawl as well as character embeddings. † indicates the usage of additional training data (GermEval) for transfer learning.

that of the downstream task (mid-1920s). Table 4 also shows the results of pre-trained language models on the ONB (1710 - 1873) dataset. The language models, that were trained on contemporary data like the German Wikipedia (Akbik et al., 2018) or multi-lingual BERT do not perform very well on the ONB dataset, which covers texts from the 18-19th century. The language model trained on the HHA corpus performs better, since there is a substantially temporal overlap with the ONB corpus. The language model trained on the WZ corpus (1703-1875) leads to the best results with a F1 score of 85.31%. This result is 6.75% better than the reported result by Riedl and Padó (2018), which again uses transfer-learning with additionally labeled training data.

4.3 Experiment 3: Synthetic Masked Language Modeling (SMLM)

We also consider the masked language modeling (MLM) objective of Devlin et al. (2018). However, this technique cannot be directly used, because they use a subword-based language model, in contrast to our character-based language model. We introduce a novel masked language modeling technique, synthetic masked language modeling (SMLM) that randomly adds noise during training.

The main motivation for using SMLM is to transfer a corpus from one domain (e.g. "clean" contemporary texts) into another (e.g. "noisy" historical texts). SMLM uses the vocabulary (characters) from the target domain and injects them into the source domain. With this technique it is possible to create a synthetic corpus, that "emulates" OCR errors or spelling mistakes without having any data from the target domain (except all possible characters as vocabulary). Furthermore, SMLM can also be seen as a kind of domain adaption.

To use SMLM we extract all vocabulary (characters) from the ONB and LFT datasets. We refer to these characters as target vocabulary. Then we obtained a corpus consisting of contemporary texts from Leipzig Corpora Collection (Goldhahn et al., 2012) for German. The resulting corpus has 388,961,352 tokens. During training, the following SMLM objective is used: Iterate overall characters in the contemporary corpus. Leave the character unchanged in 90% of the time. For the remaining 10% we employ the following strategy: in 20% of the time replace the character with a masked character, that does not exist in the target vocabulary. In 80% of the time we randomly replace the character by a symbol from the target vocabulary.

Table 4 shows that the language model trained with SMLM achieves the second best result on LFT with 77.16%. The ONB corpus is more challenging for SMLM, because it includes texts from a totally different time period (18-19th century). SMLM achieves the third best result with a F-Score of 82.15%. This result is remarkable, because the language model itself has never seen texts from the 18-19th century. The model was trained on contemporary texts with SMLM only.

5 Data Analysis

	LM	Perplexity		F-Score
		Forward	Backward	
LFT	German	8.30	8.7	76.04%
	HHA	**6.31**	**6.64**	**77.51%**
	WZ	6.72	6.97	75.60%
	Synthetic	7.87	8.20	77.16%
ONB	German	8.58	8.77	80.06%
	HHA	6.71	7.22	83.28%
	WZ	**4.72**	**4.95**	**85.31%**
	Synthetic	8.65	9.64	82.15%

Table 5: Averaged perplexity for all sentences in the test dataset for LFT for all pre-trained language models.

The usage of pre-trained character-based language models boosts performance for both LFT and ONB datasets. The results in table 4 show, that the selection of the language model corpus plays an important role: a corpus with a large degree of temporal overlap with the downstream task performs better than corpus with little to no temporal overlap. In order to compare our trained language models with each other, we measure both the perplexity of the forward language model and the backward language model on the test dataset for LFT and ONB. The perplexity for each sentence in the test dataset is calculated and averaged. The results for LFT and ONB are shown in table 5. For all language models (except one) there is a clear correlation between overall perplexity and F1 score on the test dataset: lower perplexity (both for forward and backward language model) yields better performance in terms of the F1 score on the downstream NER tasks. But this assumption does not hold for the language model that was trained on synthetic data via SMLM objective: The perplexity for this language model (both forward and backward) is relatively high compared to other language models, but the F1 score results are better than some other language models with lower perplexity. This variation can be observed

both on LFT and ONB test data. We leave this anomaly here as an open question: Is perplexity a good measure for comparing language models and a useful indicator for their results on downstream tasks?

The previous experiments show, that language model pre-training does work very well, even for domains with low data resources. Cotterell and Duh (2017) showed that using CRF-based methods outperform traditional Bi-LSTM in low-resource settings. We argue that this shortcoming can now be eliminated by using Bi-LSTMs in combination with pre-trained language models. Our experiments also showed, that pre-trained language models can also help to improve performance, even when no training data for the target domain is used (SMLM objective).

6 Conclusion

In this paper we have studied the influence of using language model pre-training for named entity recognition for Historic German. We achieve new state-of-the-art results using carefully chosen training data for language models.

For a low-resource domain like named entity recognition for Historic German, language model pre-training can be a strong competitor to CRF-only methods as proposed by Cotterell and Duh (2017). We showed that language model pre-training can be more effective than using transfer-learning with labeled datasets.

Furthermore, we introduced a new language model pre-training objective, synthetic masked language model pre-training (SMLM), that allows a transfer from one domain (contemporary texts) to another domain (historical texts) by using only the same (character) vocabulary. Results showed that using SMLM can achieve comparable results for Historic named entity recognition, even when they are only trained on contemporary texts.

Acknowledgments

We would like to thank the anonymous reviewers for their helpful and valuable comments.

References

Alan Akbik, Duncan Blythe, and Roland Vollgraf. 2018. Contextual string embeddings for sequence labeling. In *COLING 2018, 27th International Conference on Computational Linguistics*, pages 1638–1649.

Darina Benikova, Chris Biemann, and Marc Reznicek. 2014. Nosta-d named entity annotation for german: Guidelines and dataset. In *Proceedings of the Ninth International Conference on Language Resources and Evaluation (LREC-2014)*. European Language Resources Association (ELRA).

Ryan Cotterell and Kevin Duh. 2017. Low-resource named entity recognition with cross-lingual, character-level neural conditional random fields. In *Proceedings of the Eighth International Joint Conference on Natural Language Processing (Volume 2: Short Papers)*, pages 91–96. Asian Federation of Natural Language Processing.

Jacob Devlin, Ming-Wei Chang, Kenton Lee, and Kristina Toutanova. 2018. Bert: Pre-training of deep bidirectional transformers for language understanding. *arXiv preprint arXiv:1810.04805*.

Dirk Goldhahn, Thomas Eckart, and Uwe Quasthoff. 2012. Building large monolingual dictionaries at the leipzig corpora collection: From 100 to 200 languages. In *In Proceedings of the Eight International Conference on Language Resources and Evaluation (LREC12*.

Zhiheng Huang, Wei Xu, and Kai Yu. 2015. Bidirectional LSTM CRF Models for Sequence Tagging. *arXiv e-prints*, page arXiv:1508.01991.

Guillaume Lample, Miguel Ballesteros, Sandeep Subramanian, Kazuya Kawakami, and Chris Dyer. 2016a. Neural architectures for named entity recognition. In *Proceedings of the 2016 Conference of the North American Chapter of the Association for Computational Linguistics: Human Language Technologies*, pages 260–270. Association for Computational Linguistics.

Guillaume Lample, Miguel Ballesteros, Sandeep Subramanian, Kazuya Kawakami, and Chris Dyer. 2016b. Neural architectures for named entity recognition. In *Proceedings of the 2016 Conference of the North American Chapter of the Association for Computational Linguistics: Human Language Technologies*, pages 260–270, San Diego, California. Association for Computational Linguistics.

Bill Y. Lin, Frank Xu, Zhiyi Luo, and Kenny Zhu. 2017. Multi-channel bilstm-crf model for emerging named entity recognition in social media. In *Proceedings of the 3rd Workshop on Noisy User-generated Text*, pages 160–165. Association for Computational Linguistics.

Xuezhe Ma and Eduard Hovy. 2016. End-to-end sequence labeling via bi-directional lstm-cnns-crf. In *Proceedings of the 54th Annual Meeting of the Association for Computational Linguistics (Volume 1: Long Papers)*, pages 1064–1074. Association for Computational Linguistics.

Tomas Mikolov, Ilya Sutskever, Kai Chen, Greg S Corrado, and Jeff Dean. 2013. Distributed representations of words and phrases and their compositionality. In *Advances in neural information processing systems*, pages 3111–3119.

Clemens Neudecker. 2016. An open corpus for named entity recognition in historic newspapers. In *Proceedings of the Tenth International Conference on Language Resources and Evaluation (LREC 2016)*, Paris, France. European Language Resources Association (ELRA).

Jeffrey Pennington, Richard Socher, and Christopher Manning. 2014. Glove: Global vectors for word representation. In *Proceedings of the 2014 conference on empirical methods in natural language processing (EMNLP)*, pages 1532–1543.

Matthew Peters, Waleed Ammar, Chandra Bhagavatula, and Russell Power. 2017. Semi-supervised sequence tagging with bidirectional language models. In *Proceedings of the 55th Annual Meeting of the Association for Computational Linguistics (Volume 1: Long Papers)*, pages 1756–1765. Association for Computational Linguistics.

Matthew Peters, Mark Neumann, and Christopher Clark Kenton Lee Luke Zettlemoyer Mohit Iyyer, Matt Gardner. 2018a. Deep contextualized word representations. *6th International Conference on Learning Representations*.

Matthew Peters, Mark Neumann, Luke Zettlemoyer, and Wen-tau Yih. 2018b. Dissecting contextual word embeddings: Architecture and representation. In *Proceedings of the 2018 Conference on Empirical Methods in Natural Language Processing*, pages 1499–1509. Association for Computational Linguistics.

Lev Ratinov and Dan Roth. 2009. Design challenges and misconceptions in named entity recognition. In *Proceedings of the Thirteenth Conference on Computational Natural Language Learning (CoNLL-2009)*, pages 147–155. Association for Computational Linguistics.

Nils Reimers and Iryna Gurevych. 2017. Reporting score distributions makes a difference: Performance study of lstm-networks for sequence tagging. In *Proceedings of the 2017 Conference on Empirical Methods in Natural Language Processing*, pages 338–348. Association for Computational Linguistics.

Martin Riedl and Sebastian Padó. 2018. A named entity recognition shootout for german. In *Proceedings of the 56th Annual Meeting of the Association for Computational Linguistics (Volume 2: Short Papers)*, pages 120–125. Association for Computational Linguistics.

Erik F. Tjong Kim Sang and Fien De Meulder. 2003. Introduction to the conll-2003 shared task: Language-independent named entity recognition. In *Proceedings of the Seventh Conference on Natural Language Learning at HLT-NAACL 2003*.

A Supplemental Material

A.1 Language model pre-training

Table 6 shows the parameters that we used for training our language models. As our character-based language model relies on raw text, no pre-processing steps like tokenization are needed. We use 1/500 of the complete corpus for development data and another 1/500 for test data during the language model training.

Parameter	Value
LSTM hidden size	2048
LSTM layer	1
Dropout	0.1
Sequence length (characters)	250
Mini batch size	1
Epochs	1

Table 6: Parameters used for language model pre-training.

A.1.1 SMLM objective

Original sentence
Dann habe der Mann erzählt, wie er in München am Bahnhof mit Blumen begrüßt worden sei.
Sentence after SMLM transformation
Qa ¶n hab5 der MaRy erzählt nie er in MñchenIam Bahnhof mit Blumen begrüß(Corden se¶.

Figure 3: An example of the SMLM transformation for a given input sentence. The special character "¶" is used as masked character symbol.

Figure 3 shows the SMLM objective for a given input sentence and the corresponding output. We use the same parameters as shown in table 6 to train a language model with SMLM objective. We use different values of p in range of $[80, 90, 95]$ for leaving the character unchanged in the SMLM objective and found that $p = 90$ yields the best results.

A.2 Model parameters

Table 7 shows the parameters that we use for training a named entity recognition model with the FLAIR library. We reduce the learning rate by a factor of 0.5 with a patience of 3. This factor determines the number of epochs with no improvement after which learning rate will be reduced.

Parameter	Value
LSTM hidden size	512
Learning rate	0.1
Mini batch size	8
Max epochs	500
Optimizer	SGD

Table 7: Parameters used for training NER models.

A.3 BERT per-layer analysis

We experimentally found that using the last four layers as proposed in Devlin et al. (2018) for the feature-based approach does not work well. Thus, we perform a per-layer analysis that trains a model with a specific layer from the multi-lingual BERT model. Inspired by Peters et al. (2018b) we visualize the performance for each layer of the BERT model. Figure 4 shows the performance of each layer for the LFT development dataset, figure 5 for the ONB development dataset.

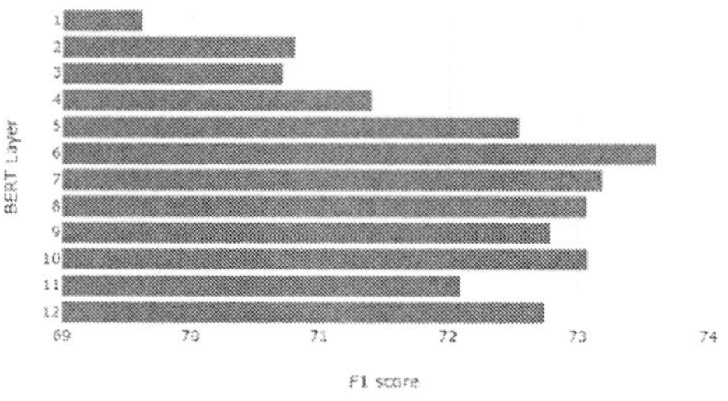

Figure 4: BERT per-layer analysis on the LFT development dataset.

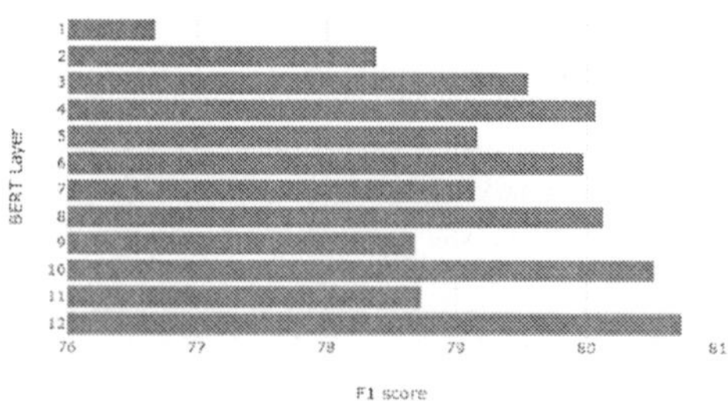

Figure 5: BERT per-layer analysis on the ONB development dataset.

A.4 Evaluation

We train all NER models with IOBES (Ratinov and Roth, 2009) tagging scheme. In the prediction step we convert IOBES tagging scheme to IOB, in order to use the offical CoNLL-2003 evaluation script[7]. For all NER models we train and evaluate 3 runs and report an averaged F1 score.

A.5 Negative Results

We briefly describe a few ideas we implemented that did not seem to be effective in initial experiments. These findings are from early initial experiments. We did not pursue these experiments further after first attempts, but some approaches could be effective with proper hyperparameter tunings.

- **FastText embeddings with subword information**: We use subword information with FastText embeddings trained on Wikipedia articles. On LFT this model was 0.81% behind a model trained with FastText embeddings without subword information. On ONB the difference was 1.56%. Using both FastText embeddings trained on Wikipedia and CommonCrawl with subword information caused out-of-memory errors on our system with 32GB of RAM.

- **ELMo Transformer**: We trained ELMo Transformer models as proposed by Peters et al. (2018b) for both HH and WZ corpus. We use the default hyperparameters as proposed by Peters et al. (2018b) and trained a ELMo Transformer model for one epoch (one iteration over the whole corpus) with a vocabulary size of 1,094,628 tokens both for the HH and WZ corpus. We use the same model architecture like in previous experiments for training a NER model on both LFT and ONB. On LFT we achieved a F1 score of 72.18%, which is 5.33% behind our new state-of-the-art result. On ONB we achieved a F1 score of 75.72%, which is 9.59% behind our new state-of-the-art result. We assume that training a ELMo Transformer model for more epochs would lead to better results.

---

[7] https://www.clips.uantwerpen.be/conll2003/ner/bin/conlleval

On Evaluating Embedding Models for Knowledge Base Completion

Yanjie Wang, Daniel Ruffinelli, Rainer Gemulla, Samuel Broscheit, Christian Meilicke
Data and Web Science Group
University of Mannheim, Germany
{ywang, rgemulla}@uni-mannheim.de,
{daniel,broscheit,christian}@informatik.uni-mannheim.de,

Abstract

Knowledge graph embedding models have recently received significant attention in the literature. These models learn latent semantic representations for the entities and relations in a given knowledge base; the representations can be used to infer missing knowledge. In this paper, we study the question of how well recent embedding models perform for the task of knowledge base completion, i.e., the task of inferring new facts from an incomplete knowledge base. We argue that the entity ranking protocol, which is currently used to evaluate knowledge graph embedding models, is not suitable to answer this question since only a subset of the model predictions are evaluated. We propose an alternative entity-pair ranking protocol that considers all model predictions as a whole and is thus more suitable to the task. We conducted an experimental study on standard datasets and found that the performance of popular embeddings models was unsatisfactory under the new protocol, even on datasets that are generally considered to be too easy. Moreover, we found that a simple rule-based model often provided superior performance. Our findings suggest that there is a need for more research into embedding models as well as their training strategies for the task of knowledge base completion.

1 Introduction

A knowledge base (KB) is a collection of relational facts, often represented as *(subject, relation, object)*-triples. KBs provide rich information for NLP tasks such as question answering (Abujabal et al., 2017) or entity linking (Shen et al., 2015). Since knowledge bases are inherently incomplete (West et al., 2014), there has been considerable interest into methods that infer missing knowledge.

In particular, a large number of *knowledge graph embedding (KGE) models* have been proposed in the recent literature (Nickel et al., 2016a). These models embed the entities and relations of a given knowledge base into a low-dimensional latent space such that the structure of the knowledge base is captured. The embeddings are subsequently used to assess whether unobserved triples constitute missing facts or are likely to be false.

To evaluate the performance of a KGE model, the most commonly adopted protocol is the *entity ranking* (ER) protocol.[1] The protocol takes as input a set of previously unobserved *test triples*, such as *(Einstein, bornIn, Ulm)*, and uses the embedding model to rank all possible answers to the questions *(?, bornIn, Ulm)* and *(Einstein, bornIn, ?)*. Model performance is then assessed based on the rank of the answer present in the test triple (*Einstein* and *Ulm*, resp.). Since each question is constructed from a test triple, the protocol ensures that questions are meaningful and always have a correct answer. Throughout this paper, we refer to the task of answering such questions as *question answering* (QA). The ER protocol is, in principle, well-suited to evaluate performance of KGE models for QA, although concerns about the benchmark datasets (Toutanova and Chen, 2015), the considered models (Kadlec et al., 2017) and the evaluation (Joulin et al., 2017) have been raised.

In this paper, we aim to study the performance of popular embedding models for the task of knowledge base completion (KBC): given a relation of a knowledge base (*bornIn*), infer true missing facts ((*Einstein, bornIn, Ulm*)). This task is different from QA (as defined above) since no information about potential missing triples is provided upfront. We argue that the ER protocol is not well-suited to assess model performance for KBC. To see this, observe that models that assign high confidence scores to incorrect triples such as

---

[1]We discuss other less adopted evaluation methods in Sec. 3.2.

Proceedings of the 4th Workshop on Representation Learning for NLP (RepL4NLP-2019), pages 104–112
Florence, Italy, August 2, 2019. ©2019 Association for Computational Linguistics

(Ulm, bornIn, Einstein) are not penalized by the ER protocol because the corresponding questions (e.g., *(Ulm, bornIn, ?)*) are never asked. Thus a model that performs well on ER may still not perform well for KBC. In fact, we argue here that some commonly used KGE models are inherently not well-suited to KBC.

We propose a simple *entity-pair ranking* (PR) protocol (PR), which is more suitable to assess model performance for KBC. Given a relation such as *bornIn*, PR uses the KGE model to rank all possible answers—i.e., all entity pairs—to the question $(?, bornIn, ?)$, and subsequently assesses model performance based on the rank of the test triples for relation *bornIn* in the answer. The protocol ensures that a model's performance is negatively affected if the model assigns high scores to false triples such as *(Ulm, bornIn, Einstein)*.

We conducted an experimental study on commonly used benchmark datasets under the ER and the PR protocols. We found that the performance of popular embeddings models was often good under the ER but unsatisfactory under the PR protocol, even on "simple" datasets that are generally considered to be too easy. Moreover, we found that a simple rule-based model often provided superior performance for PR. Our findings suggests that there is a need for more research into embedding models as well as their training strategies for the task of knowledge base completion.

2   Preliminaries

Given a set of entities $\mathcal{E}$ and a set of relations $\mathcal{R}$, a knowledge base $\mathcal{K} \subseteq \mathcal{E} \times \mathcal{R} \times \mathcal{E}$ is a set of triples (i, k, j), where $i, j \in \mathcal{E}$ and $k \in \mathcal{R}$. We refer to i, k and j as the *subject*, *relation*, and *object* to the triple, respectively.

Embedding models. A KGE model associates an *embedding* $e_i \in \mathbb{R}^{d_e}$ and $r_k \in \mathbb{R}^{d_r}$ with each entity i and relation k, resp. We refer to d_e and $d_r \in \mathbb{N}^+$ as the *size* of the embeddings. Each KGE model uses a *scoring function* $s : \mathcal{E} \times \mathcal{R} \times \mathcal{E} \to \mathbb{R}$ to associate a score $s(i, k, j)$ to each triple $(i, k, j) \in \mathcal{E} \times \mathcal{R} \times \mathcal{E}$. The scores induce a ranking: triples with high scores are considered more likely to be true than triples with low scores. Roughly speaking, the models try to find embeddings that capture the structure of the entire knowledge graph well. In this work, we consider a popular family of embedding models called bilinear models.

Bilinear KGE models. Bilinear models use the relation embedding $r_k \in \mathbb{R}^{d_r}$ to construct a *mixing matrix* $R_k \in \mathbb{R}^{d_e \times d_e}$, and they use scoring function $s(i, k, j) = e_i^T R_k e_j$. The models differ mainly in how R_k is constructed. Unless stated otherwise, the models use the same embedding sizes for entities and relations (i.e., $d_r = d_e$).

RESCAL (Nickel et al., 2011) is the most general bilinear model: it sets $d_r = d_e^2$ and stores in r_k the values of each entry of R_k. Analogy (Liu et al., 2017) constrains $R_k \in \mathbb{R}^{d_e \times d_e}$ to a block diagonal matrix in which each block is either (i) a real scalar or (ii) a 2×2 matrix of form $\begin{pmatrix} x & -y \\ y & x \end{pmatrix}$ with $x, y \in \mathbb{R}$. DistMult (Carroll and Chang, 1970; Yang et al., 2014) is a symmetric factorization model with $R_k = \text{diag}\,(r_k)$ or, equivalently, considers only case (i) of Analogy. ComplEx (Trouillon et al., 2016) and HolE (Nickel et al., 2016b) are equivalent to a model that restricts R_k to case (ii). TransE (Bordes et al., 2013) is a translation-based model with scoring function $s(i, k, j) = - \|e_i + r_k - e_j\|_2$ (or $\|\cdot\|_1$); it can also be written in bilinear form (Wang et al., 2018).

Rule learning. Rule learning methods derive logical rules that encode dependencies found in the KBs (Galárraga et al., 2013). We consider a simple rule-based model called RuleN (Meilicke et al., 2018) as baseline. The model learns (weighted) implication rules of form

$$\begin{aligned} r(i, j) &\leftarrow r_1(i, z_1) \wedge \cdots \wedge r_n(z_n, j) \\ r(i, c) &\leftarrow \exists z . r(i, z) \end{aligned}$$

where r_i are relations, c is a constant entity, and i, j, and z_i are variables quantified over entities. To perform KBC, rule-based models query the KB for instances of the bodies of each rule and interpret the corresponding head as (weighted) predicted fact.

3   Evaluation Protocols

We first review two widely used evaluation protocols for QA. We then argue that these protocols are not well-suited for assessing KBC performance, because they focus on a small subset of all possible facts for a given relation. We then introduce the entity-pair ranking (PR) protocol and discuss its advantages and potential shortcomings.

3.1 Current Evaluation Protocols

The triple classification (TC) or the entity ranking (ER) protocols are commonly used to assess KGE model performance, where ER is arguably the most widely adopted protocol. We assume throughout that only true but no false triples are available (as is commonly the case), and that the available true triples are divided into training, validation, and test triples.

Triple classification (TC) The goal of triple classification is to test the model's ability to discriminate between true and false triples (Socher et al., 2013). Since only true triples are available in practice, pseudo-negative triples are generated by randomly replacing either the subject or the object of each test triple by a random entity (that appears as a subject or object in the considered relation). All triples are then classified as positive or negative according to the KGE scores. In particular, triple (i, k, j) is classified as positive if its score $s(i, k, j)$ exceeds a relation-specific decision threshold τ_k (learned on validation data using the same procedure). Model performance is assessed by classification accuracy.

Entity ranking (ER) ER assesses model performance by testing its ability to perform QA (as defined before). In particular, for each test triple $t = (i, k, j)$, two questions $q_s = (?, k, j)$ and $q_o = (i, k, ?)$ are generated. For question q_s, all entities $i' \in \mathcal{E}$ are ranked based on the score $s(i', k, j)$. To avoid misleading results, entities $i' \neq i$ that correspond to observed triples in the dataset—i.e., (i', k, j) occurs in the training/validation/test triples—are discarded to obtain a *filtered ranking*. The same process is applied for question q_o. Model performance is evaluated based on the recorded positions of the test triples in the filtered ranking. Models that tend to rank test triples (known to be true) higher than unknown triples (assumed to be false) are thus considered superior. Usually, the micro-average of *filtered Hits@K*—i.e., the proportion of test triples ranking in the top-K—and *filtered MRR*—i.e., the mean reciprocal rank of the test triples—are used to assess model performance.

3.2 Discussion

Wang et al. (2018) found that most models achieve a TC accuracy of at least 93% on a benchmark dataset. This is because each test triple is compared against a single negative triple, and due to the high number of possible negative triples, it is unlikely that the chosen triple has a high predicted score, rendering most classification tasks "easy". Consequently, the accuracy of triple classification overestimates model performance. This protocol is less adopted in recent work.

We argue that ER is appropriate to evaluate QA performance, but may overestimate model performance for KBC. Since ER generates questions from true test triples, it only asks questions that are *known to have a correct answer*. The question itself thus provides useful information. This perfectly matches QA, but it does not match KBC where such information is not available.

To better illustrate why ER can lead to misleading assessment of a model's KBC performance, consider the DistMult model and the asymmetric relation *nominatedFor*. As described in Sec. 2, DistMult models all relations as symmetric in that $s(i, k, j) = s(j, k, i)$. Now consider triple $t = (H.\ Simon,\ nominatedFor,\ Nobel\ Prize)$, and let us suppose that the model correctly assigns t a high score $s(t)$. Then the inverse triple $t' = (Nobel\ Prize,\ nominatedFor,\ H.\ Simon)$ will also obtain a high score since $s(t') = s(t)$. Thus the score produced by DistMult does not discriminate between the true triple t and the false triple t'. In ER, however, questions about t' are never asked; there is no test triple for this relation containing either *Nobel Prize* as subject or *H. Simon* as object. The symmetry of DistMult's prediction thus barely affects its performance under the ER protocol.

For another example, consider TransE and the relation $k = marriedTo$, which is symmetric but not reflexive. One can show that for all (i, k, j), the TransE scores satisfy

$$
\begin{aligned}
&s(i, k, j) + s(j, k, i) \\
&= -\|e_i + r_k - e_j\| - \|e_j + r_k - e_i\| \\
&\leq -\|e_i + 0 - e_j\| - \|e_j + 0 - e_i\|.
\end{aligned}
$$

For symmetric relations, TransE should aim to assign high scores to both (i, k, j) and (j, k, i). To do so, TransE has the tendency to push the relation embedding r_k towards 0 as well as e_i and e_j towards each other. But when $r_k \approx 0$, then $s(i, k, i)$ is high for all i, so that the relation is treated as if it were reflexive. Again, in ER, this property only slightly influences the results: there is only one "reflexive" tuple in each filtered entity list so that the correct answer i for question $(?, k, j)$ ranks at most one position lower.

More expressive models such as RESCAL or ComplEx do not have such inherent limitations. Nevertheless, our experimental study shows that these models (at least in the way are currently trained) also tend to assign high scores to false triples.

3.3 Entity-Pair Ranking Protocol

We propose a simple alternative protocol called entity-pair ranking (PR). The protocol is more suitable to assess a model's KBC performance (although it is not without flaws either; see below). PR proceeds as follows: for each relation k, we use the KGE model to rank all triples for a specified relation k, i.e., to rank all answers to question $(?, k, ?)$. As in ER, we filter out all triples that occur in the training and validation data to obtain a filtered ranking, i.e., to only rank triples that were not used during model training. If a model tends to assign a high score to negative triples, its performance is likely to be negatively affected because it becomes harder for true triples to rank high.

Note that the number of candidate answers considered by PR is much larger than those considered by ER. Consider a relation k and let $\mathcal{T}_k$ be the set of test triples for relation k. Then ER considers $2|\mathcal{T}_k| |\mathcal{E}|$ candidates in total during evaluation, while PR considers $|\mathcal{E}|^2$ candidates. Moreover, PR considers all test triples in $\mathcal{T}_k$ simultaneously instead of sequentially. For this reason, we cannot use the MRR metric commonly used in ER. Instead, we assess model performance using weighted *MAP@K*—i.e., the weighted mean average precision in the top-K filtered results—and weighted *Hits@K*—i.e., the weighted percentage of test triples in the top-K filtered results. We weight the influence of relation k proportionally to its number of test triples (capped at K), thereby closely following ER:

$$\text{MAP@}K = \sum_{k \in \mathcal{R}} \text{AP}_k\text{@}K \times \frac{\min(K, |\mathcal{T}_k|)}{\sum_{k' \in \mathcal{R}} \min(K, |\mathcal{T}_{k'}|)}$$

$$\text{Hits@}K = \sum_{k \in \mathcal{R}} \text{Hits}_k\text{@}K \times \frac{\min(K, |\mathcal{T}_k|)}{\sum_{k' \in \mathcal{R}} \min(K, |\mathcal{T}_{k'}|)}.$$

Here $\text{AP}_k\text{@}K$ is the average precision of the top-K list (w.r.t. test triples $\mathcal{T}_k$) and $\text{Hits}_k\text{@}K$ refers to the fraction of test triples in the top-K list. Note that K should be chosen much larger for PR than

Dataset	$|\mathcal{E}|$	$|\mathcal{R}|$	$|\mathcal{T}^{train}|$	$|\mathcal{T}^{val}|$	$|\mathcal{T}^{test}|$
FB15K	14 951	1 345	483 142	50 000	59 071
FB-237	14 505	237	272 115	17 535	20 466
WN18	40 943	18	141 442	5 000	5 000
WNRR	40 559	11	86 835	2 824	2 924

Table 1: Dataset statistics

for ER since it roughly corresponds to the number of triples we aim to predict for relation k.

The PR protocol is more suited to evaluate KBC performance because it considers all model predictions. The protocol also has some disadvantages, however. First, as ER, the PR protocol may underestimate model performance due to unobserved true triples ranked high by the model. Since a larger number of candidates is considered, PR may be more sensitive to this problem than ER. We explore the effect of underestimation in our empirical study in Sec. 4.4. Another concern with PR is its potentially high computational cost. For current benchmark datasets, we found that the PR evaluation is feasible. Generally, one may argue that an embedding model is suitable for KBC only if it is feasible to determine high-scoring triples in a sufficiently efficient way. Since PR only requires the computation of the top-K predictions, performance can potentially be improved using techniques such as maximum inner-product search Shrivastava and Li (2014).

4 Experimental Study

We conducted an experimental study to assess the performance of various bilinear embedding models for KBC.[2] All datasets, experimental results, and source code are publicly available.[3] For all models, we performed evaluation under both the ER and PR protocols in order to assess their performance for the QA and KBC tasks, respectively. We found that many KGE models provided good ER but low PR performance. We also considered a simple rule-based system called *RuleN* (Meilicke et al., 2018), which provided good performance under the ER protocol, and found that RuleN performed better in both ER and PR. Our results imply that more research into KGE models for KBC is needed.

We also investigated the extent to which PR

---

[2]Some other KGE models do not support KBC directly due to their architecture; e.g., ConvE (Dettmers et al., 2018).

[3]http://www.uni-mannheim.de/dws/research/resources/kge-eval/

underestimates model performance due to unobserved true triples. We found that underestimation is not the main reason for the low PR performance of many KGE models; in fact, many KGE models ranked high clearly wrong tuples (e.g., with incorrect types).

4.1 Experimental Setup

Datasets. We used the four common KBC benchmark datasets: FB15K, WN18, FB-237, and WNRR. The latter two datasets were created since the former two datasets were considered too easy for embedding models (based on ER). Key dataset statistics are summarized in Table 1.

Negative sampling. We trained the embedding models using negative sampling to obtain pseudo-negative triples. We consider three sampling strategies in our experiments:

Perturb 1: For each training triple $t = (i, k, j)$, sample pseudo-negative triples by randomly replacing either i or j with a random entity (but such that the resulting triple is unobserved). This strategy matches ER, which is based on questions $(?, k, j)$ and $(i, k, ?)$.

Perturb 1-R: For each training triple $t = (i, k, j)$, sample pseudo-negative triples by randomly replacing either i, k or j. The generated negative samples are not compared with the training set (Liu et al., 2017).

Perturb 2: For each training triple $t = (i, k, j)$, obtain pseudo-negative triples by randomly sampling unobserved tuples for relation k. This method appears more suited to PR.

Training and implementation. We trained DistMult, ComplEx, Analogy and RESCAL with AdaGrad (Duchi et al., 2011) using binary cross-entropy loss. We used pair-wise ranking loss for TransE (as it always produces negative scores). All embeddding models are implemented on top of the code of Liu et al. (2017)[4] in C++ using OpenMP. For RuleN, we use the original implementation provided by the authors. The evaluation protocols were written in Python, with Bottleneck[5] used for efficiently obtaining the top-K entries for PR. We found PR (which took $\approx$30–90 minutes) was about 3–4 times slower than ER .

Hyperparameters. The best hyperparameters were selected based on MRR (for ER) and

MAP@100 (for PR) on the validation data. For both protocols, we performed an exhaustive grid search over the following hyperparameter settings: $d_e \in \{100, 150, 200\}$, weight of l_2-regularization $\lambda \in \{0.1, 0.01, 0.001\}$, learning rate $\eta \in \{0.01, 0.1\}$, negative sampling strategies *Perturb 1*, *Perturb 2* and *Perturb 1-R*,[6] and margin hyperparameter $\gamma \in \{0.5, 1, 2, 3, 4\}$ for TransE. For each training triple, we sampled 6 pseudo-negative triples. To keep effort tractable, we only used the most frequent relations from each dataset for hyperparameter tuning (top-5, top-5, top-15, and top-30 most frequent relations for WN18, WNRR, FB-237 and FB-15k, respectively). We trained each model for up to 500 epochs during grid search. In all cases, we evaluated model performance every 50 epochs and used the overall best-performing model. For RuleN, we used the best settings reported by the authors for ER (Meilicke et al., 2018). For PR, we learned path rules of length 2 using a sampling size of 500 for FB15K and FB-237. For WN18 and WNRR, we learned path rules of length 3 and sampling size of 500.

4.2 Performance Results with ER

Table 2 summarizes the ER results. Embedding models perform competitively with respect to RuleN on all datasets, except for their MRR performance on FB15K. Notice that this generally holds even for the more restricted models (TransE and DistMult) on the more challenging datasets, which were created after criticizing FB15K and WN18 as too easy (Toutanova and Chen, 2015; Dettmers et al., 2018). In particular, although DistMult can only model symmetric relations, and although most relations in these datasets are asymmetric, DistMult has good ER performance. Likewise, TransE achieved great performance in Hits@10 on all datasets, including WN18 which contains a large number of symmetric relations, which are not easily modeled by TransE.

4.3 Performance Results with PR

The evaluation results of PR with $K = 100$ are summarized in Table 3. Note that Tables 2 and 3 are not directly comparable: they measure different tasks. Also note that we use a different value of K, which in PR corresponds to the number of predicted facts per relation. We discuss the effect of the choice of K later.

---

[4]https://github.com/quark0/ANALOGY

[5]https://pypi.org/project/Bottleneck/

[6]We found that *Perturb-2* can be useful in both protocols.

Dataset	FB15K		FB-237		WN18		WNRR	
Model	MRR	Hits@10	MRR	Hits@10	MRR	Hits@10	MRR	Hits@10
DistMult	0.660	0.845	0.270	0.432	0.790	0.937	0.432	0.474
TransE	0.500	0.777	0.290	0.466	0.720	0.908	0.220	0.491
ComplEx	0.700	0.835	0.280	0.435	0.940	0.948	0.440	0.481
Analogy	0.700	0.836	0.270	0.433	0.941	0.942	0.440	0.486
RESCAL	0.464	0.699	0.270	0.427	0.920	0.939	0.420	0.447
RuleN	0.805	0.870	0.260	0.420	0.950	0.958	—	0.536

Table 2: Results with the entity ranking protocol (ER), which assesses QA performance

Dataset	FB15K		FB-237		WN18		WNRR	
Model	MAP@100	Hits@100	MAP@100	Hits@100	MAP@100	Hits@100	MAP@100	Hits@100
DistMult	0.013	0.104	0.030	0.042	0.079	0.097	0.141	0.178
TransE	0.211	0.363	0.079	0.176	0.223	0.315	0.020	0.013
ComplEx	0.311	0.486	0.071	0.166	0.825	0.904	0.168	0.200
Analogy	0.188	0.348	0.049	0.143	0.776	0.874	0.154	0.198
RESCAL	0.150	0.303	0.067	0.150	0.482	0.609	0.131	0.138
RuleN	0.774	0.837	0.076	0.158	0.948	0.968	0.215	0.251

Table 3: Results with the entity-pair ranking protocol (PR), which assesses KBC performance

For the embeddings, observe that with the exception of Analogy and ComplEx on WN18, the performance of all models is unsatisfactory on all datasets, especially when compared with RuleN on FB15K and WN18, which were previously considered to be too easy for embedding models. Specifically, DistMult's Hits@100 is slightly less than 10% on WN18, meaning that if we add the top 100 ranked triples to the KB, over 90% of what is added is likely false. Even when using ComplEx, the best model on FB15K, we would potentially add more than 50% false triples. This implies that embedding models cannot capture simple rules successfully. The notable exceptions are ComplEx and Analogy on WN18, although both are still behind RuleN. TransE and DistMult did not achieve competitive results on WN18. In addition, DistMult did not achieve competitive results on FB15K and FB-237 and TransE did not achieve competitive results in WNRR. In general, ComplEx and Analogy performed consistently better than other models across different datasets. When compared with the RuleN baseline, however, the performance of these models was often not satisfactory. This suggests that better KGE models and/or training strategies are needed for KBC.

RuleN did not perform well on FB-237 and WNRR, likely because the way these datasets were constructed makes them intrinsically difficult for rule-based methods (Meilicke et al., 2018). This is reflected in both ER and PR results.

To better understand the change in performance of TransE and DistMult, we investigated their predictions for the top-5 most frequent relations on WN18. Table 4 shows the number of test triples appearing in the top-100 for each relation (after filtering triples from the training and validation sets). The numbers in parentheses are discussed in Section 4.4.

We found that DistMult worked well on the symmetric relation *derivationally related form*, where its symmetry assumption clearly helps. Here 93% of the training data consists of symmetric pairs (i.e., (i, k, j) and (j, k, i)), and 88% of the test triples have its symmetric counterpart in the training set. In contrast, TransE contained no test triples for *derivationally related form* in the top-100 list. We found that the norm of the embedding vector of this relation was 0.1, which was considerably smaller than for the other relations (avg. 1.4). This supports our argument that TransE tends to push symmetric relation embeddings to $\mathbf{0}$.

Note that while *hyponymy, hypernymy, member meronym* and *member holonym* are semantically transitive, the dataset contains almost exclusively their transitive core, i.e., the dataset (both train and test) does not contain many of the transitive links of the relations. As a result, models that cannot handle transitivity well may still produce good results. This might explain why TransE performed better for these relations than for *derivationally related form*. DistMult did not perform well on

Relation	Model					
	DistMult	TransE	ComplEx	Analogy	RESCAL	RuleN
hyponymy	1 (1)	18 (32)	99 (99)	99 (99)	92 (93)	100 (100)
hypernymy	0 (0)	5 (33)	99 (99)	99 (99)	96 (98)	100 (100)
derivationally related form	100 (100)	0 (0)	100 (100)	100 (100)	6 (68)	100 (100)
member meronym	0 (0)	18 (41)	74 (84)	83 (85)	44 (63)	100 (100)
member holonym	0 (0)	16 (47)	74 (83)	83 (85)	37 (54)	100 (100)

Table 4: Number of test triples in the top-100 filtered predictions on WN18. An estimate of the number of true triples in the top-100 list is given in parentheses.

these relations (they are asymmetric). ComplEx and Analogy showed superior performance across all relations. RESCAL is in between, most likely due to difficulties in finding a good parameterization. However, it is unclear to us why TransE performed well on FB15K and FB-237.

To investigate model performance in PR for different values of K, we give the curves of Hits@K as a function of K for all datasets in Fig. 1. ComplEx and Analogy, which are universal models, performed best for large K w.r.t. other embedding models. Similarly, TransE works the best for small values of K on FB15K and FB-237. Notice that RuleN performs considerably better on FB15K, WN18 and WNRR, while it still performs competitively on FB-237.

4.4 Influence of Unobserved True Triples

Since all datasets are based on incomplete knowledge bases, all evaluation protocols may systematically underestimate model performance. In particular, any true triple t that is neither in the training, nor validation, nor test data is treated as negative during ranking-based evaluations. A model which correctly ranks t high is thus penalized. PR might be particularly sensitive to this due to the large number of candidates considered.

It is generally unclear how to design an automatic evaluation strategy that avoids this problem. Manual labeling can be used to address this, but it may sometimes be infeasible given the large number of relations, entities, and models for KBC.

To explore such underestimation effect in PR, we decoded the unobserved triples in the top-100 predictions of the 5 most frequent relations of WN18. We then checked whether those triples are implied by the symmetry and transitivity properties of each relation. In Table 4, we give the resulting number of triples in parentheses (i.e., number of test triples + implied triples). We observed that underestimation indeed happened. TransE was mostly affected, but still did not lead to competi-

tive results when compared to ComplEx and Analogy. RuleN achieves the best possible results in all 5 relations. These results suggest that (1) underestimation is indeed a concern, and (2) the results in PR can nevertheless give an indication of relative model performance.

4.5 Type Filtering

When background knowledge (BK) is available, embedding models only need to score triples consistent with the BK. We explored whether their performance can be improved by filtering out type-inconsistent triples from each model's predictions. Notice that this is inherently what rule-based approaches do, since all predicted candidates will be type-consistent. In particular, we investigated how model performance is affected when we filter out predictions that violate type constraints (domain and range of each relation). If a model's performance improves with such type filtering, it must have ranked tuples with incorrect types high in the first place. We can thus assess to what extent models capture entity types as well as the domain and range of the relations.

We extracted from Freebase type definitions for entities and domain and range constraints for relations. We also added the domain (or range) of a relation k to the type set of each subject (or object) entity which appeared in k. We obtained types for all entities in both FB datasets, and domain/range specifications for roughly 93% of relations in FB15K and 97% of relations in FB-237. The remaining relations were evaluated as before.

We report in Table 5 the Hits@100 and MAP@100 as well as their absolute improvement (in parentheses) w.r.t. Table 3. We also include the results of RuleN from Table 3, which are already type-consistent. The results show that all KGE models improve by type filtering; thus all models do predict triples with incorrect types. In particular, DistMult shows considerable improvement on both datasets. Indeed, about 90% of the

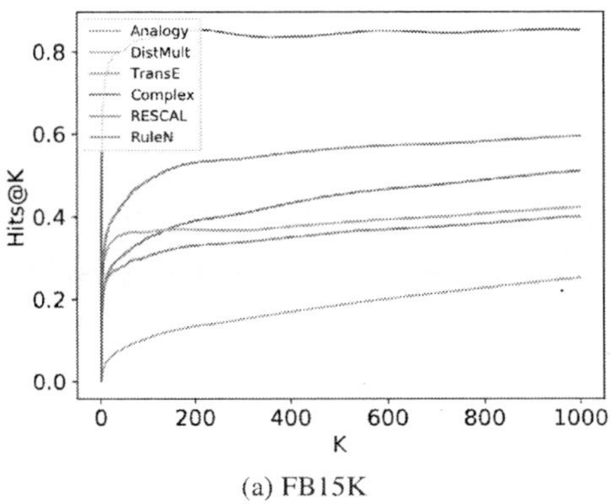

(a) FB15K

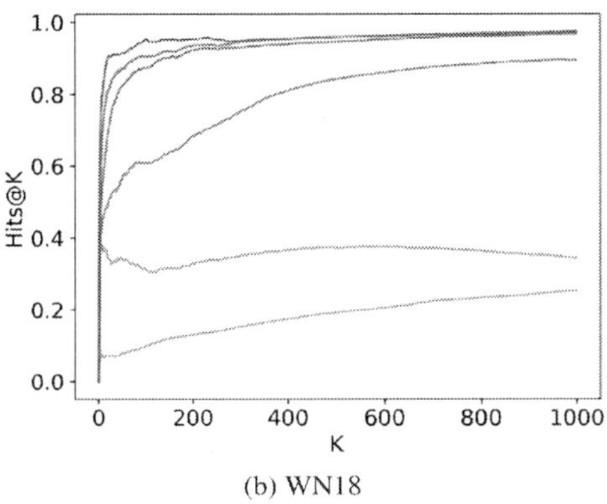

(b) WN18

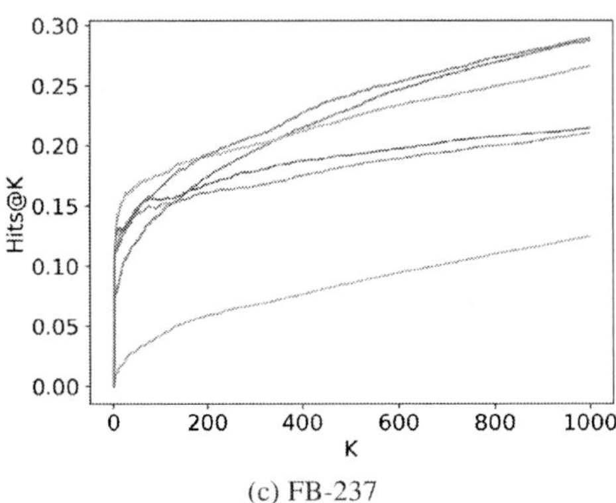

(c) FB-237

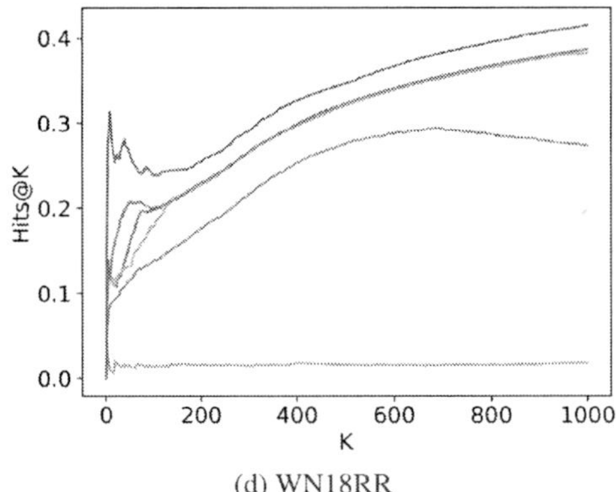

(d) WN18RR

Figure 1: Hits@K with PR as a function of K

Data	Model	MAP@K (%)		Hits@K (%)	
FB15K	DistMult	18.8	(+17.5)	36.4	(+26.0)
	TransE	25.7	(+4.5)	41.7	(+5.4)
	ComplEx	53.1	(+22.0)	69.6	(+21.0)
	Analogy	41.3	(+22.5)	61.5	(+26.7)
	RESCAL	16.7	(+1.7)	32.8	(+2.5)
	RuleN	77.4	(0.0)	83.7	(0.0)
FB-237	DistMult	9.5	(+9.2)	18.1	(+13.9)
	TransE	11.3	(+3.4)	21.2	(+3.6)
	ComplEx	11.3	(+4.2)	21.8	(+5.2)
	Analogy	10.5	(+5.6)	20.9	(+6.6)
	RESCAL	10.2	(+3.5)	19.0	(+4.0)
	RuleN	7.6	(0.0)	15.8	(0.0)

Table 5: Results with PR using type filtering (K = 100).

relations in FB15K (about 85% for FB-237) have a different type for their domain and range. As DistMult treats all relations as symmetric, it introduces a wrong triple for each true triple into the top-K list on these relations; type filtering allows us to ignore these wrong tuples. This is also consistent with DistMult's improved performance under ER, where type constraints are implicitly used since only questions with correct types are considered. Interestingly, ComplEx and Analogy improved considerably on FB15K, suggesting that the best performing embedding models on this dataset are still making a considerable number of type-inconsistent predictions. On FB15K, the relative ranking of the models with type filtering is roughly equal to the one without type filtering. On the harder FB-237 dataset, all models now perform similarly. Notice that when compared with RuleN, embedding models are still behind on FB15K, but are no longer behind on FB-237.

5 Conclusion

We investigated whether current embedding models provide good results for knowledge base completion, i.e., the task or inferring new facts from an incomplete knowledge base. We argued that the commonly-used ER evaluation protocol is not suited to answer this question, and proposed the PR evaluation protocol as an alternative. We evaluated a number of popular KGE models under the ER and PR protocols and found that most KGE models obtained good results under the ER but not the PR protocol. Therefore, more research into embedding models and their training is needed to assess whether, when, and how KGE models can be exploited for knowledge base completion.

References

Abdalghani Abujabal, Mohamed Yahya, Mirek Riedewald, and Gerhard Weikum. 2017. Automated template generation for question answering over knowledge graphs. In *Proceedings of the 26th International Conference on World Wide Web (WWW)*.

Antoine Bordes, Nicolas Usunier, Alberto García-Durán, Jason Weston, and Oksana Yakhnenko. 2013. Translating embeddings for modeling multi-relational data. In *Advances in Neural Information Processing Systems (NIPS)*.

J. Douglas Carroll and Jih-Jie Chang. 1970. Analysis of individual differences in multidimensional scaling via an n-way generalization of "Eckart-Young" decomposition. *Psychometrika*, 35(3).

Tim Dettmers, Pasquale Minervini, Pontus Stenetorp, and Sebastian Riedel. 2018. Convolutional 2D knowledge graph embeddings. In *Association for the Advancement of Artificial Intelligence (AAAI)*.

John C. Duchi, Elad Hazan, and Yoram Singer. 2011. Adaptive subgradient methods for online learning and stochastic optimization. *Journal of Machine Learning Research*, 12.

Luis Antonio Galárraga, Christina Teflioudi, Katja Hose, and Fabian Suchanek. 2013. AMIE: association rule mining under incomplete evidence in ontological knowledge bases. In *Proceedings of the 22nd international conference on World Wide Web (WWW)*.

Armand Joulin, Edouard Grave, Piotr Bojanowski, Maximilian Nickel, and Tomas Mikolov. 2017. Fast linear model for knowledge graph embeddings. *CoRR*, abs/1710.10881.

Rudolf Kadlec, Ondrej Bajgar, and Jan Kleindienst. 2017. Knowledge base completion: Baselines strike back. In *Workshop on Representation Learning for NLP (RepL4NLP@ACL)*.

Hanxiao Liu, Yuexin Wu, and Yiming Yang. 2017. Analogical inference for multi-relational embeddings. In *International Conference on Machine Learning (ICML)*.

Christian Meilicke, Manuel Fink, Yanjie Wang, Daniel Ruffinelli, Rainer Gemulla, and Heiner Stuckenschmidt. 2018. Fine-grained evaluation of rule- and embedding-based systems for knowledge graph completion. In *International Semantic Web Conference (ISWC)*.

Maximilian Nickel, Kevin Murphy, Volker Tresp, and Evgeniy Gabrilovich. 2016a. A review of relational machine learning for knowledge graphs. *Proceedings of the IEEE*, 104(1).

Maximilian Nickel, Lorenzo Rosasco, and Tomaso A. Poggio. 2016b. Holographic embeddings of knowledge graphs. In *Association for the Advancement of Artificial Intelligence (AAAI)*.

Maximilian Nickel, Volker Tresp, and Hans-Peter Kriegel. 2011. A three-way model for collective learning on multi-relational data. In *International Conference on Machine Learning (ICML)*.

Wei Shen, Jianyong Wang, and Jiawei Han. 2015. Entity linking with a knowledge base: Issues, techniques, and solutions. *IEEE Transactions on Knowledge and Data Engineering (TKDE)*, 27(2).

Anshumali Shrivastava and Ping Li. 2014. Asymmetric LSH (ALSH) for sublinear time maximum inner product search (MIPS). In *Advances in Neural Information Processing Systems (NIPS)*.

Richard Socher, Danqi Chen, Christopher D. Manning, and Andrew Y. Ng. 2013. Reasoning with neural tensor networks for knowledge base completion. In *Advances in Neural Information Processing Systems (NIPS)*.

Kristina Toutanova and Danqi Chen. 2015. Observed versus latent features for knowledge base and text inference. In *Proceedings of the 3rd Workshop on Continuous Vector Space Models and their Compositionality*.

Théo Trouillon, Johannes Welbl, Sebastian Riedel, Éric Gaussier, and Guillaume Bouchard. 2016. Complex embeddings for simple link prediction. In *International Conference on Machine Learning (ICML)*.

Yanjie Wang, Rainer Gemulla, and Hui Li. 2018. On multi-relational link prediction with bilinear models. In *Association for the Advancement of Artificial Intelligence (AAAI)*.

Robert West, Evgeniy Gabrilovich, Kevin Murphy, Shaohua Sun, Rahul Gupta, and Dekang Lin. 2014. Knowledge base completion via search-based question answering. In *International World Wide Web Conference (WWW)*.

Bishan Yang, Wen-tau Yih, Xiaodong He, Jianfeng Gao, and Li Deng. 2014. Embedding entities and relations for learning and inference in knowledge bases. International Conference on Learning Representations (ICLR).

Constructive Type-Logical Supertagging with Self-Attention Networks

Konstantinos Kogkalidis
Utrecht University
k.kogkalidis@uu.nl

Michael Moortgat
Utrecht University
m.j.moortgat@uu.nl

Tejaswini Deoskar
Utrecht University
t.deoskar@uu.nl

Abstract

We propose a novel application of self-attention networks towards grammar induction. We present an attention-based supertagger for a refined type-logical grammar, trained on constructing types inductively. In addition to achieving a high overall type accuracy, our model is able to learn the syntax of the grammar's type system along with its denotational semantics. This lifts the closed world assumption commonly made by lexicalized grammar supertaggers, greatly enhancing its generalization potential. This is evidenced both by its adequate accuracy over sparse word types and its ability to correctly construct complex types never seen during training, which, to the best of our knowledge, was as of yet unaccomplished.

1 Introduction

Categorial Grammars, in their various incarnations, posit a functional view on parsing: words are assigned simple or complex categories (or: types); their composition is modeled in terms of functor-argument relationships. Complex categories wear their combinatorics on their sleeve, which means that most of the phrasal structure is internalized within the categories themselves; performing the categorial assignment process for a sequence of words, i.e. *supertagging*, amounts to almost parsing (Bangalore and Joshi, 1999).

In machine learning literature, supertagging is commonly viewed as a particular case of sequence labeling (Graves, 2012). This perspective points to the immediate applicability of established, high-performing neural architectures; indeed, recurrent models have successfully been employed (e.g. within the context of Combinatory Categorial Grammars (CCG) (Steedman, 2000)), achieving impressive results (Vaswani et al., 2016). However, this perspective comes at a cost; the supertagger's co-domain, i.e., the different categories it may assign, is considered fixed, as defined by the set of unique categories in the training data. Additionally, some categories have disproportionately low frequencies compared to the more common ones, leading to severe sparsity issues. Since under-represented categories are very hard to learn, in practice models are evaluated and compared based on their accuracy over categories with occurrence counts above a certain threshold, a small subset of the full category set.

This practical concession has two side-effects. The first pertains to the supertagger's inability to capture rare syntactic phenomena. Although the percentage of sentences that may not be correctly analyzed due to the missing categories is usually relatively small, it still places an upper bound on the resulting parser's strength which is hard to ignore. The second, and perhaps more far reaching, consequence is the implicit constraint it places on the grammar itself. Essentially, the grammar must be sufficiently coarse while also allocating most of its probability mass on a small number of unique categories. Grammars enjoying a higher level of analytical sophistication are practically unusable, since the associated supertagger would require prohibitive amounts of data to overcome their inherent sparsity.

We take a different view on the problem, instead treating it as sequence transduction. We propose a novel supertagger based on the Transformer architecture (Vaswani et al., 2017) that is capable of constructing categories inductively, bypassing the aforementioned limitations. We test our model on a highly-refined, automatically extracted type-logical grammar for written Dutch, where it achieves competitive results for high frequency categories, while acquiring the ability to treat rare and even unseen categories adequately.

Proceedings of the 4th Workshop on Representation Learning for NLP (RepL4NLP-2019), pages 113–123
Florence, Italy, August 2, 2019. ©2019 Association for Computational Linguistics

2 Type-Logical Grammars

The type-logical strand of categorial grammar adopts a proof-theoretic perspective on natural language syntax and semantics: checking whether a phrase is syntactically well-formed amounts to a process of logical deduction deriving its type from the types of its constituent parts (Moot and Retoré, 2012). What counts as a valid deduction depends on the type logic used. The type logic we aim for is a variation on the simply typed fragment of Multiplicative Intuitionistic Linear Logic (MILL), where the type-forming operation of interest is linear implication (for a brief but instructive introduction, refer to Wadler (1993)). Types are inductively defined by the following grammar:

$$T ::= A \mid T_1 \xrightarrow{d} T_2 \tag{1}$$

where T, T_1, T_2 are types, A is an atomic type and $\xrightarrow{d}$ an implication arrow, further subcategorized by the label d.

Atomic types are assigned to phrases that are considered 'complete', e.g. NP for noun phrase, PRON for pronoun, etc. Complex types, on the other hand, are the type signatures of binary functors that compose with a single word or phrase to produce a larger phrase; for instance NP $\xrightarrow{su}$ S corresponds to a functor that consumes a noun phrase playing the subject role to create a sentence — an intransitive verb.

The logic provides *judgements* of the form $\Gamma \vdash B$, stating that from a multiset of assumptions $\Gamma = A_1, \ldots A_n$ one can derive conclusion B. In addition to the axiom $A \vdash A$, there are two rules of inference; implication elimination (2) and implication introduction (3)[1]. Intuitively, the first says that if one has a judgement of the form $\Gamma \vdash A \to B$ and a judgement of the form $\Delta \vdash A$, one can deduce that assumptions Γ and Δ together derive a proposition B. Similarly, the second says that if one can derive B from assumptions A and Γ together, then from Γ alone one can derive an implication $A \to B$.

$$\frac{\Gamma \vdash A \to B \quad \Delta \vdash A}{\Gamma, \Delta \vdash B} \to E \tag{2}$$

$$\frac{A, \Gamma \vdash B}{\Gamma \vdash A \to B} \to I \tag{3}$$

---

[1]For labeled implications $\xrightarrow{d}$, we make sure that composition is with respect to the d dependency relation.

The view of language as a linear type system offers many meaningful insights. In addition to the mentioned correspondence between parse and proof, the Curry-Howard 'proofs-as-programs' interpretation guarantees a direct translation from proofs to computations. The two rules necessary for proof construction have their computational analogues in function application and abstraction respectively, a link that paves the way to seamlessly move from a syntactic derivation to a program that computes the associated meaning in a compositional manner.

3 Constructive Supertagging

Categorial grammars assign denotational semantics to types, which are in turn defined via a set of inductive rules, as in (1). These, in effect, are the productions a simple, context-free grammar; a *grammar of types* underlying the grammar of sentences. In this light, any type may be viewed as a word of this simple type grammar's language; a regularity which we can try to exploit.

Considering neural networks' established ability of implicitly learning context-free grammars (Gers and Schmidhuber, 2001), it is reasonable to expect that, given enough representational capacity and a robust training process, a network should be able to learn a context-free grammar embedded within a wider sequence labeling task. Jointly acquiring the two amounts to learning a) how to produce types, including novel ones, and b) which types to produce under different contexts, essentially providing all of the necessary building blocks for a supertagger with unrestricted co-domain. To that end, we may represent a single type as a sequence of characters over a fixed vocabulary, defined as the union of atomic types and type forming operators (in the case of type-logical grammars, the latter being n-ary logical connectives). A sequence of types is then simply the concatenation of their corresponding representations, where type boundaries can be marked by a special separation symbol.

The problem then boils down to learning how to transduce a sequence of words onto a sequence of unfolded types. This can be pictured as a case of sequence-to-sequence translation, operating on word level input and producing character level output, with the source language now being the natural language and the target language being the language defined by the syntax and semantics of

114

our categorial grammar.

4 Related Work

Supertagging has been standard practice for lexicalized grammars with complex lexical entries since the work of Bangalore and Joshi (1999). In its original formulation, the categorial assignment process is enacted by an N-gram Markov model. Later work utilized Maximum Entropy models that account for word windows of fixed length, while incorporating expanded lexical features and POS tags as inputs (Clark and Curran, 2004). During the last half of the decade, the advent of word embeddings caused a natural shift towards neural architectures, with recurrent neural networks being established as the prime components of recent supertagging models. Xu et al. (2015) first used simple RNNs for CCG supertagging, which were gradually succeeded by LSTMs (Vaswani et al., 2016; Lewis et al., 2016), also in the context of Tree-Adjoining Grammars (Kasai et al., 2017).

Regardless of the particular implementation, the above works all fall in the same category of sequence labeling architectures. As such, the type vocabulary (i.e. the set of candidate categories) is always considered fixed and pre-specified — it is, in fact, hard coded within the architecture itself (e.g. in the network's final classification layer). The inability of such systems to account for unseen types or even consistently predict rare ones has permeated through the training and evaluation process; a frequency cut-off is usually applied on the corpus, keeping only categories that appear at least 10 times throughout the training set (Clark and Curran, 2004). This limitation has been acknowledged in the past; in the case of CCG, certain classes of syntactic constructions pose significant difficulties for parsing due to categories completely missing from the corpus (Clark et al., 2004). An attempt to address the issue was made in the form of an inference algorithm, which iteratively expands upon the lexicon with new categories for unseen words (Thomforde and Steedman, 2011) — its applicability, however, is narrow, as new categories can often be necessary even for words that have been previously encountered.

We differentiate from relevant work in not employing a type lexicon at all, fixed or adaptive. Rather than providing our system with a vocabulary of types, we seek to instead encode the type construction process directly within the network.

Type prediction is no longer a discernible part of the architecture, but rather manifested via the network's weights as a dynamic generation process, much like a language model for types that is conditioned on the input sentence.

5 Data

5.1 Corpus

The experiments reported on focus on Dutch, a language with relatively free word order that allows us to highlight the benefits of our non-directional type logic. For our data needs, we utilize the Lassy-Small corpus (van Noord et al., 2006). Lassy-Small contains approximately 65000 annotated sentences of written Dutch, comprised of over 1 million words in total. The annotations are DAGs with syntactic category labels at the nodes, and dependency labels at the edges. The possibility of re-entrancy obviates the need for abstract syntactic elements (gaps, traces, etc.) in the annotation of unbounded dependencies and related phenomena.

5.2 Extracted Grammar

To obtain type assignments from the annotation graphs, we design and apply an adaptation of Moortgat and Moot's (2002) extraction algorithm. Following established practice, we assign phrasal heads a functor (complex) type selecting for its dependents. Atomic types are instantiated by a translation table that maps part-of-speech tags and phrasal categories onto their corresponding types.

As remarked above, we diverge from standard categorial practice by making no distinction between rightward and leftward implication (slash and backslash, respectively), rather collapsing both into the direction-agnostic linear implication. We compensate for the possible loss in word-order sensitivity by subcategorizing the implication arrow into a set of distinct linear functions, the names of which are instantiated by the inventory of dependency labels present in the corpus. This decoration amounts to including the labeled dependency materialized by each head (in the context of a particular phrase) within its corresponding type, vastly increasing its informational content. In practical terms, dependency labeling is no longer treated as a task to be solved by the downstream parser; it is now internal to the grammar's type system. To consistently binarize all of our functor types, we impose an obliqueness or-

$$\cfrac{\cfrac{}{\text{geven} \vdash \text{NP} \xrightarrow{\text{obj}} \text{PRON} \xrightarrow{\text{su}} \text{S}_{\text{main}}} L \quad \cfrac{\cfrac{}{\text{enkele} \vdash \text{NP} \xrightarrow{\text{det}} \text{NP}} L \quad \cfrac{}{\text{voorbeelden} \vdash \text{NP}} L}{\text{enkele, voorbeelden} \vdash \text{NP}} \to E}{\cfrac{\text{geven, enkele, voorbeelden} \vdash \text{PRON} \xrightarrow{\text{su}} \text{S}_{\text{main}} \quad \cfrac{}{\text{we} \vdash \text{PRON}} L}{\text{we}(we), \text{geven}(give), \text{enkele}(some), \text{voorbeelden}(examples) \vdash \text{S}_{\text{main}}} \to E}$$

(a) Derivation for "we geven enkele voorbeelden" (*we give some examples*), showcasing a simple transitive verb derivation.

$$\text{Derivation (b)}$$

$$\cfrac{\cfrac{}{\text{welke} \vdash \text{N} \xrightarrow{\text{det}} (\text{N} \xrightarrow{\text{obj}} \text{SV1}) \xrightarrow{\text{body}} \text{WHQ}} L \quad \cfrac{}{\text{rol} \vdash \text{N}} L}{\text{welke, rol} \vdash (\text{N} \xrightarrow{\text{obj}} \text{SV1}) \xrightarrow{\text{body}} \text{WHQ}} \to E \qquad \cfrac{\cfrac{\cfrac{}{\text{spelen} \vdash \text{N} \xrightarrow{\text{obj}} \text{NP} \xrightarrow{\text{su}} \text{SV1}} L \quad \cfrac{}{\text{N} \vdash \text{N}} id}{\text{spelen, N} \vdash \text{NP} \xrightarrow{\text{su}} \text{SV1}} \to E \quad \cfrac{}{\text{typen} \vdash \text{NP}} L}{\cfrac{\text{spelen, typen, N} \vdash \text{SV1}}{\text{spelen, typen} \vdash \text{N} \xrightarrow{\text{obj}} \text{SV1}} \to I} \to E}{\text{welke}(which), \text{rol}(role), \text{spelen}(play), \text{typen}(types) \vdash \text{WHQ}}$$

(b) Derivation for "welke rol spelen typen" (*which role do types play*), showcasing object-relativisation via second-order types. Type SV1 stands for verb-initial sentence clause.

$$\cfrac{\cfrac{}{\text{een} \vdash \text{N} \xrightarrow{\text{det}} \text{NP}} L \quad \cfrac{\cfrac{}{\text{en} \vdash \text{ADJ}^* \xrightarrow{\text{cnj}} \text{N} \xrightarrow{\text{mod}} \text{N}} L \quad \cfrac{}{\text{eenvoudig} \vdash \text{ADJ}} L \quad \cfrac{}{\text{degelijk} \vdash \text{ADJ}} L}{\cfrac{\text{eenvoudig, en, degelijk} \vdash \text{N} \xrightarrow{\text{mod}} \text{N} \quad \cfrac{}{\text{idee} \vdash \text{N}} L}{\text{eenvoudig, en, degelijk, idee} \vdash \text{N}} \to E}}{\text{een}(a), \text{eenvoudig}(simple), \text{en}(and), \text{degelijk}(solid), \text{idee}(idea) \vdash \text{NP}} \to E$$

(c) Derivation for "een eenvoudig en degelijk idee" (*a simple and solid idea*), showcasing non-polymorphic conjunction of two adjectives forming a noun-phrase modifier.

Figure 1: Syntactic derivations of example phrases using our extracted grammar. Lexical type assignments are the proofs' axiom leaves marked L. Identity for non-lexically grounded axioms is marked id. Parentheses are right implicit. Phrasal heads are associated with complex (functor) types. Phrases are composed via function application of functors to their arguments (i.e. implication elimination: $\to E$). Hypothetical reasoning for gaps is accomplished via function abstraction of higher-order types (i.e. implication introduction: $\to I$).

dering (Dowty, 1982) over dependency roles, capturing the degree of coherence between a dependent and the head. Figure 1 presents a few example derivations, indicating how our grammar treats a selection of interesting linguistic phenomena.

The algorithm's yield is a type-logical treebank, associating a type sequence to each sentence. The treebank counts approximately 5700 unique types, made out of 22 binary connectives (one for each dependency label) and 30 atomic types (one for each part-of-speech tag or phrasal category). As Figure 2 suggests, the comprehensiveness of such a fine-grained grammar comes at the cost of a sparser lexicon. Under this regime, recognizing rare types as first-class citizens becomes imperative.

Finally, given that all our connectives are of a fixed arity, we may represent types unambiguously using polish notation (Hamblin, 1962). Polish notation eliminates the need for brackets, reducing the representation's length and succinctly encoding a type's arity in an up-front manner.

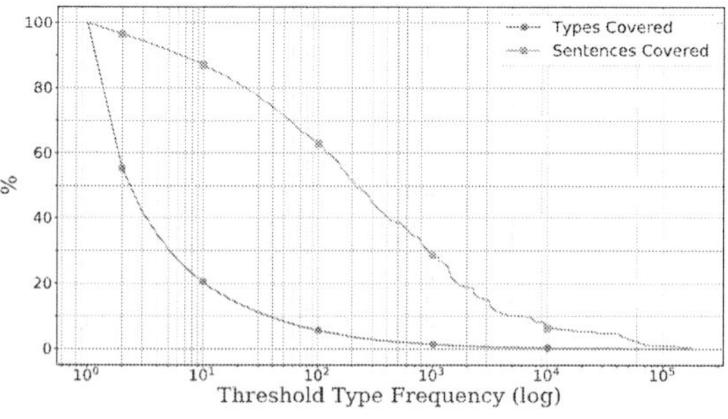

Figure 2: Percentage of types and sentences covered as a function of type frequency. The vast majority of types (80%) are rare (have less than 10 occurrences). At least one such type is present in a non-negligible part of the corpus (12% of the overall sentences). A significant portion of types (45%) appears just once throughout the corpus.

6 Model

Even though prior work suggests that both the supertagging and the CFG-generation problems are learnable (at least to an extent) in isolation, the composition of the two is less straightforward. Predicting the next atomic symbol requires for the network to be able to model local, close-range dependencies as ordained by the type-level syntax. At the same time, it needs a global receptive field in order to correctly infer full types from distant contexts, in accordance with the sentence-level syntax.

Given these two requirements, we choose to employ a variant of the Transformer for the task at hand (Vaswani et al., 2017). Transformers were originally proposed for machine translation; treating syntactic analysis as a translation task is not, however, a new idea (Vinyals et al., 2015). Transformers do away with recurrent architectures, relying only on self-attention instead, and their proven performance testifies to their strength. Self-attention grants networks the ability to selectively shift their focus over their own representations of non-contiguous elements within long sequences, based on the current context, exactly fitting the specifications of our problem formulation.

Empirical evidence points to added benefits from utilizing language models at either side of an encoder-decoder architecture (Ramachandran et al., 2017). Adhering to this, we employ a pretrained Dutch ELMo (Peters et al., 2018; Che et al., 2018) as large part of our encoder.

6.1 Network

Our network follows the standard encoder-decoder paradigm. A high-level overview of the architecture may be seen in Figure 3. The network accepts a sequence of words as input, and as output produces a (longer) sequence of tokens, where each token can be an atomic type, a logical connective or an auxiliary separation symbol that marks type boundaries. An example input/output pair may be seen in Figure 4.

Our encoder consists of a frozen ELMo followed by a single Transformer encoder layer. The employed ELMo was trained as a language model and constructs contextualized, 1024-dimensional word vectors, shown to significantly benefit downstream parsing tasks. To account for domain adaptation without unfreezing the over-parameterized ELMo, we allow for a transformer encoder layer of 3 attention heads to process ELMo's output[2].

Our decoder is a 2-layer Transformer decoder. Since the decoder processes information at a different granularity scale compared to the encoder, we break the usual symmetry by setting its number of attention heads to 8.

At timestep t, the network is tasked with modeling the probability distribution of the next atomic symbol a_t, conditional on all previous predictions $a_0, \ldots, a_{t-1}$ and the whole input sentence $w_0, \ldots, w_\tau$, and parameterized by its trainable weights θ:

$$p_\theta(a_t | a_0, \ldots, a_{t-1}, w_0, \ldots, w_\tau)$$

We make a few crucial alterations to the original Transformer formulation.

First, for the separable token transformations we use a two-layer, dimensionality preserving, feed-forward network. We replace the rectifier activation of the intermediate layer with the empirically superior Gaussian Error Linear Unit (Hendrycks and Gimpel, 2016).

Secondly, since there are no pretrained embeddings for the output tokens, we jointly train the Transformer alongside an atomic symbol embedding layer. To make maximal use of the extra parameters, we use the transpose of the embedding matrix to convert the decoder's high-dimensional output back into token class weights. We obtain the final output probability distributions by applying sigsoftmax (Kanai et al., 2018) on these weights.

6.2 Training

We train our network using the adaptive training scheme proposed by Vaswani et al (2017). We apply stricter regularization by increasing both the dropout rate and the redistributed probability mass of the Kullback-Leibler divergence loss to 0.2. The last part is of major importance, as it effectively discourages the network from simply memoizing common type patterns.

---

[2]Given that no gradient flow is allowed past the transformer encoder layer, in practice we compute the ELMo embeddings of our input sentences in advance, and feed those onto the rest of the network.

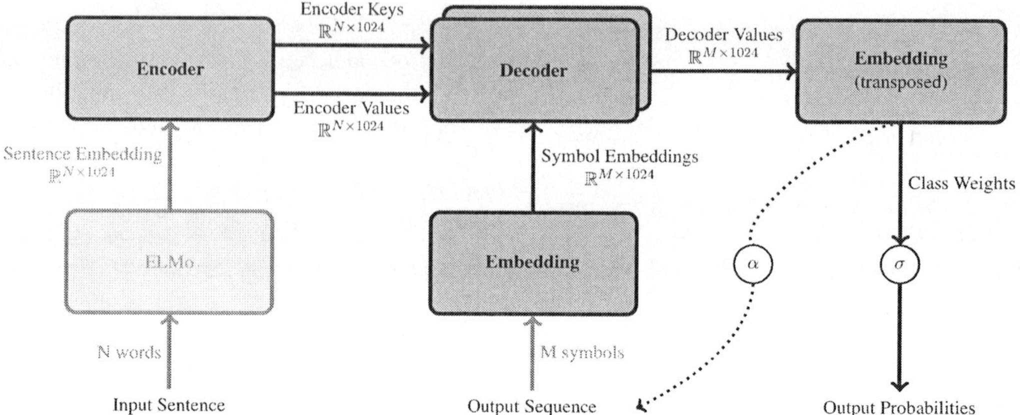

Figure 3: The model architecture, where σ and α denote the *sigsoftmax* and *argmax* functions respectively, grayed out items indicate non-trainable components and the dotted line depicts the information flow during inference.

zijn (*are*) er (*there*) toepassingen (*uses*) voor (*for*) lineaire (*linear*) logica (*logic*)

$\text{NP} \xrightarrow{\text{su}} \text{S}_{\text{main}}$ $\text{S}_{\text{main}} \xrightarrow{\text{mod}} \text{S}_{\text{main}}$ NP $\text{NP} \xrightarrow{\text{obj1}} \text{NP} \xrightarrow{\text{mod}} \text{NP}$ $\text{NP} \xrightarrow{\text{mod}} \text{NP}$ NP

$\xrightarrow{\text{su}}, \text{NP}, \text{S}_{\text{main}}, \#, \xrightarrow{\text{mod}}, \text{S}_{\text{main}}, \text{S}_{\text{main}}, \# \xrightarrow{\text{obj1}}, \text{NP}, \xrightarrow{\text{mod}}, \text{NP}, \text{NP}, \# \xrightarrow{\text{mod}}, \text{NP}, \text{NP}, \#, \text{NP}, \#$

Figure 4: Input-output example pair for the sentence "zijn er toepassingen voor lineaire logica?" (*are there applications for linear logic?*). The first two lines present the input sentence and the types that need to be assigned to each word. The third line presents the desired output sequence, with types decomposed to atomic symbol sequences under polish notation, and # used as a type separator.

7 Experiments and Results

In all described experiments, we run the model[3] on the subset of sample sentences that are at most 20 words long. We use a train/val/test split of 80/10/10[4]. We train with a batch size of 128, and pad sentences to the maximum in-batch length. Training to convergence takes, on average, eight hours & 300 epochs for our training set of 45000 sentences on a GTX1080Ti. We report averages over 5 runs.

Accuracy is reported on the type-level; that is, during evaluation, we predict atomic symbol sequences, then collapse subtype sequences into full types and compare the result against the ground truth. Notably, a single mistake within a type is counted as a completely wrong type.

7.1 Main Results

We are interested in exploring the architecture's potential at supertagging, as traditionally formulated, as well as its capacity to learn the grammar beyond the scope of the types seen in the training data. We would like to know whether the latter is at all possible (and, if so, to what degree), but also whether switching to a constructive setting has an impact on overall accuracy.

Digram Encoding Predicting type sequences one atomic symbol or connective at a time provides the vocabulary to construct new types, but results in elongated target output sequence lengths[5]. As a countermeasure, we experiment with *digram encoding*, creating new atomic symbols by iteratively applying pairwise merges of the most frequent intra-type symbol digrams (Gage, 1994), a practice already shown to improve generalization for translation tasks (Sennrich et al., 2016). To evaluate performance, we revert the merges back into their atoms after obtaining the

---

[3]The code for the model and processing scripts can be found at `https://github.com/konstantinosKokos/Lassy-TLG-Supertagging`.

[4]It is worth pointing out that the training set contains only ~85% of the overall unique types, the remainder being present only in the validation and/or test sets.

[5]Note that if lexical categories are, on average, made out of c atomic symbols, the overall output length is a constant factor of the sentence length, i.e. there is no change of complexity class with respect to a traditional supertagger.

predictions.

With no merges, the model has to construct types and type sequences using only atomic types and connectives. As more merges are applied, the model gains access to extra short-hands for sub-sequences within longer types, reducing the target output length, and thus the number of interactions it has to capture. This, however, comes at the cost of a reduced number of full-type constructions effectively seen during training, while also increasing the number of implicit rules of the type-forming context-free grammar. If merging is performed to exhaustion, all types are compressed into single symbols corresponding to the indivisible lexical types present in the treebank. The model then reduces to a traditional supertagger, never having been exposed to the internal type syntax, and loses the potential to generate new types.

We experiment with a fully constructive model employing no merges (M_0), a fully merged one i.e. a traditional supertagger, (M_∞), and three in-between models trained with 50, 100 and 200 merges (M_{50}, M_{100} and M_{200} respectively). Table 1 displays the models' accuracy. In addition to the overall accuracy, we show accuracy over different bins of type frequencies, as measured in the training data: unseen, rare (1-10), medium (10-100) and high-frequency (> 100) types.

Type Accuracy

Model	Overall	Unseen Types	Freq 1-10	Freq 10-100	Freq >100
M_0	**88.05**	**19.2**	**45.68**	**65.62**	89.93
M_{50}	88.03	15.97	43.69	64.33	**90.01**
M_{100}	87.87	15.02	41.61	63.71	89.9
M_{200}	87.54	11.7	39.56	62.4	89.64
M_∞	87.2	-	23.91	59.03	89.89

Table 1: Model performance at different merge scales, with respect to training set type frequencies. M_i denotes the model at i merges, where M_∞ means the fully merged model. For the fully merged model there is a 1 to 1 correspondence between input words and output types, so we do away with the separation symbol.

Table 1 shows that all constructive models perform overall better than M_∞, owing to a consistent increase in their accuracy over unseen, rare, and mid-frequency types. This suggests significant benefits to using a representation that is aware

Model	New Types Generated	Unique	Correct (%)
M_0	213.6	199.2	**44.39** (20.88)
M_{50}	186.6	174.2	37.89 (20.3)
M_{100}	187.8	173.4	34.31 (18.27)
M_{200}	190.4	178.8	27.46 (14.42)

Table 2: Repetition-averaged unseen type generation and precision.

of the type syntax. Additionally, the gains are greater the more transparent the view of the type syntax is, i.e. the fewer the merges. The merge-free model M_0 outperforms all other constructive models across all but the most frequent type bins, reaching an overall accuracy of 88.05% and an unseen category accuracy of 19.2%.

We are also interested in quantifying the models' "imaginative" precision, i.e., how often do they generate new types to analyze a given input sentence, and, when they do, how often are they right (Table 2). Although all constructive models are eager to produce types never seen during training, they do so to a reasonable extent. Similar to their accuracy, an upwards trend is also seen in their precision, with M_0 getting the largest percentage of generated types correct.

Together, our results indicate that the type-syntax is not only learnable, but also a representational resource that can be utilized to tangibly improve a supertagger's generalization and overall performance.

7.2 Other Models

Our preliminary experiments involved RNN-based encoder-decoder architectures. We first tried training a single-layer BiGRU encoder over the ELMo representations, connected to a single-layer GRU decoder, following Cho et al. (2014); the model took significantly longer to train and yielded far poorer results (less than 80% overall accuracy and a strong tendency towards memoizing common types). We hypothesize that the encoder's fixed length representation is unable to efficiently capture all of the information required for decoding a full sequence of atomic symbols, inhibiting learning.

As an alternative, we tried a separable LSTM decoder operating individually on the encoder's representations of each word. Even though this model was faster to train and performed marginally better compared to the previous attempt, it still showed no capacity for generalization over rarer types. This is unsurprising, as this approach assumes that the decoding task can be decomposed at the type-level; crucially, the separable decoder's prediction over a word cannot be informed by its predictions spanning other words, an information flow that evidently facilitates learning and generalization.

8 Analysis

8.1 Type Syntax

To assess the models' acquired grasp of the type syntax, we inspect type predictions in isolation. Across all merge scales and consistently over all trained models, all produced types (including unseen ones) are *well-formed*, i.e. they are indeed words of the type-forming grammar. Further, the types constructed are fully complying with our implicit notational conventions such as the obliqueness hierarchy.

Even more interestingly, for models trained on non-zero merges it is often the case that a type is put together using the correct atomic elements that together constitute a merged symbol, rather than the merged shorthand trained on. Judging from the above, it is apparent that the model gains a functionally complete understanding of the type-forming grammar's syntax, i.e. the means through which atomic symbols interact to produce types.

8.2 Sentence Syntax

Beyond the spectrum of single types, we examine type assignments in context.

We first note a remarkable ability to correctly analyze syntactically complex constructions requiring higher-order reasoning, even in the presence of unseen types. An example of such an analysis is shown in Fig 5.

For erroneous analyses, we observe a strong tendency towards self-consistency. In cases where a type construction is wrong, types that interact with that type (as either arguments or functors) tend to also follow along with the mistake. On one hand, this cascading behavior has the effect of increasing error rates as soon as a single error has been made. On the other hand, however, this is a sign of an implicitly acquired notion of phrase-wide well-typedness, and exemplifies the learned long-range interdependencies between types through the decoder's auto-regressive

formulation. On a related note, we recognize the most frequent error type as misconstruction of conjunction schemes. This was, to a degree, expected, as coordinators display an extreme level of lexical ambiguity, owing to our extracted grammar's massive type vocabulary.

8.3 Output Embeddings

Our network trains not only the encoder-decoder stacks, but also an embedding layer of atomic symbols. We can extract this layer's outputs to generate vectorial representations of atomic types and binary connectives, which essentially are high-dimensional character-level embeddings of the type language.

Considering that dense supertag representations have been shown to benefit parsing (Kasai et al., 2017), our atomic symbol embeddings may be further utilized by downstream tasks, as a highly refined source of type-level information.

8.4 Comparison

Our model's overall accuracy lies at 88%, which is comparable to the state-of-the-art in TAG supertagging (Kasai et al., 2017) but substantially lower than CCG (Clark et al., 2018). A direct numeric comparison holds little value, however, due to the different corpus, language and formalism used. To begin with, our scores are the result of a more difficult problem, since our target grammar is far more refined. Concretely, we measure accuracy over a set of 5700 types, which is one order of magnitude larger than the CCGBank test bed (425 in most published work; CCGBank itself contains a little over 1100 types) and 20% larger than the set of TAGs in the Penn Treebank. Practically, a portion of the error mass is allotted to mislabeling the implication arrow's name, which is in one-to-one correspondence with a dependency label of the associated parse tree. In that sense, our error rate is already accounting for a portion of the labeled attachment score, a task usually deferred to a parser further down the processing line. Further, the prevalence of entangled dependency structures in Dutch renders its syntax considerably more complicated than English.

9 Conclusion and Future Work

Our paper makes three novel contributions to categorial grammar parsing. We have shown that attention-based frameworks, such as the Trans-in (*to*)   hoeverre (*what-degree*)   zal (*will*)   het (*the*)

$\text{ADV} \xrightarrow{\text{obj1}} ((\text{INF} \xrightarrow{\text{mod}} \text{INF}) \to \text{SV1}) \xrightarrow{\text{body}} \text{WHQ}$ ADV $\text{INF} \xrightarrow{\text{vc}} \text{NP} \xrightarrow{\text{su}} \text{SV1}$ $\text{N} \xrightarrow{\text{det}} \text{NP}$

rapport (*report*)   dan (*then*)   nog (*still*)   een (*a*)   rol (*role*)   spelen (*play*)

N $\text{INF} \xrightarrow{\text{mod}} \text{INF}$ $\text{INF} \xrightarrow{\text{mod}} \text{INF}$ $\text{N} \xrightarrow{\text{det}} \text{NP}$ N $\text{NP} \xrightarrow{\text{obj1}} \text{INF}$

Figure 5: Type assignments for the correctly analyzed wh-question "in hoeverre zal het rapport dan nog een rol spelen" (*to what extent will the report still play a role*) involving a particular instance of *pied-piping*. The type of "in" was never seen during training; it consumes an adverb as its prepositional object, to then provide a third-order type that turns a verb-initial clause with a missing infinitive modifier into a wh-question. Such constructions are a common source of errors for supertaggers, as different instantiations require unique category assignments.

former, may act as capable and efficient supertaggers, eliminating the computational costs of recurrence. We have proposed a linear type system that internalizes dependency labels, expanding upon categorial grammar supertags and easing the burden of downstream parsing. Finally, we have demonstrated that a subtle reformulation of the supertagging task can lift the closed world assumption, allowing for unbounded supertagging and stronger grammar learning while incurring only a minimal cost in computational complexity.

Hyper-parameter tuning and network optimization were not the priority of this work; it is entirely possible that different architectures or training algorithms might yield better results under the same, constructive paradigm. This aside, our work raises three questions that we are curious to see answered. First and foremost, we are interested to examine how our approach performs under different datasets, be it different grammar specifications, formalisms or languages, as well as its potential under settings of lesser supervision. A natural continuation is also to consider how our supertags and their variable-length, content-rich vectorial representations may best be integrated with a neural parser architecture. Finally, given the close affinity between syntactic derivations, logical proofs and programs for meaning computation, we plan to investigate how insights on semantic compositionality may be gained from the vectorial representations of types and type-logical derivations.

Acknowledgments

The authors would like to thank the anonymous reviewers for their remarks and suggestions. The first two authors are supported by a NWO grant under the scope of the project "A composition calculus for vector-based semantic modelling with a localization for Dutch" (360-89-070). The first author would like to acknowledge helpful feedback and suggestions from Richard Moot and Vasilis Bountris.

References

Srinivas Bangalore and Aravind K. Joshi. 1999. Supertagging: An approach to almost parsing. *Computational Linguistics*, 25:237–265.

Wanxiang Che, Yijia Liu, Yuxuan Wang, Bo Zheng, and Ting Liu. 2018. Towards better UD parsing: Deep contextualized word embeddings, ensemble, and treebank concatenation. In *Proceedings of the CoNLL 2018 Shared Task: Multilingual Parsing from Raw Text to Universal Dependencies*, pages 55–64, Brussels, Belgium. Association for Computational Linguistics.

Kyunghyun Cho, Bart van Merrienboer, Caglar Gulcehre, Dzmitry Bahdanau, Fethi Bougares, Holger Schwenk, and Yoshua Bengio. 2014. Learning phrase representations using RNN encoder–decoder for statistical machine translation. In *Proceedings of the 2014 Conference on Empirical Methods in Natural Language Processing (EMNLP)*, pages 1724–1734, Doha, Qatar. Association for Computational Linguistics.

Kevin Clark, Minh-Thang Luong, Christopher D Manning, and Quoc V Le. 2018. Semi-supervised sequence modeling with cross-view training. *arXiv preprint arXiv:1809.08370*.

Stephen Clark and James R. Curran. 2004. The importance of supertagging for wide-coverage CCG parsing. In *Proceedings of the 20th International Conference on Computational Linguistics*, COLING '04, Stroudsburg, PA, USA. Association for Computational Linguistics.

Stephen Clark, Mark Steedman, and James R Curran. 2004. Object-extraction and question-parsing using CCG. In *Proceedings of the 2004 Conference on Empirical Methods in Natural Language Processing*, pages 111–118.

David Dowty. 1982. Grammatical relations and Montague grammar. In P. Jacobson and G. Pullum, editors, *The nature of syntactic representation*, pages 79–130. Reidel.

Philip Gage. 1994. A new algorithm for data compression. *C Users J.*, 12(2):23–38.

F. A. Gers and E. Schmidhuber. 2001. LSTM recurrent networks learn simple context-free and context-sensitive languages. *IEEE Transactions on Neural Networks*, 12(6):1333–1340.

Alex Graves. 2012. *Supervised Sequence Labelling with Recurrent Neural Networks*. Springer Berlin Heidelberg, Berlin, Heidelberg.

Charles L Hamblin. 1962. Translation to and from polish notation. *The Computer Journal*, 5(3):210–213.

Dan Hendrycks and Kevin Gimpel. 2016. Bridging nonlinearities and stochastic regularizers with gaussian error linear units. *CoRR*, abs/1606.08415.

Sekitoshi Kanai, Yasuhiro Fujiwara, Yuki Yamanaka, and Shuichi Adachi. 2018. Sigsoftmax: Reanalysis of the softmax bottleneck. In *Advances in Neural Information Processing Systems*, pages 284–294.

Jungo Kasai, Bob Frank, Tom McCoy, Owen Rambow, and Alexis Nasr. 2017. Tag parsing with neural networks and vector representations of supertags. In *Proceedings of the 2017 Conference on Empirical Methods in Natural Language Processing*, pages 1712–1722, Copenhagen, Denmark. Association for Computational Linguistics.

Mike Lewis, Kenton Lee, and Luke Zettlemoyer. 2016. LSTM CCG parsing. In *Proceedings of the 2016 Conference of the North American Chapter of the Association for Computational Linguistics: Human Language Technologies*, pages 221–231, San Diego, California. Association for Computational Linguistics.

Michael Moortgat and Richard Moot. 2002. Using the spoken Dutch corpus for type-logical grammar induction. In *Proceedings of the Third International Conference on Language Resources and Evaluation (LREC'02)*. European Language Resources Association (ELRA).

Richard Moot and Christian Retoré. 2012. *The Logic of Categorial Grammars: A Deductive Account of Natural Language Syntax and Semantics*, volume 6850. Springer.

Gertjan van Noord, Ineke Schuurman, and Vincent Vandeghinste. 2006. Syntactic annotation of large corpora in STEVIN. In *LREC 2006 Proceedings. 5th Edition of the International Conference on Language Resources and Evaluation*. European Language Resources Association (ELRA).

Matthew Peters, Mark Neumann, Mohit Iyyer, Matt Gardner, Christopher Clark, Kenton Lee, and Luke Zettlemoyer. 2018. Deep contextualized word representations. In *Proceedings of the 2018 Conference of the North American Chapter of the Association for Computational Linguistics: Human Language Technologies, Volume 1 (Long Papers)*, pages 2227–2237, New Orleans, Louisiana. Association for Computational Linguistics.

Prajit Ramachandran, Peter Liu, and Quoc Le. 2017. Unsupervised pretraining for sequence to sequence learning. In *Proceedings of the 2017 Conference on Empirical Methods in Natural Language Processing*, pages 383–391, Copenhagen, Denmark. Association for Computational Linguistics.

Rico Sennrich, Barry Haddow, and Alexandra Birch. 2016. Neural machine translation of rare words with subword units. In *Proceedings of the 54th Annual Meeting of the Association for Computational Linguistics (Volume 1: Long Papers)*, pages 1715–1725, Berlin, Germany. Association for Computational Linguistics.

Mark Steedman. 2000. *The Syntactic Process*. MIT Press/Bradford Books.

Emily Thomforde and Mark Steedman. 2011. Semi-supervised CCG lexicon extension. In *Proceedings of the Conference on Empirical Methods in Natural Language Processing*, EMNLP '11, pages 1246–1256, Stroudsburg, PA, USA. Association for Computational Linguistics.

Ashish Vaswani, Yonatan Bisk, Kenji Sagae, and Ryan Musa. 2016. Supertagging with LSTMs. In *Proceedings of the 2016 Conference of the North American Chapter of the Association for Computational Linguistics: Human Language Technologies*, pages 232–237, San Diego, California. Association for Computational Linguistics.

Ashish Vaswani, Noam Shazeer, Niki Parmar, Jakob Uszkoreit, Llion Jones, Aidan N Gomez, Łukasz Kaiser, and Illia Polosukhin. 2017. Attention is all you need. In *Advances in Neural Information Processing Systems*, pages 5998–6008.

Oriol Vinyals, Łukasz Kaiser, Terry Koo, Slav Petrov, Ilya Sutskever, and Geoffrey Hinton. 2015. Grammar as a foreign language. In C. Cortes, N. D. Lawrence, D. D. Lee, M. Sugiyama, and R. Garnett, editors, *Advances in Neural Information Processing Systems 28*, pages 2773–2781. Curran Associates, Inc.

Philip Wadler. 1993. A taste of linear logic. In *International Symposium on Mathematical Foundations of Computer Science*, pages 185–210. Springer.

Wenduan Xu, Michael Auli, and Stephen Clark. 2015. CCG supertagging with a recurrent neural network. In *Proceedings of the 53rd Annual Meeting of the Association for Computational Linguistics and the 7th International Joint Conference on Natural Language Processing (Volume 2: Short Papers)*, pages

250–255, Beijing, China. Association for Computational Linguistics.

Auto-Encoding Variational Neural Machine Translation

Bryan Eikema & Wilker Aziz
Institute for Logic, Language and Computation
University of Amsterdam
b.eikema@uva.nl, w.aziz@uva.nl

Abstract

We present a deep generative model of bilingual sentence pairs for machine translation. The model generates source and target sentences jointly from a shared latent representation and is parameterised by neural networks. We perform efficient training using amortised variational inference and reparameterised gradients. Additionally, we discuss the statistical implications of joint modelling and propose an efficient approximation to maximum a posteriori decoding for fast test-time predictions. We demonstrate the effectiveness of our model in three machine translation scenarios: in-domain training, mixed-domain training, and learning from a mix of gold-standard and synthetic data. Our experiments show consistently that our joint formulation outperforms conditional modelling (i.e. standard neural machine translation) in all such scenarios.

1 Introduction

Neural machine translation (NMT) systems (Kalchbrenner and Blunsom, 2013; Sutskever et al., 2014; Cho et al., 2014b) require vast amounts of labelled data, i.e. bilingual sentence pairs, to be trained effectively. Oftentimes, the data we use to train these systems are a byproduct of mixing different sources of data. For example, labelled data are sometimes obtained by putting together corpora from different domains (Sennrich et al., 2017). Even for a single domain, parallel data often result from the combination of documents independently translated from different languages by different people or agencies, possibly following different guidelines. When resources are scarce, it is not uncommon to mix in some synthetic data, e.g. bilingual data artificially obtained by having a model translate target monolingual data to the source language (Sennrich et al., 2016a). Translation direction,

original language, and quality of translation are some of the many factors that we typically choose not to control for (due to lack of information or simply for convenience).[1] All those arguably contribute to making our labelled data a mixture of samples from various data distributions.

Regular NMT systems do not explicitly account for latent factors of variation, instead, given a source sentence, NMT models a single conditional distribution over target sentences as a fully supervised problem. In this work, we introduce a deep generative model that generates source and target sentences jointly from a shared latent representation. The model has the potential to use the latent representation to capture global aspects of the observations, such as some of the latent factors of variation just discussed. The result is a model that accommodates members of a more complex class of marginal distributions. Due to the presence of latent variables, this model requires posterior inference, in particular, we employ the framework of amortised variational inference (Kingma and Welling, 2014). Additionally, we propose an efficient approximation to maximum a posteriori (MAP) decoding for fast test-time predictions.

Contributions We introduce a deep generative model for NMT (§3) and discuss theoretical advantages of joint modelling over conditional modelling (§3.1). We also derive an efficient approximation to MAP decoding that requires only a single forward pass through the network for prediction (§3.3). Finally, we show in §4 that our proposed model improves translation performance in at least three practical scenarios: i) in-domain

---

[1] Also note that this list is by no means exhaustive. For example, Rabinovich et al. (2017) show influence of factors such as personal traits and demographics in translation. Another clear case is presented by Johnson et al. (2017), who combine parallel resources for multiple languages to train a single encoder-decoder architecture.

Proceedings of the 4th Workshop on Representation Learning for NLP (RepL4NLP-2019), pages 124–141
Florence, Italy, August 2, 2019. ©2019 Association for Computational Linguistics

training on little data, where test data are expected to follow the training data distribution closely; ii) mixed-domain training, where we train a single model but test independently on each domain; and iii) learning from large noisy synthetic data.

2 Neural Machine Translation

In machine translation our observations are pairs of random sequences, a source sentence $x = \langle x_1, \ldots, x_m \rangle$ and a target sentence $y = \langle y_1, \ldots, y_n \rangle$, whose lengths m and n we denote by $|x|$ and $|y|$, respectively. In NMT, the likelihood of the target given the source

$$P(y|x, \theta) = \prod_{j=1}^{|y|} \mathrm{Cat}(y_j | f_\theta(x, y_{<j})) \qquad (1)$$

factorises without Markov assumptions (Sutskever et al., 2014; Bahdanau et al., 2015; Cho et al., 2014a). We have a fixed parameterised function f_θ, i.e. a neural network architecture, compute categorical parameters for varying inputs, namely, the source sentence and target prefix (denoted $y_{<j}$).

Given a dataset $\mathcal{D}$ of i.i.d. observations, the parameters θ of the model are point-estimated to attain a local maximum of the log-likelihood function, $\mathcal{L}(\theta|\mathcal{D}) = \sum_{(x,y)\in\mathcal{D}} \log P(y|x, \theta)$, via stochastic gradient-based optimisation (Robbins and Monro, 1951; Bottou and Cun, 2004).

Predictions For a trained model, predictions are performed by searching for the target sentence y that maximises the conditional $P(y|x)$, or equivalently its logarithm, with a greedy algorithm

$$\arg\max_y P(y|x, \theta) \approx \mathrm{greedy}_y \ \log P(y|x, \theta) \quad (2)$$

such as beam-search (Sutskever et al., 2014), possibly aided by a manually tuned length penalty. This *decision rule* is often referred to as MAP decoding (Smith, 2011).

3 Auto-Encoding Variational NMT

To account for a latent space where global features of observations can be captured, we introduce a random sentence embedding $z \in \mathbb{R}^d$ and model the joint distribution over observations as a marginal of $p(z, x, y|\theta)$.[2] That is, $(x, y) \in \mathcal{D}$ is assumed to be sampled from the distribution

$$P(x, y|\theta) = \int p(z) P(x, y|z, \theta) \mathrm{d}z \ . \qquad (3)$$

where we impose a standard Gaussian prior on the latent variable, i.e. $Z \sim \mathcal{N}(0, I)$, and assume $X \perp Y | Z$. That is, given a sentence embedding z, we first generate the source conditioned on z,

$$P(x|z, \theta) = \prod_{i=1}^{|x|} \mathrm{Cat}(x_i | g_\theta(z, x_{<i})) \ , \qquad (4)$$

then generate the target conditioned on x and z,

$$P(y|x, z, \theta) = \prod_{j=1}^{|y|} \mathrm{Cat}(y_j | f_\theta(z, x, y_{<j})) \ . \qquad (5)$$

Note that the source sentence is generated without Markov assumptions by drawing one word at a time from a categorical distribution parameterised by a recurrent neural network g_θ. The target sentence is generated similarly by drawing target words in context from a categorical distribution parameterised by a sequence-to-sequence architecture f_θ. This essentially combines a neural language model (Mikolov et al., 2010) and a neural translation model (§2), each extended to condition on an additional stochastic input, namely, z.

3.1 Statistical considerations

Modelling the conditional directly, as in standard NMT, corresponds to the statistical assumption that the *distribution* over source sentences can provide no information about the distribution over target sentences given a source. That is, conditional NMT assumes independence of β determining $P(y|x, \beta)$ and α determining $P(x|\alpha)$. Scenarios where this assumption is unlikely to hold are common: where x is noisy (e.g. synthetic or crowdsourced), poor quality x should be assigned low probability $P(x|\alpha)$ which in turn should inform the conditional. Implications of this assumption extend to parameter estimation: updates to the conditional are not sensitive to how exotic x is.

Let us be more explicit about how we parameterise our model by identifying 3 sets of parameters $\theta = \{\theta_{\text{emb-x}}, \theta_{\text{LM}}, \theta_{\text{TM}}\}$, where $\theta_{\text{emb-x}}$ parameterises an embedding layer for the source language. The embedding layer is shared between the two model components

$$P(x, y|z, \theta) = $$
$$P(x|\underbrace{z, \theta_{\text{emb-x}}, \theta_{\text{LM}}}_{\alpha}) P(y|x, \underbrace{z, \theta_{\text{emb-x}}, \theta_{\text{TM}}}_{\beta}) \quad (6)$$

and it is then clear by inspection that $\alpha \cap \beta = \{z, \theta_{\text{emb-x}}\}$. In words, we break the independence

---

[2] We use uppercase $P(\cdot)$ for probability mass functions and lowercase $p(\cdot)$ for probability density functions.

assumption in two ways, namely, by having the two distributions share parameters and by having them depend on a shared latent sentence representation z. Note that while the embedding layer is deterministic and global to all sentence pairs in the training data, the latent representation is stochastic and local to each sentence pair.

Now let us turn to considerations about latent variable modelling. Consider a model $P(x|\theta_{\text{emb-x}}, \theta_{\text{LM}})P(y|x, \theta_{\text{emb-x}}, \theta_{\text{TM}})$ of the joint distribution over observations that does not employ latent variables. This alternative, which we discuss further in experiments, models each component directly, whereas our proposed model (3) requires marginalisation of latent embeddings z. Marginalisation turns our directed graphical model into an undirected one inducing further structure in the marginal. See Appendix B, and Figure 2 in particular, for an extended discussion.

3.2 Parameter estimation

The marginal in Equation (3) is clearly intractable, thus precluding maximum likelihood estimation. Instead, we resort to variational inference (Jordan et al., 1999; Blei et al., 2017) and introduce a variational approximation $q(z|x, y, \lambda)$ to the intractable posterior $p(z|x, y, \theta)$. We let the approximate posterior be a diagonal Gaussian

$$
\begin{aligned}
Z|\lambda, x, y &\sim \mathcal{N}(\mathbf{u}, \text{diag}(\mathbf{s} \odot \mathbf{s})) \\
\mathbf{u} &= \mu_\lambda(x, y) \\
\mathbf{s} &= \sigma_\lambda(x, y)
\end{aligned}
\tag{7}
$$

and predict its parameters (i.e. $\mathbf{u} \in \mathbb{R}^d, \mathbf{s} \in \mathbb{R}^d_{>0}$) with neural networks whose parameters we denote by λ. This makes the model an instance of a variational auto-encoder (Kingma and Welling, 2014). See Figure 1 in Appendix B for a graphical depiction of the generative and inference models.

We can then jointly estimate the parameters of both models (generative θ and inference λ) by maximising the ELBO (Jordan et al., 1999), a lowerbound on the marginal log-likelihood,

$$
\begin{aligned}
\log P(x, y|\theta) \geq \mathcal{E}(\theta, \lambda|x, y) = \\
\mathbb{E}_{\epsilon \sim \mathcal{N}(0, I)} \left[\log P(x, y|z = \mathbf{u} + \epsilon \odot \mathbf{s}, \theta)\right] \\
- \text{KL}(\mathcal{N}(z|\mathbf{u}, \text{diag}(\mathbf{s} \odot \mathbf{s}))||\mathcal{N}(z|0, I)),
\end{aligned}
\tag{8}
$$

where we have expressed the expectation with respect to a fixed distribution—a reparameterisation available to location-scale families such as the Gaussian (Kingma and Welling, 2014; Rezende

et al., 2014). Due to this reparameterisation, we can compute a Monte Carlo estimate of the gradient of the first term via back-propagation (Rumelhart et al., 1986; Schulman et al., 2015). The KL term, on the other hand, is available in closed form (Kingma and Welling, 2014, Appendix B).

3.3 Predictions

In a latent variable model, MAP decoding (9a) requires searching for y that maximises the marginal $P(y|x, \theta) \propto P(x, y|\theta)$, or equivalently its logarithm. In addition to approximating exact search with a greedy algorithm, other approximations are necessary in order to achieve fast prediction. First, rather than searching through the true marginal, we search through the evidence lowerbound. Second, we replace the approximate posterior $q(z|x, y)$ by an auxiliary distribution $r(z|x)$. As we are searching through the space of target sentences, not conditioning on y circumvents combinatorial explosion and allows us to drop terms that depend on x alone (9b). Finally, instead of approximating the expectation via MC sampling, we condition on the expected latent representation and search greedily (9c).

$$
\begin{aligned}
&\arg\max_y \ \log P(y|x) &&\text{(9a)} \\
&\approx \arg\max_y \ \mathbb{E}_{r(z|x)}[\log P(y|z, x)] &&\text{(9b)} \\
&\approx \text{greedy}_y \ \log P(y|\mathbb{E}_{r(z|x)}[z], x) &&\text{(9c)}
\end{aligned}
$$

Together, these approximations enable prediction with a single call to an $\arg\max$ solver, in our case a standard greedy search algorithm, which leads to prediction times that are very close to that of the conditional model. This strategy, and (9b) in particular, suggests that a good auxiliary distribution $r(z|x)$ should approximate $q(z|x, y)$ closely.

We parameterise this *prediction model* using a neural network and investigate different options to estimate its parameters. As a first option, we restrict the approximate posterior to conditioning on x alone, i.e. we approach posterior inference with $q_\lambda(z|x)$ rather than $q_\lambda(z|x, y)$, and thus, we can use $r(z|x) = q_\lambda(z|x)$ for prediction.[3] As a second option, we make $r_\phi(z|x)$ a diagonal Gaussian and estimate parameters ϕ to make $r_\phi(z|x)$ close to the approximate posterior $q_\lambda(z|x, y)$ as measured by

---

[3] Note that this does not stand in contrast to our motivation for joint modelling, as we still tie source and target through z in the generative model, but it does limit the context available for posterior inference.

$D(r_\phi, q_\lambda)$. For as long as $D(r_\phi, q_\lambda) \in \mathbb{R}_{\geq 0}$ for every choice of ϕ and λ, we can estimate ϕ jointly with θ and λ by maximising a modified ELBO

$$\log P(x, y|\theta) \geq \mathcal{E}(\theta, \lambda|x, y) - D(r_\phi, q_\lambda) \quad (10)$$

which is loosened by the gap between r_ϕ and q_λ. In experiments we investigate a few options for $D(r_\phi, q_\lambda)$, all available in closed form for Gaussians, such as $\mathrm{KL}(r_\phi \| q_\lambda)$, $\mathrm{KL}(q_\lambda \| r_\phi)$, as well as the Jensen-Shannon (JS) divergence.

Note that r_ϕ is used only for prediction as a decoding *heuristic* and as such need not be stochastic. We can, for example, design $r_\phi(x)$ to be a point estimate of the posterior mean and optimise

$$\mathcal{E}(\theta, \lambda|x, y) - \left\| r_\phi(x) - \mathbb{E}_{q_\lambda(z|x,y)}[z] \right\|_2^2 \quad (11)$$

which remains a lowerbound on log-likelihood.

4   Experiments

We investigate two translation tasks, namely, WMT's translation of news (Bojar et al., 2016) and IWSLT's translation of transcripts of TED talks (Cettolo et al., 2014), and concentrate on translations for German (DE) and English (EN) in either direction. In this section we aim to investigate scenarios where we expect observations to be representative of various data distributions. As a sanity check, we start where training conditions can be considered in-domain with respect to test conditions. Though note that this does not preclude the potential for appreciable variability in observations as various other latent factors still likely play a role (see §1). We then mix datasets from these two remarkably different translation tasks and investigate whether performance can be improved across tasks with a single model. Finally, we investigate the case where we learn from synthetic data in addition to gold-standard data. For this investigation we derive synthetic data from observations that are close to the domain of the test set in an attempt to avoid further confounders.

Data   For bilingual data we use News Commentary (NC) v12 (Bojar et al., 2017) and IWSLT 2014 (Cettolo et al., 2014), where we assume NC to be representative of the test domain of the WMT News task. The datasets consist of $255, 591$ training sentences and $153, 326$ training sentences respectively. In experiments with synthetic data, we subsample 10^6 sentences from the News Crawl 2016 articles (Bojar et al., 2017) for either German

or English depending on the target language. For the WMT task, we concatenate `newstest2014` and `newstest2015` for validation/development ($5, 172$ sentence pairs) and report test results on `newstest2016` ($2, 999$ sentence pairs). For IWSLT, we use the split proposed by Ranzato et al. (2016) who separated $6, 969$ training instances for validation/development and reported test results on a concatenation of `dev2010`, `dev2012` and `tst2010-2012` ($6, 750$ sentence pairs).

Pre-processing   We tokenized and truecased all data using standard scripts from the Moses toolkit (Koehn et al., 2007), and removed sentences longer than 50 tokens. For computational efficiency and to avoid problems with closed vocabularies, we segment the data using BPE (Sennrich et al., 2016b) with $32, 000$ merge operations independently for each language. For training the truecaser and the BPEs we used a concatenation of all the available bilingual and monolingual data for German and all bilingual data for English.

Systems   We develop all of our models on top of Tensorflow NMT (Luong et al., 2017). Our baseline system is a standard implementation of conditional NMT (COND) (Bahdanau et al., 2015). To illustrate the importance of latent variable modelling, we also include in the comparison a simpler attempt at JOINT modelling where we do not induce a shared latent space. Instead, the model is trained in a fully-supervised manner to maximise what is essentially a combination of two nearly independent objectives,

$$\mathcal{L}(\theta|\mathcal{D}) = \sum_{(x,y)\in\mathcal{D}} \sum_{i=1}^{|x|} \log P(x_i|x_{<i}, \theta_{\text{emb-x}}, \theta_{\text{LM}})$$
$$+ \sum_{j=1}^{|y|} \log P(y_j|x, y_{<j}, \theta_{\text{emb-x}}, \theta_{\text{TM}}) , \quad (12)$$

namely, a language model and a conditional translation model. Note that the two components of the model share very little, i.e. an embedding layer for the source language. Finally, we aim at investigating the effectiveness of our auto-encoding variational NMT (AEVNMT).[4] Appendix A contains a detailed description of the architectures that parameterise our systems.[5]

---

[4] Code available from `github.com/Roxot/AEVNMT`.

[5] In comparison to COND, AEVNMT requires additional components: a source language model, an inference network,

	NC	IWSLT
Dropout	30%	30%
Word dropout rate	10%	20%
KL annealing steps	80,000	80,000
KL$(q(z)\|\|p(z))$ on EN-DE	5.94	8.01

Table 1: Strategies to promote use of latent representation along with the validation KL achieved.

Objective	BLEU $\uparrow$
$\mathrm{ELBO}_{x,y} - \mathrm{KL}(r_\phi(z\|x)\|\|q_\lambda(z\|x,y))$	14.7
$\mathrm{ELBO}_{x,y} - \mathrm{KL}(q_\lambda(z\|x,y)\|\|r_\phi(z\|x))$	14.8
$\mathrm{ELBO}_{x,y} - \mathrm{JS}(r_\phi(z\|x)\|\|q_\lambda(z\|x,y))$	14.9
$\mathrm{ELBO}_{x,y} - \left\|\right. r_\phi(x) - \mathbb{E}_{q_\lambda(z\|x,y)}[Z] \left.\right\|_2^2$	14.8
ELBO_x	14.9

Table 2: EN-DE validation results for NC training. ELBO_x means we condition on the source alone for posterior inference, i.e. the variational approximation $q_\lambda(z|x)$ is used for training and for predictions. In all other cases, we condition on both observations for training, i.e. $q_\lambda(z|x,y)$, and train either a distribution $r_\phi(z|x)$ or a point estimate $r_\phi(x)$ for predictions.

Hyperparameters Our recurrent cells are 256-dimensional GRU units (Cho et al., 2014b). We train on batches of 64 sentence pairs with Adam (Kingma and Ba, 2015), learning rate 3×10^{-4}, for at least T updates. We then perform convergence checks every 500 batches and stop after 20 checks without any improvement measured by BLEU (Papineni et al., 2002). For in-domain training we set $T = 140,000$, and for mixed-domain training, as well as training with synthetic data, we set $T = 280,000$. For decoding we use a beam width of 10 and a length penalty of 1.0. We investigate the use of dropout (Srivastava et al., 2014) for the conditional baseline with rates from 10% to 60% in increments of 10%. Best validation performance on WMT required a rate of 40% for EN-DE and 50% for DE-EN, while on IWSLT it required 50% for either translation direction. To spare resources, we also use these rates for training the simple JOINT model.

Avoiding collapsing to prior Many have noticed that VAEs whose observation models are parameterised by *strong generators*, such as recurrent neural networks, learn to ignore the latent representation (Bowman et al., 2016; Higgins et al., 2017; Sønderby et al., 2016; Alemi et al., 2018). In such cases, the approximate posterior "collapses" to the prior, and where one has a fixed prior, such as our standard Gaussian, this means that the posterior becomes independent of the data, which is obviously not desirable. Bowman et al. (2016) proposed two techniques to counter this effect, namely, "KL annealing", and target word dropout. KL annealing consists in incorporating the KL term of Equation (8) into the objective gradually, thus allowing the posterior to move away from the prior more freely at early stages of training. After

a number of annealing steps, the KL term is incorporated in full and training continues with the actual ELBO. In our search we considered annealing for $20,000$ to $80,000$ training steps. Word dropout consists in randomly masking words in observed target prefixes at a given rate. The idea is to harm the potential of the decoder to capitalise on correlations internal to the structure of the observation in the hope that it will rely more on the latent representation instead. We considered rates from 20% to 40% in increments of 10%. Table 1 shows the configurations that achieve best validation results on EN-DE. To spare resources, we reuse these hyperparameters for DE-EN experiments. With these settings, we attain a non-negligible validation KL (see, last row of Table 1), which indicates that the approximate posterior is different from the prior at the end of training.

ELBO variants We investigate the effect of conditioning on target observations for posterior inference during training against a simpler variant that conditions on the source alone. Table 2 suggests that conditioning on x is sufficient and thus we opt to continue with this simpler version. Do note that when we use both observations for posterior inference, i.e. $q_\lambda(z|x,y)$, and thus train an approximation r_ϕ for prediction, we have additional parameters to estimate (e.g. due to the need to encode y for q_λ and x for r_ϕ), thus it may be the case that for these variants to show their potential we need larger data and/or prolonged training.

4.1 Results

In this section we report test results in terms of BLEU (Papineni et al., 2002) and BEER (Stanojević and Sima'an, 2014), but in Appendix E

---

and possibly a prediction network. However, this does not add much sequential computation: the inference network can run in parallel with the source encoder, and the source language model runs in parallel with the target decoder.

Task	Model	EN-DE		DE-EN	
		BLEU ↑	BEER ↑	BLEU ↑	BEER ↑
IWSLT14	COND	23.0 (0.1)	58.6 (0.1)	27.3 (0.2)	59.8 (0.1)
	JOINT	23.2	58.7	27.5	59.8
	AEVNMT	**23.4 (0.1)**	**58.8 (0.1)**	**28.0 (0.1)**	**60.1 (0.1)**
WMT16	COND	17.8 (0.2)	53.1 (0.1)	20.1 (0.1)	**53.7 (0.1)**
	JOINT	17.9	53.4	20.1	**53.7**
	AEVNMT	**18.4 (0.2)**	**53.5 (0.1)**	**20.6 (0.2)**	53.6 (0.1)

Table 3: Test results for in-domain training on IWSLT (top) and NC (bottom): we report average (1std) across 5 independent runs for COND and AEVNMT, but a single run of JOINT.

we additionally report METEOR (Denkowski and Lavie, 2011) and TER (Snover et al., 2006). We de-truecase and de-tokenize our system's predictions and compute BLEU scores using Sacre-BLEU (Post, 2018).[6] For BEER, METEOR and TER, we tokenize the results and test sets using the same tokenizer as used by SacreBLEU. We make use of BEER 2.0, and for METEOR and TER use MULTEVAL (Clark et al., 2011). In Appendix D we report validation results, in this case in terms of BLEU alone as that is what we used for model selection. Finally, to give an indication of the degree to which results are sensitive to initial conditions (e.g. random initialisation of parameters), and to avoid possibly misleading significance testing, we report the average and standard deviation of 5 independently trained models. To spare resources we do not report multiple runs for JOINT, but our experience is that its performance varies similarly to that of the conditional baseline.

We start with the case where we can reasonably assume training data to be in-domain with respect to test data. Table 3 shows in-domain training performance. First, we remark that our conditional baseline for the IWSLT14 task (IWSLT training) is very close to an external baseline trained on the same data (Bahdanau et al., 2017).[7] The results on IWSLT show benefits from joint modelling and in particular from learning a shared latent space. For the WMT16 task (NC training), BLEU shows a similar trend, namely, joint modelling with a shared latent space (AEVNMT) outperforms both conditional modelling and the simple joint model.

We now consider the scenario where we know for a fact that observations come from two different data distributions, which we realise by training our models on a concatenation of IWSLT and NC. In this case, we perform model selection once on the concatenation of both development sets and evaluate the same model on each domain separately. We can see in Table 4 that conditional modelling is never preferred, JOINT performs reasonably well, especially for DE-EN, and that in every comparison our AEVNMT outperforms the conditional baseline both in terms of BLEU and BEER.

Another common scenario where two very distinct data distributions are mixed is when we capitalise on the abundance of monolingual data and train on a concatenation of gold-standard bilingual data (we use NC) and synthetic bilingual data derived from target monolingual corpora via back-translation (Sennrich et al., 2016a) (we use News Crawl). In such a scenario the latent variable might be able to inform the translation model of the amount of noise present in the source sentence. Table 5 shows results for both baselines and AEVNMT. First, note that synthetic data greatly improves the conditional baseline, in particular translating into English. Once again AEVNMT consistently outperforms conditional modelling and joint modelling without latent variables.

By mixing different sources of data we are trying to diagnose whether the generative model we propose is robust to unknown and diverse sources of variation mixed together in one training set (e.g. NC + IWSLT or gold-standard + synthetic data). However, note that a point we are certainly not trying to make is that the model has been designed to perform *domain adaptation*. Nonetheless, in Appendix C we try to shed light on what happens when we use the model to translate genres

---

[6]Version string: `BLEU+case.mixed+numrefs.1+smooth.exp+tok.13a+version.1.2.12`

[7]Bahdanau et al. (2017) report 27.56 on the same test set for DE-EN, though note that they train on words rather than BPEs and use a different implementation of BLEU.

Training	Model	WMT16		IWSLT14	
		BLEU ↑	BEER ↑	BLEU ↑	BEER ↑
En-De	Cond	17.6 (0.4)	53.9 (0.2)	23.9 (0.3)	59.3 (0.1)
	Joint	18.1	54.3	**24.2**	**59.5**
	AEVNMT	**18.4 (0.2)**	**54.5 (0.2)**	24.1 (0.3)	**59.5 (0.2)**
De-En	Cond	21.6 (0.2)	55.5 (0.2)	29.1 (0.2)	60.9 (0.1)
	Joint	**22.3**	**55.6**	**29.2**	61.2
	AEVNMT	**22.3 (0.1)**	**55.6 (0.1)**	**29.2 (0.1)**	61.1 (0.1)

Table 4: Test results for mixed-domain training: we report average (1std) across 5 independent runs for Cond and AEVNMT, but a single run of Joint.

it has never seen. On a dataset covering various unseen genres, we observe that both Cond and AEVNMT perform considerably worse showing that without taking domain adaptation seriously both models are inadequate. In terms of BLEU, differences range from −0.3 to 0.8 (En-De) and 0.3 to 0.7 (De-En) and are mostly in favour of AEVNMT (17/20 comparisons).

Remarks It is intuitive to expect latent variable modelling to be most useful in settings containing high variability in the data, i.e. mixed-domain and synthetic data settings, though in our experiments AEVNMT shows larger improvements in the in-domain setting. We speculate two reasons for this: i) it is conceivable that variation in the mixed-domain and synthetic data settings are too large to be well accounted by a diagonal Gaussian; and ii) the benefits of latent variable modelling may diminish as the amount of available data grows.

4.2 Probing latent space

To investigate what information the latent space encodes we explore the idea of training simple *linear probes* or *diagnostic classifiers* (Alain and Bengio, 2017; Hupkes et al., 2018). With simple Bayesian logistic regression we have managed to predict from $Z \sim q(z|x)$ domain indicators (i.e. newswire vs transcripts) and gold-standard vs synthetic data at performance above 90% accuracy on development set. However, a similar performance is achieved from the deterministic average state of the bidirectional encoder of the conditional baseline. We have also been able to predict from $Z \sim q(z|x)$ the level of noise in back-translated data measured on the development set at the sentence level by an automatic metric, i.e. METEOR, with performance above what can be done with

random features. Though again, the performance is not much better than what can be done with a conditional baseline. Still, it is worth highlighting that these aspects are rather coarse, and it is possible that the performance gains we report in §4.1 are due to far more nuanced variations in the data. At this point, however, we do not have a good qualitative assessment of this conjecture.

5 Related Work

Joint modelling In similar work, Shah and Barber (2018) propose a joint generative model whose probabilistic formulation is essentially identical to ours. Besides some small differences in architecture, our work differs in two regards: motivation and strategy for predictions. Their goal is to jointly learn from multiple language pairs by sharing a single polyglot architecture (Johnson et al., 2017). Their strategy for prediction is based on a form of stochastic hill-climbing, where they sample an initial z from the standard Gaussian prior and decode via beam search in order to obtain a draft translation $\tilde{y} = \text{greedy}_y P(y|z,x)$. This translation is then iteratively refined by encoding the pair $\langle x, \tilde{y} \rangle$, re-sampling z, though this time from $q(z|x, \tilde{y})$, and re-decoding with beam search. Unlike our approach, this requires multiple calls to the inference network and to beam search. Moreover, the inference model, which is trained on gold-standard observations, is used on noisy target sentences.

Cotterell and Kreutzer (2018) interpret back-translation as a single iteration of a wake-sleep algorithm (Hinton et al., 1995) for a joint model of bitext $P(x, y|\theta) = P(y|x, \theta)P_\star(x)$. They sample directly from the data distribution $P_\star(x)$ and learn two NMT models, a generative $P(y|x, \theta)$ and an auxiliary model $Q(x|y, \phi)$, each trained

WMT16	En-De		De-En	
	BLEU ↑	BEER ↑	BLEU ↑	BEER ↑
Cond	17.8 (0.2)	53.1 (0.1)	20.1 (0.1)	53.7 (0.1)
+ synthetic data	22.3 (0.3)	**57.0 (0.2)**	26.9 (0.2)	58.5 (0.1)
Joint + synthetic data	22.2	**57.0**	26.7	58.6
AEVNMT + synthetic data	**22.5 (0.2)**	**57.0 (0.1)**	**27.4 (0.2)**	**58.8 (0.1)**

Table 5: Test results for training on NC plus synthetic data (back-translated News Crawl): we report average (1std) across 5 independent runs for Cond and AEVNMT, but a single run of Joint.

on a separate objective. Zhang et al. (2018) propose a joint model of bitext trained to incorporate the back-translation heuristic as a trainable component in a formulation similar to that of Cotterell and Kreutzer (2018). In both cases, joint modelling is done without a shared latent space and without a source language model.

Multi-task learning An alternative to joint learning is to turn to multi-task learning and explore parameter sharing across models trained on different, though related, data with different objectives. For example, Cheng et al. (2016) incorporate both source and target monolingual data by multi-tasking with a non-differentiable auto-encoding objective. They jointly train a source-to-target and target-to-source system that act as encoder and decoder respectively. Zhang and Zong (2016) combine a source language model objective with a source-to-target conditional NMT objective and shared the source encoder in a multi-task learning fashion.

Variational LMs and NMT Bowman et al. (2016) first proposed to augment a neural language model with a prior over latent space. Our source component is an instance of their model. More recently, Xu and Durrett (2018) proposed to use a hyperspherical uniform prior rather than a Gaussian and showed the former leads to better representations. Zhang et al. (2016) proposed the first VAE for NMT. They augment the conditional with a Gaussian sentence embedding and model observations as draws from the marginal $P(y|x, \theta) = \int p(z|x, \theta) P(y|x, z, \theta) \mathrm{d}z$. Their formulation is a conditional deep generative model (Sohn et al., 2015) that does not model the source side of the data, where, rather than a fixed standard Gaussian, the latent model is itself parameterised and depends on the data. Schulz et al. (2018) extend the model of Zhang et al. (2016) with a

Markov chain of latent variables, one per timestep, allowing the model to capture greater variability.

Latent domains In the context of statistical MT, Cuong and Sima'an (2015) estimate a joint distribution over sentence pairs while marginalising discrete latent domain indicators. Their model factorises over word alignments and is not used directly for translation, but rather to improve word and phrase alignments, or to perform data selection (Hoang and Sima'an, 2014), prior to training. There is a vast literature on domain adaptation for statistical machine translation (Cuong and Sima'an, 2017), as well as for NMT (Chu and Wang, 2018), but a full characterisation of this exciting field is beyond the scope of this paper.

6 Discussion and Future Work

We have presented a joint generative model of translation data that generates both observations conditioned on a shared latent representation. Our formulation leads to questions such as *why joint learning?* and *why latent variable modelling?* to which we give an answer based on statistical facts about conditional modelling and marginalisation as well as empirical evidence of improved performance. Our model shows moderate but consistent improvements across various settings and over multiple independent runs.

In future work, we shall investigate datasets annotated with demographics and personal traits in an attempt to assess how far we can go in capturing fine grained variation. Though note that if such factors of variation vary widely in distribution, it may be naïve to expect we can model them well with a simple Gaussian prior. If that turns out to be the case, we will investigate mixing Gaussian components (Miao et al., 2016; Srivastava and Sutton, 2017) and/or employing a hierarchical prior (Goyal et al., 2017).

Acknowledgements

 This project has received funding from the Dutch Organization for Scientific Research VICI Grant No 277-89-002 and from the European Union's Horizon 2020 research and innovation programme under grant agreement No 825299 (GoURMET). We also thank Philip Schulz, Khalil Sima'an, and Joost Bastings for comments and helpful discussions. A Titan Xp card used for this research was donated by the NVIDIA Corporation.

References

G. Alain and Y. Bengio. 2017. Understanding intermediate layers using linear classifier probes. In *ICLR, 2017*, Toulon, France.

A. Alemi, B. Poole, I. Fischer, J. Dillon, R. A. Saurous, and K. Murphy. 2018. Fixing a broken ELBO. In *Proceedings of ICML, 2018*, pages 159–168, Stockholm, Sweden.

D. Bahdanau, P. Brakel, K. Xu, A. Goyal, R. Lowe, J. Pineau, A. Courville, and Y. Bengio. 2017. An actor-critic algorithm for sequence prediction. In *ICLR, 2017*, Toulon, France.

D. Bahdanau, K. Cho, and Y. Bengio. 2015. Neural Machine Translation by Jointly Learning to Align and Translate. In *ICLR, 2015*, San Diego, USA.

D. M. Blei, A. Kucukelbir, and J. D. McAuliffe. 2017. Variational inference: A review for statisticians. *JASA*, 112(518):859–877.

O. Bojar, R. Chatterjee, C. Federmann, Y. Graham, B. Haddow, S. Huang, M. Huck, P. Koehn, Q. Liu, V. Logacheva, C. Monz, M. Negri, M. Post, R. Rubino, L. Specia, and M. Turchi. 2017. Findings of the 2017 conference on machine translation (wmt17). In *Proceedings of WMT, 2017*, pages 169–214, Copenhagen, Denmark.

O. Bojar, R. Chatterjee, C. Federmann, Y. Graham, B. Haddow, M. Huck, A. Jimeno Yepes, P. Koehn, V. Logacheva, C. Monz, M. Negri, A. Neveol, M. Neves, M. Popel, M. Post, R. Rubino, C. Scarton, L. Specia, M. Turchi, K. Verspoor, and M. Zampieri. 2016. Findings of the 2016 conference on machine translation. In *Proceedings of WMT, 2016*, pages 131–198, Berlin, Germany.

L. Bottou and Y. L. Cun. 2004. Large scale online learning. In S. Thrun, L. K. Saul, and B. Schölkopf, editors, *NIPS, 2004*, pages 217–224. Vancouver, Canada.

S. R. Bowman, L. Vilnis, O. Vinyals, A. Dai, R. Jozefowicz, and S. Bengio. 2016. Generating sentences from a continuous space. In *Proceedings of CoNLL, 2016*, pages 10–21, Berlin, Germany.

M. Cettolo, J. Niehues, S. Stüker, L. Bentivogli, and M. Federico. 2014. Report on the 11th iwslt evaluation campaign, iwslt 2014. In *Proceedings of IWSLT, 2014*, Lake Tahoe, USA.

Y. Cheng, W. Xu, Z. He, W. He, H. Wu, M. Sun, and Y. Liu. 2016. Semi-supervised learning for neural machine translation. In *Proceedings of ACL, 2016*, pages 1965–1974, Berlin, Germany.

K. Cho, B. van Merrienboer, D. Bahdanau, and Y. Bengio. 2014a. On the Properties of Neural Machine Translation: Encoder-Decoder Approaches. In *Proceedings of SSST, 2014*, pages 103–111, Doha, Qatar.

K. Cho, B. van Merrienboer, C. Gulcehre, D. Bahdanau, F. Bougares, H. Schwenk, and Y. Bengio. 2014b. Learning phrase representations using rnn encoder–decoder for statistical machine translation. In *Proceedings of EMNLP, 2014*, pages 1724–1734, Doha, Qatar.

C. Chu and R. Wang. 2018. A survey of domain adaptation for neural machine translation. In *Proceedings of COLING, 2018*, pages 1304–1319, Santa Fe, USA.

J. H. Clark, C. Dyer, A. Lavie, and N. A. Smith. 2011. Better hypothesis testing for statistical machine translation: Controlling for optimizer instability. In *Proceedings of ACL, 2011*, pages 176–181, Portland, USA.

R. Cotterell and J. Kreutzer. 2018. Explaining and generalizing back-translation through wake-sleep. *arXiv preprint arXiv:1806.04402*.

H. Cuong and K. Sima'an. 2015. Latent domain word alignment for heterogeneous corpora. In *Proceedings of NAACL-HLT, 2015*, pages 398–408, Denver, Colorado.

H. Cuong and K. Sima'an. 2017. A survey of domain adaptation for statistical machine translation. *Machine Translation*, 31(4):187–224.

H. Cuong, K. Sima'an, and I. Titov. 2016. Adapting to all domains at once: Rewarding domain invariance in smt. *TACL*, 4:99–112.

M. Denkowski and A. Lavie. 2011. Meteor 1.3: Automatic metric for reliable optimization and evaluation of machine translation systems. In *Proceedings of WMT, 2011*, pages 85–91, Edinburgh, Scotland.

P. Goyal, Z. Hu, X. Liang, C. Wang, E. P. Xing, and C. Mellon. 2017. Nonparametric variational autoencoders for hierarchical representation learning. In *ICCV, 2017*, pages 5104–5112, Venice, Italy.

I. Higgins, L. Matthey, A. Pal, C. Burgess, X. Glorot, M. Botvinick, S. Mohamed, and A. Lerchner. 2017. beta-VAE: Learning basic visual concepts with a constrained variational framework. In *ICLR, 2017*, Toulon, France.

G. E. Hinton, P. Dayan, B. J. Frey, and R. M. Neal. 1995. The" wake-sleep" algorithm for unsupervised neural networks. *Science*, 268(5214):1158–1161.

C. Hoang and K. Sima'an. 2014. Latent domain translation models in mix-of-domains haystack. In *Proceedings of COLING, 2014*, pages 1928–1939, Dublin, Ireland.

D. Hupkes, S. Veldhoen, and W. Zuidema. 2018. Visualisation and 'diagnostic classifiers' reveal how recurrent and recursive neural networks process hierarchical structure. *JAIR*, 61:907–926.

M. Johnson, M. Schuster, Q. Le, M. Krikun, Y. Wu, Z. Chen, N. Thorat, F. a. Viégas, M. Wattenberg, G. Corrado, M. Hughes, and J. Dean. 2017. Google's multilingual neural machine translation system: Enabling zero-shot translation. *TACL*, 5:339–351.

M. Jordan, Z. Ghahramani, T. Jaakkola, and L. Saul. 1999. An introduction to variational methods for graphical models. *Machine Learning*, 37(2):183–233.

N. Kalchbrenner and P. Blunsom. 2013. Recurrent continuous translation models. In *Proceedings of EMNLP, 2013*, pages 1700–1709, Seattle, USA.

D. P. Kingma and J. Ba. 2015. Adam: A method for stochastic optimization. In *ICLR, 2015*, San Diego, USA.

D. P. Kingma and M. Welling. 2014. Auto-encoding variational bayes. In *ICLR, 2014*, Banff, Canada.

P. Koehn, H. Hoang, A. Birch, C. Callison-Burch, M. Federico, N. Bertoldi, B. Cowan, W. Shen, C. Moran, R. Zens, C. Dyer, O. Bojar, A. Constantin, and E. Herbst. 2007. Moses: open source toolkit for statistical machine translation. In *Proceedings of ACL, 2007*, pages 177–180, Prague, Czech Republic.

D. Koller and N. Friedman. 2009. *Probabilistic Graphical Models*. MIT Press.

A. Kucukelbir, D. Tran, R. Ranganath, A. Gelman, and D. M. Blei. 2017. Automatic differentiation variational inference. *JMLR*, 18(1):430–474.

M. Luong, E. Brevdo, and R. Zhao. 2017. Neural machine translation (seq2seq) tutorial. *https://github.com/tensorflow/nmt*.

Y. Miao, L. Yu, and P. Blunsom. 2016. Neural variational inference for text processing. In *ICML, 2016*, pages 1727–1736, New York, USA.

T. Mikolov, M. Karafiát, L. Burget, J. Černocký, and S. Khudanpur. 2010. Recurrent neural network based language model. In *ISCA, 2010*, Kyoto, Japan.

V. Nair and G. E. Hinton. 2010. Rectified linear units improve restricted boltzmann machines. In *Proceedings of ICML, 2010*, Haifa, Israel.

K. Papineni, S. Roukos, T. Ward, and W.-J. Zhu. 2002. BLEU: a method for automatic evaluation of machine translation. In *Proceedings of ACL, 2002*, pages 311–318, Philadelphia, USA.

M. Post. 2018. A call for clarity in reporting BLEU scores. In *Proceedings of WMT, 2018*, pages 186–191, Brussels, Belgium.

E. Rabinovich, R. N. Patel, S. Mirkin, L. Specia, and S. Wintner. 2017. Personalized machine translation: Preserving original author traits. In *Proceedings of EACL, 2017*, pages 1074–1084, Valencia, Spain.

M. Ranzato, S. Chopra, M. Auli, and W. Zaremba. 2016. Sequence level training with recurrent neural networks. In *ICLR, 2016*, San Juan, Puerto Rico.

D. J. Rezende, S. Mohamed, and D. Wierstra. 2014. Stochastic backpropagation and approximate inference in deep generative models. In *Proceedings of ICML, 2014*, 2, pages 1278–1286, Bejing, China.

H. Robbins and S. Monro. 1951. A stochastic approximation method. *Ann. Math. Statist.*, 22(3):400–407.

D. E. Rumelhart, G. E. Hinton, and R. J. Williams. 1986. Parallel distributed processing: Explorations in the microstructure of cognition, vol. 1. *Nature*, 323.

J. Schulman, N. Heess, T. Weber, and P. Abbeel. 2015. Gradient estimation using stochastic computation graphs. In *NIPS, 2015*, pages 3528–3536. Montreal, Canada.

P. Schulz, W. Aziz, and T. Cohn. 2018. A stochastic decoder for neural machine translation. In *Proceedings of ACL, 2018*, Melbourne, Australia.

R. Sennrich, A. Birch, A. Currey, U. Germann, B. Haddow, K. Heafield, A. V. Miceli Barone, and P. Williams. 2017. The university of edinburgh's neural mt systems for wmt17. In *Proceedings of WMT, 2017*, pages 389–399, Copenhagen, Denmark.

R. Sennrich, B. Haddow, and A. Birch. 2016a. Improving neural machine translation models with monolingual data. In *Proceedings of ACL, 2016*, pages 86–96, Berlin, Germany.

R. Sennrich, B. Haddow, and A. Birch. 2016b. Neural machine translation of rare words with subword units. In *Proceedings of ACL, 2016*, pages 1715–1725, Berlin, Germany.

H. Shah and D. Barber. 2018. Generative neural machine translation. In S. Bengio, H. Wallach, H. Larochelle, K. Grauman, N. Cesa-Bianchi, and R. Garnett, editors, *NIPS, 2018*, pages 1352–1361. Montreal, Canada.

N. A. Smith. 2011. *Linguistic Structure Prediction*. Morgan and Claypool.

M. Snover, B. J. Dorr, R. Schwartz, L. Micciulla, and J. Makhoul. 2006. A study of translation edit rate with targeted human annotation. *Proceedings of AMTA, 2006*, pages 223 – 231.

K. Sohn, H. Lee, and X. Yan. 2015. Learning structured output representation using deep conditional generative models. In *NIPS, 2015*, pages 3483–3491, Montreal, Canada.

C. K. Sønderby, T. Raiko, L. Maaløe, S. K. Sønderby, and O. Winther. 2016. Ladder variational autoencoders. In *NIPS, 2016*, pages 3738–3746, Barcelona, Spain.

A. Srivastava and C. Sutton. 2017. Autoencoding variational inference for topic models. In *ICLR, 2017*, Toulon, France.

N. Srivastava, G. Hinton, A. Krizhevsky, I. Sutskever, and R. Salakhutdinov. 2014. Dropout: A simple way to prevent neural networks from overfitting. *JMLR*, 15:1929–1958.

M. Stanojević and K. Sima'an. 2014. Fitting sentence level translation evaluation with many dense features. In *Proceedings of EMNLP, 2014*, pages 202–206, Doha, Qatar.

I. Sutskever, O. Vinyals, and Q. V. V. Le. 2014. Sequence to sequence learning with neural networks. In Z. Ghahramani, M. Welling, C. Cortes, N. Lawrence, and K. Weinberger, editors, *NIPS, 2014*, pages 3104–3112. Montreal, Canada.

J. Xu and G. Durrett. 2018. Spherical latent spaces for stable variational autoencoders. In *Proceedings of EMNLP, 2018*, pages 4503–4513, Brussels, Belgium.

B. Zhang, D. Xiong, j. su, H. Duan, and M. Zhang. 2016. Variational neural machine translation. In *Proceedings of EMNLP, 2016*, pages 521–530, Austin, USA.

J. Zhang and C. Zong. 2016. Exploiting source-side monolingual data in neural machine translation. In *Proceedings of EMNLP, 2016*, pages 1535–1545, Austin, Texas.

Z. Zhang, S. Liu, M. Li, M. Zhou, and E. Chen. 2018. Joint training for neural machine translation models with monolingual data. In *Proceedings of AAAI, 2018*, pages 555–562, New Orleans, USA.

A Architectures

Here we describe parameterisation of the different models presented in §3. Rather than completely specifying standard blocks, we use the notation block(inputs; parameters), where we give an indication of the relevant parameter set. This makes it easier to visually track which model a component belongs to.

A.1 Source Language Model

The source language model consists of a sequence of categorical draws for $i = 1, \ldots, |x|$

$$X_i | z, x_{<i} \sim \mathrm{Cat}(g_\theta(z, x_{<i})) \qquad (13)$$

parameterised by a single-layer recurrent neural network using GRU units:

$$\mathbf{f}_i = \mathrm{emb}(x_i; \theta_{\text{emb-x}}) \qquad (14\text{a})$$

$$\mathbf{h}_0 = \tanh(\mathrm{affine}(z; \theta_{\text{init-lm}})) \qquad (14\text{b})$$

$$\mathbf{h}_i = \mathrm{GRU}(\mathbf{h}_{i-1}, \mathbf{f}_{i-1}; \theta_{\text{gru-lm}}) \qquad (14\text{c})$$

$$g_\theta(z, x_{<i}) = \mathrm{softmax}(\mathrm{affine}(\mathbf{h}_i; \theta_{\text{out-x}})) . \qquad (14\text{d})$$

We initialise the GRU cell with a transformation (14b) of the stochastic encoding z. For the simple joint model baseline we initialise the GRU with a vector of zeros as there is no stochastic encoding we can condition on in that case.

A.2 Translation Model

The translation model consists of a sequence of categorical draws for $j = 1, \ldots, |y|$

$$Y_j | z, x, y_{<j} \sim \mathrm{Cat}(f_\theta(z, x, y_{<j})) \qquad (15)$$

parameterised by an architecture that roughly follows Bahdanau et al. (2015). The encoder is a bidirectional GRU encoder (16b) that shares source embeddings with the language model (14a) and is initialised with its own projection of the latent representation put through a tanh activation. The decoder, also initialised with its own projection of the latent representation (16d), is a single-layer recurrent neural network with GRU units (16f). At any timestep the decoder is a function of the previous state, previous output word embedding, and a context vector. This context vector (16e) is a weighted average of the bidirectional source encodings, of which the weights are computed by a Bahdanau-style attention mechanism. The output of the GRU decoder is projected to the target vocabulary size and mapped to the simplex using a softmax activation (17) to obtain the categorical parameters:

$$\mathbf{s}_0 = \tanh(\mathrm{affine}(z; \theta_{\text{init-enc}})) \qquad (16\text{a})$$

$$\mathbf{s}_1^m = \mathrm{BiGRU}(\mathbf{f}_1^m, \mathbf{s}_0; \theta_{\text{bigru-x}}) \qquad (16\text{b})$$

$$\mathbf{e}_j = \mathrm{emb}(y_j; \theta_{\text{emb-y}}) \qquad (16\text{c})$$

$$\mathbf{t}_0 = \tanh(\mathrm{affine}(z; \theta_{\text{init-dec}})) \qquad (16\text{d})$$

$$\mathbf{c}_j = \mathrm{attention}(\mathbf{s}_1^m, \mathbf{t}_{j-1}; \theta_{\text{bahd}}) \qquad (16\text{e})$$

$$\mathbf{t}_j = \mathrm{GRU}(\mathbf{t}_{j-1}, [\mathbf{c}_j, \mathbf{e}_{j-1}]; \theta_{\text{gru-dec}}) , \qquad (16\text{f})$$

and

$$f_\theta(z, x, y_{<j}) = \mathrm{softmax}(\mathrm{affine}([\mathbf{t}_j, \mathbf{e}_{j-1}, \mathbf{c}_j]; \theta_{\text{out-y}})) . \qquad (17)$$

In baseline models, recurrent cells are initialised with a vector of zeros as there is no stochastic encoding we can condition on.

A.3 Inference Network

The inference model $q(z | x, y, \lambda)$ is a diagonal Gaussian

$$Z | x, y \sim \mathcal{N}(\mathbf{u}, \mathrm{diag}(\mathbf{s} \odot \mathbf{s})) \qquad (18)$$

whose parameters are computed by an *inference network*. We use two bidirectional GRU encoders to encode the source and target sentences separately. To spare memory, we reuse embeddings from the generative model (19a-19b), but we prevent updates to those parameters based on gradients of the inference network, which we indicate with the function detach. To obtain fixed-size representations for the sentences, GRU encodings are averaged (19c-19d) .

$$\mathbf{f}_1^m = \mathrm{detach}(\mathrm{emb}(x_1^m; \theta_{\text{emb-x}})) \qquad (19\text{a})$$

$$\mathbf{e}_1^n = \mathrm{detach}(\mathrm{emb}(y_1^n; \theta_{\text{emb-y}})) \qquad (19\text{b})$$

$$\mathbf{h}_x = \mathrm{avg}\left(\mathrm{BiGRU}\left(\mathbf{f}_1^m; \lambda_{\text{gru-x}}\right)\right) \qquad (19\text{c})$$

$$\mathbf{h}_y = \mathrm{avg}\left(\mathrm{BiGRU}\left(\mathbf{e}_1^n; \lambda_{\text{gru-y}}\right)\right) \qquad (19\text{d})$$

$$\mathbf{h}_{xy} = \mathrm{concat}(\mathbf{h}_x, \mathbf{h}_y) \qquad (19\text{e})$$

$$\mathbf{h}_u = \mathrm{ReLU}(\mathrm{affine}(\mathbf{h}_{xy}; \lambda_{\text{u-hid}})) \qquad (19\text{f})$$

$$\mathbf{h}_s = \mathrm{ReLU}(\mathrm{affine}(\mathbf{h}_{xy}; \lambda_{\text{s-hid}}) \qquad (19\text{g})$$

$$\mathbf{u} = \mathrm{affine}(\mathbf{h}_u; \lambda_{\text{u-out}}) \qquad (19\text{h})$$

$$\mathbf{s} = \mathrm{softplus}(\mathrm{affine}(\mathbf{h}_s; \lambda_{\text{s-out}})) \qquad (19\text{i})$$

We use a concatenation $\mathbf{h}_{xy}$ of the average source and target encodings (19e) as inputs to compute the parameters of the Gaussian approximate posterior, namely, d-dimensional location and scale vectors. Both transformations use ReLU hidden activations (Nair and Hinton, 2010), but locations live in $\mathbb{R}^d$ and therefore call for linear output activations (19h), whereas scales live in $\mathbb{R}^d_{>0}$ and call for strictly positive outputs (19i), we follow Kucukelbir et al. (2017) and use softplus. The complete set of parameters used for inference is thus $\lambda = \{\lambda_{\text{gru-x}}, \lambda_{\text{gru-y}}, \lambda_{\text{u-hid}}, \lambda_{\text{u-out}}, \lambda_{\text{s-hid}}, \lambda_{\text{s-out}}\}$.

A.4 Prediction Network

The *prediction network* parameterises our prediction model $r(z|x, \phi)$, a variant of the inference model that conditions on the source sentence alone. In §4 we explore several variants of the ELBO using different parameterisations of r_ϕ. In the simplest case we do not condition on the target sentence during training, thus we can use the same network both for training and prediction. The network is similar to the one described in A.3, except that there is a single bidirectional GRU and we use the average source encoding (19c) as input to the predictors for $\mathbf{u}$ and $\mathbf{s}$ (20c-20d).

$$\mathbf{h}_u = \text{ReLU}(\text{affine}(\mathbf{h}_x; \lambda_{\text{u-hid}})) \tag{20a}$$

$$\mathbf{h}_s = \text{ReLU}(\text{affine}(\mathbf{h}_x; \lambda_{\text{s-hid}})) \tag{20b}$$

$$\mathbf{u} = \text{affine}(\mathbf{h}_u; \lambda_{\text{u-out}}) \tag{20c}$$

$$\mathbf{s} = \text{softplus}(\text{affine}(\mathbf{h}_s; \lambda_{\text{s-out}})) \tag{20d}$$

In all other cases we use $q(z|x, y, \lambda)$ parameterised as discussed in A.3 for training, and design a separate network to parameterise r_ϕ for prediction. Much like the inference model, the prediction model is a diagonal Gaussian

$$Z|x \sim \mathcal{N}(\hat{\mathbf{u}}, \text{diag}(\hat{\mathbf{s}} \odot \hat{\mathbf{s}})) \tag{21}$$

also parameterised by d-dimensional location and scale vectors, however in predicting $\hat{\mathbf{u}}$ and $\hat{\mathbf{s}}$ (22d-22e) it can only access an encoding of the source (22a).

$$\mathbf{h}_x = \text{avg}\left(\text{BiGRU}\left(\mathbf{f}_1^m; \phi_{\text{gru-x}}\right)\right) \tag{22a}$$

$$\mathbf{h}_u = \text{ReLU}(\text{affine}(\mathbf{h}_x; \phi_{\text{u-hid}})) \tag{22b}$$

$$\mathbf{h}_s = \text{ReLU}(\text{affine}(\mathbf{h}_x; \phi_{\text{s-hid}})) \tag{22c}$$

$$\hat{\mathbf{u}} = \text{affine}(\mathbf{h}_u; \phi_{\text{u-out}}) \tag{22d}$$

$$\hat{\mathbf{s}} = \text{softplus}(\text{affine}(\mathbf{h}_s; \phi_{\text{s-out}})) \tag{22e}$$

The complete set of parameters is then $\phi = \{\phi_{\text{gru-x}}, \phi_{\text{u-hid}}, \phi_{\text{u-out}}, \phi_{\text{s-hid}}, \phi_{\text{s-out}}\}$. For the deterministic variant, we use $\hat{\mathbf{u}}$ (22d) alone to approximate $\mathbf{u}$ (19h), i.e. the posterior mean of Z.

B Graphical models

Figure 1 is a graphical depiction of our AEVNMT model. Circled nodes denote random variables while uncircled nodes denote deterministic quantities. Shaded random variables correspond to observations and unshaded random variables are latent. The plate denotes a dataset of $|\mathcal{D}|$ observations.

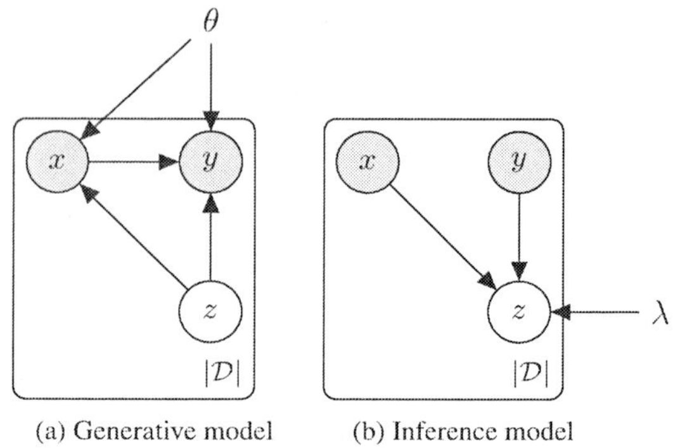

(a) Generative model   (b) Inference model

Figure 1: On the left we have AEVNMT, a generative model parameterised by neural networks. On the right we show an independently parameterised model used for approximate posterior inference.

In Figure 2a, we illustrate the precise statistical assumptions of AEVNMT. Here plates iterate over words in either the source or the target sentence. Note that the arrow from x_i to y_j states that the jth target word depends on all of the source sentence, not on the ith source word alone, and that is the case because x_i is within the source plate. In Figure 2b, we illustrate the statistical dependencies induced in the marginal distribution upon marginalisation of latent variables. Recall that the marginal is the distribution which by assumption produced the observed data. Now compare that to the distribution modelled by the simple JOINT model (Figure 2c). Marginalisation induces undirected dependencies amongst random variables creating more structure in the marginal distribution. In graphical models literature this is known as *moralisation* (Koller and Friedman, 2009).

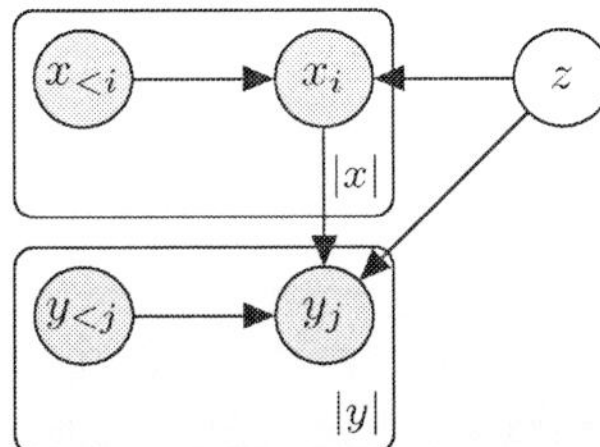

(a) Joint distribution of AEVNMT

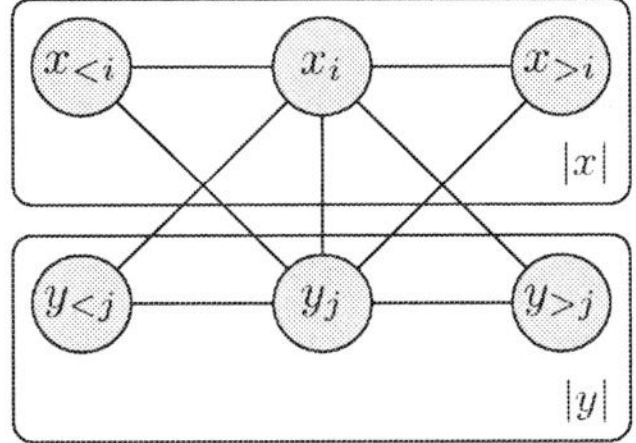

(b) Marginal distribution of AEVNMT

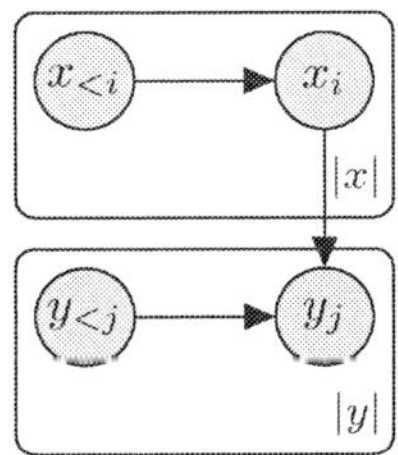

(c) Joint distribution modelled without latent variables

Figure 2: Here we zoom in into the model of Figure 1a to show the statistical dependencies between observed variables. In the joint distribution (top), we have the directed dependency of a source word on all of the previous source words, and similarly, of a target word on all of the previous target words in addition to the complete source sentence. Besides, all observations depend directly on the latent variable Z. Marginalisation of Z (middle) ties all variables together through undirected connections. At the bottom we show the distribution we get if we model the data distribution directly without latent variables.

C Robustness to out-of-domain data

We use our stronger models, those trained on gold-standard NC bilingual data and synthetic News data, to translate test sets in various unseen genres. These data sets are collected and distributed by TAUS,[8] and have been used in scenarios of adapation to all domains at once (Cuong et al., 2016). Table 6 shows the performance of AEVNMT and the conditional baseline. The first thing to note is the remarkable drop in performance showing that without taking domain adaptation seriously both models are inadequate. In terms of BLEU, differences range from -0.3 to 0.8 (EN-DE) and 0.3 to 0.7 (DE-EN) and are mostly in favour of AEVNMT, though note the increased standard deviations.

---

[8]TAUS Hardware, TAUS Software, TAUS Industrial Electronics, TAUS Professional & Business Services, and TAUS Legal available from TAUS data cloud `http://tausdata.org/`.

Model	Domain	EN-DE				DE-EN			
		BLEU ↑	METEOR ↑	TER ↓	BEER ↑	BLEU ↑	METEOR ↑	TER ↓	BEER ↑
COND	Computer Hardware	8.7 (0.3)	23.6 (0.2)	82.3 (4.0)	44.2 (0.3)	13.0 (0.4)	20.8 (0.1)	73.5 (3.6)	49.2 (0.1)
	Computer Software	7.9 (0.2)	22.9 (0.1)	83.6 (3.2)	44.1 (0.3)	11.8 (0.8)	20.4 (0.3)	80.8 (7.0)	**48.6 (0.3)**
	Industrial Electronics	7.6 (0.3)	21.8 (0.2)	89.6 (5.5)	42.7 (0.3)	10.1 (1.0)	17.6 (0.4)	85.7 (9.7)	46.0 (0.4)
	Professional & Business Services	**8.1 (0.4)**	**23.3 (0.4)**	**75.6 (0.4)**	**43.1 (0.4)**	11.1 (0.2)	20.5 (0.1)	73.8 (1.4)	44.9 (0.1)
	Legal	12.3 (0.1)	29.7 (0.3)	75.3 (0.5)	49.6 (0.1)	14.2 (0.3)	23.0 (0.3)	67.3 (2.1)	50.8 (0.3)
AEVNMT	Computer Hardware	**9.1 (0.3)**	**23.9 (0.4)**	**79.4 (1.3)**	**44.7 (0.2)**	13.6 (0.3)	**21.0 (0.2)**	**70.6 (1.4)**	**49.3 (0.2)**
	Computer Software	**8.3 (0.1)**	**23.2 (0.2)**	**81.4 (0.7)**	**44.5 (0.2)**	12.2 (0.5)	**20.7 (0.3)**	**77.0 (3.7)**	48.6 (0.3)
	Industrial Electronics	**8.1 (0.2)**	**22.2 (0.3)**	**85.2 (1.0)**	**43.1 (0.2)**	10.8 (0.6)	**17.9 (0.3)**	**79.9 (4.9)**	**46.3 (0.2)**
	Professional & Business Services	7.8 (0.7)	23.0 (0.7)	75.7 (1.0)	43.0 (0.5)	**11.5 (0.2)**	**20.6 (0.2)**	**73.1 (0.7)**	**45.1 (0.1)**
	Legal	**13.1 (0.2)**	**30.5 (0.3)**	74.4 (0.6)	49.9 (0.2)	**14.5 (0.2)**	**23.2 (0.2)**	66.1 (1.3)	**50.9 (0.3)**

Table 6: Performance of models trained with NC and back-translated News on various TAUS test sets: we report average (1std) across 5 independent runs.

D Validation results

	WMT16		IWSLT14	
	EN-DE	DE-EN	EN-DE	DE-EN
COND	14.5 (0.2)	16.9 (0.2)	25.1 (0.1)	30.8 (0.1)
JOINT	**14.8**	17.1	25.2	31.0
AEVNMT	**14.8 (0.2)**	**17.4 (0.2)**	**25.7 (0.0)**	**31.4 (0.0)**

Table 7: Validation results reported in BLEU for in-domain training on NC and IWSLT: we report average (1std) across 5 independent runs for COND and AEVNMT, but a single run of JOINT.

WMT & IWSLT	EN-DE	DE-EN
COND	20.5 (0.1)	25.9 (0.1)
JOINT	20.7	**26.1**
AEVNMT	**20.8 (0.1)**	**26.1 (0.1)**

Table 8: Validation results reported in BLEU for mixed-domain training: we report average (1std) across 5 independent runs for COND and AEVNMT, but a single run of JOINT. The validation set used is a concatenation of the development sets from WMT and IWSLT.

WMT16	EN-DE	DE-EN
COND	14.5 (0.2)	16.9 (0.2)
+ synthetic data	17.4 (0.1)	21.8 (0.1)
JOINT + synthetic data	17.3	21.8
AEVNMT + synthetic data	**17.6 (0.1)**	**22.1 (0.1)**

Table 9: Validation results reported in BLEU for training on NC plus synthetic data: we report average (1std) across 5 independent runs for COND and AEVNMT, but a single run of JOINT.

IWSLT14	En-De				De-En			
	BLEU ↑	METEOR ↑	TER ↓	BEER ↑	BLEU ↑	METEOR ↑	TER ↓	BEER ↑
Cond	23.0 (0.1)	42.4 (0.1)	56.0 (0.1)	58.6 (0.1)	27.3 (0.2)	30.3 (0.1)	52.4 (0.5)	59.8 (0.1)
Joint	23.2	**42.8**	56.1	58.7	27.5	30.3	52.7	59.8
AEVNMT	**23.4 (0.1)**	**42.8 (0.2)**	**55.5 (0.3)**	**58.8 (0.1)**	**28.0 (0.1)**	**30.6 (0.1)**	**51.2 (0.6)**	**60.1 (0.1)**

Table 10: Test results for in-domain training on IWSLT: we report average (1std) across 5 independent runs for Cond and AEVNMT, but a single run of Joint.

WMT16	En-De				De-En			
	BLEU ↑	METEOR ↑	TER ↓	BEER ↑	BLEU ↑	METEOR ↑	TER ↓	BEER ↑
Cond	17.8 (0.2)	35.9 (0.2)	65.2 (0.4)	53.1 (0.1)	20.1 (0.1)	**26.0 (0.1)**	62.0 (0.3)	**53.7 (0.1)**
Joint	17.9	36.2	64.1	53.4	20.1	**26.0**	62.7	**53.7**
AEVNMT	**18.4 (0.2)**	**36.6 (0.2)**	**64.0 (0.4)**	**53.5 (0.1)**	**20.6 (0.2)**	**26.0 (0.1)**	**60.7 (0.8)**	53.6 (0.1)

Table 11: Test results for in-domain training on NC: we report average (1std) across 5 independent runs for Cond and AEVNMT, but a single run of Joint.

WMT16	En-De				De-En			
	BLEU ↑	METEOR ↑	TER ↓	BEER ↑	BLEU ↑	METEOR ↑	TER ↓	BEER ↑
Cond	17.8 (0.2)	35.9 (0.2)	65.2 (0.4)	53.1 (0.1)	20.1 (0.1)	26.0 (0.1)	62.0 (0.3)	53.7 (0.1)
+ synthetic data	22.3 (0.3)	40.9 (0.2)	58.5 (0.5)	**57.0 (0.2)**	26.9 (0.2)	30.4 (0.1)	53.0 (0.5)	58.5 (0.1)
Joint + synthetic data	22.2	40.8	**58.1**	**57.0**	26.7	30.2	52.1	58.6
AEVNMT + synthetic data	**22.5 (0.2)**	**41.0 (0.1)**	58.1 (0.2)	57.0 (0.1)	**27.4 (0.2)**	**30.6 (0.1)**	**52.0 (0.1)**	**58.8 (0.1)**

Table 12: Test results for training on NC plus synthetic data (back-translated News Crawl): we report average (1std) across 5 independent runs for Cond and AEVNMT, but a single run of Joint.

EN-DE

Training	Model	WMT16				IWSLT14			
		BLEU ↑	METEOR ↑	TER ↓	BEER ↑	BLEU ↑	METEOR ↑	TER ↓	BEER ↑
EN-DE	COND	17.6 (0.4)	35.7 (0.3)	61.9 (0.7)	53.9 (0.2)	23.9 (0.3)	43.1 (0.3)	54.7 (0.2)	59.3 (0.1)
	JOINT	18.1	36.3	61.4	54.3	**24.2**	43.4	54.5	**59.5**
	AEVNMT	**18.4 (0.2)**	**36.6 (0.3)**	**60.9 (0.4)**	**54.5 (0.2)**	24.1 (0.3)	**43.5 (0.3)**	**54.0 (0.3)**	**59.5 (0.2)**
DE-EN	COND	21.6 (0.2)	27.4 (0.1)	59.9 (0.7)	55.5 (0.2)	29.1 (0.2)	**31.5 (0.1)**	50.9 (0.5)	60.9 (0.1)
	JOINT	**22.3**	27.4	58.8	**55.6**	29.2	31.5	49.2	**61.2**
	AEVNMT	**22.3 (0.1)**	**27.5 (0.1)**	**57.8 (0.6)**	**55.6 (0.1)**	**29.2 (0.1)**	31.5 (0.0)	49.2 (0.4)	61.1 (0.1)

Table 13: Test results for mixed-domain training: we report average (1std) across 5 independent runs for COND and AEVNMT, but a single run of JOINT.

Learning Bilingual Word Embeddings Using Lexical Definitions

Weijia Shi[1], Muhao Chen[1], Yingtao Tian[2], Kai-Wei Chang[1]
[1]Department of Computer Science, University of California, Los Angeles
[2]Department of Computer Science, Stony Brook University
{swj0419, muhaochen, kw2c}@cs.ucla.edu; {yittian}@cs.stonybrook.edu

Abstract

Bilingual word embeddings, which represent lexicons of different languages in a shared embedding space, are essential for supporting semantic and knowledge transfers in a variety of cross-lingual NLP tasks. Existing approaches to training bilingual word embeddings require often require pre-defined seed lexicons that are expensive to obtain, or parallel sentences that comprise coarse and noisy alignment. In contrast, we propose BilLex that leverages publicly available lexical definitions for bilingual word embedding learning. Without the need of predefined seed lexicons, BilLex comprises a novel word pairing strategy to automatically identify and propagate the precise fine-grained word alignment from lexical definitions. We evaluate BilLex in word-level and sentence-level translation tasks, which seek to find the cross-lingual counterparts of words and sentences respectively. BilLex significantly outperforms previous embedding methods on both tasks.

1 Introduction

Bilingual word embeddings are the essential components of multilingual NLP systems. These embeddings capture cross-lingual semantic transfers of words and phrases from bilingual corpora, and are widely deployed in many NLP tasks, such as machine translation (Conneau et al., 2018), cross-lingual Wikification (Tsai and Roth, 2016), knowledge alignment (Chen et al., 2018) and semantic search (Vulić and Moens, 2015).

A variety of approaches have been proposed to learn bilingual word embeddings (Duong et al., 2017; Luong et al., 2015; Coulmance et al., 2015). Many such approaches rely on the use of aligned corpora. Such corpora could be seed lexicons that provide word-level mappings between two languages (Mikolov et al., 2013a; Xing et al., 2015),

or parallel corpora that align sentences and documents (Klementiev et al., 2012; Gouws et al., 2015). However, these methods critically suffer from several deficiencies. First, seed-lexicon-based approaches are often hindered by the limitedness of seeds (Vulić and Korhonen, 2016), which is an intractable barrier since high-quality seed lexicons require extensive human efforts to obtain (Zhang et al., 2017). Second, parallel corpora provide coarse alignment that does not often accurately infer fine-grained semantic transfers of lexicons (Ruder et al., 2017).

Unlike the existing methods, we propose to use publicly available dictionaries[1] for bilingual word embedding learning. Dictionaries, such as Wiktionary and Merriam-Webster, contain large collections of lexical definitions, which are clean linguistic knowledge that naturally connects word semantics within and across human languages. Hence, dictionaries provide valuable information to bridge the lexicons in different languages. However, cross-lingual learning from lexical definitions is a non-trivial task. A straightforward approach based on aligning the target word embedding to the aggregated embedding of words in the definition might work, but not all words in a definition are semantically related to the defined target word (Fig. 1(a)). Therefore, a successful model has to effectively identify the most related lexicons from the multi-granular and asymmetric alignment of lexical definitions. Besides, how to leverage both bilingual and monolingual dictionaries for cross-lingual learning is another challenge.

In this paper, we propose BilLex (**Bi**lingual Word Embeddings Based on **Lex**ical Definitions) to learn bilingual word embeddings. BilLex constitutes a carefully designed two-stage mechanism

---

[1]We refer to *dictionary* in its regular meaning, i.e. the collections of word definitions. This is different from some papers that refer to dictionaries as seed lexicons.

Proceedings of the 4th Workshop on Representation Learning for NLP (RepL4NLP-2019), pages 142–147
Florence, Italy, August 2, 2019. ©2019 Association for Computational Linguistics

to automatically cultivate, propagate and leverage lexicon pairs of high semantic similarity from lexical definitions in dictionaries. It first extracts *bilingual strong word pairs* from bilingual lexical definitions of which the words contribute to the cross-lingual definitions of each other. On top of that, our model automatically exploits *induced word pairs*, which utilize monolingual dictionaries and the aforementioned strong pairs to exploit semantically related word pairs. This automated word pair induction process enables BilLex to capture abundant high-quality lexical alignment information, based on which the cross-lingual semantic transfer of words is easily captured in a shared embedding space. Experimental results on word-level and sentence-level translation tasks show that BilLex drastically outperforms various baselines that are trained on parallel or seed-lexicon corpora, as well as state-of-the-art unsupervised methods.

2   Related Work

Prior approaches to learning bilingual word embeddings often rely on word or sentence alignment (Ruder et al., 2017). In particular, seed lexicon methods (Mikolov et al., 2013a; Faruqui and Dyer, 2014; Guo et al., 2015) learn transformations across different language-specific embedding spaces based on predefined word alignment. The performance of these approaches is limited by the sufficiency of seed lexicons. Besides, parallel corpora methods (Gouws et al., 2015; Coulmance et al., 2015) leverage the aligned sentences in different languages and force the representations of corresponding sentence components to be similar. However, aligned sentences merely provide weak alignment of lexicons that do not accurately capture the one-to-one mapping of words, while such a mapping is well-desired by translation tasks (Upadhyay et al., 2016). In addition, a few unsupervised approaches alleviate the use of bilingual resources (Chen and Cardie, 2018; Conneau et al., 2018). These models require considerable effort to train and rely heavily on massive monolingual corpora.

Monolingual lexical definitions have been used for weak supervision of monolingual word similarities (Tissier et al., 2017). Our work demonstrates that dictionary information can be extended to a cross-lingual scenario, for which we develop a simple yet effective induction method to populate fine-grain word alignment.

3   Modeling

We first provide the formal definition of bilingual dictionaries. Let $\mathcal{L}$ be the set of languages and $\mathcal{L}^2$ be the set of ordered language pairs. For a language $l \in \mathcal{L}$, we use V_l to denote its vocabulary, where for each word $w \in V_l$, $\mathbf{w} \in \mathbb{R}^k$ denotes its embedding vector. A dictionary denoted as D_{l_i, l_j} contains words in language l_i and their definitions in l_j. In particular, D_{l_i, l_j} is a monolingual dictionary if $l_i = l_j$ and is a bilingual dictionary if $l_i \neq l_j$. A dictionary D_{l_i, l_j} contains dictionary entries $(w^i, Q^j(w^i))$, where $w^i \in V_{l_i}$ is the word being defined and $Q^j(w^i)$ is a sequence of words in l_j describing the meaning of the word w^i. Fig. 1(a) shows an entry from an English-French dictionary, and one from a French-English dictionary.

BilLex allows us to exploit semantically related word pairs in two stages. We first use bilingual dictionaries to construct bilingual strong pairs, which are similar to those monolingual word pairs in (Tissier et al., 2017). Then based on the given strong word pairs and monolingual dictionaries, we provide two types of induced word pairs to further enhance the cross-lingual learning.

3.1   Bilingual Strong Pairs

A bilingual strong pair contains two words with high semantic relevance. Such a pair of words that mutually contribute to the cross-lingual definitions of each other is defined as below.

Definition (Bilingual Strong Pairs) $P^S_{l_i, l_j}$ *is the set of bilingual strong pairs in* $(l_i, l_j) \in \mathcal{L}^2$ $(l_i \neq l_j)$, *where each word pair is defined as:*
$$(w^i, w^j) \in P^S_{l_i, l_j} \Leftrightarrow w^i \in Q^i(w^j) \wedge w^j \in Q^j(w^i)$$

Intuitively, if w^i appears in the cross-lingual definition of w^j and w^j appears in the cross-lingual definition of w^i, then w^i and w^j should be semantically close to each other. Particularly, $P^S_{l_i, l_j}$ denotes monolingual strong pairs if $l_i = l_j$. For instance, *(car, véhicule)* depicted in Fig. 1(a) form a bilingual strong pair. Note that Tissier et al. also introduce the monolingual weak pairs by pairing the target word with the other words from its definition, which do not form strong pairs with it. However, we do not extend such weak pairs to the bilingual setting, as we find them to be inaccurate to represent cross-lingual corresponding words.

3.2   Induced Word Pairs

Since bilingual lexical definitions cover only limited numbers of words in two languages, we in-

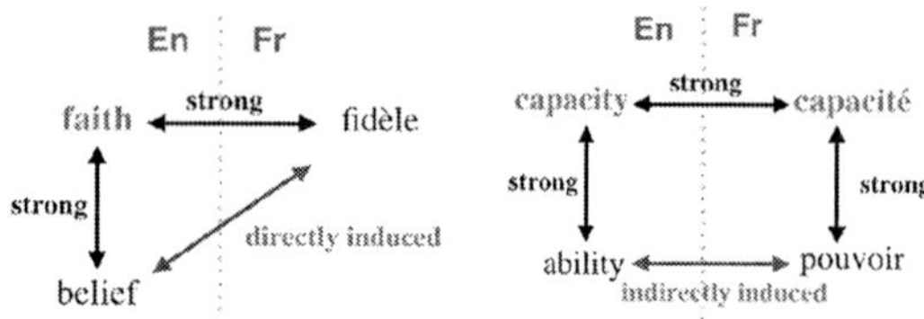

(a) Bilingual strong pair

(b) Directly induced pair   (c) Indirectly induced pair

Figure 1: Examples of three types of word pairs. The blue words in (b-c) are pivot words of the induced pairs.

corporate both monolingual and bilingual strong pairs, from which we induce two types of word pairs with different confidence: *directly induced pairs* and *indirectly induced pairs*.

Definition (Bilingual Directly Induced Pairs) $P^D_{l_i,l_j}$ *is the set of bilingual directly induced pairs in* $(l_i, l_j) \in \mathcal{L}^2$, *where each word pair is defined as:* $(w^i, w^j) \in P^D_{l_i,l_j} \Leftrightarrow \exists w^i_p, (w^i, w^i_p) \in P^S_{l_i,l_i} \wedge (w^i_p, w^j) \in P^S_{l_i,l_j}$

Intuitively, a bilingual induced pair (w^i, w^j) indicates that we can find a pivot word that forms a monolingual strong pair with one word from (w^i, w^j) and a bilingual strong pair with the other.

Definition (Bilingual Indirectly Induced Pairs) $P^I_{l_i,l_j}$ *is the set of bilingual indirectly induced pairs in* $(l_i, l_j) \in \mathcal{L}^2$, *where each word pair is defined as:* $(w^i, w^j) \in P^I_{l_i,l_j} \Leftrightarrow \exists (w^i_p, w^j_p) \in P^S_{l_i,l_j}, (w^i, w^i_p) \in P^S_{l_i,l_i} \wedge (w^j, w^j_p) \in P^S_{l_j,l_j}$

A bilingual indirectly induced pair (w^i, w^j) indicates that there exists a pivot bilingual strong pair (w^i_p, w^j_p), such that w^i_p forms a monolingual strong pair with w_i and w^j_p forms a monolingual strong pair with w^j. Fig. 1(b-c) shows examples of the two types of induced word pairs.

3.3 Training

Our model jointly learns three word-pair-based cross-lingual objectives Ω_K to align the embedding spaces of two languages, and two monolingual monolingual Skip-Gram losses (Mikolov et al., 2013b) L_{l_i}, L_{l_j} to preserve monolingual word similarities. Given a language pair $(l_i, l_j) \in$

$\mathcal{L}^2$, the learning objective of BilLex is to minimize the following joint loss function:

$$J = L_{l_i} + L_{l_j} + \sum_{K \in \{P^S, P^D, P^I\}} \lambda_K \Omega_K$$

Each λ_K ($K \in \{P^S, P^D, P^I\}$) thereof, is the hyperparameter that controls how much the corresponding type of word pairs contributes to cross-lingual learning. For alignment objectives, we use word pairs in both directions of an ordered language pair $(l_i, l_j) \in \mathcal{L}^2$ to capture the cross-lingual semantic similarity of words, such that $P^S = P^S_{l_i,l_j} \cup P^S_{l_j,l_i}$, $P^D = P^D_{l_i,l_j} \cup P^D_{l_j,l_i}$ and $P^I = P^I_{l_i,l_j} \cup P^I_{l_j,l_i}$. Then for each $K \in \{P^S, P^D, P^I\}$, the alignment objective Ω_K is defined as below, where σ is the sigmoid function.

$$\Omega_K = -\frac{1}{|K|} \sum_{(w^i, w^j) \in K} \left(\log \sigma(\mathbf{w}^{i\top} \mathbf{w}^j) \right.$$
$$\left. + \sum_{(w_a, w_b) \in N_i(w^j) \cup N_j(w^i)} \log \sigma(-\mathbf{w}_a^{\top} \mathbf{w}_b) \right)$$

For each word pair (w^i, w^j), we use the unigram distribution raised to the power of 0.75 to select a number of words in l_j (or l_i) for w^i (or w^j) to form a negative sample set $N_i(w^j)$ (or $N_j(w^i)$). Without loss of generality, we define the negative sample set as $N_i(w^j) = \{(w^i_n, w^j)|w^i_n \sim U_i(w) \wedge (w^i_n, w^j) \notin P^S \cup P^D \cup P^I\}$, where $U_i(w)$ is the distribution of words in l_i.

4   Experiment

We evaluate BilLex on two bilingual tasks: *word translation* and *sentence translation retrieval*. Following the convention (Gouws et al., 2015; Mogadala and Rettinger, 2016), we evaluate BilLex between English-French and English-Spanish. Accordingly, we extract word pairs from both directions of bilingual dictionaries in Wiktionary for these language pairs. To support the induced word pairs, we also extract monolingual lexical definitions in the three languages involved, which include 238k entries in English, 107k entries in French and 49k entries in Spanish. The word pair extraction process of BilLex excludes stop words and punctuation in the lexical definitions. The statistics of three types of extracted word pairs are reported in Table 1.

4.1   Word translation

This task aims to retrieve the translation of a source word in the target language. We use the

144

Lang	#Def	S	I_D	I_I
En&Fr	108,638	52,406	48,524	62,488
En&Es	56,239	32,210	29,857	37,952

Table 1: Statistics of dictionaries and word pair sets.

Language	En-Fr		Fr-En		En-Es		Es-En	
Metric	$P@1$	$P@5$	$P@1$	$P@5$	$P@1$	$P@5$	$P@1$	$P@5$
BiCVM	41.8	56.6	42.6	58.4	37.8	52.8	39.9	54.2
BilBOWA	42.3	59.7	45.2	59.2	37.6	50.3	45.8	53.7
BiSkip	44.0	58.4	45.9	60.2	41.2	58.0	45.4	56.9
Supervised MUSE	74.9	89.8	76.1	90.9	77.4	93.8	77.3	93.6
Unsupervised MUSE	**78.1**	**94.3**	**78.2**	**93.0**	**81.7**	**94.4**	**83.3**	**96.6**
BilLex(P^S)	62.4	79.2	61.8	77.4	64.3	78.4	61.9	78.0
BilLex(P^S+P^D)	73.6	87.3	75.3	87.7	73.7	88.7	76.0	90.2
BilLex(P^S+P^D+P^I)	**82.5**	**96.2**	**83.8**	**96.0**	**82.0**	**96.5**	**85.1**	**96.8**

Table 2: Results of the word translation task.

Language	En-Fr		Fr-En	
Metric	$P@1$	$P@5$	$P@1$	$P@5$
BiCVM	24.4	40.5	32.3	43.8
BilBOWA	27.7	41.4	31.5	47.0
BiSkip	25.3	38.8	26.4	40.4
Supervised MUSE	**63.2**	**76.9**	**74.9**	85.4
Unsupervised MUSE	60.0	76.3	73.7	**87.6**
BilLex(P^S)	47.4	59.7	57.2	69.6
BilLex(P^S+P^D)	58.7	73.8	67.6	78.9
BilLex(P^S+P^D+P^I)	**64.9**	**78.2**	**76.3**	**89.7**

Table 3: Results of sentence translation retrieval.

test set provided by Conneau et al. (2018), which selects the most frequent 200k words of each language as candidates for 1.5k query words. We translate a query word by retrieving its k nearest neighbours in the target language, and report $P@k$ ($k = 1, 5$) to represent the fraction of correct translations that are ranked not larger than k.

Evaluation protocol. The hyperparameters of BilLex are tuned based on a small validation set of 1k word pairs provided by Conneau et al. (2018). We allocate 128-dimensional word embeddings with pre-trained BilBOWA (Gouws et al., 2015). and use the standard configuration to Skip-Gram (Mikolov et al., 2013b) on monolingual Wikipedia dumps. We set the negative sampling size of bilingual word pairs to 4, which is selected from 0 to 10 with the step of 1. λ_{PS} is set to 0.9, which is tuned from 0 to 1 with the step of 0.1. As we assume that the strong pair relations between words are independent, we empirically set $\lambda_{PD} = (\lambda_{PS})^2 = 0.81$ and $\lambda_{PI} = (\lambda_{PS})^3 = 0.729$. We minimize the loss function using AMSGrad (Reddi et al., 2018) with a learning rate of 0.001. The training is terminated based on early stopping. We limit the vocabularies as the 200k most frequent words in each language, and exclude the bilingual strong pairs that have appeared in the test set. The baselines we compare against include BiCVM (Hermann and Blunsom, 2014), BilBOWA (Gouws et al., 2015), Biskip (Luong et al., 2015), supervised and unsupervised MUSE (Conneau et al., 2018).

Results. Results are summarized in Table 2, where the performance of BilLex is reported for three variants: (i) training with bilingual strong pairs only BilLex(P^S), (ii) with directly induced pair added BilLex(P^S+P^D), and (iii) with all three types of word pairs BilLex(P^S+P^D+P^I). BilLex(P^S+P^D+P^I) thereof, offers consistently better performance in all settings, which implies that the induced word pairs are effective in improving the cross-lingual learning of lexical semantics. Among the baseline models, the unsupervised MUSE outperforms the other four supervised ones. We also discover that for the word translation task, the supervised models with coarse alignment such as BiCVM and BilBOWA do not perform as well as the models with word-level supervision, such as BiSkip and supervised MUSE. Our best BilLex outperforms unsupervised MUSE by 4.4~5.7% of $P@1$ between En and Fr, and by 0.3~1.8% between En and Es. The reason why the settings between En and Fr achieve better performance is that there are much fewer bilingual definitions between En and Es.

4.2 Sentence translation retrieval

This task focuses on retrieving the sentence in the target language space with the tf-idf weighted sentence representation approach. We follow the experiment setup in (Conneau et al., 2018) with 2k source sentence queries and 200k target sentences from the Europarl corpus for English and French. We carry forward model configurations from the previous experiment, and report $P@k$ ($k = 1, 5$). **Results.** The results are reported in Table 3. Overall, our best model variant BilLex(P^S+P^D+P^I) performs better than the best baseline with a noticeable increment of $P@1$ by 1.4~1.7% and P@5 by 1.3~2.1%. This demonstrates that BilLex is suitable for transferring sentential semantics.

5 Conclusion

In this paper, we propose BilLex, a novel bilingual word embedding model based on lexical definitions. BilLex is motivated by the fact that openly available dictionaries offer high-quality linguistic knowledge to connect lexicons across languages. We design the word pair induction method to capture semantically related lexicons in dictionaries, which serve as alignment information in joint training. BilLex outperforms state-of-the-art methods on word and sentence translation tasks.

References

Muhao Chen, Yingtao Tian, Kai-Wei Chang, Steven Skiena, et al. 2018. Co-training embeddings of knowledge graphs and entity descriptions for cross-lingual entity alignment. In *Proceedings of the 27th International Joint Conference on Artificial Intelligence*, pages 3998–4004.

Xilun Chen and Claire Cardie. 2018. Unsupervised multilingual word embeddings. In *Proceedings of the 2018 Conference on Empirical Methods in Natural Language Processing*, pages 261–270.

Alexis Conneau, Guillaume Lample, Marc'Aurelio Ranzato, Ludovic Denoyer, and Hervé Jégou. 2018. Word translation without parallel data. *ICLR*.

Jocelyn Coulmance, Jean-Marc Marty, Guillaume Wenzek, and Amine Benhalloum. 2015. Transgram, fast cross-lingual word-embeddings.

Long Duong, Hiroshi Kanayama, Tengfei Ma, Steven Bird, and Trevor Cohn. 2017. Multilingual training of crosslingual word embeddings. In *Proceedings of the 15th Conference of the European Chapter of the Association for Computational Linguistics: Volume 1, Long Papers*, volume 1, pages 894–904.

Manaal Faruqui and Chris Dyer. 2014. Improving vector space word representations using multilingual correlation. In *Proceedings of the 14th Conference of the European Chapter of the Association for Computational Linguistics*, pages 462–471.

Stephan Gouws, Yoshua Bengio, and Greg Corrado. 2015. Bilbowa: Fast bilingual distributed representations without word alignments. In *Inter National Conference on Machine Learning*.

Jiang Guo, Wanxiang Che, David Yarowsky, Haifeng Wang, and Ting Liu. 2015. Cross-lingual dependency parsing based on distributed representations. In *Proceedings of the 53rd Annual Meeting of the Association for Computational Linguistics and the 7th International Joint Conference on Natural Language Processing (Volume 1: Long Papers)*, volume 1, pages 1234–1244.

Karl Moritz Hermann and Phil Blunsom. 2014. Multilingual models for compositional distributed semantics. In *Proceedings of the 52nd Annual Meeting of the Association for Computational Linguistics (Volume 1: Long Papers)*, volume 1, pages 58–68.

Alexandre Klementiev, Ivan Titov, and Binod Bhattarai. 2012. Inducing crosslingual distributed representations of words. In *Proceedings of COLING 2012*.

Thang Luong, Hieu Pham, and Christopher D Manning. 2015. Bilingual word representations with monolingual quality in mind. In *Proceedings of NAACL-HLT*, pages 151–159.

Tomas Mikolov, Quoc V Le, and Ilya Sutskever. 2013a. Exploiting similarities among languages for machine translation. *CoRR,abs/1309.4168.*

Tomas Mikolov, Ilya Sutskever, Kai Chen, Greg S Corrado, and Jeff Dean. 2013b. Distributed representations of words and phrases and their compositionality. In *Advances in neural information processing systems*, pages 3111–3119.

Aditya Mogadala and Achim Rettinger. 2016. Bilingual word embeddings from parallel and non-parallel corpora for cross-language text classification. In *Proceedings of the 2016 Conference of the North American Chapter of the Association for Computational Linguistics: Human Language Technologies*, pages 692–702.

Sashank J Reddi, Satyen Kale, and Sanjiv Kumar. 2018. On the convergence of adam and beyond. In *ICLR*.

Sebastian Ruder, Ivan Vulić, and Anders Søgaard. 2017. A survey of cross-lingual word embedding models. *Journal of Artificial Intelligence Research*.

Julien Tissier, Christophe Gravier, and Amaury Habrard. 2017. Dict2vec: Learning word embeddings using lexical dictionaries. In *Conference on Empirical Methods in Natural Language Processing (EMNLP 2017)*, pages 254–263.

Chen-Tse Tsai and Dan Roth. 2016. Cross-lingual wikification using multilingual embeddings. In *Proceedings of the 2016 Conference of the North American Chapter of the Association for Computational Linguistics: Human Language Technologies*, pages 589–598.

Shyam Upadhyay, Manaal Faruqui, Chris Dyer, and Dan Roth. 2016. Cross-lingual models of word embeddings: An empirical comparison. In *Proceedings of the 54th Annual Meeting of the Association for Computational Linguistics (Volume 1: Long Papers)*, volume 1, pages 1661–1670.

Ivan Vulić and Anna Korhonen. 2016. On the role of seed lexicons in learning bilingual word embeddings. In *Proceedings of the 54th Annual Meeting of the Association for Computational Linguistics (Volume 1: Long Papers)*, volume 1, pages 247–257.

Ivan Vulić and Marie-Francine Moens. 2015. Monolingual and cross-lingual information retrieval models based on (bilingual) word embeddings. In *Proceedings of the 38th international ACM SIGIR conference on research and development in information retrieval*, pages 363–372. ACM.

Chao Xing, Dong Wang, Chao Liu, and Yiye Lin. 2015. Normalized word embedding and orthogonal transform for bilingual word translation. In *Proceedings of the 2015 Conference of the North American Chapter of the Association for Computational Linguistics: Human Language Technologies*, pages 1006–1011.

Meng Zhang, Haoruo Peng, Yang Liu, Huan-Bo Luan, and Maosong Sun. 2017. Bilingual lexicon induction from non-parallel data with minimal supervision. In *AAAI*, pages 3379–3385.

An Empirical study on Pre-trained Embeddings and Language Models for Bot Detection

Andres Garcia-Silva
Expert System
Calle Profesor Waksman 10
28036, Madrid, Spain
agarcia@expertsystem.com

Cristian Berrio
Expert System
Calle Profesor Waksman 10
28036, Madrid, Spain
cberrio@expertsystem.com

Jose Manuel Gomez-Perez
Expert System
Calle Profesor Waksman 10
28036, Madrid, Spain
jmgomez@expertsystem.com

Abstract

Fine-tuning pre-trained language models has significantly advanced the state of art in a wide range of downstream NLP tasks. Usually, such language models are learned from large and well-formed text corpora from e.g. encyclopedic resources, books or news. However, a significant amount of the text to be analyzed nowadays is Web data, often from social media. In this paper we consider the research question: How do standard pre-trained language models generalize and capture the peculiarities of rather short, informal and frequently automatically generated text found in social media? To answer this question, we focus on bot detection in Twitter as our evaluation task and test the performance of fine-tuning approaches based on language models against popular neural architectures such as LSTM and CNN combined with pre-trained and contextualized embeddings. Our results also show strong performance variations among the different language model approaches, which suggest further research.

1 Introduction

Recently, transfer learning techniques (Pan and Yang, 2010) based on language models have successfully delivered breaktrough accuracies in all kinds of downstream NLP tasks. Approaches like ULMFiT (Howard and Ruder, 2018), Open AI GPT (Radford et al., 2018) and BERT (Devlin et al., 2018) have in common the generation of pre-trained models learned from very large text corpora. The resulting language models are then fine-tuned for the specific domain and task, continuously advancing the state of the art across the different evaluation tasks and benchmarks commonly used by the NLP community.

Transfer learning approaches based on language models are therefore the NLP analogue to similar approaches in other fields of AI like Computer Vision, where the availability of large datasets like ImageNet (Deng et al., 2009) enabled the development of state of the art pre-trained models. Before language models, common practice for transfer learning in NLP was based on pre-trained context-independent embeddings. These are also learned from large corpora and encode different types of syntactic and semantic relations that can be observed when operating on the vector space. However, their use is limited to the input layer of neural architectures, and hence the amount of data and training effort necessary to learn a high performance task-related model is high since it is still necessary to train the whole network. Pre-trained language models, on the other hand, attempt to learn in the network structure the word inter-relations that can be leveraged during the fine-tuning step, usually by just learning a feed forward network for the specific task. The network architecture varies depending on the approach, including transformers (Vaswani et al., 2017) based on decoders, encoders and attention mechanisms, and bi-directional long-short term memory networks (Hochreiter and Schmidhuber, 1997).

Language models are usually learnt from high quality, grammatically correct and curated text corpora, such as Wikipedia (ULMFiT), BookCorpus (Open AI GPT), a combination of Wikipedia and BookCorpus (BERT) or News (ELMo). However, a very significant amount of the text to be analyzed nowadays is Web data, frequently from social media. The question that immediately arises is therefore whether such language models also capture the nuances of the short and informal language often found in social media channels.

In this paper we explore this question and empirically study how pre-trained embeddings and language models perform when used to analyze text from social media. To this purpose, we focus

Proceedings of the 4th Workshop on Representation Learning for NLP (RepL4NLP-2019), pages 148–155
Florence, Italy, August 2, 2019. ©2019 Association for Computational Linguistics

on bot detection in Twitter as evaluation task for two main reasons. First, the intrinsic relevance of the task for counteracting the automatic spreading of disinformation and bias on social media. Second, because in this context the gap, in terms of the quality and overall characteristics of the language used, between the corpora used to learn the language models and the task-specific text to be analyzed (automatically generated in a social media, micro-blogging context) can be particularly representative.

In our experiments, prior to evaluating the behavior of pre-trained language models, we test pre-trained embeddings as a baseline learned from general corpora, social media and informal vocabularies. We choose two popular NLP neural architectures for our binary classification task: Long Short Term memory networks (LSTM; Hochreiter and Schmidhuber, 1997) and convolutional networks (CNN; LeCun et al., 1998). We also pre-processed our Twitter dataset, observing a positive effect on our CNN and LSTM classifiers while on the other hand such effect was actually negative on some of the tested pre-trained language models.

In general, our results indicate that fine-tuned pre-trained language models outperform pre-trained and contextualized embeddings used in conjunction with CNN or LSTM for the task at hand. This shows evidence that language models actually capture much of the peculiarities of social media and bot language or at least are flexible enough to generalize during fine-tuning in such context. From the different language models we evaluated, Open AI GPT beats BERT (base) and ULMFit in the bot/no bot classification task, suggesting that a forward and unidirectional language model is more appropriated for social media messages than other language modeling architectures, which is relatively surprising. Nevertheless, the considerable experimentation we carried out has raised a number of additional questions that will need further research. During the workshop, we aim at sharing and discussing these questions with the participants.

The rest of the paper is structured as follows. Section 2 describes the state of the art about the different models and embeddings used in the experiments. Next, the experimental setup is presented in section 3, where the learning objective is defined as well as the dataset and the used

pre-trained embeddings. Section 4 and 5 present the experiments using CNN and LSTM and different combinations of pre-trained, contextualized and dynamically generated embeddings learnt during training of the bot/no bot classification model. Then, section 6 describes the experiments with pre-trained language models. Finally, a discussion about the results is presented in section 7.

2 State of the Art

Mikolov's word2vec (Mikolov et al., 2013) approach that proposes an efficient way to learn embeddings by predicting words based on their context using negative sampling sparkled a new generation of embedding learning methods like GloVe (Pennington et al., 2014), Swivel (Shazeer et al., 2016) and FastText (Joulin et al., 2016). These embeddings capture semantic and syntactic relations between words that were mapped to vector operations in the multidimensional space. Nevertheless these approaches generate static, context-independent embeddings for words in the vocabulary. ELMo (Peters et al., 2018) overcome this limitation by generating representations for each word as a function of the input sentence. In addition, while pre-trained embeddings are used as input for neural networks, ELMo allows the end-task model to learn a contextualized linear combination of its internal representation.

Pre-trained embeddings are used as the first layer of models or as additional features to neural architectures. However as the models are initialized randomly a lot of training data was still required to get a high performance. To alleviate this problem ULMFiT (Howard and Ruder, 2018) proposes a transfer learning method that pre-trains a language model on a large corpus using 3-layer LSTM architecture that is then fine-tuned on the target task. In fact, the fine tuning is done at the language model level to reflect the target task distribution and at the task level.

In the same vein the Open AI Generative Pre-trained Transformer (GPT) (Radford et al., 2018) learns a language model on a large corpus using a multi-layer transformer decoder, and supervised fine-tuning to adapt the parameters to the target task. For tasks other than text classification the input is transformed into an ordered sequence that the pre-trained model can process. In contrast, BERT uses a bidirectional transformer (Devlin et al., 2018), also known as a transformer encoder, that learns representations jointly conditioned on left and right context in all layers. Similar to ELMo, ULMFiT and Open AI GPT which pre-train language models, BERT learning objective is a masked language model and a binarized next sentence prediction tasks. For a classification process all of the parameters of BERT and the classification layer are fine-tuned jointly to maximize the log-probability of the correct label.

Our contribution is an empirical study on the fitness of the fine-tuning of pre-trained language models when tested against text from social media and the target task is classification. We also show how pre-processing of the target task corpus can affect the performance of the pre-trained models, and compare them with the use of pre-trained and contextualized embeddings as inputs of CNN and BiLSTM for the classification task.

3 Experiments

To evaluate pre-trained language models with Twitter data we focus on the relevant problem of detecting bots in social media. Bots are automatic agents that publish information for a variety of purposes such as weather and natural hazards updates, and news, but also for spreading misinformation and fake news. In fact, as of 2017 it has been estimated that as 9% to 15% of twitter accounts are bots (Varol et al., 2017) which means that out of the 321 million active user accounts[1] the number of automatic agents range from 28 to 48 million.

Detecting bots can be addressed as a binary classification problem focusing only in the tweet textual content since our main target are language models, regardless of the other features that might be drawn from the social network, such user metadata, network features based on the follower and followee relations, and tweet and retweet activity.

3.1 Dataset

To generate a dataset of tweets generated by bots or humans we rely on an existing dataset of bot and human accounts published by Gilani et al. (2017). We create a balanced dataset containing tweets labelled as bot or human according to the account label. In total our dataset comprises 500,000 tweets

where 279,495 tweets were created by 1,208 human accounts, and 220,505 tweets were tweeted from 722 bot accounts.

In this sample, bots tend to be more prolific than humans since they average 305 tweets per account which contrasts with the human average of 231. In addition, bots tend to use more URL (0.8313 URL per tweet) and hash tags (0.4745 hashtags per tweets) in their tweets than humans (0.5781 URL and 0.2887 hashtags per tweet). This shows that bots aim at maximizing visibility (hashtags) and to redirect traffic to other sources (URL). Finally, we found that bots display more egoistic behaviour than humans since they mention other users in their tweets (0.4371 user mentions per tweet) less frequently than humans (0.5781 user mentions per tweet).

3.2 Pre-trained embeddings

We use pre-trained embeddings to train the classifiers rather than doing it from scratch. We use pre-trained embeddings learned from Twitter itself, urban dictionary definitions to accommodate the informal vocabulary often used in the social network, and common crawl as a general source of information:

- glove.twitter[2]: 200 dimension embeddings generated from Twitter (27B tokens, 1.2M vocabulary) using GloVe (Pennington et al., 2014).
- word2vec.urban[3]: 100 dimension embeddings generated from Urban Dictionary definitions (568K vocabulary) using Word2Vec (Mikolov et al., 2013).
- fastText.crawl[4]: 300 dimension embeddings generated from Common Crawl (600B tokens, 1.9M vocabulary) using fastText (Mikolov et al., 2018)

4 CNN for text classification

We use convolutional neural networks (CNN; LeCun et al., 1998) for the bot detection task inspired by Kim's work (Kim, 2014) that showed how this architecture achieved good performance in several sentence classification tasks, and other reports like (Yin et al., 2017) that show good results in NLP tasks. The neural network architecture uses

---

[1]Twitter 4th quarter and fiscal year 2018 results: https://www.prnewswire.com/news-releases/twitter-announces-fourth-quarter-and-fiscal-year-2018-results-300791624.html

[2]https://nlp.stanford.edu/projects/glove/
[3]https://data.world/jaredfern/urban-dictionary-embedding
[4]https://fasttext.cc/docs/en/english-vectors.html

3 convolutional layers and a fully connected layer. Each convolutional layer has 128 filters of size 5, relu was used as activation function and max pooling was applied in each layer. The fully connected layer uses softmax as activation function to predict the probability of each message being written by a bot or a human. All the experiments reported hereinafter use a vocabulary size of 20k tokens, sequence size 200, learning rate 0.001, 5 epochs, 128 batch size, static embeddings unless otherwise stated, and 10-fold cross validation.

First we train the CNN classifier on our dataset using pre-trained embeddings and compare them with randomly generated embeddings. In addition, we pre-process our dataset using the same pre-processing script[5] that was applied when learning the GloVe Twitter embeddings. This pre-processing replaces, for example, URL, numbers, user mentions, hashtags and some ascii emoticons with the corresponding tags. Evaluation results are presented in table 1.

Embeddings	Dim.	Pre-proc.	Precision	Recall	F-Measure
random	300	No	0.7567	0.7551	0.7517
glove.twitter	200	No	0.7641	0.7618	0.7587
		Yes	0.7834	0.7790	0.7750
word2vec.urban	100	No	0.7122	0.7119	0.7075
		Yes	0.7601	0.7565	0.7522
fastText.crawl	300	No	*0.7679*	*0.7659*	*0.7627*
		Yes	**0.7858**	**0.7849**	**0.7829**

Table 1: Evaluation of CNN classifiers using random and pre-trained embeddings. Bold and italics are used for best classifiers using pre-processing or not pre-processing respectively.

In this setting, the best classifiers, according to the f-measure, is learned using fastText common crawl embeddings and the pre-processed dataset, followed by the classifier that uses GloVe Twitter embeddings also with pre-processing. In general pre-processing improves all the classifiers and evaluation metrics. Also notice that the CNN with word2vec urban dictionary embeddings without pre-processing underperformed the classifier that uses random embeddings, however when using pre-processing the metrics are better for the former.

4.1 Contextualized embeddings

In addition to static pre-trained embeddings we train CNN classifiers with dinamically-generated

[5]https://nlp.stanford.edu/projects/glove/pre-process-twitter.rb

embeddings using ELMo. ELMo embeddings were generated from our dataset, however none of the trainable parameters (i.e., linear combination weights) were modified in the process. Due to the high dimension of these embeddings (dim=1024) we reduced the sequence size to 50 to avoid memory errors. Evaluation results, reported in table 2, shows that when the corpus was not pre-processed ELMo embeddings produced the best classifier, in terms of f-measure, when compared with classifiers learned from pre-trained embedddings and a dataset without pre-processing (see results in table 1 for comparison).

Embeddings	Dim	Preproc.	Precision	Recall	F-Measure
ELMo	1024	No	0.7766	0.7719	0.7675
		Yes	0.7859	0.7827	0.7798

Table 2: Evaluation of CNN classifiers using contextualized embeddings.

However, when the corpus was pre-processed the classifier learned from ELMo embeddings underperforms with respect to the best classifier learned from fastText common crawl embeddings, while outperforms the classifiers learned from GloVe and Urban dictionary. Nevertheless, in this setting ELMo embeddings produces the classifier with highest precision. Another important finding is that ELMo embeddings always generates the classifier with highest precision, regardless of data pre-processings.

4.2 Combining embeddings

We experiment by concatenating different pre-trained embeddings in the input layer of the CNN. Since fastText embeddings learned the best classifiers we pivot around them. Results in table 3 show that the best classifier is learned using fastText common crawl and GloVe Twitter embeddings with data pre-processing, and this classifier is better than any of the previous classifiers reported in tables 1 and 2.

Nevertheless, if we consider the results without pre-processing the combination of these embeddings with ELMo generates the best classifier, which is compatible with what we found above when ELMo embeddings help to learn the best classifier when the dataset was not pre-processed (see table 2). Similarly, this combination of embeddings helps to learn the classifier with highest precision regardless data pre-proccessing.

Embeddings	Pre-proc.	Precision	Recall	F-Measure
fastText.crawl+glove.twitter	No	0.7724	0.7704	0.7672
	Yes	0.7906	**0.7887**	**0.7862**
fastText.crawl+word2vec.urban	No	0.7598	0.7566	0.7526
	Yes	0.7826	0.7798	0.7767
fastText.crawl + glove.twitter	No	0.7675	0.7644	0.7606
+ word2vec.urban	Yes	0.7806	0.7782	0.775
fastText.crawl + glove.twitter	No	*0.7787*	*0.7771*	*0.7744*
+ ELMo	Yes	**0.7925**	0.7861	0.7816

Table 3: Evaluation of CNN classifiers using concatenations of pre-trained and contextualized embeddings. Bold and italics are used for best classifiers using pre-processing or not pre-processing respectively.

4.3 Dynamic and pre-trained embeddings

Another option to improve these classifiers is to allow the CNN to adjust dynamically the embeddings or part of them in the learning process. To do so, we generate 300 dimension embeddings initialized randomly and configure the CNN to make them trainable. In addition, we concatenate these random and trainable embeddings to the pre-trained and ELMo embeddings, which were not modified in the learning process. In this round of experiments we always use pre-processing since in the previous sections this option always improved the classifiers.

Table 4 shows that dynamic embeddings by themselves help to learn a classifier better than all the previous reported. Nevertheless, there exists the risk of over-fitting since the embeddings are tailored to the classification task, and that is why it makes sense to combine them with embeddings learned from other corpora. In this case, the combination of dynamic and ELMo embeddings generates the best classifier. Another interesting finding is that for the first time a classifier using word2vec urban dictionary is better than the others using GloVe twitter and fastText common crawl. We think that the reduced dimensionality of urban dictionary embeddings (100 dim) compared to Twitter and common crawl embeddings (200 dim and 300dim) allows the dynamic embeddings (300 dim) to influence more the learning process, and achieve better results.

Embeddings	Precision	Recall	F-Measure
dynamic	0.7956	0.7957	0.7950
dynamic + glove.twitter	0.8051	0.8042	0.8027
dynamic + fastText.crawl	0.8013	0.8016	0.8009
dynamic + word2vec.urban	0.8066	0.8053	0.8034
dynamic + ELMo	**0.8125**	**0.8097**	**0.8073**

Table 4: Evaluation of CNN classifiers using dynamic embeddings and pre-trained and contextualized embeddings using a pre-processed dataset

In addition, as shown in table 5 we evaluate different combination of the dynamic embeddings and concatenations of the pre-trained and contextualized embeddings. None of these attempts generate a better classifier than the one using the combination of dynamic embeddings and ELMo. Nevertheless, concatenating more embeddings never worsens the evaluation results, and most of the time improves them, with the exception of ELMo embeddings.

Embeddings	Precision	Recall	F-Measure
dynamic + glove.twitter + word2vec.urban	0.8067	0.8056	0.8041
dynamic + fastText.crawl +glove.twitter	0.8057	0.8045	0.8027
dynamic + fastText.crawl + glove .twitter + word2vec.urban	0.8092	0.8078	0.8060
dynamic + fastText.crawl + ELMo	0.8118	0.8093	0.8070
dynamic + fastText.crawl + glove .twitter+ELMo	0.8105	0.8088	0.8070
dynamic + fastText.crawl + glove .twitter+word2vec.urban+ELMo	0.8131	0.8096	0.8069

Table 5: Evaluation of CNN classifiers using dynamic embeddings and concatenations of to pre-trained and contextualized embeddings.

Figure 1 presents an overview of all the CNN classifiers evaluated so far using pre-processing sorted in descending order by f-measure. This figure shows how different classifiers were generated by using initially single pre-trained embeddings and combinations of them. The upper part of the figure is dominated by classifiers that use dynamic and pre-trained embeddings where ELMo embeddings are always involved.

5 Bidirectional long short term memory networks

In addition to CNN we test Long Short Term Memory networks LSTM (Hochreiter and Schmidhuber, 1997), a neural architecture that is also often used in NLP tasks (Yin et al., 2017). LSTM are sequential networks that are able to learn long-term dependencies. In our experiments we use a bidirectional LSTM that processes the sequence of text forward and backward to learn the model. The architecture of the BiLSTM comprises an embedding layer, the BiLSTM layer with 50 processing cells, and a fully connected layer that uses softmax as activation function to predict the probability of each message being written by a bot or a human. The rest of hyperparameters are set with the same values that we use for the CNN experiments.

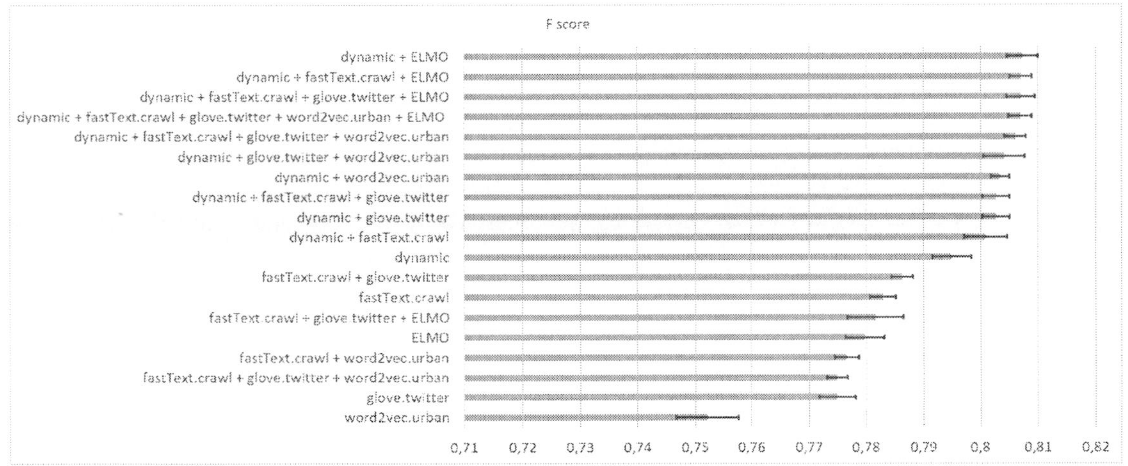

Figure 1: Evaluation of CNN classifiers learned from the single and concatenated pre-trained, contextualized and dynamic embeddings. The results are sorted in descending order by f-measure

In our experiments we test the embeddings combination that generates the best CNN classifiers: dynamic and ELMo embeddings, and also this combination enriched with fastText common crawl embeddings. Evaluation presented in table 6 shows that the best BiLSTM classifier learned from dynamic and ELMo emdeddings performs is very similar to the corresponding CNN. In fact, despite a slightly higher f-measure the individual values of precision and recall reported for the CNN are higher. In this experiment we do not find relevant differences between the CNN classifiers and their BiLSTM counterparts.

Embeddings	Precision	Recall	F-Measure
dynamic + ELMo	0.8095	0.8088	0.8074
dynamic+fastText.crawl + ELMo	0.8093	0.8087	0.8073

Table 6: Evaluation of BiLSTM classifiers using dynamic and pre-trained embeddings and a pre-processed corpus.

6 Pre-trained languages models and fine-tuning

In this section we present the evaluation results for the bot detection task using pre-trained language models and fine-tuning approaches. We follow the fine-tune procedures available for ULMFit[6], Open AI GPT[7], and BERT[8]. In all cases we use the default hyper-parameters:

- BERT base: 3 epochs, batch size of 32, and a learning rate of 2e-5
- Open AI GPT: 3 epochs, batch size of 8, and a learning rate of 6.25e-5
- ULMFiT: 2 epochs for the language model fine-tuning and 3 epochs for the classifier, batch size of 32, and a variable learning rate.

The classifiers evaluation results are presented in table 7. Considering f-measure the best classifier is learned by Open AI GPT, followed by BERT base model classifier. Transformer based approaches are more up to deal with social media messages. While Open AI GPT learns a classifier with highest recall, BERT base model does it with the highest precision. ULMFiT, on the other hand, achieves a high precision, although lower than the rest, and a low recall hence the low f-measure. Both, Open AI GPT and BERT base improve f-measure with respect to the best classifier learned previously by a BiLSTM using dynamic and ELMo embeddings (see table 6).

In addition, we evaluate how data pre-processing affects the pre-trained language models and fine-tuning approaches. Evaluation results presented in table 8 shows that while ULMFiT performance improves, Open AI GPT and BERT base worsen. Nevertheless, ULMFiT classifier is

---

[6]https://docs.fast.ai/text.html#Fine-tuning-a-language-model

[7]https://github.com/tingkai-zhang/pytorch-openai-transformer_clas

[8]https://github.com/google-research/bert#fine-tuning-with-bert

Pre-trained Language model	Precision	Recall	F-Measure
BERT base	**0.8572**	0.8213	0.8388
ULMFiT	0.8471	0.6902	0.7606
Open AI GPT	0.8567	**0.8546**	**0.8533**

Table 7: Pre-trained language models and fine-tuning without data pre-processing

still worse than Open AI and BERT base classifiers. Similarly to what we found above BERT base has the highest precisions while Open AI GPT the highest recall. Note that none of these classifiers beats the Open AI GPT learned from a non pre-processed dataset (see table 7).

Pre-trained Language model	Precision	Recall	F-Measure
BERT base	**0.8481**	0.7948	0.8206
ULMFiT	0.8096	0.7510	0.8123
Open AI GPT	0.8257	**0.8243**	**0.8229**

Table 8: Pre-trained Language models and fine tuning with data pre-processing

7 Discussion

In this paper we use a classification task to validate whether the improvement that transfer learning approaches based on fine-tuning pre-trained language models have brought to NLP tasks can be also achieved with social media text. The challenge for these models is that they have been learned from corpora like Wikipedia, News, or Books, where text is well written, grammatically correct and contextualized. On the other hand, social media messages are short and full of acronyms, hashtags, user mentions, urls, and misspellings. Our learning objective is detecting bots in Twitter messages since as automated agents the generated text is potentially different than the text sources used to pre-trained the language models.

We first present experimental results using classifiers trained with CNN and BiLSTM neural architectures along pre-trained, contextualized and dynamic embeddings. From the experiment results we conclude that using a concatenation of dynamically adjusted embeddings in the training process plus contextualized embeddings generated by ELMo helps to learn the best classifiers. Nevertheless, the models using ELMo embeddings exclusively were penalized when the training data was pre-processed. This was an unexpected result since ELMo works at the character level allowing

it to work with unseen tokens like the tags that we use to replace the actual tokens in the messages.

Next, we fine-tune pre-trained language models generated with ULMFit, BERT base and Open AI GPT, showing that the last two approaches generate classifiers that outperform the best classifiers generated by the CNN and BiLSTM respectively, while ULMFit performance only improves over these classifiers when the data was pre-processed. In addition, BERT always learns the classifier with the highest precision while Open AI GPT learns the classifier with highest recall.

These results open many questions that need more research such as:

- Are unidirectional language models such as Open AI GPT more fitted for short and informal text?
- Is the bidirectional approach used in BERT contributing to the highest precision, while the masked tokens are decreasing its recall?
- Why does the BiLSTM approach used in UMLFiT perform better with pre-processed data in contrast to the other approaches or is this a result of the techniques used in the fine-tuning steps (gradual unfreezing, discriminative fine-tuning, and slanted triangular learning rates) ?

We expect to discuss these questions within the workshop to get more insights about the presented experimental work.

Acknowledgments

This work has been partially supported by LETSCROWD and The European Language Grid projects funded by the European Unions Horizon 2020 research and innovation programme under grant agreements No 740466 and No 825627, respectively. Special thanks to Ronald Denaux for discussion and technical support.

References

J. Deng, W. Dong, R. Socher, L.-J. Li, K. Li, and L. Fei-Fei. 2009. ImageNet: A Large-Scale Hierarchical Image Database. In *CVPR09*.

Jacob Devlin, Ming-Wei Chang, Kenton Lee, and Kristina Toutanova. 2018. Bert: Pre-training of deep bidirectional transformers for language understanding. *arXiv preprint arXiv:1810.04805*.

Zafar Gilani, Ekaterina Kochmar, and Jon Crowcroft. 2017. Classification of twitter accounts into automated agents and human users. In *Proceedings of the 2017 IEEE/ACM International Conference on Advances in Social Networks Analysis and Mining 2017*, ASONAM '17, pages 489–496, New York, NY, USA. ACM.

Sepp Hochreiter and Jürgen Schmidhuber. 1997. Long short-term memory. *Neural Comput.*, 9(8):1735–1780.

Jeremy Howard and Sebastian Ruder. 2018. Fine-tuned language models for text classification. *CoRR*, abs/1801.06146.

Armand Joulin, Edouard Grave, Piotr Bojanowski, and Tomas Mikolov. 2016. Bag of tricks for efficient text classification. *CoRR*, abs/1607.01759.

Yoon Kim. 2014. Convolutional neural networks for sentence classification. In *Proceedings of the 2014 Conference on Empirical Methods in Natural Language Processing, EMNLP 2014, October 25-29, 2014, Doha, Qatar, A meeting of SIGDAT, a Special Interest Group of the ACL*, pages 1746–1751.

Yann LeCun, Léon Bottou, Yoshua Bengio, and Patrick Haffner. 1998. Gradient-based learning applied to document recognition. *Proceedings of the IEEE*, 86(11):2278–2324.

Tomas Mikolov, Kai Chen, Greg Corrado, and Jeffrey Dean. 2013. Efficient estimation of word representations in vector space. *CoRR*, abs/1301.3781.

Tomas Mikolov, Edouard Grave, Piotr Bojanowski, Christian Puhrsch, and Armand Joulin. 2018. Advances in pre-training distributed word representations. In *Proceedings of the International Conference on Language Resources and Evaluation (LREC 2018)*.

Sinno Jialin Pan and Qiang Yang. 2010. A survey on transfer learning. *IEEE Trans. on Knowl. and Data Eng.*, 22(10):1345–1359.

Jeffrey Pennington, Richard Socher, and Christopher D Manning. 2014. Glove: Global vectors for word representation. In *EMNLP*, volume 14, pages 1532–1543.

Matthew Peters, Mark Neumann, Mohit Iyyer, Matt Gardner, Christopher Clark, Kenton Lee, and Luke Zettlemoyer. 2018. Deep contextualized word representations. In *Proceedings of the 2018 Conference of the North American Chapter of the Association for Computational Linguistics: Human Language Technologies, Volume 1 (Long Papers)*, pages 2227–2237. Association for Computational Linguistics.

Alec Radford, Karthik Narasimhan, Tim Salimans, and Ilya Sutskever. 2018. Improving language understanding by generative pre-training. *URL https://s3-us-west-2. amazonaws. com/openai-assets/research-covers/languageunsupervised/language understanding paper. pdf.*

Noam Shazeer, Ryan Doherty, Colin Evans, and Chris Waterson. 2016. Swivel: Improving Embeddings by Noticing What's Missing. *arXiv preprint.*

Onur Varol, Emilio Ferrara, Clayton A. Davis, Filippo Menczer, and Alessandro Flammini. 2017. Online human-bot interactions: Detection, estimation, and characterization. In *ICWSM*.

Ashish Vaswani, Noam Shazeer, Niki Parmar, Jakob Uszkoreit, Llion Jones, Aidan N. Gomez, Lukasz Kaiser, and Illia Polosukhin. 2017. Attention is all you need. *CoRR*, abs/1706.03762.

Wenpeng Yin, Katharina Kann, Mo Yu, and Hinrich Schtze. 2017. Comparative study of cnn and rnn for natural language processing.

Probing Multilingual Sentence Representations With X-PROBE

Vinit Ravishankar
Language Technology Group
Department of Informatics
University of Oslo
vinitr@ifi.uio.no

Lilja Øvrelid
Language Technology Group
Department of Informatics
University of Oslo
liljao@ifi.uio.no

Erik Velldal
Language Technology Group
Department of Informatics
University of Oslo
erikve@ifi.uio.no

Abstract

This paper extends the task of probing sentence representations for linguistic insight in a multilingual domain. In doing so, we make two contributions: first, we provide datasets for multilingual probing, derived from Wikipedia, in five languages, viz. English, French, German, Spanish and Russian. Second, we evaluate six sentence encoders for each language, each trained by mapping sentence representations to English sentence representations, using sentences in a parallel corpus. We discover that cross-lingually mapped representations are often better at retaining certain linguistic information than representations derived from English encoders trained on natural language inference (NLI) as a downstream task.

1 Introduction

In recent years, there has been a considerable amount of research into attempting to represent contexts longer than single words with fixed-length vectors. These representations typically tend to focus on attempting to represent sentences, although phrase- and paragraph-centric mechanisms do exist. These have moved well beyond relatively naïve compositional methods, such as additive and multiplicative methods (Mitchell and Lapata, 2008), one of the earlier papers on the subject. There have been several proposed approaches to learning these representations since, both unsupervised and supervised. Naturally, this has also sparked interest in evaluation methods for sentence representations; the focus of this paper is on *probing*-centric evaluations, and their extension to a multilingual domain.

In Section 2, we provide a literature review of prior work in the numerous domains that our paper builds upon. Section 3 motivates the principle of cross-lingual probing and describes our goals. In Section 4, we describe our probing tasks and relevant modifications, if any. Section 5 describes our sentence encoders, as well as the procedure we follow for training, mapping and probing. Section 6 describes our data and relevant preprocessing methods we applied. Section 7 presents a detailed evaluation from several perspectives, which we discuss in Section 8. We conclude, as well as describe avenues for future work, in Section 9. Our hyperparameters are described in Appendix A.1, and further detailed results that are not critical to the paper are tabulated in A.2.

2 Background

2.1 Sentence representation learning

Numerous methods for learning sentence representations exist. Many of these methods are unsupervised, and thus do not have much significant annotation burden. Most of these methods are, however, structured: they rely on the sentences in training data being ordered and not randomly sampled. The aptly named *SkipThoughts* (Kiros et al., 2015) is a well-known earlier work, and uses recurrent encoder-decoder models to 'decode' sentences surrounding the encoded sentence, using the final encoder state as the encoded sentence's representation. Cer et al. (2018) evaluate two different encoders, a deep averaging network and a transformer, on unsupervised data drawn from a variety of web sources. Hill et al. (2016) describe a model based on denoising auto-encoders, and a simplified variant of SkipThoughts, that sums up source word embeddings, that they dub (*FastSent*). Another SkipThoughts variant (Logeswaran and Lee, 2018) uses a multiple-choice objective for contextual sentences, over the more complicated decoder-based objective.

Several supervised approaches to building representations also exist. An earlier work is Chara-

Proceedings of the 4th Workshop on Representation Learning for NLP (RepL4NLP-2019), pages 156–168
Florence, Italy, August 2, 2019. ©2019 Association for Computational Linguistics

gram (Wieting et al., 2016), which uses paraphrase data and builds on character representations to arrive at sentence representations. More recent papers use a diverse variety of target tasks to ground representations, such as visual data (Kiela et al., 2017), machine translation data (McCann et al., 2017), and even multiple tasks, in a multi-task learning framework (Subramanian et al., 2018). Relevant to this paper is Conneau et al.'s (2017a) *InferSent*, that uses natural language inference (NLI) data to ground representations: they learn these representations on the well-known SNLI dataset (Bowman et al., 2015).

2.2 Multilingual representations

Whilst sentence representation is a thriving research domain, there has been relatively less work on multilingualism in the context of sentence representation learning: most prior work has been focussed on multilingual word representation. For sentence representations, an early work (Schwenk and Douze, 2017) proposes a seq2seq-based objective, using machine learning encoders to map source sequences to fixed-length vectors. Along similar lines, Conneau et al. (2018b) propose using machine translation data to transfer sentence representations pre-trained on NLI, using a mean squared error (MSE) loss - this is the approach we follow.

Artetxe and Schwenk (2018) present a 'language agnostic' sentence representation system learnt over machine translation; the agnosticism refers to the joint BPE vocabulary that they construct over all languages, giving their encoders no language information, whilst their decoders are told what language to generate. Similarly, Lample and Conneau (2019) present pre-trained cross-lingual models (XLM), based on modern pretraining mechanisms; specifically, a variant of the masked LM pretraining scheme used in BERT (Devlin et al., 2018).

Contemporaneous with this work, Aldarmaki and Diab (2019) present an evaluation of three cross-lingual sentence transfer methods. Their methods include joint cross-lingual modelling methods that extend monolingual objectives to cross-lingual training, representation transfer learning methods that attempt to 'optimise' sentence representations to be similar to parallel representations in another language, and sentence mapping methods based on orthogonal word embedding transfer: the authors use a parallel corpus as a 'seed dictionary' to fit a transformation matrix between their source and target languages.

2.3 On evaluation

Work on evaluating sentence representations was encouraged by the release of the SentEval toolkit (Conneau and Kiela, 2018), which provided an easy-to-use framework that sentence representations could be 'plugged' into, for rapid downstream evaluation on numerous tasks: these include several classification tasks, textual entailment and similarity tasks, a paraphrase detection task, and caption/image retrieval tasks. Conneau et al. (2018a) also created a set of 'probing tasks', a variant on the theme of diagnostic classification (Hupkes et al., 2017; Belinkov et al., 2017), that would attempt to quantify precisely what sort of linguistic information was being retained by sentence representations. The authors, whose work focussed on evaluating representations for English, provided Spearman correlations between the performance of a particular representation mechanism on being probed for specific linguistic properties, and the downstream performance on a variety of NLP tasks. Along similar lines, and contemporaneously with this work, Liu et al. (2019) probe three pretrained contextualised word representation models – ELMo (Peters et al., 2018), BERT (Devlin et al., 2018) and the OpenAI transformer (Radford et al., 2018) – with a "suite of sixteen diverse probing tasks".

On a different note, Saphra and Lopez (2018) present a CCA-based method to compare representation learning dynamics across time and models, without explicitly requiring annotated probing corpora. They motivate the use of SVCCA (Raghu et al., 2017) to quantify precisely what an encoder learns by comparing the representations it generates with representations generated by an architecture trained specifically for a certain task, with the intuition that a higher similarity between the representations generated by the generic encoder and the specialised representations would indicate that the encoder is capable of encapsulating more task-relevant information. Their method has numerous advantages over traditional diagnostic classification, such as the elimination of the classifier, which reduces the risk of an additional component obfuscating results.

A visible limitation of the datasets provided by

these probing tasks is that most of them were created with the idea of evaluating representations built for English language data. In this spirit, what we propose is analogous to Abdou et al.'s (2018) work on generating multilingual evaluation corpora for word representations. Within the realm of evaluating *multilingual* sentence representations, Conneau et al. (2018b) describe the XNLI dataset, a set of translations of the development and test portions of the multi-genre MultiNLI inference dataset (Williams et al., 2018). This, in a sense, is an extension of a predominantly monolingual task to the multilingual domain; the authors evaluate sentence representations derived by *mapping* non-English representations to an English representation space.

The original XNLI paper provides a baseline representation mapping technique, based on minimising the mean-squared error (MSE) loss between sentence representations across a parallel corpus. Their English language sentence representations are derived from an encoder trained on NLI data (Conneau et al., 2017a), and their target language representations are randomly initialised for a parallel sentence. While this system does perform reasonably well, a more naive machine-translation based approach performs better.

3   Multilingual evaluation

The focus of this paper is twofold. First, we provide five datasets for probing mapped sentence representations, in five languages (including an additional dataset for English), drawn from a different domain to Conneau et al.'s probing dataset: specifically, from Wikipedia. Second, we probe a selection of mapped sentence representations, in an attempt to answer precisely what linguistic features are retained, and to what extent, post mapping. The emphasis of this evaluation is therefore, crucially, not a probing-oriented analysis of representations *trained* on different languages, but an analysis of the effects of MSE-based mapping procedures on the ability of sentence representations to retain linguistic features. In this sense, our focus is less on the correlation between probing performance and downstream performance, and more on the relative performance of our representations on probing tasks.

Despite having described (in Section 2) numerous methods, both for learning monolingual sentence representations, and for mapping them

cross-linguistically, we restrict our work to a smaller subset of these. Specifically, we evaluate six encoders, each trained in a supervised fashion on NLI data.

Whilst our choice of languages could have been more typologically diverse, we were restricted by three factors:

1. the availability of a parallel corpus with English for our mapping procedure

2. the availability of a large enough Wikipedia to allow us to extract sufficient data (for instance, the Arabic Wikipedia was not large enough to fully extract data for all our tasks)

3. the inclusion of the language in XNLI. Despite not being necessary, we believed it would be interesting to have a 'real' downstream task to compare to.

4   Probing

We use most of the probing tasks described in Conneau et al. (2018a). Due to the differences in corpus domain, we alter some of their word-frequency parameters. We also exclude the top constituent (**TopConst**) task; we noticed that Wikipedia tended to have far less diversity in sentence structure than the original Toronto Books corpus, due to the more encyclopaedic style of writing. A brief description of the tasks follows, although we urge the reader to refer to the original paper for more detailed descriptions.

1. Sentence length: In **SentLen**, sentences are divided into multiple bins based on their length; the job of the classifier is to predict the appropriate bin, creating a 6-way classification task.

2. Word count: In **WC**, we sample sentences that feature exactly one amongst a thousand mid-frequency words, and train the classifier to predict the word: this is the most 'difficult' task, in that it has the most possible classes.

3. Tree depth: The **TreeDepth** task simply asks the representation to predict the depth of the sentence's syntax tree. Unlike the original paper, we use the depth the of the dependency tree instead of the constituency tree: this has the added benefit of being faster to extract,

due to the relative speed of dependency parsing, as well as having better multilingual support. We also replace the authors' sentence-length-decorrelation procedure with a naïver one, where we sample an equal number of d-depth trees for each sentence length bin.

4. Bigram shift: In **BiShift**, for half the sentences in the dataset, the order of words in a randomly sampled bigram is reversed. The classifier learns to predict whether or not the sentence contains a reversal.

5. Subject number: The **SubjNum** task asks the classifier to predict the number of the subject of the head verb of the sentence. Only sentences with exactly one subject (annotated with the `nsubj` relation) attached to the root verb were considered.

6. Object number: **ObjNum**, similar to the subject number task, was annotated with the number of the direct object of the head verb (annotated with the `obj` relation).

7. Coordination inversion: In **CoordInv**, two main clauses joined by a coordinating conjunction (annotated with the `cc` and `conj` relations) have their orders reversed, with a probability of one in two. Only sentences with exactly two top-level conjuncts are considered.

8. (Semantic) odd man out: **SOMO**, one of the more difficult tasks in the collection, replaces a randomly sampled word with another word with comparable corpus bigram frequencies, for both bigrams formed with the preceding and the succeeding words. We defined 'comparable' as having a log-frequency difference not greater than 1.

9. Tense prediction: The **Tense** prediction asks the classifier to predict the tense of the main verb: the task uses a rather simple division of tenses; two tenses, `Past` and `Pres`. Tense information was extracted from UD morphological annotation.

5 Encoders

The NLI-oriented training approach for all our encoders is based on *InferSent* (Conneau et al., 2017a). Our first encoder is an RNN-based encoder (specifically, an LSTM); we use two variants of this encoder, one that uses max-pooling over bidirectional RNN states, and another that uses the last recurrent state. Our second encoder is a self-attention based encoder Lin et al. (2017), with the same max-pool/last-state variants. Finally, we include a convolutional sentence representation model inspired by Gan et al. (2016); this model has an order of magnitude fewer parameters than the RNN- and attention-based variants. A variant of this CNN-based encoder has the maximum pooling replaced with average pooling.

5.1 Representation learning

We train all our encoders to represent sentences using the same NLI-based objective followed by Conneau et al. (2017a). More precisely, we first convert the word indices for both our premise and our hypothesis into dense word representations using pretrained fastText word embeddings (Bojanowski et al., 2016). These representations are then passed to our encoder of choice, which returns two fixed-length vectors: u for the premise, and v for the hypothesis. These vectors are combined and concatenated, as $[u, v, u * v, \mid u - v \mid]$, and then passed through a classifier with a softmax layer that outputs a probability distribution over the three NLI labels.

5.2 Mapping

Our procedure for mapping our encoders cross-linguistically broadly follows the principled mapping approach described in Conneau et al. (2018b). The procedure begins by mapping our *word* representations to the same vector space. Unlike the original paper, we use the supervised variant of VecMap (Artetxe et al., 2016) for representation mapping; however, we use seed dictionaries described in Conneau et al. (2017b). Having mapped our word representations, we proceed to map our sentence representations. To do so, we first build an English-language encoder, using (frozen) word representations and (frozen) encoder weights obtained in Section 5.1. We then build a target language encoder, using word embeddings mapped to the same space as the English embeddings. The sentence encoder itself is initialised with random parameters.

We then encode the source and target sentences in an en-trg machine translation corpus, where trg is our target language. Our English encoder re-

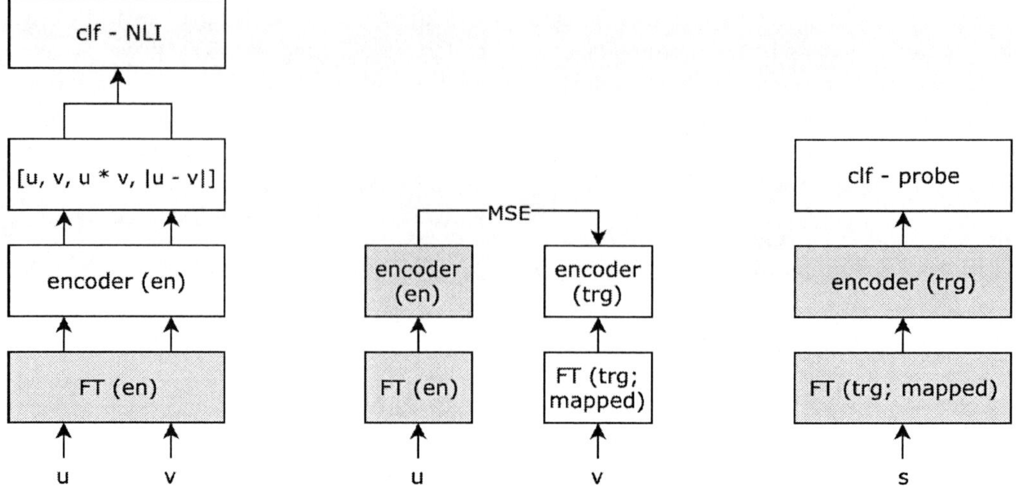

Figure 1: (a) an English-language encoder is trained on NLI data; (b) parallel sentences are encoded in English and the target language, and the MSE loss between them is minimised; (c) the mapped target encoders are used downstream in probing. Greyed-out blocks represent 'frozen' components that do not further adjust their parameters.

turns a 'meaningful' representation: recall that the encoder has weights trained on NLI data. We then use a mean-square error loss function to reduce the distance between our target-language representation and the English representation; the system then backpropagates through the target language encoder to obtain better parameters.

Our MSE loss function, similar to Conneau et al.'s function, attempts to minimise the distance between representations of parallel sentences, whilst simultaneously maximising the distance between random sentences sampled from either language in the pair. Mathematically, the alignment loss is given by:

$$\mathcal{L}_{align} = ||\mathbf{x} - \mathbf{y}||_2 - \lambda(||\mathbf{x_c} - \mathbf{y}||_2 + ||\mathbf{x} - \mathbf{y_c}||_2)$$

where λ is a hyperparameter.

We evaluate our mapped encoder on the relevant validation data section from the XNLI corpus per epoch, and terminate the mapping procedure when our validation accuracy does not improve for two consecutive epochs.

5.3 Multilingual probing

Having obtained our mapped sentence representation encoder, we proceed to plug the encoder into our probing architecture downstream, and evaluate classifier performance.

First, we load our mapped word representations for the language that we intend to analyse. We use these word representations to build sentence representations, using the encoder architecture of choice. We then add a simple multi-layer perceptron (MLP) that learns to predict the appropriate label for each task: the MLP consists of a dense layer, a non-linearity (we use the sigmoid function), and another dense layer that we softmax over to arrive at per-class probabilities. During training, we keep the encoder's parameters fixed. Mathematically, therefore, given an encoder f with parameters θ, and word representations $\mathbf{w_k}$ for each word k:

$$\mathbf{s} = f(\mathbf{w_0}, \mathbf{w_1}, ..., \mathbf{w_n}; \theta)$$
$$\mathbf{z} = \mathrm{MLP}(\mathbf{s})$$
$$\mathbf{y} = \mathrm{softmax}(\mathbf{z})$$

where 'MLP' refers to a multi-layer perceptron with one sigmoid hidden layer.

Finally, we evaluate our representations on the relevant test portion. Whilst Conneau et al. used grid search to determine the best hyperparameters for each probing task, we did not do so, due to both time constraints, and in an attempt to ensure classifier uniformity across languages. We describe our probing results in Section 7.

6 Data

6.1 Probing data

We build our probing datasets using the relevant language's Wikipedia dump as a corpus. Specifically, we use Wikipedia dumps (dated 2019-02-01), which we process using the WikiExtractor

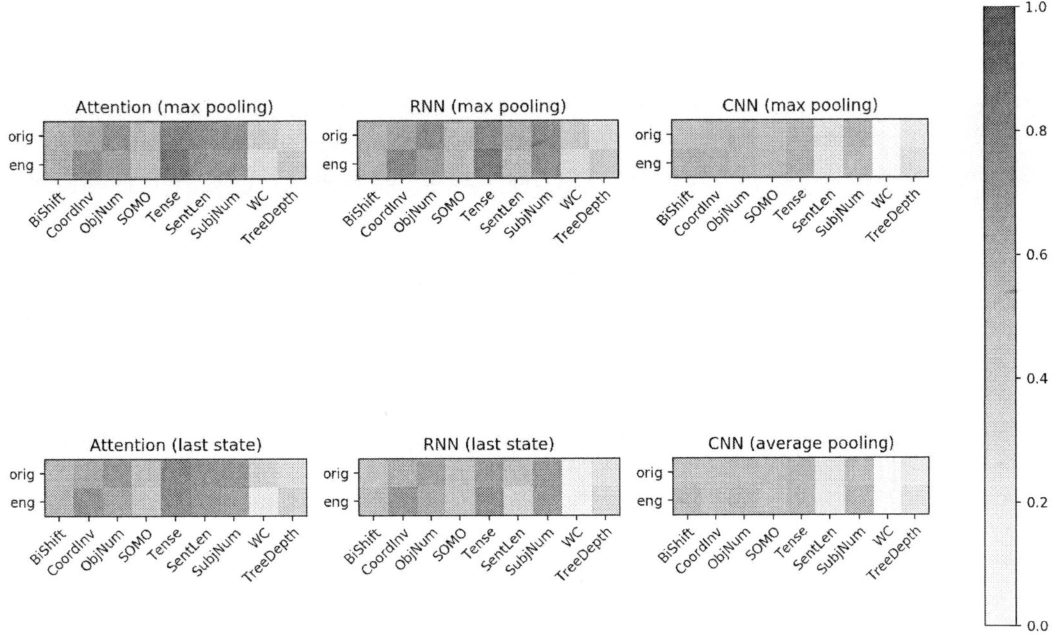

Figure 2: Probing accuracies for our six encoders on Conneau et al.'s dataset (`orig`), compared to our Wikipedia-derived dataset (`eng`)

utility[1]. We use the Punkt tokeniser (Kiss and Strunk, 2006) to segment our Wikipedia dumps into discrete sentences. For Russian, which lacked a Punkt tokenisation model, we used the UD-Pipe (Straka and Straková, 2017) toolkit to perform segmentation.

Having segmented our data, we used the Moses (Koehn et al., 2007) tokeniser for the appropriate language, falling back to English tokenisation when unavailable: this was similar to XNLI's tokenisation schema, and therefore necessary for appropriate evaluation on XNLI.

Next, we obtained dependency parses for our sentences, again using the UDPipe toolkit's pretrained models, trained on Universal Dependencies treebanks (Nivre et al., 2015). We then processed these dependency parsed corpora to extract the appropriate sentences; each task had 120k extracted sentences, divided into training/validation/test splits with 100k, 10k and 10k sentences respectively.

6.2 Mapping data

For mapping our sentence representations, we were restricted by the availability of large parallel corpora we could use for our mapping procedure. We used two such corpora: the Europarl corpus (Koehn, 2005), a multilingual collection of European Parliament proceedings, and the MultiUN corpus (Tiedemann, 2012), a collection of translated documents from the United Nations. We used Europarl for the official EU languages we analysed: German and Spanish. For Russian, we used MultiUN. We used both corpora for French, to attempt to analyse what, if any, effect the mapping corpus would have. We also truncated our MultiUN cororpora to 2 million sentences, to keep the corpus size roughly equivalent to Europarl, and also due to time and resource constraints: mapping representations on the complete 10 million sentence corpus would have required significant amounts of time.

Both our corpora were pre-segmented: we followed the same Moses-based tokenisation scheme that we did for our probing corpora, falling back to English for languages that lacked appropriate tokeniser models.

<hr>

[1]`https://github.com/attardi/
wikiextractor/`

7 Evaluation

As a preface to this section, we reiterate that the goal of this work was not to attempt to reach state-of-the-art on the tasks we describe; our goal was primarily to study the effect of transfer on sentence representations.

Our first step during evaluation, therefore, was to probe all our encoders using Conneau et al.'s original probing corpus, and compare these results to our English-language results on our Wikipedia-generated corpus. We present these results in the form of a heatmap in Figure 2.

Similarities between results on our corpora are instantly visible; these also appear to hold across encoders. Tasks with minor visible differences include **WC**, the most 'difficult' classification task (1k classes), and **TreeDepth**, where we use dependency tree depth instead of constituency tree depth, as well as a different sampling mechanism.

Next, we present Spearman correlations between the performance of our encoders on probing tasks and on the only 'true' cross-lingual downstream task we evaluated our systems on: cross-lingual natural language inference, via the XNLI (Conneau et al., 2018b) corpus. A caveat here is that we make no claims about the statistical significance of these results; given just six data points per language per task, our p-values tend to be well below acceptable for statistical significance. We refer the reader to Conneau et al.'s original probing work, where despite having results for 30 encoders, correlations between many downstream and probing tasks were not statistically significant. Our correlations are presented, again in the form of a heatmap, in Figure 3. Our absolute results on XNLI are presented in the appendix. These are not a focus for this work: we did not attempt to obtain state-of-the-art, nor, indeed, perform any sort of hyperparameter optimisation to get the 'best' possible results. Given these caveats, we draw the reader's attention to the fact that the overwhelming majority of correlations are negative.

Finally, and most importantly, we measure downstream performance on probing tasks for all our cross-lingually mapped encoders. For visualisation relevant to our goals, and for brevity, we present these results, in Figure 4, as a heatmap of probing results *relative* to (our) English probing results; a full table with numeric results is presented in Appendix A.2.

8 Discussion

Our cross-lingual results display some very interesting characteristics, that we enumerate and attempt to explain in this section. These results can be analysed along three dimensions: that of language, encoder mechanism, and the probing task itself.

8.1 Language

Whilst our results are broadly similar across languages, Russian appears to be an exception to this: our probing performance for most tasks is considerably worse when transferred to Russian than other languages. Transfer corpus does not appear to be a factor in this case: most of our encoders perform very similarly on both the Europarl and the UN variants of our transferred French representations. These are interesting preliminary results, that would require further analysis: as we mentioned in an earlier section, we were rather limited in our choice of languages, however, we foresee a possible extension to this work including more typologically diverse languages. One possible explanation for the relatively poor results on Russian is the nature of the word embeddings themselves: whilst we did not use the same methods, we did map our embeddings to the same space using the same dictionaries as Conneau et al. (2017b). The results they describe for word translation retrieval are considerably poorer for English and Russian than they are for English and Spanish, French or German.

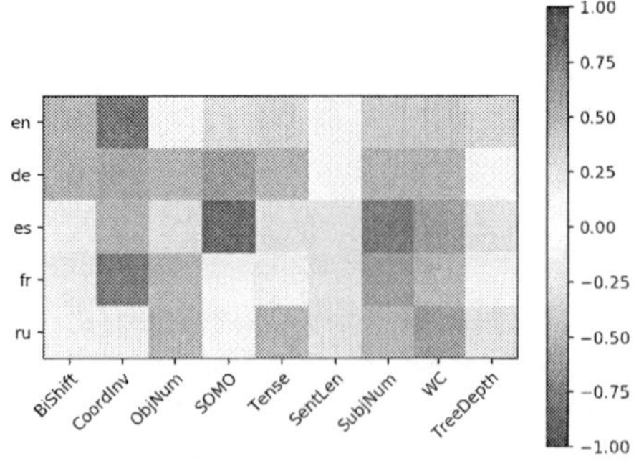

Figure 3: Spearman correlation between probing performance and XNLI; results are not statistically significant.

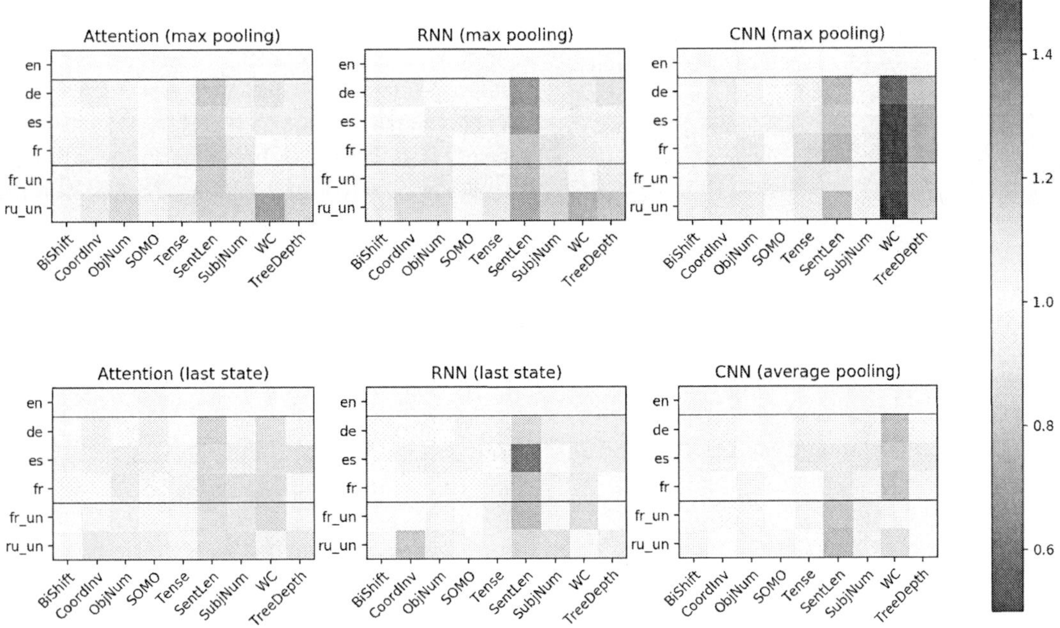

Figure 4: Probing results for each encoder relative to results on English. The second horizontal line indicates a switch in corpora. A white square indicates a value of 1, i.e. a parity in performance

8.2 Probing task

An immediate surprising takeaway from our results is the (perhaps counter-intuitive) fact that transferred representations are not necessarily worse at probing tasks than trained representations are. To help with the analysis of Figure 4, we present Table 1, where several trends are easily visible. In particular, a task that appears to stand out is **SentLen**, with transferred encoders displaying considerably improved performance in five out of six cases.

Apart from sentence length, both number prediction tasks – **SubjNum** and **ObjNum** – show noticeable improvements when transferred to a non-English language. The fact that this improvement is consistent across both number tasks likely also rules out mere coincidence. We hypothesise that the explanation for these three tasks in particular showing improvements on transfer lies in the specific nature of the mapping task. While it is plausible that this is due to these specific phenomena being less critical to NLI (on which our English encoders were trained) than to the attempt made by our target encoders to *emulate* these English representations, it is not immediately clear how these encoders are capable of exceeding the predictive capabilities of the encoders they are attempting to emulate.

Another interesting observation is the variance in performance for the word content (**WC**) task, which also happens to be the 'hardest' task with the most output classes. We further note that, regrettably, none of our encoders were able to learn anything on **SOMO**.

Task	μ	σ
BiShift	0.558	0.013
CoordInv	0.656	0.111
ObjNum	0.605	0.073
SOMO	0.505	0.011
Tense	0.708	0.124
SentLen	0.523	0.259
SubjNum	0.643	0.099
WC	0.152	0.115
TreeDepth	0.330	0.082

Table 1: Mean and standard deviations for the absolute performance for each probing task, across languages and encoders

8.3 Encoder

All our encoders do appear to display very distinctive probing patterns, with variants of each encoder being more similar to each other than to different encoders. We enumerate some of the key observations:

1. Both our CNNs appear to perform worse than attentive or recurrent mechanisms; this is, however, perfectly understandable, as our CNN-based models had an order of magnitude fewer parameters than the recurrent ones. The choice of pooling mechanism, however, appears to have a more significant effect on convolutional encoders than on others.

2. Attentive encoders appear to be better at probing in general, whilst recurrent encoders show extremely strong performance on certain tasks, such as sentence length.

3. The max-pooled CNN is the only encoder that shows considerably worse performance on sentence length. This is also true for English, as is visible from Figure 2. We hypothesise that the fixed-length filters used in convolutional encoders do not store much information about sentence length, as they only observe chunks of the sentence. A max-pooling mechanism further compounds this inability to store length by eliminating possible compositional length information that mean-pooling does ignore.

9 Conclusions

Our analysis reveals several interesting patterns that appear to hold during cross-lingual transfer. Several of our probing tasks give us clearer insight into the sentence representations that we have generated by cross-lingual mapping, which is much needed: the principle of learning a sentence representation in parallel, combined with the fact that these representations actually appear to 'work' downstream, raises a lot of questions both about what information sentence representations hold, but more interestingly, in a cross-lingual context, about what *mutual* information a sentence and its translation contain.

We open-source both our training code and the probing datasets (that we dub X-PROBE)[2] that we

generated in the hope that the domain of cross-lingual analysis sees further work. There are several avenues for expansion, the most obvious being a probing-oriented analysis of more complex contextualisers, such as BERT, as well as of massively multilingual or language agnostic model.

We also hypothesise that more can be said about probing with a different selection of probing tasks; indeed, Liu et al. (2019) do provide a set of tasks that do not overlap with the tasks we have used. Selecting probing tasks that might tell allow us to better interpret cross-lingual modelling is another logical path one might follow. On a similar theme, an interesting research direction also involve adaptations of simple probing tasks describing linguistic phenomena to specialised architectures, for better comparison using SVCCA-style analyses (Saphra and Lopez, 2018).

Finally, we would also like to expand these datasets to more typologically diverse languages. A challenge in doing so is the availability of corpora that are large enough; none of our probing tasks have any sentences in common, which, given the size of each task's corpus, requires a fairly large corpus for extraction. However, this process could possibly be simplified massively by removing this mutual exclusivity requirement, which would vastly simplify the process.

References

Mostafa Abdou, Artur Kulmizev, and Vinit Ravishankar. 2018. MGAD: Multilingual Generation of Analogy Datasets. In *Proceedings of the 11th Language Resources and Evaluation Conference*, Miyazaki, Japan. European Language Resource Association.

Hanan Aldarmaki and Mona Diab. 2019. Scalable Cross-Lingual Transfer of Neural Sentence Embeddings. *arXiv:1904.05542 [cs]*. ArXiv: 1904.05542.

Mikel Artetxe, Gorka Labaka, and Eneko Agirre. 2016. Learning principled bilingual mappings of word embeddings while preserving monolingual invariance. In *Proceedings of the 2016 Conference on Empirical Methods in Natural Language Processing*, pages 2289–2294.

Mikel Artetxe and Holger Schwenk. 2018. Massively Multilingual Sentence Embeddings for Zero-Shot Cross-Lingual Transfer and Beyond. *arXiv:1812.10464 [cs]*. ArXiv: 1812.10464.

Yonatan Belinkov, Nadir Durrani, Fahim Dalvi, Hassan Sajjad, and James Glass. 2017. What do Neural

---

[2] https://github.com/ltgoslo/xprobe

Machine Translation Models Learn about Morphology? In *Proceedings of the 55th Annual Meeting of the Association for Computational Linguistics (Volume 1: Long Papers)*, pages 861–872, Vancouver, Canada. Association for Computational Linguistics.

Piotr Bojanowski, Edouard Grave, Armand Joulin, and Tomas Mikolov. 2016. Enriching Word Vectors with Subword Information. *arXiv:1607.04606 [cs]*. ArXiv: 1607.04606.

Samuel R. Bowman, Gabor Angeli, Christopher Potts, and Christopher D. Manning. 2015. A large annotated corpus for learning natural language inference. *arXiv:1508.05326 [cs]*. ArXiv: 1508.05326.

Daniel Cer, Yinfei Yang, Sheng-yi Kong, Nan Hua, Nicole Limtiaco, Rhomni St John, Noah Constant, Mario Guajardo-Cespedes, Steve Yuan, and Chris Tar. 2018. Universal sentence encoder. *arXiv preprint arXiv:1803.11175*.

Alexis Conneau and Douwe Kiela. 2018. SentEval: An Evaluation Toolkit for Universal Sentence Representations. *arXiv:1803.05449 [cs]*. ArXiv: 1803.05449.

Alexis Conneau, Douwe Kiela, Holger Schwenk, Loic Barrault, and Antoine Bordes. 2017a. Supervised Learning of Universal Sentence Representations from Natural Language Inference Data. *arXiv:1705.02364 [cs]*. ArXiv: 1705.02364.

Alexis Conneau, German Kruszewski, Guillaume Lample, Loc Barrault, and Marco Baroni. 2018a. What you can cram into a single vector: Probing sentence embeddings for linguistic properties. *arXiv:1805.01070 [cs]*. ArXiv: 1805.01070.

Alexis Conneau, Guillaume Lample, Marc'Aurelio Ranzato, Ludovic Denoyer, and Herv Jgou. 2017b. Word Translation Without Parallel Data. *arXiv:1710.04087 [cs]*. ArXiv: 1710.04087.

Alexis Conneau, Guillaume Lample, Ruty Rinott, Adina Williams, Samuel R. Bowman, Holger Schwenk, and Veselin Stoyanov. 2018b. XNLI: Evaluating Cross-lingual Sentence Representations. *arXiv:1809.05053 [cs]*. ArXiv: 1809.05053.

Jacob Devlin, Ming-Wei Chang, Kenton Lee, and Kristina Toutanova. 2018. Bert: Pre-training of deep bidirectional transformers for language understanding. *arXiv preprint arXiv:1810.04805*.

Zhe Gan, Yunchen Pu, Ricardo Henao, Chunyuan Li, Xiaodong He, and Lawrence Carin. 2016. Learning generic sentence representations using convolutional neural networks. *arXiv preprint arXiv:1611.07897*.

Felix Hill, Kyunghyun Cho, and Anna Korhonen. 2016. Learning Distributed Representations of Sentences from Unlabelled Data. In *Proceedings of the 2016 Conference of the North American Chapter of the Association for Computational Linguistics: Human Language Technologies*, pages 1367–1377, San Diego, California. Association for Computational Linguistics.

Dieuwke Hupkes, Sara Veldhoen, and Willem Zuidema. 2017. Visualisation and 'diagnostic classifiers' reveal how recurrent and recursive neural networks process hierarchical structure. *arXiv:1711.10203 [cs]*. ArXiv: 1711.10203.

Douwe Kiela, Alexis Conneau, Allan Jabri, and Maximilian Nickel. 2017. Learning Visually Grounded Sentence Representations. *arXiv:1707.06320 [cs]*. ArXiv: 1707.06320.

Ryan Kiros, Yukun Zhu, Ruslan Salakhutdinov, Richard S. Zemel, Antonio Torralba, Raquel Urtasun, and Sanja Fidler. 2015. Skip-Thought Vectors. *arXiv:1506.06726 [cs]*. ArXiv: 1506.06726.

Tibor Kiss and Jan Strunk. 2006. Unsupervised multilingual sentence boundary detection. *Computational Linguistics*, 32(4):485–525.

Philipp Koehn. 2005. Europarl: A parallel corpus for statistical machine translation. In *MT summit*, volume 5, pages 79–86.

Philipp Koehn, Hieu Hoang, Alexandra Birch, Chris Callison-Burch, Marcello Federico, Nicola Bertoldi, Brooke Cowan, Wade Shen, Christine Moran, Richard Zens, et al. 2007. Moses: Open source toolkit for statistical machine translation. In *Proceedings of the 45th annual meeting of the association for computational linguistics companion volume proceedings of the demo and poster sessions*, pages 177–180.

Guillaume Lample and Alexis Conneau. 2019. Cross-lingual Language Model Pretraining. *arXiv:1901.07291 [cs]*. ArXiv: 1901.07291.

Zhouhan Lin, Minwei Feng, Cicero Nogueira dos Santos, Mo Yu, Bing Xiang, Bowen Zhou, and Yoshua Bengio. 2017. A Structured Self-attentive Sentence Embedding. *arXiv:1703.03130 [cs]*. ArXiv: 1703.03130.

Nelson F Liu, Matt Gardner, Yonatan Belinkov, Matthew E Peters, and Noah A Smith. 2019. Linguistic Knowledge and Transferability of Contextual Representations. page 22.

Lajanugen Logeswaran and Honglak Lee. 2018. An efficient framework for learning sentence representations. *arXiv:1803.02893 [cs]*. ArXiv: 1803.02893.

Bryan McCann, James Bradbury, Caiming Xiong, and Richard Socher. 2017. Learned in Translation: Contextualized Word Vectors.

Jeff Mitchell and Mirella Lapata. 2008. Vector-based Models of Semantic Composition. In *Proceedings of ACL-08: HLT*, pages 236–244, Columbus, Ohio. Association for Computational Linguistics.

Joakim Nivre, Željko Agić, Maria Jesus Aranzabe, Masayuki Asahara, Aitziber Atutxa, Miguel Ballesteros, John Bauer, Kepa Bengoetxea, Riyaz Ahmad Bhat, Cristina Bosco, Sam Bowman, Giuseppe G. A. Celano, Miriam Connor, Marie-Catherine de Marneffe, Arantza Diaz de Ilarraza, Kaja Dobrovoljc, Timothy Dozat, Tomaž Erjavec, Richárd Farkas, Jennifer Foster, Daniel Galbraith, Filip Ginter, Iakes Goenaga, Koldo Gojenola, Yoav Goldberg, Berta Gonzales, Bruno Guillaume, Jan Hajič, Dag Haug, Radu Ion, Elena Irimia, Anders Johannsen, Hiroshi Kanayama, Jenna Kanerva, Simon Krek, Veronika Laippala, Alessandro Lenci, Nikola Ljubešić, Teresa Lynn, Christopher Manning, Cătălina Mărănduc, David Mareček, Héctor Martínez Alonso, Jan Mašek, Yuji Matsumoto, Ryan McDonald, Anna Missilä, Verginica Mititelu, Yusuke Miyao, Simonetta Montemagni, Shunsuke Mori, Hanna Nurmi, Petya Osenova, Lilja Øvrelid, Elena Pascual, Marco Passarotti, Cenel-Augusto Perez, Slav Petrov, Jussi Piitulainen, Barbara Plank, Martin Popel, Prokopis Prokopidis, Sampo Pyysalo, Loganathan Ramasamy, Rudolf Rosa, Shadi Saleh, Sebastian Schuster, Wolfgang Seeker, Mojgan Seraji, Natalia Silveira, Maria Simi, Radu Simionescu, Katalin Simkó, Kiril Simov, Aaron Smith, Jan Štěpánek, Alane Suhr, Zsolt Szántó, Takaaki Tanaka, Reut Tsarfaty, Sumire Uematsu, Larraitz Uria, Viktor Varga, Veronika Vincze, Zdeněk Žabokrtský, Daniel Zeman, and Hanzhi Zhu. 2015. Universal dependencies 1.2. LINDAT/CLARIN digital library at the Institute of Formal and Applied Linguistics (ÚFAL), Faculty of Mathematics and Physics, Charles University.

Matthew E Peters, Mark Neumann, Mohit Iyyer, Matt Gardner, Christopher Clark, Kenton Lee, and Luke Zettlemoyer. 2018. Deep contextualized word representations. *arXiv preprint arXiv:1802.05365*.

Alec Radford, Karthik Narasimhan, Tim Salimans, and Ilya Sutskever. 2018. Improving language understanding by generative pre-training.

Maithra Raghu, Justin Gilmer, Jason Yosinski, and Jascha Sohl-Dickstein. 2017. Svcca: Singular vector canonical correlation analysis for deep learning dynamics and interpretability. In *Advances in Neural Information Processing Systems*, pages 6076–6085.

Naomi Saphra and Adam Lopez. 2018. Understanding Learning Dynamics Of Language Models with SVCCA. *arXiv:1811.00225 [cs]*. ArXiv: 1811.00225.

Holger Schwenk and Matthijs Douze. 2017. Learning Joint Multilingual Sentence Representations with Neural Machine Translation. *arXiv:1704.04154 [cs]*. ArXiv: 1704.04154.

Milan Straka and Jana Straková. 2017. Tokenizing, pos tagging, lemmatizing and parsing ud 2.0 with udpipe. In *Proceedings of the CoNLL 2017 Shared Task: Multilingual Parsing from Raw Text to Universal Dependencies*, pages 88–99, Vancouver, Canada. Association for Computational Linguistics.

Sandeep Subramanian, Adam Trischler, Yoshua Bengio, and Christopher J. Pal. 2018. Learning General Purpose Distributed Sentence Representations via Large Scale Multi-task Learning. *arXiv:1804.00079 [cs]*. ArXiv: 1804.00079.

Jrg Tiedemann. 2012. Parallel data, tools and interfaces in opus. In *Proceedings of the Eight International Conference on Language Resources and Evaluation (LREC'12)*, Istanbul, Turkey. European Language Resources Association (ELRA).

John Wieting, Mohit Bansal, Kevin Gimpel, and Karen Livescu. 2016. Charagram: Embedding Words and Sentences via Character n-grams. In *Proceedings of the 2016 Conference on Empirical Methods in Natural Language Processing*, pages 1504–1515, Austin, Texas. Association for Computational Linguistics.

Adina Williams, Nikita Nangia, and Samuel Bowman. 2018. A Broad-Coverage Challenge Corpus for Sentence Understanding through Inference. In *Proceedings of the 2018 Conference of the North American Chapter of the Association for Computational Linguistics: Human Language Technologies, Volume 1 (Long Papers)*, pages 1112–1122, New Orleans, Louisiana. Association for Computational Linguistics.

A Appendices

A.1 Hyperparameters

Component	Layer	Value
Global	Embeddings	300 (FastText)
	Batch size	10
	Optimiser	Adam
	Learning rate	10^{-3}
RNN	biLSTM dim	512
	biLSTM layers	2
	Dropout	10%
CNN	Filter sizes	(3, 4, 5)
	Padding	(1, 2, 2)
	Channels	800
	Projection dim	1024
Attention	biLSTM dim	512
	biLSTM layers	2
	Dropout	10%
	MLP dim	150
	Activation	tanh
	Attn. heads	60
Mapper	λ	0.25
Probe classifier	Hidden dim	150
	Activation	σ

Table 2: Hyperparameters, divided by the 'component' that each layer belongs to. Note that biRNN dims are per direction.

A.2 Additional results

Encoder	Language					
	English	German	Spanish	French	French (UN)	Russian
RNN (maxpool)	**0.71**	**0.66**	0.68	0.68	0.65	0.61
RNN (last)	0.66	0.63	0.65	0.65	0.63	0.59
CNN (maxpool)	0.51	0.39	0.41	0.36	0.44	0.43
CNN (avg. pool)	0.51	0.50	0.51	0.50	0.50	0.48
Attn. (maxpool)	**0.71**	0.64	0.67	0.67	0.67	0.60
Attn. (last)	0.70	0.65	**0.69**	**0.69**	**0.66**	**0.62**

Table 3: Language-specific results on relevant XNLI splits for each encoder

English	BiShift	CoordInv	ObjNum	SOMO	Tense	SentLen	SubjNum	WC	TreeDepth
Attention (maxpool)	0.57	0.73	0.65	0.5	0.82	0.7	0.7	0.27	0.41
Attention (last)	0.56	0.74	0.64	0.49	0.8	0.74	0.7	0.22	0.4
RNN (maxpool)	0.54	0.74	0.65	0.5	0.82	0.51	0.73	0.3	0.42
RNN (last)	0.55	0.73	0.62	0.5	0.74	0.38	0.68	0.11	0.34
CNN (maxpool)	0.55	0.55	0.53	0.51	0.57	0.22	0.52	0.01	0.26
CNN (avg. pool)	0.55	0.51	0.54	0.5	0.54	0.21	0.56	0.02	0.24

German	BiShift	CoordInv	ObjNum	SOMO	Tense	SentLen	SubjNum	WC	TreeDepth
Attention (maxpool)	0.56	0.76	0.63	0.5	0.8	0.85	0.66	0.24	0.39
Attention (last)	0.56	0.79	0.63	0.52	0.81	0.87	0.68	0.25	0.39
RNN (maxpool)	0.57	0.8	0.64	0.51	0.82	0.68	0.69	0.28	0.37
RNN (last)	0.54	0.74	0.61	0.52	0.71	0.44	0.63	0.11	0.31
CNN (maxpool)	0.54	0.51	0.51	0.5	0.55	0.17	0.53	0.0	0.21
CNN (avg. pool)	0.54	0.5	0.53	0.5	0.57	0.21	0.54	0.01	0.23

Spanish	BiShift	CoordInv	ObjNum	SOMO	Tense	SentLen	SubjNum	WC	TreeDepth
Attention (maxpool)	0.57	0.72	0.69	0.51	0.85	0.82	0.73	0.25	0.44
Attention (last)	0.58	0.71	0.7	0.51	0.84	0.85	0.74	0.25	0.45
RNN (maxpool)	0.55	0.75	0.69	0.53	0.85	0.67	0.76	0.28	0.44
RNN (last)	0.55	0.7	0.65	0.52	0.75	0.54	0.68	0.12	0.36
CNN (maxpool)	0.55	0.5	0.51	0.49	0.52	0.18	0.51	0.0	0.19
CNN (avg. pool)	0.55	0.5	0.54	0.5	0.6	0.23	0.51	0.01	0.26

French	BiShift	CoordInv	ObjNum	SOMO	Tense	SentLen	SubjNum	WC	TreeDepth
Attention (maxpool)	0.56	0.76	0.7	0.5	0.85	0.84	0.76	0.27	0.42
Attention (last)	0.58	0.76	0.71	0.5	0.84	0.86	0.79	0.26	0.41
RNN (maxpool)	0.53	0.78	0.7	0.5	0.84	0.61	0.8	0.31	0.4
RNN (last)	0.55	0.72	0.65	0.49	0.71	0.47	0.71	0.12	0.34
CNN (maxpool)	0.55	0.52	0.49	0.51	0.5	0.17	0.51	0.0	0.2
CNN (avg. pool)	0.55	0.51	0.52	0.5	0.54	0.23	0.54	0.01	0.23

French (UN)	BiShift	CoordInv	ObjNum	SOMO	Tense	SentLen	SubjNum	WC	TreeDepth
Attention (maxpool)	0.57	0.74	0.7	0.5	0.82	0.83	0.76	0.27	0.42
Attention (last)	0.57	0.76	0.69	0.5	0.83	0.83	0.78	0.26	0.41
RNN (maxpool)	0.56	0.78	0.7	0.5	0.83	0.62	0.79	0.3	0.39
RNN (last)	0.55	0.73	0.65	0.5	0.68	0.47	0.71	0.13	0.34
CNN (maxpool)	0.55	0.51	0.51	0.49	0.52	0.2	0.52	0.0	0.21
CNN (avg. pool)	0.55	0.52	0.52	0.5	0.52	0.25	0.53	0.02	0.24

Russian	BiShift	CoordInv	ObjNum	SOMO	Tense	SentLen	SubjNum	WC	TreeDepth
Attention (maxpool)	0.58	0.66	0.56	0.52	0.74	0.82	0.6	0.2	0.35
Attention (last)	0.58	0.66	0.57	0.53	0.76	0.84	0.6	0.2	0.35
RNN (maxpool)	0.57	0.65	0.57	0.51	0.76	0.65	0.61	0.22	0.33
RNN (last)	0.57	0.57	0.56	0.52	0.68	0.45	0.59	0.11	0.3
CNN (maxpool)	0.57	0.51	0.5	0.5	0.55	0.17	0.51	0.0	0.21
CNN (avg. pool)	0.57	0.51	0.52	0.52	0.56	0.26	0.53	0.01	0.24

Table 4: Complete set of absolute results per probing task, per encoder, per language. For English, these numbers are for unmapped, NLI-based encoders; for all other languages, these are post-mapping numbers

Fine-Grained Entity Typing in Hyperbolic Space

Federico López*   Benjamin Heinzerling   Michael Strube
*Research Training Group AIPHES
Heidelberg Institute for Theoretical Studies
`firstname.lastname@h-its.org`

Abstract

How can we represent hierarchical information present in large type inventories for entity typing? We study the ability of hyperbolic embeddings to capture hierarchical relations between mentions in context and their target types in a shared vector space. We evaluate on two datasets and investigate two different techniques for creating a large hierarchical entity type inventory: from an expert-generated ontology and by automatically mining type co-occurrences. We find that the hyperbolic model yields improvements over its Euclidean counterpart in some, but not all cases. Our analysis suggests that the adequacy of this geometry depends on the *granularity* of the type inventory and the way hierarchical relations are inferred.[1]

1 Introduction

Entity typing classifies textual mentions of entities according to their semantic class. The task has progressed from finding company names (Rau, 1991), to recognizing coarse classes (*person, location, organization,* and *other,* Tjong Kim Sang and De Meulder, 2003), to fine-grained inventories of about one hundred types, with finer-grained types proving beneficial in applications such as relation extraction (Yaghoobzadeh et al., 2017) and question answering (Yavuz et al., 2016). The trend towards larger inventories has culminated in *ultra-fine* and *open* entity typing with thousands of classes (Choi et al., 2018; Zhou et al., 2018).

However, large type inventories pose a challenge for the common approach of casting entity typing as a multi-label classification task (Yogatama et al., 2015; Shimaoka et al., 2016), since exploiting inter-type correlations becomes more

---

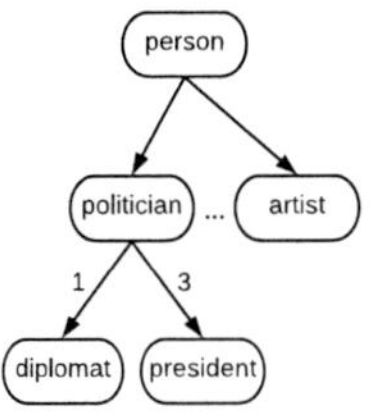

Sentence	Annotation
...when the **president** said...	politician, president
...during the negotiation, **he**...	politician, diplomat
...after the last meeting, **she**...	politician, president
...the **president** argued...	politician, president

Figure 1: Examples of annotations and hierarchical type inventory with co-occurrence frequencies.

difficult as the number of types increases. A natural solution for dealing with a large number of types is to organize them in hierarchy ranging from general, *coarse* types such as "person" near the top, to more specific, *fine* types such as "politician" in the middle, to even more specific, *ultra-fine* entity types such as "diplomat" at the bottom (see Figure 1). By virtue of such a hierarchy, a model learning about diplomats will be able to transfer this knowledge to related entities such as politicians.

Prior work integrated hierarchical entity type information by formulating a hierarchy-aware loss (Ren et al., 2016; Murty et al., 2018; Xu and Barbosa, 2018) or by representing words and types in a joint Euclidean embedding space (Shimaoka et al., 2017; Abhishek et al., 2017). Noting that it is impossible to embed arbitrary hierarchies in Euclidean space, Nickel and Kiela (2017) propose hyperbolic space as an alternative and show that hyperbolic embeddings accurately encode hierarchical information. Intuitively (and as explained in more detail in Section 2), this is because distances in hyperbolic space grow exponentially as one moves away from the origin, just like the number of elements in a hierarchy grows exponentially with its depth.

While the intrinsic advantages of hyperbolic embeddings are well-established, their usefulness in downstream tasks is, so far, less clear. We be

Proceedings of the 4th Workshop on Representation Learning for NLP (RepL4NLP-2019), pages 169–180
Florence, Italy, August 2, 2019. ©2019 Association for Computational Linguistics

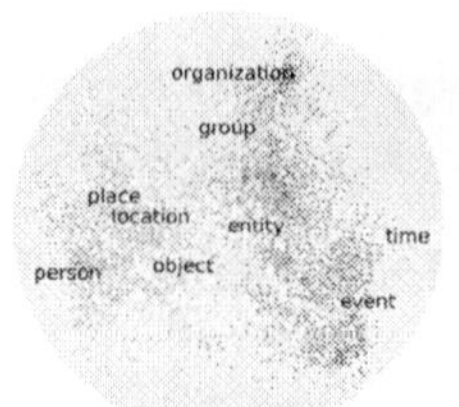 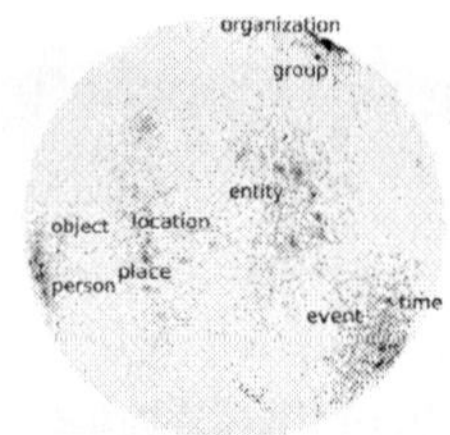

(a) Euclidean Space.   (b) Hyperbolic Space.

Figure 2: Type inventory of the Ultra-Fine dataset aligned to the WordNet noun hierarchy and projected on two dimensions in different spaces.

lieve this is due to two difficulties: First, incorporating hyperbolic embeddings into a neural model is non-trivial since training involves optimization in hyperbolic space. Second, it is often not clear what the best hierarchy for the task at hand is.

In this work, we address both of these issues. Using ultra-fine grained entity typing (Choi et al., 2018) as a test bed, we first show how to incorporate hyperbolic embeddings into a neural model (Section 3). Then, we examine the impact of the hierarchy, comparing hyperbolic embeddings of an expert-generated ontology to those of a large, automatically-generated one (Section 4). As our experiments on two different datasets show (Section 5), hyperbolic embeddings improve entity typing in some but not all cases, suggesting that their usefulness depends both on the type inventory and its hierarchy. In summary, we make the following contributions:

1. We develop a fine-grained entity typing model that embeds both entity types and entity mentions in hyperbolic space.

2. We compare two different entity type hierarchies, one created by experts (WordNet) and one generated automatically, and find that their adequacy depends on the dataset.

3. We study the impact of replacing the Euclidean geometry with its hyperbolic counterpart in an entity typing model, finding that the improvements of the hyperbolic model are noticeable on *ultra-fine* types.

2 Background: Poincaré Embeddings

Hyperbolic geometry studies non-Euclidean spaces with constant negative curvature. Two-dimensional hyperbolic space can be modelled as the open unit disk, the so-called *Poincaré disk*, in which the unit circle represents infinity, i.e., as a

point approaches infinity in hyperbolic space, its norm approaches one in the Poincaré disk model. In the general n-dimensional case, the disk model becomes the Poincaré ball (Chamberlain et al., 2017) $\mathcal{B}^n = \{x \in \mathbb{R}^n \mid \|x\| < 1\}$, where $\| \cdot \|$ denotes the Euclidean norm. In the Poincaré model the distance between two points $u, v \in \mathcal{B}^n$ is given by:

$$d_H(\mathbf{u}, \mathbf{v}) = \operatorname{arcosh}(1 + 2\frac{\|\mathbf{u} - \mathbf{v}\|^2}{(1 - \|\mathbf{u}\|^2)(1 - \|\mathbf{v}\|^2)}) \quad (1)$$

If we consider the origin O and two points, x and y, moving towards the outside of the disk, i.e. $\|x\|, \|y\| \to 1$, the distance $d_H(x, y)$ tends to $d_H(x, O) + d_H(O, y)$. That is, the path between x and y is converges to a path through the origin. This behaviour can be seen as the continuous analogue to a (discrete) tree-like hierarchical structure, where the shortest path between two sibling nodes goes through their common ancestor.

As an alternative intuition, note that the hyperbolic distance between points grows exponentially as points move away from the center. This mirrors the exponential growth of the number of nodes in trees with increasing depths, thus making hyperbolic space a natural fit for representing trees and hence hierarchies (Krioukov et al., 2010; Nickel and Kiela, 2017).

By embedding hierarchies in the Poincaré ball so that items near the top of the hierarchy are placed near the origin and lower items near infinity (intuitively, embedding the "vertical" structure), and so that items sharing a parent in the hierarchy are close to each other (embedding the "horizontal" structure), we obtain Poincaré embeddings (Nickel and Kiela, 2017). More formally, this means that embedding norm represents depth in the hierarchy, and distance between embeddings the similarity of the respective items.

Figure 2 shows the results of embedding the WordNet noun hierarchy in two-dimensional Euclidean space (left) and the Poincaré disk (right). In the hyperbolic model, the types tend to be located near the boundary of the disk. In this region the space grows exponentially, which allows related types to be placed near one another and far from unrelated ones. The actual distance in this model is not the one visualized in the figure but the one given by Equation 1.

170

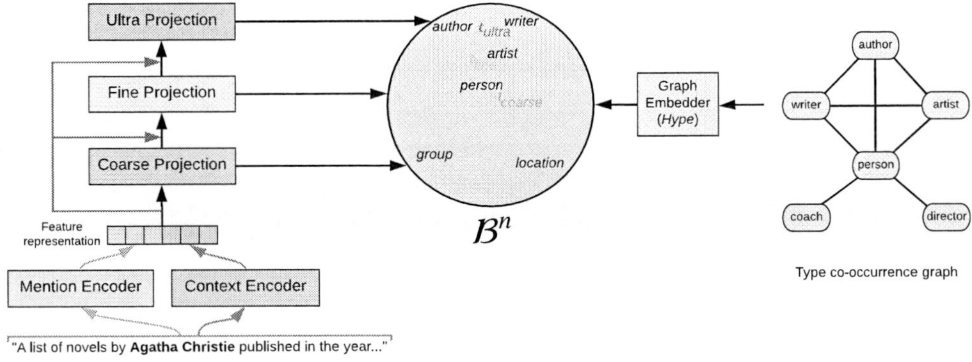

(a) Projection layers.

(b) Incorporation of hierarchical information.

Figure 3: Overview of the proposed model to predict types of a mention within its context.

3 Entity Typing in Hyperbolic Space

3.1 Task Definition

The task we consider is, given a context sentence c containing an entity mention m, predict the correct type labels t_m that describe m from a type inventory T, which includes more than 10,000 types (Choi et al., 2018). The mention m can be a named entity, a nominal, or a pronoun. The ground-truth type set t_m may contain multiple types, making the task a multi-label classification problem.

3.2 Objective

We aim to analyze the effects of hyperbolic and Euclidean spaces when modeling hierarchical information present in the type inventory, for the task of fine-grained entity typing. Since hyperbolic geometry is naturally equipped to model hierarchical structures, we hypothesize that this enhanced representation will result in superior performance. With the goal of examining the relation between the metric space and the hierarchy, we propose a regression model. We learn a function that maps feature representations of a mention and its context onto a vector space such that the instances are embedded closer to their target types.

The ground-truth type set contains a varying number of types per instance. In our regression setup, however, we aim to predict a fixed amount of labels for all the instances. This imposes strong upper bounds to the performance of our proposed model. Nonetheless, as the strict accuracy of state-of-the-art methods for the Ultra-Fine dataset is below 40% (Choi et al., 2018; Xiong et al., 2019), the evaluation we perform is still informative in qualitative terms, and enables us to gain better intuitions with regard to embedding hierarchical structures in different metric spaces.

3.3 Method

Given the encoded feature representations of a mention m and its context c, noted as $e(m, c) \in \mathbb{R}^{n'}$ our goal is to learn a mapping function $f : \mathbb{R}^{n'} \to \mathcal{S}^n$, where $\mathcal{S}^n$ is the target vector space. We intend to approximate embeddings of the type labels t_m, previously projected into the space. Subsequently, we perform a search of the nearest type embeddings of the embedded representation in order to assign the categorical label corresponding to the mention within that context. Figure 3 presents an overview of the model.

The label distribution on the dataset is diverse and fine-grained. Each instances is annotated with three levels of granularity, namely *coarse*, *fine* and *ultra-fine*, and on the development and test set there are, on average, five labels per item. This poses a challenging problem for learning and predicting with only one projection. As a solution, we propose three different projection functions, f_{coarse}, f_{fine}, and f_{ultra}, each one of them fine-tuned to predict labels of a specific granularity.

We hypothesize that the complexity of the projection increases as the granularity becomes *finer*, given that the target label space per granularity increases. Inspired by Sanh et al. (2019), we arrange the three projections in a hierarchical manner that reflects these difficulties. The *coarse* projection task is set at the bottom layer of the model and more complex (*finer*) interactions at higher layers. With the projected embedding of each layer, we aim to introduce an inductive bias in the next projection that will help to guide it into the correct region of the space. Nevertheless, we use shortcut connections so that top layers can have access to the encoder layer representation.

3.4 Mention and Context Representations

To encode the context c containing the mention m, we apply the encoder schema of Choi et al. (2018) based on Shimaoka et al. (2016). We replace the location embedding of the original encoder with a word position embedding p_i to reflect relative distances between the i-th word and the entity mention. This modification induces a bias on the attention layer to focus less on the mention and more on the context. Finally we apply a standard Bi-LSTM and a self-attentive encoder (McCann et al., 2017) on top to get the context representation $C \in \mathbb{R}^{d_c}$.

For the mention representation we derive features from a character-level CNN, concatenate them with the Glove word embeddings (Pennington et al., 2014) of the mention, and combine them with a similar self-attentive encoder. The mention representation is denoted as $M \in \mathbb{R}^{d_m}$. The final representation is achieved by the concatenation of mention and context $[M; C] \in \mathbb{R}^{d_m + d_c}$.

3.5 Projecting into the Ball

To learn a projection function that embeds our feature representation in the target space, we apply a variation of the re-parameterization technique introduced in Dhingra et al. (2018). The re-parameterization involves computing a direction vector r and a norm magnitude λ from $e(m, c)$ as follows:

$$\overline{r} = \varphi_{dir}(e(m, c)), \quad r = \frac{\overline{r}}{\|\overline{r}\|},$$
$$\overline{\lambda} = \varphi_{norm}(e(m, c)), \quad \lambda = \sigma(\overline{\lambda}), \quad (2)$$

where $\varphi_{dir} : \mathbb{R}^{n'} \to \mathbb{R}^n$, $\varphi_{norm} : \mathbb{R}^{n'} \to \mathbb{R}$ can be arbitrary functions, whose parameters will be optimized during training, and σ is the sigmoid function that ensures the resulting norm $\lambda \in (0, 1)$. The re-parameterized embedding is defined as $v = \lambda r$, which lies in $\mathcal{S}^n$.

By making use of this simple technique, the embeddings are guaranteed to lie in the Poincaré ball. This avoids the need to correct the gradient or the utilization of Riemannian-SGD (Bonnabel, 2011). Instead, it allows the use of any optimization method in deep learning, such as Adam (Kingma and Ba, 2014).

We parameterize the direction function $\varphi_{dir} : \mathbb{R}^{d_m + d_c} \to \mathbb{R}^n$ as a multi-layer perceptron (MLP) with a single hidden layer, using rectified linear units (ReLU) as nonlinearity, and dropout. We do not apply the ReLU function after the output layer in order to allow negative values as components of the direction vector. For the norm magnitude function $\varphi_{norm} : \mathbb{R}^{d_m + d_c} \to \mathbb{R}$ we use a single linear layer.

3.6 Optimization of the Model

We aim to find projection functions f_i that embed the instance representations closer to the respective target types, in a given vector space $\mathcal{S}^n$. As target space $\mathcal{S}^n$ we use the Poincaré Ball $\mathcal{B}^n$ and compare it with the Euclidean unit ball $\mathbb{R}^n$. Both $\mathcal{B}^n$ and $\mathbb{R}^n$ are metric spaces, therefore they are equipped with a distance function, namely the hyperbolic distance d_H defined in Equation 1, and the Euclidean distance d_E respectively, which we intend to minimize. Moreover, since the Poincaré Model is a conformal model of the hyperbolic space, *i.e.* the angles between Euclidean and hyperbolic vectors are equal, the cosine distance $d_{\cos}$ can be used, as well.

We propose to minimize a combination of the distance defined by each metric space and the cosine distance to approximate the embeddings. Although formally this is not a distance metric since it does not satisfy the Cauchy-Schwarz inequality, it provides a very strong signal to approximate the target embeddings accounting for the main concepts modeled in the representation: *relatedness*, captured via the distance and orientation in the space, and *generality*, via the norm of the embeddings.

To mitigate the instability in the derivative of the hyperbolic distance[2] we follow the approach proposed in Sala et al. (2018) and minimize the square of the distance, which does have a continuous derivative in $\mathcal{B}^n$. Thus, in the Poincaré Model we minimize the distance for two points $u, v \in \mathcal{B}^n$ defined as:

$$d_{\mathcal{B}}(u, v) = \alpha(d_H(u, v))^2 + \beta d_{\cos}(u, v) \quad (3)$$

Whereas in the Euclidean space, for $x, y \in \mathbb{R}^n$ we minimize:

$$d_{\mathbb{R}}(x, y) = \alpha d_E(x, y) + \beta d_{\cos}(x, y) \quad (4)$$

The hyperparameters α and β are added to compensate the bounded image of the cosine distance function in $[0, 1]$.

---

[2] $\lim_{y \to x} \partial_x |d_H(x, y)| \to \infty \; \forall x \in \mathcal{B}^n$

Split	Coarse	Fine	Ultra-fine
Train	2,416,593	4,146,143	3,997,318
Dev	1,918	1,289	7,594
Test	1,904	1,318	7,511

Table 1: Type instances in the dataset grouped by split and granularity.

4 Hierarchical Type Inventories

In this section, we investigate two methods for deriving a hierarchical structure for a given type inventory. First, we introduce the datasets on which we perform our study since we exploit some of their characteristics to construct a hierarchy.

4.1 Data

We focus our analysis on the the Ultra-Fine entity typing dataset introduced in Choi et al. (2018). Its design goals were to increase the diversity and coverage entity type annotations. It contains 10,331 target types defined as free-form noun phrases and divided in three levels of granularity: *coarse*, *fine* and *ultra-fine*. The data consist of 6,000 crowdsourced examples and approximately 6M training samples in the open-source version[3], automatically extracted with distant supervision, by entity linking and nominal head word extraction. Our evaluation is done on the original crowdsourced dev/test splits.

To gain a better understanding of the proposed model under different geometries, we also experiment on the OntoNotes dataset (Gillick et al., 2014) as it is a standard benchmark for entity typing.

4.2 Deriving the Hierarchies

The two methods we analyze to derive a hierarchical structure from the type inventory are the following.

Knowledge base alignment: Hierarchical information can be provided explicitly, by aligning the type labels to a knowledge base schema. In this case the types follow the tree-like structure of the ontology curated by experts. On the Ultra-Fine dataset, the type vocabulary T (*i.e.* noun phrases) is extracted from WordNet (Miller, 1992). Nouns in WordNet are organized into a deep hierarchy, defined by hypernym or "IS A" relationships. By aligning the type labels to the hypernym structure existing in WordNet, we obtain a type hierarchy. In this case, all paths lead to the root type *entity*.

In the OntoNotes dataset the annotations follow a pre-established, much smaller, hierarchical taxonomy based on "IS A" relations, as well.

Type co-occurrences: Although in practical scenarios hierarchical information may not always be available, the distribution of types has an implicit hierarchy that can be inferred automatically. If we model the ground-truth labels as nodes of a graph, its adjacency matrix can be drawn and weighted by considering the co-occurrences on each instance. That is, if t_1 and t_2 are annotated as true types for a training instance, we add an edge between both types. To weigh the edge we explore two variants: the frequency of observed instances where this co-relation holds, and the *pointwise mutual information* (pmi), as a measure of the association between the two types[4]. By mining type co-occurrences present in the dataset as an affinity score, the hierarchy can be inferred. This method alleviates the need for a type inventory explicitly aligned to an ontology or pre-defined label correlations.

To embed the target type representations into the different metric spaces we make use of the library *Hype*[5] (Nickel and Kiela, 2018). This library allows us to embed graphs into low-dimensional continuous spaces with different metrics, such as hyperbolic or Euclidean, ensuring that related objects are closer to each other in the space. The learned embeddings capture notions of both similarity, through the relative distance among each other, and hierarchy, through the distance to the origin, i.e. the norm. The projection of the hierarchy derived from WordNet is depicted in Figure 2.

5 Experiments

We perform experiments on the Ultra-Fine (Choi et al., 2018) and OntoNotes (Gillick et al., 2014) datasets to evaluate which kind of hierarchical information is better suited for entity typing, and under which geometry the hierarchy can be better exploited.

5.1 Setup

For evaluation we run experiments on the Ultra-Fine dataset with our model projecting onto the hyperbolic space, and compare to the same setting in Euclidean space. The type embeddings are

---

[3]Choi et al. (2018) uses the licensed Gigaword to build part of the dataset resulting in about 25.2M training samples.

[4]We adapt pmi in order to satisfy the condition of non-negativity.

[5]https://github.com/facebookresearch/poincare-embeddings/

Model	Space	Coarse		Fine		Ultra-fine		Coarse + Ultra		Variation	
		MaF1	MiF1	MaF1	MiF1	MaF1	MiF1	MaF1	MiF1	MaF1	MiF1
MULTITASK	-	60.6	58.0	37.8	34.7	13.6	11.7	-	-	-	-
WORDNET	Hyper	45.9	44.3	22.5	21.5	7.0	6.7	41.8	37.2	-4.1	-7.1
	Euclid	56.1	54.2	26.6	25.3	7.2	6.5	56.6	48.5	0.6	-5.7
WORDNET + FREQ	Hyper	54.6	52.8	18.4	18.0	11.3	10.8	46.5	40.6	-8.0	-12.2
	Euclid	**56.7**	**54.9**	**27.3**	**26.0**	12.1	11.5	55.8	49.1	-0.9	-5.8
FREQ	Hyper	56.5	54.6	26.8	25.7	**16.0**	15.2	59.7	**53.5**	3.2	**-1.1**
	Euclid	56.1	54.2	25.8	24.4	12.1	11.4	**60.0**	53.0	**3.9**	-1.3
PMI	Hyper	54.7	53.0	26.9	25.8	**16.0**	**15.4**	57.5	51.8	2.8	-1.2
	Euclid	56.5	54.6	26.9	25.6	12.2	11.5	59.7	53.0	3.2	-1.5

(a) Results on the same three granularities analyzed by Choi et al. (2018).

(b) Comparison to previous *coarse* results.

Table 2: Results on the test set for different hierarchies and spaces. The best results of our models are marked in bold. On (b) we report the comparison of adding the closest *coarse* label to the *ultra-fine* prediction, with respect to the *coarse* results on (a).

created based on the following hierarchical structures derived from the dataset: the type vocabulary aligned to the WordNet hierarchy (WORDNET), type co-occurrence frequency (FREQ), *pointwise mutual information* among types (PMI), and finally, the combination of WordNet's transitive closure of each type with the co-occurrence frequency graph (WORDNET + FREQ).

We compare our model to the multi-task model of Choi et al. (2018) trained on the open-source version of their dataset (MULTITASK). The final type predictions consist of the closest neighbor from the *coarse* and *fine* projections, and the three closest neighbors from the *ultra-fine* projection. We report Loose Macro-averaged and Loose Micro-averaged F1 metrics computed from the precision/recall scores over the same three granularities established by Choi et al. (2018). For all models we optimize Macro-averaged F1 on *coarse* types on the validation set, and evaluate on the test set. All experiments project onto a target space of 10 dimensions. The complete set of hyperparameters is detailed in the Appendix.

6 Results and Discussion

6.1 Comparison of the Hierarchies

Results on the test set are reported in Table 2. From comparing the different strategies to derive the hierarchies, we can see that FREQ and PMI substantially outperform MULTITASK on the *ultra-fine* granularity (17.5% and 29.8% relative improvement in Macro F1 and Micro F1, respectively, with the hyperbolic model). Both hierarchies show a substantially better performance over the WORDNET hierarchy on this granularity as

well (MaF1 16.0 and MiF1 15.4 for PMI vs 7.0 and 6.7 for WORDNET on the Hyperbolic model), indicating that these structures, created solely from the dataset statistics, better reflect the type distribution in the annotations. On FREQ and PMI, types that frequently co-occur on the training set are located closer to each other, improving the prediction based on nearest neighbor.

All the hierarchies show very low performance on *fine* when compared to the MULTITASK model. This exhibits a weakness of our regression setup. On the test set there are 1,998 instances but only 1,318 *fine* labels as ground truth (see Table 1). By forcing a prediction on the *fine* level for all instances, precision decreases notably. More details in Section 6.3.

The combined hierarchy WORDNET + FREQ achieves marginal improvements on *coarse* and *fine* granularities, while it degrades the performance on *ultra-fine* when compared to FREQ.

By imposing a hierarchical structure over the type vocabulary we can infer types that are located higher up in the hierarchy from the predictions of the lower ones. To analyze this, we add the closest *coarse* label to the *ultra-fine* prediction of each instance. Results are reported in Table 2b. The improvements are noticeable on the Macro score (up to 3.9 F1 points difference on FREQ) whereas Micro decreases. Since we are adding types to the prediction, this technique improves recall and penalizes precision. Macro is computed on the entity level, while Micro provides an overall score, showing that per instance the prediction tends to be better. The improvements can be observed on FREQ and PMI given that their predictions over

a) Example	Rin, Kohaku and Sesshomaru Rin befriends Kohaku, the demonslayer Sango's younger brother, while Kohaku acts as her guard when Naraku is using her for bait to lure Sesshomaru into **battle**.
Annotation	*event, conflict, war, fight, battle, struggle, dispute, group_action*
Prediction	FREQ: event, conflict, war, fight, battle;
	WORDNET: event, conflict, difference, engagement, assault
b) Example	**The UN mission in Afghanistan** dispatched its own investigation, expressing concern about reports of civilian casualties and calling for them to be properly cared for.
Annotation	*organization, team, mission*
Prediction	FREQ: organization, team, mission, activity, operation;
	WORDNET: group, institution, branch, delegation, corporation
c) Example	Brazilian President Luiz Inacio Lula da Silva and Turkish Prime Minister Recep Tayyip Erdogan talked about designing a strategy different from sanctions at **a meeting** Monday, Amorim said.
Annotation	*event, meeting, conference, gathering, summit*
Prediction	FREQ: event, meeting, conference, film, campaign;
	WORDNET: entity, meeting, gathering, structure, court

Table 3: Qualitative analysis of instances taken from the development set. The predictions are generated with the hyperbolic models of FREQ and WORDNET. Correct predictions are marked in blue color.

6.2 Comparison of the Spaces

ultra-fine types are better.

When comparing performances with respect to the metric spaces, the hyperbolic models for PMI and FREQ outperform all other models on *ultra-fine* granularity. Compared to its Euclidean counterpart, PMI brings considerable improvements (16.0 vs 12.2 and 15.4 vs 11.5 for Macro and Micro F1 respectively). This can be explained by the exponential growth of this space towards the boundary of the ball, combined with a representation that reflects the type co-occurrences in the dataset. Figure 4 shows a histogram of the distribution of ground-truth types as closest neighbors to the prediction.

On both Euclidean and hyperbolic models, the type embeddings for *coarse* and *fine* labels are located closer to the origin of the space. In this region, the spaces show a much more similar behavior in terms of the distance calculation, and this similarity is reflected on the results as well.

The low performance of the hyperbolic model of WORDNET on *coarse* can be explained by the fact that *entity* is the root node of the hierarchy, therefore it is located closer to the center of the space. Elements placed in the vicinity of the origin have a norm closer to zero, thus their distance to other types tends to be shorter (does not grow exponentially). This often misleads the model into assign *entity* as the *coarse*. See Table 3c for an example.

This issue is alleviated on WORDNET + FREQ. Nevertheless, it appears again when using the *ultra-fine* prediction to infer the *coarse* label. The

drop in performance can be seen in Table 2b: Macro F1 decreases by 8.0 and Micro F1 by 12.2.

6.3 Error analysis

We perform an error analysis on samples from the development set and predictions from two of our proposed hyperbolic models. We show three examples in Table 3. Overall we can see that predictions are reasonable, suggesting synonyms or related words.

In the proposed regression setup, we predict a fixed amount of labels per instance. This schema has drawbacks as shown in example a), where all predicted types by the FREQ model are correct though we can not predict more, and b), where we predict more related types that are not part of the annotations.

In examples b) and c) we see how the FREQ model predicts the *coarse* type correctly whereas the model that uses the WordNet hierarchy predicts *group* and *entity* since these labels are considered more general (*organization* IS A *group*) thus located closer to the origin of the space.

To analyse precision and recall more accurately, we compare our model to the one of Shimaoka et al. (2016) (ATTNER) and the multi-task model of Choi et al. (2018) (MULTI). We show the results for macro-averaged metrics in Table 4. Our model is able to achieve higher recall but lower precision. Nonetheless we are able to outperform ATTNER with a regression model even though they apply a classifier to the task.

Model	Dev			Test		
	P	**R**	**F1**	**P**	**R**	**F1**
ATTNER	**53.7**	15.0	23.5	**54.2**	15.2	23.7
FREQ	24.8	**25.9**	25.4	25.6	**26.8**	26.2
MULTI	48.1	23.2	**31.3**	47.1	24.2	**32.0**

Table 4: Combined performance over the three granularities. Results are extracted from Choi et al. (2018).

Model	Sp	Coarse		Fine		Ultra	
		Ma	**Mi**	**Ma**	**Mi**	**Ma**	**Mi**
ONTO	Hy	**83.0**	81.9	24.0	23.9	2.0	2.0
	Eu	82.2	**82.2**	28.8	28.7	2.4	2.4
FREQ	Hy	81.7	81.8	27.1	27.1	**4.2**	**4.2**
	Eu	81.7	81.7	**30.6**	**30.6**	3.8	3.8

Table 5: Macro and micro F1 results on OntoNotes.

6.4 Analysis Case: OntoNotes

To better understand the effects of the hierarchy and the metric spaces we also perform an evaluation on OntoNotes (Gillick et al., 2014). We compare the original hierarchy of the dataset (ONTO), and one derived from the type co-occurrence frequency extracted from the data augmented by Choi et al. (2018) with this type inventory. The results for the three granularities are presented in Table 5.

The FREQ model on the hyperbolic geometry achieves the best performance for the *ultra-fine* granularity, in accordance with the results on the Ultra-Fine dataset. In this case the improvements of the frequency-based hierarchy are not so remarkable when compared to the ONTO model given that the type inventory is much smaller, and the annotations follow a hierarchy where there is only one possible path for every label to its *coarse* type.

The low results on the *ultra-fine* granularity are

due to the reduced multiplicity of the annotated types (See Table 8). Most instances have only one or two types, setting very restrictive upper bounds for this setup.

7 Related Work

Type inventories for the task of fine-grained entity typing (Ling and Weld, 2012; Gillick et al., 2014; Yosef et al., 2012) have grown in size and complexity (Del Corro et al., 2015; Murty et al., 2017; Choi et al., 2018). Systems have tried to incorporate hierarchical information on the type distribution in different manners. Shimaoka et al. (2017) encode the hierarchy through a sparse matrix. Xu and Barbosa (2018) model the relations through a hierarchy-aware loss function. Ma et al. (2016) and Abhishek et al. (2017) learn embeddings for labels and feature representations into a joint space in order to facilitate information sharing among them. Our work resembles Xiong et al. (2019) since they derive hierarchical information in an unrestricted fashion, through type co-occurrence statistics from the dataset. These models operate under Euclidean assumptions. Instead, we impose a hyperbolic geometry to enrich the hierarchical information.

Hyperbolic spaces have been applied mostly on complex and social networks modeling (Krioukov et al., 2010; Verbeek and Suri, 2016). In the field of Natural Language Processing, they have been employed to learn embeddings for Question Answering (Tay et al., 2018), in Neural Machine Translation (Gulcehre et al., 2019), and to model language (Leimeister and Wilson, 2018; Tifrea et al., 2019). We build upon the work of Nickel and Kiela (2017) on modeling hierarchical link structure of symbolic data and adapt it with the parameterization method proposed by Dhingra et al. (2018) to cope with feature representations of text.

8 Conclusions

Incorporation of hierarchical information from large type inventories into neural models has become critical to improve performance. In this work we analyze expert-generated and data-driven hierarchies, and the geometrical properties provided by the choice of the vector space, in order to model this information. Experiments on two different datasets show consistent improvements of hyperbolic embedding over Euclidean baselines

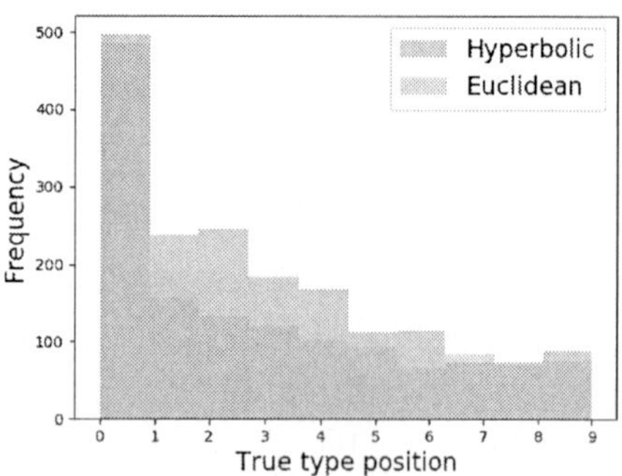

Figure 4: Histogram of ground-truth type neighbor positions for *ultra-fine* predictions in Hyperbolic and Euclidean spaces on the test set.

on very fine-grained labels when the hierarchy reflects the annotated type distribution.

Acknowledgments

We would like to thank the anonymous reviewers for their valuable comments and suggestions, and we also thank Ana Marasović, Mareike Pfeil, Todor Mihaylov and Mark-Christoph Müller for their helpful discussions. This work has been supported by the German Research Foundation (DFG) as part of the Research Training Group Adaptive Preparation of Information from Heterogeneous Sources (AIPHES) under grant No. GRK 1994/1 and the Klaus Tschira Foundation, Heidelberg, Germany.

References

Abhishek Abhishek, Ashish Anand, and Amit Awekar. 2017. Fine-grained entity type classification by jointly learning representations and label embeddings. In *Proceedings of the 15th Conference of the European Chapter of the Association for Computational Linguistics: Volume 1, Long Papers*, pages 797–807, Valencia, Spain. Association for Computational Linguistics.

Silvre Bonnabel. 2011. Stochastic gradient descent on riemannian manifolds. *IEEE Transactions on Automatic Control*, 58.

Benjamin Paul Chamberlain, James Clough, and Marc Peter Deisenroth. 2017. Neural embeddings of graphs in hyperbolic space. *CoRR*, abs/1705.10359.

Eunsol Choi, Omer Levy, Yejin Choi, and Luke Zettlemoyer. 2018. Ultra-fine entity typing. In *Proceedings of the 56th Annual Meeting of the Association for Computational Linguistics (Volume 1: Long Papers)*, pages 87–96, Melbourne, Australia. Association for Computational Linguistics.

Luciano Del Corro, Abdalghani Abujabal, Rainer Gemulla, and Gerhard Weikum. 2015. Finet: Context-aware fine-grained named entity typing. In *Proceedings of the 2015 Conference on Empirical Methods in Natural Language Processing*, pages 868–878, Lisbon, Portugal. Association for Computational Linguistics.

Bhuwan Dhingra, Christopher Shallue, Mohammad Norouzi, Andrew Dai, and George Dahl. 2018. Embedding text in hyperbolic spaces. In *Proceedings of the Twelfth Workshop on Graph-Based Methods for Natural Language Processing (TextGraphs-12)*, pages 59–69, New Orleans, Louisiana, USA. Association for Computational Linguistics.

Dan Gillick, Nevena Lazic, Kuzman Ganchev, Jesse Kirchner, and David Huynh. 2014. Context-Dependent Fine-Grained Entity Type Tagging. *ArXiv e-prints*.

Caglar Gulcehre, Misha Denil, Mateusz Malinowski, Ali Razavi, Razvan Pascanu, Karl Moritz Hermann, Peter Battaglia, Victor Bapst, David Raposo, Adam Santoro, and Nando de Freitas. 2019. Hyperbolic attention networks. In *International Conference on Learning Representations*.

Diederik P. Kingma and Jimmy Ba. 2014. Adam: A method for stochastic optimization. *International Conference on Learning Representations*, abs/1412.6980.

Dmitri Krioukov, Fragkiskos Papadopoulos, Maksim Kitsak, Amin Vahdat, and Marin Bogu. 2010. Hyperbolic geometry of complex networks. *Physical review. E, Statistical, nonlinear, and soft matter physics*, 82:036106.

Matthias Leimeister and Benjamin J. Wilson. 2018. Skip-gram word embeddings in hyperbolic space. *CoRR*, abs/1809.01498.

Xiao Ling and Daniel S. Weld. 2012. Fine-grained entity recognition. In *Proceedings of the Twenty-Sixth AAAI Conference on Artificial Intelligence*, AAAI'12, pages 94–100. AAAI Press.

Yukun Ma, Erik Cambria, and SA GAO. 2016. Label embedding for zero-shot fine-grained named entity typing. In *Proceedings of COLING 2016, the 26th International Conference on Computational Linguistics: Technical Papers*, pages 171–180, Osaka, Japan.

Bryan McCann, James Bradbury, Caiming Xiong, and Richard Socher. 2017. Learned in translation: Contextualized word vectors. In *Advances in Neural Information Processing Systems*, pages 6297–6308.

George A. Miller. 1992. Wordnet: A lexical database for english. In *Speech and Natural Language: Proceedings of a Workshop Held at Harriman, New York, February 23-26, 1992*.

Shikhar Murty, Patrick Verga, Luke Vilnis, and Andrew McCallum. 2017. Finer grained entity typing with typenet. In *31st Conference on Neural Information Processing Systems (NIPS 2017)*, Long Beach, CA, USA.

Shikhar Murty, Patrick Verga, Luke Vilnis, Irena Radovanovic, and Andrew McCallum. 2018. Hierarchical losses and new resources for fine-grained entity typing and linking. In *Proceedings of the 56th Annual Meeting of the Association for Computational Linguistics (Volume 1: Long Papers)*, pages 97–109, Melbourne, Australia. Association for Computational Linguistics.

Maximilian Nickel and Douwe Kiela. 2017. Poincaré embeddings for learning hierarchical representations. In I. Guyon, U. V. Luxburg, S. Bengio, H. Wallach, R. Fergus, S. Vishwanathan, and R. Garnett, editors, *Advances in Neural Information Processing Systems 30*, pages 6341–6350. Curran Associates, Inc.

Maximillian Nickel and Douwe Kiela. 2018. Learning continuous hierarchies in the Lorentz model of hyperbolic geometry. In *Proceedings of the 35th International Conference on Machine Learning*, volume 80 of *Proceedings of Machine Learning Research*, pages 3779–3788, Stockholmsmssan, Stockholm Sweden. PMLR.

Jeffrey Pennington, Richard Socher, and Christopher Manning. 2014. Glove: Global vectors for word representation. In *Proceedings of the 2014 Conference on Empirical Methods in Natural Language Processing (EMNLP)*, pages 1532–1543, Doha, Qatar. Association for Computational Linguistics.

Lisa F Rau. 1991. Extracting company names from text. In *Artificial Intelligence Applications, 1991. Proceedings., Seventh IEEE Conference on*, volume 1, pages 29–32. IEEE.

Xiang Ren, Wenqi He, Meng Qu, Clare R. Voss, Heng Ji, and Jiawei Han. 2016. Label noise reduction in entity typing by heterogeneous partial-label embedding. In *Proceedings of the 22Nd ACM SIGKDD International Conference on Knowledge Discovery and Data Mining*, KDD '16, pages 1825–1834, New York, NY, USA. ACM.

Frederic Sala, Chris De Sa, Albert Gu, and Christopher Re. 2018. Representation tradeoffs for hyperbolic embeddings. In *Proceedings of the 35th International Conference on Machine Learning*, volume 80 of *Proceedings of Machine Learning Research*, pages 4460–4469, Stockholmsmssan, Stockholm Sweden. PMLR.

Victor Sanh, Thomas Wolf, and Sebastian Ruder. 2019. A hierarchical multi-task approach for learning embeddings from semantic tasks. In *AAAI*, volume abs/1811.06031.

Sonse Shimaoka, Pontus Stenetorp, Kentaro Inui, and Sebastian Riedel. 2016. An attentive neural architecture for fine-grained entity type classification. In *Proceedings of the 5th Workshop on Automated Knowledge Base Construction*, pages 69–74, San Diego, CA. Association for Computational Linguistics.

Sonse Shimaoka, Pontus Stenetorp, Kentaro Inui, and Sebastian Riedel. 2017. Neural architectures for fine-grained entity type classification. In *Proceedings of the 15th Conference of the European Chapter of the Association for Computational Linguistics: Volume 1, Long Papers*, pages 1271–1280, Valencia, Spain. Association for Computational Linguistics.

Yi Tay, Luu Anh Tuan, and Siu Cheung Hui. 2018. Hyperbolic representation learning for fast and efficient neural question answering. In *Proceedings of the Eleventh ACM International Conference on Web Search and Data Mining*, WSDM '18, pages 583–591, New York, NY, USA. ACM.

Alexandru Tifrea, Gary Becigneul, and Octavian-Eugen Ganea. 2019. Poincare glove: Hyperbolic word embeddings. In *International Conference on Learning Representations*.

Erik F. Tjong Kim Sang and Fien De Meulder. 2003. Introduction to the CoNLL-2003 shared task: Language-independent named entity recognition. In *Proceedings of the Seventh Conference on Natural Language Learning at HLT-NAACL 2003 - Volume 4*, CONLL '03, pages 142–147, Stroudsburg, PA, USA. Association for Computational Linguistics.

Kevin Verbeek and Subhash Suri. 2016. Metric embedding, hyperbolic space, and social networks. *Computational Geometry*, 59:1 – 12.

Wenhan Xiong, Jiawei Wu, Deren Lei, Mo Yu, Shiyu Chang, Xiaoxiao Guo, and William Yang Wang. 2019. Imposing label-relational inductive bias for extremely fine-grained entity typing. In *Proceedings of NAACL-HLT 2019*.

Peng Xu and Denilson Barbosa. 2018. Neural fine-grained entity type classification with hierarchy-aware loss. In *Proceedings of the 2018 Conference of the North American Chapter of the Association for Computational Linguistics: Human Language Technologies, Volume 1 (Long Papers)*, pages 16–25, New Orleans, Louisiana. Association for Computational Linguistics.

Yadollah Yaghoobzadeh, Heike Adel, and Hinrich Schütze. 2017. Noise mitigation for neural entity typing and relation extraction. In *Proceedings of the 15th Conference of the European Chapter of the Association for Computational Linguistics: Volume 1, Long Papers*, pages 1183–1194, Valencia, Spain. Association for Computational Linguistics.

Semih Yavuz, Izzeddin Gur, Yu Su, Mudhakar Srivatsa, and Xifeng Yan. 2016. Improving semantic parsing via answer type inference. In *Proceedings of the 2016 Conference on Empirical Methods in Natural Language Processing*, pages 149–159, Austin, Texas. Association for Computational Linguistics.

Dani Yogatama, Daniel Gillick, and Nevena Lazic. 2015. Embedding methods for fine grained entity type classification. In *Proceedings of the 53rd Annual Meeting of the Association for Computational Linguistics and the 7th International Joint Conference on Natural Language Processing (Volume 2: Short Papers)*, pages 291–296, Beijing, China. Association for Computational Linguistics.

Mohamed Amir Yosef, Sandro Bauer, Johannes Hoffart, Marc Spaniol, and Gerhard Weikum. 2012.

HYENA: Hierarchical type classification for entity names. In *Proceedings of COLING 2012: Posters*, pages 1361–1370, Mumbai, India.

Ben Zhou, Daniel Khashabi, Chen-Tse Tsai, and Dan Roth. 2018. Zero-shot open entity typing as type-compatible grounding. In *Proceedings of the 2018 Conference on Empirical Methods in Natural Language Processing*, pages 2065–2076, Brussels, Belgium. Association for Computational Linguistics.

A Appendix

A.1 Hyperparameters

Both hyperbolic and Euclidean models were trained with the following hyperparameters.

Parameter	Value
Word embedding dim	300
Max mention tokens	5
Max mention chars	25
Context length (per side)	10
Char embedding dim	50
Position embedding dim	25
Context LSTM dim	200
Attention dim	100
Mention dropout	0.5
Context dropout	0.2
Max gradient norm	10
Projection hidden dim	500
Optimizer	Adam
Learning rate	0.001
Batch size	1024
Epochs	50

Table 6: Model hyperparameters.

A.2 Dataset statistics

Split	Samples	Coarse	Fine	Ultra-fine
Train	6,240,105	2,148,669	2,664,933	3,368,607
Dev	1,998	1,612	947	1,860
Test	1,998	1,598	964	1,864

Table 7: Amount of samples with at least one label of the granularity organized by split on Ultra-Fine Dataset.

Split	Samples	Coarse	Fine	Ultra
Train	793,487	828,840	735,162	301,006
Dev	2,202	2,337	869	76
Test	8,963	9,455	3,521	417

Table 8: Samples and label distribution by split on OntoNotes Dataset.

Learning Multilingual Meta-Embeddings for
Code-Switching Named Entity Recognition

Genta Indra Winata, Zhaojiang Lin, Pascale Fung
Center for Artificial Intelligence Research (CAiRE)
Department of Electronic and Computer Engineering
The Hong Kong University of Science and Technology, Clear Water Bay, Hong Kong
{giwinata,zlinao}@connect.ust.hk, pascale@ece.ust.hk

Abstract

In this paper, we propose Multilingual Meta-Embeddings (MME), an effective method to learn multilingual representations by leveraging monolingual pre-trained embeddings. MME learns to utilize information from these embeddings via a self-attention mechanism without explicit language identification. We evaluate the proposed embedding method on the code-switching English-Spanish Named Entity Recognition dataset in a multilingual and cross-lingual setting. The experimental results show that our proposed method achieves state-of-the-art performance on the multilingual setting, and it has the ability to generalize to an unseen language task.

1 Introduction

Learning a representation through embedding is a fundamental technique to capture latent word semantics (Clark, 2015). Practically, word-level representation has been extensively explored to improve many downstream natural language processing (NLP) tasks (Mikolov et al., 2013; Pennington et al., 2014; Grave et al., 2018). A new wave of "meta-embeddings" research aims to learn how to effectively combine pre-trained word embeddings in supervised training into a single dense representation (Yin and Schütze, 2016; Muromägi et al., 2017; Bollegala et al., 2018; Coates and Bollegala, 2018; Kiela et al., 2018). This method is known to be effective to overcome domain and modality limitations. However, the generalization ability of previous works has been limited to monolingual tasks, so we aim to extend the method to multilingual contexts which benefits the processing of code-switching text.

In multilingual societies, speakers tend to move back and forth from one language to another during the same conversation, which is commonly

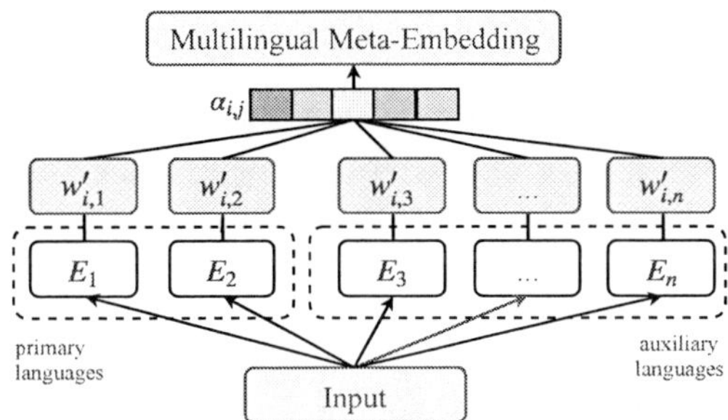

Figure 1: Multilingual Meta-Embeddings. The inputs are word embeddings and the output is a single word representation.

called "*code-switching*". Code-Switching is produced in both written text and speech in a discourse. Recent studies in code-switching has been mainly focused on natural language tasks, such as language modeling (Winata et al., 2018a; Pratapa et al., 2018; Garg et al., 2018), named entity recognition (Aguilar et al., 2018), and language identification (Solorio et al., 2014; Molina et al., 2016; Barman et al., 2014). Code-Switching is considered as a challenging task because words from different languages may co-exist within a sequence, and models are required to recognize the context of mixed-language sentences. Meanwhile, some words with the same spelling may have entirely different meanings (e.g., cola in English and Spanish) (Winata et al., 2018b). Language identifiers were commonly used to solve the word ambiguity issue in mixed-language sentences. However, it may not reliably cover all code-switching cases, and it creates a bottleneck that would require large-scale crowdsourcing to annotate language identifiers in code-switching data correctly.

To overcome the code-switching problem, we introduce a multilingual meta-embedding model learned from different languages. Our approach can be seen as a method to create a universal mul-

Proceedings of the 4th Workshop on Representation Learning for NLP (RepL4NLP-2019), pages 181–186
Florence, Italy, August 2, 2019. ©2019 Association for Computational Linguistics

tilingual meta-embedding learned in a supervised way with code-switching contexts by gathering information from monolingual sources. Concurrently, this is a language-agnostic approach where it does not require any language information of each word. We show the possibility of transferring information from multiple languages to unseen languages, and this approach can also be useful for a low-resource setting. To effectively leverage the embeddings, we use FastText subwords information to solve out-of-vocabulary (OOV) issues. By applying this method, our model can align the words with the corresponding languages. Our contributions are two-fold:

- We propose to generate multilingual meta-representations from pre-trained monolingual word embeddings. The model can learn how to construct the best word representation by mixing multiple sources without explicit language identification.

- We evaluate our multilingual meta-embedding on English-Spanish code-switching Named Entity Recognition (NER). The result shows the effectiveness of the method on multilingual setting and demonstrates that our meta-embedding can generalize to unseen languages in a cross-lingual setting.

2   Meta-Embeddings

Word embedding pre-training is a well-known method to transfer the knowledge from previous tasks to a target task that has fewer high-quality training data. Word embeddings are commonly used as features in supervised learning problems. We propose to generate a single word representation by extracting information from different pre-trained embeddings. We extend the idea of meta-embeddings from Kiela et al. (2018) to solve a multilingual task. We define a sentence that consists of m words $\{\mathbf{x}_j\}_{j=1}^m$, and $\{\mathbf{w}_{i,j}\}_{j=1}^n$ word vectors from n pre-trained word embeddings.

2.1   Baselines

We compare our method to two baselines: (1) concatenation and (2) linear ensembles.

Concatenation   We concatenate word embeddings by merging the dimensions of word representations. This is the simplest way to utilize all

sources of information; however, it is very inefficient due to the high-dimensional input:

$$\mathbf{w}_i^{CONCAT} = [\mathbf{w}_{i,1}, ..., \mathbf{w}_{i,n}]. \quad (1)$$

Linear Ensembles   We sum all word embeddings into a single word vector with an equal weight. This method is efficient since it does not increase the dimensionality of the input. We apply a projection layer through $\mathbf{w}_{i,j}$ to have equal dimension before we sum:

$$\mathbf{w}_i^{LINEAR} = \sum_{j=0}^n \mathbf{w}'_{i,j}, \quad (2)$$

$$\mathbf{w}'_{i,j} = \mathbf{a}_j \cdot \mathbf{w}_{i,j} + b_j, \quad (3)$$

where $\mathbf{a}_j \in \mathbb{R}^{l \times d}$ and $b_j \in \mathbb{R}^d$ are trainable parameters, and l and d are the original dimensions of the pre-trained embeddings and projected dimensions respectively.

2.2   Multilingual Meta-Embedding

We generate a multilingual vector representation for each word by taking a weighted sum of monolingual embeddings. Each embedding $\mathbf{w}_{i,j}$ is projected with a fully connected layer with a non-linear scoring function ϕ (e.g., tanh) into a d-dimensional vector, and an attention mechanism to calculate attention weight $\alpha_{i,j} \in \mathbb{R}^d$:

$$\mathbf{w}_i^{MME} = \sum_{j=1}^n \alpha_{i,j} \mathbf{w}'_{i,j}, \quad (4)$$

$$\alpha_{i,j} = \frac{e^{\phi(\mathbf{w}'_{i,j})}}{\sum_{j=1}^n e^{\phi(\mathbf{w}'_{i,j})}}. \quad (5)$$

3   Named Entity Recognition

Our proposed model is based on a self-attention mechanism from a transformer encoder (Vaswani et al., 2017) followed by a Conditional Random Field (CRF) layer (Lafferty et al., 2001).

Encoder Architecture   We apply a multi-layer transformer encoder as our sentence encoder:

$$h_0 = \text{Concat}(\mathbf{w}_0, \mathbf{w}_1, \ldots, \mathbf{w}_m)\mathbf{W}_t + \mathbf{W}_p, \quad (6)$$

$$h_l = \text{Transformer\_blocks}(h_0), \quad (7)$$

$$o = h_l \mathbf{W}_o + b_o, \quad (8)$$

where $\mathbf{W}_t$ is the projection matrix, $\mathbf{W}_p$ is the positional encoding matrix, $\mathbf{W}_o$ is the output layer, h_0 is the first layer hidden states, and h_l is the output representation from the final transformer layer. The output of the final layer is logits o.

Conditional Random Field This model calculates the dependencies across tag labels. NER requires a stronger constraint where `I-PERSON` should follow only after `B-PERSON`. We use CRF to learn the correlations between the current label and its neighbors (Lafferty et al., 2001). We consider $\mathbf{A} \in \mathbb{R}^{(k+2)\times(k+2)}$ as a trainable matrix, transition scores of the tags, where k is the number of tags. $\mathbf{A}_{i,j}$ denotes the transition score from tag i to tag j. We include a start tag and an end tag in the matrix, and calculate the score of a tag sequence $\mathbf{y}$ given o as follows:

$$s(o, \mathbf{y}) = \sum_{i=0}^{n} \mathbf{A}_{\mathbf{y}_i, \mathbf{y}_{i+1}} + \sum_{i=0}^{n} \mathbf{P}_{i, \mathbf{y}_i}, \qquad (9)$$

where $\mathbf{P}_{i, \mathbf{y}_i} \in \mathbb{R}^{n \times k}$ represents the output probability of the tags. We use the Viterbi algorithm to select the best sequence.

4 Experiments

4.1 Dataset

For our experiment, we use English-Spanish tweets data provided by Aguilar et al. (2018). There are nine entity labels. The labels use IOB format, where every token is labeled as a `B-label` in the beginning and then an `I-label` if it is a named entity, or `O` otherwise.

4.2 Experimental Setup

We use pre-trained FastText [1] English *(EN)* and Spanish *(ES)* word embeddings (Grave et al., 2018) as our primary language embeddings, and pre-trained FastText Catalan *(CA)* and Portuguese *(PT)* word embeddings as our auxiliary language embeddings. We opt for *CA* and *PT* because they come from the same Romance language family as Spanish. We also include GloVe Twitter English embedding *(GLOVE_EN)* (Pennington et al., 2014).[2] Experiments are conducted in two different settings. In the multilingual setting, we learn our meta-embedding from primary languages and auxiliary languages, while in the cross-lingual setting only auxiliary languages are used. We run all experiments five times and calculate the average and standard deviation. To improve our final predictions, we ensemble all five experiments and take the results from a majority consensus.

---

[1] https://fasttext.cc/docs/en/crawl-vectors.html
[2] https://nlp.stanford.edu/projects/glove/

Approaches	F1
Trivedi et al. (2018) (Single)	61.89
Wang et al. (2018) (Single)	62.39
Wang et al. (2018) (Ensemble)	62.67
Winata et al. (2018b) (Single)	62.76
Trivedi et al. (2018) (Ensemble)	63.76
MONOLINGUAL	
EN	62.75 ± 0.66
ES	62.91 ± 1.07
CONCAT	
EN + ES	65.30 ± 0.38
EN + ES + CA	65.36 ± 0.85
EN + ES + PT	65.53 ± 0.79
EN + ES + CA + PT	64.99 ± 1.06
LINEAR	
EN + ES + CA + PT (Single)	65.33 ± 0.87
EN + ES + CA + PT (Ensemble)	67.03
MME	
EN + ES	65.43 ± 0.67
EN + ES + CA	65.69 ± 0.83
EN + ES + PT	65.65 ± 0.48
EN + ES + CA + PT (Single)	$\mathbf{66.63 \pm 0.94}$
EN + ES + CA + PT (Ensemble)	**68.34**

Table 1: Multilingual results (mean and standard deviation from five experiments). *EN*: both English FastText and GloVe word embeddings.

Implementation Details Our model is trained using a Noam optimizer with a dropout of 0.1 for multilingual setting and 0.3 for the cross-lingual setting. Our model contains four layers of transformer blocks with a hidden size of 200 and four heads. We start the training with a learning rate of 0.1. We replace user hashtags (#user) and mentions (@user) with `<USR>`, and URL (https://domain.com) with `<URL>`, similarly to Winata et al. (2018b).

5 Results

Multilingual experimental results are shown in Table 1. Interestingly, both concatenation and linear ensemble are strong baselines since they can achieve higher performance compared to any existing works that use more complicated features, such as character-based features using a bidirectional long short-term memory (LSTM) (Winata et al., 2018b; Wang et al., 2018) or a convolutional neural network (CNN) with additional gazetteers (Trivedi et al., 2018). Overall, our transformer encoder using a single word embedding achieves better performance compared to the LSTM encoder

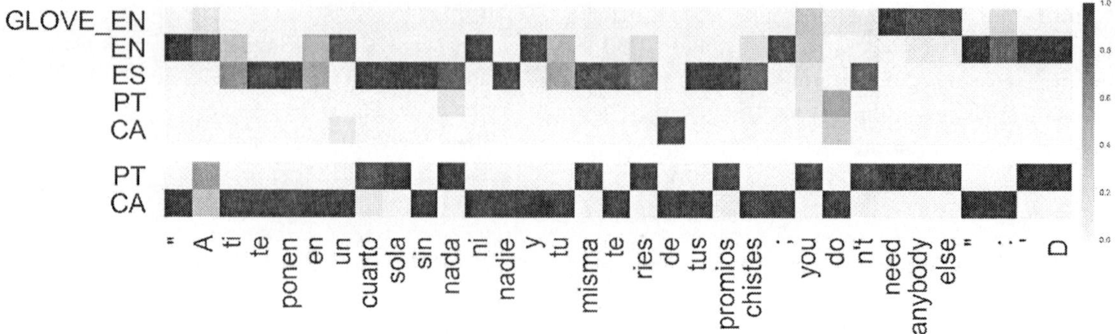

Figure 2: An example of attention weights on a development sample evaluated from a multilingual model **(top)** and a cross-lingual model **(bottom)**. Darker color shows higher attention scores.

Approaches	F1
MONOLINGUAL	
CA	53.96 ± 1.42
PT	54.86 ± 4.10
CONCAT	
CA + PT	58.28 ± 2.66
LINEAR	
CA + PT (Single)	60.72 ± 0.84
CA + PT (Ensemble)	62.9
MME	
CA + PT (Single)	**61.75 ± 0.56**
CA + PT (Ensemble)	**63.66**

Table 2: Cross-lingual results (mean and standard deviation from five experiments).

structure used by Winata et al. (2018b); Trivedi et al. (2018); Wang et al. (2018). More importantly, MME outperforms the two baselines on different language combinations, which shows its effectiveness. The results also show that the two baselines cannot effectively exploit the information from auxiliary languages. Here we note that the main advantage of MME is that it dynamically weights the different language pre-trained embeddings for each input token, while the concatenation and linear ensemble approaches always score the weights equally.

In the cross-lingual setting, our model does not perform well when we only use one auxiliary language, as seen in Table 2. A significant improvement is shown after we combine both languages, and MME shows a similar performance to the previous state-of-the-art result (Trivedi et al., 2018). This implies that our approach can effectively generalize word representations on an unseen language task by transferring information from lan-

guages that come from the same root as the primary languages.

We inspect the assigned weights on word embeddings to see which embedding our model attends. Figure 2 visualizes the weights for the multilingual and cross-lingual cases. It appears that our model can align words to their languages (e.g., Spanish words, such as *"ti"*, *"te"*, and *"ponen"* attend to *ES*) with strong confidences. In most cases, our model strongly attends to a single language and takes a small proportion of information from other languages. It shows the potential to automatically learn how to construct a multilingual embedding from semantically similar embeddings without requiring any language labels.

6   Related Work

Early studies on named entity recognition heavily relied on language-specific knowledge resources, such as hand-crafted features or gazetteers (Lafferty et al., 2001; Ratinov and Roth, 2009; Tsai et al., 2016). However, this approach was costly for new languages and domains. Thus, end-to-end approaches that do not rely on any external knowledge were proposed. Sobhana et al. (2010) proposed to use a CRF without any external resources, to leverage the label dependencies. Then, neural-based approaches, such as LSTM with a CRF (Lample et al., 2016; Lin et al., 2017; Greenberg et al., 2018) and LSTM with a CNN (Chiu and Nichols, 2016) showed a significant improvement in performance. Liu et al. (2018); Trivedi et al. (2018) proposed a character-level LSTM to capture the underlying style and structure, such as word boundaries and spellings. Finally, word-embedding ensemble techniques and preprocessing techniques, such as tokenization and normalization have been introduced to reduce OOV issues (Winata et al., 2018b; Wang et al., 2018).

7 Conclusion

In this paper, we propose a novel approach to learn multilingual representations by leveraging monolingual pre-trained embeddings. MME solves the dependencies on the language identification in code-switching Named Entity Recognition task since it utilizes more information from semantically similar embeddings. The experiment results show that our method surpasses previous works and baselines, achieving the state-of-the-art performance. Moreover, cross-lingual setting experiments demonstrate the generalization ability of MME to an unseen language task.

Acknowledgments

We want to thank Samuel Cahyawijaya for insightful discussions about this project. This work has been partially funded by ITF/319/16FP and MRP/055/18 of the Innovation Technology Commission, the Hong Kong SAR Government, and School of Engineering Ph.D. Fellowship Award, the Hong Kong University of Science and Technology, and RDC 1718050-0 of EMOS.AI.

References

Gustavo Aguilar, Fahad AlGhamdi, Victor Soto, Mona Diab, Julia Hirschberg, and Thamar Solorio. 2018. Named entity recognition on code-switched data: Overview of the calcs 2018 shared task. In *Proceedings of the Third Workshop on Computational Approaches to Linguistic Code-Switching*, pages 138–147, Melbourne, Australia. Association for Computational Linguistics.

Utsab Barman, Amitava Das, Joachim Wagner, and Jennifer Foster. 2014. Code mixing: A challenge for language identification in the language of social media. In *Proceedings of the first workshop on computational approaches to code switching*, pages 13–23.

Danushka Bollegala, Kohei Hayashi, and Ken-Ichi Kawarabayashi. 2018. Think globally, embed locally: locally linear meta-embedding of words. In *Proceedings of the 27th International Joint Conference on Artificial Intelligence*, pages 3970–3976. AAAI Press.

Jason PC Chiu and Eric Nichols. 2016. Named entity recognition with bidirectional lstm-cnns. *Transactions of the Association for Computational Linguistics*, 4:357–370.

Stephen Clark. 2015. Vector space models of lexical meaning. *Handbook of Contemporary Semantics*, 10:9781118882139.

Joshua Coates and Danushka Bollegala. 2018. Frustratingly easy meta-embedding–computing meta-embeddings by averaging source word embeddings. In *Proceedings of the 2018 Conference of the North American Chapter of the Association for Computational Linguistics: Human Language Technologies, Volume 2 (Short Papers)*, pages 194–198.

Saurabh Garg, Tanmay Parekh, and Preethi Jyothi. 2018. Code-switched language models using dual rnns and same-source pretraining. In *Proceedings of the 2018 Conference on Empirical Methods in Natural Language Processing*, pages 3078–3083.

Edouard Grave, Piotr Bojanowski, Prakhar Gupta, Armand Joulin, and Tomas Mikolov. 2018. Learning word vectors for 157 languages. In *Proceedings of the International Conference on Language Resources and Evaluation (LREC 2018)*.

Nathan Greenberg, Trapit Bansal, Patrick Verga, and Andrew McCallum. 2018. Marginal likelihood training of bilstm-crf for biomedical named entity recognition from disjoint label sets. In *Proceedings of the 2018 Conference on Empirical Methods in Natural Language Processing*, pages 2824–2829.

Douwe Kiela, Changhan Wang, and Kyunghyun Cho. 2018. Dynamic meta-embeddings for improved sentence representations. In *Proceedings of the 2018 Conference on Empirical Methods in Natural Language Processing*, pages 1466–1477.

John D. Lafferty, Andrew McCallum, and Fernando Pereira. 2001. Conditional random fields: Probabilistic models for segmenting and labeling sequence data. In *ICML*.

Guillaume Lample, Miguel Ballesteros, Sandeep Subramanian, Kazuya Kawakami, and Chris Dyer. 2016. Neural architectures for named entity recognition. In *Proceedings of the 2016 Conference of the North American Chapter of the Association for Computational Linguistics: Human Language Technologies*, pages 260–270.

Bill Y Lin, Frank Xu, Zhiyi Luo, and Kenny Zhu. 2017. Multi-channel bilstm-crf model for emerging named entity recognition in social media. In *Proceedings of the 3rd Workshop on Noisy User-generated Text*, pages 160–165.

Liyuan Liu, Jingbo Shang, Xiang Ren, Frank Fangzheng Xu, Huan Gui, Jian Peng, and Jiawei Han. 2018. Empower sequence labeling with task-aware neural language model. In *Thirty-Second AAAI Conference on Artificial Intelligence*.

Tomas Mikolov, Ilya Sutskever, Kai Chen, Greg S Corrado, and Jeff Dean. 2013. Distributed representations of words and phrases and their compositionality. In *Advances in neural information processing systems*, pages 3111–3119.

Giovanni Molina, Fahad AlGhamdi, Mahmoud Ghoneim, Abdelati Hawwari, Nicolas Rey-Villamizar, Mona Diab, and Thamar Solorio. 2016. Overview for the second shared task on language identification in code-switched data. In *Proceedings of the Second Workshop on Computational Approaches to Code Switching*, pages 40–49.

Avo Muromägi, Kairit Sirts, and Sven Laur. 2017. Linear ensembles of word embedding models. In *Proceedings of the 21st Nordic Conference on Computational Linguistics*, pages 96–104.

Jeffrey Pennington, Richard Socher, and Christopher Manning. 2014. Glove: Global vectors for word representation. In *Proceedings of the 2014 conference on empirical methods in natural language processing (EMNLP)*, pages 1532–1543.

Adithya Pratapa, Gayatri Bhat, Monojit Choudhury, Sunayana Sitaram, Sandipan Dandapat, and Kalika Bali. 2018. Language modeling for code-mixing: The role of linguistic theory based synthetic data. In *Proceedings of the 56th Annual Meeting of the Association for Computational Linguistics (Volume 1: Long Papers)*, volume 1, pages 1543–1553.

Lev Ratinov and Dan Roth. 2009. Design challenges and misconceptions in named entity recognition. In *Proceedings of the thirteenth conference on computational natural language learning*, pages 147–155. Association for Computational Linguistics.

N Sobhana, Pabitra Mitra, and SK Ghosh. 2010. Conditional random field based named entity recognition in geological text. *International Journal of Computer Applications*, 1(3):143–147.

Thamar Solorio, Elizabeth Blair, Suraj Maharjan, Steven Bethard, Mona Diab, Mahmoud Ghoneim, Abdelati Hawwari, Fahad AlGhamdi, Julia Hirschberg, Alison Chang, et al. 2014. Overview for the first shared task on language identification in code-switched data. In *Proceedings of the First Workshop on Computational Approaches to Code Switching*, pages 62–72.

Shashwat Trivedi, Harsh Rangwani, and Anil Kumar Singh. 2018. Iit (bhu) submission for the acl shared task on named entity recognition on code-switched data. In *Proceedings of the Third Workshop on Computational Approaches to Linguistic Code-Switching*, pages 148–153.

Chen-Tse Tsai, Stephen Mayhew, and Dan Roth. 2016. Cross-lingual named entity recognition via wikification. In *Proceedings of The 20th SIGNLL Conference on Computational Natural Language Learning*, pages 219–228.

Ashish Vaswani, Noam Shazeer, Niki Parmar, Jakob Uszkoreit, Llion Jones, Aidan N Gomez, Łukasz Kaiser, and Illia Polosukhin. 2017. Attention is all you need. In *Advances in neural information processing systems*, pages 5998–6008.

Changhan Wang, Kyunghyun Cho, and Douwe Kiela. 2018. Code-switched named entity recognition with embedding attention. In *Proceedings of the Third Workshop on Computational Approaches to Linguistic Code-Switching*, pages 154–158.

Genta Indra Winata, Andrea Madotto, Chien-Sheng Wu, and Pascale Fung. 2018a. Code-switching language modeling using syntax-aware multi-task learning. In *Proceedings of the Third Workshop on Computational Approaches to Linguistic Code-Switching*, pages 62–67.

Genta Indra Winata, Chien-Sheng Wu, Andrea Madotto, and Pascale Fung. 2018b. Bilingual character representation for efficiently addressing out-of-vocabulary words in code-switching named entity recognition. In *Proceedings of the Third Workshop on Computational Approaches to Linguistic Code-Switching*, pages 110–114.

Wenpeng Yin and Hinrich Schütze. 2016. Learning word meta-embeddings. In *Proceedings of the 54th Annual Meeting of the Association for Computational Linguistics (Volume 1: Long Papers)*, volume 1, pages 1351–1360.

Investigating sub-word embedding strategies
for the morphologically rich and free phrase-order Hungarian

Bálint Döbrössy[1], Márton Makrai[2], Balázs Tarján[1], and György Szaszák[1]

[1]Dept of Telecommunications and Media Info, Budapest University of Technology and Econ
[2] Research Institute for Linguistics of the Hungarian Academy of Sciences
[1] `balint.dobrossy@gmail.com`, `{tarjanb, szaszak}@tmit.bme.hu`
[2]`makrai.marton@nytud.mta.hu`

Abstract

For morphologically rich languages, word embeddings provide less consistent semantic representations due to higher variance in word forms. Moreover, these languages often allow for less constrained word order, which further increases variance. For the highly agglutinative Hungarian, semantic accuracy of word embeddings measured on word analogy tasks drops by 50-75% compared to English. We observed that embeddings learn morphosyntax quite well instead.

Therefore, we explore and evaluate several sub-word unit based embedding strategies – character n-grams, lemmatization provided by an NLP-pipeline, and segments obtained in unsupervised learning (`morfessor`) – to boost semantic consistency in Hungarian word vectors. The effect of changing embedding dimension and context window size have also been considered. Morphological analysis based lemmatization was found to be the best strategy to improve embeddings' semantic accuracy, whereas adding character n-grams was found consistently counterproductive in this regard.

1 Introduction

Word embeddings show amazing capabilities in representing semantic relations, which has been demonstrated in analogical reasoning tasks (Mikolov et al., 2013b; Gladkova and Drozd, 2016). They are also capable of learning morphosyntax, showing again a consistent mapping of grammatical operations, i.e. inflections (see Section 2). Word embeddings obtain such semantic and syntactic capabilities by matching the words to their observed contexts (or vice versa). Since the size of the word vector table is the vocabulary size times the embedding dimension, for languages with rich morphology (especially aggluti-

native ones), this results in huge matrices (Takala, 2016). The vocabulary needs to be increased for morphologically rich languages to ensure a high enough coverage for the overall occurring words. Furthermore, to obtain a reliable estimate of word vectors, a larger training corpus is required so that theoretically the same convergence of the estimation can be reached than for a non agglutinative language. Finally, morphologically rich languages can express grammatical relations through suffixes (i.e. case endings) and hence let the word order becoming less constrained than in configurational languages. This can result in higher context variability, which translates again into less accurate estimates (i.e. the effect of migrating words outside the context window can be imagined as a kind of smoothing, making representation more blurred). Augmenting the size of the context window is not a effective counter-measure, as it will result again in higher variability of the context.

Bojanowski et al. (2017) proposes character level enhancement for word embeddings to overcome difficulties caused by unseen or rare words. It is demonstrated for a large set of languages that adding character n-grams to the embeddings can be a powerful way of generating word vectors for unseen words, and this augments both semantic and syntactic consistency (and accuracy) of the embeddings. However, Bojanowski et al. (2017) tests no highly agglutinative language for their embeddings' syntactic and semantic accuracies with and without n-grams.

We conduct proper evaluation on an analogy set for Hungarian (Makrai, 2015) designed according to the standard Mikolov et al. (2013a), and show that the already weak baseline semantic accuracy consistently decreases when character n-grams are added. On the other hand, embeddings learn the complex Hungarian morphosyntax quite

Proceedings of the 4th Workshop on Representation Learning for NLP (RepL4NLP-2019), pages 187–193
Florence, Italy, August 2, 2019. ©2019 Association for Computational Linguistics

well. Our ambition in this work is to address these issues emerging from large vocabulary and less constrained word order. We systematically investigate and analyze sub-word embedding strategies for the very highly agglutinating Hungarian language. We are basically interested in benchmarking syntactic and semantic accuracies with each of the methods, therefore we are primarily engaged in testing morphological analysis, lemmatization and stemming based alternatives.

2 Related work

The closest work to ours is a concurrent study (Zhu et al., 2019) of subword models especially for morphologically rich languages across different tasks. Unfortunately they miss Hungarian, which leaved a huge gap, as they find that performance is both language- and task-dependent. They find that unsupervised segmentation (e.g., BPE, Morfessor, see later in this section) is sometimes comparable to or even outperform supervised word segmentation.

Morphology in word embeddings The morphologically informed approach to compositionally gained word embedding vectors start with Lazaridou et al. (2013) and Luong et al. (2013), who train a Recursive Neural Network, which builds representations for morphologically complex words from their morphemes.

The work of Soricut and Och (2015) can be regarded as the unsupervised counterpart of Mikolov et al. (2013b)-style analogical questions. Soricut induces morphological relations as the systematic difference of embedding vectors in an unsupervised manner. They evaluate on word-similarity.

Relying on existing morphological resources, Cotterell et al. (2016) introduce a latent-variable morphological model that extrapolates vectors for unseen words, and smoothes those of observed words over several languages.

Cao and Rei (2016) introduce a joint model for unsupervised segmentation and weighted character-level composition. Cotterell et al. (2018) compute supervised models for the same two sub-tasks of morphological analysis, also induces a canonical form (i.e. models orthographic changes).

Language modeling and characters Morphologically compositional language modeling proper begins with Botha and Blunsom (2014)'s decoder

in machine translation to morphologically rich languages, which is unsupervised with respect to morphological segmentation. Cotterell and Schütze (2015) augment the log-bilinear language model (LM) (Mnih and Hinton, 2007) with a multi-task objective for morphological tags along with the next word.

Character n-gram features proved to be powerful as the basis of Facebook's fastText classifier (Joulin et al., 2016). Subword units based on byte-pair encoding have been found to be particularly useful for machine translation (Sennrich et al., 2016), and even in models based on matrix factorization (Salle and Villavicencio, 2018).

Hungarian In their de-glutinatve method, Borbély et al. (2016) and Nemeskey (2017) split all inflectional prefixes into separate tokens for better morphological generalization. Nemeskey opts for supervised morphological knowledge because of linguistic interpretability. Lévai and Kornai (2019) analyze Hungarian word embedding vectors grouped by the morphological tag of the corresponding word. They investigate whether the coherence of these classes correlate with the specificity or the frequency of the tag.

3 Experiments

3.1 Corpus, segmentation, and embeddings

For training the word vector models, we rely on the fastText (Joulin et al., 2016) tool, which also allows for augmentation with character n-grams, if desired. We do not use stemming, but go instead for some more sophisticated analysis. As we explained, our primary goal is benchmarking the individual approaches.

For a true morphological analysis, we use the magyarlánc (Zsibrita et al., 2013) toolkit, which provides lemmatization in the form of a stem plus a suffix series, also decomposed into individual component morphemes. Although some disambiguation capability arises from sentence level part-of-speech tagging, magyarlánc may end up with several hypotheses for the morphological composition of the input word. Fortunately this happens rarely at the lemma level. If still, the shortest lemma is used.

For unsupervised pseudo-morphemic analysis, we use Morfessor (Virpioja et al., 2013). Morfessor has been used to provide subword unit tokens for Automatic Speech Recognition in heav-

Parameter	Value range
Frequency cut-off	5
Min length of char ngram	none or 3
Max length of char ngram	none or 6
Embedding dimension	100-200
Context window	5–25
Learning rate (α)	0.05
α update interval	100
Number of epochs	15
Negative sampling loss	yes
Negative samples	5
Pretraining	none

Table 1: Embedding vector trainer parameters.

ily agglutinative languages, with improved accuracy (Enarvi et al., 2017) over word based vocabularies and models. Morfessor is based on statistical machine learning. In order to reflect that the provided subword units are not true morphemes in the grammatical sense, they are called morfs.

The text corpus we use is a contemporary dump of Hungarian language web pages constructed for this paper, which covers mostly online newspapers in various fields from years 2014-2018. The corpus has over 70 M word tokens. Text normalization is performed with a Python script.

3.2 Analogical questions

Our approach is to train word embeddings in different scenarios and assess syntactic and semantic accuracies based on a Hungarian analogy test (Makrai, 2015) that has been constructed according to (Mikolov et al., 2013a). For the semantic accuracy, we use `country-capital` and `country-currency` pairs. For the syntactic accuracy we use `singular-plural` for nouns, `present-past tense` for verbs and `base vs comparative forms` for adjectives.

3.3 Fasttext settings

There are three main parameters which are controlled during the experiments: (i) whether we use character n-gram augmentation or not; (ii) the size of the context window; and (iii) the target dimension of the resulting embedding vectors. We preferred to preserve all other parameters of fastText at their default value. The most important of these parameters are summarized in Table 1.

3.4 Embedding strategies

Word vectors (W) This constitutes our baseline. A standard word embedding is trained with fastText, no prior stop word filtering is applied.

Lemma vectors (L) The magyarlánc toolkit is used for morphological analysis. Lemmas are identified and used as embedded entities. Note that whereas ambiguity on the entire morphological composition may arise, ambiguity affecting the lemma's surface form is rare. If this still occurs, the shortest form is used.

Morf vectors (M) Running Morfessor yields a morf based split-up. Morfs become the modeling unit (subword unit). As an alternative, using the **root (R)** yielded by Morfessor is evaluated as well. The word embedding is trained on the corpus with words divided into segments (as if they were separate words). During testing in analogical questions, query words are also spitted to segments, and their vectors are computed as the sum of the segments' vectors.

Vector dimension is changed between 100 and 200. We did not consider using higher dimensions to avoid making down-stream applications heavy.

More experimental details and related work can be found in a longer version of this paper, which appeared at Repl4NLP 2019. We will refer to the individual setups by specifying the unit out of {W, L, M, R} and the dimension, e.g. L200 will refer to lemma as unit and 200-dimensional embeddings.

4 Results

4.1 Extending the context window

As we pointed out in Section 1, using wider context may help in overcoming the difficulties resulting from the less constrained word order of Hungarian. A wider context window allows for capturing words further apart, but it may have an adverse effect as well, because the context becomes more noisy (variable). Relative data sparsity may also be a problem when a larger context is considered. So basically our research question related to the context of a word is that whether the benefits of capturing further apart words can be superior compared to the negative effect of increasing variance w.r.t the occurring context words.

It has been reported (Lebret and Collobert, 2015) that semantic analogical questions benefit

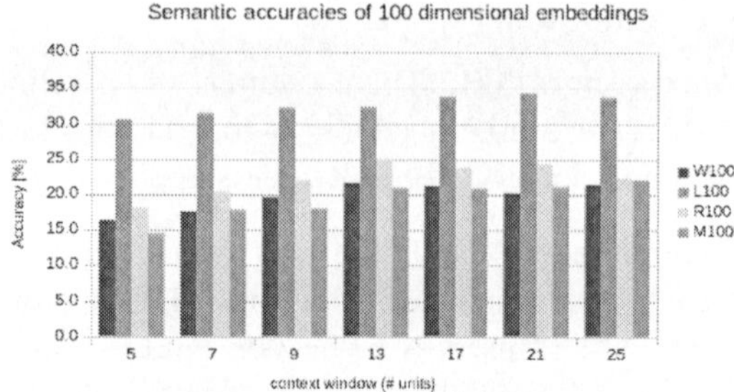

Figure 1: Semantic accuracies of Hungarian 100 dimensional embeddings with different strategies.

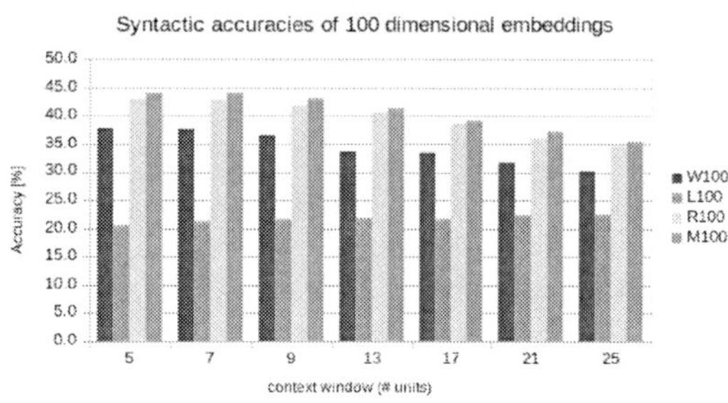

Figure 2: Syntactic accuracies of Hungarian 100 dimensional embeddings with different strategies.

from larger windows, while syntactic ones do not. On the contrary, experimenting with SVD models and different window sizes, Gladkova and Drozd (2016) find that all categories of analogical questions are best detected between window sizes 2–4, although a handful of them yield equally good performance in larger windows. They find no one-on-one correspondence between semantics and larger windows. We consider unusually large contexts of up to 25 words (see Table 1). i

Semantic and syntactic accuracies with 100 dimensional embeddings are shown in Figures 1 and 2, respectively. Comparing strategies, using the lemma (L) for embedding is yielding the highest semantic accuracy. Regarding the context window, our hypothesis that long context windows may be a better fit is confirmed. All the four strategies consistently show increasing semantic accuracy as context window is extended to cover 21 units. Compared to W, L embeddings yield higher semantic accuracy by 75%. Nevertheless, syntactic accuracies decrease tendentiously when extending the context window, which is a negative effect, most likely resulting from the higher variation seen in a larger window.

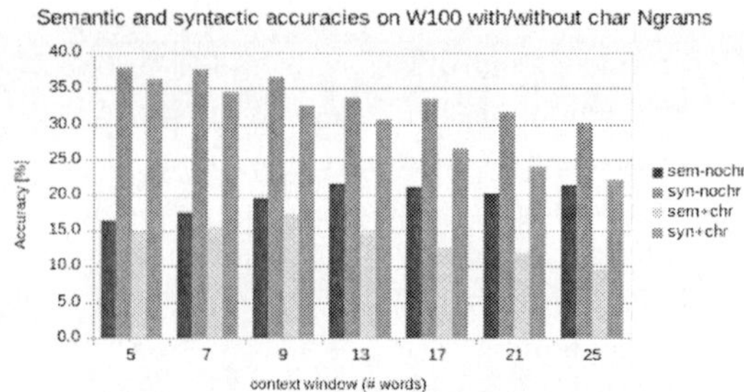

Figure 3: Semantic and syntactic accuracies of Hungarian 100 dimensional word embeddings with (chr) and without (nochr) character n-grams.

4.2 Adding character n-grams

We have already mentioned in the Introduction that in contrast to many other languages (Bojanowski et al., 2016), the very highly agglutinative Hungarian cannot profit from adding character n-grams to the embeddings: semantic (but also syntactic) accuracy gets lower. We suppose that this happens because agglutination is frequent and hence word vectors become universal (i.e. they cannot specialize for the context). The less constrained word order interplays in this, too.

Figure 3 shows how semantic and syntactic accuracies change when adding character n-grams (sem+chr and syn+chr, respectively) in the W100 case. We present again a trend with increasing context window size on the horizontal axis to allow for easy comparison with the previous results.

Regarding semantic accuracies, no benefit is registered when adding character n-grams with any of the 4 investigated embedding strategies.

Adding character n-grams becomes helpful at the syntax level in some cases, syntactic accuracies augment for the L100, L200 and R200 scenarios. Nevertheless, the basis is very low as for using the lemmas or morf roots, most of the morphosyntactic information is lost. Not surprisingly, semantics improves with a large window, while morphosyntax does not.

4.3 Embedding dimension

Figure 4 compares semantic accuracies of 100 and 200 dimensional scenarios with a context window of 21. Increasing the embedding dimension has a positive effect on semantic accuracies, as far as up to 50% relative increase in accuracy. Accuracy in individual relations (whose importance has been shown by Gladkova and Drozd (2016)) are

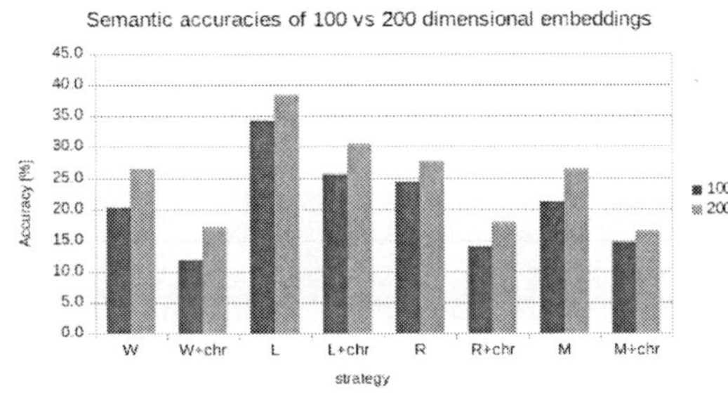

Figure 4: Semantic accuracies of Hungarian 100 and 200 dimensional embeddings with different strategies; context window covers 21 units.

capital-common-countries	66.0% (101/153)
capital-world	40.3% (2595/6441)
county-center	18.2% (12/66)
currency	6.4% (26/406)
family	16.5% (15/91)
Semantic	38.41% (2749/7157)

Table 2: Results in individual semantic relations with the best setting (magyarlánc, window 21, dimension 200, no character n-grams).

reported in Table 2. We can again observe that adding character n-grams consistently results in decreased semantic accuracy.

Increasing embedding dimensions above 200 could be expected to yield further improvement is semantic accuracies, but we did not address this issue in our current work, which focuses mostly on the modeling unit and its optimal context.

5 Conclusions

In this work, we analyzed embedding strategies for the morphologically very rich Hungarian language. Unlike may other languages, Hungarian cannot profit from character n-gram enhancement of word embeddings, whereas rich morphology results in very large vocabulary and less constrained word order, both contributing to very high variation in the data used for training the embeddings. Therefore we analyzed subword embedding strategies above the character level. Results showed that using the lemmas instead of the words was by far the most effective approach by maximizing semantic accuracy of the embeddings. Using the roots yielded by the `morfessor` tool also contributed to an increase in semantic accuracy, but to a smaller extent compared to lemmas learned

in a supervised fashion. Obviously, syntactic accuracies were found decreasing when switching to lemma units. Adding character n-grams was counterproductive with any investigated strategy w.r.t semantic accuracy. Analyzing the effect of extending the context window showed that despite the higher variance of units seen in a larger context, embeddings can still profit from these to increase their semantic consistence. This founding was consistent with all investigated sub-word strategies, and is therefore an efficient way of dealing with the weakly constrained word order.

Future work may investigate whether results generalize to other embedding algorithms (besides fastText, the original and the enhanced (Mikolov et al., 2018) word2vec and the GloVe (Řehůřek and Sojka, 2010) implementations of the *continuous bag of words* and the *skip-gram* models could be tried); extend the ablation over dimensionality up to a few hundred dimensions; and analyze other morphologically rich languages (e.g. Finnish, Turkish, or Slavic languages). The bottleneck is that we are restricted to languages to which the analogical questions have been translated. As a reviewer noted, the semantic part of the Mikolov-style analogical questions consist of a handful of semantic relations between named entities. It is questionable how appropriate it is to use them for the evaluation of the embedding strategies, especially that of encoding lexical semantic relations and not the world knowledge. Gladkova and Drozd (2016) examine Mikolov et al. (2013b)-style analogical questions systematically, finding that different systems shine at different sub-categories of the morphological and semantic tasks. They publish a test set which is more difficult than existing ones. Translating this test set to morphologically rich languages would be very useful.

Acknowledgments

This work was supported by the Hungarian National Research, Development and Innovation Office under contract ID FK-124413: 'Enhancement of deep learning based semantic representations with acoustic-prosodic features for automatic spoken document summarization and retrieval'. Márton Makrai was partially supported by project found 2018-1.2.1-NKP-00008: Exploring the Mathematical Foundations of Artificial Intelligence and National Research, Development and Innovation Office grant #120145.

References

Oded Avraham and Yoav Goldberg. 2017. The interplay of semantics and morphology in word embeddings. *arXiv preprint arXiv:1704.01938.*

Piotr Bojanowski, Edouard Grave, Armand Joulin, and Tomas Mikolov. 2017. Enriching word vectors with subword information. *Transactions of the Association for Computational Linguistics*, 5:135–146.

Piotr Bojanowski, Armand Joulin, and Tomas Mikolov. 2016. Alternative structures for character-level rnns. In *International Conference on Learning Representations, Workshop track (ICLR 2016).*

Gábor Borbély, András Kornai, Dávid Nemeskey, and Marcus Kracht. 2016. Denoising composition in distributional semantics. In *DSALT: Distributional Semantics and Linguistic Theory.* Poster.

Jan A Botha and Phil Blunsom. 2014. Compositional morphology for word representations and language modelling. In *ICML*, pages 1899–1907.

Kris Cao and Marek Rei. 2016. A joint model for word embedding and word morphology. In *Repl4NLP.*

Ryan Cotterell, Christo Kirov, John Sylak-Glassman, Géraldine Walther, Ekaterina Vylomova, Arya D. McCarthy, Katharina Kann, Sebastian Mielke, Garrett Nicolai, Miikka Silfverberg, David Yarowsky, Jason Eisner, and Mans Hulden. 2018. The CoNLL–SIGMORPHON 2018 shared task: Universal morphological reinflection. In *Proceedings of the CoNLL–SIGMORPHON 2018 Shared Task: Universal Morphological Reinflection*, Brussels, Belgium. Association for Computational Linguistics.

Ryan Cotterell, Christo Kirov, John Sylak-Glassman, David Yarowsky, Jason Eisner, and Mans Hulden. 2016. The SIGMORPHON 2016 shared task— morphological reinflection. In *Proceedings of the 2016 Meeting of SIGMORPHON*, Berlin, Germany. Association for Computational Linguistics.

Ryan Cotterell and Hinrich Schütze. 2015. Morphological word-embeddings. In *Proceedings of the 2015 Conference of the North American Chapter of the Association for Computational Linguistics: Human Language Technologies*, pages 1287–1292.

Seppo Enarvi, Peter Smit, Sami Virpioja, Mikko Kurimo, Seppo Enarvi, Peter Smit, Sami Virpioja, and Mikko Kurimo. 2017. Automatic speech recognition with very large conversational finnish and estonian vocabularies. *IEEE/ACM Transactions on Audio, Speech and Language Processing (TASLP)*, 25(11):2085–2097.

Anna Gladkova and Aleksandr Drozd. 2016. Intrinsic evaluations of word embeddings: What can we do better? In *Proc. RepEval (this volume).* ACL.

Armand Joulin, Edouard Grave, Piotr Bojanowski, and Tomas Mikolov. 2016. Bag of tricks for efficient text classification. ArXiv preprint arXiv:1607.01759.

Angeliki Lazaridou, Marco Marelli, Roberto Zamparelli, and Marco Baroni. 2013. Compositional-ly derived representations of morphologically complex words in distributional semantics. In *ACL (1)*, pages 1517–1526.

Rémi Lebret and Ronan Collobert. 2015. Rehabilitation of count-based models for word vector representations. In *International Conference on Intelligent Text Processing and Computational Linguistics*, pages 417–429. Springer.

Thang Luong, Richard Socher, and Christopher D. Manning. 2013. Better word representations with recursive neural networks for morphology. In *CoNLL*, pages 104–113.

Dániel Lévai and András Kornai. 2019. The impact of inflection on word vectors. In *XV. Magyar Számítógépes Nyelvészeti Konferencia.*

Márton Makrai. 2015. Comparison of distributed language models on medium-resourced languages. In *XI. Magyar Számítógépes Nyelvészeti Konferencia (MSZNY 2015).*

Tomas Mikolov, Kai Chen, G.s. Corrado, and Jeffrey Dean. 2013a. Efficient estimation of word representations in vector space. In *Proceedings of Workshop at ICLR*, volume 2013.

Tomas Mikolov, Edouard Grave, Piotr Bojanowski, Christian Puhrsch, and Armand Joulin. 2018. Advances in pre-training distributed word representations. In *Language Resources and Evaluation Conference (LREC).*

Tomas Mikolov, Wen-tau Yih, and Geoffrey Zweig. 2013b. Linguistic regularities in continuous space word representations. In *Proceedings of the 2013 Conference of the North American Chapter of the Association for Computational Linguistics: Human Language Technologies (NAACL-HLT 2013)*, pages 746–751, Atlanta, Georgia. Association for Computational Linguistics.

Andriy Mnih and Geoffrey Hinton. 2007. Three new graphical models for statistical language modelling. In *Proceedings of the 24th international conference on Machine learning*, pages 641–648. ACM.

Dávid Márk Nemeskey. 2017. `emMorph` a hungarian language modeling baseline. In *XIII. Magyar Számítógépes Nyelvészeti Konferencia (MSZNY2017)*, pages 91–102, Szeged.

Radim Řehůřek and Petr Sojka. 2010. Software Framework for Topic Modelling with Large Corpora. In *Proceedings of the LREC 2010 Workshop on New Challenges for NLP Frameworks*, pages 45–50, Valletta, Malta. ELRA.

Alexandre Salle and Aline Villavicencio. 2018. Incorporating subword information into matrix factorization word embeddings. *arXiv preprint arXiv:1805.03710.*

Rico Sennrich, Barry Haddow, and Alexandra Birch. 2016. Neural machine translation of rare words with subword units. In *Proceedings of the 54th Annual Meeting of the Association for Computational Linguistics (Volume 1: Long Papers)*, pages 1715–1725, Berlin, Germany. Association for Computational Linguistics.

Radu Soricut and Franz Och. 2015. Unsupervised morphology induction using word embeddings. In *Proceedings of NAACL*, pages 1627–1637, Denver, Colorado.

Pyry Takala. 2016. Word embeddings for morphologically rich languages. In *Proceedings of European Symposium on Artificial Neural Networks, Computational Intelligence and Machine Learning*.

Sami Virpioja, Peter Smit, Stig-Arne Grönroos, Mikko Kurimo, et al. 2013. Morfessor 2.0: Python implementation and extensions for morfessor baseline.

Yi Zhu, Ivan Vulić, and Anna Korhonen. 2019. A systematic study of leveraging subword information for learning word representations. In *NAACL*. ArXiv:1904.07994.

János Zsibrita, Veronika Vincze, and Richárd Farkas. 2013. magyarlanc: A tool for morphological and dependency parsing of hungarian. In *Proceedings of the International Conference Recent Advances in Natural Language Processing (RANLP 2013)*, pages 763–771, Hissar, Bulgaria. INCOMA Ltd. Shoumen.

A Self-Training Approach for Short Text Clustering

Amir Hadifar   **Lucas Sterckx**   **Thomas Demeester**   **Chris Develder**

Ghent University – imec, IDLab

Department of Information Technology

`firstname.lastname@ugent.be`

Abstract

Short text clustering is a challenging problem when adopting traditional bag-of-words or TF-IDF representations, since these lead to sparse vector representations for short texts. Low-dimensional continuous representations or embeddings can counter that sparseness problem: their high representational power is exploited in deep clustering algorithms. While deep clustering has been studied extensively in computer vision, relatively little work has focused on NLP. The method we propose, learns discriminative features from both an autoencoder and a sentence embedding, then uses assignments from a clustering algorithm as supervision to update weights of the encoder network. Experiments on three short text datasets empirically validate the effectiveness of our method.

1 Introduction

Text clustering groups semantically similar text without using supervision or manually assigned labels. Text clusters have proven to be beneficial in many applications including news recommendation (Wang et al., 2010), language modeling (Liu and Croft, 2004), query expansion (Amini and Usunier, 2007), visualization (Cadez et al., 2003), and corpus summarization (Schutze and Silverstein, 1997).

Due to the popularity of social media and online fora such as Twitter and Reddit, texts containing only few words have become prevalent on the web. Compared to clustering of long documents, Short Text Clustering (STC) introduces additional challenges. Traditionally, text is represented as a bag-of-words (BOW) or term-frequency inverse-document-frequency (TF-IDF) vectors, after which a clustering algorithm such as k-means is applied to partition the texts into homogeneous groups (Xu et al., 2017). Due to the short lengths of such texts, their vector representations tend to become very sparse. As a result, traditional measures for similarity, which rely on word overlap or distance between high-dimensional vectors, become ineffective (Xu et al., 2015).

Previous work on STC enriched short text representations by incorporating features from external resources. Hu et al. (2009) and Banerjee et al. (2007) extended short texts using articles from Wikipedia. In similar fashion, Hotho et al. (2003) and Wei et al. (2015) proposed different methods to enrich text representation using ontologies. More recently, low-dimensional representations have shown potential to counter the sparsity problem in STC. Combined with neural network architectures, embeddings of words (Mikolov et al., 2013; Pennington et al., 2014), sentences (Le and Mikolov, 2014; Kiros et al., 2015) and documents (Dai et al., 2015) were proven to be effective on a variety of tasks in machine learning for NLP.

Deep clustering methods first embed the high-dimensional data into a lower dimensional space, after which a clustering algorithm is applied. These methods either perform clustering after having trained the embedding transformation (Tian et al., 2014; De Boom et al., 2016), or jointly optimize both the embedding and clustering (Yang et al., 2016), and we situate our method in the former. Closely related to our work is the method of Deep Embedded Clustering (DEC) (Xie et al., 2016), which learns feature representations and cluster assignments using deep neural networks. DEC learns a mapping from the data space to a lower-dimensional feature space while iteratively optimizing a clustering objective. The self-taught convolutional neural network (STC^2) framework proposed by Xu et al. (2017) uses a dimensionality reduction technique to generate auxiliary targets for a neural network architecture. A convolutional neural network (CNN) learns feature rep-

Proceedings of the 4th Workshop on Representation Learning for NLP (RepL4NLP-2019), pages 194–199

Florence, Italy, August 2, 2019. ©2019 Association for Computational Linguistics

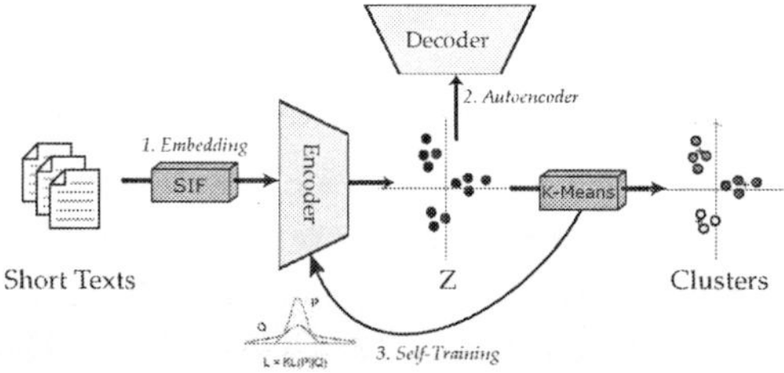

Figure 1: Short text clustering using SIF embedding, an autoencoder architecture and self-training.

resentations in order to reconstruct these auxiliary targets. Trained representations from the CNN are clustered using the k-means algorithm. Two recent surveys provide an overview of research on deep clustering methods (Aljalbout et al., 2018; Min et al., 2018).

Similar to Xie et al. (2016), we follow a multi-phase approach and train a neural network (which we will refer to as the encoder) to transform embeddings to a latent space before clustering. However, we apply two crucial modifications. As opposed to CNN-based encoders (Xu et al., 2017), we propose the use of Smooth Inverse Frequency (SIF) embeddings (Arora et al., 2017) in order to simplify and make clustering more efficient while maintaining performance.

During the second stage of clustering, we apply self-training using soft cluster assigments to fine-tune the encoder before applying a final clustering. We describe our methodology in more detail in Section 2. In Section 3, we evaluate our method using three short text datasets, measuring for clustering accuracy and normalized mutual information. Our model matches or produces better results compared to more sophisticated neural network architectures.

2   Methodology

Our model for short text clustering includes three steps: (1) Short texts are embedded using SIF embeddings (Section 2.1); (2) During a pre-training phase, a deep *autoencoder* is applied to encode and reconstruct the short text SIF embeddings (Section 2.2); (3) In a self-training phase, we use soft cluster assignments as an auxiliary target distribution, and jointly fine-tune the encoder weights and the clustering assignments (Section 2.3). The described setup is illustrated in Figure 1.

2.1   SIF Embedding

We apply a relatively simple and yet effective strategy for embedding short texts, called Smooth Inverse Frequency (SIF) embeddings. For SIF embedding, first, a weighted average of pre-trained word embeddings is computed. The contribution of each word is calculated as $\frac{a}{a+p(w)}$ with a being a hyperparameter and $p(w)$ being the empirical word frequency in the text corpus. SIF embeddings are then produced by computing the first principal component of all the resulting vectors and removing it from the weighted embeddings.

2.2   Autoencoder

The parameters of the encoder network are initialized using a deep autoencoder architecture such as the one used by Hinton and Salakhutdinov (2006). The mean squared error is used to measure reconstruction loss after the encoded embeddings are decoded by the decoder subnetwork (see Fig. 1). This *non-clustering* loss is independent of the clustering algorithm and controls preservation of the original text representations. Yang et al. (2017) demonstrated that the absence of such a non-clustering loss can lead to worse representations, or trivial solutions where the clusters all collapse into a single representation.

2.3   Self-Training

After pre-training using the autoencoder architecture, we obtain an initial estimate of the non-linear mapping from the SIF embedding to a low-dimensional representation, on which a cluster algorithm is applied. Next, we improve clustering using a second *self-training* phase: we assign initial cluster centroids after which we alternate between two steps: (i) first, the probability of assigning a data point to each cluster is computed; (ii) second, an auxiliary probability distribution is calculated and used as target for the encoder network. Network weights and cluster centroids are updated iteratively until a stopping criterion is met.

For Step (i), we compute a *soft cluster assignment* for each data point. Maaten and Hinton (2008) propose the Student's t-distribution Q with a single degree of freedom to measure the similarity between embedded points z_i and centroids μ_j:

$$q_{ij} = \frac{(1 + \|z_i - \mu_j\|^2)^{-1}}{\sum_{j'}(1 + \|z_i - \mu_{j'}\|^2)^{-1}}, \qquad (1)$$

in which q_{ij} can be interpreted as the probability of assigning sample i to cluster j. Then q_{ij} can be used as a soft assignment of embeddings to centroids. The encoder is then fine-tuned to match this soft assignment q_i to a target distribution p_j.

For Step (ii), as Xie et al. (2016), we use an auxiliary target distribution P which has "stricter" probabilities compared to the similarity score q_{ij}, with the aim to improve cluster purity and put more emphasis on data points assigned with high confidence. This prevents large clusters from distorting the hidden feature space. The probabilities p_{ij} in the proposed distribution P are calculated as:

$$p_{ij} = \frac{q_{ij}^2/\sum_{i'} q_{i'j}}{\sum_{j'}(q_{ij'}^2/\sum_{i'} q_{i'j'})}, \tag{2}$$

in which the squared summation terms q_{ij}^2 are normalized by the soft cluster frequencies ($\sum_{i'} q_{i'j}$).

The KL-divergence between the two probability distributions P and Q is then used as training objective, i.e., the training loss L is defined as:

$$L = \mathrm{KL}(P\|Q) = \sum_i \sum_j p_{ij} \log \frac{p_{ij}}{q_{ij}}. \tag{3}$$

The strategy outlined above can be seen as a form of self-supervision (Nigam and Ghani, 2000). Centroids of a standard clustering algorithm (e.g., k-means) are used to intialize the weights of the clustering layer, after which high confidence predictions are used to fine-tune the encoder and centroids. After convergence of this procedure, short texts are encoded and final cluster assignments are made using k-means.

3 Experimental Results

After describing the datasets (Section 3.1) and the experiment design (Section 3.2), we will present the results of these experiments (Section 3.3).

3.1 Data

We replicate the test setting used by Xu et al. (2017) and evaluate our model on three datasets for short text clustering: (1) **SearchSnippets:** a text collection comprising Web search snippets categorized in 8 different topics (Phan et al., 2008). (2) **Stackoverflow:** a collection of posts from question and answer site stackoverflow, published as part of a Kaggle challenge.[1] This subset contains question titles from 20 different categories selected by Xu et al. (2017). (3) **Biomedical,** a snapshot of one year of PubMed data distributed by BioASQ for evaluation of large-scale online biomedical semantic indexing.[2] Table 2 provides an overview of the main characteristics of the presented short text datasets.

3.2 Experimental Setup

We compare our method to baselines for STC including clustering of TF and TF-IDF representations, Skip-thought Vectors (Kiros et al., 2015) and the best reported STC[2] model by Xu et al. (2017). Following (Van Der Maaten, 2009; Xie et al., 2016), we set sizes of hidden layers to d:500:500:2000:20 for all datasets, where d is the short text embedding dimension for all datasets. We used pre-trained word2vec embeddings[3] with fixed $\alpha = 0.1$ value for all corpora. We set the batch size to 64 and pre-trained the autoencoder for 15 epochs. We initialized stochastic gradient descent with a learning rate of 0.01 and momentum value of 0.9.

During experiments, the choice of initial centroids had considerable impact on clustering performance when applying the k-means algorithm. To reduce this influence of initialization, we restarted k-means 100 times with different initial centroids, as Huang et al. (2014); Xu et al. (2017), and selected the best centroids, which obtained the lowest sum of squared distances of samples to their closest cluster center. Similar to Xu et al. (2017), results are averaged over 5 trials and we also report the standard deviation on the scores.

3.3 Results and Discussion

We evaluate clustering performance based on the correspondence between clusters and partitions as per the ground truth class labels assigned to each of the short texts. We report two widely used performance metrics, the clustering accuracy (ACC) and the normalized mutual information (NMI) (Huang et al., 2014; Xu et al., 2017).

NMI measures the information shared between the predicted assignments A, and the ground truth

---

196

| | SearchSnippets | | Stackoverflow | | Biomedical | |
Method	ACC	NMI	ACC	NMI	ACC	NMI
TF	24.7±2.22	9.0±2.30	13.5±2.18	7.8±2.56	15.2±1.78	9.4±2.04
TF-IDF	33.8±3.92	21.4±4.35	20.3±3.95	15.6±4.68	28.0±2.83	25.4±3.23
Skip-Thought	33.6±1.95	13.8±0.78	9.3±0.24	2.7±0.34	16.3±0.33	10.7±0.46
SIF	53.4±1.86	36.9±0.90	30.5±0.28	28.9±0.17	33.7±2.35	30.1±0.64
STC^2	77.0±4.1	**62.9±1.7**	51.14±2.9	49.0±1.5	43.0±1.3	38.1±0.5
SIF + Aut., Self-Train.	**77.1±1.1**	56.7±1.0	**59.8±1.9**	**54.8±1.0**	**54.8±2.3**	**47.1±0.8**

Table 1: Clustering results (accuracy ACC and normalized mutal information NMI) for three short text collections using various representations and self-training methods. STC^2 and our method involve additional fine-tuning of encoders, others apply k-means directly on short text representations. Performance results are average and standard deviations over 5 runs.

Dataset	C	N	T	$|V|$
SearchSnippets	8	12.3k	17.9	31k
StackOverflow	20	20k	8.3	23k
Biomedical	20	20k	12.9	19k

Table 2: Statistics for the short text clustering datasets as used by Xu et al. (2017): number of classes (C), number of short texts (N), average number of tokens per text (T) and vocabulary size ($|V|$).

assignments B, and is defined as

$$NMI(A,B) = \frac{I(A,B)}{\sqrt{H(A)H(B)}}, \qquad (4)$$

where I is the mutual information and H is the entropy. When data is partitioned perfectly, the NMI score is 1, and when A and B are independent, it becomes 0.

The clustering accuracy is defined as

$$ACC = \frac{\sum_{i=1}^{N} \delta(y_i = map(c_i))}{N}, \qquad (5)$$

where $\delta()$ is an indicator function, c_i is the clustering label for x_i, $map()$ transforms the clustering label c_i to its group label by the Hungarian algorithm (Papadimitriou and Steiglitz, 1982), and y_i is the true group label of x_i. Results for NMI and accuracy of existing work and the presented model are shown in Table 1.

While generic, low-dimensional representations such as Skip-Thought or SIF embeddings have demonstrated to be beneficial for NLP on many tasks, for STC, additional fine-tuning and self-training leads to improved cluster quality. The evaluation results show the superiority of our approach, compared to the STC^2 model, on all but one of the metrics.

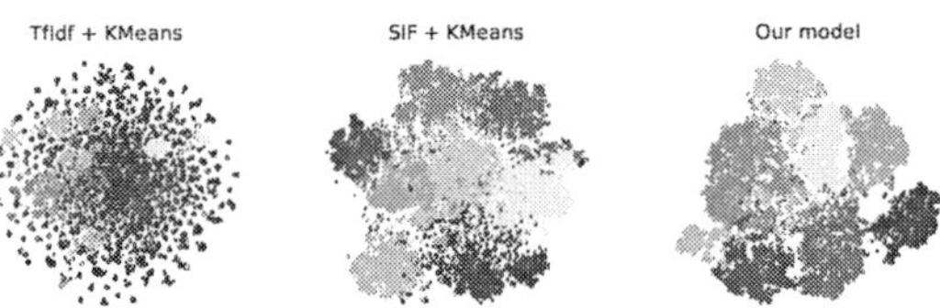

Figure 2: Two dimensional representations of *Search-Snippets* short texts before application of k-means. Colors indicate the $C = 8$ different ground truth labels.

Qualitatively, the improved cluster quality is also visually apparent in Figure 2, which shows a two-dimensional t-SNE (Maaten and Hinton, 2008) representation of the *SearchSnippets* short texts before clustering.

The source code of our model, implemented using Tensorflow, is publicly available to encourage further research on STC.[4]

4 Conclusion

We proposed a method for clustering of short texts using sentence embeddings and a multi-phase approach, starting from unsupervised SIF embeddings for the short texts. Our STC model then adopts an autoencoder architecture which is fine-tuned for clustering using self-training. Our empirical evaluation on three short text clustering datasets demonstrates resulting accuracies ranging from at least as good up to 12 percentage points, compared to the state-of-the-art STC^2 method.

Acknowledgments

The authors would like to thank the anonymous reviewers for their constructive feedback.

[4]https://github.com/hadifar/
stc_clustering

References

Elie Aljalbout, Vladimir Golkov, Yawar Siddiqui, Maximilian Strobel, and Daniel Cremers. 2018. Clustering with deep learning: Taxonomy and new methods. *arXiv preprint arXiv:1801.07648.*

Massih R Amini and Nicolas Usunier. 2007. A contextual query expansion approach by term clustering for robust text summarization. In *Proceedings of DUC*, pages 48–55.

Sanjeev Arora, Yingyu Liang, and Tengyu Ma. 2017. A simple but tough-to-beat baseline for sentence embeddings. In *Proceedings of ICLR*.

Somnath Banerjee, Krishnan Ramanathan, and Ajay Gupta. 2007. Clustering short texts using Wikipedia. In *Proceedings of SIGIR*, pages 787–788. ACM.

Igor Cadez, David Heckerman, Christopher Meek, Padhraic Smyth, and Steven White. 2003. Model-based clustering and visualization of navigation patterns on a web site. *Data Mining and Knowledge Discovery*, 7:399–424.

Andrew M. Dai, Christopher Olah, and Quoc V. Le. 2015. Document embedding with paragraph vectors. *CoRR*, abs/1507.07998.

Cedric De Boom, Steven Van Canneyt, Thomas Demeester, and Bart Dhoedt. 2016. Representation learning for very short texts using weighted word embedding aggregation. *Pattern Recogn. Lett.*, pages 150–156.

Geoffrey E. Hinton and Ruslan R. Salakhutdinov. 2006. Reducing the dimensionality of data with neural networks. *Science*, pages 504–507.

Andreas Hotho, Steffen Staab, and Gerd Stumme. 2003. Ontologies improve text document clustering. In *Proceedings of ICDM*, pages 541–544. IEEE.

Xiaohua Hu, Xiaodan Zhang, Caimei Lu, Eun K. Park, and Xiaohua Zhou. 2009. Exploiting Wikipedia as external knowledge for document clustering. In *Proceedings of SIGKDD*, pages 389–396. ACM.

Peihao Huang, Yan Huang, Wei Wang, and Liang Wang. 2014. Deep embedding network for clustering. In *Proceedings of ICPR*, pages 1532–1537. IEEE.

Ryan Kiros, Yukun Zhu, Ruslan R Salakhutdinov, Richard Zemel, Raquel Urtasun, Antonio Torralba, and Sanja Fidler. 2015. Skip-thought vectors. In *Proceedings of the NIPS*, pages 3294–3302.

Quoc Le and Tomas Mikolov. 2014. Distributed representations of sentences and documents. In *Proceedings of the ICML*, pages 1188–1196.

Xiaoyong Liu and W. Bruce Croft. 2004. Cluster-based retrieval using language models. In *Proceedings of SIGIR*, pages 186–193. ACM.

Laurens van der Maaten and Geoffrey Hinton. 2008. Visualizing data using t-SNE. *Journal of machine learning research*, 9:2579–2605.

Tomas Mikolov, Ilya Sutskever, Kai Chen, Greg S Corrado, and Jeff Dean. 2013. Distributed representations of words and phrases and their compositionality. In *Proceedings of NIPS*, pages 3111–3119.

Erxue Min, Xifeng Guo, Qiang Liu, Gen Zhang, Jianjing Cui, and Jun Long. 2018. A survey of clustering with deep learning: From the perspective of network architecture. *IEEE Access*, 6:39501–39514.

Kamal Nigam and Rayid Ghani. 2000. Analyzing the effectiveness and applicability of co-training. In *Proceedings of CIKM*, pages 86–93.

Christos H. Papadimitriou and Kenneth Steiglitz. 1982. *Combinatorial Optimization: Algorithms and Complexity*. Prentice-Hall.

Jeffrey Pennington, Richard Socher, and Christopher D. Manning. 2014. GloVe: Global vectors for word representation. In *Proceedings of EMNLP*, pages 1532–1543.

Xuan-Hieu Phan, Le-Minh Nguyen, and Susumu Horiguchi. 2008. Learning to classify short and sparse text & web with hidden topics from large-scale data collections. In *Proceedings of WWW*, pages 91–100. ACM.

Hinrich Schutze and Craig Silverstein. 1997. Projections for efficient document clustering. In *Proceedings of SIGIR*, pages 74–81.

Fei Tian, Bin Gao, Qing Cui, Enhong Chen, and Tie-Yan Liu. 2014. Learning deep representations for graph clustering. In *Proceedings of AAAI*, page 1293–1299.

Laurens Van Der Maaten. 2009. Learning a parametric embedding by preserving local structure. In *Proceedings of AIStats*, pages 384–391.

Jia Wang, Qing Li, Yuanzhu Peter Chen, and Zhangxi Lin. 2010. Recommendation in internet forums and blogs. In *Proceedings of ACL*, pages 257–265. ACL.

Tingting Wei, Yonghe Lu, Huiyou Chang, Qiang Zhou, and Xianyu Bao. 2015. A semantic approach for text clustering using WordNet and lexical chains. *Expert Systems with Applications*, 42:2264–2275.

Junyuan Xie, Ross Girshick, and Ali Farhadi. 2016. Unsupervised deep embedding for clustering analysis. In *Proceedings of ICML*, pages 478–487.

Jiaming Xu, Peng Wang, Guanhua Tian, Bo Xu, Jun Zhao, Fangyuan Wang, and Hongwei Hao. 2015. Short text clustering via convolutional neural networks. In *Workshops at the ACL Conference*, pages 62–69. ACL.

Jiaming Xu, Bo Xu, Peng Wang, Suncong Zheng, Guanhua Tian, and Jun Zhao. 2017. Self-taught convolutional neural networks for short text clustering. *Neural Networks*, 88:22–31.

Bo Yang, Xiao Fu, Nicholas D Sidiropoulos, and Mingyi Hong. 2017. Towards k-means-friendly spaces: Simultaneous deep learning and clustering. In *Proceedings of ICML*, pages 3861–3870.

Jianwei Yang, Devi Parikh, and Dhruv Batra. 2016. Joint unsupervised learning of deep representations and image clusters. In *Proceedings of CVPR*, pages 5147–5156.

Improving Word Embeddings Using Kernel PCA

Vishwani Gupta **Sven Giesselbach** **Stefan Rüping** **Christian Bauckhage**

Fraunhofer IAIS, Sankt Augustin, Germany

`firstname.lastname@iais.fraunhofer.de`

Abstract

Word-based embedding approaches such as Word2Vec capture the meaning of words and relations between them, particularly well when trained with large text collections; however, they fail to do so with small datasets. Extensions such as fastText reduce the amount of data needed slightly, however, the joint task of learning meaningful morphology, syntactic and semantic representations still requires a lot of data. In this paper, we introduce a new approach to warm-start embedding models with morphological information, in order to reduce training time and enhance their performance. We use word embeddings generated using both word2vec and fastText models and enrich them with morphological information of words, derived from kernel principal component analysis (KPCA) of word similarity matrices. This can be seen as explicitly feeding the network morphological similarities and letting it learn semantic and syntactic similarities. Evaluating our models on word similarity and analogy tasks in English and German, we find that they not only achieve higher accuracies than the original skip-gram and fastText models but also require significantly less training data and time. Another benefit of our approach is that it is capable of generating a high-quality representation of infrequent words as, for example, found in very recent news articles with rapidly changing vocabularies. Lastly, we evaluate the different models on a downstream sentence classification task in which a CNN model is initialized with our embeddings and find promising results.

1   Introduction

Continuous vector representations of words learned from unstructured text corpora are an effective way of capturing semantic relationships among words. Approaches to computing word embeddings are typically based on the context of words, their morphemes, or corpus-wide co-occurrence statistics. As of this writing, arguably the most popular approaches are the *Word2Vec* skip-gram model (Mikolov et al., 2013a) and the fastText model (Bojanowski et al., 2017). The skip-gram model generates embeddings based on windowed word contexts. While it incorporates semantic information, it ignores word morphology. Yet, the latter might be beneficial especially for morphologically rich languages such as German and Turkish. Bojanowski et al. (2017) therefore introduced *fastText* which builds on the Word2Vec approach but also incorporates morphology by considering sub-word units and representing a word by a sum of its character n-grams as well as the word itself.

To learn high-quality embeddings, Word2Vec requires huge text corpora with billions of words and still fails to generate high-quality vector representations for less frequent or unknown words. Although fastText improves the results by incorporating subword information, it still fails in many cases. This is particularly evident in the news domain where frequently new words such as names occur over time which, in turn, impacts the performance of downstream applications. In this paper, we therefore propose an alternative approach which not only makes use of morphological information but also performs well when trained on smaller datasets or domains with rapidly changing vocabulary. Research questions we answer in this paper are:

1. Can high-quality word embeddings be trained on small datasets?

2. Can high-quality embeddings be generated for infrequent words?

3. Can the use of morphological information increase the efficiency of learning semantic and syntactic similarities?

Proceedings of the 4th Workshop on Representation Learning for NLP (RepL4NLP-2019), pages 200–208
Florence, Italy, August 2, 2019. ©2019 Association for Computational Linguistics

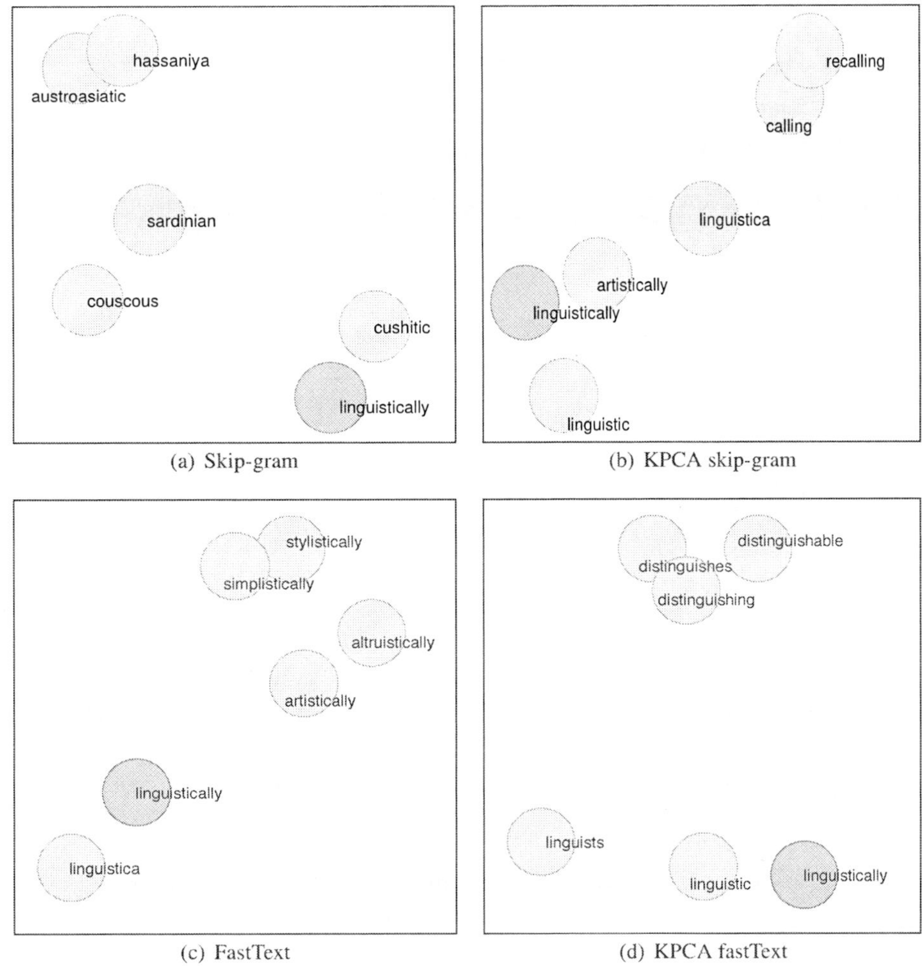

<table>
<tr><td>(a) Skip-gram</td><td>(b) KPCA skip-gram</td></tr>
<tr><td>(c) FastText</td><td>(d) KPCA fastText</td></tr>
</table>

Figure 1: Visualization of 5-nearest neighbors for the word "Linguistically".

2   Related work

Mikolov et al. (2013a) proposed log-bilinear models to learn vector representations of words from the context in which they appear in large corpora. These are the Continuous Bag-of-Words Model (CBOW) and the Continuous Skip-gram Model (skip-gram) which predict target words from source context words and source context words from target words, respectively. An extension proposed by Mnih and Kavukcuoglu (2013) involves training lightweight log-bilinear language models with noise-contrastive estimation and achieves results comparable to the best previous models with one quarter of the training data and in less computing time.

There are some recent works which try to incorporate morphological structures into the computation of embeddings. Soricut and Och (2015) learn vector representation of morphological transformations and are able to obtain representations for unseen words. Cotterell et al. (2016) presented a morpheme-based post-processor for word embeddings. They proposed a Gaussian graphical model which can be extended to continuous representations for unknown words as well as helps in smoothing the representations of the observed words in the training dataset. Bhatia et al. (2016) proposed a new unified probabilistic framework in which they combine morphological and distributional information. The word embeddings act as a latent variable for which morphological information provides a prior distribution. This in turn condition a likelihood function over an observed dataset. Bojanowski et al. (2017) proposed *fastText*, an extension of the skip-gram model, which learns word representations by including sub-word information. This is achieved by not only representing words with vectors but also the subword parts they consist of. Word vector representations are finally built as the sum of their sub-word vectors and their own representation.

3 KPCA-based skip-gram and fastText models

In this section, we propose a general extension to word embedding methods which we evaluate on the skip-gram model as well as on the fast-Text model. We propose pre-training embeddings with a kernel PCA computed on word similarity matrices, generated using a string similarity function, for words in a vocabulary and then injecting the pre-trained embeddings in the Word2Vec and fastText embeddings by initializing them with the KPCA word and subword embeddings. This seamlessly incorporates sub-word structures in Word2Vec and yields a better starting point for fastText training. It is especially useful for morphologically rich languages because their semantically similar words often share some common morphemes such as roots, affixes, and syllables.

3.1 Kernel PCA on string similarities

Embedding words according to morphological similarities can be seen as a clustering problem in a higher dimensional feature space which can be tackled using Kernel PCA (Schölkopf et al., 1997), a nonlinear form of principal component analysis. Suppose a vocabulary V of words w_i, a string similarity measure $\mathcal{S}$ (e.g. the n-gram similarity (Brito et al., 2017)), and a non-linear kernel function $\mathcal{K}$ (e.g. the Gaussian) to be given. This allows us to compute a $|V| \times |V|$ word similarity matrix $\mathbf{K}$ where

$$K_{ij} = \mathcal{K}\big(\mathcal{S}(w_i, w_j)\big) \tag{1}$$

Centering this kernel matrix (Schölkopf et al., 1997) yields a feature space representation of words in V, because column vector $\mathbf{k}_i$ of $\mathbf{K}$ can be seen as a $|V|$-dimensional representation of w_i. Performing PCA in this feature space then allows for selecting the first $d < |V|$ nonlinear principal components $\mathbf{v_i}$ which, in turn, allow for projecting word vectors into lower dimensional spaces. Using projection matrix,

$$\mathbf{P} = \left[\frac{\mathbf{v_1}}{\lambda_1}, ..., \frac{\mathbf{v_d}}{\lambda_d}\right] \tag{2}$$

generated by selecting d eigenvectors $\mathbf{v_1}$ to $\mathbf{v_d}$ corresponding to the highest eigenvalues, λ_1 to λ_d, the d-dimensional projections are

$$\mathbf{e}_i = \mathbf{P}^\mathsf{T}\mathbf{k}_i. \tag{3}$$

3.2 Models with KPCA embeddings

Computing Kernel PCA for a large vocabulary is computationally demanding. We thus restrict our vocabulary V to contain only the most frequent words of a text corpus. For any *new* or *out of vocabulary word* s_{new} not contained in V, we can compute its kernel vector

$$\mathbf{k}_{new} = \mathcal{K}\big(\mathcal{S}(s_{new}, V)\big) \tag{4}$$

and obtain a lower dimensional representation as

$$\mathbf{e}_{new} = \mathbf{P}^\mathsf{T}\mathbf{k}_{new}. \tag{5}$$

Note that word embeddings computed this way only encode morphological similarity. To incorporate semantic similarities, we initialize Word2Vec and fastText models with the pre-trained KPCA embeddings. We train the Word2Vec skip-gram model with negative sampling (Mikolov et al., 2013b) on our morphological embeddings using the C implementation of Word2vec package[1].

To initialize the fastText model with morphological embeddings, we also compute the KPCA vectors for the subword units in the dictionary, as fastText also has vector representations for character n-grams contained in words. We train the fastText model initialized with our morphological embeddings using the C++ implementation of fastText [2]. After training both the models, we obtain embeddings encoded with semantic, syntactic and morphological similarities whose practical merits we evaluate in the next section.

4 Experimental Results

To evaluate our models' performance when trained on datasets of different sizes, we consider English and German datasets such as *Text8* [3], *20 News*

---

[1]https://code.google.com/p/word2vec/
[2]https://github.com/facebookresearch/
fastText/
[3]http://mattmahoney.net/dc/text8.zip

Dataset name	Language	Corpus size (words)	Vocab Size (words)
20 Newsgroups	English	1 million	$\approx 19,000$
Text8	English	10 million	$\approx 70,000$
English Wiki 2016	English	1,192 million	$\approx 330,000$
German news 2013	German	183 million	$\approx 247,000$

Table 1: Details of the datasets used for evaluation.

groups [4], *English Wiki 2016* and *German news 2013* [5] for training. Each dataset contains articles crawled from news websites or Wikipedia. These raw text corpora contain a large amount of irrelevant text and are pre-processed using a script by Mahoney[6]. In Table 1, we list all the datasets that we have used to train the models.

4.1 Baseline

One of our main results is the observation that the KPCA fastText model and the KPCA skip-gram model generate high-quality word embeddings even when trained only on small datasets when compared to fastText or skip-gram model respectively. To compare how well our models perform in comparison to the original skip-gram model and fastText model, we consider both of them as the baselines in all our experiments and use the same parameters and datasets for generating and evaluating embeddings for all models.

4.2 Evaluation

We evaluate our models using *intrinsic evaluation tasks* which assess how well the vectors capture meanings of and relationships between words. In particular, we evaluate all the models with respect to

1. *Word similarity tasks* which include finding a word's nearest neighbors.

2. *Word analogy tasks* which include calculating the semantic and the syntactic similarities between words and their relations.

3. *Performance in a downstream application* which illustrates how well the embeddings

work for subsequent processing steps such as a sentence classification task (Kim, 2014).

4.3 Word similarity Evaluation

Word similarity tasks evaluate word embeddings in terms of their k-nearest neighbors. For selected words, we show nearest neighbors according to cosine similarity for vectors trained using the proposed models as well as the baseline models. Here we illustrate how the models performed for frequent as well as for infrequent words. Table 2 presents examples for all the models obtained after being trained for an epoch on the small *Text8* dataset.

The table illustrates that for the frequent words, all the models learn a good representation and are able to produce relevant nearest neighbors. For the infrequent words, the skip-gram did not learn a very good representation as there are not enough examples for the word to learn from. In these cases the nearest neighbor of the skip-gram model are not very meaningful, e.g. it places firecracker close to "prochnow", while the KPCA fastText model places it closer to "cracker" and "fire" related words. Since the fastText model uses sub-word information, it achieves better performance at this task compared to the skip-gram model. It finds meaningful neighbors for "placental", however it fails for words such as "cruel". KPCA skip-gram gets a warm start with the morphological information learned from KPCA, which helps in learning a better representation for scarce words, thus producing better k-nearest neighbors for words such as "cruel".

When we compare KPCA skip-gram with KPCA fastText, we observe that KPCA fastText generally generates better neighbors. We assume this is because of the fact that it benefits from the fastText approach of jointly refining subword and word representations. Comparing fastText with the better initialized KPCA fastText model, KPCA produces decidedly better neighbors, especially for "scrubbing", "firecracker", "linguistically" and

Word (frequency)	Model	k-nearest neighbors (sorted by similarity)
three (114,775)	Skip-gram	four, five, seven, eight, runways
	KPCA skip-gram	four, seven, five, eight, nine
	fastText	four, five, seven, zero, eight
	KPCA fastText	seven, five, four, eight, nine
history (12,623)	Skip-gram	overview, timeline, prehistory, origins, beginnings
	KPCA skip-gram	article, origins, pamphlets, references, offshoot
	fastText	prehistory, historique, historica, historiques, historiography
	KPCA fastText	historical, prehistory, histories, historiography, historic
april (3,069)	Skip-gram	june, march, august, february, november
	KPCA skip-gram	august, march, june, february, december
	fastText	february, january, october, september, november
	KPCA fastText	february, august, june, october, november
biblical (703)	Skip-gram	talmud, josephus, apocrypha, tanakh, commentaries
	KPCA skip-gram	judaica, mythical, mexica, metaphysical, micah
	fastText	evangelical, biblically, bibliographical, noncanonical, mythological
	KPCA fastText	bible, bibles, bibl, testament, biblically
moscow (622)	Skip-gram	warsaw, armistice, versailles, hostage, daoud
	KPCA skip-gram	kabul, prague, beirut, bonn, cpsu
	fastText	mosby, mokhehle, moonwalks, mocha, rsfsr
	KPCA fastText	borisovich, soviet, helsinki, denisovich, warsaw
cruel (140)	Skip-gram	injustice, urge, fears, zeal, appease
	KPCA skip-gram	cruelty, foes, lawful, imbued, idols
	fastText	cruzi, crusoe, crux, cruijff, duel
	KPCA fastText	cruelty, cruelly, ruelle, cruzi, duel
linguistically (46)	Skip-gram	cushitic, hassaniya, couscous, austroasiatic, sardinian
	KPCA skip-gram	linguistic, recalling, artistically, calling, linguistics
	fastText	simplistically, altruistically, stylistically, artistically ,linguistica
	KPCA fastText	linguistic, linguists, distinguishes, distinguishing, distinguishable
placental (30)	Skip-gram	intestine, condense, spikes, greasy, sideways
	KPCA skip-gram	placenta, centaurus, labiodental, centaur, centaurs
	fastText	placentals, placenta, dental, placement, placement, segmental
	KPCA fastText	placentals, placenta, parental, placement, concentrates
firecracker (5)	Skip-gram	prochnow, caff, gwen, hillis, horovitz
	KPCA skip-gram	mccracken, racked, wracked, rackets, racket
	fastText	cracker, nutcracker, acker, thacker, skywalker
	KPCA fastText	cracker, crackers, fireplace, firestrom, firewall
scrubbing (5)	Skip-gram	underpowered, transceivers, refineries, heliport, gasification
	KPCA skip-gram	ingot, ingots, xing, mcing, plying
	fastText	scrying, dubbing, rubbing, ebing, screwing
	KPCA fastText	rubbing, clubbing, scrubbed, scraping, scrying

Table 2: The $k = 5$-nearest neighbors of word embeddings in $\mathbb{R}^{128}$, trained on the *Text8* dataset.

"cruel". In figure 1, we can visualize the t-SNE 2-D representation of the nearest neighbors for the word "linguistically".

Epoch No.	Model	Total	Semantic	Syntactic
	Skip-gram	7.84%	3.92%	11.24%
1	KPCA skip-gram	15.74%	2.96%	26.71%
	fastText	36.89%	0.89%	67.80%
	KPCA fastText	38.04%	1.12%	69.76%
	Skip-gram	17.09%	9.59%	23.50%
2	KPCA skip-gram	21.14%	7.26%	33.07%
	fastText	41.19%	1.60%	75.19%
	KPCA fastText	40.48%	2.10%	73.43%
	Skip-gram	24.21%	19.28%	28.45%
5	KPCA skip-gram	26.20%	15.56%	35.34%
	fastText	43.60%	5.51%	76.31%
	KPCA fastText	43.42%	7.37%	74.39%
	Skip-gram	26.68%	24.61%	28.45%
10	KPCA skip-gram	28.65%	22.22%	34.18%
	fastText	44.49%	12.10%	71.75%
	KPCA fastText	44.68%	13.17%	72.29%

Table 3: Analogy accuracies of embeddings in $\mathbb{R}^{128}$ trained for different epochs on *Text8* dataset.

Epoch No.	Model	Total	Semantic	Syntactic
	Skip-gram	0.18%	0.20%	0.17%
1	KPCA skip-gram	15.47%	0.66%	19.80%
	fastText	3.07%	0.26%	3.89%
	KPCA fastText	33.66%	0.79%	43.26.%
	Skip-gram	0.99%	1.26%	0.91%
2	KPCA skip-gram	14.83%	1.65%	18.68%
	fastText	28.52%	0.33%	36.76%
	KPCA fastText	45.85%	1.19%	58.91%
	Skip-gram	0.96%	1.46%	0.81%
3	KPCA skip-gram	14.07%	1.92%	17.62%
	fastText	44.84%	0.79%	57.71%
	KPCA fastText	47.44%	1.39%	60.90%

Table 4: Analogy accuracies of embeddings in $\mathbb{R}^{128}$ trained for different epochs on *20 Newsgroups* dataset.

4.4 Word Analogy Evaluation

Pre-trained word vectors are available for a dataset of 100 billion words from Google News. Mikolov et al. (2013a) observed that, when word vectors are trained on such a large dataset, they are able to answer very subtle relationships between words. Yet, for the news data or for a small dataset such results cannot be achieved. Warm-starting the models with our KPCA embeddings, however, yields good performance in such settings, too.

To assess accuracies in the word analogy task, we use a comprehensive test set provided by Mikolov et al. (2013a). This test consists of semantic and syntactic similarity questions which include relationships like adjective-to-adverb, currency, plural-verbs, city-in-state, comparative, superlative relationships, and others. A question is assumed to be correctly answered only if the closest word to the vector is exactly the same as the correct word in the question; synonyms are considered as mistakes. In order to use this evaluation to compare our models' results to those of the skip-gram and the fastText models, we train the models on the different datasets shown in Table 1. Results are reported in Tables 3, 4, 5 and 6.

A comparison of 300-dimensional and 128-dimensional embeddings on the analogy tasks on the *text8* and *20-Newsgroups* datasets showed that all models (including baselines) perform best when we picked 128-dimensional embeddings. For the sake of simplicity we used 128-dimensions in all tasks. From Table 4, it is evident that our KPCA fastText model outperforms the skip-gram as well as the fastText model when trained on a small dataset. KPCA skip-gram as well as KPCA fastText models have better accuracies for both semantic and syntactic questions in the initial epochs compared to their cold-start counterparts. One question arising in this context is whether the skip-gram or the fastText models can also learn from smaller datasets. The answer for the *20 Newsgroup* as well as for the *text8* datasets is "yes", but only if they are trained for several epochs.

The results for the *20 Newsgroups* dataset in Table 4 also show that the skip-gram models completely fail to learn analogies on this dataset. The KPCA fastText embeddings benefit from their warm-start and show a quicker convergence rate. We make the following observations from the accuracies obtained after each epoch of training. During the 1st epoch, the skip-gram and the fastText model do not perform well. However, after the 2nd epoch, the fastText model starts performing better on the syntactic questions. Meanwhile KPCA skip-gram and KPCA fastText models still achieve higher accuracies than the respective skip-gram and fastText models. Hence, considering accuracies from the initial epochs, we can conclude that training of our model converges faster than the training of the fastText model and the skip-gram model.

From Table 3, we observe that the skip-gram model always seems to perform better on the semantic questions but when we compare these accuracies with the nearest neighbors results from Table 2, it can be observed that although KPCA models seem to work badly on semantic tasks, they generate better k-nearest neighbors than the respective skip-gram and fastText models.

We also compare the accuracies achieved by the models when trained for one epoch on a large data set, namely *English Wikipedia* dataset. The results in Table 5, illustrate the performance of the different models when training them on a large training dataset size. When compared to fastText, KPCA skip-gram performs better on semantic questions, but worse on syntactic questions. Noticeably KPCA fastText performs better on semantic questions than all the other models. However plain fastText outperforms it on the syntactic questions. The overall accuracy of fastText is also slightly higher than for KPCA fastText model.

We also report accuracies for the analogy task when the models are trained on the *German news* dataset for morphologically rich German language. We use the German version of the semantic/syntactic analogy dataset, introduced by (Köper et al., 2015) for evaluation. Table 6 shows how different models perform on the analogies tasks. We note that morphological information

Epochs	Model	Total	Sem	Syn
	Skip-gram	70.95%	85.29%	66.67%
1	KPCA skip-gram	75.00%	85.29%	71.93%
	fastText	81.43%	82.35%	80.46%
	KPCA fastText	80.41%	88.24%	78.07%

Table 5: Analogy accuracies of embeddings in $\mathbb{R}^{128}$ trained for one epoch on *English Wiki 2016* dataset.

Epochs	Model	Total	Sem	Syn
	Skip-gram	34.43%	35.89%	31.69%
1	KPCA skip-gram	35.71%	37.72%	31.94%
	fastText	29.56%	14.34%	58.20%
	KPCA fastText	30.15%	14.54%	59.56%

Table 6: Analogy accuracies of embeddings in $\mathbb{R}^{128}$ trained for one epoch on *German news 2012* dataset.

Dataset	Model	Accuracies
	Skip-gram	72.82%
20 Newsgroups	KPCA Skip-gram	73.57%
	fastText	72.07%
	KPCA fastText	72.73%
	Skip-gram	73.90%
english Wiki 2016	KPCA Skip-gram	74.56%
	fastText	73.96%
	KPCA fastText	74.09%

Table 7: Sentence classification task trained using pre-trained embeddings obtained from different models after 10 epochs of training.

significantly improves the syntactic tasks when we compare KPCA fastText and fastText with KPCA skip-gram and skip-gram. While the semantic accuracy degrades for both KPCA fastText and fastText. Initializing the skip-gram and fastText with KPCA embeddings has improved the performance of both the models. The KPCA skip-gram model shows the overall best performance. This shows that the initialization of the models with morphological information, is beneficial for the German language as well.

4.5 Evaluation of performance on downstream applications

Finally, we investigate how well the embeddings obtained from the different models and different datasets perform on a downstream task in a neural network architecture. We choose the convolutional neural network proposed in (Kim, 2014) and evaluate it with the embeddings in a sentence classification task. We initialize the CNN with the embeddings obtained from the different embedding models and keep the embeddings static during training. Initializing the word vectors with the pre-trained word embeddings instead of random embeddings improves the performance as noted by (Collobert et al., 2011) and (Iyyer et al., 2014).

In our experiment, the classification task is a sentiment classification task, i.e. detecting whether reviews are positive or negative. The dataset used for it, consists of movie reviews[7] with one sentence per review. We use embeddings generated by training the embedding models on the *20 Newsgroups* and *English Wikipedia* datasets. The CNN network is trained for 10 epochs.

In Table 7, we list the accuracies for the model trained with different embeddings obtained from the two datasets. In both cases, the model initialized with embeddings generated using KPCA skip-gram model and the KPCA fastText outperform the models initialized with the respective cold-start embeddings, albeit with a small margin. The models initialized with the KPCA skip-gram model achieve the best results in both cases.

5 Conclusion

In this paper, we explored a simple method to improve models for computing word embeddings and evaluated it with the popular skip-gram and fastText models.

Our approach relies on string similarity matrices computed from small vocabularies which, in a first step, are subjected to kernel PCA (KPCA) in order to generate non-linear, morphologically informed word embeddings. In a second step, the KPCA-based vector representations of words are used as input to the skip-gram model in order to obtain embeddings that also account for word contexts.

In practical experiments, we evaluated the quality of our embeddings using intrinsic measures such as word similarity and word analogy. In our experiments the KPCA skip-gram and KPCA fastText were found to outperform the original continuous skip-gram and fastText model. In particular, we found that the continuous skip-gram model can learn similarity among words

only when it has seen a sufficiently large number of examples. When feeding the models with morphologically informed vector representations of words, they seem to be able to learn from a better starting point when computing semantically informed embeddings. Using KPCA fastText or KPCA skip-gram model, we found that it is possible to obtain high-quality word vectors even when training with small datasets and fewer epochs.

6 Future Work

Future work concerns deeper analysis of how to choose words in the vocabulary to construct the projection matrix used to generate Kernel PCA embeddings. We would like to explore different string similarity functions which would help in creating better clusters of the similar words.
We would also like to extend our experiments to different embeddings such as GloVe as well as to further downstream tasks such as Named Entity Recognition or Relation Extraction.

7 Acknowledgements

This work was funded by the German Federal Ministry of Education and Research under the Competence Center Machine Learning Rhine-Ruhr ML2R, Foerderkennzeichen 01S18038B.

References

Parminder Bhatia, Robert Guthrie, and Jacob Eisenstein. 2016. Morphological priors for probabilistic neural word embeddings. *arXiv preprint arXiv:1608.01056*.

Piotr Bojanowski, Edouard Grave, Armand Joulin, and Tomas Mikolov. 2017. Enriching word vectors with subword information. *Transactions of the Association for Computational Linguistics*, pages 135–146.

Eduardo Brito, Rafet Sifa, Kostadin Cvejoski, Cesar Ojeda, and Christian Bauckhage. 2017. Towards german word embeddings: A use case with predictive sentiment analysis. In *Proceedings of Data Science, Analytics, and Applications*, pages 59–62.

Ronan Collobert, Jason Weston, Léon Bottou, Michael Karlen, Koray Kavukcuoglu, and Pavel Kuksa. 2011. Natural language processing (almost) from scratch. *Journal of machine learning research*, 12(Aug):2493–2537.

Ryan Cotterell, Hinrich Schütze, and Jason Eisner. 2016. Morphological smoothing and extrapolation of word embeddings. In *Proceedings of the*

---

[7]http://www.cs.cornell.edu/people/
pabo/movie-review-data/

54th Annual Meeting of the Association for Computational Linguistics (Volume 1: Long Papers), pages 1651–1660.

Mohit Iyyer, Peter Enns, Jordan Boyd-Graber, and Philip Resnik. 2014. Political ideology detection using recursive neural networks. In *Proceedings of the 52nd Annual Meeting of the Association for Computational Linguistics (Volume 1: Long Papers)*, pages 1113–1122.

Yoon Kim. 2014. Convolutional neural networks for sentence classification. In *Proceedings of the 2014 Conference on Empirical Methods in Natural Language Processing*, pages 1746–1751.

Maximilian Köper, Christian Scheible, and Sabine Schulte im Walde. 2015. Multilingual reliability and semantic structure of continuous word spaces. In *Proceedings of the 11th International Conference on Computational Semantics (IWCS)*.

Tomas Mikolov, Kai Chen, Greg Corrado, and Jeffrey Dean. 2013a. Efficient estimation of word representations in vector space. *arXiv preprint arXiv:1301.3781*.

Tomas Mikolov, Ilya Sutskever, Kai Chen, Greg Corrado, and Jeffrey Dean. 2013b. Distributed representations of words and phrases and their compositionality. In *Advances in neural information processing systems*, pages 3111–3119.

Andriy Mnih and Koray Kavukcuoglu. 2013. Learning word embeddings efficiently with noise-contrastive estimation. In *Advances in neural information processing systems*, pages 2265–2273.

Bernhard Schölkopf, Alexander Smola, and Klaus-Robert Müller. 1997. Kernel principal component analysis. In *International conference on artificial neural networks*, pages 583–588.

Radu Soricut and Franz Och. 2015. Unsupervised morphology induction using word embeddings. In *Proceedings of the 2015 Conference of the North American Chapter of the ACL: Human Language Technologies*, pages 1627–1637.

Assessing incrementality in sequence-to-sequence models

Dennis Ulmer
University of Amsterdam
dennis.ulmer@gmx.de

Dieuwke Hupkes
University of Amsterdam
d.hupkes@uva.nl

Elia Bruni
Universitat Pompeu Fabra
elia.bruni@gmail.com

Abstract

Since their inception, encoder-decoder models have successfully been applied to a wide array of problems in computational linguistics. The most recent successes are predominantly due to the use of different variations of attention mechanisms, but their cognitive plausibility is questionable. In particular, because past representations can be revisited at any point in time, attention-centric methods seem to lack an incentive to build up incrementally more informative representations of incoming sentences. This way of processing stands in stark contrast with the way in which humans are believed to process language: continuously and rapidly integrating new information as it is encountered. In this work, we propose three novel metrics to assess the behavior of RNNs with and without an attention mechanism and identify key differences in the way the different model types process sentences.

1 Introduction

Incrementality – that is, building up representations "as rapidly as possible as the input is encountered" (Christiansen and Chater, 2016) – is considered one of the key ingredients for humans to process language efficiently and effectively.

Christiansen and Chater (2016) conjecture how this trait is realized in human cognition by identifying several components which either make up or are implications of their hypothesized *Now-or-Never bottleneck*, a set of fundamental constraints on human language processing, which include a limited amount of available memory and time pressure. First of all, one of the implications of the now-or-never bottleneck is anticipation, implemented by a mechanism called *predictive processing*. As humans have to process sequences of inputs fast, they already try to anticipate the next element before it is being uttered. This is hypothesized to be the reason why people struggle with

so-called garden path sentences like "The horse race past the barn fell", where the last word encountered, "fell", goes against the representation of the sentence built up until this point. Secondly, another strategy being employed by humans in processing language seems to be *eager processing*: the cognitive system encodes new input into "rich" representations as fast as possible. These are build up in chunks and then processed into more and more abstract representations, an operation Christiansen and Chater (2016) call *Chunk-and-pass processing*.

In this paper, we aim to gain a better insight into the inner workings of recurrent models with respect to incrementality while taking inspiration from and drawing parallels to this psycholinguistic perspective. To ensure a successful processing of language, the human brain seems to be forced to employ an encoding scheme that seems highly reminiscent of the encoder in today's encoder-decoder architectures. Here, we look at differences between a recurrent-based encoder-decoder model with and without attention. We analyze the two model variants when tasked with a navigation instruction dataset designed to assess the compositional abilities of sequence-to-sequence models (Lake and Baroni, 2018).

The key contributions of this work can be summarized as follows:

- We introduce three new metrics for incrementality that help to understand the way that recurrent-based encoder-decoder models encode information;

- We conduct an in-depth analysis of how incrementally recurrent-based encoder-decoder models with and without attention encode sequential information;

- We confirm existing intuitions about

Proceedings of the 4th Workshop on Representation Learning for NLP (RepL4NLP-2019), pages 209–217
Florence, Italy, August 2, 2019. ©2019 Association for Computational Linguistics

attention-based recurrent models but also highlight some new aspects that explain their superiority over most attention-less recurrent models.

2   Related Work

Sequence-to-Sequence models that rely partly or fully on attention have gained much popularity in recent years (Bahdanau et al. (2015), Vaswani et al. (2017)). Although this concept can be related to the prioritisation of information in the human visual cortex (Hassabis et al., 2017), it seems contrary to the incremental processing of information in a language context, as for instance recently shown empirically for the understanding of conjunctive generic sentences (Tessler et al., 2019).

In machine learning, the idea of incrementality has already played a role in several problem statements, such as inferring the tree structure of a sentence (Jacob et al., 2018), parsing (Köhn and Menzel, 2014), or in other problems that are naturally equipped with time constraints like real-time neural machine translation (Neubig et al., 2017; Dalvi et al., 2018a), and speech recognition (Baumann et al., 2009; Jaitly et al., 2016; Graves, 2012). Other approaches try to encourage incremental behavior implictly by modifying the model architecture or the training objective: Guan et al. (2018) introduce an encoder with an incremental self-attention scheme for story generation. Wang (2019) try to encourage a more incremental attention behaviour through masking for text-to-speech, while Hupkes et al. (2018a) guide attention by penalizing deviation from a target pattern.

The significance of the encoding process in sequence-to-sequence models has also been studied extensively by Conneau et al. (2018). Proposals exploring how to improve the resulting approaches include adding additional loss terms (Serdyuk et al., 2018) or a second decoder (Jiang and Bansal, 2018; Korrel et al., 2019).

3   Metrics

In this section, we present three novel metrics called *Diagnostic Classifier Accuracy* (Section 3.1), *Integration Ratio* (Section 3.2) and *Representational Similarity* (Section 3.3) to assess the ability of models to process information incrementally. These metrics are later evaluated themselves in Section 5.2 and differ from traditional ones used to assess the incrementality of models, e.g. as the

ones summarized by Köhn and Menzel (2014), as they focus on the role of the encoder in sequence-to-sequence models. It further should be noted that the "optimal" score of these measures with respect to downstream applications cannot defined explicity; they rather serve as a mean to uncover insights about the ways that attention changes a model's behavior, which might aid the development of new architectures.

3.1   Diagnostic Classifier Accuracy

Several works have utilized linear classifiers to predict the existence of certain features in the hidden activations[1] of deep neural networks (Hupkes et al., 2018b; Dalvi et al., 2018b; Conneau et al., 2018). Here we follow the nomenclature of Hupkes et al. (2018b) and call these models *Diagnostic Classifiers* (DCs).

We hypothesize that the hidden activations of an incremental model contain more information about previous tokens inside the sequence. This is based on the assumption that attention-based models have no incentive to encode inputs recurrently, as previous representations can always be revisited. To test this assumption, we train a DC on every time step $t > 1$ in a sequence $t \in [1, \ldots T]$ to predict the k most frequently occuring input tokens for all time steps $t' < t$ (see Figure 1). For a sentence of length T, this results in $\sum_{t=2}^{T} \sum_{t'=t-1}^{t} k$ trained DCs. To then generate the corresponding training set for one of these classifiers, all activations from the network on a test set are extracted and the corresponding tokens recorded. Next, all activations from time step t are used as the training samples and all tokens to generate binary labels based on whether the target token x_k occured on target time step t'. As these data sets are highly unbalanced, class weights are also computed and used during training.

Applying this metric to a model, the accuracies of all classifiers after training are averaged on a given test set, which we call *Diagnostic Classifier Accuracy* (DC Accuracy). We can test this way how much information about specific inputs is lost and whether that even matters for successful model performance, should it employ an encoding procedure of increasing abstraction like in *Chunk-and-pass processing*. On the other hand, one might assume that a more powerful model

---

[1] In this work, the terms *hidden representation* and *hidden activations* are used synonymously.

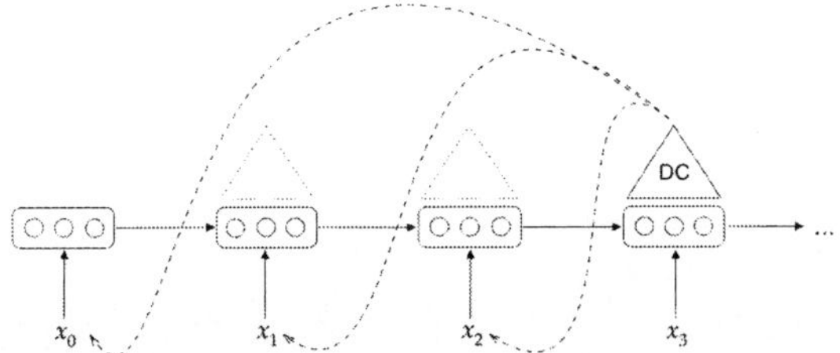

Figure 1: For the Diagnostic Classifier Accuracy, DCs are trained on the hidden activations to predict previously occuring tokens. The accuracies are averaged and potentially weighed by the distance between the hidden activations used for training the occurrence of the token to predict.

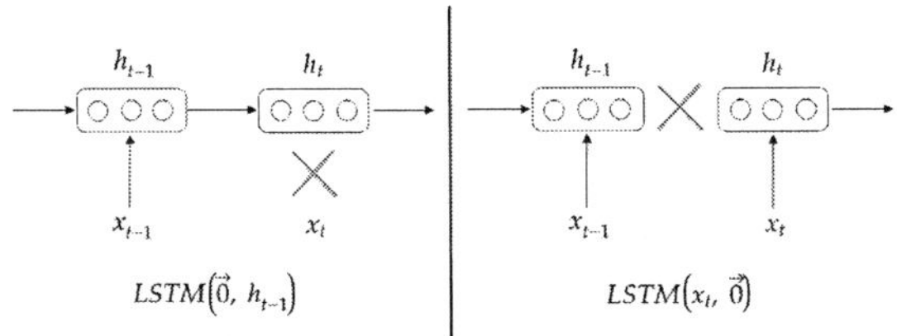

Figure 2: Illustration of a thought experiment about two types of extreme recurrent models. (*Left*) The model completely ignores the current token and bases its new hidden state entirely on the previous one. (*Right*) The model forgets the whole history and just encodes the current input.

might require to retain information about an input even if the same occured several time steps ago. To account for this fact, we introduce a modified version of this metric called *Weighed Diagnostic Classifier Accuracy* (Weighed DC Accuracy), where we weigh the accuracy of a classifier based on the distance $t - t'$.

3.2 Integration Ratio

Imagine an extreme attention-based model that does not encode information recurrently but whose hidden state $\mathbf{h}_t$ is solely based on the current token $\mathbf{x}_t$ (see right half of Figure 2). If we formalize an LSTM as a recurrent function $f_\theta : \mathbb{R}^n, \mathbb{R}^m \mapsto \mathbb{R}^m$ parameterized by weights θ that maps two continuous vector representations, in our case the n-dimensional representation of the current token $\mathbf{x}_t \in \mathbb{R}^n$ and the m-dimensional previous hidden state representation $\mathbf{h}_{t-1} \in \mathbb{R}^m$ to a new hidden state $\mathbf{h}_t \in \mathbb{R}^m$, we can formalize the mentioned scenario as a recurrent function that completely ignores the pevious hidden state, which we can denote using a zero-vector $\vec{0} \in \mathbb{R}^m$: $\mathbf{h}_t = f_\theta(\mathbf{x}_t, \vec{0})$.

In a more realistic setting, we can exploit this thought experiment to quantify the amount of new information that is integrated into the current hidden representation by subtracting this hypothetical value from the actual value at timestep t:

$$\Delta \mathbf{x}_t = ||\mathbf{h}_t - f_\theta(\mathbf{x}_t, \vec{0})||^2, \qquad (1)$$

where $|| \dots ||^2$ denotes the l_2-norm. Conversely, we can quantify the amount of information that was lost from previous hidden states with:

$$\Delta \mathbf{h}_t = ||\mathbf{h}_t - f_\theta(\vec{0}, \mathbf{h}_{t-1})||^2. \qquad (2)$$

In the case of the extreme attention-based model, we would expect $\Delta \mathbf{x}_t = 0$, as no information from $\mathbf{h}_{t-1}$ has been used in the transformation of $\mathbf{x}_t$ by f_θ. Likewise, the "ignorant" model would produce a value of $\Delta \mathbf{h}_t = 0$, as any new hidden representation completely originates from a transformation of the previous one.

Using these two quanitities, we can formulate a metric expressing the average ratio between them throughout a sequence which we call *Integration Ratio*:

$$\phi_{int} = \frac{1}{T-1} \sum_{t=2}^{T} \frac{\Delta \mathbf{x}_t}{\Delta \mathbf{h}_t} \qquad (3)$$

This metric provides an intuitive insight into the (average) model behavior during the encoding process: For $\phi_{int} < 1$ it holds that $\Delta \mathbf{x}_t < \Delta \mathbf{h}_t$, signifying that the model prefers to integrate new information into the hidden state. Vice versa, $\phi_{int} > 1$ and therefore $\Delta \mathbf{x}_t > \Delta \mathbf{h}_t$ implies a preference to maintain a representation of preceding inputs, possibly at the cost of encoding the current token $\mathbf{x}_t$ in an incomplete manner.

To account for the fact that integrating new information is more important at the beginning of a sequence – as no inputs have been processed yet – and maintaining a representation of the sentence is more plausile towards the end of a sentence, we introduce two linear weighing terms with $\alpha_{\Delta \mathbf{x}_t} = \frac{T-t}{T}$ and $\alpha_{\Delta \mathbf{h}_t} = \frac{t}{T}$ for $\Delta \mathbf{x}_t$ and $\Delta \mathbf{h}_t$, respectively, which simplify to a single term α_t:

$$\phi_{int} = \frac{1}{Z} \sum_{t=2}^{T} \alpha_t \frac{\Delta \mathbf{x}_t}{\Delta \mathbf{h}_t} = \frac{1}{Z} \sum_{t=2}^{T} \frac{T-t}{t} \frac{\Delta \mathbf{x}_t}{\Delta \mathbf{h}_t}, \quad (4)$$

where Z corresponds to a new normalizing factor such that $Z = \sum_{t=2}^{T} \frac{T-t}{t}$. It should be noted that the ideal score for this metric is unknown. The motivation for this score merely lies in gaining inside into a model's behaviour, showing us whether it engages in a similar kind of *eager processing* while having to handle memory constraints (in this case realized in the constant dimensionality of hidden representations) like in human cognition.

3.3   Representational Similarity

The sentences "I saw a cat" and "I saw a feline" only differ in terms of word choice, but essentially encode the same information. An incremental model, based on the Chunk-and-Pass processing described by Christiansen and Chater (2016), should arrive at the same or at least a similar, abstract encoding of these phrases.[2] While the exact wording might be lost in the process, the information encoded should still describe an encounter with a feline creature. We therefore hypothesize that an incremental model should map the hidden activations of similar sequences of tokens into similar regions of the hidden activation space. To test this assumption, we compare the representations produced by a model after encoding the same sequence of tokens - or *history* - using their average pairwise distance based on a distance measure like the l_2 norm or cosine similarity. We call the length of the history the *order* of the *Representational Similarity*.

To avoid models to score high on this model metric by substituting most or all of a hidden representation with an encoding of the current token,[3] we only gather the hidden states for comparison after encoding another, arbitrary token (see Figure 3). We can therefore interpret the score as the ability to "remember" the same sequence of tokens in the past through the encoding.

The procedure is repeated for the n most common histories of a specified order occuring in the test corpus over all time steps and, to obtain the final score, results are averaged.

4   Setup

We test our metric on two different architectures, trained on the SCAN dataset proposed by Lake and Baroni (2018). We explain both below.

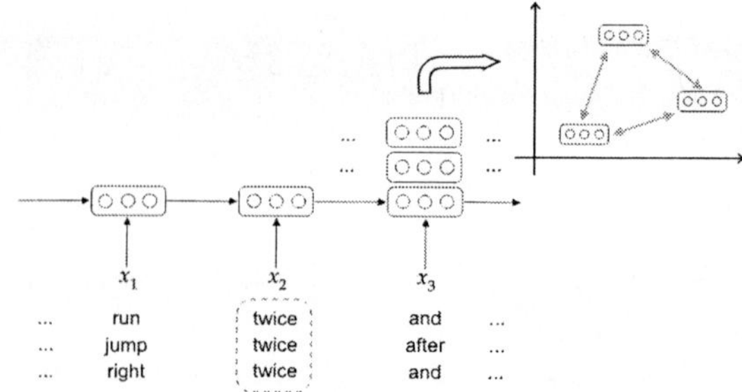

Figure 3: *Representational Similarity* measures the average pair-wise distance of hidden representations after encoding the same subsequence of tokens (in this case the history is only of first order, i.e. x_2) as well as one arbitrary token x_3.

4.1   Data

We use the SCAN data set proposed by Lake and Baroni (2018): It is a simplified version of the CommAI Navigation task, where the objective is to translate an order in natural language into a sequence of machine-readable commands, e.g. "jump thrice and look" into `I_JUMP I_JUMP I_JUMP I_LOOK`. We focus on the `add_prim_jump_split` (Loula et al., 2018), where the model has to learn to generalize from seeing a command like `jump` only in primitive forms (i.e. by itself) to seeing it in composite forms during test time (e.g. `jump twice`), where the remainder of the composite forms has been encountered in the context of other primitive commands during training.

The SCAN dataset has been proposed to assess the *compositional* abilities of a model, which we believe to be deeply related with the concept of *incrementality*, which is the target of our research.

4.2   Models

We test two seasoned architectures used in sequence processing, namely a Long-Short Term Memory (LSTM) network (Hochreiter and Schmidhuber, 1997) and an LSTM network with attention (Bahdanau et al., 2015). The attention mechanism creates a time-dependent context vector c_i for every decoder time step i that is used together with the previous decoder hidden state. This vector is a weighted average of the output of the encoder, where the weights are calculated based on some sort of similarity measure. More specifically, we first calculate the energy e_{it} between the last decoder hidden state s_{i-1} and

---

[2]In fact, given that humans built up sentence representations in a compositional manner, the same should hold for sentence pairs like "I saw a cat" and "A feline was observed by me", which is beyond the limits of the metric proposed here.

[3]$\Delta \mathbf{x}_t = 0$ in the framework introduced in the previous Section 3.2.

any encoder hidden state $\mathbf{h}_t$ using some function $a(\cdot)$

$$e_{it} = a(\mathbf{s}_{i-1}, \mathbf{h}_t) \tag{5}$$

We then normalize the energies using the softmax function and use the normalised attention weights α_{it} to create the context vector $\mathbf{c}_t$:

$$\mathbf{c}_i = \sum_{t=1}^{T} \alpha_{it} \mathbf{h}_t \tag{6}$$

In this work, we use a simple attention function, namely a dot product a_{dot}:

$$a_{dot}(\mathbf{s}_{i-1}, \mathbf{h}_t) = \mathbf{s}_{i-1}^T \mathbf{h}_t, \tag{7}$$

matching the setup originally introduced by Bahdanau et al. (2015).

4.3 Training

For both architectures, we train 15 single-layer uni-directional models, with an embedding and hidden layer size of 128. We use the same hyperparameters for both architectures, to ensure compatibility. More specifically, both models were trained for 50 epochs using the Adam optimizer (Kingma and Ba, 2015) with the AMSgrad correction (Reddi et al., 2018) and a learning rate of 0.001 and a batch size of 128.

5 Results

We compute metric values for all 30 models (15 per architecture) that resulted from the training procedure described above.[4] We plot the metric values, averaged over all runs for both models, in Figure 4. For the representational similarity score, we use all instances of the $n = 5$ most frequently occuring histories of length 2 at all available time steps. The unweighted DC accuracies are not depicted, as they do not differ substantially from their weighted counter part, for which we also try to detect the $k = 5$ most frequently occuring inputs at every time step.

5.1 Metric scores

As expected, the standard attention model significantly outperforms the vanilla model in terms of

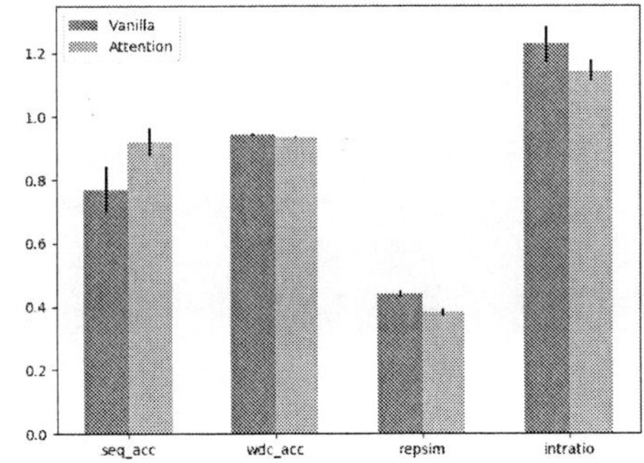

Figure 4: Results on SCAN `add_prim_left` with $n = 15$. Abbreviations stand for sequence accuracy, weighed diagnostic classifier accuracy, integration ratio and representational similarity, respectively. All differences are statistically significant (using a Student's t-test with $p = 0.05$).

sequence accuracy. Surprisingly, both models perform very similarly in terms of weighed DC accuracy. While one possible conclusion is that both models display a similar ability to store information about past tokens, we instead hypothesize that this can be explained by the fact that all sequences in our test set are fairly short (6.8 tokens on average). Therefore, it is easy for both models to store information about tokens over the entire length of the input even under the constrained capacity of the hidden representations. Bigger differences might be observed on corpora that contain longer sequences.

From the integration ratio scores (last column in Figure 4), it seems that, while both models prefer to maintain a history of previous tokens, the attention-based model contains a certain bias to add new information about the current input token. This supports our suspicion that this model is less incentivized to build up expressive representations over entire sequences, as the encoder representation can always be revisited later via the attention mechanism. Counterintuitively and perhaps surprisingly, it appears that the attention model produces representations that are more similar than the vanilla model, judging from the representational similarity score. To decode successfully, the vanilla model has to include information about the entire input sequence in the last encoder hidden state, making the encodings of similar subsequences more distinct because of their different prefixes.[5] In contrast, the representations of the at-

---

[4]The code used in this work is available online under `https://github.com/i-machine-think/incremental_encoding`.

[5]Remember that to obtain these scores, identical subsequences of only length 2 were considered.

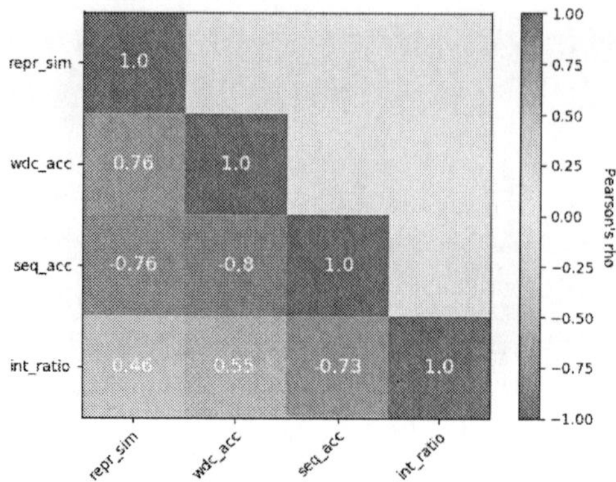

Figure 5: Correlations between metrics as heatmap of Pearson's rho values. 1 indicates a strong positive correlation, −1 a negative one. Abbreviations correspond to the same metrics as in Figure 4. Best viewed in color.

tention model is able to only contain information about the most recent tokens, exclusively encoding the current input at a given time step in the extreme case, as the attention mechanism can select the required representations on demand. These results will be revisited in more detail in section 5.3.

5.2 Metrics Comparison

To further understand the salience of our new metrics, we use *Pearson's correlation coefficient* to show their correlation with each other and with sequence accuracy. A heat map showing Pearson's ρ values between all metric pairs is given in Figure 5.

We can observe that representational similarity and weighed DC accuracy display a substantial negative correlation with sequence accuracy. In the first case, this implies that the more similar representations of the same subsequences produced by the model's encoder are, the better the model itself performs later.[6] Surprisingly, we can infer from the latter case that storing more information about the previous inputs does not lead to better performance. At this point we should disentangle correlation from causation, as it is to be assumed that our hypothesis about the attention mechanism applies here as well: The attention is always able to revisit the encodings later during the decoding process, thus a hidden representation does not need to contain information about all pre-

___

[6]The representational similarity score actually expresses a degree of dissimilarity, i.e. a lower score results from more similar representations, therefore we identify a negative correlation here.

vious tokens and the weighed DC accuracy suffers. Therefore, as the attention model performs better in terms of sequence accuracy, a negative correlation score is observed. The same trend can be observed for the sequence accuracy - integration ratio pair, where the better performance of the attention model creates a significant negative correlation.

The last noteworthy observation can be found looking at the high positive correlation between the weighed DC accuracy and representational similarity, which follows from the line of thought in Section 5.1: As the vanilla model has to squeeze information about the whole history into the hidden representation at every time step, encodings for a shorter subsequence become more distinct, while the attention model only encodes the few most recent inputs and are therefore able to produce more homogenous representations.

5.3 Qualitative Analysis

We scrutinize the models' behavior when processing the same sequence by recording the integration ratio per time step and contrasting them in plots, which are shown in Figure 6. Figure 6a and 6b are thereby indicative of a trend which further reinforces our hypothesis about the behavior of attention-based models: As the orange curve lies below the vanilla model's blue curve in the majority of cases, we can even infer on a case by case basis that these models tend to integrate more information at every time step than a vanilla LSTM. Interestingly, these distinct behaviors when processing information do not always lead to the models finding different solutions. In Figure 6 however, we present three error cases in which the models' results do diverge.

In Figure 6a, we can see that the vanilla model decodes a second and redundant TURN−LEFT in the beginning of the sequence. Although this happens right at the start, the corresponding part in the input sequence is actually encountered right at the end of the encoding process in the form of "turn left", where "after" in front of it constitutes an inversion of the sequence of operations. Therefore, when the vanilla model starts decoding based on the last encoder hidden state, "left" is actually the most recently encoded token. We might assume that, due to this reason, the vanilla model might contain some sort of recency bias, which seems to corrupt some count information and leads

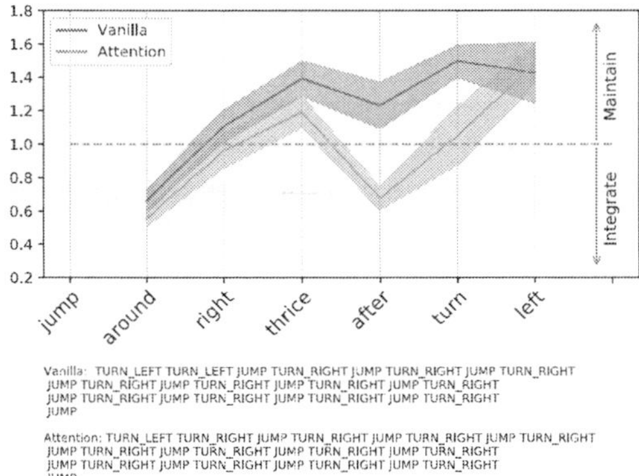

Vanilla: TURN_LEFT TURN_LEFT JUMP TURN_RIGHT JUMP TURN_RIGHT JUMP TURN_RIGHT JUMP TURN_RIGHT JUMP TURN_RIGHT JUMP TURN_RIGHT JUMP TURN_RIGHT JUMP TURN_RIGHT JUMP

Attention: TURN_LEFT TURN_RIGHT JUMP TURN_RIGHT JUMP TURN_RIGHT JUMP TURN_RIGHT JUMP TURN_RIGHT JUMP TURN_RIGHT JUMP TURN_RIGHT JUMP TURN_RIGHT JUMP TURN_RIGHT JUMP

(a) The vanilla model adds a redundant TURN-LEFT in the beginning.

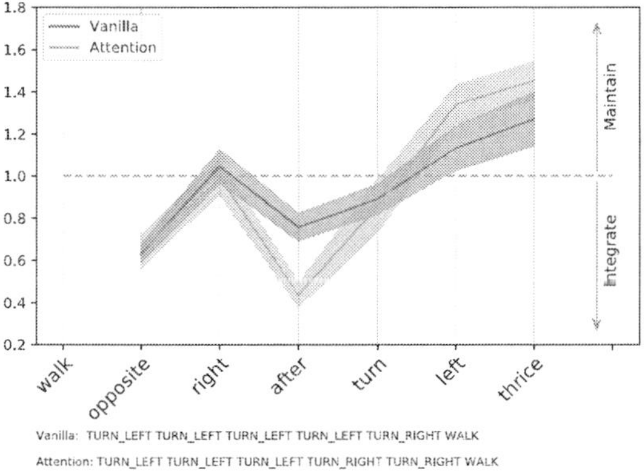

Vanilla: TURN_LEFT TURN_LEFT TURN_LEFT TURN_LEFT TURN_RIGHT WALK

Attention: TURN_LEFT TURN_LEFT TURN_LEFT TURN_RIGHT TURN_RIGHT WALK

(b) The vanilla model confuses left and right when decoding opposite.

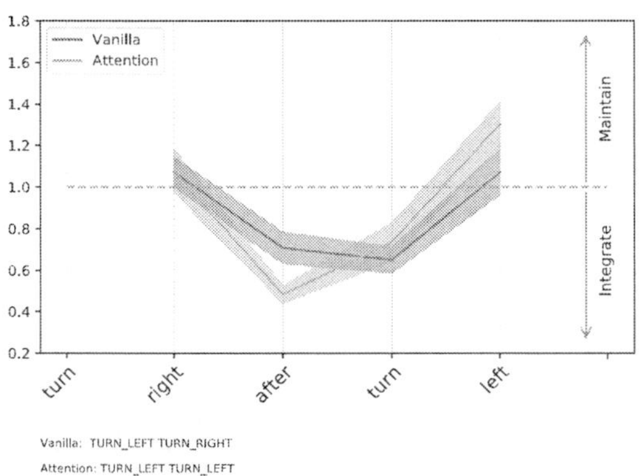

Vanilla: TURN_LEFT TURN_RIGHT

Attention: TURN_LEFT TURN_LEFT

(c) The attention model fails on a trivial sequence.

Figure 6: Qualitative analysis about the models' encoding behavior. Bounds show the standard deviation of integration ratio scores per time step. Decoded sentences are produced by having each model decode the sequence individually and then consolidating the solution via a majority vote. Resulting sequences have been slightly simplified for readability. Best viewed in color.

to a duplicate in the output sequence. The attention model seems to be able to avoid this issue by erasing a lot of its prior encoded information when processing "after", as signified by the drop in the graph. Afterwards, only very little information seems to be integrated by the model.

The vanilla model commits a slightly different error in Figure 6b: After both models decode three TURN-LEFT correctly, it choses to decode "opposite" as TURN-LEFT TURN-RIGHT in contrast to the corect TURN-RIGHT TURN-RIGHT supplied by the attention model. It is to be assumed here that the last half of the input, "turn left thrice" had the vanilla model overwrite some critical information about the initial command. Again, the attention model is able to evade this problem by erasing a lot of its representation when encoding "after" and can achieve a correct decoding this critical part by attending to the representation produced at "right" later. "turn left thrice" can followingly be encoded without having to loose any past information.

Lastly, we want to shed some light on one of the rare failure cases of the *attention model*, as given in Figure 6c. Both models display very similar behavior when encoding this trivial sequence, yet only the vanilla model is able to decode it correctly. A possible reason for this could be found in the model's energy function: When deciding which encoded input to attend to for the next decoding step, the model scores potential candidates based on the last decoder hidden state (see eq. 7), which was decoded as TURN-LEFT. Therefore the most similar inputs token might appear to be TURN-LEFT as well. Notwithstanding this explanation, it falls short of giving a conclusive reason why the model does not err in similar ways in other examples.

Looking at all three examples, it should furthermore be noted that the encoder of the attention model seems to anticipate the mechanism's behavior and learns to erase much of its representation after encoding one contiguous chunk of information, as exemplified by the low integration ratio after finishing the first block of commands in an input sequence. This freedom seems to enable the encoder to come up with more homogenous representations, i.e. that no information has to be overwritten and possibly being corrupted to process later, less related inputs, which also explains the lower representational similarity score in 5.1.

6   Conclusion

In this work, we introduced three novel metrics that try to shine a light on the incremental abilities of the encoder in a sequence-to-sequence model and tested them on a LSTM-RNN with and without an attention mechanism. We showed how these metrics relate to each other and how they can be employed to better understand the encoding behavior of models and how these difference lead to performance improvements in the case of the attention-based model.

We confirm the general intuition that using an attention mechanism, due to its ability to operate on the whole encoded input sequence, prefers to integrate new information about the current token and is less pressured to maintain a representation for the whole input sequence, which seems to lead to some corruptions of the encoded information in case of the vanilla model. Moreover, our qualitative analysis suggests that the encoder of the attention model learns to chunk parts of the input sequence into salient blocks, a behavior that is reminiscent of the Chunk-and-Pass processing described by Christiansen and Chater (2016) and one component that is hypothesized to enable incremental processing in humans. In this way, the attention model most surprisingly seems to display a more incremental way of processing than the vanilla model.

These results open up several lines of future research: Although we tried to assess incrementality in sequence-to-sequence models in a quantitative manner, the notion of incremental processing lacks a formal definition within this framework. Thus, such definition could help to confirm our findings and aid in developing more incremental architectures. It furthermore appears consequential to extend this methodology to deeper models and other RNN-variants as well as other data sets in order to confirm this work's findings.

Although we were possibly able to identify one of the components that build the foundation of human language processing (as defined by Christiansen and Chater, 2016) in attention models, more work needs to be done to understand how these dynamics play out in models that solely rely on attention like the Transformer (Vaswani et al., 2017) and how the remaining components could be realized in future models.

Based on these reflections, future work should attack this problem from a solid foundation: A formalization of incrementality in the context of sequence-to-sequence modelling could help to develop more expressive metrics. These metrics in turn could then be used to assess possible incremental models in a more unbiased way. Further thought should also be given to a fairer comparison of candidate models to existing baselines: The attention mechanism by Bahdanau et al. (2015) and models like the Transformer operate without the temporal and memory pressure that is claimed to fundamentally shape human cognition Christiansen and Chater (2016). Controlling for this factor, it can be better judged whether incremental processing has a positive impact on the model's performance. We hope that these steps will lead to encoders that create richer representations that can followingly be used back in regular sequence-to-sequence modelling tasks.

Acknowledgements

DH is funded by the Netherlands Organization for Scientific Research (NWO), through a Gravitation Grant 024.001.006 to the Language in Interaction Consortium. EB is funded by the European Union's Horizon 2020 research and innovation program under the Marie Sklodowska-Curie grant agreement No 790369 (MAGIC).

References

Dzmitry Bahdanau, Kyunghyun Cho, and Yoshua Bengio. 2015. Neural machine translation by jointly learning to align and translate. In *3rd International Conference on Learning Representations, ICLR 2015, San Diego, CA, USA, May 7-9, 2015, Conference Track Proceedings*.

Timo Baumann, Michaela Atterer, and David Schlangen. 2009. Assessing and improving the performance of speech recognition for incremental systems. In *Proceedings of Human Language Technologies: The 2009 Annual Conference of the North American Chapter of the Association for Computational Linguistics*, pages 380–388. Association for Computational Linguistics.

Morten H Christiansen and Nick Chater. 2016. The now-or-never bottleneck: A fundamental constraint on language. *Behavioral and Brain Sciences*, 39.

Alexis Conneau, Germán Kruszewski, Guillaume Lample, Loïc Barrault, and Marco Baroni. 2018. What you can cram into a single \\$&!#* vector: Probing sentence embeddings for linguistic properties. In *Proceedings of the 56th Annual Meeting of the Association for Computational Linguistics, ACL*

2018, Melbourne, Australia, July 15-20, 2018, Volume 1: Long Papers*, pages 2126–2136.

Fahim Dalvi, Nadir Durrani, Hassan Sajjad, and Stephan Vogel. 2018a. Incremental decoding and training methods for simultaneous translation in neural machine translation. In *Proceedings of the 2018 Conference of the North American Chapter of the Association for Computational Linguistics: Human Language Technologies, NAACL-HLT, New Orleans, Louisiana, USA, June 1-6, 2018, Volume 2 (Short Papers)*, pages 493–499.

Fahim Dalvi, Nadir Durrani, Hassan Sajjad, and Stephan Vogel. 2018b. Incremental decoding and training methods for simultaneous translation in neural machine translation. In *Proceedings of the 2018 Conference of the North American Chapter of the Association for Computational Linguistics: Human Language Technologies, NAACL-HLT, New Orleans, Louisiana, USA, June 1-6, 2018, Volume 2 (Short Papers)*, pages 493–499.

Alex Graves. 2012. Sequence transduction with recurrent neural networks. *CoRR*, abs/1211.3711.

Jian Guan, Yansen Wang, and Minlie Huang. 2018. Story ending generation with incremental encoding and commonsense knowledge. *CoRR*, abs/1808.10113.

Demis Hassabis, Dharshan Kumaran, Christopher Summerfield, and Matthew Botvinick. 2017. Neuroscience-inspired artificial intelligence. *Neuron*, 95(2):245–258.

Sepp Hochreiter and Jürgen Schmidhuber. 1997. Long short-term memory. *Neural computation*, 9(8):1735–1780.

Dieuwke Hupkes, Anand Singh, Kris Korrel, Germán Kruszewski, and Elia Bruni. 2018a. Learning compositionally through attentive guidance. *CoRR*, abs/1805.09657.

Dieuwke Hupkes, Sara Veldhoen, and Willem Zuidema. 2018b. Visualisation and'diagnostic classifiers' reveal how recurrent and recursive neural networks process hierarchical structure. *Journal of Artificial Intelligence Research*, 61:907–926.

Athul Paul Jacob, Zhouhan Lin, Alessandro Sordoni, and Yoshua Bengio. 2018. Learning hierarchical structures on-the-fly with a recurrent-recursive model for sequences. In *Proceedings of The Third Workshop on Representation Learning for NLP*, pages 154–158.

Navdeep Jaitly, Quoc V Le, Oriol Vinyals, Ilya Sutskever, David Sussillo, and Samy Bengio. 2016. An online sequence-to-sequence model using partial conditioning. In *Advances in Neural Information Processing Systems*, pages 5067–5075.

Yichen Jiang and Mohit Bansal. 2018. Closed-book training to improve summarization encoder memory. In *Proceedings of the 2018 Conference on Empirical Methods in Natural Language Processing, Brussels, Belgium, October 31 - November 4, 2018*, pages 4067–4077.

Diederik P. Kingma and Jimmy Ba. 2015. Adam: A method for stochastic optimization. In *3rd International Conference on Learning Representations, ICLR 2015, San Diego, CA, USA, May 7-9, 2015, Conference Track Proceedings*.

Arne Köhn and Wolfgang Menzel. 2014. Incremental predictive parsing with turboparser. In *Proceedings of the 52nd Annual Meeting of the Association for Computational Linguistics (Volume 2: Short Papers)*, volume 2, pages 803–808.

Kris Korrel, Dieuwke Hupkes, Verna Dankers, and Elia Bruni. 2019. Transcoding compositionally: using attention to find more generalizable solutions. *BlackboxNLP 2019, ACL*.

Brenden Lake and Marco Baroni. 2018. Generalization without systematicity: On the compositional skills of sequence-to-sequence recurrent networks. In *International Conference on Machine Learning*, pages 2879–2888.

João Loula, Marco Baroni, and Brenden M Lake. 2018. Rearranging the familiar: Testing compositional generalization in recurrent networks. *arXiv preprint arXiv:1807.07545*.

Graham Neubig, Kyunghyun Cho, Jiatao Gu, and Victor O. K. Li. 2017. Learning to translate in real-time with neural machine translation. In *Proceedings of the 15th Conference of the European Chapter of the Association for Computational Linguistics, EACL 2017, Valencia, Spain, April 3-7, 2017, Volume 1: Long Papers*, pages 1053–1062.

Sashank J Reddi, Satyen Kale, and Sanjiv Kumar. 2018. On the convergence of adam and beyond.

Dmitriy Serdyuk, Nan Rosemary Ke, Alessandro Sordoni, Adam Trischler, Chris Pal, and Yoshua Bengio. 2018. Twin networks: Matching the future for sequence generation. In *6th International Conference on Learning Representations, ICLR 2018, Vancouver, BC, Canada, April 30 - May 3, 2018, Conference Track Proceedings*.

Michael Henry Tessler, Karen Gu, and Roger Philip Levy. 2019. Incremental understanding of conjunctive generic sentences.

Ashish Vaswani, Noam Shazeer, Niki Parmar, Jakob Uszkoreit, Llion Jones, Aidan N Gomez, Łukasz Kaiser, and Illia Polosukhin. 2017. Attention is all you need. In *Advances in Neural Information Processing Systems*, pages 5998–6008.

Gary Wang. 2019. Deep text-to-speech system with seq2seq model. *CoRR*, abs/1903.07398.

On Committee Representations of Adversarial Learning Models for Question-Answer Ranking

Sparsh Gupta
University of California San Diego
San Diego, CA
spg005@ucsd.edu

Vitor Carvalho
Intuit AI
San Diego, CA
vitor_carvalho@intuit.com

Abstract

Adversarial training is a process in Machine Learning that explicitly trains models on adversarial inputs (inputs designed to deceive or trick the learning process) in order to make it more robust or accurate. In this paper we investigate how representing adversarial training models as committees can be used to effectively improve the performance of Question-Answer (QA) Ranking. We start by empirically probing the effects of adversarial training over multiple QA ranking algorithms, including the state-of-the-art Multihop Attention Network model. We evaluate these algorithms on several benchmark datasets and observe that, while adversarial training is beneficial to most baseline algorithms, there are cases where it may lead to overfitting and performance degradation. We investigate the causes of such degradation, and then propose a new representation procedure for this adversarial learning problem, based on committee learning, that not only is capable of consistently improving all baseline algorithms, but also outperforms the previous state-of-the-art algorithm by as much as 6% in NDCG (Normalized Discounted Cumulative Gain).

1 Introduction

Question Answer (QA) ranking, or the task of accurately ranking the best answers to an input question, has been a long-standing research pursuit with practical applications in a variety of domains. Popular examples of such applications are customer support chat-bots, community question answering portals, and digital assistants like Siri or Alexa Yih and Ma (2016).

Early work on QA ranking relied heavily on linguistic knowledge (such as parse-trees), feature engineering or external resources (Wang and Manning, 2010; Wang et al., 2007; Yih et al., 2013). Yih et al. (2013) constructed semantic features from WordNet and paired semantically related words based on these features and relations. Wang and Manning (2010); Wang et al. (2007) used syntactic matching between question and answer parse trees for answer selection. Other proposals used minimal edit sequences between dependency parse trees as a matching score between question and answer (Heilman and Smith, 2010; Severyn and Moschitti, 2013; Yao et al., 2013).

The majority of the recent developments for QA ranking algorithms are based on deep learning techniques, and fall into two different classes of models: *representation-based* or *interaction-based*. In *representation-based* models, both question and answer are mapped to the same representation space via network layers with shared weights, and a final relevance or matching score is computed from these representations (Bowman et al., 2015; Tan et al., 2015; Huang et al., 2013; Tan et al., 2016; Wang et al., 2016). In *interaction-based* models, the network attempts to capture multiple levels of interaction (or similarity) between question and answer (Hu et al., 2014; Pang et al., 2016; Yu et al., 2018). The final relevance/matching score can be computed out of the partial similarities derived from the multiple interactions.

Recent results have indicated that representation-based models, when used with attention layers to focus on relevant parts of the question and answer, tend to outperform interaction-based models (Tan et al., 2016; Wang et al., 2016). The recently proposed Multihop Attention Network (MAN) model (Tran and Niederee, 2018) currently achieves state-of-the-art performance on ranking tasks by using sequential attention (Brarda et al., 2017) over multiple attention layers. This model is discussed in detail in Section 2.2.

Adversarial training and Generative Adversarial Networks (GANs) (Goodfellow et al., 2014) have been successfully applied to Computer Vision (Karras et al., 2017; Isola et al., 2017; Zhu et al., 2017; Kelkar et al., 2018) and Natural Language Processing (Lin et al., 2017) applications, but only sparsely studied in Information Retrieval

Proceedings of the 4th Workshop on Representation Learning for NLP (RepL4NLP-2019), pages 218–223
Florence, Italy, August 2, 2019. ©2019 Association for Computational Linguistics

tasks. As described by Wang et al. (2017), adversarial training in Information Retrieval can be approached by having a *generator model* to sample difficult adversarial examples which are passed to a *discriminator model* that learns to rank on increasingly difficult adversarial examples. This adversarial training process in principle can lead to increased robustness and accuracy of the final ranking model.

We show that in general most models do benefit from adversarial training, with a clear increase in ranking metrics. However, we also observed that not all types of models benefit from straightforward adversarial training. For instance, Multihop Attention Network often displayed worse results with adversarial training. In such cases, we observed that the model was excessively compensating to the current adversarial training data batch and often forgetting previous batches, thus reducing its performance on test data.

To help address this issue, we propose a novel committee representation to adversarial modeling for QA ranking that can be applied to any underlying ranking algorithm. Not only does it address the observed "overfitting" that may occur during adversarial training, but provides an improvement to all baseline QA ranking models we tested. In particular, we introduce a new state-of-the-art model *AdvCom-MAN* (**Adv**ersarial **Com**mittee - **M**ultihop **A**ttention **N**etwork) for QA ranking that displays, to the best of our knowledge, state-of-the-art results on four different datasets for QA Ranking.

2 Approaches

We introduce in this section the various algorithms and techniques that we use to investigate the use of adversarial training to QA ranking.

2.1 Baselines

We used two recently proposed interaction based models as baselines, meaning that these models work on interaction (lexical similarities) between the question and answer text.

- **Match Pyramid -** Proposed by Pang et al. (2016), this model uses convolution layers on the "interaction matrix" formed by taking the dot product of embeddings of question words with answer words.
- **Deep Matching Net -** This model was proposed by Yang et al. (2018) and was originally meant for multi-turn conversations, but we adapted a version of it for single turn conversation which can also work as QA ranking. Similar to Match Pyramid in most aspects, this model uses 2 interaction matrices, the second one being constructed in a similar fashion of dot products between embeddings obtained by a Bi-directional Gated Recurrent Unit (Bi-GRU).

2.2 Multihop Attention Network (MAN)

This model was recently proposed by Tran and Niederee (2018) as state-of-the-art in QA ranking tasks. A bi-directional LSTM layer first generates the representations of question and answer words. Following this, multiple "hops" or multiple layers of attention are used to get attended representations of the question and answer at each attention layer. This is accomplished by using sequential attention (Brarda et al., 2017) at every layer. The intuition for this architecture is to compare and analyze the question and answer from different points of view by focusing on different parts of the text in each hop. At each attention hop, cosine similarity is computed between the question and answer representations. The final matching score is calculated by summing the cosine similarities at each layer (Equation 1).

$$sim(q, a) = \sum_k \cos \left(o_q^{(k)}, o_a^{(k)} \right) \qquad (1)$$

Here $o_q^{(k)}$ and $o_a^{(k)}$ refer to the question and answer representations after the kth hop in the network. All the models are trained by minimizing the Hinge Loss (Equation 2) with L2 regularization.

$$L = \max\{0, M - sim(q, a_+) + sim(q, a_-)\} \qquad (2)$$

where M is the margin, q is the input question, and a_+ and a_- are correct and incorrect answers to q respectively.

2.3 Vanilla Adversarial Learning

IRGAN (Information Retrieval Generative Adversarial Networks) has been recently proposed as a generic adversarial learning framework for several Information Retrieval tasks (Wang et al., 2017). In this paper we focus the adaptation of IRGAN to pairwise cases, which adapt well to the QA ranking problem.

IRGAN uses the same minimax game idea as a Generative Adversarial Network (GAN) (Goodfellow et al., 2014) but uses different objective functions for the generator and discriminator. The generator and discriminator of a GAN are initialized with a model pre-trained on original training dataset. In a ranking task setting, the job of generator is to sample difficult incorrect answers given an input question and correct answers for it. The discriminator then learns to rank this difficult dataset.

Since sampling is a non-differentiable operation, the generator cannot be trained using backpropagation by error signal from the discriminator. Hence a Reinforcement Learning strategy (Williams, 1992; Yu et al., 2017) is used to train the generator where the objective of the generator is to maximize its reward (Equation 3).

$$L_{Gen} = \frac{1}{K} \sum_{k=1}^{K} \log\left(g_\theta(d_k|q)\right) \times reward \quad (3)$$

$$L_{Dis} = \frac{1}{K} \sum_{k=1}^{K} hinge(q, a_+, d_k) \quad (4)$$

where d_k is the kth adversarial incorrect answer, g_θ is the generator score for kth answer and question q, and $reward$ is given by Equation 5.

$$reward = 2\left(\sigma\left(hinge(q, a_+, d_k)\right) - 0.5\right) \quad (5)$$

and $hinge(q, a_+, d_k)$ is hinge loss (Equation 2). Detailed derivation of these equations has been given in the paper that proposes IRGAN (Wang et al., 2017) and has not been delineated here to focus on more relevant aspects of the paper.

2.4 Adversarial Committee Learning

In Section 3 we present details on our adversarial training experiments. Surprisingly, a number of experiments showed results with high variance that seemed somewhat contradictory to the expectation that adversarial training should boost model performance (or at least not deteriorate it). After careful observation, we noticed that as adversarial training progresses, some models may start overfitting to the adversarial examples in the current batch, and partially forgetting the original training data, which consequently leads to a deterioration of test data ranking performance.

This led to the development of a novel adversarial committee learning strategy that boosts the model performance, irrespective of the nature of model itself. The idea is to sample the model at regular intervals during adversarial training, including the pre-trained model and the fully trained model after adversarial training. The intuition behind this strategy is that the sampled models have decision boundaries that are fit to different proportions of the original dataset and the adversarial dataset, consequently creating a committee of diverse decision makers. This idea is very similar to the work of Elsas et al. (2008) where perceptrons are sampled during training to be a part of the decision making committee. This work uses the original dataset to form the committee, as opposed to adversarial dataset which is used in our model.

During prediction, given a question q and a candidate answer a, the matching score between them $score(q, a)$ is computed as shown in equation 6.

$$score(q, a) = \sum_{i=1}^{N} w_i h_i(q, a) \quad (6)$$

where $h_i(q, a)$ is the matching score between q and a given by ith model, and w_i is the weight assigned to ith model. This weight is computed by first recording the performance metric (MRR, MAP, NDCG@5, etc.) on the validation dataset for all models, and then normalizing them to 1. We sampled these N models at regular intervals during adversarial training process. For our experiments, we sampled the models at every 3rd epoch to be a part of the committee. We tried different sampling strategies but this one worked out to be the best trade-off between committee performance and run-time during prediction.

The results show that this strategy works for all types of models and it overcomes the overfitting issues observed with vanilla adversarial training.

3 Experiments

3.1 Datasets

We use four datasets, belonging to factoid and non factoid categories to evaluate the proposed strategy. **WikiQA** is an open domain question answering dataset that was introduced by Yang et al. (2015) and has now become a very popular benchmark dataset for QA ranking systems. Feng et al. (2015) recently released a large nonfactoid QA dataset for insurance domain - **Insurance QA**. Like Tran and Niederee (2018), we use

Model	WikiQA (19k/ 2.5k/ 5.8k)		Insurance QA (926k/ 724k/ 650k)		FiQA (700k/ 300k/ 300k)		Tax Domain QA (42k/ 14k/ 14k)
	NDCG@5	MRR	test-1	test-2	NDCG@5	MRR	prec@1
Match Pyramid	0.6628	0.6258	0.4571	0.4036	0.3423	0.4571	0.5767
+ Vanilla Adversarial	0.6939	0.6675	0.5269	0.4602	0.3715	0.4859	0.6437
+ Adversarial Committee	0.6987	0.6748	0.5307	0.4751	0.3812	0.4866	0.6568
Deep Matching Net	0.6922	0.6533	0.6135	0.5498	0.3972	0.4963	0.6601
+ Vanilla Adversarial	0.6952	0.6692	0.6464	0.6007	0.4114	0.5149	0.6636
+ Adversarial Committee	0.7051	0.67	0.688	0.625	0.4157	0.5191	0.6863
MAN	0.7328	0.7134	0.7032	0.668	0.4312	0.5153	0.7927
+ Vanilla Adversarial	0.7337	0.711	0.6951	0.6509	0.3844	0.465	0.7975
+ Adversarial Committee	**0.7402**	**0.7205**	**0.7267**	**0.6814**	**0.4601**	**0.5318**	**0.8029**

Table 1: Experimental results of adversarial learning on different datasets; Models have been evaluated on NDCG@5 and MRR for WikiQA and FiQA, and on Precision@1 for Insurance QA test sets 1 and 2, and Tax Domain QA

version 1 of this dataset which is divided into a training, validation and 2 test sets. **FiQA**, the financial domain non-factoid dataset[1] was released recently and built by crawling data from Reddit, StockTwits and StackExchange. **Tax Domain QA** dataset was obtained from a popular tax domain question answering platform. Each question had only one correct answer, so we create an answer pool for each question by randomly sampling incorrect answers from the entire collection of answers. Table 1 shows the size of these datasets in terms of QA pairs in the (train/ validation/ test) format.

We evaluate these datasets on different metrics. For the datasets that have only 1 correct answer in the answer pool associated with every question, we use precision@1 since it it the the most suitable metric. For datasets that have multiple correct answers, more comprehensive metrics such as Mean Reciprocal Rank (MRR) and NDCG@5 have been used that evaluate the model's ability to retrieve not only the most relevant, but all relevant answers.

3.2 Results

In this Section we present our experimental results on running adversarial training techniques over different QA ranking baseline algorithm (from Section 2) on multiple QA datasets (from Section 3.1). For all the models, we use the prefix Adv- when we refer to their variants trained by vanilla adversarial learning, and AdvCom- when they are trained by adversarial committee learning.

From Table 1 it can be seen that the metrics show fairly similar trends across all datasets [2].

Based on the results from all our experiments, we observed that the overall performance of Multihop Attention Network and its variants was the best of the three model types, followed by Deep Matching Network and its variants. Match Pyramid and its variants had the lowest performance scores in general, except for a few anomalous cases where AdvCom-Match Pyramid performed better than few variants of Deep Matching Network on some of the datasets. Furthermore, the results also show that while vanilla adversarial learning provides a significant boost in model performance for Match Pyramid and Deep Matching Network, the performance boost by adversarial committee learning was much better. However for MAN, vanilla adversarial learning significantly worsens the base model performance for most datasets. Our hypothesis is that since MAN has a higher capacity, it overfitted to adversarial training samples thereby forgetting some of its knowledge from original dataset. Adversarial committee learning however addresses this issue and improves the performance of base MAN by creating a committee of diverse decision makers that contain knowledge from both original and adversarial dataset. Consequently, the AdvCom-MAN establishes new state-of-the-art standards for QA ranking models on almost all datasets.

---

[2]All row differences are statistically significant based on 95% bootstrap confidence interval

4 Discussion and Conclusion

In this work we provided a large empirical investigation on the effects of adversarial training applied to deep QA ranking models. We explored both interaction-based and representation-based QA ranking models, including the previous state-of-the-art Multihop Attention Network algorithm. While in most cases adversarial training proved to be indeed beneficial to QA ranking, we observed that in some cases overfitting to the adversarial training data during adversarial learning could lead to lower than expected ranking performance.

We then proposed a new adversarial learning representation based on a committee strategy to improve QA ranking performance. We showed that the adversarial committee technique was able to boost the performance of all models and in all datasets. As a result, an adversarial committee applied to the MAN algorithm presented the new state-of-the-art results for QA ranking on all datasets tested on this paper, including WikiQA, InsuranceQA and FiQA.

References

Samuel R. Bowman, Gabor Angeli, Christopher Potts, and Christopher D. Manning. 2015. A large annotated corpus for learning natural language inference. In *Proceedings of the 2015 Conference on Empirical Methods in Natural Language Processing (EMNLP)*, pages 632–642. ACL.

Sebastian Brarda, Philip Yeres, and Samuel R. Bowman. 2017. Sequential attention: A context-aware alignment function for machine reading. In *Proceedings of the 2nd Workshop on Representation Learning for NLP*, pages 75–80. ACL.

Jonathan L. Elsas, Vitor R. Carvalho, and Jaime G. Carbonell. 2008. Fast learning of document ranking functions with the committee perceptron. In *Proceedings of the 1st ACM International Conference on Web Search and Data Mining*. ACM.

Minwei Feng, Bing Xiang, Michael R. Glass, Lidan Wang, and Bowen Zhou. 2015. Applying deep learning to answer selection: A study and an open task. In *Workshop on Automatic Speech Recognition and Understanding*, pages 813–820. IEEE.

Ian Goodfellow, Jean Pouget-Abadie, Mehdi Mirza, Bing Xu, David Warde-Farley, Sherjil Ozair, Aaron Courville, and Yoshua Bengio. 2014. Generative adversarial nets. In *Advances in Neural Information Processing Systems*, pages 2672–2680.

Michael Heilman and Noah A. Smith. 2010. Tree edit models for recognizing textual entailments, paraphrases and answers to questions. In *Human Language Technologies: The 2010 Annual Conference of the North American Chapter of the Association for Computational Linguistics*, pages 1011–1019. ACL.

Baotian Hu, Zhengdong Lu, Hang Li, and Qingcai Chen. 2014. Convolutional neural network architectures for matching natural language sentences. In *Advances in Neural Information Processing Systems*.

Po-Sen Huang, Xiaodong He, Jianfeng Gao, Li Deng, Alex Acero, and Larry P. Heck. 2013. Learning deep structured semantic models for web search using clickthrough data. In *Proceedings of the 36th ACM International Conference on Information and Knowledge Management*, pages 2333–2338. ACM.

Philip Isola, Jun-Yan Zhu, Tinghui Zhou, and Alexi A. Efros. 2017. Image-to-image translation with conditional adversarial networks. *2017 IEEE Conference on Computer Vision and Pattern Recognition (CVPR)*, pages 5967–5976.

Tero Karras, Timo Aila, Samuli Laine, and Jaakko Lehtinen. 2017. Progressive growing of gans for improved quality, stability, and variation. *CoRR*, abs/1710.10196.

Sachin Kelkar, Chetanya Rastogi, Sparsh Gupta, and G.N. Pillai. 2018. Squeezegan: Image to image translation with minimum parameters. In *2018 IEEE International Joint Conference on Neural Networks (IJCNN)*, pages 1–6.

Kevin Lin, Dianqi Li, Xiaodong He, Zhengyou Zhang, and Ming-Ting Sun. 2017. Adversarial ranking for language generation. In *Advances in Neural Information Processing Systems*, pages 3155–3165.

Liang Pang, Yanyan Lan, Jiafeng Guo, Jun Xu, Shengxian Wan, and Xueqi Cheng. 2016. Text matching as image recognitionm. In *Proceedings of the 30th AAAI Conference on Artificial Intelligence*, pages 2793–2799. AAAI.

Aliaksei Severyn and Alessandro Moschitti. 2013. Automatic feature engineering for answer selection and extraction. In *Proceedings of the 2013 Conference on Empirical Methods in Natural Language Processing (EMNLP)*, pages 458–467. ACL.

Ming Tan, Cicero dos Santos, Bing Xiang, and Bowen Zhou. 2015. Lstm-based deep learning models for non-factoid answer selection. *CoRR*, abs/1511.04108.

Ming Tan, Cicero dos Santos, Bing Xiang, and Bowen Zhou. 2016. Improved representation learning for question answer matching. In *Proceedings of the 54th Annual Meeting of the Association for Computational Linguistics (Volume 1: Long Papers)*, pages 464–473. ACL.

Nam Khanh Tran and Claudia Niederee. 2018. Multi-hop attention networks for question answer matching. In *Proceedings of the 41st International ACM SIGIR Conference on Research and Development in Information Retrieval*, pages 325–334. ACM.

Bingning Wang, Kang Liu, and Jun Zhao. 2016. Inner attention based recurrent neural networks for answer selection. In *Proceedings of the 54th Annual Meeting of the Association for Computational Linguistics (Volume 1: Long Papers)*, pages 1288–1297. ACL.

Jun Wang, Lantao Yu, Weinan Zhang, Yu Gong, Yinghui Xu, Benyou Wang, Peng Zhang, and Dell Zhang. 2017. Irgan: A minimax game for unifying generative and discriminative information retrieval models. In *Proceedings of the 40th International ACM SIGIR Conference on Research and Development in Information Retrieval*, pages 515–524. ACM.

Mengqiu Wang and Christopher Manning. 2010. Probabilistic tree-edit models with structured latent variables for textual entailment and question answering. In *Proceedings of the 23rd International Conference on Computational Linguistics (Coling 2010)*, pages 1164–1172. ICCL.

Mengqiu Wang, Noah A. Smith, and Teruko Mitamura. 2007. What is the jeopardy model? a quasi-synchronous grammar for qa. In *Proceedings of the 2007 Joint Conference on Empirical Methods in Natural Language Processing and Computational Natural Language Learning (EMNLP-CoNLL)*, pages 22–32. ACL.

Ronald J. Williams. 1992. Simple statistical gradient-following algorithms for connectionist reinforcement learning. *Machine Learning*, 8:3-4:229–256.

Liu Yang, Minghui Qiu, Chen Qu, Jiafeng Guo, Yongfeng Zhang, W. Bruce Croft, Jun Huang, and Haiqing Chen. 2018. Response ranking with deep matching networks and external knowledge in information-seeking conversation systems. In *Proceedings of the 41st International ACM SIGIR Conference on Research and Development in Information Retrieval*, pages 245–254. ACM.

Yi Yang, Wen-tau Yih, and Christopher Meek. 2015. Wikiqa: A challenge dataset for open-domain question answering. In *Proceedings of the 2015 Conference on Empirical Methods in Natural Language Processing (EMNLP)*, pages 2013–2018. ACL.

Xuchen Yao, Benjamin Van Durme, Chris Callison Burch, and Peter Clark. 2013. Answer extraction as sequence tagging with tree edit distance. In *Proceedings of the 2013 Conference of the North American Chapter of the Association for Computational Linguistics: Human Language Technologies*, pages 858–867. ACL.

Wen-tau Yih, Ming-Wei Chang, Christopher Meek, and Andrzej Pastusiak. 2013. Question answering using enhanced lexical semantic models. In *Proceedings of the 51st Annual Meeting of the Association for Computational Linguistics (Volume 1: Long Papers)*, pages 1744–1753. ACL.

Wen-tau Yih and Hao Ma. 2016. Question answering with knowledge base, web and beyond. In *Proceedings of the 39th International ACM SIGIR Conference on Research and Development in Information Retrieval*, SIGIR '16, pages 1219–1221, New York, NY, USA. ACM.

Jianfei Yu, Minghui Qiu, Jing Jiang, Jun Huang, Shuangyong Song, Wei Chu, and Haiqing Chen. 2018. Modelling domain relationships for transfer learning on retrieval-based question answering systems in e-commerce. In *Proceedings of the 11th ACM International Conference on Web Search and Data Mining*, pages 682–690. ACM.

Lantao Yu, Weinan Zhang, Jun Wang, and Yong Yu. 2017. Seqgan: Sequence generative adversarial nets with policy gradient. In *Proceedings of the 31st AAAI Conference on Artificial Intelligence*. AAAI.

Jun-Yan Zhu, Taesung Park, Phillip Isola, and Alexei A Efros. 2017. Unpaired image-to-image translation using cycle-consistent adversarial networks. In *Computer Vision (ICCV), 2017 IEEE International Conference on*.

Meta-Learning Improves Lifelong Relation Extraction

Abiola Obamuyide
Department of Computer Science
University of Sheffield
avobamuyide1@sheffield.ac.uk

Andreas Vlachos
Dept. of Computer Science and Technology
University of Cambridge
andreas.vlachos@cst.cam.ac.uk

Abstract

Most existing relation extraction models assume a fixed set of relations and are unable to adapt to exploit newly available supervision data to extract new relations. In order to alleviate such problems, there is the need to develop approaches that make relation extraction models capable of continuous adaptation and learning. We investigate and present results for such an approach, based on a combination of ideas from lifelong learning and optimization-based meta-learning. We evaluate the proposed approach on two recent lifelong relation extraction benchmarks, and demonstrate that it markedly outperforms current state-of-the-art approaches.

1 Introduction

The majority of existing supervised relation extraction models can only extract a fixed set of relations which has been specified at training time. They are unable to detect an evolving set of novel relations observed after training without substantial retraining, which can be computationally expensive and may lead to catastrophic forgetting of previously learned relations. Zero-shot relation extraction approaches (Rocktäschel et al., 2015; Demeester et al., 2016; Levy et al., 2017; Obamuyide and Vlachos, 2018) can extract unseen relations, but at lower performance levels, and are unable to continually exploit newly available supervision to improve performance without considerable retraining. These limitations also extend to approaches to extracting relations in other limited supervision settings, for instance in the one-shot setting (Obamuyide and Vlachos, 2017). It is therefore desirable for relation extraction models to have the capability to learn continuously without catastrophic forgetting of previously learned relations. This would enable them exploit newly

available supervision to both identify novel relations and improve performance without substantial retraining.

Recently, Wang et al. (2019) introduced an embedding alignment approach to enable continual learning for relation extraction models. They consider a setting with streaming tasks, where each task consists of a number of distinct relations, and proposed to align the representation of relation instances in the embedding space to enable continual learning of new relations without forgetting knowledge from past relations. While they obtained promising results, a key weakness of the approach is that the use of an alignment model introduces additional parameters to already over-parameterized relation extraction models, which may in turn lead to an increase in the quantity of supervision required for training. In addition, the approach can only align embeddings between observed relations, and does not have any explicit objective that encourages the model to transfer and exploit knowledge gathered from previously observed relations to facilitate the efficient learning of yet to be observed relations.

In this work, we extend the work of Wang et al. (2019) by exploiting ideas from both lifelong learning and meta-learning. We propose to consider lifelong relation extraction as a meta-learning challenge, to which the machinery of current optimization-based meta-learning algorithms can be applied. Unlike the use of a separate alignment model as proposed in Wang et al. (2019), the proposed approach does not introduce additional parameters. In addition, the proposed approach is more data efficient since it explicitly optimizes for the transfer of knowledge from past relations, while avoiding the catastrophic forgetting of previously learned relations. Empirically, we evaluate on lifelong versions of the datasets by Bordes et al. (2015) and Han et al. (2018) and demonstrate con-

224

Proceedings of the 4th Workshop on Representation Learning for NLP (RepL4NLP-2019), pages 224–229
Florence, Italy, August 2, 2019. ©2019 Association for Computational Linguistics

siderable performance improvements over prior state-of-the-art approaches.

2 Background

Lifelong Learning In the lifelong learning setting, also referred to as continual learning (Ring, 1994; Thrun, 1996; Zhao and Schmidhuber, 1996), a model f_θ is presented with a sequence of tasks $\{\mathcal{T}_t\}_{t=1,2,3..,T}$, one task per round, and the goal is to learn model parameters $\{\theta_t\}_{t=1,2,3,..,T}$ with the best performance on the observed tasks. Each task $\mathcal{T}$ can be a conventional supervised task with its own distinct train ($\mathcal{T}^{train}$), development ($\mathcal{T}^{dev}$) and test ($\mathcal{T}^{test}$) splits. At each round t, the model is allowed to exploit knowledge gained from the previous $t-1$ tasks to enhance performance on the current task. In addition, the model is also allowed to have a small-sized buffer memory B, which can be used to store a limited amount of data from previously observed tasks. A prominent line of work in lifelong learning research is developing approaches that enable models learn new tasks without forgetting knowledge from previous tasks, i.e. avoiding catastrophic forgetting of old tasks (McCloskey and Cohen, 1989; Ratcliff, 1990; McClelland et al., 1995; French, 1999). Approaches proposed to address this problem include memory-based approaches (Lopez-Paz and Ranzato, 2017; Rebuffi et al., 2017; Chaudhry et al., 2019); parameter consolidation approaches (Kirkpatrick et al., 2017; Zenke et al., 2017); and dynamic model architecture approaches (Xiao et al., 2014; Rusu et al., 2016; Fernando et al., 2017).

Meta-Learning Meta-learning, or learning to learn (Schmidhuber, 1987; Naik and Mammone, 1992; Thrun and Pratt, 1998), aims to develop algorithms that learn a generic knowledge of how to solve tasks from a given distribution of tasks, by generalizing from solving related tasks from that distribution. Given tasks $\mathcal{T}$ sampled from a distribution of tasks $p(\mathcal{T})$, and a learner model $f(\mathbf{x}; \theta)$ parameterized by θ, gradient-based meta-learning methods, such as *MAML* (Finn et al., 2017), learn a prior initialization of the parameters of the model which, at meta-test time, can be quickly adapted to achieve good performance on a new task using a few steps of gradient descent. During adaptation to the new task, the model parameters θ are updated to task-specific parameters θ' with good performance on the task. Formally, the meta-learning algorithms optimize for the meta-objective:

$$\min_\theta \mathbb{E}_{\mathcal{T}\sim p(\mathcal{T})}\left[\mathcal{L}_\mathcal{T}\left(\theta'\right)\right] =$$
$$\min_\theta \mathbb{E}_{\mathcal{T}\sim p(\mathcal{T})}\left[\mathcal{L}_\mathcal{T}\left(\mathcal{U}\left(\mathcal{D}_\mathcal{T}; \theta\right)\right)\right] \qquad (1)$$

where $\mathcal{L}_\mathcal{T}$ is the loss and $\mathcal{D}_\mathcal{T}$ is training data from task $\mathcal{T}$, and $\mathcal{U}$ is a fixed gradient descent learning rule, such as vanilla SGD. While these algorithms were proposed and evaluated in the context of few-shot learning, here we demonstrate their effectiveness when utilized in the lifelong learning setting for relation extraction, following similar intuition as recent work by Finn et al. (2019).

3 Meta-Learning for Lifelong Relation Extraction

It can be inferred from the previous section that a lot of lifelong learning research has focused on approaches to avoid catastrophic forgetting (i.e. negative backward transfer of knowledge) while recent meta-learning studies have focused on effective approaches for positive forward transfer of knowledge (for few-shot tasks). Given the complementary strengths of the approaches from the two learning settings, we propose to embed meta-learning into the lifelong learning process for relation extraction.

While we can utilize the MAML algorithm to directly optimize the meta-objective in Equation 1 for our purpose, doing so requires the computation of second-order derivatives, which can be computationally expensive. Nichol et al. (2018) proposed *REPTILE*, a first-order alternative to MAML, which uses only first-order derivatives. Similar to MAML, REPTILE works by repeatedly sampling tasks, training on those tasks and moving the initialization towards the adapted weights on those tasks. Here we adopt the REPTILE algorithm for meta-learning. Our algorithm for lifelong relation extraction is illustrated in Algorithm 1.

We start by randomly initializing the parameters of the relation extraction model (the *learner*) (line 1). Then, as new tasks arrive, we augment their training set with randomly sampled task exemplars from the buffer memory B (lines 2-9). We then sample a batch of relations from the augmented training set (line 10). Then for each sampled relation $\mathcal{R}_i$, we sample a batch of supervision instances $\mathcal{D}^{train}_{\mathcal{R}_i}$ from its training set (line 11-12).

We then obtain the adapted model parameters θ_t^i on the relation by first computing the gradient of the training loss on the sampled relation instances (line 13) and backpropagating the gradients with a gradient-based optimization algorithm (such as *SGD* or *Adagrad* (Duchi et al., 2011)) (line 14). At the end of the learning iteration, the adapted parameters on all sampled relations in the batch are averaged, and an update is made on the task parameters θ_t (line 16). This is done until convergence on the current task, after which exemplars of the current task are added to the buffer memory (line 18). Task exemplars are obtained by first clustering all training instances of the current task into 50 clusters using K-Means, then selecting an instance from each cluster with a representation closest to the cluster prototype. Finally, the model parameters are updated to the current task's adapted parameters (line 19).

Algorithm 1 Meta-Learning for Lifelong Relation Extraction (*MLLRE*)

Require: Stream of incoming tasks $\mathcal{T}_1, \mathcal{T}_2, \mathcal{T}_3, \ldots$
Require: Relation extraction function f_θ
Require: Optimization algorithm (e.g. *SGD*)
Require: Step size ϵ, learning rate α
Require: Buffer memory B

1: Randomly initialize θ
2: **while** there are still tasks **do**
3:     Retrieve next task $\mathcal{T}_t$ from stream
4:     Initialize $\theta_t \leftarrow \theta$
5:     **repeat**
6:         **if** B is not empty **then**
7:             Retrieve exemplars $\mathcal{E}$ of random task from B
8:             Update task training set $\mathcal{D}_t^{train} = \mathcal{D}_t^{train} \cup \mathcal{E}$
9:         **end if**
10:        Sample random relations $\{\mathcal{R}_i\}_{i=1}^N$ from $\mathcal{D}_t^{train}$
11:        **for** each $\mathcal{R}_i$ **do**
12:            Sample train instances $\mathcal{D}_{\mathcal{R}_i}^{train}$ of $\mathcal{R}_i$
13:            Evaluate $\nabla_{\theta_t}\mathcal{L}_{\mathcal{R}_i}(f_{\theta_t})$ using $\mathcal{D}_{\mathcal{R}_i}^{train}$
14:            Compute adapted parameters:
             $\theta_t^i = SGD(\theta_t, \nabla_{\theta_t}\mathcal{L}_{\mathcal{R}_i}(f_{\theta_t}), \alpha)$
15:        **end for**
16:        Update task parameters:
$$\theta_t = \theta_t - \epsilon \frac{1}{N}\sum_{i=1}^N (\theta_t^i - \theta_t)$$
17:     **until** *Convergence*
18:     Add exemplars of $\mathcal{T}_t$ to B
19:     Update $\theta \leftarrow \theta_t$
20: **end while**

---

4   Relation Classification Model

In principle the learner model f_θ could be any gradient-optimized relation extraction model. In order to use the same number of parameters and ensure fair comparison to Wang et al. (2019), we adopt as the relation extraction model f_θ the Hier-

Method	FewRel		SimpleQuestions	
	$ACC_w.$	$ACC_a.$	$ACC_w.$	$ACC_a.$
Origin	0.189	0.208	0.632	0.569
GEM	0.492	0.598	0.841	0.796
AGEM	0.361	0.425	0.776	0.722
EWC	0.271	0.302	0.672	0.590
EA-EMR (Full)	0.566	0.673	0.878	0.824
EA-EMR (w/o Sel.)	0.564	0.674	0.857	0.812
EA-EMR (w/o Align.)	0.526	0.632	0.869	0.820
EMR	0.510	0.620	0.852	0.808
MLLRE	**0.602**	**0.741**	**0.880**	**0.842**

Table 1: Accuracy on the test set of all tasks ACC_{whole} (denoted $ACC_w.$) and average accuracy on the test set of only observed tasks ACC_{avg} (denoted $ACC_a.$) on the *Lifelong FewRel* and *Lifelong SimpleQuestions* datasets. Best results are in bold. Except for *MLLRE*, results for other models are obtained from Wang et al. (2019).

arachical Residual BiLSTM (*HR-BiLSTM*) model of Yu et al. (2017), which is the same model used by Wang et al. (2019) for their experiments. The *HR-BILSTM* is a relation classifier which accepts as input a sentence and a candidate relation, then utilizes two Bidirectional Long Short-Term Memory (Hochreiter and Schmidhuber, 1997; Graves and Schmidhuber, 2005) (BiLSTM) units with shared parameters to process the Glove (Pennington et al., 2014) embeddings of words in the sentence and relation names, then selects the relation with the maximum cosine similarity to the sentence as its response.

Hyperparameters Apart from the hyperparameters specific to meta-learning (such as the step size ϵ), all other hyperparameters we use for the learner model are the same as used by Wang et al. (2019). We also use the same buffer memory size (50) for each task. Note that the meta-learning algorithm uses SGD as the update rule ($\mathcal{U}$), and does not add any additional trainable parameters to the learner model.

5   Experiments

5.1   Setup

We conduct experiments in two settings. In the full supervision setting, we provide all models with all supervision available in the training set of each task. In the second, we limit the amount of supervision for each task to measure how the models are able to cope with limited supervision. Each experiment is run five (5) times and we report the

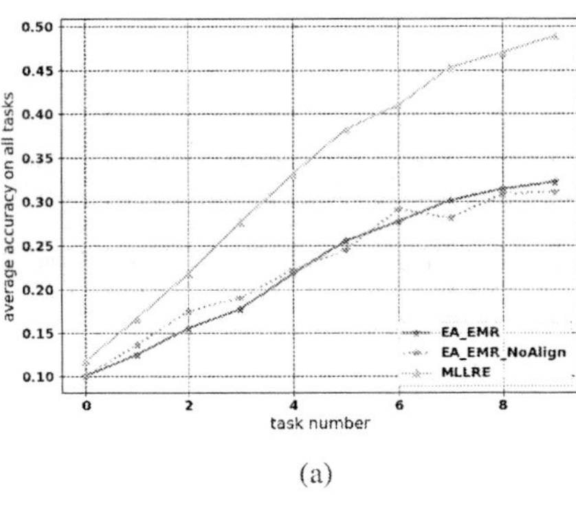

(a)

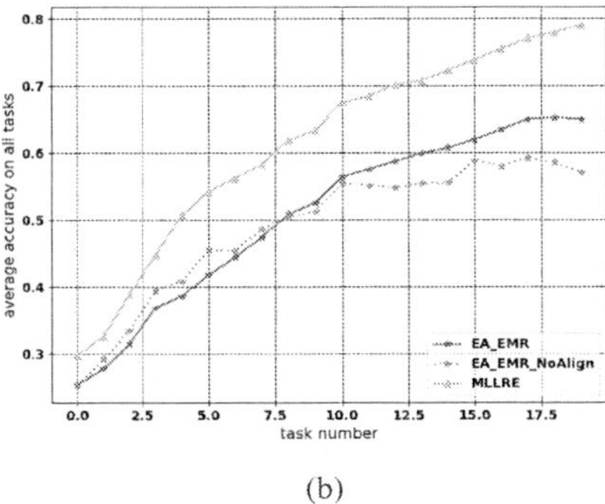

(b)

Figure 1: Results obtained using 100 training instances for each task on (a) *Lifelong FewRel* and (b) *Lifelong SimpleQuestions* datasets.

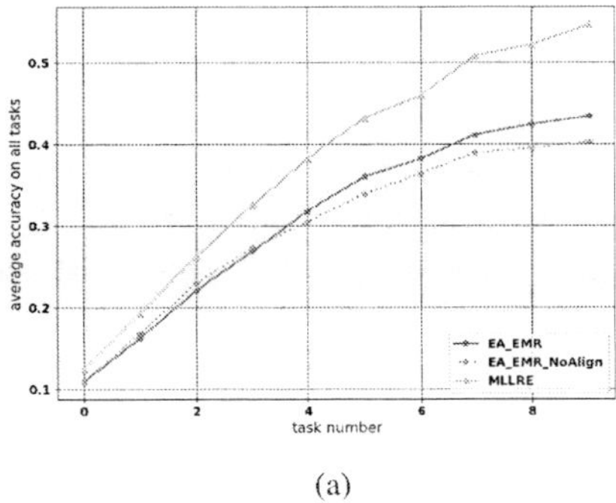

(a)

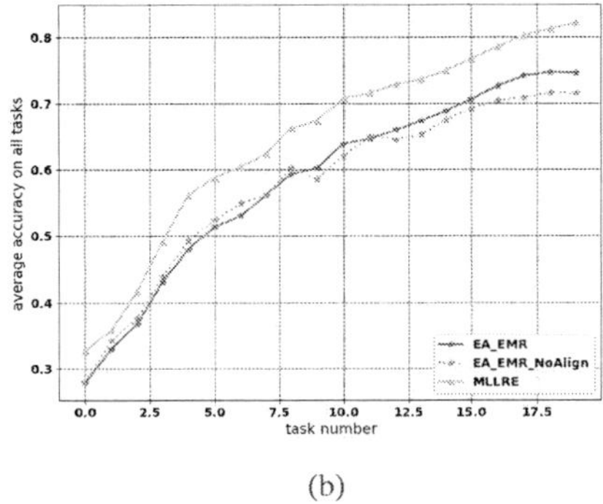

(b)

Figure 2: Results obtained using 200 training instances for each task on (a) *Lifelong FewRel* and (b) *Lifelong SimpleQuestions* datasets.

average result.

5.2 Datasets

We conduct experiments on *Lifelong FewRel* and *Lifelong SimpleQuestions* datasets, both introduced in Wang et al. (2019). *Lifelong FewRel* is derived from the *FewRel* (Han et al., 2018) dataset, by partitioning its 80 relations into 10 distinct clusters made up of 8 relations each, with each cluster serving as a task where a sentence must be labeled with the correct relation. The 8 relations in each cluster were obtained by clustering the averaged Glove word embeddings of the relation names in the *FewRel* dataset. Each instance of the dataset contains a sentence, the relation it expresses and a set of randomly sampled negative relations. *Lifelong SimpleQuestions* was similarly obtained from the *SimpleQuestions* (Bordes et al., 2015) dataset, and is made up of 20 clusters of relations, with each cluster serving as a task.

5.3 Evaluation Metrics

We report two measures, ACC_{whole} and ACC_{avg}, both introduced in Wang et al. (2019). ACC_{whole} measures accuracy on the test set of all tasks and gives a balanced measure of model performance on both observed (seen) and unobserved (unseen) tasks, and is the primary metric we report for all experiments. We also report ACC_{avg}, which measures the average accuracy on the test set of only observed (seen) tasks.

5.4 Results and Discussion

Full Supervision Results Table 1 gives both the ACC_{whole} and ACC_{avg} results of our approach compared to other approaches including Episodic Memory Replay (EMR) and its various embedding-aligned variants *EA-EMR* as proposed in Wang et al. (2019). Across all metrics, our approach outperforms the previous approaches, demonstrating its effectiveness in this setting. This result is likely because our approach is able to efficiently learn new relations by exploiting knowledge from previously observed relations.

Limited Supervision Results The aim of our limited supervision experiments is to compare the use of an alignment module as proposed by Wang et al. (2019) to using our approach when only limited supervision is available for all tasks. We compare three approaches, Full *EA-EMR* (which uses their alignment module), its variant without the alignment module (*EA-EMR_NoAlign*) and our approach (*MLLRE*). Figures 1(a) and 1(b) show results obtained using 100 supervision instances for each task on *Lifelong FewRel* and *Lifelong SimpleQuestions*. Figures 2(a) and 2(b) show the corresponding plots using 200 supervision instances for each task. From the figures, we observe that the use of a separate alignment model results in only minor gains when supervision for the tasks is limited, whereas the use of our approach leads to wide gains on both datasets.

In summary, because our approach explicitly encourages the model to learn to share and transfer knowledge between relations (by means of the meta-learning objective), the model is able to learn to exploit common structures across relations in different tasks to efficiently learn new relations over time. This leads to the performance improvements obtained by our approach.

6 Conclusion

We investigated the effectiveness of utilizing a gradient-based meta-learning algorithm within a lifelong learning setting to enable relation extraction models that are able to learn continually. We show the effectiveness of this approach, both when provided full supervision for new tasks and when provided limited supervision for new tasks, and demonstrated that the proposed approach outperformed current state-of-the-art approaches.

Acknowledgements

The authors acknowledge support from the EU H2020 SUMMA project (grant agreement number 688139).

References

Antoine Bordes, Nicolas Usunier, Sumit Chopra, and Jason Weston. 2015. Large-scale simple question answering with memory networks. *CoRR*, abs/1506.02075.

Arslan Chaudhry, MarcAurelio Ranzato, Marcus Rohrbach, and Mohamed Elhoseiny. 2019. Efficient lifelong learning with a-gem. In *International Conference on Learning Representations*.

Thomas Demeester, Tim Rocktäschel, and Sebastian Riedel. 2016. Lifted Rule Injection for Relation Embeddings. *Proceedings of the 2016 Conference on Empirical Methods in Natural Language Processing (EMNLP)*, pages 1389–1399.

John Duchi, Elad Hazan, and Yoram Singer. 2011. Adaptive subgradient methods for online learning and stochastic optimization. *Journal of Machine Learning Research*, 12:2121–2159.

Chrisantha Fernando, Dylan Banarse, Charles Blundell, Yori Zwols, David Ha, Andrei A Rusu, Alexander Pritzel, and Daan Wierstra. 2017. Pathnet: Evolution channels gradient descent in super neural networks. *arXiv preprint arXiv:1701.08734*.

Chelsea Finn, Pieter Abbeel, and Sergey Levine. 2017. Model-agnostic meta-learning for fast adaptation of deep networks. In *Proceedings of the 34th International Conference on Machine Learning*, volume 70 of *Proceedings of Machine Learning Research*, pages 1126–1135, International Convention Centre, Sydney, Australia.

Chelsea Finn, Aravind Rajeswaran, Sham Kakade, and Sergey Levine. 2019. Online meta-learning. In *Proceedings of the 36th International Conference on Machine Learning*.

Robert M French. 1999. Catastrophic forgetting in connectionist networks. *Trends in cognitive sciences*, 3(4):128–135.

Alex Graves and Jürgen Schmidhuber. 2005. Framewise phoneme classification with bidirectional LSTM networks. In *Proceedings of the International Joint Conference on Neural Networks*, volume 4, pages 2047–2052.

Xu Han, Hao Zhu, Pengfei Yu, Ziyun Wang, Maosong Sun, Yuan Yao, and Zhiyuan Liu. 2018. FewRel : A Large-Scale Supervised Few-Shot Relation Classification Dataset with State-of-the-Art Evaluation. In *Emnlp*, pages 4803–4809, Brussels, Belgium. Association for Computational Linguistics.

Sepp Hochreiter and Jürgen Schmidhuber. 1997. Long Short-Term Memory. *Neural Computation*, 9(8):1735–1780.

James Kirkpatrick, Razvan Pascanu, Neil Rabinowitz, Joel Veness, Guillaume Desjardins, Andrei A Rusu, Kieran Milan, John Quan, Tiago Ramalho, Agnieszka Grabska-Barwinska, and Others. 2017. Overcoming catastrophic forgetting in neural networks. *Proceedings of the national academy of sciences*, 114(13):3521–3526.

Omer Levy, Minjoon Seo, Eunsol Choi, and Luke Zettlemoyer. 2017. Zero-shot relation extraction via reading comprehension. In *Proceedings of the 21st Conference on Computational Natural Language*

Learning (CoNLL 2017), pages 333–342, Vancouver, Canada. Association for Computational Linguistics.

David Lopez-Paz and Marc'Aurelio Ranzato. 2017. Gradient episodic memory for continual learning. In *Advances in Neural Information Processing Systems*.

James L McClelland, Bruce L McNaughton, and Randall C O'reilly. 1995. Why there are complementary learning systems in the hippocampus and neocortex: insights from the successes and failures of connectionist models of learning and memory. *Psychological review*, 102(3):419.

Michael McCloskey and Neal J Cohen. 1989. Catastrophic interference in connectionist networks: The sequential learning problem. In *Psychology of learning and motivation*, volume 24, pages 109–165.

Devang K Naik and R J Mammone. 1992. Meta-neural networks that learn by learning. In *Proceedings of the International Joint Conference on Neural Networks*, volume 1, pages 437–442.

Alex Nichol, Joshua Achiam, and John Schulman. 2018. On first-order meta-learning algorithms. *CoRR*, abs/1803.02999.

Abiola Obamuyide and Andreas Vlachos. 2017. Contextual pattern embeddings for one-shot relation extraction. In *Proceedings of the NeurIPS 2017 Workshop on Automated Knowledge Base Construction (AKBC)*.

Abiola Obamuyide and Andreas Vlachos. 2018. Zero-shot relation classification as textual entailment. In *Proceedings of the EMNLP 2018 Workshop on Fact Extraction and VERification (FEVER)*, pages 72–78, Brussels, Belgium. Association for Computational Linguistics.

Jeffrey Pennington, Richard Socher, and Christopher D Manning. 2014. GloVe: Global Vectors for Word Representation. In *Empirical Methods in Natural Language Processing (EMNLP)*, pages 1532–1543.

Roger Ratcliff. 1990. Connectionist models of recognition memory: constraints imposed by learning and forgetting functions. *Psychological review*, 97(2):285.

Sylvestre-Alvise Rebuffi, Alexander Kolesnikov, Georg Sperl, and Christoph H Lampert. 2017. icarl: Incremental classifier and representation learning. In *Proceedings of the IEEE Conference on Computer Vision and Pattern Recognition*, pages 2001–2010.

Mark Bishop Ring. 1994. *Continual learning in reinforcement environments*. Ph.D. thesis, University of Texas at Austin Austin, Texas 78712.

Tim Rocktäschel, Sameer Singh, and Sebastian Riedel. 2015. Injecting Logical Background Knowledge into Embeddings for Relation Extraction. *North American Association for Computational Linguistics*, pages 1119–1129.

Andrei A Rusu, Neil C Rabinowitz, Guillaume Desjardins, Hubert Soyer, James Kirkpatrick, Koray Kavukcuoglu, Razvan Pascanu, and Raia Hadsell. 2016. Progressive neural networks. *arXiv preprint arXiv:1606.04671*.

Jurgen Schmidhuber. 1987. Evolutionary principles in self-referential learning. *On learning how to learn: The meta-meta-... hook.) Diploma thesis, Institut f. Informatik, Tech. Univ. Munich.*

Sebastian Thrun. 1996. Is learning the n-th thing any easier than learning the first? In *Advances in neural information processing systems*, pages 640–646.

Sebastian Thrun and Lorien Pratt. 1998. Learning to Learn: Introduction and Overview. In *Learning to Learn*, pages 3–17. Springer US, Boston, MA.

Hong Wang, Wenhan Xiong, Mo Yu, Xiaoxiao Guo, Shiyu Chang, and William Yang Wang. 2019. Sentence embedding alignment for lifelong relation extraction. In *Proceedings of the 2019 Conference of the North American Chapter of the Association for Computational Linguistics: Human Language Technologies, Volume 1 (Long and Short Papers)*, pages 796–806, Minneapolis, Minnesota. Association for Computational Linguistics.

Tianjun Xiao, Jiaxing Zhang, Kuiyuan Yang, Yuxin Peng, and Zheng Zhang. 2014. Error-driven incremental learning in deep convolutional neural network for large-scale image classification. In *Proceedings of the 22nd ACM international conference on Multimedia*, pages 177–186.

Mo Yu, Wenpeng Yin, Kazi Saidul Hasan, Cicero dos Santos, Bing Xiang, and Bowen Zhou. 2017. Improved neural relation detection for knowledge base question answering. In *Proceedings of the 55th Annual Meeting of the Association for Computational Linguistics (Volume 1: Long Papers)*, pages 571–581, Vancouver, Canada. Association for Computational Linguistics.

Friedemann Zenke, Ben Poole, and Surya Ganguli. 2017. Continual Learning Through Synaptic Intelligence. In *Proceedings of the 34th International Conference on Machine Learning*, volume 70 of *Proceedings of Machine Learning Research*, pages 3987–3995, International Convention Centre, Sydney, Australia.

Jieyu Zhao and Jurgen Schmidhuber. 1996. Incremental self-improvement for life-time multi-agent reinforcement learning. In *From Animals to Animats 4: Proceedings of the Fourth International Conference on Simulation of Adaptive Behavior, Cambridge, MA*, pages 516–525.

Best Practices for Learning Domain-Specific Cross-Lingual Embeddings

Lena Shakurova[1,2], Beata Nyari[1], Chao Li[1], Mihai Rotaru[1]

1 Textkernel B.V., Amsterdam, Netherlands
2 Radboud University, Nijmegen, Netherlands
{shakurova,nyari,chaoli,rotaru}@textkernel.nl

Abstract

Cross-lingual embeddings aim to represent words in multiple languages in a shared vector space by capturing semantic similarities across languages. They are a crucial component for scaling tasks to multiple languages by transferring knowledge from languages with rich resources to low-resource languages. A common approach to learning cross-lingual embeddings is to train monolingual embeddings separately for each language and learn a linear projection from the monolingual spaces into a shared space, where the mapping relies on a small seed dictionary. While there are high-quality generic seed dictionaries and pre-trained cross-lingual embeddings available for many language pairs, there is little research on how they perform on specialised tasks. In this paper, we investigate the best practices for constructing the seed dictionary for a specific domain. We evaluate the embeddings on the sequence labelling task of Curriculum Vitae parsing and show that the size of a bilingual dictionary, the frequency of the dictionary words in the domain corpora and the source of data (task-specific vs generic) influence the performance. We also show that the less training data is available in the low-resource language, the more the construction of the bilingual dictionary matters, and demonstrate that some of the choices are crucial in the zero-shot transfer learning case.

1 Introduction

Expanding Natural Language Processing (NLP) models to new languages typically involves creating completely new data sets for each language which comes with challenges such as acquiring and annotating the data. To avoid these tedious and costly tasks, one can use cross-lingual embeddings to enable knowledge transfer from languages with sufficient training data to low-resource languages.

Cross-lingual embeddings aim to represent words in multiple languages in a shared vector space by capturing semantic similarities across languages. Based on the assumption that the embedding spaces of different languages exhibit a similar structure (Mikolov et al., 2013), previous work proposed to learn a linear transformation which projects independently learned monolingual spaces into a single shared space, using a seed translation dictionary (Faruqui and Dyer, 2014). Although more advanced techniques involving jointly optimising monolingual and cross-lingual objectives were proposed, most of these solutions require some form of cross-lingual supervision via parallel data (Guo et al., 2015; Klementiev et al., 2012; Xiao and Guo, 2014; Hermann and Blunsom, 2014; Søgaard et al., 2015; Vulic and Moens, 2015). However, for applications targeting a specific domain (in our case, human resources) there is often little to no parallel data available, so simple alignment-based methods relying on only a small translation dictionary remain an attractive choice.

We adopt the Multilingual CCA framework (Ammar et al., 2016), and evaluate the cross-lingual embedding on a sequence labelling task in Curriculum Vitae parsing domain. We use this framework as it only requires an easier to acquire seed dictionary. Previous work has shown that the quality of this dictionary influences the cross-lingual embeddings (Vulić and Korhonen, 2016). However, to the best of our knowledge, there has been no extensive research on the choice of a seed dictionary in a non-generic domain. In addition, little attention was paid to how the quality of the bilingual dictionary affects performance as some labelled data from the target language is added.

In this paper, we investigate the best practices to create a seed dictionary for training domain-specific cross-lingual embeddings. We measure the impact of different choices of the dictionary creation on the downstream task: the dictionary

Proceedings of the 4th Workshop on Representation Learning for NLP (RepL4NLP-2019), pages 230–234
Florence, Italy, August 2, 2019. ©2019 Association for Computational Linguistics

size, the source of the words and their frequency, in both zero-shot and joint training scenarios.

2   Related work

Offline linear map induction methods The earliest approach to induce a linear mapping from the monolingual embedding spaces into a shared space was introduced in (Mikolov et al., 2013). They propose to learn the mapping by optimising the least squares objective on the monolingual embedding matrices corresponding to translational equivalent pairs. Subsequent research aimed to improve the mapping quality by optimising different objectives such as max-margin (Lazaridou et al., 2015) and by introducing an orthogonality constraint to the bilingual map to enforce self-consistency (Xing et al., 2015; Smith et al., 2017). (Artetxe et al., 2016) provide a theoretical analysis to existing approaches and in a follow-up research (Artetxe et al., 2018) they propose to learn principled bilingual mappings via a series of linear transformations.

An extensive survey of different approaches, including offline and online methods can be found in (Ruder, 2017).

The role of bilingual dictionary A common way to select a bilingual dictionary is by using either automatic translations of frequent words or word alignments. For instance, (Faruqui and Dyer, 2014) select the target word to which the source word is most frequently aligned in parallel corpora. (Mikolov et al., 2013) use the 5,000 most frequent words from the source language with their translations. To investigate the impact of the dictionary on the embedding quality, (Vulić and Korhonen, 2016) evaluate different factors and conclude that carefully selecting highly reliable symmetric translation pairs improves the performance of benchmark word-translation tasks. The authors also demonstrate that increasing the lexicon size over 10,000 pairs show a slow and steady decrease in performance.

3   Task

In this work, we look at the Curriculum Vitae (CV) parsing task: extraction of relevant information (e.g. name, job titles, etc) from a given CV and converting it into a structured format. This task can be cast as a cascaded sequence labelling problem (Yu et al., 2005) consisting of two steps: section segmentation and extraction of pre-defined entities, similar to named entity recognition task (NER). In the first step, a model segments the entire CV into sections such as personal information, education, experience or skills. In the second step, for each section, a dedicated model extracts entities specific to that section such as name, phone number, etc. from personal section and degree level, institution, etc. from education section. For all models, we use the standard BIO approach (Begin, Inside, Outside) to sequence labelling (Ramshaw and Marcus, 1995). For brevity, in this paper, we present the results of extracting 2 entities from the experience section: job title and organisation name.

4   Methodology

We conduct the experiments for German-English and Dutch-English cross-lingual embeddings. Given a bilingual seed dictionary, we use the learned CCA linear projection (see Section 2) between the monolingual vector spaces to project German/Dutch embeddings into the English space. The projected embeddings are then fed into the sequence labelling model. The sequence labelling model is always trained in the English space using either English training data (zero-shot) or English training data combined with projected German/Dutch training data. The model is tested using projected German/Dutch embeddings and German/Dutch test data. We experiment with several factors in the construction of the bilingual dictionary: source of data, size, and the frequency of the bilingual dictionary entries in the domain corpus.

4.1   Training data

Monolingual embeddings For each language, we train monolingual word2vec embeddings (Mikolov et al., 2013) on normalised CV data. The dimension of embeddings is 150, vocabulary size is 169k, 503k and 286k for English, German and Dutch respectively (minimum frequency 5).

Corpora In our experiments, we use English as high resource language and German and Dutch as low resource. The number of annotated documents is 4342 for English, 1947 for German and 2383 for Dutch. Having enough resources for German/Dutch also allows us to study the impact of increasing the amount of training data. Each document contains on average 11 entities. We split our data into train, development and test set with proportions of 70, 15 and 15% accordingly.

4.2 Bilingual dictionary factors

Source of data (IDP vs MUSE vs domain): We want to investigate the impact of constructing the bilingual dictionary from domain-specific words versus employing generic seed dictionaries: 1) from Facebook's MUSE project [1] 2) from The Internet Dictionary Project (IDP) [2]. MUSE dictionaries were specifically created for developing cross-lingual embeddings (Lample et al., 2017), whereas IDP dictionaries were produced for the purpose of making royalty-free translating dictionaries accessible to the Internet community. For the domain-specific dictionary, we picked top frequent words (see below) from the source monolingual corpus (German/Dutch) and translated the selected words into English using Yandex Translate API [3]. Stop words were removed and the words shorter than three characters were filtered out due to their unreliable translation.

Frequency of bilingual dictionary entries (high vs lower): We compared choosing most frequent words to those selected from a lower frequency range (between top 5-10%) in our domain-specific corpus. It has been observed by previous research that due to the fact that frequent terms are over-represented in commonly used seed dictionaries, the performance of cross-lingual mappings is much lower on rare words (Nakashole, 2018). Motivated by this finding we wanted to analyse the downstream effect of adding rarer terms to the dictionary.

Size of bilingual dictionary (1k vs 5k vs 10k): We compared seed dictionaries of different size: 1.000, 5.000 and 10.000. Understanding the impact of this factor is important as larger dictionaries are more expensive to create.

Validation: Previous research suggests using back-translation as a verification step for a translation pair. We skipped this because we noticed that certain words are crucial to be included in the seed dictionary and despite their translation being correct often they would be invalidated because of synonyms or suffixes (e.g. *persönliche* → *personal* → *persönlich*). Instead, we filter words whose translations do not reach a frequency

threshold in the English corpus, where this threshold is tuned on a validation set.

4.3 Model Architecture

Our sequence labelling model is a stacked Bidirectional LSTM with a CRF layer based on (Huang et al., 2015) with a pre-trained embedding layer. We used Adam optimiser and trained for 150 epochs. The network's hyperparameters are tuned on the English development set.

4.4 Evaluation metrics

As extrinsic evaluation metric of the cross-lingual embeddings, we use the average F1 score across the 2 entities we extract (job title and organisation name). As intrinsic evaluation metric, we use the precision at 1 (P@1) measured on the MUSE test sets consisting of 1,500 translation pairs.

5 Results and discussion

Table 1 presents our results on how the 3 bilingual dictionary factors influence the downstream task performance and the precision@1 score. We start with the best practices from previous work (top 5k frequent words) and change one factor at a time choosing the best performing setting when moving to the next factor.

From the first set of rows, we see that using in-domain seed words improves the task performance over generic dictionaries. This effect is amplified in the zero-shot transfer learning scenario. We also see that using a bilingual dictionary (MUSE) employed by previous NLP research performs much better than typical free online resource dictionary (IDP). These observations are particularly important in industry settings where it is a common practice to use free open-source resources. We also see that the intrinsic metric (P@1) yields very low scores and it is uncorrelated with the task metric e.g. it ranks MUSE and IDP in the reverse order. This highlights the importance of verifying cross-lingual embeddings on the downstream task.

We also observe that choosing less frequent seed words degrades the performance in the zero-shot case. Qualitative analysis shows that including certain high-frequency words can be crucial for our task: these words are typically section header words (e.g. *Persönliche Angaben* (Personal Information)) or common context words of the entities of interest (e.g. *Erfahrung* (experience)). Since these words tend to occur in similar contexts

---

[1] https://github.com/facebookresearch/MUSE

[2] http://www.june29.com/IDP/

[3] https://pypi.org/project/yandex-translater/

Factor combinations	DE - EN			NL-EN		
	Joint training	Zero shot	P@1	Joint training	Zero shot	P@1
IDP + 5k	79.5	61.5	1.1	-	-	-
MUSE + 5k	80.4	72.1	0.8	81.4	77.2	2.1
domain + 5k + high freq	81.1	75.8	1.7	81.5	79.1	2.5
domain + 5k + **high freq**	81.1	75.8	1.7	81.4	79.1	2.5
domain + 5k + **lower freq**	81.0	70.2	1.0	80.9	71.6	1.9
domain + **10k** + high freq	81.5	76.8	1.2	81.6	79.3	2.8
domain + **5k** + high freq	81.1	75.8	1.7	81.4	79.1	2.5
domain + **1k** + high freq	80.1	72.2	1.2	79.3	77.8	1.6

Table 1: Average F1 and precision@1 score for bilingual dictionary experiments. Joint training uses 200 documents from the low resource language.

Low resource data	DE - EN		NL - EN	
	Monolingual	Cross-lingual gain	Monolingual	Cross-lingual gain
None (zero-shot)	-	+75.8	-	+79.1
200 CVs	77.0	+4.1	75.1	+6.3
500 CVs	83.9	+0.2	80.9	+1.3
Full set	87.1	+0.0	83.5	+0.3

Table 2: Gain from knowledge transfer, averaged F1 score. Full set is 1363 for German and 1678 for Dutch.

as the entities, they tend to be confused with these entities in the zero-shot setting if they are not in the dictionary. Being common words, their meaning is quickly picked up when jointly training with some German/Dutch data.

In terms of vocabulary size, we notice that even with a smaller 1k domain-specific dictionary we tend to get a competitive performance. Using 5k terms seems sufficient, although in line with (Vulić and Korhonen, 2016) we observe that a larger vocabulary (10k) gives only a slight improvement.

By analysing neighbourhoods of non-seed German words projected in the English space, we noticed that even though the nearest English neighbours are related words (e.g. job title words), often the distances are quite big. Our intuition is that, specifically for sequence labelling tasks, adding some training data from the low-resource language allows the BLSTM model to the learn about these nearby neighbourhoods and account for the leeway created by imperfect cross-lingual projections.

We investigate the impact of increasing the size of low-resource language data in Table 2. For these experiments, we use the best performing seed dictionary (5k high-frequency words from domain corpus). The results demonstrate that with a strong English-only CV parsing model and cross-lingual embeddings we achieve comparable results to a model trained on only 15% of the low-resource language. We also observe that the gain of transfer learning diminishes as we jointly train with an increasing amount of German data.

6 Conclusions and future work

In this paper, we investigate the best practices for constructing a bilingual dictionary for learning domain-specific cross-lingual embeddings. We show that for our CV parsing task, the dictionary should be created from top frequency domain-specific words. A dictionary size of 5k tends to be sufficient, with limited gains coming from adding more words. We also show that the less training data is available in the low-resource language, the more these best practices matter.

In future work, we plan to extend our research to cover other language pairs (e.g. Slavic languages) or more distant pairs (e.g. English-Russian). We also plan to look at cross-lingual subwords embeddings which become crucial for languages with more complex morphology.

References

Waleed Ammar, George Mulcaire, Yulia Tsvetkov, Guillaume Lample, Chris Dyer, and Noah A. Smith.

2016. Massively Multilingual Word Embeddings. *arXiv e-prints*, page arXiv:1602.01925.

Mikel Artetxe, Gorka Labaka, and Eneko Agirre. 2016. Learning principled bilingual mappings of word embeddings while preserving monolingual invariance. pages 2289–2294.

Mikel Artetxe, Gorka Labaka, and Eneko Agirre. 2018. Generalizing and improving bilingual word embedding mappings with a multi-step framework of linear transformations. In *Proceedings of the Thirty-Second AAAI Conference on Artificial Intelligence*, pages 5012–5019.

Manaal Faruqui and Chris Dyer. 2014. Improving vector space word representations using multilingual correlation. In *Proceedings of the 14th Conference of the European Chapter of the Association for Computational Linguistics*, pages 462–471. Association for Computational Linguistics.

Jiang Guo, Wanxiang Che, David Yarowsky, Haifeng Wang, and Ting Liu. 2015. Cross-lingual dependency parsing based on distributed representations. In *Proceedings of the 53rd Annual Meeting of the Association for Computational Linguistics and the 7th International Joint Conference on Natural Language Processing (Volume 1: Long Papers)*, pages 1234–1244, Beijing, China. Association for Computational Linguistics.

Karl Moritz Hermann and Phil Blunsom. 2014. Multilingual distributed representations without word alignment. In *ICLR 2014*.

Zhiheng Huang, Wei Xu, and Kai Yu. 2015. Bidirectional lstm-crf models for sequence tagging. Cite arxiv:1508.01991.

Alexandre Klementiev, Ivan Titov, and Binod Bhattarai. 2012. Inducing crosslingual distributed representations of words. In *Proceedings of COLING 2012*, pages 1459–1474, Mumbai, India. The COLING 2012 Organizing Committee.

Guillaume Lample, Alexis Conneau, Ludovic Denoyer, and Marc'Aurelio Ranzato. 2017. Unsupervised machine translation using monolingual corpora only. *arXiv preprint arXiv:1711.00043*.

Angeliki Lazaridou, Georgiana Dinu, and Marco Baroni. 2015. Hubness and pollution: Delving into cross-space mapping for zero-shot learning. In *ACL*.

Tomas Mikolov, Kai Chen, Greg Corrado, and Jeffrey Dean. 2013. Efficient estimation of word representations in vector space. *CoRR*, abs/1301.3781.

Tomas Mikolov, Quoc V. Le, and Ilya Sutskever. 2013. Exploiting Similarities among Languages for Machine Translation. *arXiv e-prints*, page arXiv:1309.4168.

Tomas Mikolov, Ilya Sutskever, Kai Chen, Greg Corrado, and Jeffrey Dean. 2013. Distributed representations of words and phrases and their compositionality. *CoRR*, abs/1310.4546.

Ndapa Nakashole. 2018. NORMA: Neighborhood sensitive maps for multilingual word embeddings. In *Proceedings of the 2018 Conference on Empirical Methods in Natural Language Processing*, pages 512–522, Brussels, Belgium. Association for Computational Linguistics.

Lance A. Ramshaw and Mitchell P. Marcus. 1995. Text chunking using transformation-based learning. *CoRR*, cmp-lg/9505040.

Sebastian Ruder. 2017. A survey of cross-lingual embedding models. *CoRR*, abs/1706.04902.

Samuel L. Smith, David H. P. Turban, Steven Hamblin, and Nils Y. Hammerla. 2017. Offline bilingual word vectors, orthogonal transformations and the inverted softmax.

Anders Søgaard, Željko Agić, Héctor Martínez Alonso, Barbara Plank, Bernd Bohnet, and Anders Johannsen. 2015. Inverted indexing for cross-lingual NLP. In *Proceedings of the 53rd Annual Meeting of the Association for Computational Linguistics and the 7th International Joint Conference on Natural Language Processing (Volume 1: Long Papers)*, pages 1713–1722, Beijing, China. Association for Computational Linguistics.

Ivan Vulić and Anna Korhonen. 2016. On the role of seed lexicons in learning bilingual word embeddings. In *Proceedings of the 54th Annual Meeting of the Association for Computational Linguistics (Volume 1: Long Papers)*, pages 247–257, Berlin, Germany. Association for Computational Linguistics.

Ivan Vulic and Marie-Francine Moens. 2015. Bilingual distributed word representations from document-aligned comparable data. *CoRR*, abs/1509.07308.

Min Xiao and Yuhong Guo. 2014. Distributed word representation learning for cross-lingual dependency parsing. In *Proceedings of the Eighteenth Conference on Computational Natural Language Learning*, pages 119–129, Ann Arbor, Michigan. Association for Computational Linguistics.

Chao Xing, Dong Wang, Chao Liu, and Yiye Lin. 2015. Normalized word embedding and orthogonal transform for bilingual word translation. In *HLT-NAACL*.

Kun Yu, Gang Guan, and Ming Zhou. 2005. Resume information extraction with cascaded hybrid model. In *Proceedings of the 43rd Annual Meeting on Association for Computational Linguistics*, ACL '05, pages 499–506, Stroudsburg, PA, USA. Association for Computational Linguistics.

Effective Dimensionality Reduction for Word Embeddings

Vikas Raunak
Carnegie Mellon University
vraunak@cs.cmu.edu

Vivek Gupta
University of Utah
vgupta@cs.utah.edu

Florian Metze
Carnegie Mellon University
fmetze@cs.cmu.edu

Abstract

Pre-trained word embeddings are used in several downstream applications as well as for constructing representations for sentences, paragraphs and documents. Recently, there has been an emphasis on improving the pre-trained word vectors through post-processing algorithms. One improvement area is reducing the dimensionality of word embeddings. Reducing the size of word embeddings can improve their utility in memory constrained devices, benefiting several real-world applications. In this work, we present a novel technique that efficiently combines PCA based dimensionality reduction with a recently proposed post-processing algorithm (Mu and Viswanath, 2018), to construct effective word embeddings of lower dimensions. Empirical evaluations on several benchmarks show that our algorithm efficiently reduces the embedding size while achieving similar or (more often) better performance than original embeddings. To foster reproducibility, we have released the source code along with paper [1].

1 Introduction

Word embeddings such as Glove (Pennington et al., 2014) and word2vec Skip-Gram (Mikolov et al., 2013) obtained from unlabeled text corpora can represent words in distributed dense real-valued low dimensional vectors which geometrically capture the semantic *'meaning'* of a word. These embeddings capture several linguistic regularities such as analogy relationships. Such embeddings are of a pivotal role in several natural language processing tasks.

Recently, there has been an emphasis on applying post-processing algorithms on the pre-trained word vectors to further improve their quality. For example, algorithm in (Mrkšic et al., 2016) tries

to inject antonymy and synonymy constraints into vector representations, while (Faruqui et al., 2015) tries to refine word vectors by using relational information from semantic lexicons such as Word-Net (Miller, 1995). (Bolukbasi et al., 2016) tries to remove the biases (e.g. gender biases) present in word embeddings and (Nguyen et al., 2016) tries to *'denoise'* word embeddings by strengthening salient information and weakening noise. In particular, the post-processing algorithm in (Mu and Viswanath, 2018) tries to improve word embeddings by projecting the embeddings away from the most dominant directions and considerably improves their performance by making them more discriminative. However, a major issue related with word embeddings is their size (Ling et al., 2016), e.g., loading a word embedding matrix of 2.5 M tokens takes up to 6 GB memory (for 300-dimensional vectors, on a 64-bit system). Such large memory requirements impose significant constraints on the practical use of word embeddings, especially on mobile devices where the available memory is often highly restricted. In this work we combine the simple dimensionality reduction technique, PCA with the post processing technique of (Mu and Viswanath, 2018), as discussed above.

In Section 2, we first explain the post processing algorithm (Mu and Viswanath, 2018) and then our novel algorithm and describe with an example the choices behind its design. The evaluation results are presented in section 3. In section 4, we discuss the related works, followed by the conclusion.

2 Proposed Algorithm

We first explain the post-processing algorithm from (Mu and Viswanath, 2018) in section 2.1. Our main algorithm, along with the motivations is explained next, in the section 2.2.

---

[1] https://github.com/vyraun/Half-Size

Proceedings of the 4th Workshop on Representation Learning for NLP (RepL4NLP-2019), pages 235–243
Florence, Italy, August 2, 2019. ©2019 Association for Computational Linguistics

2.1 Post-Processing Algorithm

(Mu and Viswanath, 2018) presents a simple post-processing algorithm that renders off-the-shelf word embeddings even stronger, as measured on a number of lexical-level and sentence-level tasks. The algorithm is based on the geometrical observations that the word embeddings (across all representations such as Glove, word2vec etc.) have a large mean vector and most of their energy, after subtracting the mean vector is located in a subspace of about 8 dimensions. Since, all embeddings share a common mean vector and all embeddings have the same dominating directions, both of which strongly influence the representations, eliminating them makes the embeddings stronger. Detailed description of the post-processing algorithm is presented in Algorithm 1 (PPA).

Algorithm 1: Post Processing Algorithm PPA(X, D)

Data: Word Embedding Matrix X, Threshold Parameter D
Result: Post-Processed Word Embedding Matrix X
/* Subtract Mean Embedding   */
1   $X = X - \overline{X}$;
/* Compute PCA Components   */
2   $u_i = PCA(X)$, where i = 1,2, . . . ,d. ;
/* Remove Top-D Components   */
3   **for** *all v in X* **do**
4    $v = v - \sum_{i=1}^{D}(u_i^T \cdot v)u_i$
5   **end**

Figure 1 demonstrates the impact of the post-processing algorithm (PPA, with D= 7) as observed on wiki pre-trained Glove embeddings (300-dimensions). It compares the fraction of variance explained by the top 20 principal components of the original and post-processed word vectors respectively [2]. In the post-processed word embeddings none of the top principal components are disproportionately dominant in terms of explaining the data, which implies that the post-processed word vectors are not as influenced by the common dominant directions as the original embeddings. This makes the individual word vectors more *'discriminative'*, hence, improving their quality, as validated on several benchmarks in (Mu and Viswanath, 2018).

2.2 Proposed Algorithm

This section explains our algorithm, 2 that effectively uses the the PPA algorithm, along with PCA for constructing lower dimensional embeddings.

---

[2] the total sum of explained variances over the 300 principal components is equal to 1.0

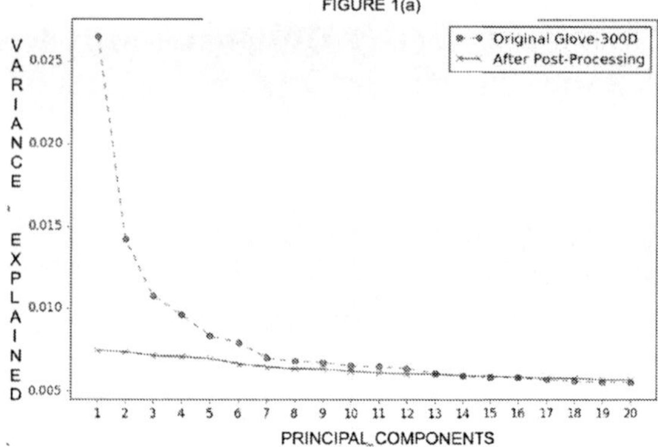

Figure 1: Comparison of the fraction of variance explained by top 20 principal components of the Original and Post-Processing (PPA) applied Glove embeddings (300D).

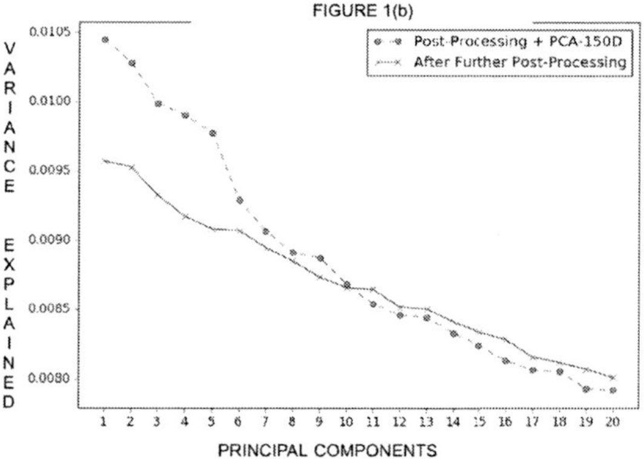

Figure 2: Comparison of the fraction of variance explained by top 20 principal components of the PPA + PCA-150D baseline and Further Post-Processed Glove embedding (150D).

We first apply the algorithm 1 (PPA) of (Mu and Viswanath, 2018) on the original word embedding, to make it more *'discriminative'*. We then construct a lower dimensional representation of the post processed *'purified'* word embedding using Principal Component Analysis (PCA (Shlens, 2014)) based dimensionality reduction technique. Lastly, we again *'purify'* the reduced word embedding by applying the algorithm 1 (PPA) of (Mu and Viswanath, 2018) on the reduced word embedding to get our final word embeddings.

To explain the last step of applying the algorithm 1 (PPA) on the reduced word embedding, consider the Figure 2. It compares the variance explained by the top 20 principal components for the embeddings constructed by first post-processing the Glove-300D embeddings according by Algorithm 1 (PPA) and then transforming the embeddings to 150 dimensions with PCA (labeled as Post-Processing + PCA); against a further post-processed version by again applying the Algorithm 1 (PPA) of the reduced word embeddings [3]. We observe that even though PCA has been applied on post-processed embeddings which had their dominant directions eliminated, the variance in the reduced embeddings is still explained disproportionately by a few top principal components. The re-emergence of this geometrical behavior implies that further post-processing (Algorithm 1 (PPA)) could improve the embeddings further. Thus, for constructing lower-dimensional word embeddings, we apply the post-processing algorithm on either side of a PCA dimensionality reduction of the word vectors in our algorithm.

Finally, from Figures 1 and 2, it is also evident that the extent to which the top principal components explain the data in the case of the reduced embeddings is not as great as in the case of the original 300 dimensional embeddings. Hence, multiple levels of post-processing at different levels of dimensionality will yield diminishing returns as the influence of common dominant directions decreases on the word embeddings. Details of reduction technique is given in Algorithm 2.

Algorithm 2: Dimensionality Reduction Algorithm

Data: Word Embedding Matrix X, New Dimension N, Threshold Parameter D
Result: Word Embedding Matrix of Reduced Dimension N: X

```
   /* Apply Algorithm 1 (PPA)        */
1  X = PPA(X, D);
   /* Transform X using PCA          */
2  X = PCA(X);
   /* Apply Algorithm 1 (PPA)        */
3  X = PPA(X, D);
```

---

3 Experimental Results

In this section, we evaluate our proposed algorithm on standard word similarity benchmarks and across a range of downstream tasks. For all our experiments, we used pre-trained Glove embeddings of dimensions 300, 200 and 100, trained on Wikipedia 2014 and Gigaword 5 corpus (400K vocabulary) (Pennington et al., 2014) [4] and fastText embeddings of 300 dimensions trained on Wikipedia using the Skip-Gram model described in (Bojanowski et al., 2017) (with 2.5M vocabu-

lary) [5]. The next subsection also presents results using word2vec embeddings trained on Google News dataset [6].

3.1 Word Similarity Benchmarks

We use the standard word similarity benchmarks summarized in (Faruqui and Dyer, 2014) for evaluating the word vectors.

Dataset: The datasets (Faruqui and Dyer, 2014) have word pairs (WP) that have been assigned similarity rating by humans. While evaluating word vectors, the similarity between the words is calculated by the cosine similarity of their vector representations. Then, Spearman's rank correlation coefficient (Rho $\times$ 100) between the ranks produced by using the word vectors and the human rankings is used for the evaluation. The reported metric in our experiments is Rho $\times$ 100. Hence, for better word similarity, the evaluation metric will be higher.

Baselines: To evaluate the performance of our algorithm, we compare it against different schemes of combining the post-processing algorithm with PCA [7] as following baselines:

- **PCA**: Transform word vectors using PCA.

- **P+PCA**: Apply PPA (Algorithm 1) and then transform word vectors using PCA.

- **PCA+P**: Transform word vectors using PCA and then apply PPA.

These baselines can also be regarded as ablations on our algorithm and can shed light on whether our intuitions in developing the algorithm were correct. In the comparisons ahead, we represent our algorithm as Algo-N ,where N is the reduced dimensionality of word embeddings. We use the scikit-learn (Pedregosa et al., 2011) PCA implementation.

Evaluation Results: First we evaluate our algorithm on the same embeddings against the 3 baselines, we then evaluate our algorithm across word embeddings of different dimensions and different types. In all the experiments, the threshold parameter D in the PPA algorithm was set to 7 and the new dimensionality after applying the dimensionality reduction algorithms, N was set to $\frac{d}{2}$, where

---

[3] the total sum of explained variances over the 150 principal components is equal to 1.0
[4] nlp.stanford.edu/projects/glove/

[5] github.com/facebookresearch/fastText/
[6] https://code.google.com/archive/p/word2vec/   [7] Generic non-linear dimensionality-reduction techniques performed worse than baselines, presumably because they fail to exploit the unique geometrical property of word embeddings discussed in section 2.

Table 1: Performance (Rho × 100) of Algo. 2 on different embedding and dimensions across multiple datasets. Bold represent the best value in each column.

Dataset	M Turk -771	WS 353 SIM	M Turk -287	VE RB -143	WS -353 -ALL	RW Stan ford	Men -TR -3K	RG -65	MC -30	Sim Lex -999	WS -353 -Rel	YP -130
Glove-300D	65.01	66.38	63.32	30.51	60.54	41.18	73.75	**76.62**	70.26	**37.05**	57.26	**56.13**
PCA-150D	52.47	52.69	56.56	28.52	46.52	27.46	63.35	71.71	70.03	27.21	41.82	36.72
P+PCA-150D	**65.59**	70.03	63.38	39.04	66.23	**43.17**	75.34	73.62	69.21	36.71	62.02	55.42
PCA-150D+P	63.86	70.87	**64.62**	40.14	66.85	40.79	75.37	74.27	72.35	33.81	60.5	50.2
Algo-150D	64.58	**71.61**	63.01	**42.24**	**67.41**	42.21	75.8	75.71	**74.8**	35.57	**62.09**	55.91
FastText-300D	66.89	**78.12**	**67.93**	**39.73**	**73.69**	**48.66**	**76.37**	79.74	81.23	**38.03**	68.21	**53.33**
Algo-150D	**67.29**	77.4	66.17	34.24	73.16	47.19	76.36	**80.95**	**86.41**	35.47	**69.96**	50.9
Glove-200D	**62.12**	62.91	61.99	28.45	57.42	38.95	71.01	71.26	66.56	34.03	54.48	52.21
Algo-100D	61.99	**68.43**	**63.55**	**36.82**	**65.41**	**39.8**	**74.44**	**71.53**	**69.83**	**34.19**	**61.56**	**49.94**
Glove-100D	58.05	60.35	61.93	30.23	52.9	**36.64**	68.09	69.07	62.71	**29.75**	49.55	**45.43**
Algo-50D	**58.85**	**66.27**	**64.09**	**33.04**	**62.05**	**36.64**	**70.93**	**64.56**	**68.79**	29.13	**59.55**	41.95

d is the original dimensionality. The value of parameter D was set to 7, because from Figure 1, we observe that the top 7 components are disproportionately contributing to the variance. Choosing a lower D will not eliminate the disproportionately dominant directions, while choosing a higher D will eliminate useful discriminative information from the word vectors. We choose $N = \frac{d}{2}$ as we observed that going below half the dimensions ($N < \frac{d}{2}$) significantly hurts performance of all embeddings.

Results Across Different Baselines: Table 1 shows the results of different baselines on the 12 datasets. As expected from discussions in Section 2, our algorithm achieves the best results on 6 out of 12 datasets when compared across all other baselines. In particular, the 150-dimension word embeddings constructed with our algorithm performs better than the 300-dimension embeddings in 7 out of 12 datasets with an average improvement of 2.74% across the 12 datasets, thus performing significantly better than PCA, PCA+P baselines and beating P+PCA baseline in 8 out of the 12 tasks.

Results Across Different Embeddings: Table 1 also shows the results of our algorithm on 300-dimension fastText embeddings, 100-dimension Glove embeddings and 200-dimension Glove embeddings. In fastText embeddings, the 150-dimension word vectors constructed using our algorithm gets better performance on 4 out of 12 datasets when compared to the 300-dimension embeddings. Overall, the 150-dimension word vectors have a cumulative score of 765.5 against the 771.93 of the 300-dimension vectors. The performance is similar to the 300-dimension embeddings with an average performance decline of 0.53% across the 12 datasets. With Glove embeddings of 100 and 200 dimensions, our algorithm leads to significant gains, with average performance improvements of 2.6% and 3% respectively over the original embeddings and achieves much better performance on 8 and 10 datasets respectively. Another observation is the embeddings generated by reducing Glove-200D to 100 dimensions using our algorithm outperform the original Glove-100D embeddings, with an average performance improvement of 6% across all 12 datasets. Hence, empirical results validate that our algorithm is effective in constructing lower dimension word embeddings, while maintaining similar or better performance than the original embeddings.

3.2 Downstream Tasks

Embeddings obtained using the proposed dimensionality reduction algorithm can be used as direct features for downstream supervised tasks. We experimented with textual similarity tasks (27 datasets) and text classification tasks (9 data-sets) to show the effectiveness of our algorithm. We used the SentEval (Conneau and Kiela, 2018) toolkit for all our experiments. In all cases, sentences were represented as the mean of their words' embeddings and in the classification tasks, logistic regression was used as the classifier. Table 2 give an overview of the downstream tasks we evaluated our reduced representation.

Table 2: Downstream Task Overview

Task	# of Datasets
Textual Classification Task	9
Sentence Similarity Task	5 (27)

Sentence Similarity Task: We further evaluate our algorithm against the baselines on the SemEval dataset (2012-2016) which involved 27 semantic textual similarity (STS) tasks (2012 - 2016) (Agirre et al., 2012), (Agirre et al., 2013), (Agirre et al., 2014), (Agirre et al., 2015), and (Agirre et al., 2016). The objectives of these tasks are to predict the similarity between two sentences. We used the average Spearmans rank correlation coefficient (Rho $\times$ 100) between the predicted scores and the ground-truth scores as the evaluation metric. Table 4 show performance of all reduction methods with varying reduction dimensions. Figure 3 - 8 compare performance of all reduction methods with varying reduction dimensions (in all these figures, X-axis represents the number of dimensions of reduced embeddings while Y-axis represents the score: Rho $\times$ 100). Similar to previous observations[8] our reduction technique outperforms all other baselines.

Textual Classification Task: We also performed the experiments on several textual classification tasks using SentEval (Conneau and Kiela, 2018) toolkit, which includes binary classification (MR, CR, SUBJ, MPQA), multiclass classification (SST-FG, TREC), entailment (SICK-E), semantic relatedness (STS-B) and Paraphrase detection (MRPC) tasks, across a range of domains (such as sentiment, product reviews etc). We observe that our embedding is effective on downstream classification tasks and can effectively reduce the input size and the model parameters without distinctively reducing the performance ($<= 1.0\%$). Table 3 compares the accuracy of reduced embeddings for multiple dimensions to the original embeddings on classification for several datasets. It can be clearly seen that the reduced embeddings at 200-D perform comparable to the orignal embeddings. The results confirm that [9] one can effectively reduce the input size and the model parameters without distinctively reducing the performance ($<= 1.0\%$).

3.3 Analysis and Discussion

The performance of reduced embeddings matches that of unreduced embeddings in a range of word

---

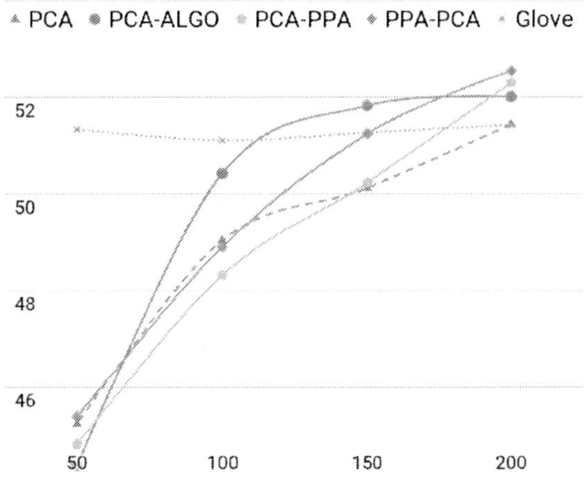

Figure 3: STS-12

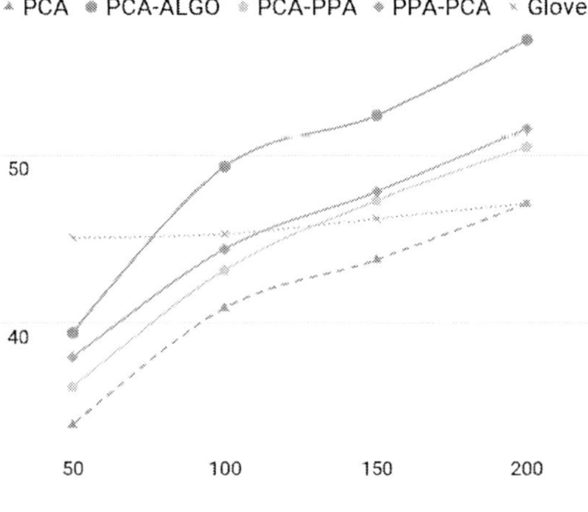

Figure 4: STS-13

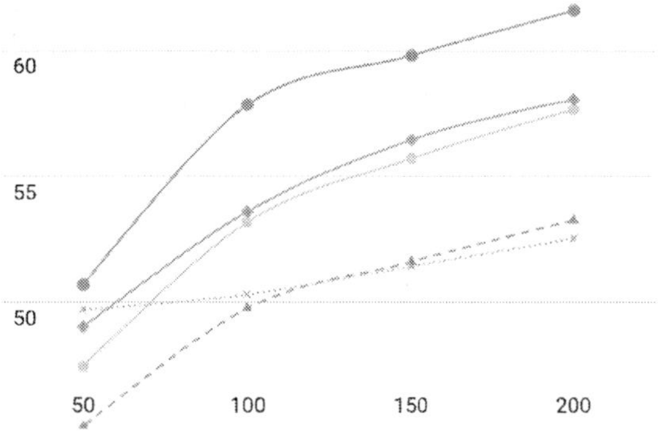

Figure 5: STS-14

Table 3: Comparison of performance (in terms of test accuracy) on several classification datasets with original embeddings and the reduced embeddings obtained using the proposed algorithm. Bold represents the reduced embeddings performance with is within <= 1% of the original 300D dimensional embeddings.

Model	MR	CR	SUBJ	MPQA	STS-B	SST -FG	TREC	SICK-E	MRPC
Glove-300D	75.59	78.31	91.58	86.88	78.03	41	**68**	78.49	71.48
Algo-50D	66.52	70.49	85.6	77.5	68.92	35.48	50	73.25	71.01
Algo-100D	70.43	75.34	88.31	82.3	71.99	38.42	55	75.6	71.42
Algo-150D	73.45	77.43	89.86	85.59	76.33	40.18	59.6	76.76	71.54
Algo-200D	**75.23**	**78.17**	**90.61**	**86.51**	**78.09**	**41.36**	65.4	**77.35**	**73.1**
word2vec-300D	77.65	**79.26**	90.76	**88.3**	61.42	42.44	**83**	**78.24**	72.58
Algo-50D	71.84	72.79	88.1	83.53	54.89	39.37	64.6	73.03	71.07
Algo-100D	73.89	75.65	89.56	84.81	59.54	39.95	69	74.97	71.42
Algo-150D	75.88	77.06	**90.01**	86.13	**61.42**	41.27	73.4	76.42	71.19
Algo-200D	**76.77**	77.88	**90.15**	86.9	**61.5**	**41.45**	77.4	76.98	**71.77**
fastText-300D	78.23	80.4	92.52	87.67	**68.33**	45.02	**85.8**	**79.2**	73.04
Algo-50D	71.23	75.36	87.88	82.25	57.01	38.87	66.8	71.91	72.06
Algo-100D	73.94	77.64	89.88	84.34	62.67	40.86	72.8	74.79	73.16
Algo-150D	75.52	78.2	90.96	86.18	63.46	41.4	75.2	75.06	73.39
Algo-200D	**77.18**	**79.76**	**91.6**	**86.64**	64.32	**43.48**	77.4	76.76	**72.93**

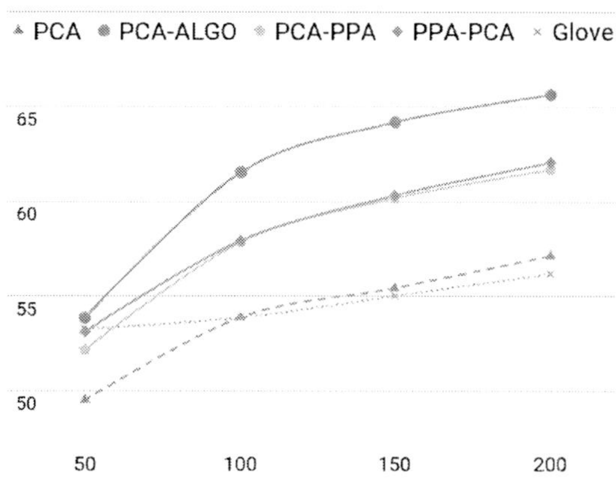

Figure 6: STS-15

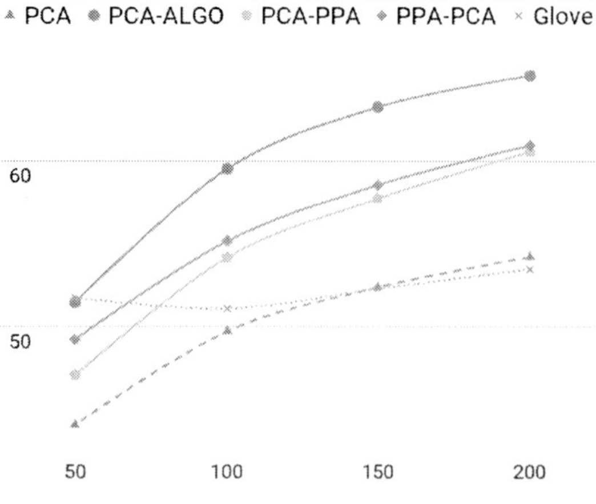

Figure 7: STS-16

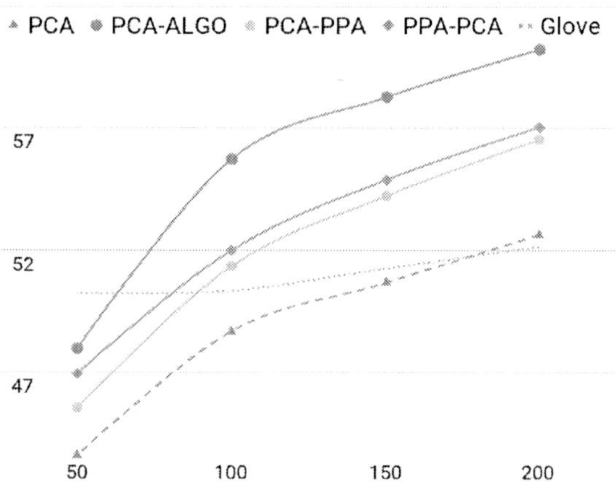

Figure 8: STS Average

and sentence similarity tasks. Considering the fact that semantic textual similarity (Majumder et al., 2016) is an important task across several fields, the resulting gains in efficiency, resulting from an efficient embeddings reduction, can prove useful to a range of applications. We obtain good performance on the similarity tasks since the proposed algorithm effectively exploits the geometry of the word embeddings (Mu and Viswanath, 2018) to reduce irrelevant noise in the word representations. In the sentence classification tasks, the reduced embeddings suffer from a slight performance loss in terms of test accuracy, which we suspect is due to the limitation of variance based techniques themselves in the context of word embeddings, i.e. owing to the disproprortionate distribution of linguistic features across the principal components themselves. Therefore, the loss of

STS-12	200	150	100	50
PCA	51.32	50.39	48.68	46.15
ALGO	**53.76**	**53.34**	**51.56**	**48.46**
PCA-PPA	51.76	51.26	49.12	42.45
PPA-PCA	51.91	50.91	49.27	46.73
Glove	51.42	51.26	51.1	51.33
STS-13	**200**	**150**	**100**	**50**
PCA	46.51	44.16	40.8	35.47
ALGO	**58.47**	**58.08**	**53.51**	**48.42**
PCA-PPA	56.71	54.26	50.11	43.46
PPA-PCA	56.98	55.12	52.43	45.94
Glove	47.1	46.19	45.27	45.06
STS-14	**200**	**150**	**100**	**50**
PCA	53.33	51.66	49.86	44.95
ALGO	**62.33**	**62.32**	**60.85**	**56.4**
PCA-PPA	61.62	61.04	58.59	54.24
PPA-PCA	61.66	61.13	58.84	54.67
Glove	52.56	51.44	50.31	49.71
STS-15	**200**	**150**	**100**	**50**
PCA	57.11	55.82	53.81	49.91
ALGO	**68.1**	**67.35**	**66.46**	**60.95**
PCA-PPA	65.49	64.78	61.17	56.23
PPA-PCA	65.48	64.92	62.49	57.55
Glove	56.18	55.04	53.89	53.29
STS-16	**200**	**150**	**100**	**50**
PCA	54.32	52.86	49.16	44.56
ALGO	**67.3**	**66.89**	**64.48**	**60.01**
PCA-PPA	65.06	63.86	60.07	55.27
PPA-PCA	65.36	64.12	61.16	54.89
Glove	53.52	52.33	51.14	51.8
STS Average	**200**	**150**	**100**	**50**
PCA	52.52	50.98	48.29	35.31
ALGO	**61.99**	**61.6**	**59.37**	**54.85**
PCA-PPA	60.13	59.04	55.81	50.33
PPA-PCA	60.28	59.24	56.84	51.96
Glove	52.16	51.25	50.34	50.24

Table 4: Performance in terms of (Rho × 100) between the predicted scores and the ground-truth scores for STS tasks.

information which is decorrelated with principal components (or the amount of variance explained) leads to decline in performance, since those properties of the embedding space are lost upon dimensionality reduction.

Another interesting analysis is to compare the performance of the reduced embeddings against state-of-the-art neural techniques on each of the datasets in Tables 3 and 4. In particular, the performance of the reduced embeddings of 200 dimensions (using Glove) obtained using the proposed algorithm suffers from an average drop of 4.1% in Spearman's Rank correlation scores (x 100) across the five sentence similarity datasets in Table 4, when compared against 4096 (**20X more**) dimensional sentence encoding obtained using InferSent [10] (Conneau et al., 2017). In the 9 sentence classification datasets, described in Table 3, the 200 dimensional reduced embeddings lead to an average drop of 7.3% in accuracy scores when compared against the 4096 dimensional Infersent encodings. If we exclude TREC (on which all pre-trained embeddings perform poorly), then the 200 dimensional embeddings lead to an average drop of 5.4% when compared against the 4096 dimensional InferSent encodings, across the remaining 8 sentence classification tasks in Table 3.

4   Comparison with Related Work

Most of the existing work on word embedding size reduction focuses on quantization (e.g. (Lam, 2018), which requires retraining with a different training objective), compression or limited precision training. In particular, (Ling et al., 2016) tries to reduce the embeddings' memory footprint by using limited precision representation during word embedding use and training while (Andrews, 2016) tries to compress word embeddings using different compression algorithms and (Shu and Nakayama, 2017) uses compositional coding approach for constructing embeddings with fewer parameters. There hasn't been much study on dimensionality reduction for word embeddings, with a general consensus on the use of publicly released pre-trained word embeddings of 300 dimensions, trained on large corpora (Yin and Shen, 2018). A recent work (Yin and Shen, 2018) has addressed the issue of exploring optimal dimensionality by changing the training objective, instead of dimensionality reduction. However, in this paper we mainly focus on the dimensionality reduction of the widely used pre-trained word embeddings (word2vec, Glove, fastText) and show that we can half the standard dimensionality by effectively exploiting the geometry of the embedding space. Therefore, our work is the first to extensively explore directly reducing the dimensionality of existing/pre-trained word embeddings, making it both different and complementary to the existing methods.

---

[10] https://github.com/facebookresearch/InferSent

5 Conclusions and Future Work

Empirical results show that our method is effective in constructing lower dimension word embeddings, having similar or (more often) better performance than the original embeddings. This could allow the use of word embeddings in memory-constrained environments. In future, an interesting area to explore would be the application of compressed and limited precision representations on top of dimensionality reduction to further reduce the size of the word embeddings. Deriving an algorithm to choose D, N and the levels of post-processing automatically, while optimizing for performance could also make the dimensionality reduction pipeline simpler for downstream applications. Further, owing to the growing popularity of contextualized embeddings such as ElMo (Peters et al., 2018) and BERT (Devlin et al., 2018), it would be interesting to explore whether the geometric intuitions used for developing the proposed algorithm for word embedding dimensionality reduction could be leveraged for contextualized embeddings as well.

References

Eneko Agirre, Carmen Banea, Claire Cardie, Daniel Cer, Mona Diab, Aitor Gonzalez-Agirre, Weiwei Guo, Inigo Lopez-Gazpio, Montse Maritxalar, Rada Mihalcea, et al. 2015. Semeval-2015 task 2: Semantic textual similarity, english, spanish and pilot on interpretability. In *(SemEval 2015)*, pages 252–263.

Eneko Agirre, Carmen Banea, Claire Cardie, Daniel Cer, Mona Diab, Aitor Gonzalez-Agirre, Weiwei Guo, Rada Mihalcea, German Rigau, and Janyce Wiebe. 2014. Semeval-2014 task 10: Multilingual semantic textual similarity. In *(SemEval 2014)*, pages 81–91.

Eneko Agirre, Carmen Banea, Daniel Cer, Mona Diab, Aitor Gonzalez-Agirre, Rada Mihalcea, German Rigau, and Janyce Wiebe. 2016. Semeval-2016 task 1: Semantic textual similarity, monolingual and cross-lingual evaluation. In *(SemEval-2016)*, pages 497–511.

Eneko Agirre, Daniel Cer, Mona Diab, Aitor Gonzalez-Agirre, and Weiwei Guo. 2013. * sem 2013 shared task: Semantic textual similarity. In *(SemEval 2013)*, volume 1, pages 32–43.

Eneko Agirre, Mona Diab, Daniel Cer, and Aitor Gonzalez-Agirre. 2012. Semeval-2012 task 6: A pilot on semantic textual similarity. In *(SemEval 2012)*, pages 385–393. Association for Computational Linguistics.

Martin Andrews. 2016. Compressing word embeddings. In *International Conference on Neural Information Processing*, pages 413–422. Springer.

Piotr Bojanowski, Edouard Grave, Armand Joulin, and Tomas Mikolov. 2017. Enriching word vectors with subword information. *Transactions of the Association of Computational Linguistics*, 5(1):135–146.

Tolga Bolukbasi, Kai-Wei Chang, James Y Zou, Venkatesh Saligrama, and Adam T Kalai. 2016. Man is to computer programmer as woman is to homemaker? debiasing word embeddings. In *Advances in Neural Information Processing Systems*, pages 4349–4357.

Alexis Conneau and Douwe Kiela. 2018. Senteval: An evaluation toolkit for universal sentence representations. *arXiv preprint arXiv:1803.05449*.

Alexis Conneau, Douwe Kiela, Holger Schwenk, Loic Barrault, and Antoine Bordes. 2017. Supervised learning of universal sentence representations from natural language inference data. *arXiv preprint arXiv:1705.02364*.

Jacob Devlin, Ming-Wei Chang, Kenton Lee, and Kristina Toutanova. 2018. Bert: Pre-training of deep bidirectional transformers for language understanding. *arXiv preprint arXiv:1810.04805*.

Manaal Faruqui, Jesse Dodge, Sujay Kumar Jauhar, Chris Dyer, Eduard Hovy, and Noah A Smith. 2015. Retrofitting word vectors to semantic lexicons. In *NAACL-HLT 2015*, pages 1606–1615.

Manaal Faruqui and Chris Dyer. 2014. Improving vector space word representations using multilingual correlation. In *Proceedings of the 14th Conference of the European Chapter of the Association for Computational Linguistics*, pages 462–471.

Maximilian Lam. 2018. Word2bits-quantized word vectors. *arXiv preprint arXiv:1803.05651*.

Shaoshi Ling, Yangqiu Song, and Dan Roth. 2016. Word embeddings with limited memory. In *Proceedings of the 54th Annual Meeting of the Association for Computational Linguistics (Volume 2: Short Papers)*, volume 2, pages 387–392.

Goutam Majumder, Partha Pakray, Alexander Gelbukh, and David Pinto. 2016. Semantic textual similarity methods, tools, and applications: A survey. *Computación y Sistemas*, 20(4):647–665.

Tomas Mikolov, Ilya Sutskever, Kai Chen, Greg S Corrado, and Jeff Dean. 2013. Distributed representations of words and phrases and their compositionality. In *Advances in neural information processing systems*, pages 3111–3119.

George A Miller. 1995. Wordnet: a lexical database for english. *Communications of the ACM*, 38(11):39–41.

Nikola Mrkšic, Diarmuid OSéaghdha, Blaise Thomson, Milica Gašic, Lina Rojas-Barahona, Pei-Hao Su, David Vandyke, Tsung-Hsien Wen, and Steve Young. 2016. Counter-fitting word vectors to linguistic constraints. In *Proceedings of NAACL-HLT*, pages 142–148.

Jiaqi Mu and Pramod Viswanath. 2018. All-but-the-top: Simple and effective postprocessing for word representations. In *International Conference on Learning Representations*.

Kim Anh Nguyen, Sabine Schulte im Walde, and Ngoc Thang Vu. 2016. Neural-based noise filtering from word embeddings. In *Proceedings of COLING 2016, the 26th International Conference on Computational Linguistics: Technical Papers*, pages 2699–2707.

Fabian Pedregosa, Gaël Varoquaux, Alexandre Gramfort, Vincent Michel, Bertrand Thirion, Olivier Grisel, Mathieu Blondel, Peter Prettenhofer, Ron Weiss, Vincent Dubourg, et al. 2011. Scikit-learn: Machine learning in python. *Journal of machine learning research*, 12(Oct):2825–2830.

Jeffrey Pennington, Richard Socher, and Christopher Manning. 2014. Glove: Global vectors for word representation. In *Proceedings of the 2014 conference on empirical methods in natural language processing (EMNLP)*, pages 1532–1543.

Matthew E Peters, Mark Neumann, Mohit Iyyer, Matt Gardner, Christopher Clark, Kenton Lee, and Luke Zettlemoyer. 2018. Deep contextualized word representations. *arXiv preprint arXiv:1802.05365*.

Jonathon Shlens. 2014. A tutorial on principal component analysis. *arXiv preprint arXiv:1404.1100*.

Raphael Shu and Hideki Nakayama. 2017. Compressing word embeddings via deep compositional code learning. In *International Conference on Neural Information Processing*, page arXiv:1711.01068. arXiv preprint.

Zi Yin and Yuanyuan Shen. 2018. On the dimensionality of word embedding. In *Advances in Neural Information Processing Systems*, pages 895–906.

Learning Word Embeddings without Context Vectors

Alexey Zobnin
Yandex,
National Research University
Higher School of Economics,
Moscow, Russia
azobnin@hse.ru

Evgenia Elistratova
Moscow State University,
Moscow, Russia
evg3307@yandex.ru

Abstract

Most word embedding algorithms such as word2vec or fastText construct two sort of vectors: for words and for contexts. Naive use of vectors of only one sort leads to poor results. We suggest using indefinite inner product in skip-gram negative sampling algorithm. This allows us to use only one sort of vectors without loss of quality. Our "context-free" cf algorithm performs on par with SGNS on word similarity datasets.

1 Introduction

Vector representation of words are widely used in NLP tasks. Two approaches to word embeddings are usually contrasted: implicit (word2vec-like) and explicit (SVD-like). Implicit models are usually faster and consume less memory than their explicit analogues.

Typically, word embedding algorithms produce two matrices both for "words" and "contexts". Usually, contexts are the words themselves. It is believed that word and context vectors cannot be equated to each other.

In practice, however, only the vectors of one sort are considered. For example, typical solutions to word similarity or analogy problems use only the inner products of word vectors.

We present a modified skip-gram negative sampling algorithm that produces related word and context vectors. One may say that some components of our word and context vectors are equal, while other components have different signs. Another point of view is to say that word and context vectors are completely equal, but the inner product between them is indefinite. This relation was suggested by the properties of explicit SVD embeddings.

2 Preliminaries

We briefly recall the skip-gram negative sampling (SGNS) algorithm implemented in popular programs word2vec (Mikolov et al., 2013a,b) and fastText (Bojanowski et al., 2017). Given row vectors of a current word w, its context c_0 and negative context samples $c_1, \ldots, c_k$, SGNS algorithm computes the loss

$$\mathcal{L} = -\ln \sigma(wc_0^T) - \sum_{j=1}^{k} \ln \sigma(-wc_j^T), \quad (1)$$

where $\sigma(x) = \frac{1}{1+e^{-x}}$ is the sigmoid function. Starting from random initial approximation of word vectors, the algorithm uses stochastic gradient descent (SGD) for optimization. The intuition is the following: the word vector should be similar to the true context vector and dissimilar to random negative contexts. Due to the properties of $\sigma(x)$, the gradient and update formulas look simple.

Let n be the size of the vocabulary, and d be the dimension of embeddings. Let W and C be $n \times d$ matrices of word (respectively, context) vectors written in rows. The SGNS loss (1) depends only on elements of WC^T, and does not depend on W or C separately. The optimal solution of SGNS is not unique: the transformation $W \mapsto WS$, $C \mapsto C(S^{-1})^T$ for an invertible $d \times d$-matrix S, gives an equivalent solution. However, such transformation could change the inner products between word vectors dramatically if S is not orthogonal. Nevertheless, SGNS produces a "good" solution without any regularization. This phenomenon is not well understood, and can be seen as "implicit regularization" of SGD.

Levy and Goldberg showed that the implicit matrix $M = WC^T$ tends to the shifted PMI matrix $\mathcal{M}$ when d is sufficiently large (Levy and Goldberg, 2014). Here $\mathcal{M}_{i,j} = \text{PMI}(w_i, w_j) - \log k$,

Proceedings of the 4th Workshop on Representation Learning for NLP (RepL4NLP-2019), pages 244–249
Florence, Italy, August 2, 2019. ©2019 Association for Computational Linguistics

where

$$\mathrm{PMI}(w_i, w_j) = \log \frac{P(w_i w_j)}{P(w_i) P(w_j)}$$

is the pointwise mutual information of the pair of words w_i, w_j, and k is the amount of negative samples. Thus, SGNS can be considered as an implicit matrix factorization problem.

We recall that a (compact) singular value decomposition (SVD) of a real-valued $m \times n$-matrix M of rank r is a decomposition $M = U\Sigma V^T$, where U and V are respectively $m \times r$ and $n \times r$ matrices with orthogonal columns, and Σ is $r \times r$ diagonal matrix with non-zero singular values on diagonal. We refer to (Golub and Van Loan, 2012) for details. SVD embeddings are obtained from truncated SVD decomposition $M \approx U_d \Sigma_d V_d^T$, where only d top singular values and vectors are kept. The common way is to take $W = U_d \sqrt{\Sigma_d}$ and $C = V_d \sqrt{\Sigma_d}$.

3 Main result

First of all, we make an observation about SVD embeddings. We shall use it further to modify the SGNS algorithm.

3.1 SVD of real symmetric matrices

Proposition. *Let M be a real-valued symmetric $n \times n$-matrix.*

1. *There exists a decomposition $M = WDW^T$, where $D = \mathrm{diag}(\pm 1)$.*

2. *There exists a compact SVD $M = U\Sigma V^T$ such that $V = UD$.*

3. *If all singular values of M are different, then all singular value decompositions of M have this form[1].*

In other words, the corresponding columns of U and V either coincide, or differ in sign.

Proof. All eigenvalues of a real symmetric matrix are real. Moreover, M has an eigendecomposition $M = C\Lambda C^T$, where $\Lambda = \mathrm{diag}(\lambda_i)$ is a diagonal matrix of eigenvalues, and C is an orthogonal matrix. Let r be the rank of M. We may remove columns in C and Λ that correspond to zero eigenvalues and assume that C is $n \times r$-matrix and

Λ is $r \times r$-matrix with non-zero eigenvalues on diagonal. Note that non-zero singular values σ_i of M are absolute values of λ_i.

1. Let $\Sigma = \mathrm{diag}(\sigma_i)$ be a diagonal matrix of non-zero singular values. Then $\Lambda = \Sigma D = \sqrt{\Sigma} D \sqrt{\Sigma}$, where

$$D_{ii} = \begin{cases} 1, & \text{if } \lambda_i > 0, \\ -1, & \text{if } \lambda_i < 0. \end{cases}$$

Now take $W = C\sqrt{\Sigma}$.

2. Write M as $C\Sigma DC^T$ and take $U = C$, $V = CD$.

3. If all singular values are different, then SVD is determined uniquely up to a simultaneous change of signs in some columns of U and V. Take the SVD constructed above and note that the relation $V = UD$ is preserved after these transformations. $\square$

We denote by q the amount of -1 in D. Due to the Sylvester's law of inertia, it is uniquely determined by M and equals to the amount of negative eigenvalues of M.

3.2 Negative eigenvalues of word relation matrices

Consider an $n \times n$-matrix $M = (f(w_i, w_j))$ describing the relation between the words w_i and w_j. For example, $f(w_i, w_j)$ may be the shifted PPMI, as suggested in (Levy and Goldberg, 2014):

$$f(w_i, w_j) = \max(0, \mathrm{PMI}(w_i, w_j) - \log k).$$

As a rule, the relation f is symmetric, and hence M is symmetric too.

Let's look at the SVD embeddings obtained from this matrix. Let $M = U\Sigma V^T$ be an SVD, and $M \approx M_d = U_d \Sigma_d V_d^T$ be its truncated approximation. Then symmetric SVD embeddings are $W = U_d \sqrt{\Sigma_d}$ and $C = V_d \sqrt{\Sigma_d}$. In the following, we will naturally assume that top d singular values of M are different and non-zero: all real cases are just like that. By the proposition we have that some columns of W and C coincide, while the others differ in sign. As a consequence, we obtain that for such SVD embeddings word and context vectors are equally good in applied problems, because inner products $(w_i w_j)$ and $(c_i c_j)$ are the same. We would like to construct implicit SGNS-like embeddings with similar properties.

---

[1] This is also valid for a more general case when equal singular values of M correspond to the eigenvalues of the same sign.

The amount of negative eigenvalues of M measures the deviation from the positive definiteness in some sense. To estimate it, we construct shifted PPMI matrices for Wikipedia corpora in three different languages (English, French and Russian). Each corpus contains 1M articles. We measure the amount of negative eigenvalues among top by magnitude eigenvalues. The results for $k = 1$ (pure PPMI matrix, no shift) and for $k = 5$ are presented in Tables 1 and 2, respectively. We see that the rate of negative eigenvalues is about 11–13% for $k = 1$ and about 7–8% for $k = 5$. Surprisingly, this rate actually does not depend on the language.

corpus \ dimension	100	200	300
English Wikipedia	15	27	39
French Wikipedia	10	22	34
Russian Wikipedia	11	22	31

Table 1: Amount of negative eigenvalues in the truncated SVD of PPMI matrix ($k = 1$, i. e., no shift).

corpus \ dimension	100	200	300
English Wikipedia	9	16	24
French Wikipedia	7	15	22
Russian Wikipedia	7	14	20

Table 2: Amount of negative eigenvalues in the truncated SVD of shifted PMI matrix with $k = 5$.

3.3 Context-free SGNS algorithm

Recall that SGNS loss depends on the inner products of words and contexts. Let's fix the matrix

$$D = \mathrm{diag}(\underbrace{-1, \ldots, -1}_{q}, \underbrace{1, 1, \ldots, 1}_{p=d-q})$$

specifying indefinite inner product in the embedding space. The amount of minus ones in this matrix, q, will be a hyperparameter of our algorithm. Next, we equate word and context vectors to each other. This corresponds to the implicit factorization WDW^T instead of WC^T.

Thus, we replace the initial SGNS loss (1) with

$$\mathcal{L}_q = -\ln \sigma(wDw_0^T) - \sum_{j=1}^{k} \ln \sigma(-wDw_j^T).$$

The solution of this new optimization problem is also not unique. Replacing W with WS for any matrix S that preserves D, i. e., such that $SDS^T = D$, yields another solution. Nevertheless, the solution set in our case is "smaller" in some sense than in the pure SGNS case, where S may be any invertible matrix.

Since we got rid of context vectors, we call this algorithm *context-free SGNS*[2] and denote it `cf`.

4 Experimental results

4.1 Training setup

We train word embeddings on the English Wikipedia dump. We preprocess this dump using gensim.corpora.wikicorpus package[3] and take a subsample of 100K articles. Our corpus consists of approximately 175M words with $n \approx 312000$. We use fastText[4] skipgram mode with the default values of parameters and without ngrams (`-maxn 0`) as a vanilla SGNS implementation. We implement our model by modifying the C++ implementation of fastText[5]. We learn `cf` vectors of dimension $d = 100$ and $100 + q$ for $q = 0, 5, 10, 15, 20, 25$. Vectors of dimension $100 + q$ were projected to 100 "positive" components.

4.2 Datasets

Datasets for word similarity evaluation consist of pairs of words rated by humans. We use the following well-known English similarity datasets: MEN-3k (Bruni et al., 2014), MTurk-287 (Halawi et al., 2012), RW-STANFORD (Luong et al., 2013), SimLex-999 (Hill et al., 2015), SimVerb-3500 (Gerz et al., 2016), VERB-143 (Baker et al., 2014), and WS-353 (Finkelstein et al., 2002) splitted into similarity and relatedness parts (Agirre et al., 2009). We use the evaluation code (Faruqui and Dyer, 2014) for computing Spearman rank correlation ρ between the similarity scores and the annotated ratings.

4.3 Results

Table 3 shows the results for word vectors of dimension 100 with q negative components in D. The best results are written in bold, and the best `cf` results are underlined. We see that $q = 0$, i. e., the case of positive semidefinite approximation, has the worst performance. The better perfor-

---

[2]Not to be confused with context-free grammars.
[3]`https://radimrehurek.com/gensim/corpora/wikicorpus.html`.
[4]`https://fasttext.cc/`.
[5]`https://github.com/jen1995/fastText/tree/sgns-loss`.

Dataset	SGNS	$q = 0$	$q = 5$	$q = 10$	$q = 15$	$q = 20$	$q = 25$
MEN-TR-3k	**.7314**	.6790	<u>.7234</u>	.7185	.7165	.7124	.7092
MTurk-287	.6668	.6335	.6574	.6604	.6615	.6609	**.6725**
RW-STANFORD	.3801	.2862	.4094	.4202	**.4223**	.4151	.4090
SIMLEX-999	**.3323**	.2520	.3141	.3194	.3126	.3098	<u>.3226</u>
SimVerb-3500	**.2022**	.1317	.1890	.1948	<u>.1975</u>	.1942	.1965
VERB-143	.3000	.2995	.3323	.3304	.3498	**.3834**	.3595
WS-353-REL	**.6648**	.6142	.6372	<u>.6594</u>	.6389	.6306	.6296
WS-353-SIM	**.7612**	.7079	.7508	<u>.7538</u>	.7525	.7506	.7332
average	.4380	.3700	.4346	**.4384**	.4382	.4345	.4340

Table 3: Word similarity for $d = 100$.

Dataset	SGNS	$q = 0$	$q = 5$	$q = 10$	$q = 15$	$q = 20$	$q = 25$
MEN-TR-3k	.7314	.6790	.7333	.7348	.7351	**.7371**	.7370
MTurk-287	.6668	.6335	.6612	.6697	.6719	**.6746**	.6645
RW-STANFORD	.3801	.2862	.4015	**.4091**	.4069	.4022	.3999
SIMLEX-999	**.3323**	.2520	.3138	.3127	.3199	.3166	<u>.3235</u>
SimVerb-3500	**.2022**	.1317	<u>.1926</u>	.1917	.1894	.1905	.1914
VERB-143	.3000	.2995	**.3362**	.3148	.3141	.3285	.3315
WS-353-REL	.6648	.6142	.6673	.6714	**.6765**	.6718	.6741
WS-353-SIM	.7612	.7079	**.7627**	.7476	.7577	.7554	.7480
average	.4380	.3700	.4382	**.4394**	**.4394**	.4392	**.4394**

Table 4: Word similarity for $p = 100$ (only "positive" components of $p + q$-dimensional `cf` vectors were taken).

mance of `cf` is achieved at $q = 10$ or $q = 15$. This argees with empirical results of Subsection 3.2. In general, `cf` is either on par with SGNS, or slightly loses. In the second experiment we learn `cf` vectors of higher dimension $100 + q$ and projected them to 100 "positive" components. These results are shown in Table 4. Starting from $q = 5$, they are slightly better than SGNS.

5 Related work

There were several attempts to establish a connection between word and context vectors. In (Li et al., 2017) a PMI matrix is approximated by a positive semidefinite matrix of the form WW^T. Dependencies between word and context vectors for word2vec SGNS model were studied in (Mimno and Thompson, 2017).

In (Allen et al., 2018) it is suggested that word and context vectors should be conjugated in the complex space. Our model can be reformulated in terms of complex vectors too in the case $p = q$, but we prefer to stay in reals. One of the problems with complex embedding is that $\sigma(z)$ is not holomorphic in the whole complex plane, and should be replaced with $\sigma(|z|)$ or $\sigma(\mathrm{Re}\,z)$. Complex-valued embeddings are also discussed in (Trouillon et al., 2016), where a complex decomposition like $M = \mathrm{Re}\,U\Lambda\bar{U}^T$ is suggested.

In (Assylbekov and Takhanov, 2019) it was conjectured that context vectors are reflections of word vectors in half the dimensions. Our result is similar, but we suggest using lower amount of reflections. Perhaps this difference is due to the fact that we consider shifted PPMI matrices, while they consider pure PMI matrices.

Embeddings in hyperbolic space with Minkowski metric was suggested in (Leimeister and Wilson, 2018). In (Soleimani and Matwin, 2018) there is an erroneous statement that a thresholded PMI matrix, as well as any symmetric matrix, has SVD decomposition $U\Sigma U^T$: in fact it is true only for positive semidefinite matrices.

Non-uniqueness of SGNS solutions was addressed in (Fonarev et al., 2017) and (Mu et al., 2018), resulting in new models. Implicit regularization of SGD in neural networks and in matrix factorization problems was studied in (Gunasekar et al., 2017; Neyshabur et al., 2017; Ma et al., 2018), but SGNS loss was not considered directly in these works.

6   Conclusion

We proposed cf, an alternative to SGNS algorithm that do not use context vectors. Instead, indefinite inner product between word vectors is used. Our algorithm shows similar results compared to SGNS.

The phenomenon of implicit regularization of SGNS, as well as the problem of finding the linguistic interpretation of "negative" components of word vectors in our algorithm, deserve further investigation.

Acknowledgements

The authors thank Anna Potapenko for fruitful discussions and anonymous referees for valuable comments.

References

Eneko Agirre, Enrique Alfonseca, Keith Hall, Jana Kravalova, Marius Paşca, and Aitor Soroa. 2009. A study on similarity and relatedness using distributional and wordnet-based approaches. In *Proceedings of Human Language Technologies: NAACL-2009*, pages 19–27. ACL.

Carl Allen, Ivana Balažević, and Timothy Hospedales. 2018. What the vec? Towards probabilistically grounded embeddings. *arXiv:1805.12164*.

Zhenisbek Assylbekov and Rustem Takhanov. 2019. Context vectors are reflections of word vectors in half the dimensions. *arXiv:1902.09859*.

Simon Baker, Roi Reichart, and Anna Korhonen. 2014. An unsupervised model for instance level subcategorization acquisition. In *Proceedings of the 2014 Conference on Empirical Methods in Natural Language Processing (EMNLP)*, pages 278–289.

Piotr Bojanowski, Edouard Grave, Armand Joulin, and Tomas Mikolov. 2017. Enriching word vectors with subword information. *Transactions of the Association for Computational Linguistics*, 5:135–146.

Elia Bruni, Nam-Khanh Tran, and Marco Baroni. 2014. Multimodal distributional semantics. *Journal of Artificial Intelligence Research*, 49:1–47.

Manaal Faruqui and Chris Dyer. 2014. Community evaluation and exchange of word vectors at wordvectors. org. In *Proceedings of 52nd Annual Meeting of ACL: System Demonstrations*, pages 19–24.

Lev Finkelstein, Evgeniy Gabrilovich, Yossi Matias, Ehud Rivlin, Zach Solan, Gadi Wolfman, and Eytan Ruppin. 2002. Placing search in context: The concept revisited. *ACM Transactions on information systems*, 20(1):116–131.

Alexander Fonarev, Oleksii Grinchuk, Gleb Gusev, Pavel Serdyukov, and Ivan Oseledets. 2017. Riemannian optimization for skip-gram negative sampling. In *Proceedings of the 55th Annual Meeting of the ACL (Volume 1: Long Papers)*, pages 2028–2036.

Daniela Gerz, Ivan Vulić, Felix Hill, Roi Reichart, and Anna Korhonen. 2016. Simverb-3500: A large-scale evaluation set of verb similarity. In *Proceedings of the 2016 Conference on Empirical Methods in Natural Language Processing*, pages 2173–2182.

Gene H Golub and Charles F Van Loan. 2012. *Matrix computations*, volume 3. JHU press.

Suriya Gunasekar, Blake E Woodworth, Srinadh Bhojanapalli, Behnam Neyshabur, and Nati Srebro. 2017. Implicit regularization in matrix factorization. In *Advances in Neural Information Processing Systems*, pages 6151–6159.

Guy Halawi, Gideon Dror, Evgeniy Gabrilovich, and Yehuda Koren. 2012. Large-scale learning of word relatedness with constraints. In *Proceedings of the 18th ACM SIGKDD international conference on Knowledge discovery and data mining*, pages 1406–1414. ACM.

Felix Hill, Roi Reichart, and Anna Korhonen. 2015. Simlex-999: Evaluating semantic models with (genuine) similarity estimation. *Computational Linguistics*, 41(4):665–695.

Matthias Leimeister and Benjamin J Wilson. 2018. Skip-gram word embeddings in hyperbolic space. *arXiv:1809.01498*.

Omer Levy and Yoav Goldberg. 2014. Neural word embedding as implicit matrix factorization. In *Advances in Neural Information Processing Systems*, pages 2177–2185.

Shaohua Li, Jun Zhu, and Chunyan Miao. 2017. Psdvec: A toolbox for incremental and scalable word embedding. *Neurocomputing*, 237:405–409.

Thang Luong, Richard Socher, and Christopher Manning. 2013. Better word representations with recursive neural networks for morphology. In *Proceedings of the 17th Conference on Computational Natural Language Learning*, pages 104–113.

Cong Ma, Kaizheng Wang, Yuejie Chi, and Yuxin Chen. 2018. Implicit regularization in nonconvex statistical estimation: Gradient descent converges linearly for phase retrieval and matrix completion. In *Proceedings of the 35th International Conference on Machine Learning*, volume 80.

Tomas Mikolov, Kai Chen, Greg Corrado, and Jeffrey Dean. 2013a. Efficient estimation of word representations in vector space. *arXiv:1301.3781*.

Tomas Mikolov, Ilya Sutskever, Kai Chen, Greg S Corrado, and Jeff Dean. 2013b. Distributed representations of words and phrases and their compositionality. In *Advances in neural information processing systems*, pages 3111–3119.

David Mimno and Laure Thompson. 2017. The strange geometry of skip-gram with negative sampling. In *Proceedings of the 2017 Conference on Empirical Methods in Natural Language Processing*, pages 2873–2878.

Cun Mu, Guang Yang, and Zheng Yan. 2018. Revisiting skip-gram negative sampling model with rectification. *arXiv:1804.00306*.

Behnam Neyshabur, Ryota Tomioka, Ruslan Salakhutdinov, and Nathan Srebro. 2017. Geometry of optimization and implicit regularization in deep learning. *arXiv:1705.03071*.

Behrouz Haji Soleimani and Stan Matwin. 2018. Spectral word embedding with negative sampling. In *32nd AAAI Conference on Artificial Intelligence*.

Théo Trouillon, Johannes Welbl, Sebastian Riedel, Éric Gaussier, and Guillaume Bouchard. 2016. Complex embeddings for simple link prediction. In *International Conference on Machine Learning*, pages 2071–2080.

Learning Cross-Lingual Sentence Representations via a
Multi-task Dual-Encoder Model

**Muthuraman Chidambaram,[*] Yinfei Yang,[*] Daniel Cer,[*] Steve Yuan,
Yun-Hsuan Sung, Brian Strope, Ray Kurzweil**
Google AI, Mountain View, CA, USA
{mutty, yinfeiy, cer}@google.com

Abstract

The scarcity of labeled training data across many languages is a significant roadblock for multilingual neural language processing. We approach the lack of in-language training data using sentence embeddings that map text written in different languages, but with similar meanings, to nearby embedding space representations. The representations are produced using a dual-encoder based model trained to maximize the representational similarity between sentence pairs drawn from parallel data. The representations are enhanced using multitask training and unsupervised monolingual corpora. The effectiveness of our multilingual sentence embeddings are assessed on a comprehensive collection of monolingual, cross-lingual, and zero-shot/few-shot learning tasks.

1 Introduction

Sentence embeddings are broadly useful for a diverse collection of downstream natural language processing tasks (Cer et al., 2018; Conneau et al., 2017; Kiros et al., 2015; Logeswaran and Lee, 2018; Subramanian et al., 2018). Sentence embeddings evaluated on downstream tasks in prior work have been trained on monolingual data, preventing them from being used for cross-lingual transfer learning. However, recent work on learning multilingual sentence embeddings has produced representations that capture semantic similarity even when sentences are written in different languages (Eriguchi et al., 2018; Guo et al., 2018; Schwenk and Douze, 2017; Singla et al., 2018). *We explore multi-task extensions of multilingual models for cross-lingual transfer learning.*

We present a novel approach for cross-lingual representation learning that combines methods for multi-task learning of monolingual sentence representations (Cer et al., 2018; Subramanian et al., 2018) with recent work on dual encoder methods for obtaining multilingual sentence representations for bi-text retrieval (Guo et al., 2018; Yang et al., 2019). By doing so, we learn representations that maintain strong performance on the original monolingual language tasks, while *simultaneously* obtaining good performance using zero-shot learning on the same task in another language. For a given language pair, we construct a multi-task training scheme using native source language tasks, native target language tasks, and a *bridging translation task* to encourage sentences with identical meanings, but written in different languages, to have similar embeddings.

We evaluate the learned representations on several monolingual and cross-lingual tasks, and provide a graph-based analysis of the learned representations. Multi-task training using additional monolingual tasks is found to improve performance over models that only make use of parallel data on both cross-lingual semantic textual similarity (STS) (Cer et al., 2017) and cross-lingual eigen-similarity (Søgaard et al., 2018). For European languages, the results show that the addition of monolingual data improves the embedding alignment of sentences and their translations. Further, we find that cross-lingual training with additional monolingual data leads to far better cross-lingual transfer learning performance.[1]

---

[*]equal contribution

[1]Models based on this work are available at `https://tfhub.dev/` as: universal-sentence-encoder-xling/en-de, universal-sentence-encoder-xling/en-fr, and universal-sentence-encoder-xling/en-es. A large multilingual model is available as universal-sentence-encoder-xling/many.

Proceedings of the 4th Workshop on Representation Learning for NLP (RepL4NLP-2019), pages 250–259
Florence, Italy, August 2, 2019. ©2019 Association for Computational Linguistics

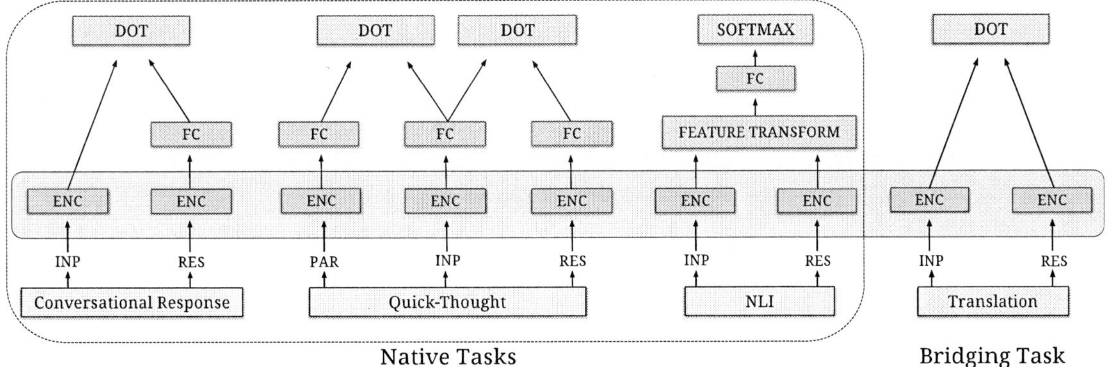

Figure 1: Multi-task dual-encoder model with native tasks and a bridging translation task. The terms PAR, INP, RES refer to parent, input, and response respectively. ENC refers to the shared encoder g, FC refers to fully connected layers, and DOT refers to dot product. Finally, FEATURE TRANSFORM refers to the feature vector used for natural language inference.

2 Multi-Task Dual-Encoder Model

The core of our approach is multi-task training over problems that can be modeled as ranking input-response pairs encoded via dual-encoders (Cer et al., 2018; Henderson et al., 2017; Yang et al., 2018). Cross-lingual representations are obtained by incorporating a *translation bridge task* (Gouws et al., 2015; Guo et al., 2018; Yang et al., 2019). For input-response ranking, we take an input sentence s_i^I and an associated response sentence s_i^R, and we seek to rank s_i^R over all other possible response sentences $s_j^R \in \mathcal{S}^R$. We model the conditional probability $P(s_i^R \mid s_i^I)$ as:

$$P(s_i^R \mid s_i^I) = \frac{e^{\phi(s_i^I, s_i^R)}}{\sum_{s_j^R \in \mathcal{S}^R} e^{\phi(s_i^R, s_j^R)}} \quad (1)$$

$$\phi(s_i^I, s_j^R) = g^I(s_i^I)^\top g^R(s_j^R)$$

Where g^I and g^R are the input and response sentence encoding functions that compose the dual-encoder. The normalization term in eq. 1 is computationally intractable. We follow Henderson et al. (2017) and instead choose to model an approximate conditional probability $\widetilde{P}(s_i^R \mid s_i^I)$:

$$\widetilde{P}(s_i^R \mid s_i^I) = \frac{e^{\phi(s_i^I, s_i^R)}}{\sum_{j=1}^{K} e^{\phi(s_i^R, s_j^R)}} \quad (2)$$

Where K denotes the size of a single batch of training examples, and the s_j^R corresponds to the response sentences associated with the other input sentences in the same batch as s_i^I. We realize g^I and g^R as deep neural networks that are trained to

maximize the approximate log-likelihood, $\widetilde{P}(s_i^R \mid s_i^I)$, for each task.

To obtain a single sentence encoding function g for use in downstream tasks, we share the first k layers of the input and response encoders and treat the final output of these shared layers as g. The shared encoders are used with the ranking formulation above to support conversational response ranking (Henderson et al., 2017), a modified version of quick-though (Logeswaran and Lee, 2018), and a supervised NLI task for representation learning similar to InferSent (Conneau et al., 2017). To learn cross-lingual representations, we incorporate translation ranking tasks using parallel corpora for the source-target pairs: English-French (en-fr), English-Spanish (en-es), English-German (en-de), and English-Chinese (en-zh).

The resulting model structure is illustrated in Figure 1. We note that the conversational response ranking task can be seen as a special case of Contrastive Predictive Coding (CPC) (van den Oord et al., 2018) that only makes predictions one step into the future.

2.1 Encoder Architecture

Word and Character Embeddings. Our sentence encoder makes use of word and character n-gram embeddings. Word embeddings are learned end-to-end.[2] Character n-gram embeddings are learned in a similar manner and are combined at the word-level by summing their representations and then passing the resulting vector to a single

---

[2]Using pre-trained embeddings, did not improve performance during preliminary experiments.

feedforward layer with $tanh$ activation. We average the word and character embeddings before providing them as input to g.

Transformer Encoder. The architecture of the shared encoder g consists of three stacked transformer sub-networks,[3] each containing the feedforward and multi-head attention sub-layers described in Vaswani et al. (2017). The transformer output is a variable-length sequence. We average encodings of all sequence positions in the final layer to obtain our sentence embeddings. This embedding is then fed into different sets of feedforward layers that are used for each task. For our transformer layers, we use 8 attentions heads, a hidden size of 512, and a filter size of 2048.

2.2 Multi-task Training Setup

We employ four unique task types for each language pair in order to learn a function g that is capable of strong cross-lingual semantic matching and transfer learning performance for a source-target language pair while also maintaining monolingual task transfer performance. Specifically, we employ: *(i) conversational response prediction, (ii) quick thought, (iii) a natural language inference*, and *(iv) translation ranking* as the bridge task. For models trained on a single language pair (e.g., en-fr), six total tasks are used in training, as the first two tasks are mirrored across languages.[4]

Conversational Response Prediction. We model the conversational response prediction task in the same manner as Yang et al. (2018). We minimize the negative log-likelihood of $\widetilde{P}(s_i^R \mid s_i^I)$, where s_i^I is a single comment and s_i^R is its associated response comment. For the response side, we model $g^R(s_i^R)$ as $g(s_i^R)$ followed by two fully-connected feedforward layers of size 320 and 512 with $tanh$ activation. For the input representation, however, we simply let $g^I(s_i^I) = g(s_i^I)$.[5]

Quick Thought. We use a modified version of the Quick Thought task detailed by Logeswaran and Lee (2018). We minimize the sum of the negative log-likelihoods of $\widetilde{P}(s_i^R \mid s_i^I)$ and $\widetilde{P}(s_i^P \mid s_i^I)$,

---

[3] We tried up to six stacked transformers, but did not notice a significant difference beyond three.

[4] We note that our architecture can scale to models trained on > 2 languages. Preliminary experiments using more than two languages achieve promising results, but we consider fully evaluating models trained on larger collections of languages to be outside the scope of the current work.

[5] In early experiments, letting the optimization of the conversational response task more directly influence the parameters of the underlying sentence encoder g led to better downstream task performance.

where s_i^I is a sentence taken from an article and s_i^P and s_i^R are its predecessor and successor sentences, respectively. For this task, we model all three of $g^P(s_i^P)$, $g^I(s_i^I)$, and $g^R(s_i^R)$ by g followed by separate, fully-connected feedforward layers of size 320 and 512 and using $tanh$ activation.

Natural Language Inference (NLI). We also include an *English-only* natural language inference task (Bowman et al., 2015). For this task, we first encode an input sentence s_i^I and its corresponding response hypothesis s_i^R into vectors u_1 and u_2 using g. Following Conneau et al. (2017), the vectors u_1, u_2 are then used to construct a relation feature vector $(u_1, u_2, |u_1 - u_2|, u_1 * u_2)$, where $(\cdot)$ represents concatenation and $*$ represents element-wise multiplication. The relation vector is then fed into a single feedforward layer of size 512 followed by a softmax output layer that is used to perform the 3-way NLI classification.

Translation Ranking. Our translation task setup is identical to the one used by Guo et al. (2018) for bi-text retrieval. We minimize the negative log-likelihood of $\widetilde{P}(s_i \mid t_i)$, where (s_i, t_i) is a source-target translation pair. Since the translation task is intended to align the sentence representations of the source and target languages, we do not use any kind of task-specific feedforward layers and instead use g as both g^I and g^R. Following Guo et al. (2018), we append 5 incorrect translations that are semantically similar to the correct translation for each training example as "hard-negatives". Similarity is determined via a version of our model trained only on the translation ranking task. We did not see additional gains from using more than 5 hard-negatives.

3 Experiments

3.1 Corpora

Training data is composed of Reddit, Wikipedia, Stanford Natural Language Inference (SNLI), and web mined translation pairs. For each of our datasets, we use 90% of the data for training, and the remaining 10% for development/validation.

3.2 Model Configuration

In all of our experiments, multi-task training is performed by cycling through the different tasks (translation pairs, Reddit, Wikipedia, NLI) and performing an optimization step for a single task at a time. We train all of our models with a batch

Model	MR	CR	SUBJ	MPQA	TREC	SST	STS Bench (dev / test)
Cross-lingual Multi-task Models							
en-fr	77.9	82.9	95.5	<u>89.3</u>	95.3	84.0	0.803 / 0.763
en-es	<u>80.1</u>	<u>85.9</u>	94.6	86.5	96.2	<u>85.2</u>	<u>0.809</u> / <u>0.770</u>
en-de	78.8	84.0	**95.9**	87.6	96.1	85.0	0.802 / 0.764
en-zh	76.1	83.4	93.0	86.4	**97.7**	81.4	0.791 / <u>0.770</u>
Translation-ranking Models							
en-fr	68.7	79.3	87.0	81.8	89.4	74.2	0.668 / 0.558
en-es	67.7	75.7	83.5	86.0	94.4	72.6	0.669 / 0.631
en-de	67.8	75.2	84.4	83.6	86.8	74.6	0.673 / 0.632
en-zh	73.6	78.5	88.1	88.2	96.1	77.1	0.779 / 0.761
Prior Work							
CPC (van den Oord et al., 2018)	76.9	80.1	91.2	87.7	<u>96.8</u>	--	--
USE Trans. (Cer et al., 2018)	**81.4**	**87.4**	93.9	87.0	92.5	85.4	**0.814 / 0.782**
QT (Logeswaran and Lee, 2018)	82.4	86.0	<u>94.8</u>	**90.2**	92.4	**87.6**	
InferSent (Conneau et al., 2017)	81.1	86.3	92.4	**90.2**	88.2	84.6	0.801 / 0.758
ST LN (Kiros et al., 2015)	79.4	83.1	93.7	89.3	—	—	

Table 1: Performance on classification transfer tasks from SentEval (Conneau and Kiela, 2018).

size of 100 using stochastic gradient descent with a learning rate of 0.008. All of our models are trained for 30 million steps. All input text is treebank style tokenized prior to being used for training. We build a vocab containing 200 thousand unigram tokens with 10 thousand hash buckets for out-of-vocabulary tokens. The character n-gram vocab contains 200 thousand hash buckets used for 3 and 4 grams. Both the word and character n-gram embedding sizes are 320. All hyperparameters are tuned based on the development portion (random 10% slice) of our training sets. As an additional training heuristic, we multiply the gradient updates to the word and character embeddings by a factor of 100.[6] We found that using this embedding gradient multiplier alleviates vanishing gradients and greatly improves training.

We compare the proposed cross-lingual multi-task models, subsequently referred to simply as "multi-task", with baseline models that are trained using only the translation ranking task, referred to as "translation-ranking" models.

3.3 Model Performance on English Downstream Tasks

We first evaluate all of our cross-lingual models on several downstream English tasks taken from SentEval (Conneau and Kiela, 2018) to verify the impact of cross-lingual training. Evaluations are performed by training single hidden-layer feedforward networks on top of the 512-dimensional em-

beddings taken from the frozen models. Results on the tasks are summarized in Table 1. We note that cross-lingual training does not hinder the effectiveness of our encoder on English tasks, as the multi-task models are close to state-of-the-art in each of the downstream tasks. For the Text REtrieval Conference (TREC) eval, we actually find that our multi-task models outperform the previous state-of-the-art by a sizable amount.

We observe the en-zh translation-ranking models perform significantly better on the downstream tasks than the European language pair translation-ranking models. The en-zh models are possibly less capable of exploiting grammatical and other superficial similarities and are forced to rely on semantic representations. Exploring this further may present a promising direction for future research.

3.4 Cross-lingual Retrieval

We evaluate both the multi-task and translation-ranking models' efficacy in performing cross-lingual retrieval by using held-out translation pair data. Following Guo et al. (2018) and Henderson et al. (2017), we use precision at N (P@N) as our evaluation metric. Performance is scored by checking if a source sentence's target translation ranks[7] in the top N scored candidates when considering K other randomly selected target sentences. We set K to 999. Similar to Guo et al. (2018), we observe using a small value of K, such as $K = 99$ from Henderson et al. (2017), results

---

[6] We tried different orders of magnitude for the multiplier and found 100 to work the best.

[7] Translation ranking scores are obtained by the dot product of source and target representations

Model	STS Benchmark (dev / test)				
	en	fr	es	de	zh
Multi-task en-fr	0.803 / 0.763	**0.777 / 0.738**	–	–	–
Trans.-ranking en-fr	0.668 / 0.558	0.641 / 0.579	–	–	–
Multi-task en-es	**0.809 / 0.770**	–	**0.779 / 0.744**	–	–
Trans.-ranking en-es	0.669 / 0.631	–	0.622 / 0.611	–	–
Multi-task en-de	0.802 / 0.764	–	–	**0.768 / 0.722**	–
Trans.-ranking en-de	0.673 / 0.632	–	–	0.630 / 0.526	–
Multi-task en-zh	0.791 / **0.770**	–	–	–	0.730 / **0.705**
Trans.-ranking en-zh	0.779 / 0.761	–	–	–	**0.733** / 0.701

Table 2: Pearson's correlation coefficients on STS Benchmark (dev / test). The first column shows the results on the original STS Benchmark data in English. French, Spanish

in all metrics quickly obtaining $> 99\%$ P@1.[8]

The translation-ranking model is a strong baseline for identifying correct translations, with 95.4%, 87.5%, 97.5%, and 99.7% P@1 for en-fr, en-es, en-de, and en-zh retrieval tasks, respectively. The multi-task model performs almost identical with 95.1%, 88.8%, 97.8%, and 99.7% P@1, which provides empirical justification that it is possible to maintain cross-lingual embedding space alignment despite training on additional monolingual tasks for each individual language.[9] Both model types surprisingly achieve particularly strong ranking performance on en-zh. Similar to the task transfer experiments, this may be due to the en-zh models having an implicit inductive bias to rely more heavily on semantics rather than more superficial aspects of sentence pair similarity.

3.5 Multilingual STS

Cross-lingual representations are evaluated on semantic textual similarity (STS) in French, Spanish, German, and Chinese. To evaluate Spanish-Spanish (es-es) STS, we use data from track 3 of the SemEval-2017 STS shared task (Cer et al., 2017), containing 250 Spanish sentence pairs. We evaluate English-Spanish (en-es) STS using STS 2017 track 4(a),[10] which contains 250 English-Spanish sentence pairs.

Beyond English and Spanish, however, there are no standard STS datasets available for the other languages explored in this work. As such, we perform an additional evaluation on a translated version of the STS Benchmark (Cer et al., 2017) for French, Spanish, German, and Chinese. We use Google's translation system to translate the STS Benchmark sentences into each of these languages. We believe the results on the translated STS Benchmark evaluation sets are a reasonable indicator of multilingual semantic similarly performance, particularly since the NMT encoder-decoder architecture for translation differs significantly from our dual-encoder approach.

Following Cer et al. (2018), we first compute the sentence embeddings u, v for an STS sentence pair, and then score the sentence pair similarity based on the angular distance between the two embedding vectors, $- \arccos\left(\frac{uv}{||u||\,||v||}\right)$. Table 2 shows Pearson's r on the STS Benchmark for all models. The first column shows the trained model performance on the original English STS Benchmark. Columns 2 to 5 provide the performance on the remaining languages. Multi-task models perform better than the translation ranking models on our multilingual STS Benchmark evaluation sets. Table 3 provides the results from the en-es models on the SemEval-2017 STS *-es tracks. The multi-task models achieve 0.827 Pearson's r for the es-es task and 0.769 for the en-es task. As a point of reference, we also list the two best performing STS systems, ECNU (Tian et al., 2017) and BIT (Wu et al., 2017), as reported in Cer et al. (2017). Our results are very close to these state-of-the-art feature engineered and mixed systems.

---

[8]999 is smaller than the 10+ million used by Guo et al. (2018), but it allows for good discrimination between models without requiring a heavier and slower evaluation framework

[9]We also experimented with P@3 and P@10, the results are identical.

[10]The en-es task is split into track 4(a) and track 4(b). We only use track 4(a) here. Track 4(b) contains sentence pairs from WMT with only one annotator for each pair. Previously reported numbers are particularly low for track 4(b), which may suggest either distributional or annotation differences between this track and other STS datasets.

Model	STS (SemEval 2017)	
	es-es	**en-es**
Multi-task	<u>0.827</u>	<u>0.769</u>
Trans.-ranking	0.642	0.587
ECNU	**0.856**	**0.813**
BIT	0.846	0.749

Table 3: Pearson's r on track 3 (es-es) and track 4(a) (en-es) of the SemEval-2017 STS shared task.

4 Zero-shot Classification

To evaluate the cross-lingual transfer learning capabilities of our models, we examine performance of the multi-task and translation-ranking encoders on zero-shot and few-shot classification tasks.

4.1 Multilingual NLI

We evaluate the zero-shot classification performance of our multi-task models on two multilingual natural language inference (NLI) tasks. However, prior to doing so, we first train a modified version[11] of our multi-task models that also includes training on the English Multi-genre NLI (MultiNLI) dataset of Williams et al. (2018) in addition to SNLI. We train with MultiNLI to be consistent with the baselines from prior work.

We make use of the professionally translated French and Spanish SNLI subset created by Agić and Schluter (2018) for an initial cross-lingual zero-shot evaluation of French and Spanish. We refer to these translated subsets as SNLI-X. There are 1,000 examples in the subset for each language. To evaluate, we feed the French and Spanish examples into the pre-trained English NLI subnetwork of our multi-task models.

We additionally make use of the XNLI dataset of Conneau et al. (2018), which provides multilingual NLI evaluations for Spanish, French, German, Chinese and more. There are 5,000 examples in each XNLI test set, and zero-shot evaluation is once again done by feeding non-English examples into the pre-trained English NLI sub-network.

Table 4 lists the accuracy on the English SNLI test set as well as on SNLI-X and XNLI for all of our multi-task models. The original English SNLI accuracies are around 84% for all of our multi-task models, indicating that English SNLI performance remains stable in the multi-task training setting.

The zero-shot accuracy on SNLI-X is around 74% for both the en-fr and en-es models. The zero-shot accuracy on XNLI is around 65% for en-es, en-fr, and en-de, and around 63% for en-zh, thereby significantly outperforming the pretrained sentence encoding baselines (X-CBOW) described in Conneau et al. (2018). The X-CBOW baselines use fixed sentence encoders that are the result of averaging tuned multilingual word embeddings.

Row 4 of Table 4 shows the zero-shot French NLI performance of Eriguchi et al. (2018), which is a state-of-the-art zero-shot NLI classifier based on multilingual NMT embeddings. Our multi-task model shows comparable performance to the NMT-based model in both English and French.

4.2 Amazon Reviews

Zero-shot Learning. We also conduct a zero-shot evaluation based on the Amazon review data extracted by Prettenhofer and Stein (2010). Following Prettenhofer and Stein (2010), we preprocess the Amazon reviews and convert the data into a binary sentiment classification task by considering reviews with strictly more than three stars as positive and less than three stars as negative. Reviews contain a summary field and a text field, which we concatenate to produce a single input. Since our models are trained with sentence lengths clipped to 64, we only take the first 64 tokens from the concatenated text as the input. There are 6,000 training reviews in English, which we split into 90% for training and 10% for development.

We first encode inputs using the pre-trained multi-task and translation-ranking encoders and feed the encoded vectors into a 2-layer feedforward network culminating in a softmax layer. We use hidden layers of size 512 with $tanh$ activation functions. We use Adam for optimization with an initial learning rate of 0.0005 and a learning rate decay of 0.9 at every epoch during training. We use a batch size of 16 and train for 20 total epochs in all experiments. We freeze the cross-lingual encoder during training. The model architecture and parameters are tuned on the development set.

We first train the classifier on English data, and then evaluate it on the 6,000 French and German Amazon review test examples. The results are summarized in Table 5. On the English test set, accuracy of the en-fr model is 87.4% with the en-de model achieving 87.1%. Both mod-

---

[11]Training with additional MultiNLI data did not significantly impact SNLI or downstream task performance.

Model	SNLI-X			XNLI				
	en	fr	es	en	fr	es	de	zh
Multi-task en-fr	84.2	**74.0**	–	**71.6**	**64.4**	–	–	–
Multi-task en-es	83.9	–	75.9	70.2	–	65.2	–	–
Multi-task en-de	84.1	–	–	71.5	–	–	65.0	–
Multi-task en-zh	83.7	–	–	69.2	–	–	–	62.8
NMT en-fr (Eriguchi et al., 2018)	**84.4**	73.9	–		–	–	–	–
XNLI-CBOW zero-shot (Conneau et al., 2018)	–	–	–	64.5	60.3	60.7	61.0	58.8
Non zero-shot baselines								
XNLI-BiLSTM-last (Conneau et al., 2018)	–	–	–	71.0	65.2	67.8	66.6	63.7
XNLI-BiLSTM-max (Conneau et al., 2018)	–	–	–	**73.7**	**67.7**	**68.7**	**67.7**	**65.8**

Table 4: Zero-shot classification accuracy (%) on SNLI-X and XNLI datasets. Cross-lingual transfer models are training on English only NLI data and then evaluated on French (fr), Spanish (es), German (de) and Chinese (zh) evaluation sets.

Model	en	fr	de
Multi-task en-fr	**87.4**	**82.3**	–
Translation-ranking en-fr	74.4	66.3	–
Multi-task en-de	**87.1**	–	**81.0**
Translation-ranking en-de	73.8	–	67.0
Eriguchi et al. (2018) (NMT en-fr)	83.2	81.3	–

Table 5: Zero-shot sentiment classification accuracy(%) on non-English Amazon review test data after training on English only Amazon reviews.

els achieve zero-shot accuracy on their respective non-English datasets that is above 80%. The translation-ranking models again perform worse on all metrics. Once again we compare the proposed model with Eriguchi et al. (2018), and find that our zero-shot performance has a reasonable gain on the French test set.[12]

Few-shot Learning. We further evaluate the proposed multi-task models via few-shot learning, by training on English reviews and only a portion of French and German reviews. Our few-shot models are compared with baselines trained on French and German reviews only. Table 6 provides the classification accuracy of the few-shot models, where the second row indicates the percent of French and German data that is used when training each model. With as little as 20% of the French or German training data, the few-shot models perform nearly as well compare to the baseline models trained on 100% of the French and German data. Adding more French and German training data leads to further improvements in few-

shot model performance, with the few-shot models reaching 85.8% accuracy in French and 84.5% accuracy in German, when using all of the French and German data. The French model notably performs +0.9% better when being trained on a combination of the English and French reviews rather than on the French reviews alone.

5 Analysis of Cross-lingual Embedding Spaces

Motivated by the recent work of Søgaard et al. (2018) studying the graph structure of multilingual word representations, we perform a similar analysis for our learned cross-lingual sentence representations. We take N samples of size K from the language pair translation data and then encode these samples using the corresponding multi-task and translation-ranking models. We then compute pairwise distance matrices within each sampled set of encodings, and use these distance matrices to construct graph Laplacians.[13] We obtain the similarity $\Psi(S, T)$ between each model's source and target language embedding by comparing the eigenvalues of the source language graph Laplacians to the eigenvalues of the target language graph Laplacians:

$$\Psi(S, T) = \frac{1}{N} \sum_{i=1}^{N} \sum_{j=1}^{K} (\lambda_j(L_i^{(s)}) - \lambda_j(L_i^{(t)}))^2 \quad (3)$$

Where $L_i^{(s)}$ and $L_i^{(t)}$ refer to the graph Laplacians of the source language and target language sentences obtained from the ith sample of

---

[12]Eriguchi et al. (2018) also train a shallow classifier, but use only review text and truncate their inputs to 200 tokens. Our setup is slightly different, as our models can take a maximum of only 64 tokens.

[13]See Zhang (2011) for an overview of graph Laplacians.

Target Language	Model		0%	10%	20%	40%	80%	100%
		% available fr/de data						
French	Few-shot	100% en + X% fr	82.3	**84.4**	**84.4**	**84.8**	**85.2**	**85.8**
	Monolingual	0% en + X% fr	–	79.2	80.0	82.7	84.3	84.9
German	Few-shot	100% en + X% de	81.0	**81.6**	**83.3**	**84.0**	**84.7**	**84.5**
	Monolingual	0% en + X% de	–	75.5	77.7	81.6	83.5	84.4

Table 6: Sentiment classification accuracy(%) on target language Amazon review test data after training on English Amazon review data and a portion of French of German data. The second row shows the percent of French (fr) or German (de) data is used for training in each model.

source-target translation pairs. A smaller value of $\Psi(S, T)$ indicates higher eigen-similarity between the source language and target language embedding subsets. Following Søgaard et al. (2018) we use a sample size of $K = 10$ translation pairs, but we choose to draw $N = 1,000$ samples instead of $N = 10$, as was done in Søgaard et al. (2018). We found $\Psi(S, T)$ has very high variance at $N = 10$. The computed values of $\Psi(S, T)$ for our multi-task and translation-ranking models are summarized in Table 7.

We find that the source and target embedding subsets constructed from the multi-task models exhibit greater average eigen-similarity than those resulting from the translation-ranking models for the European source-target language pairs, and observe the opposite for the English-Chinese models (en-zh). As a curious discrepancy, we believe further experiments looking at eigen-similarity across languages could yield interesting results and language groupings.

Eigen-similarity trends with better performance for the European language pair multi-task models on the cross-lingual transfer tasks. A potential direction for future work could be to introduce regularization penalties based on graph similarity during multi-task training. Interestingly, we also observe that the eigen-similarity gaps between the multi-task and translation-ranking models are not uniform across language pairs. Thus, another direction could be to further study differences in the difficulty of aligning different source-target language embeddings.

5.1 Discussion on Input Representations

Our early explorations using a combination of character n-gram embeddings and word embeddings vs. word embeddings alone as the model input representation suggest using word-embeddings only performs just slightly worse (one

Model	en-fr	en-es	en-de	en-zh
multi-task	**0.592**	**0.526**	**0.761**	2.366
trans.-ranking	1.036	0.572	2.187	**0.393**

Table 7: Average eigen-similarity values of source and target embedding subsets.

to two absolute percentage points) on the dev sets for the training tasks. The notable exception is the word-embedding only English-German models tend to perform much worse on the dev sets for the training tasks involving German. This is likely due to the prevalence of compound words in German and represents an interesting difference for future exploration.

We subsequently explored training versions of our cross-lingual models using a SentencePiece vocabulary (Kudo and Richardson, 2018), a set of largely sub-word tokens (characters and word chunks) that provide good coverage of an input dataset. Multilingual models for a single language pair (e.g., en-de) trained with SentencePiece performed similarly on the training dev sets to the models using character n-grams. However, when more languages are included in a single model (e.g., a single model that covers en, fr, de, es, and zh), SentencePiece tends to perform worse than using a combination of word and character n-gram embeddings. Within a larger joint model, SentencePiece is particularly problematic for languages like zh, which end up getting largely tokenized into individual characters.

6 Conclusion

Cross-lingual multi-task dual-encoder models are found to learn representations that achieve strong within language and cross-lingual transfer learning performance. By training English-French, English-Spanish, English-German, and English-

Chinese multi-task models, we achieve near-state-of-the-art or state-of-the-art performance on a variety of English tasks, while also being able to produce similar caliber results in zero-shot cross-lingual transfer learning tasks. Further, cross-lingual multi-task training is shown to improve performance on some downstream English tasks (TREC). We believe that there are many possibilities for future explorations of cross-lingual model training and that such models will be foundational as language processing systems are tasked with increasing amounts of multilingual data.

Acknowledgments

We thank the anonymous reviewers and our teammates from Descartes and other Google groups for their feedback and suggestions.

References

Željko Agić and Natalie Schluter. 2018. Baselines and test data for cross-lingual inference. In *Proceedings of the 11th Language Resources and Evaluation Conference*, Miyazaki, Japan. European Language Resource Association.

Samuel R. Bowman, Gabor Angeli, Christopher Potts, and Christopher D. Manning. 2015. A large annotated corpus for learning natural language inference. In *Proceedings of the 2015 Conference on Empirical Methods in Natural Language Processing*, pages 632–642. Association for Computational Linguistics.

Daniel Cer, Mona Diab, Eneko Agirre, Inigo Lopez-Gazpio, and Lucia Specia. 2017. Semeval-2017 task 1: Semantic textual similarity multilingual and crosslingual focused evaluation. In *Proceedings of the 11th International Workshop on Semantic Evaluation (SemEval-2017)*, pages 1–14, Vancouver, Canada. Association for Computational Linguistics.

Daniel Cer, Yinfei Yang, Sheng-yi Kong, Nan Hua, Nicole Limtiaco, Rhomni St. John, Noah Constant, Mario Guajardo-Cespedes, Steve Yuan, Chris Tar, Brian Strope, and Ray Kurzweil. 2018. Universal sentence encoder for English. In *Proceedings of the 2018 Conference on Empirical Methods in Natural Language Processing: System Demonstrations*, pages 169–174, Brussels, Belgium. Association for Computational Linguistics.

Alexis Conneau and Douwe Kiela. 2018. SentEval: An evaluation toolkit for universal sentence representations. In *Proceedings of the 11th Language Resources and Evaluation Conference*, Miyazaki, Japan. European Language Resource Association.

Alexis Conneau, Douwe Kiela, Holger Schwenk, Loïc Barrault, and Antoine Bordes. 2017. Supervised learning of universal sentence representations from natural language inference data. In *Proceedings of the 2017 Conference on Empirical Methods in Natural Language Processing*, pages 670–680. Association for Computational Linguistics.

Alexis Conneau, Ruty Rinott, Guillaume Lample, Adina Williams, Samuel Bowman, Holger Schwenk, and Veselin Stoyanov. 2018. XNLI: Evaluating cross-lingual sentence representations. In *Proceedings of the 2018 Conference on Empirical Methods in Natural Language Processing*, pages 2475–2485, Brussels, Belgium. Association for Computational Linguistics.

Akiko Eriguchi, Melvin Johnson, Orhan Firat, Hideto Kazawa, and Wolfgang Macherey. 2018. Zero-shot cross-lingual classification using multilingual neural machine translation. *CoRR*, abs/1809.04686.

Stephan Gouws, Yoshua Bengio, and Greg Corrado. 2015. Bilbowa: Fast bilingual distributed representations without word alignments. In *Proceedings of the 32Nd International Conference on International Conference on Machine Learning - Volume 37*, ICML'15, pages 748–756. JMLR.org.

Mandy Guo, Qinlan Shen, Yinfei Yang, Heming Ge, Daniel Cer, Gustavo Hernandez Abrego, Keith Stevens, Noah Constant, Yun-Hsuan Sung, Brian Strope, and Ray Kurzweil. 2018. Effective parallel corpus mining using bilingual sentence embeddings. In *Proceedings of the Third Conference on Machine Translation: Research Papers*, pages 165–176, Belgium, Brussels. Association for Computational Linguistics.

Matthew Henderson, Rami Al-Rfou, Brian Strope, Yun-Hsuan Sung, László Lukács, Ruiqi Guo, Sanjiv Kumar, Balint Miklos, and Ray Kurzweil. 2017. Efficient natural language response suggestion for smart reply. *CoRR*, abs/1705.00652.

Ryan Kiros, Yukun Zhu, Ruslan Salakhutdinov, Richard S. Zemel, Antonio Torralba, Raquel Urtasun, and Sanja Fidler. 2015. Skip-thought vectors. In *Proceedings of the 28th International Conference on Neural Information Processing Systems - Volume 2*, NIPS'15, pages 3294–3302, Cambridge, MA, USA. MIT Press.

Taku Kudo and John Richardson. 2018. Sentence-Piece: A simple and language independent subword tokenizer and detokenizer for neural text processing. In *Proceedings of the 2018 Conference on Empirical Methods in Natural Language Processing: System Demonstrations*, pages 66–71, Brussels, Belgium. Association for Computational Linguistics.

Lajanugen Logeswaran and Honglak Lee. 2018. An efficient framework for learning sentence representations. In *International Conference on Learning Representations*.

Aäron van den Oord, Yazhe Li, and Oriol Vinyals. 2018. Representation learning with contrastive predictive coding. *CoRR*, abs/1807.03748.

Peter Prettenhofer and Benno Stein. 2010. Cross-Language Text Classification using Structural Correspondence Learning. In *48th Annual Meeting of the Association of Computational Linguistics (ACL 10)*, pages 1118–1127. Association for Computational Linguistics.

Holger Schwenk and Matthijs Douze. 2017. Learning joint multilingual sentence representations with neural machine translation. In *Proceedings of the 2nd Workshop on Representation Learning for NLP*, pages 157–167, Vancouver, Canada. Association for Computational Linguistics.

Karan Singla, Dogan Can, and Shrikanth Narayanan. 2018. A multi-task approach to learning multilingual representations. In *Proceedings of the 56th Annual Meeting of the Association for Computational Linguistics (Volume 2: Short Papers)*, pages 214–220. Association for Computational Linguistics.

Anders Søgaard, Sebastian Ruder, and Ivan Vulić. 2018. On the limitations of unsupervised bilingual dictionary induction. In *Proceedings of the 56th Annual Meeting of the Association for Computational Linguistics (Volume 1: Long Papers)*, pages 778–788, Melbourne, Australia. Association for Computational Linguistics.

Sandeep Subramanian, Adam Trischler, Yoshua Bengio, and Christopher J Pal. 2018. Learning general purpose distributed sentence representations via large scale multi-task learning. In *International Conference on Learning Representations*.

Junfeng Tian, Zhiheng Zhou, Man Lan, and Yuanbin Wu. 2017. ECNU at SemEval-2017 task 1: Leverage kernel-based traditional NLP features and neural networks to build a universal model for multilingual and cross-lingual semantic textual similarity. In *Proceedings of the 11th International Workshop on Semantic Evaluation (SemEval-2017)*, pages 191–197, Vancouver, Canada. Association for Computational Linguistics.

Ashish Vaswani, Noam Shazeer, Niki Parmar, Jakob Uszkoreit, Llion Jones, Aidan N Gomez, Ł ukasz Kaiser, and Illia Polosukhin. 2017. Attention is all you need. In I. Guyon, U. V. Luxburg, S. Bengio, H. Wallach, R. Fergus, S. Vishwanathan, and R. Garnett, editors, *Advances in Neural Information Processing Systems 30*, pages 5998–6008. Curran Associates, Inc.

Adina Williams, Nikita Nangia, and Samuel Bowman. 2018. A broad-coverage challenge corpus for sentence understanding through inference. In *Proceedings of the 2018 Conference of the North American Chapter of the Association for Computational Linguistics: Human Language Technologies, Volume 1 (Long Papers)*, pages 1112–1122. Association for Computational Linguistics.

Hao Wu, Heyan Huang, Ping Jian, Yuhang Guo, and Chao Su. 2017. BIT at SemEval-2017 task 1: Using semantic information space to evaluate semantic textual similarity. In *Proceedings of the 11th International Workshop on Semantic Evaluation (SemEval-2017)*, pages 77–84, Vancouver, Canada. Association for Computational Linguistics.

Yinfei Yang, Gustavo Hernández Ábrego, Steve Yuan, Mandy Guo, Qinlan Shen, Daniel Cer, Yun-Hsuan Sung, Brian Strope, and Ray Kurzweil. 2019. Improving multilingual sentence embedding using bi-directional dual encoder with additive margin softmax. In *Proceedings International Joint Conference on Artificial Intelligence (IJCAI)*.

Yinfei Yang, Steve Yuan, Daniel Cer, Sheng-Yi Kong, Noah Constant, Petr Pilar, Heming Ge, Yun-hsuan Sung, Brian Strope, and Ray Kurzweil. 2018. Learning semantic textual similarity from conversations. In *Proceedings of The Third Workshop on Representation Learning for NLP*, pages 164–174. Association for Computational Linguistics.

X.-D. Zhang. 2011. The Laplacian eigenvalues of graphs: a survey. *CoRR*, abs/1111.2897.

Modality-based Factorization for Multimodal Fusion

Elham J. Barezi, Pascale Fung
Center for Artificial Intelligence Research (CAiRE)
Department of Computer Science and Engineering
The Hong Kong University of Science and Technology, Clear Water Bay, Hong Kong
`ejs@cse.ust.hk,pascale@ust.hk`

Abstract

We propose a novel method, Modality-based Redundancy Reduction Fusion (MRRF), for understanding and modulating the relative contribution of each modality in multimodal inference tasks. This is achieved by obtaining an $(M+1)$-way tensor to consider the high-order relationships between M modalities and the output layer of a neural network model. Applying a modality-based tensor factorization method, which adopts different factors for different modalities, results in removing information present in a modality that can be compensated by other modalities, with respect to model outputs. This helps to understand the relative utility of information in each modality. In addition it leads to a less complicated model with less parameters and therefore could be applied as a regularizer avoiding overfitting. We have applied this method to three different multimodal datasets in sentiment analysis, personality trait recognition, and emotion recognition. We are able to recognize relationships and relative importance of different modalities in these tasks and achieves a 1% to 4% improvement on several evaluation measures compared to the state-of-the-art for all three tasks.

1 Introduction

Multimodal data fusion is a desirable method for many machine learning tasks where information is available from multiple source modalities, typically achieving better predictions through integration of information from different modalities. Multimodal integration can handle missing data from one or more modalities. Since some modalities can include noise, it can also lead to more robust prediction. Moreover, since some information may not be visible in some modalities or a single modality may not be powerful enough for a specific task, considering multiple modalities often improves perfor-

mance (Potamianos et al., 2003; Soleymani et al., 2012; Kampman et al., 2018).

For example, humans assign personality traits to each other, as well as to virtual characters by inferring personality from diverse cues, both behavioral and verbal, suggesting that a model to predict personality should take into account multiple modalities such as language, speech, and visual cues.

Our method, Modality-based Redundancy Reduction multimodal Fusion (MRRF), builds on recent work in mutimodal fusion utilizing first an outer product tensor of input modalities to better capture inter-modality dependencies (Zadeh et al., 2017) and a recent approach to reduce the number of elements in the resulting tensor through low rank factorization (Liu et al., 2018). Whereas the factorization used in (Liu et al., 2018) utilizes a single compression rate across all modalities, we instead use Tuckers tensor decomposition (see the Methodology section), which allows different compression rates for each modality. This allows the model to adapt to variations in the amount of useful information between modalities. Modality-specific factors are chosen by maximizing performance on a validation set.

Applying a modality-based factorization method results in removing redundant information duplicated across modalities and leading to fewer parameters with minimal information loss. Through maximizing performance on a validation set, our method can work as a regularizer, leading to a less complicated model and reducing overfitting. In addition, our modality-based factorization approach helps to understand the differences in useful information between modalities for the task at hand.

We evaluate the performance of our approach using sentiment analysis, personality detection, and emotion recognition from audio, text and video frames. The method reduces the number of pa-

Proceedings of the 4th Workshop on Representation Learning for NLP (RepL4NLP-2019), pages 260–269
Florence, Italy, August 2, 2019. ©2019 Association for Computational Linguistics

rameters which requires fewer training samples, providing efficient training for the smaller datasets, and accelerating both training and prediction. Our experimental results demonstrate that the proposed approach can make notable improvements, in terms of accuracy, mean average error (MAE), correlation, and F_1 score, especially for the applications with more complicated inter-modality relations.

We further study the effect of different compression rates for different modalities. Our results on the importance of each modality for each task supports the previous results on the usefulness of each modality for personality recognition, emotion recognition and sentiment analysis.

In the sequel, we first describe related work. We elaborate on the details of our proposed method in Methodology section. In the following section we go on to describe our experimental setup. In the Results section, we compare the performance of MRRF and state-of-the-art baselines on three different datasets and discuss the effect of compression rate on each modality. Finally, we provide a brief conclusion of the approach and the results. Supplementary materials describe the methodology in greater detail.

Notation The operator $\otimes$ is the outer product operator where $z_1 \otimes \ldots \otimes z_M$ for $z_i \in \mathbb{R}^{d_i}$ leads to a M-way tensor in $\mathbb{R}^{d_1 \times \ldots \times d_M}$. The operator $\times_k$, for a given k, is k-mode product of a tensor $R \in \mathbb{R}^{r_1 \times r_2 \times \ldots \times r_M}$ and a matrix $W \in \mathbb{R}^{d_k \times r_k}$ as $W \times_k R$, which results in a tensor $\bar{R} \in \mathbb{R}^{r_1 \times \ldots \times r_{k-1} \times d_k \times r_{k+1} \times \ldots \times r_M}$.

2   Related Work

Multimodal Fusion: Multimodal fusion (Ngiam et al., 2011) has a very broad range of applications, including audio-visual speech recognition (Potamianos et al., 2003), classification of images and their captions (Srivastava and Salakhutdinov, 2012), multimodal emotion recognition (Soleymani et al., 2012), medical image analysis (James and Dasarathy, 2014), multimedia event detection (Lan et al., 2014), personality trait detection (Kampman et al., 2018), and sentiment analysis (Zadeh et al., 2017).

According to the recent work by (Baltrušaitis et al., 2018), the techniques for multimodal fusion can be divided into early, late and hybrid approaches. Early approaches combine the multimodal features immediately by simply concatenating them (D'mello and Kory, 2015). Late fusion

combines the decision for each modality (either classification, or regression), by voting (Morvant et al., 2014), averaging (Shutova et al., 2016) or weighted sum of the outputs of the learned models (Glodek et al., 2011; Shutova et al., 2016). The hybrid approach combines the prediction by early fusion and unimodal predictions.

It has been observed that early fusion (feature level fusion) concentrates on the inter-modality information rather than intra-modality information (Zadeh et al., 2017) due to the fact that inter-modality information can be more complicated at the feature level and dominates the learning process. On the other hand, these fusion approaches are not powerful enough to extract the inter-modality integration model and they are limited to some simple combining methods (Zadeh et al., 2017).

Zadeh et al. (2017) proposed combining n modalities by computing an n-way tensor as a tensor product of the n different modality representations followed by a flattening operation, in order to include 1-st order to n-th order inter modality relations. This is then fed to a neural network model to make predictions. The authors show that their proposed method improves the accuracy by considering both inter-modality and intra-modality relations. However, the generated representation has a very large dimension which leads to a very large hidden layer and therefore a huge number of parameters.

The authors of (Poria et al., 2017a,b; Zadeh et al., 2018a,b) introduce attention mechanisms utilizing the contextual information available from the utterances for each speaker. They require additional information like the identity of the speaker, the sequence of the utterance-sentiments while integrating the multimodal data. Since these methods, despite our proposed method, need additional information might not be available in the general scenario, we do not include them in our experiments.

Low Rank Factorization: Recently (Liu et al., 2018) proposed a factorization approach in order to achieve a factorized version of the weight matrix which leads to fewer parameters while maintaining model accuracy. They use a CAN-DECOMP/PARAFAC decomposition (Carroll and Chang, 1970; Harshman, 1970) which follows Eq. 1 in order to decompose a tensor $W \in \mathbb{R}^{d_1 \times \ldots d_M}$

to several 1-dimensional vectors $w_m^i \in \mathbb{R}^{d_k}$:

$$
\begin{aligned}
W &= \sum_{i=1}^{r} \lambda_i w_1^i \otimes w_2^i \otimes \ldots \otimes w_M^i \\
&= \sum_{i=1}^{r} \lambda_i \otimes_{m=1}^{M} w_m^i
\end{aligned}
\tag{1}
$$

where $\otimes$ is the outer product operator, $\lambda_i s$ are scalar weights to combine rank 1 decompositions. This approach used the same compression rate for all modalities, i.e. r is shared for all the modalities, and is not able to allow for varying compression rates between modalities. Previous studies have found that some modalities are more informative than others (De Silva et al., 1997; Kampman et al., 2018), suggesting that allowing different compression rates for different modalities should improve performance.

3 Methodology

3.1 Tucker Factorization for Multimodal Learning

Modality-based Redundancy Reduc- tion Fusion (MRRF): We have used Tucker's tensor decomposition method (Tucker, 1966; Hitchcock, 1927) which decomposes an M-way tensor $W \in \mathbb{R}^{d_1 \times d_2 \times \ldots \times d_M}$ to a core tensor $R \in \mathbb{R}^{r_1 \times r_2 \times \ldots \times r_M}$ and M matrices $W_i \in \mathbb{R}^{r_i \times d_i}$, with $r_i \leq d_i$, as it can be seen in Eq. 2.

$$
\begin{aligned}
W &= R \times_1 W_1 \times_2 W_2 \times_3 \ldots \times_M W_M, \\
W &\in \mathbb{R}^{d_1 \times d_2 \times \ldots \times d_M} \\
R &\in \mathbb{R}^{r_1 \times r_2 \times \ldots \times r_M}, \\
W_i &\in \mathbb{R}^{d_i \times r_i}
\end{aligned}
\tag{2}
$$

The operator $\times_k$ is a k-mode product of a tensor $R \in \mathbb{R}^{r_1 \times r_2 \times \ldots \times r_M}$ and a matrix $W \in \mathbb{R}^{d_k \times r_k}$ as $R \times_k W_k$, which results in a tensor $\bar{R} \in \mathbb{R}^{r_1 \times \ldots \times r_{k-1} \times d_k \times r_{k+1} \times \ldots \times r_M}$.

For M modalities with representations D_1, D_2, $\ldots$ and D_M of size d_1, d_2, $\ldots$ and d_M, an M-modal tensor fusion approach as proposed by the authors of (Zadeh et al., 2017) leads to a tensor $D = D_1 \otimes D_2 \otimes \ldots \otimes D_m \in \mathbb{R}^{d_1 \times d_2 \times \ldots \times d_M}$. The authors proposed flattening the tensor layer in the deep network which results in loss of the information included in the tensor structure. In this paper, we propose to avoid the flattening and follow Eq. 3 with weight tensor $W \in \mathbb{R}^{h \times d_1 \times d_2 \times \ldots \times d_M}$, where leads to an output layer H of size h.

$$
H = WD
\tag{3}
$$

The above equation suffers from a large number of parameters ($O(\prod_{i=1} d_i h)$) which requires a large number of the training samples, huge time and space, and easily overfits. In order to reduce the number of parameters, we propose to use Tucker's tensor decomposition (Tucker, 1966; Hitchcock, 1927) as shown in Eq. 4, which works as a low-rank regularizer (Fazel, 2002).

$$
\begin{aligned}
W &= R \times_1 W_1 \times_2 W_2 \times_3 \ldots \times_{M+1} W_{M+1}, \\
W &\in \mathbb{R}^{h \times d_1 \times d_2 \times \ldots d_M}, \\
R &\in \mathbb{R}^{r_1 \times r_2 \times r_3 \times \ldots \times r_M}, \\
W_i &\in \mathbb{R}^{r_i \times d_i}, \; i = \{1, \ldots, M\}, \\
W_{M+1} &\in \mathbb{R}^{r_{M+1} \times h}
\end{aligned}
\tag{4}
$$

The non-diagonal core tensor R maintain inter-modality information after compression, despite the factorization proposed by (Liu et al., 2018) which loses part of inter-modality information.

3.2 Proposed MRRF framework

We propose Modality-based Redundancy Reduction Fusion (MRRF), a tensor fusion and factorization method allowing for modality specific compression rates, combining the power of tensor fusion methods with a reduced parameter complexity. Without loss of generality, we will consider the number of modalities to be 3 in this discussion.

Our method first forms an outer product tensor from input modalities D, then projects this via a tensor W to a feature vector H passed as input to a neural network which performs the desired inference task.

$$
H = WD
\tag{5}
$$

The trainable projection tensor W represents a large number of parameters, and in order to reduce this number, we propose to use Tucker's tensor decomposition (Tucker, 1966; Hitchcock, 1927), which works as a low-rank regularizer (Fazel, 2002). This results in a decomposition of W into a core tensor R of reduced dimensionality and three modality specific matrices W_i.

$$
W = R \times_1 W_1 \times_2 W_2 \times_3 W_3
\tag{6}
$$

where $\times_k$ is a k-mode product of a tensor and a matrix. Equation 5 can then be re-written

$$
\begin{aligned}
Z &= W_1 \times_1 W_2 \times_2 W_3 \times_3 D \\
H &= ZR
\end{aligned}
\tag{7}
$$

See Figure 1 for an overview of this process for the case of three separate channels for audio, text, and video. In practice we flatten tensors Z and R to reduce this last operation to a matrix multiplication. Further details of the decomposition strategy can be found in the supplementary materials.

Note that a simple outer product of the input features leads only to the high-order trimodal dependencies. In order to also obtain the unimodal and bimodal dependencies, the input feature vectors for each modality are padded by 1. This also provides a constant element whose corresponding factors in W act as a bias vector.

Algorithm 1 shows the whole MRRF process.

Algorithm 1 Tensor Factorization Layer.

Input: n input modalities $D_1, D_2, \ldots, D_n$ of size $d_1, d_2, \ldots, d_n$, correspondingly.

Initialization: factorization size for each modality $r_1, r_2, \ldots, r_n$.

1: Compute tensor $D = D_1 \otimes D_2 \otimes \ldots \otimes D_n$
2: Generate the layers for $out = WD$ which $W = \hat{R} \times_1 W_1 \times_2 \ldots \times_M W_M$ in order to transform the high-dimensional tensor D to the output h.
3: Use Adam optimizer for the differentiable tensor factorization layer to find the unknown parameters $W_1, W_2, \ldots, W_n, \hat{R}$.

Output: Factors for Weight Matrix W: $W_1, W_2, \ldots, W_n, R$.

The original tensor fusion approach as proposed in (Zadeh et al., 2017) flattened the tensor D which results in loss of the information included in the tensor structure, which is avoided in our approach. Liu et al. (2018) developed a similar approach to ours using a diagonal core tensor R, losing much inter-modality information. Our non-diagonal core tensor maintains key inter-modality information after compression.

Note that the factorization step is task dependent, included in the deep network structure and learned during network training. Thus, for follow-up learning tasks, we would learn a new factorization specific to the task at hand, typically also estimating optimal compression ratios as described in the discussion section. In this process, any shared, helpful information is retained, as demonstrated by our results.

Analysis of parameter complexity: Following our proposed approach, we have decomposed the trainable W tensor to four substantially smaller trainable matrices (W_1, W_2, W_3, R) leading to $O(\sum_{i=1}^{M} (d_i * r_i) + \prod_{i=1}^{M} r_i * h)$ parameters. Concat fusion (CF) leads to a layer size of $O(\sum_{i=1}^{M} d_i)$ and $O(\sum_{i=1}^{M} d_i * h)$ parameters.

The tensor fusion approach (TF), leads to a layer size of $O(\prod_{i=1}^{M} d_i)$, and $O(\prod_{i=1}^{M} d_i * h)$ parameters. The LMF approach (Liu et al., 2018) requires training $O(\sum_{i=1}^{M} r * h * d_i)$ parameters, where r is the rank used for all the modalities.

It can be seen that the number of parameters in the proposed approach is substantially fewer than the simple tensor fusion (TF) approach and comparable to the LMF approach.

4 Experimental Setup

4.1 Datasets

We perform our experiments on the following multimodal datasets: CMU-MOSI (Zadeh et al., 2016), POM (Park et al., 2014), and IEMOCAP (Busso et al., 2008) for sentiment analysis, speaker traits recognition, and emotion recognition, respectively. These tasks can be done by integrating both verbal and nonverbal behaviors of the persons.

The CMU-MOSI dataset is annotated on a seven-step scale as highly negative, negative, weakly negative, neutral, weakly positive, positive, highly positive which can be considered as a 7 class classification problem with 7 labels in the range $[-3, +3]$. The dataset is an annotated dataset of 2199 opinion utterances from 93 distinct YouTube movie reviews, each containing several opinion segments. Segments average of 4.2 seconds in length.

The POM dataset is composed of 903 movie review videos. Each video is annotated with the following speaker traits: confident, passionate, voice pleasant, dominant, credible, vivid, expertise, entertaining, reserved, trusting, relaxed, outgoing, thorough, nervous, persuasive and humorous.

The IEMOCAP dataset is a collection of 151 videos of recorded dialogues, with 2 speakers per session for a total of 302 videos across the dataset. Each segment is annotated for the presence of 9 emotions (angry, excited, fear, sad, surprised, frustrated, happy, disgust and neutral).

Each dataset consists of three modalities, namely language, visual, and acoustic. The visual and acoustic features are calculated by taking the average of their feature values over the word time

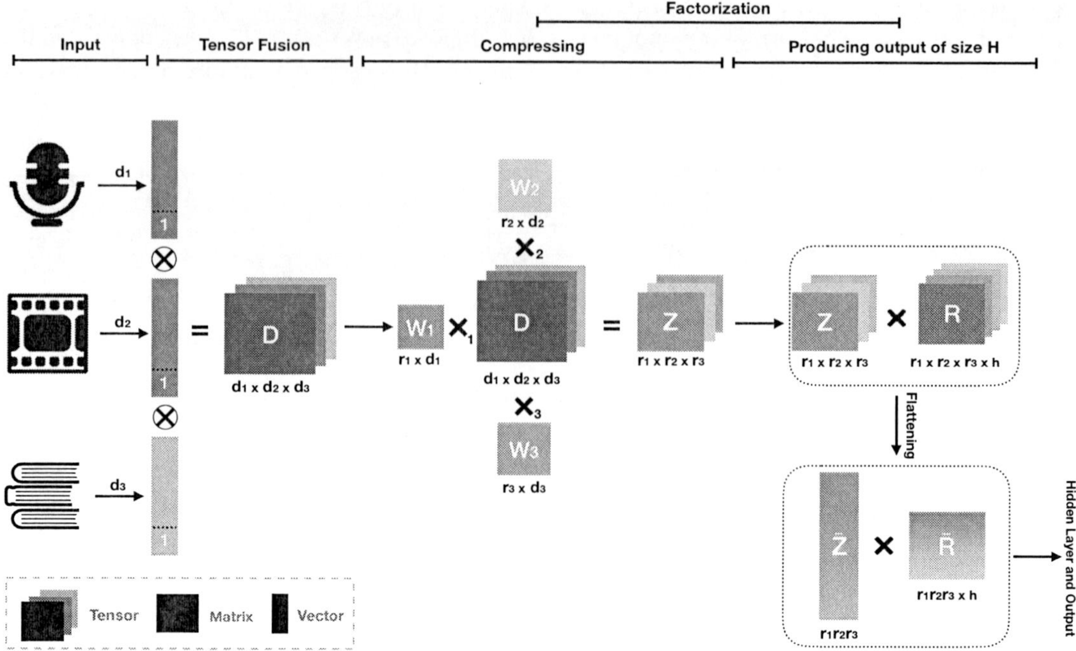

Figure 1: Diagram of Modality-based Redundancy Reduction Multimodal Fusion (MRRF).

interval (Chen et al., 2017). In order to perform time alignment across modalities, the three modalities are aligned using P2FA (Yuan and Liberman, 2008) at the word level.

Pre-trained 300-dimensional Glove word embeddings (Chen et al., 2017) were used to extract the language feature representations, which encodes a sequence of the transcribed words into a sequence of vectors.

Visual features for each frame (sampled at 30Hz) are extracted using the library Facet[1] which includes 20 facial action units, 68 facial landmarks, head pose, gaze tracking and HOG features (Zhu et al., 2006).

COVAREP acoustic analysis framework (Degottex et al., 2014) is used to extract low-level acoustic features, including 12 Mel frequency cepstral coefficients (MFCCs), pitch, voiced/unvoiced segmentation, glottal source, peak slope, and maxima dispersion quotient features.

To evaluate model generalization, all datasets are split into training, validation, and test sets such that the splits are speaker independent, i.e., no speakers from the training set are present in the test sets. Table 1 illustrates the data splits for all the datasets in detail.

Dataset Level	CMU-MOSI Segment	IEMOCAP Segment	POM Video
Train	1284	6373	600
Valid	229	1775	100
Test	686	1807	203

Table 1: The speaker independent data splits for training, validation, and test sets

4.2 Model Architecture

Similarly to (Liu et al., 2018), we use a simple model architecture for extracting the representations for each modality. We used three unimodal sub-embedding networks to extract representations z_a, z_v and z_l for each modality, respectively. For acoustic and visual modalities, the sub-embedding network is a simple 2-layer feed-forward neural network, and for language, we used a long short-term memory (LSTM) network (Hochreiter and Schmidhuber, 1997).

We tuned the layer sizes, the learning rates and the compression rates, by checking the mean average error for the validation set by grid search. We trained our model using the Adam optimizer (Kingma and Ba, 2014). All models were implemented with Pytorch (Paszke et al., 2017).

[1] goo.gl/1rh1JN

| Dataset | CMU-MOSI | | | | | POM | | | IEMOCAP | | | |
Metric	MAE	Corr	Acc-2	F1	Acc-7	MAE	Corr	Acc	F1-Happy	F1-Sad	F1-Angry	F1-Neutral
CF	1.140	0.52	72.3	72.1	26.5	0.865	0.142	34.1	81.1	81.2	65.1	44.1
TFN	0.970	0.633	73.9	73.4	32.1	0.886	0.093	31.6	83.6	82.8	84.2	65.4
LMF	0.912	0.668	76.4	75.7	32.8	0.796	0.396	42.8	85.8	85.9	89.0	71.7
MRRF	0.912	0.772	77.46	76.73	33.02	0.69	0.44	43.02	87.71	85.9	90.02	73.7

Table 2: Results for Sentiment Analysis on CMU-MOSI, emotion recognition on IEMOCAP and personality trait recognition on POM. (CF, TF, and LMF stand for concat, tensor and low-rank fusion respectively).

5 Experimental Results and Comparing with State-of-the-art

We compared our proposed method with three baseline methods. Concat fusion (CF) (Baltrušaitis et al., 2018) proposes a simple concatenation of the different modalities followed by a linear combination. The tensor fusion approach (TF) (Zadeh et al., 2017) computes a tensor including uni-modal, bi-modal, and tri-modal combination information. LMF (Liu et al., 2018) is a tensor fusion method that performs tensor factorization using the same rank for all the modalities in order to reduce the number of parameters. Our proposed method aims to use different factors for each modality.

In Table 2, we present mean average error (MAE), the correlation between prediction and true scores, binary accuracy (Acc-2), multi-class accuracy (Acc-7) and F1 measure. The proposed approach outperforms baseline approaches in nearly all metrics, with marked improvements in Happy and Neutral recognition. The reason is that the inter-modality information for these emotions is more complicated than the other emotions and requires a non-diagonal core tensor to extract the complicated information. It is worth to note that for the equivalent setting and equal ranks for all the modalities, the result of the proposed method is always marginally better than LMF method.

5.1 Investigating the Effect of Compression Rate on Each Modality

In this section, we aim to investigate the amount of redundant information in each modality. To do this, after obtaining a tensor which includes the combinations of all modalities with the equivalent size, we factorize a single dimension of the tensor while keeping the size for the other modalities fixed. By observing how the performance changes by compression rate, one can find how much redundant information is contained in the corresponding modality relative to the other modalities.

The results can be seen in Fig. 2, 3 and 4. The horizontal axis is the compressed size and the vertical axis shows the accuracy for each modality. Note that due to the padding of each D_i with 1, we have used $r_i + 1$ as the new embedding size.

The first point that could be perceived clearly from the different modality diagrams is that each of the modalities changes in a different way when getting compressed, which means they each have a different amount of information that can not be compensated by the non-compressed modalities. In other words, a high accuracy when a modality is highly compressed means that there is a lot of redundant information in this modality — the information loss resulting from factorization could be compensated by the other modalities so performance was not reduced.

Fig. 2 shows results for the CMU-MOSI sentiment analysis dataset. For this dataset, a notable decrease in accuracy can be seen by compressing the video modality, while the audio and text modalities are not notably sensitive to compression. This shows that for sentiment analysis based on CMU-MOSI dataset, the information in Video modality cannot be compensated by other modalities, however most information in the audio and language modalities is covered in video modality. In other words, the video contains essential information for this task whereas information from audio and language can be recovered from video.

Fig. 3 shows the average accuracy over 16 personality types for the POM personality trait recognition dataset. For this dataset also, each of the modalities has a different behavior for different compression rates. We can see that the audio modality includes more non-redundant information for personality recognition as accuracy is highly affected by audio compression. In addition, there is a notable accuracy reduction when the language modality is highly compressed, which shows a small amount of non-redundant information for this task. Note that the POM data does not contain sufficient information for an effective analysis of the 16 personality sub types individually.

Fig. 4 shows the results for the IEMOCAP emo-

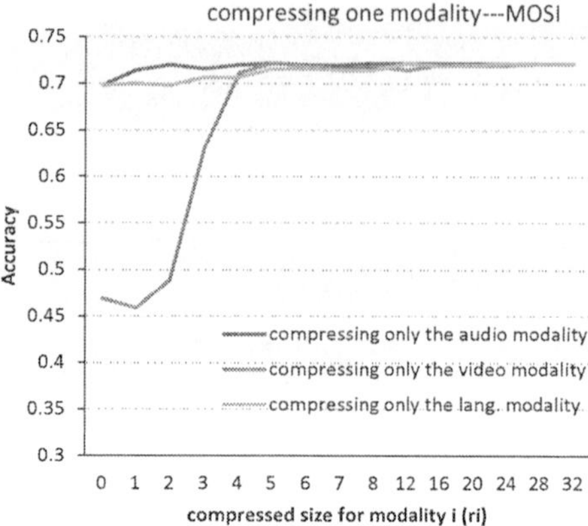

Figure 2: CMU-MOSI sentiment analysis dataset: Effect of different compression rates on accuracy for single modalities.

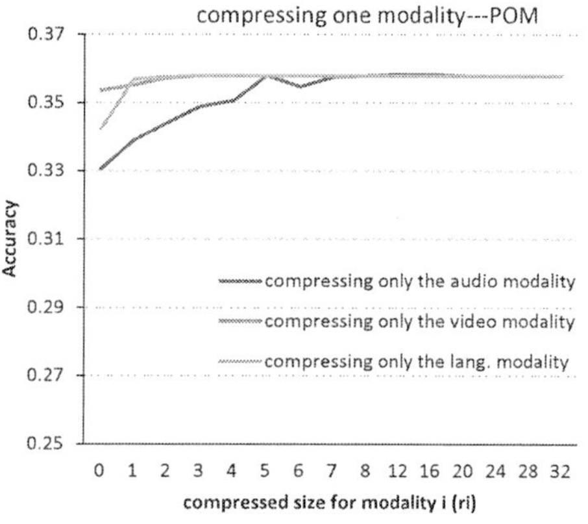

Figure 3: POM personality recognition dataset: Effect of different compression rates on accuracy for single modalities.

tion recognition dataset for each of the four emotional categories: happy, angry, sad, and neutral. Looking at the sad category, we see notable accuracy reduction for small sizes (high compression) for all the modalities, showing that each contains at least some non-redundant information. However, high compression of audio and especially language modalities results in strong accuracy reduction whereas video compression results in relatively minor reduction. It can be concluded that for this emotion, the language modality has the most non-redundant information and the video modality very little — it's information can be compensated by the other two modalities. Moving on to the angry emotion, small sizes (high compression) result in accuracy reduction for audio and language modalities, showing that they contain some non-redundant information, with the audio modality containing more. Again the information in video can be almost completely compensated by the other two modalities.

By comparing the highest accuracy values for various emotion categories, it is observed that neutral is hard to predict in comparison to the other categories. Again, the audio and Language modalities both include non-redundant information leading to a severe accuracy reduction with high compression of these modalities, with video containing almost no information not compensated by audio and language.

The happy category is the easiest to predict emotion, and it slightly suffers for very small sizes of audio and video and language modalities, indicating a small amount of non-redundant information in all modalities.

6 Conclusion

We proposed a tensor fusion method for multimodal media analysis by obtaining an $M + 1$-way tensor to consider the high-order relationships between M input modalities and the output layer. Our modality-based factorization method removes the redundant information in this high-order dependency structure and leads to fewer parameters with minimal loss of information. In addition, a modality-based factorization approach helps to understand the relative quantities of non-redundant information in each modality through investigation sensitivity to modality-specific compression rates. As the proposed compression method leads to a less complicated model, it can be applied as a regularizer which avoiding overfitting.

We have provided experimental results for combining acoustic, text, and visual modalities for three different tasks: sentiment analysis, personality trait recognition, and emotion recognition. We have seen that the modality-based tensor compression approach improves the results in comparison to the simple concatenation method, the tensor fusion method and tensor fusion using the same factorization rank for all modalities, as proposed in the LMF method. In other words, the proposed method enjoys the same benefits as the tensor fusion method and avoids suffering from having a large number of parameters, which leads to a more complex model, needs many training samples and is more prone to overfitting. We have investigated the effect of the compression rate on single modalities while

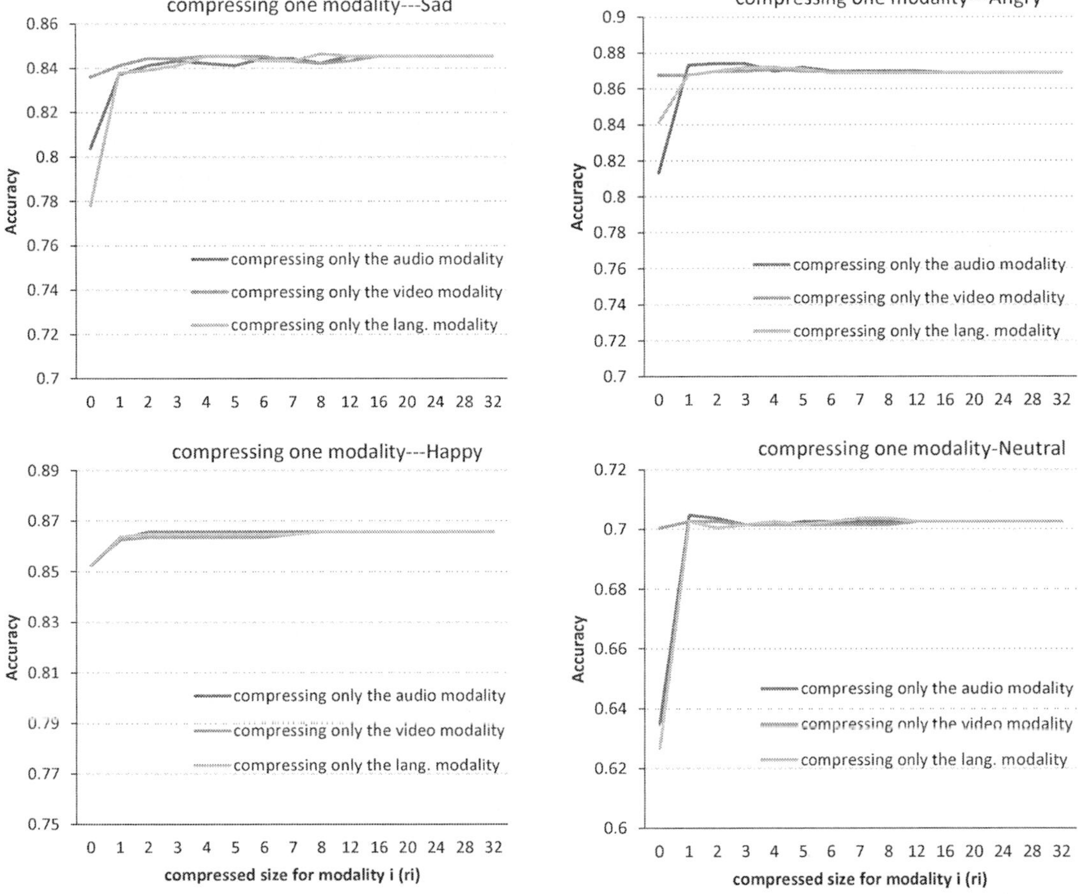

Figure 4: IEMOCAP Emotion Recognition Dataset: Effect of different compression rates on accuracy for single modalities.

fixing the other modalities helping to understand the amount of useful non-redundant information in each modality. Moreover, we have evaluated our method by comparing the results with state-of-the-art methods, achieving a 1% to 4% improvement across multiple measures for the different tasks.

In future work, we will investigate the relation between dataset size and compression rate by applying our method to larger datasets. This will help to understand the trade-off between the model size and available training data, allowing more efficient training and avoiding under- and overfitting.

As the availability of data with more and more modalities increases, both finding a trade-off between cost and performance and effective and efficient utilization of available modalities will be vital. Exploring compression methods promises to help identify and remove highly redundant modalities.

Acknowledgments

This work was partially funded by grants #16214415 and #16248016 of the Hong Kong Research Grants Council, ITS/319/16FP of Innovation Technology Commission, and RDC 1718050-0 of EMOS.AI. Thanks to Dr. Ian D. Wood and Peyman Momeni for their helpful commnets.

References

Tadas Baltrušaitis, Chaitanya Ahuja, and Louis-Philippe Morency. 2018. Multimodal machine learning: A survey and taxonomy. *IEEE Transactions on Pattern Analysis and Machine Intelligence*.

Carlos Busso, Murtaza Bulut, Chi-Chun Lee, Abe Kazemzadeh, Emily Mower, Samuel Kim, Jeannette N Chang, Sungbok Lee, and Shrikanth S Narayanan. 2008. Iemocap: Interactive emotional dyadic motion capture database. *Language resources and evaluation*, 42(4):335.

J Douglas Carroll and Jih-Jie Chang. 1970. Analysis of individual differences in multidimensional scaling via an n-way generalization of eckart-young decomposition. *Psychometrika*, 35(3):283–319.

Minghai Chen, Sen Wang, Paul Pu Liang, Tadas Baltrušaitis, Amir Zadeh, and Louis-Philippe Morency. 2017. Multimodal sentiment analysis with word-level fusion and reinforcement learning. In *Proceedings of the 19th ACM International Conference on Multimodal Interaction*, pages 163–171. ACM.

Liyanage C De Silva, Tsutomu Miyasato, and Ryohei Nakatsu. 1997. Facial emotion recognition using multi-modal information. In *Information, Communications and Signal Processing, 1997. ICICS., Proceedings of 1997 International Conference on*, volume 1, pages 397–401. IEEE.

Gilles Degottex, John Kane, Thomas Drugman, Tuomo Raitio, and Stefan Scherer. 2014. Covarepa collaborative voice analysis repository for speech technologies. In *Acoustics, Speech and Signal Processing (ICASSP), 2014 IEEE International Conference on*, pages 960–964. IEEE.

Sidney K D'mello and Jacqueline Kory. 2015. A review and meta-analysis of multimodal affect detection systems. *ACM Computing Surveys (CSUR)*, 47(3):43.

Maryam Fazel. 2002. *Matrix rank minimization with applications*. Ph.D. thesis, PhD thesis, Stanford University.

Michael Glodek, Stephan Tschechne, Georg Layher, Martin Schels, Tobias Brosch, Stefan Scherer, Markus Kächele, Miriam Schmidt, Heiko Neumann, Günther Palm, et al. 2011. Multiple classifier systems for the classification of audio-visual emotional states. In *Affective Computing and Intelligent Interaction*, pages 359–368. Springer.

RA Harshman. 1970. Foundations of the parafac procedure: Models and conditions for an" explanatory" multimodal factor analysis. *UCLA Working Papers in Phonetics*, 16:1–84.

Frank L Hitchcock. 1927. The expression of a tensor or a polyadic as a sum of products. *Studies in Applied Mathematics*, 6(1-4):164–189.

Sepp Hochreiter and Jürgen Schmidhuber. 1997. Long short-term memory. *Neural computation*, 9(8):1735–1780.

Alex Pappachen James and Belur V Dasarathy. 2014. Medical image fusion: A survey of the state of the art. *Information Fusion*, 19:4–19.

Onno Kampman, Elham J Barezi, Dario Bertero, and Pascale Fung. 2018. Investigating audio, video, and text fusion methods for end-to-end automatic personality prediction. In *Proceedings of the 56th Annual Meeting of the Association for Computational Linguistics (Volume 2: Short Papers)*, volume 2, pages 606–611.

Diederik Kingma and Jimmy Ba. 2014. Adam: A method for stochastic optimization. *arXiv preprint arXiv:1412.6980*.

Zhen-Zhong Lan, Lei Bao, Shoou-I Yu, Wei Liu, and Alexander G Hauptmann. 2014. Multimedia classification and event detection using double fusion. *Multimedia tools and applications*, 71(1):333–347.

Zhun Liu, Ying Shen, Varun Bharadhwaj Lakshminarasimhan, Paul Pu Liang, Amir Zadeh, and Louis-Philippe Morency. 2018. Efficient low-rank multimodal fusion with modality-specific factors. *arXiv preprint arXiv:1806.00064*.

Emilie Morvant, Amaury Habrard, and Stéphane Ayache. 2014. Majority vote of diverse classifiers for late fusion. In *Joint IAPR International Workshops on Statistical Techniques in Pattern Recognition (SPR) and Structural and Syntactic Pattern Recognition (SSPR)*, pages 153–162. Springer.

Jiquan Ngiam, Aditya Khosla, Mingyu Kim, Juhan Nam, Honglak Lee, and Andrew Y. Ng. 2011. Multimodal deep learning. In *Proceedings of the 28th International Conference on Machine Learning (ICML-11)*, ICML '11, pages 689–696, New York, NY, USA. ACM.

Sunghyun Park, Han Suk Shim, Moitreya Chatterjee, Kenji Sagae, and Louis-Philippe Morency. 2014. Computational analysis of persuasiveness in social multimedia: A novel dataset and multimodal prediction approach. In *Proceedings of the 16th International Conference on Multimodal Interaction*, pages 50–57. ACM.

Adam Paszke, Sam Gross, Soumith Chintala, Gregory Chanan, Edward Yang, Zachary DeVito, Zeming Lin, Alban Desmaison, Luca Antiga, and Adam Lerer. 2017. Automatic differentiation in pytorch.

Soujanya Poria, Erik Cambria, Devamanyu Hazarika, Navonil Majumder, Amir Zadeh, and Louis-Philippe Morency. 2017a. Context-dependent sentiment analysis in user-generated videos. In *Proceedings of the 55th Annual Meeting of the Association for Computational Linguistics (Volume 1: Long Papers)*, pages 873–883.

Soujanya Poria, Erik Cambria, Devamanyu Hazarika, Navonil Mazumder, Amir Zadeh, and Louis-Philippe Morency. 2017b. Multi-level multiple attentions for contextual multimodal sentiment analysis. In *2017 IEEE International Conference on Data Mining (ICDM)*, pages 1033–1038. IEEE.

Gerasimos Potamianos, Chalapathy Neti, Guillaume Gravier, Ashutosh Garg, and Andrew W Senior. 2003. Recent advances in the automatic recognition of audiovisual speech. *Proceedings of the IEEE*, 91(9):1306–1326.

Ekaterina Shutova, Douwe Kiela, and Jean Maillard. 2016. Black holes and white rabbits: Metaphor identification with visual features. In *Proceedings of the*

2016 Conference of the North American Chapter of the Association for Computational Linguistics: Human Language Technologies, pages 160–170.

Mohammad Soleymani, Maja Pantic, and Thierry Pun. 2012. Multimodal emotion recognition in response to videos. *IEEE transactions on affective computing*, 3(2):211–223.

Nitish Srivastava and Ruslan R Salakhutdinov. 2012. Multimodal learning with deep boltzmann machines. In *Advances in Neural Information Processing Systems 25*, pages 2222–2230. Curran Associates, Inc.

Ledyard R Tucker. 1966. Some mathematical notes on three-mode factor analysis. *Psychometrika*, 31(3):279–311.

Jiahong Yuan and Mark Liberman. 2008. Speaker identification on the scotus corpus. *Journal of the Acoustical Society of America*, 123(5):3878.

Amir Zadeh, Minghai Chen, Soujanya Poria, Erik Cambria, and Louis-Philippe Morency. 2017. Tensor fusion network for multimodal sentiment analysis. *arXiv preprint arXiv:1707.07250*.

Amir Zadeh, Paul Pu Liang, Navonil Mazumder, Soujanya Poria, Erik Cambria, and Louis-Philippe Morency. 2018a. Memory fusion network for multi-view sequential learning. In *Thirty-Second AAAI Conference on Artificial Intelligence*.

Amir Zadeh, Paul Pu Liang, Soujanya Poria, Prateek Vij, Erik Cambria, and Louis-Philippe Morency. 2018b. Multi-attention recurrent network for human communication comprehension. In *Thirty-Second AAAI Conference on Artificial Intelligence*.

Amir Zadeh, Rowan Zellers, Eli Pincus, and Louis-Philippe Morency. 2016. Mosi: multimodal corpus of sentiment intensity and subjectivity analysis in online opinion videos. *arXiv preprint arXiv:1606.06259*.

Qiang Zhu, Mei-Chen Yeh, Kwang-Ting Cheng, and Shai Avidan. 2006. Fast human detection using a cascade of histograms of oriented gradients. In *Computer Vision and Pattern Recognition, 2006 IEEE Computer Society Conference on*, volume 2, pages 1491–1498. IEEE.

Leveraging Pre-Trained Embeddings for Welsh Taggers

Ignatius Ezeani[1]   **Scott Piao**[1]   **Steven Neale**[2]   **Paul Rayson**[1]   **Dawn Knight**[2]
[1]School of Computing and Communications, Lancaster University, UK.
{i.ezeani, s.piao, p.rayson}@lancaster.ac.uk
[2]School of English, Communication and Philosophy, Cardiff University, UK.
{NealeS2, knightd5}@cardiff.ac.uk

Abstract

While the application of word embedding models to downstream Natural Language Processing (NLP) tasks has been shown to be successful, the benefits for low-resource languages is somewhat limited due to lack of adequate data for training the models. However, NLP research efforts for low-resource languages have focused on constantly seeking ways to harness pre-trained models to improve the performance of NLP systems built to process these languages without the need to re-invent the wheel. One such language is Welsh and therefore, in this paper, we present the results of our experiments on learning a simple multi-task neural network model for part-of-speech and semantic tagging for Welsh using a pre-trained embedding model from *Fast-Text*. Our model's performance was compared with those of the existing rule-based stand-alone taggers for part-of-speech and semantic taggers. Despite its simplicity and capacity to perform both tasks simultaneously, our tagger compared very well with the existing taggers.

1 Introduction

The Welsh language can easily be classified as low resourced in the context of natural language processing because the lack of the commonly used resources in language research such as large annotated corpora as well as the standard computational tools and techniques for processing these resources.

There is still a long way to go for Welsh, but the situation is improving. For instance, Welsh is fortunate to have a fund that supports an on-going inter-disciplinary and multi-institutional project, the National Corpus of Contemporary Welsh (Corpws Cenedlaethol Cymraeg Cyfoes - *CorCenCC*)[1], which has been building a large-scale open-source language resource for contemporary Welsh language.

Existing Welsh part-of-speech (sections 2.1) and semantic (section 2.2) taggers produce good results, but their heavy dependence on hand-crafted rules and hard-coded resources may pose a maintenance challenge in future. Also, considering the speed with which languages evolve, especially on the internet, and the huge amount of unannotated corpora that can be collected from the web, we urgently need a system that is capable of learning from unstructured text in order to guarantee the generalisability and scalability of tagging tools.

Given the potential challenges with the existing approaches and considering the similarities between the tasks of part-of-speech (POS) and semantic (SEM) annotation, we propose to train a single neural network model that can jointly learn both of the tasks. We aim at requiring as little human annotation effort as possible and leveraging the linguistic patterns acquired from unsupervised language models like word embeddings. The main contributions of this research includes: (1) The first application of multi-task learning to POS and semantic tagging for any language that we know of, (2) The ability to improve OOV coverage for the Welsh language using pre-trained embeddings for semantic category extension, (3) Public release of two sets of manually checked gold-standard corpora for POS and semantic tagging of Welsh, (4) Inter-annotator agreement scores for Welsh semantic tagging, (5) Public release of the first Welsh semantic tagger (CySemTagger) (6) The first demonstration of multi-task learning to improve NLP task accuracy for Welsh, and (7) A demonstration of the usefulness of multi-task learning in a mono-lingual setting for a low re-

---

[1]http://www.corcencc.org/

Proceedings of the 4th Workshop on Representation Learning for NLP (RepL4NLP-2019), pages 270–280
Florence, Italy, August 2, 2019. ©2019 Association for Computational Linguistics

source language.[2]

2 Background

POS tagging is a well studied NLP task. Much recent work on this task has moved away from English and European languages to other major languages such as Arabic (Aldarmaki and Diab, 2015), Chinese (Sun and Wan, 2016), dialects thereof (Darwish et al., 2018), and text types containing more noise such as historical (Yang and Eisenstein, 2016; Janssen et al., 2017), learner language (Nagata et al., 2018), code switching (Vyas et al., 2014) and social media varieties (Horsmann and Zesch, 2016; van der Goot et al., 2017). More recently, joint and multi-task learning approaches have been applied to link POS tagging and other tasks such as segmentation or tokenisation (Al-Gahtani and McNaught, 2015; Shao et al., 2017), dependency parsing (Nguyen and Verspoor, 2018) and lemmatisation (Arakelyan et al., 2018).

Besides being applied to other NLP applications and levels, multi-task learning has been applied with promising results to the semantic level in various scenarios, including cross-lingual sentiment analysis (Wang et al., 2018), opinion and semantic role labelling (Marasović and Frank, 2018), semantic parsing (Bordes et al., 2012), emotion prediction (Buechel and Hahn, 2018), irony detection (Wu et al., 2018) and rumour verification (Kochkina et al., 2018). However, there is very little research that applies multi-task learning to link Word Sense Disambiguation (WSD) or semantic tagging with another task. Here, we refer to the semantic tagging as coarse-grained word sense disambiguation based on an existing taxonomy of categories, e.g. in USAS (Rayson et al., 2004). Previously, semantic tagging in multiple languages has been shown to greatly benefit from POS tagging in the NLP pipeline, since it can help to filter out inapplicable semantic fields from the set of possible candidates (Piao et al., 2015).

Over the past few years, researchers started to port NLP tools and methods into low resource languages using a various approaches, such as porting lexicons from one language to another using bilingual dictionaries and parallel corpora (Piao et al., 2016) and cross-lingual word embeddings (Adams et al., 2017; Sharoff, 2018). Multi-task learning has also been proved useful in transferring the learning across languages in a multilingual setting where one of the languages has only sparse resources available (Junczys-Dowmunt et al., 2018; Lin et al., 2018; Choi et al., 2018), although less successful in named entity recognition settings (Enghoff et al., 2018). In our experiments, we focus on a low-resource mono-lingual setting with a small manually corrected corpus, and combine the Welsh POS and SEM annotation for the first time.

2.1 *CyTag*

The rule-based POS tagger under consideration in our work, *CyTag* (Neale et al., 2018), was built based on Constraint Grammar (CG) (Karlsson, 1990), in particular built around the latest version of the software, VISL CG-3[3]. The *CyTag* tagset[4] contains 145 fine-grained POS tags that can collapse into 13 *EAGLES*[5]-conformant broader categories.

CyTag utilises three steps to assign POS tags to tokens:

- A list of candidate POS tags is produced for each token.

- The list of candidate tags for each token is pruned to as few as possible (ideally one) using CG-formatted rules.

- The optimal tag for each token is selected, helped by some small additional processing steps for any cases that were still ambiguous after post-CG.

In the second step listed above, *CyTag* makes use of a CG-formatted 'grammar' file – currently containing 243 hand-crafted and hard-coded rules – to 'prune' the list of candidate tags to one for ambiguous tokens. The rules are formatted as follows:

action (reading) if (neighbour (features))

whereby *action* refers to the 'operation' to be performed on the *reading* e.g. ('selecting or 'removing'); *neighbour* is a nearby token of interest to the target token on whose *features* the *action* depends. *CyTag* was evaluated using a gold-standard annotated corpus containing 611 sentences (14,876 tokens), as will be described in subsection 3.1.

---

[3]`http://visl.sdu.dk/cg3.html`
[4]`http://cytag.corcencc.org/tagset`
[5]`http://www.ilc.cnr.it/EAGLES/browse.html`

Another recently-developed POS tagger for Welsh is the *WNLT-Tagger*, which forms part of the *Welsh Natural Language Toolkit (WNLT)*[6]. *WNLT-Tagger* is one of the four main modules in *WNLT*, which is itself built on the *GATE (General Architecture for Text Engineering)* framework (Cunningham, 2002).

2.2 *CySemTagger*: The Welsh Semantic tagger

CyTag is a precursor to *CySemTagger* (Piao et al., 2018) which is an automatic semantic annotation tool that depends on the POS tagged output to assign semantic tags to tokens in Welsh texts. *CySemTagger* employs the semantic tagset of Lancaster University's *UCREL Semantic Analysis System*, USAS[7]. The semantic tagset, which was originally derived from Tom McArthur's *Longman Lexicon of Contemporary English* (McArthur and McArthur, 1981), has 21 major discourse fields and 232 tags.

The *CySemTagger* is a knowledge-based and rule-based system with the following key components:

- lexicon look-up (both for single words and MWEs)

- part-of-speech tagging (*CyTag* and *WNLT-Tagger*)

- semantic category disambiguation

- output formatting and display

The *CySemTagger* tagger is designed to work with any POS-tagger but its performance was assessed so far only on the *coverage* of the Welsh text presented to it, i.e. the fraction of the tokens it is able to assign at least one of the valid semantic tags. The experiment presented in (Piao et al., 2018) indicates that, on the text coverage evaluation, the *CySemTagger* works better with *CyTag* than with *WNLT-Tagger*, as shown by the respective text coverage scores of 91.78% and 72.92% with both POS taggers.

3 Experiments

The *CyTag* and the *CySemTagger* are separate tools that use rule-based methods to achieve their

results. The semantic tagger relies heavily on a part-of-speech tagger to function. The key aim of this paper is to implement a tagging system that:

- learns from unstructured data,

- leverages available embedding models,

- performs both tasks, POS and semantic tagging, simultaneously using a multi-task learning set up.

3.1 Experimental data

As mentioned earlier in section 2.1, the instances for training the POS and semantic taggers were extracted from the manually annotated gold standard evaluation corpus that has been constructed in the CorCenCC project, i.e. the data used for the *CyTag* and *CySemTagger* development. This training data comprises 611 tagged sentences (14,876 tokens) stored in eight input files that contain excerpts from a variety of existing Welsh corpora, including *Kynulliad314* (Welsh Assembly proceedings), *Meddalwedd15* (translations of software instructions), *Kwici16* (Welsh Wikipedia articles), *LERBIML17* (multi-domain spoken corpora) and some short abstracts of three additional Welsh Wikipedia articles. The fully manually checked version of the gold standard data, i.e. with the POS and SEM tags, will be released along with the multi-task model for parts-of-speech and semantic tagging.

The dataset used for training the multi-task model was built with the data instances extracted from the fully tagged version of the gold standard data. These data instances do not contain unambiguous tokens (e.g. punctuation and numbers) and those categorised as *unknown* are removed from the training data. The basic statistics from the data used in our experiment are shown in Table 1.

Although the data used in this experiment is comparatively smaller than what is often used by typical neural network projects, we assume it is sufficient for an exploratory research that aims to build a prototypical framework to support further developments for the Welsh language tools.

3.2 Embedding model

A key contribution of this work to Welsh NLP research is the application of pre-trained embeddings to build the model. Although most deep-learning frameworks provide an embedding layer

Key item	Counts
sentences	611
tokens	14876
vocab length	3902
model vocab	3821
model vecsize	300
model oov	81
tagset size	392
punctuation	1667
unknown tags	44

Table 1: Basic statistics from the training data and embedding model used in this experiment.

that allows one to create embeddings from the training data, it is more beneficial to leverage existing models trained with much larger Welsh text data than to only rely on what is currently available. To that effect, we used the Welsh pre-trained embedding models built by the *FastText Project*[8] (Grave et al., 2018).

3.3 Design of experiment

The key input data to our pipeline consists of the 611 sentences that are jointly annotated with the POS and semantic tags. The combination of the annotation tags on the gold standard data makes it possible to extract the data in the different formats, as shown in Table 3. However, the format used for this experiment is the last one, *3-BOTH*, in which each token is tagged with a concatenation of the POS and semantic tags.

The extraction of the instance features for each token is carried out in two stage process which involves the *chunking* of the target word along with its three previous tokens (i.e. 4 words in total), as well as the *vectorisation* of the features. The chunking process proceeds with a sliding window along the sentence, with the target word being the rightmost in the chunk. The *vectorisation* then replaces each word in the chunk with its vector representation from a word-embedding model, forming a matrix of values that represent each training instance. The label for each instance is the *tag-ID* i.e. a unique integer number assigned to each of the tags.

3.4 Model architecture and training setup

The model we used is a simple neural network with only one hidden layer. Each instance is a con-

[8] https://dl.fbaipublicfiles.com/
fasttext/vectors-crawl/cc.cy.300.vec.gz

	Training		Evaluation	
	Accuracy	*Loss*	*Accuracy*	*Loss*
-Vector size				
10	72.44	1.160	70.26	3.517
50	99.09	0.036	94.51	5.313
100	99.04	0.032	94.76	4.775
200	99.09	0.027	95.23	4.650
300	99.05	0.030	95.38	4.994
-Mini-batch size				
8	99.08	0.032	95.29	4.450
16	99.10	0.030	95.55	4.552
32	99.04	0.034	95.03	4.758
64	99.13	0.030	94.97	4.905
-Dropout rates				
10	99.11	0.033	95.38	3.807
20	98.60	0.051	94.80	3.873
30	97.68	0.083	94.27	3.434
40	95.92	0.137	92.85	3.362
50	93.08	0.232	90.32	3.280

Table 2: Parameter optimisation: Training and Evaluation of scores on *Accuracy* and *Loss*. Parameter values in **bold** were chosen.

Tagtype	Example
0 - None	A fydd rhywfaint o 'r arian hwn yn cael ei ddefnyddio i sicrhau bod modd defnyddio tocynnau rhatach yn Lloegr yn ogystal ag yng Nghymru ?
1 - POS	A/Rha fydd/B rhywfaint/E o/Ar 'r/YFB arian/E hwn/Rha yn/U cael/B ei/Rha ddefnyddio/B i/Ar sicrhau/B ...
2 - SEM	A/Z5 fydd/A3 rhywfaint/N5 o/Z5 'r/Z5 arian/I1 hwn/A3 yn/Z5 cael/A9 ei/Z8 ddefnyddio/A1 i/Z5 sicrhau/A7 ...
3 - BOTH	A/Rha/Z5 fydd/B/A3 rhywfaint/E/N5 o/Ar/Z5 'r/YFB/Z5 arian/E/I1 hwn/Rha/A3 yn/U/Z5 cael/B/A9 ei/Rha/Z8 ddefnyddio/B/A1 i/Ar/Z5 sicrhau/B/A7 ...

Table 3: Different annotation formats for the experimental data. We used the *3-BOTH* format which combines the POS and semantic tags.

catenation of the embedding vectors of the target word and the three previous words. So the size of the input layer is the same as the length of the concatenated vectors. The key parameters required for the model training and evaluation are *vector size*, *mini-batch size* and *dropout rate*, and different values of each parameter are tested over runs of 50 epochs for each as shown in Table 2.

The output layer is the size of the tagset extracted from the training data. From the annotation format used, each token's tag is a combination of the POS and semantic tags and, as shown in Table 1, the total tagset size is 392. This is comparatively large but it will help facilitate the multi-task learning, which this work aims to achieve.

The model architecture is shallow, as only one hidden layer is used. Ideally, the size of the hidden layer should be somewhere between the sizes of both the input and the output layers (Reed and Marks, 1999). However, in order to reduce the number of parameters in this model, the size of 256 was arbitrarily chosen. For the hidden layer, the *Adam* optimiser (Kingma and Ba, 2014) was used with the *rectified linear unit (ReLu)* activation function (Nair and Hinton, 2010) as implemented in the integrated *TensorFlow-Keras* (Abadi et al., 2016), (Chollet et al., 2015) framework.

3.4.1 Vector size

Given the small size of the training data, and in order not to have too many parameters that can cause over-fitting, we tested the model with different vector sizes, (i.e. 10, 50, 100, 200, 300), averaged across a range of other parameters values for the *mini-batch* and *dropout*. The training and evaluation for parameter optimisation was performed over 50 epochs.

With regards to the evaluation accuracy, as shown in Figure 1, apart from $nvecs = 10$, all other vector sizes could converge within the first 30 to 40 epochs. However, the evaluation loss begins to rise within the first 10 epochs, with most $nvecs$ hitting nearly above 4.5 before reaching the 50th epoch. To balance this, a vector size of 100 was used, i.e. only the first 100 values were taken from each embedding vector to build the input layer, as suggested in (Brownlee, 2017). This produced an input layer size of 400.

3.4.2 Mini-batch size

The training set was chunked into *mini-batches* as described in (Ruder, 2016), with 8 instances per batch. The *mini-batch* values 8, 16, 32 and 64 were tested across other parameter values (see Figure 2). Their average performances indicate that, while there is only a small change in evaluation accuracies across the values, there is a slightly lower loss value with a mini-batch of 8 than the others.

3.4.3 Dropout rate

Given the small quantity of the training data, the architecture also implemented *dropout* regularisation (Srivastava et al., 2014) on the hidden layer to reduce the expected likelihood of *over-fitting*. Different dropout rates (10%, 20%, 30%, 40% and 50%) were tested as shown in Figure 3, and dropout rate of 30% was chosen to jointly mitigate the impact of on both the evaluation accuracy and the loss.

3.4.4 Batch Normalisation

Batch normalisation addresses the problem of *internal covariate shift* (Ioffe and Szegedy, 2015) by normalising the inputs to the model layers, thereby increasing the training speed. In some cases, it acts as a regulariser. Therefore, a version of the model architecture described above implements batch normalisation. This is because, during training, improvement rates in the model's evaluation accuracy slow down after the first 50 epochs while the loss continues to escalate. Techniques that speed up the learning were considered to investigate the combined impact of speed and regularisation on evaluation accuracy and loss.

3.4.5 Loss Function

As a multi-class classification task, the standard loss function is the *cross-entropy* with the $softmax$ logistic activation function, as described in equation 3.4.5 (Mannor et al., 2005).

$$-\frac{1}{N}\sum_{i=1}^{N}\sum_{t=1}^{T} log(p(y|X_i)_t)1[y_i = t] \qquad (1)$$

where N is the number of instances in the training batch, T is the number of unique tags while X_i, and y_i are a set of input values and the corresponding label respectively.

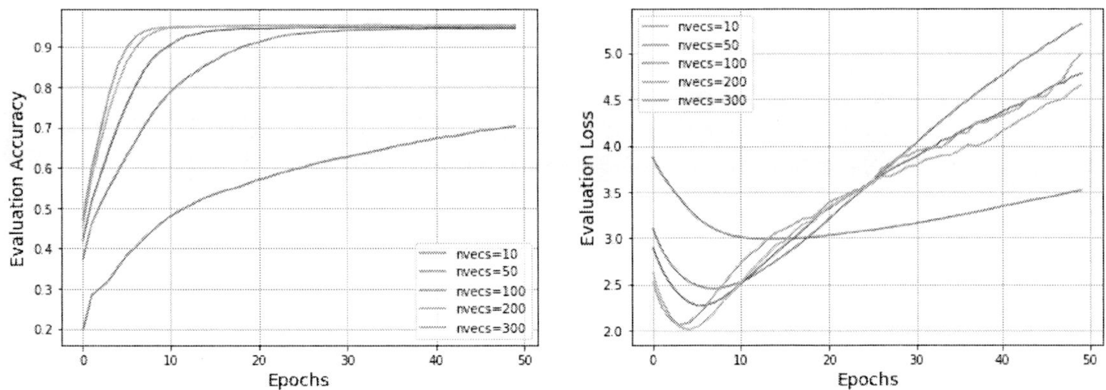

Figure 1: *Accuracy* vs *Loss* for different vector sizes

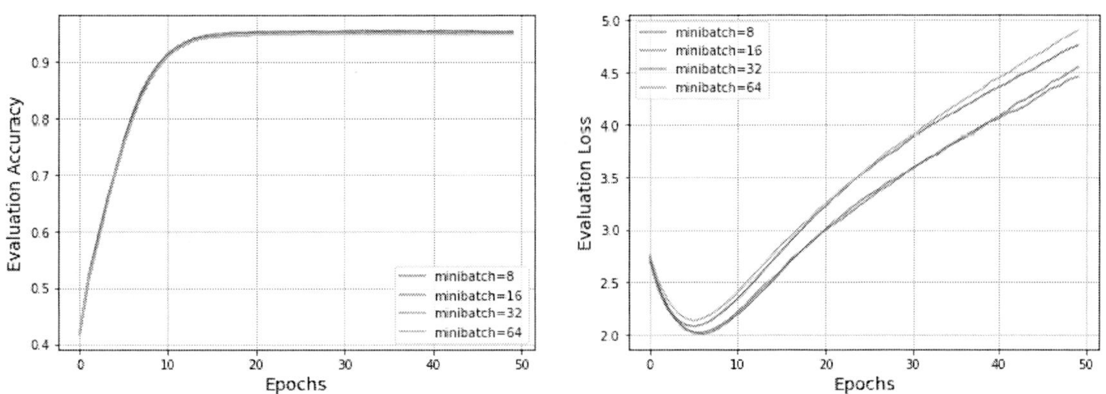

Figure 2: *Accuracy* vs *Loss* for different mini-batch sizes

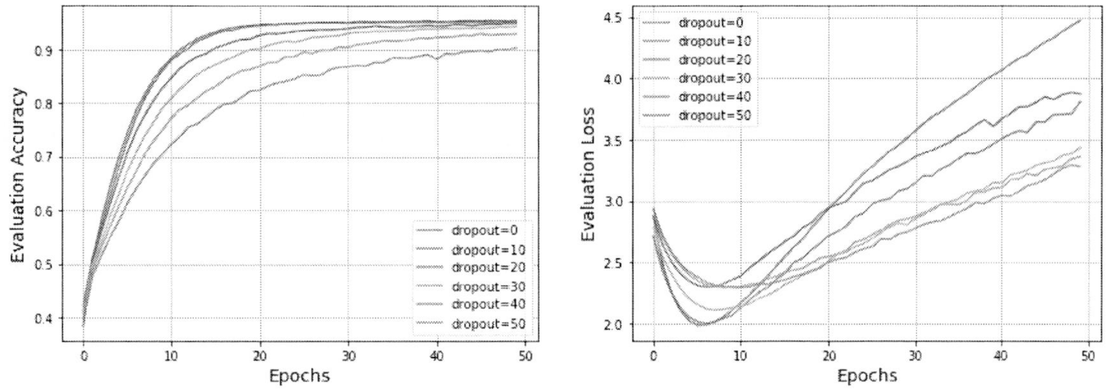

Figure 3: *Accuracy* vs *Loss* for different dropout rates

	Training		**Evaluation**	
	Accuracy	*Loss*	*Accuracy*	*Loss*
-dropout,-batchnorm	99.23	0.021	95.24	6.161
-dropout,+batchnorm	95.51	0.144	92.57	3.837
+dropout,-batchnorm	98.36	0.050	94.89	4.880
+dropout,+batchnorm	88.88	0.350	86.66	2.682

Table 4: Result summary for training and evaluation of accuracy and loss with or without dropout and batch normalisation

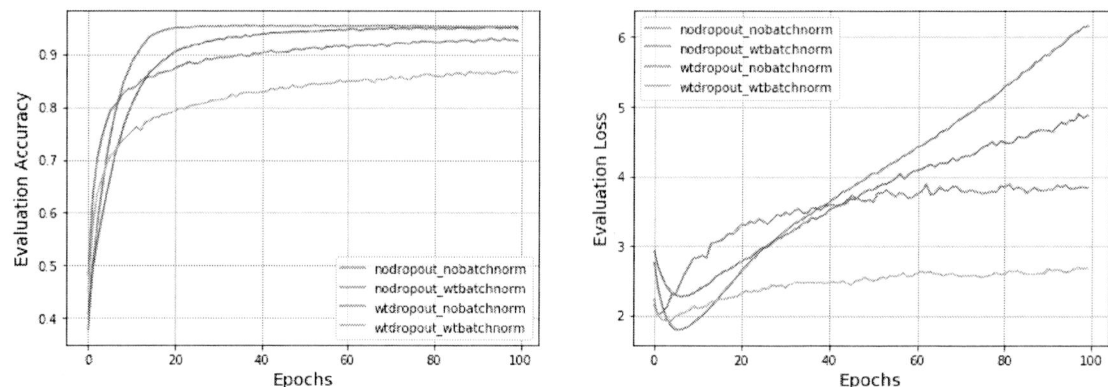

Figure 4: Evaluation graph for both accuracy and loss with and without dropout and/or batch normalisation.

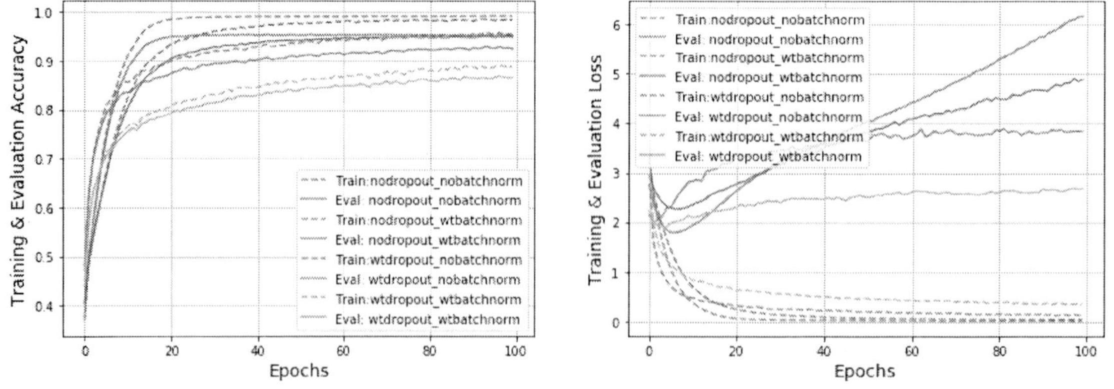

Figure 5: Training and evaluation graphs for accuracy and loss with and without dropout and/or batch normalisation.

4 Evaluation and discussion

With the *accuracy* of 93.64% and the *F1* of 95.06% reported previously for the *CyTag*, it represented the state-of-the-art in Welsh POS-tagging. Also, although the *CySemTagger* did not report those specific metrics, it is currently the only semantic tagger for Welsh language that we are aware of. Therefore, the evaluation results from the multi-tagger built in this experiment, which simultaneously performs both POS- and SEM-tagging, were compared against these tools.

The effects of dropout regularisation and batch normalisation were examined with the previously selected parameters for *vector size=100, mini-batches=8* and *dropout rate=30%*. As shown in Table 4, the results indicate that, at the detriment of accuracy, both dropout and the batch normalisation achieved significant reductions in evaluation loss. Without them, the training accuracy and loss scores for the multi-task tagger are 99.23% and 0.021 respectively while the evaluation scores are 95.24% and 6.161. However, with only dropout, training accuracy and loss scores are 98.36% and 0.050 while those of evaluation are 94.89% and 4.880.

Batch normalisation without dropout produced accuracy and loss scores of 95.51% and 0.144 respectively while those of evaluation produced 92.57% and 3.837 respectively. The combination of them achieved a significant reduction in evaluation loss (2.682), but with relatively poorer accuracy scores for training (88.88%) and evaluation (86.66%).

Figures 4 and 5 show that, as used in this experiment, the batch normalisation had a more regularising effect than the dropout, thereby slowing down convergence and avoiding over-fitting.

5 Conclusion

The main motivation for this work is to contribute a useful tool to the fledgling Welsh NLP research effort. There are two key objectives of this work: a) To build a multi-task classifier that can match the performance of the existing rule-based systems for Welsh POS and semantic taggers with as little human input as possible. b) To leverage existing language models such as word embedding created using unsupervised methods. Our work has demonstrated that these objectives can be achieved, although our results of a small-scale experiment can not be conclusive. The results obtained in this work compare favourably with those obtained from the existing rule-based models. We have also shown that, in a low resource setting, multi-task framework can also bring improvements to mono-lingual tasks, which is complementary to the previous findings from multi-lingual multi-task learning scenarios.

In our experiment, the neural network architecture was configured using pre-existing tools and frameworks, following suggestions from the literature. In future, we will focus on optimising the system parameters to improve the training efficiency and performance of the tagging models, as well as constructing larger training data.

References

Martín Abadi, Paul Barham, Jianmin Chen, Zhifeng Chen, Andy Davis, Jeffrey Dean, Matthieu Devin, Sanjay Ghemawat, Geoffrey Irving, Michael Isard, Manjunath Kudlur, Josh Levenberg, Rajat Monga, Sherry Moore, Derek G. Murray, Benoit Steiner, Paul Tucker, Vijay Vasudevan, Pete Warden, Martin Wicke, Yuan Yu, and Xiaoqiang Zheng. 2016. Tensorflow: A system for large-scale machine learning. In *Proceedings of the 12th USENIX Conference on Operating Systems Design and Implementation*, OSDI'16, pages 265–283, Berkeley, CA, USA. USENIX Association.

Oliver Adams, Adam Makarucha, Graham Neubig, Steven Bird, and Trevor Cohn. 2017. Cross-lingual word embeddings for low-resource language modeling. In *Proceedings of the 15th Conference of the European Chapter of the Association for Computational Linguistics: Volume 1, Long Papers*, pages 937–947. Association for Computational Linguistics.

Hanan Aldarmaki and Mona Diab. 2015. Robust part-of-speech tagging of Arabic text. In *Proceedings of the Second Workshop on Arabic Natural Language Processing*, pages 173–182. Association for Computational Linguistics.

Shabib AlGahtani and John McNaught. 2015. Joint Arabic segmentation and part-of-speech tagging. In *Proceedings of the Second Workshop on Arabic Natural Language Processing*, pages 108–117. Association for Computational Linguistics.

Gor Arakelyan, Karen Hambardzumyan, and Hrant Khachatrian. 2018. Towards jointud: Part-of-speech tagging and lemmatization using recurrent neural networks. In *Proceedings of the CoNLL 2018 Shared Task: Multilingual Parsing from Raw Text to Universal Dependencies*, pages 180–186. Association for Computational Linguistics.

Antoine Bordes, Xavier Glorot, Jason Weston, and Yoshua Bengio. 2012. Joint learning of words and meaning representations for open-text semantic parsing. In *Artificial Intelligence and Statistics*, pages 127–135.

Jason Brownlee. 2017. How to use word embedding layers for deep learning with keras. `https://machinelearningmastery.com/use-word-embedding-layers-deep-\learning-keras/`.

Sven Buechel and Udo Hahn. 2018. Word emotion induction for multiple languages as a deep multi-task learning problem. In *Proceedings of the 2018 Conference of the North American Chapter of the Association for Computational Linguistics: Human Language Technologies, Volume 1 (Long Papers)*, pages 1907–1918. Association for Computational Linguistics.

Gyu Hyeon Choi, Jong Hun Shin, and Young Kil Kim. 2018. Improving a multi-source neural machine translation model with corpus extension for low-resource languages. In *Proceedings of the Eleventh International Conference on Language Resources and Evaluation (LREC-2018)*. European Language Resource Association.

François Chollet et al. 2015. Keras. `https://github.com/fchollet/keras`.

Hamish Cunningham. 2002. Gate, a general architecture for text engineering. *Computers and the Humanities*, 36(2):223–254.

Kareem Darwish, Hamdy Mubarak, Ahmed Abdelali, Mohamed Eldesouki, Younes Samih, Randah Alharbi, Mohammed Attia, Walid Magdy, and Laura Kallmeyer. 2018. Multi-dialect Arabic POS Tagging: A CRF approach. In *Proceedings of the Eleventh International Conference on Language Resources and Evaluation (LREC-2018)*. European Language Resource Association.

Jan Vium Enghoff, Søren Harrison, and Željko Agić. 2018. Low-resource named entity recognition via multi-source projection: Not quite there yet? In *Proceedings of the 2018 EMNLP Workshop W-NUT: The 4th Workshop on Noisy User-generated Text*, pages 195–201. Association for Computational Linguistics.

Rob van der Goot, Barbara Plank, and Malvina Nissim. 2017. To normalize, or not to normalize: The impact of normalization on part-of-speech tagging. In *Proceedings of the 3rd Workshop on Noisy User-generated Text*, pages 31–39. Association for Computational Linguistics.

Edouard Grave, Piotr Bojanowski, Prakhar Gupta, Armand Joulin, and Tomas Mikolov. 2018. Learning word vectors for 157 languages. In *Proceedings of the International Conference on Language Resources and Evaluation (LREC 2018)*.

Tobias Horsmann and Torsten Zesch. 2016. Ltl-ude $@$ empirist 2015: Tokenization and pos tagging of social media text. In *Proceedings of the 10th Web as Corpus Workshop*, pages 120–126. Association for Computational Linguistics.

Sergey Ioffe and Christian Szegedy. 2015. Batch normalization: Accelerating deep network training by reducing internal covariate shift. *arXiv preprint arXiv:1502.03167*.

Maarten Janssen, Josep Ausensi, and Josep Fontana. 2017. Improving POS Tagging in Old Spanish Using TEITOK. In *Proceedings of the NoDaLiDa 2017 Workshop on Processing Historical Language*, pages 2–6. Linköping University Electronic Press.

Marcin Junczys-Dowmunt, Roman Grundkiewicz, Shubha Guha, and Kenneth Heafield. 2018. Approaching neural grammatical error correction as a low-resource machine translation task. In *Proceedings of the 2018 Conference of the North American Chapter of the Association for Computational Linguistics: Human Language Technologies, Volume 1 (Long Papers)*, pages 595–606. Association for Computational Linguistics.

Fred Karlsson. 1990. Constraint grammar as a framework for parsing running text. In *Karlgren, Hans (ed.), Proceedings of 13th International Conference on Computational Linguistics*, volume 3, pages 168–173, Finland. Helsinki.

Diederik P. Kingma and Jimmy Ba. 2014. Adam: A method for stochastic optimization. *CoRR*, abs/1412.6980.

Elena Kochkina, Maria Liakata, and Arkaitz Zubiaga. 2018. All-in-one: Multi-task learning for rumour verification. In *Proceedings of the 27th International Conference on Computational Linguistics*, pages 3402–3413. Association for Computational Linguistics.

Ying Lin, Shengqi Yang, Veselin Stoyanov, and Heng Ji. 2018. A multi-lingual multi-task architecture for low-resource sequence labeling. In *Proceedings of the 56th Annual Meeting of the Association for Computational Linguistics (Volume 1: Long Papers)*, pages 799–809. Association for Computational Linguistics.

Shie Mannor, Dori Peleg, and Reuven Rubinstein. 2005. The cross entropy method for classification. In *Proceedings of the 22Nd International Conference on Machine Learning*, ICML '05, pages 561–568, New York, NY, USA. ACM.

Ana Marasović and Anette Frank. 2018. Srl4orl: Improving opinion role labeling using multi-task learning with semantic role labeling. In *Proceedings of the 2018 Conference of the North American Chapter of the Association for Computational Linguistics: Human Language Technologies, Volume 1 (Long Papers)*, pages 583–594. Association for Computational Linguistics.

Tom McArthur and Thomas G McArthur. 1981. *Longman lexicon of contemporary English*. Longman London.

Ryo Nagata, Tomoya Mizumoto, Yuta Kikuchi, Yoshifumi Kawasaki, and Kotaro Funakoshi. 2018. A POS tagging model adapted to learner English. In *Proceedings of the 2018 EMNLP Workshop W-NUT: The 4th Workshop on Noisy User-generated Text*, pages 39–48. Association for Computational Linguistics.

Vinod Nair and Geoffrey E. Hinton. 2010. Rectified linear units improve restricted boltzmann machines. In *Proceedings of the 27th International Conference on International Conference on Machine Learning*, ICML'10, pages 807–814, USA. Omnipress.

Steve Neale, Kevin Donnelly, Gareth Watkins, and Dawn Knight. 2018. Leveraging lexical resources and constraint grammar for rule-based part-of-speech tagging in Welsh. In *Proceedings of the 11th Edition of Language Resources and Evaluation Conference (LREC 2018) May 7-12, 2018.*, volume 3, pages 168–173, Japan. Miazaki.

Dat Quoc Nguyen and Karin Verspoor. 2018. An improved neural network model for joint POS tagging and dependency parsing. In *Proceedings of the CoNLL 2018 Shared Task: Multilingual Parsing from Raw Text to Universal Dependencies*, pages 81–91. Association for Computational Linguistics.

Scott Piao, Francesca Bianchi, Carmen Dayrell, Angela D'Egidio, and Paul Rayson. 2015. Development of the multilingual semantic annotation system. In *Proceedings of the 2015 Conference of the North American Chapter of the Association for Computational Linguistics: Human Language Technologies*, pages 1268–1274. Association for Computational Linguistics.

Scott Piao, Paul Rayson, Dawn Archer, Francesca Bianchi, Carmen Dayrell, Mahmoud El-Haj, Ricardo-Mara Jimnez, Dawn Knight, Michal Ken, Laura Lfberg, Rao Muhammad Adeel Nawab, Jawad Shafi, Phoey Lee Teh, and Olga Mudraya. 2016. Lexical coverage evaluation of large-scale multilingual semantic lexicons for twelve languages. In *Proceedings of the Tenth International Conference on Language Resources and Evaluation (LREC 2016)*, Paris, France. European Language Resources Association (ELRA).

Scott Piao, Paul Rayson, Dawn Knight, and Gareth Watkins. 2018. Towards a Welsh Semantic Annotation System. In *Proceedings of the Eleventh International Conference on Language Resources and Evaluation (LREC 2018)*, Miyazaki, Japan. European Language Resources Association (ELRA).

Paul Rayson, Dawn Archer, Scott Piao, and Tony McEnery. 2004. The UCREL semantic analysis system. In *Proceedings of the beyond named entity recognition semantic labelling for NLP tasks workshop, LREC2004*, pages 7–12.

Russell D. Reed and Robert J. Marks. 1999. *Neural Smithing: Supervised Learning in Feedforward Artificial Neural Networks*. MIT Press.

Sebastian Ruder. 2016. An overview of gradient descent optimization algorithms. *arXiv preprint arXiv:1609.04747*.

Yan Shao, Christian Hardmeier, Jörg Tiedemann, and Joakim Nivre. 2017. Character-based joint segmentation and POS Tagging for Chinese using Bidirectional RNN-CRF. In *Proceedings of the Eighth International Joint Conference on Natural Language Processing (Volume 1: Long Papers)*, pages 173–183. Asian Federation of Natural Language Processing.

Serge Sharoff. 2018. Language adaptation experiments via cross-lingual embeddings for related languages. In *Proceedings of the Eleventh International Conference on Language Resources and Evaluation (LREC-2018)*. European Language Resource Association.

Nitish Srivastava, Geoffrey Hinton, Alex Krizhevsky, Ilya Sutskever, and Ruslan Salakhutdinov. 2014. Dropout: a simple way to prevent neural networks from overfitting. *The Journal of Machine Learning Research*, 15(1):1929–1958.

Weiwei Sun and Xiaojun Wan. 2016. Towards accurate and efficient Chinese part-of-speech tagging. *Computational Linguistics*, 42(3):391–419.

Yogarshi Vyas, Spandana Gella, Jatin Sharma, Kalika Bali, and Monojit Choudhury. 2014. POS Tagging of English-Hindi Code-Mixed Social Media Content. In *Proceedings of the 2014 Conference on Empirical Methods in Natural Language Processing (EMNLP)*, pages 974–979. Association for Computational Linguistics.

Weichao Wang, Shi Feng, Wei Gao, Daling Wang, and Yifei Zhang. 2018. Personalized microblog sentiment classification via adversarial cross-lingual multi-task learning. In *Proceedings of the 2018 Conference on Empirical Methods in Natural Language Processing*, pages 338–348. Association for Computational Linguistics.

Chuhan Wu, Fangzhao Wu, Sixing Wu, Junxin Liu, Zhigang Yuan, and Yongfeng Huang. 2018. Thu_ngn at semeval-2018 task 3: Tweet irony detection with densely connected lstm and multi-task learning. In *Proceedings of The 12th International Workshop on Semantic Evaluation*, pages 51–56. Association for Computational Linguistics.

Yi Yang and Jacob Eisenstein. 2016. Part-of-speech tagging for historical English. In *Proceedings of the 2016 Conference of the North American Chapter of the Association for Computational Linguistics: Human Language Technologies*, pages 1318–1328. Association for Computational Linguistics.

A   Appendices

A.1   The Basic *CyTag* Tagset

The list of the coarse-grained (*basic*) *CyTag* part-of-speech categories used in this work is as shown below.

R han Ymadrodd	CYTAG(ENG)
Enw (Noun)	E (NN)
Y Fannod Benodol (Article)	YFB (ART)
Arddodiad (Preposition)	Ar PRE
Cysylltair (Conjunction)	Cys (CJN)
Rhifeiriau (Numeral)	Rhi (NUM)
Ansoddair (Adjective)	Ans (ADJ)
Adferf (Adverb)	Adf (ADV)
Berf (Verb)	B (VRB)
Rhagenw (Pronoun)	Rha (PRN)
Unigryw (Unique)	U UNI)
Ebychiad (Interjection)	Ebych (ITJ)
Gweddilliol (Others)	Gw (OTH)
Atalnodiad(Punctuation)	Atd (PUN)

A.2   The *USAS* Semantic Tagset

Below is a list and the descriptions of the USAS semantic top level categories:

Domain	Description
A	General and abstract terms
B	The body and the individual
C	Arts and crafts
E	Emotion
F	Food and farming
G	Government and public
H	Architecture, housing and the home
I	Money and commerce in industry
K	Entertainment, sports and games
L	Life and living things
M	Movement, location, travel and transport
N	Numbers and measurement
O	Substances, materials, objects and equipment
P	Education
Q	Language and communication
S	Social actions, states and processes
T	Time
W	World and environment
X	Psychological actions, states and processes
Y	Science and technology
Z	Names and grammar

Author Index

Association for Computational Linguistics
209 N. Eighth Street
Stroudsburg, Pennsylvania 18360

ISBN 978-1-5108-9114-2